UNIX® SYSTEM ADMINISTRATION HANDBOOK

SECOND EDITION

Evi Nemeth
Garth Snyder
Scott Seebass
Trent R. Hein

Prentice Hall PTR
Englewood Cliffs, New Jersey 07632

Library of Congress Cataloging-in-Publication Data

Acquisitions Editor: Mike Meehan
Cover Design: Lundgren Graphics
Cover Illustration and Interior Cartoons: Tyler Stevens

The publisher offers discounts on this book when ordered in bulk quantities.
For more information, contact:

Corporate Sales Department
PTR Prentice Hall
113 Sylvan Avenue
Englewood Cliffs, NJ 07632
Phone: 800-382-3419
FAX: 201-592-2249
E-mail: dan_rush@prenhall.com

Printed in the United States of America

10 9 8 7 6 5 4 3 2

ISBN 0-13-151051-7

Prentice-Hall International (UK) Limited, London
Prentice-Hall of Australia Pty. Limited, Sydney
Prentice-Hall of Canada, Inc., Toronto
Prentice-Hall Hispanoamericana S.A., Mexico
Prentice-Hall of India Private Limited, New Delhi
Prentice-Hall of Japan, Inc., Tokyo
Simon & Schuster Asia Pte. Ltd., Singapore
Editora Prentice-Hall do Brasil, Ltda., Rio de Janeiro

Table of Contents

BASIC ADMINISTRATION

CHAPTER 1 WHERE TO START

i

CHAPTER 2 BOOTING AND SHUTTING DOWN

CHAPTER 6   ADDING NEW USERS

CHAPTER 7   DEVICES AND DRIVERS

CHAPTER 8   SERIAL DEVICES

CHAPTER 9   ADDING A DISK

CHAPTER 10 PERIODIC PROCESSES

CHAPTER 11 BACKUPS

NETWORKING

Chapter 14   TCP/IP and Routing

CHAPTER 16   THE DOMAIN NAME SYSTEM

CHAPTER 17   THE NETWORK FILE SYSTEM

Chapter 18 Sharing System Files

Chapter 19 SLIP and PPP

CHAPTER 20   THE INTERNET

CHAPTER 21   ELECTRONIC MAIL

CHAPTER 22 NETWORK MANAGEMENT

CHAPTER 23   SECURITY

BUNCH O' STUFF

CHAPTER 24   USENET NEWS

CHAPTER 29   PERFORMANCE ANALYSIS

CHAPTER 30   UUCP

Foreword

There are a lot of books about system administration out there. Why is this one special? We can think of two reasons.

First, it's good. The authors do real system administration on real systems with a lot of users, a lot of networking, and a lot of special connectivity. They've been at it long enough that they can still recall what a Unibus adaptor was and what was wrong with the DZ11 (no interrupts). They've lived in a "dirty" world with lots of different systems from lots of different vendors and lots of different versions of the operating system. They've been bitten by alligators of every type and persuasion. This is not a nice, neat book written for a nice, clean world. It's a nasty book written for a nasty world.

Second, it's comprehensive. There are a lot of good books about specific UNIX® topics (we know of a great book on **sendmail**, for example), but few books on the general problem of system administration that are worth their weight in dead trees.[1] The initial draft of the first edition of this book was called *UNIX System Administration Made Difficult*, which seemed appropriate: the "… Made Simple" style of books always seemed to gloss over so many details that they actually made the job harder.

The fact is that system administration *is* difficult. UNIX systems are tremendously powerful, and with power comes some measure of complexity. PCs get complicated too, when you start connecting them to networks, modems, printers, and third-party disks, and when you real-

---

1. UNIX is a registered trademark in the United States and other countries, licensed exclusively through X/Open Company Limited.

ize that you need to worry about topics such as backups and security. Suddenly, managing a PC starts to look a lot like administering a UNIX box: "It's easy! Just click here, then you have to turn off the printer to use the network (select here, pull down this menu, and click on "Disable" and "Apply"), then pull down this menu, then select the selector, type in your hostname here, then click here, here, and double-click here (dismiss that dialog box, it always gives that, I don't know why…), then pop up here, select that menu, enable the network, then go over there to start up the TCP/IP application, then—Woops! We forgot to set the network mask; no problem, just go back to the third menu selection and change the mask—Drat, that disabled the network, just fix that (click, drag, click)… Great, now start up the TCP/IP application again (click), and now you can use **telnet**! See, easy!"

By contrast, UNIX boxes have the network installed by default. It is set up once, and most users never see how the configuration is done. Unfortunately, system administrators are not "most users" and so we get to go through the messy process of setting it up.

The authors also have something to offer for those rare, calm moments when you have the chance to reflect on how to improve your environment to make your life a bit easier. For example, this book will help you tune your network to maximize throughput, minimize delay, and avoid single points of failure. It will also give you hints on how to let the good guys in while keeping the bad guys out.

Some people do have isolated UNIX boxes without networks, printers, modems, or maybe even third-party disk drives. If you are one of these rare birds, or you feel that your vendor's point-and-click graphical interface fills all your needs (and you aren't curious about what goes on behind the curtain), you may not need this book. It goes into detail about obscure things you may never need to know.

However, such simple environments make up a tiny and dwindling fraction of the real world. This is a book for the rest of us.

Eric Allman
Marshall Kirk McKusick

August, 1994

Foreword to the First Edition

The administration of UNIX systems has always been a somewhat neglected subject. I think this happened for several reasons, all connected to various aspects of its unusual history.

First, the creation and early spread of the system took place among devotees, people who soon became knowledgeable of its nooks and crannies. These groups were often irritated by the formalities and procedures common in the big computer centers that were the chief computational resources during the 1970s, and they were ingenious in developing their own wizardly administrative recipes, instead of relying on cookbooks.

Second, a typical UNIX system inhabits a computing niche unusual until recently. Most commonly, such systems are either medium-size machines serving a single department in a company or university, or workstations used by a single person, but connected by a network to many other systems. For the most part—though there are now exceptions—UNIX systems are not big machines with professional, on-site staff from the manufacturer or a big computer center, nor personal computers owned by isolated individuals.

For a large machine, it is expected that professionals will provide the support. For the personal computer, the manufacturer is expected to write the administrative cookbook for the limited range of uses to which the machine will be put. The purchasers of a mid-range machine may find themselves suddenly nominated to be the staff; this can make them feel nearly as much on their own as if they had bought a personal computer, but they must face the complexities of keeping an eye on multiple users, dealing with one or more networks, and handling all the other daunting conundrums that turn up.

Finally, UNIX systems come from a variety of sources. Although there is a common core of useful administrative tools and procedures, not all suppliers provide a useful degree of support. Also, many sites import substantial amounts of software from university distributions, Usenet, or other places that provide the programs, but little else.

Despite the problems, many of the purveyors of UNIX systems do a good job of telling their customers how to run them. Nevertheless, a comprehensive book discussing administration is clearly needed. The manufacturer's theory of what you want to do is not necessarily your own, and the documentation may be scattered; your supplier may be more talented at building hardware than at generating useful manuals; or you may be using popular software that didn't come in the box.

Therefore, this book is most welcome.

Dennis Ritchie

October, 1988

Preface

INTRODUCTION

When we were writing the first edition of this book in the mid-1980s, we were eager to compare our manuscript with other books about UNIX system administration. To our delight, we could find only three.

These days, you have your choice of at least fifty. Here are the features that distinguish our book:

- We take a practical approach. Our purpose is not to restate the contents of your manuals, but rather to give you the benefit of our collective experience in system administration. This book contains plenty of war stories and a wealth of pragmatic advice.

- We cover UNIX networking in detail. It is the most difficult aspect of UNIX system administration, and the area in which we can most likely be of help to you.

- We do not oversimplify the material. Our examples reflect true-life situations, with all their warts and unsightly complications. In most cases, the examples have been taken directly from production systems.

- We emphasize the use of software tools. Every piece of software mentioned in the text is either a standard UNIX tool, or is included on the CD-ROM at the back of this book—sometimes both, since many vendors don't do a perfect job of keeping up with new releases.

- We cover all the major variants of UNIX.

OUR SIX EXAMPLE SYSTEMS

There are two main flavors of UNIX: one from AT&T ("original") and one from the University of California, Berkeley ("extra crispy"). Neither AT&T nor Berkeley is still active in the UNIX marketplace, but the terms "AT&T UNIX" and "Berkeley UNIX" survive for historical reasons.

This book covers six different operating systems:

- Solaris 2.4
- SunOS 4.1.3
- HP-UX 9.0
- DEC's OSF/1 2.0
- IRIX 5.2
- BSD/OS 1.1

We chose these systems because they are among the most popular, and because they illustrate a broad range of approaches to UNIX administration. The systems in the left column are predominantly derived from AT&T UNIX, while those on the right are more like Berkeley UNIX.

We provide detailed information about each of these example systems for every topic that we discuss. Comments specific to a particular operating system are marked with the manufacturer's logo.[1]

There are many other versions of UNIX. Most fall within the range of variation defined by these six systems, but a few (such as AIX and SCO) are so beautifully strange that they must be taken on their own terms.

THE ORGANIZATION OF THIS BOOK

This book is divided into three large chunks: Basic Administration, Networking, and Bunch o' Stuff.

Basic Administration provides a broad overview of UNIX from a system administrator's perspective. The chapters in this section cover most of the facts and techniques needed to run a stand-alone UNIX system.

The Networking section describes the protocols used on UNIX systems and the techniques used to set up, extend, and maintain networks. High-level network software is also covered here. Among the featured topics are the Domain Name System, the Network File System, network routing, and **sendmail**.

Bunch o' Stuff includes a variety of supplemental information. Some chapters discuss optional software packages such as UUCP and the UNIX printing system. Others give sage advice on topics ranging from hardware maintenance to disk space management to the politics of running a UNIX installation.

1. Permission to reprint the copyrighted and trademarked ▣◪▣ logo which appears in this publication has been granted by the copyright and registered trademark owner, Open Software Foundation, Inc.

ABOUT THE CD-ROM

The CD-ROM contains software and reference information that we recommend for system administrators. Most of the items on the CD-ROM are available over the Internet, but you may find the CD-ROM faster and more convenient to use.

The CD-ROM uses the ISO-9660 format, which is supported by most computers (including our six example systems). This format does not allow filenames longer than eight characters, so we have packaged up the tools using the standard UNIX **tar** command. Decoding instructions are included at the back of this book.

The CD-ROM will be updated on an approximately yearly basis. To determine the age of your copy, check the date printed on the CD-ROM itself. To order the most recent version, send email to

```
cd-order@admin.com
```

You can also order updates by calling 1-800-ADMIN-CD.

CONTACT INFORMATION

Please send suggestions, comments, typos, and bug reports to

```
sa-book@admin.com
```

We answer all mail, but please be patient; it is sometimes a few days before one of us is able to respond. We hope you enjoy this book, and good luck with your adventures in system administration!

Evi Nemeth
Garth Snyder
Scott Seebass
Trent R. Hein

November, 1994

Acknowledgments

Since the first edition of this book was published, hundreds of readers have sent us bug fixes, comments, and criticisms. We would like to thank everyone who took the time to write us, and we hope that we've successfully incorporated the feedback we received.

Many thanks go to Tyler Stevens, our faithful copy editor. Tyler also remained onboard from the first edition as our staff cartoonist.

We also thank Jim Lane, who loaned his energy and expertise to the project of assembling the CD-ROM and documenting its contents.

System administration for UNIX has become more complex over the last five years, and the technical breadth of this text has grown proportionately. Our technical reviewers read various portions of the book, ranging from one paragraph to the entire manuscript. These distinguished volunteers provided valuable advice on everything from historical and technical details to attempts at humor that failed:

Rick Adams	Chris Hall	Herb Morreale
Eric Allman	Mike Karels	Laszlo Nemeth
Keith Bostic	Rob Kolstad	Pat Parseghian
Bob Bubon	Don Libes	Joel O. Rem
Bob Coggeshall	Lennart Lövstrand	Andy Rudoff
Bryan Costales	Bob Manchek	Donn Seeley
Mark Dadgar	Alan Marcum	Dave Slattengren
Barb Dijker	Jamie Marks	Russell Snyder
Randy Else	Lynda McGinley	Bob Sutterfield
Jeff Forys	Kirk McKusick	Paul Vixie
Bob Gray	Dave Menges	Philip Zimmermann

We give special thanks to Pat Parseghian for her comprehensive review of the complete manuscript, and to Jeff Forys for digging up technical nits where we were sure that none remained. Thanks also to Bob Gray and Andy Rudoff, who inspected the galley proofs.

The backstage area at a four-author circus can be filled with tempers, unrealistic deadlines, and general chaos. Many thanks to Beth McElroy, Vincent Cawley, and Dotty Foerst, who assisted us with various aspects of the production process.

Thanks also to the editor of the first edition, John Wait.

Finally, the Computer Science Department at the University of Colorado deserves many thanks for providing computing resources, production assistance, and numerous "test subjects."

SECTION ONE
BASIC ADMINISTRATION

1 *Where to Start*

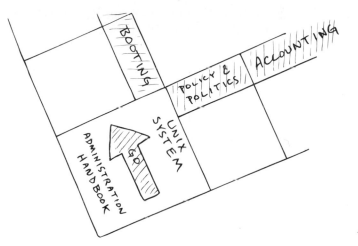

1.1 THE SORDID HISTORY OF UNIX

UNIX originated as a research project at AT&T Bell Labs in 1969. Bell
Labs' Sixth Edition, known commonly as V6, was released in 1976 and
was available free to universities. Version Seven was released three
years later; it was the first version to be widely distributed (primarily to
universities and research labs), and became the basis for most later versions of UNIX. It cost $100 for universities and $21,000 for everyone else.

After the release of V7, AT&T created its UNIX Support Group (USG,
later spun off as Unix System Laboratories, USL) to deploy UNIX as a
commercial product. Bell Labs and USG both continued the development of UNIX, but the two groups' efforts diverged. USL's releases, System III and System V, were widely distributed and have had a proportionately greater impact on modern systems.

In 1992, AT&T sold its UNIX operations to Novell, which has repackaged
System V as a not-very-popular product called UnixWare. Since most
versions of UNIX are ultimately derived from AT&T's code, Novell also
receives a royalty from other vendors' UNIX sales.[1]

Berkeley UNIX began in 1977, when the Computer Systems Research
Group (CSRG) at the University of California, Berkeley licensed the V6
code from AT&T. Berkeley's releases (called BSD, for Berkeley Software

---

1. However, Sun Microsystems has made a large one-time payment instead.

Distribution) began in 1977 with 1BSD for the PDP-11 and culminated in 1993 with 4.4BSD. Since BSD was based on AT&T's UNIX, a license from AT&T was required to use it.

AT&T's source licenses were always expensive for government laboratories and commercial entities. At first they were cheap for universities, but as UNIX gained commercial acceptance, the price rose rapidly. Eventually, Berkeley set the long-term goal of removing AT&T's code from BSD, a tedious and time-consuming process. Before the work could be completed, Berkeley lost funding for operating systems research and the CSRG was disbanded.

Before collapsing, the CSRG released its second collection of AT&T-free code, known as Net/2. Several companies, most notably BSDI (Berkeley Software Design, Inc.), took that release, supplied the missing pieces, and began to market it as a cheap but real implementation of UNIX. Meanwhile, AT&T and Berkeley took to slapping each other with lawsuits: AT&T's mostly for trade secret and copyright infringement, and Berkeley's for contract violation (e.g. failure to give due credit). At the same time, AT&T sued BSDI for using Net/2 as the basis for its product.

In February, 1994, Novell (which by that time had acquired UNIX from AT&T) and the University of California agreed to drop their mutual lawsuits. The suits involving BSDI were also quickly settled. While details of the settlements were not made public, Berkeley stopped distributing the Net/2 release and announced a more mature package, 4.4BSD-Lite. This package is "freely redistributable," and is blessed by both Novell and the University of California. BSDI has announced plans to migrate their product to 4.4BSD-Lite by mid-1995.[2]

Throughout the 80s, workstation vendors hacked away at their own versions of UNIX. Typically, a vendor would start with a vanilla AT&T or BSD system, then proceed to develop it independently. Some vendors didn't want to commit to one flavor of UNIX and supported both, or developed hybrids that combined both sets of features.

When the chaos seemed like it could get no worse, rival standards organizations arose to combat the proliferation of UNIX variants. All of a sudden there were UNIX standards galore, each supported by a fragile coalition of a few vendors. But instead of simplifying the UNIX market, these standards only served to introduce more versions of UNIX. DEC is the only major vendor to ever discontinue development of its own version of UNIX in favor of a standard.[3]

---

2. O'Reilly & Associates sells the 4.4BSD manual set and the raw (unbootable) 4.4BSD-Lite code (on CD-ROM) for a reasonable fee.

3. Even so, DEC has substantially customized the "standard" release.

1.2 CONTEMPORARY UNIX PRODUCTS

In this book, we use the abbreviations ATT and BSD to identify versions of UNIX as being more AT&T-like or more Berkeley-like, respectively. By virtue of lineage, Novell's UnixWare and BSDI's BSD/OS are the most generic systems relative to our terminology.

Sun Microsystems' Solaris 2.X is an ATT UNIX with many extensions. SunOS, an older operating system from Sun, is a BSD-based system, also with many extensions. Sun publications sometimes refer to SunOS as Solaris 1.X. Do not be alarmed; this is just Sun's way of editing history to serve current marketing needs. Due to popular demand, Sun has agreed to support both operating systems, at least for a while.

DEC uses the OSF/1 standard, which is in turn based on the Mach operating system developed at Carnegie-Mellon University. Mach is derived from BSD (though the kernel and UNIX interface are structured differently), and OSF/1 systems behave much like BSD machines from an administrative point of view. NeXT Computer's NEXTSTEP is also an extended Mach, though it is not of the OSF/1 ilk. You might also encounter DEC machines that run DEC's previous UNIX, called Ultrix; it is more or less a vanilla BSD system.

IBM, backward as ever, flogs a weirdo product called AIX, which they deny stands for "Ain't UNIX." It's, ah, UNIX-compatible?

Silicon Graphics provides IRIX, which is similar to ATT. Early versions had all the good BSD extensions, but IRIX has been steadily creeping towards ATT-land ever since. SCO, the Santa Cruz Operation, sells a popular but perverse PC UNIX based on an older version of AT&T UNIX, SVR3.2. It has been extensively modified. HP's system is called HP-UX; it is mostly ATT-ish but with odd surprises of its own.

Several free UNIX systems are available for PC hardware. The most popular is called Linux. It was originally written by Linus Torvalds of Helsinki, but now has a large and growing developer community. It requires a 386 PC with 4MB of memory and a 40MB hard disk. Linux internals and system administration are BSD-ish (probably closest to SunOS); its programming interface is more like ATT.

NetBSD, 386BSD, and FreeBSD are PC UNIX implementations based on Net/2 from Berkeley. They require similar hardware.

1.3 HOW TO USE THIS BOOK

This book is designed to complement, not replace, your system's documentation. For obvious reasons, we cannot condense six sets of 3,000-page manuals into one book. Luckily, the manuals that come with UNIX systems are generally pretty good, and they are certainly authoritative.

We encourage you to familiarize yourself with your manuals and to refer to them frequently.

This book will help you in five ways:

- It will give you an overview of the major administrative systems, identifying the different pieces of each and explaining how they work together.

- It will introduce general administrative techniques that we have found, through experience, to be worthwhile.

- It will help you choose solutions that continue to work well as your site grows in size and complexity.

- It will help you sort good ideas from bad ideas and educate you about various atrocities of taste committed by vendors.

- It will summarize common procedures so that you don't have to dig through the excessive detail of the manuals to accomplish simple tasks.

It's impossible to perform these functions with perfect objectivity. Instead of pretending to be impartial, we simply wear our biases on our sleeves. We hope you'll take it all with a grain of salt.

System Administration 101

We assume that you have a certain amount of UNIX experience. In particular, you should have a general concept of how UNIX looks and feels from the user's perspective before jumping into administration. There are several good books that can get you up to speed; see the reading list on page 12.

Most administrative tasks are performed by editing configuration files and writing scripts, so you must be familiar with a text editor. We strongly recommend that you learn **vi**. It is standard on all UNIX systems, and though it may appear a bit pale when compared with glitzier offerings such as **emacs**, it is perfectly usable. If you become addicted to another editor, you will soon tire of dragging it along with you to install on every new system.

One of the mainstays of UNIX system administration (and a theme that runs throughout this book) is the use of shell scripts to automate administrative tasks. You *must* be able to read and modify **sh** scripts. Scripts that you write from scratch can be written in the shell or scripting language of your choice.

If you want to be a true power scripter, you may want to learn **perl**. As a programming language, it is a little strange. However, it does include many features that are useful for administrators. We also recommend that you learn **expect**, which is discussed in a bit more detail starting on page 390. **expect** can be picked up quite rapidly.

Notation and Typographical Conventions

Filenames, commands, and literal arguments to commands are shown in Courier bold (**like this**). Place holders (e.g., command arguments that should not be taken literally) are in Courier italic (*like this*). For example, in the command

```
cp file directory
```

you're supposed to replace *file* and *directory* with the names of an actual file and an actual directory.

The output of commands and excerpts from scripts and configuration files are shown in plain Courier. Sometimes, we annotate interactive sessions with italic text. For example:

```
% grep arth /pub/phonelist    /* Look up Garth's phone # */
Garth Snyder 555 2834
Sharon Seyfarth 555-2311
```

In general, we use the same conventions as the UNIX manual pages for indicating the syntax of commands:

* Anything between square brackets ("[" and "]") is optional.
* Anything followed by an ellipsis ("...") can be repeated.
* Curly braces ("{" and "}") indicate that you should select one of the items separated by vertical bars ("|").

For example, the specification

```
bork [-x] {on|off} filename ...
```

would match any of the following commands:

```
bork on /etc/passwd
bork -x off /etc/passwd /etc/termcap
bork off /usr/lib/tmac
```

We use shell-style globbing characters for pattern matching:

* A star ("*") matches zero or more characters.
* A question mark ("?") matches one character.
* A tilde ("~") means the home directory of the current user.
* *~user* means the home directory of *user*.

For example, we sometimes refer to the BSD startup scripts

```
/etc/rc.boot
/etc/rc
/etc/rc.local
```

with the shorthand pattern `/etc/rc*`.

Other special words (such as hostnames and usernames) are not specially marked unless the context makes them ambiguous; in this case, they are double-quoted.

Sometimes, text within quotation marks has a precise technical meaning. In these cases, we flout the normal rules of English and put punctuation outside the quotation marks so that there can be no confusion about what's included and what's not.

System-Specific Information

Information in this book generally applies to all six of our example systems unless a specific attribution is given. Details peculiar to one system are marked with the vendor's logo:

Solaris 2.4   IRIX 5.2   DEC's OSF/1 2.0

HP-UX 9.0   SunOS 4.1.3   BSD/OS 1.1

These logos are used with the permission of their respective owners. However, the vendors have neither reviewed nor endorsed the contents of this book.

We discuss the systems in order they are shown here (reading down and to the right), from most ATT-ish (Solaris) to most BSD-ish (BSD/OS). The features that we identify as ATT-ish are most likely to apply to Solaris, HP-UX, and IRIX. The other systems are BSD-ish.

1.4   HOW TO USE YOUR MANUALS

The UNIX manuals contain all the information needed to keep the system running, yet that information is sometimes hard to find and often cryptic. You *must* have a complete set of manuals for the particular version of UNIX you are using. If you need additional copies, it is usually cheaper to buy them than to make photocopies.

UNIX systems typically come with two types of documentation: "man pages" and supplemental articles. Man pages (so called because they are designed for use with the **man** command) are concise descriptions of individual commands, file formats, or library routines. They are usually kept on-line, but may also be supplied in a printed form.

Articles are longer documents that describe systems at a deeper level or that adopt a tutorial or procedural approach. Many pieces of software have both a man page and an article. For example, the man page for **vi** tells you about the command-line arguments that **vi** understands, but you have to go to the supplement to learn how to actually edit a file.

In early versions of the manuals, man pages were placed in volume one. The longer tutorials and installation guides were put in volume two. ATT manuals had volumes 2A and 2B, and BSD added volume 2C. On older BSD systems, volume two was kept on-line in /usr/doc; however, this practice is now quite rare.

Since the man pages are closely tied to the software they describe, vendors tend not to change them very much unless they modify the software itself.[4] Not so with the supplements; that is an area in which vendors go in all different directions. Many vendors have entirely replaced the traditional manuals with new books and documents.

 All IRIX documentation is kept on-line. Printed manuals are not even supplied anymore. The rationale is to save a tree and to avoid the delay and cost of printing. This may become a common practice in the future.

Organization of the Man Pages

All UNIX systems divide the man pages into sections. However, ATT and BSD have done things a bit differently. The basic organization of the man pages is shown in Table 1.1.

Table 1.1   Sections of the UNIX man pages

ATT	BSD	Contents
1	1	User-level commands and applications
2	2	System calls and kernel error codes
3	3	Library calls
4	5	Standard file formats
5	7	Miscellaneous files and documents
6	6	Games and demonstrations
7	4	Device drivers and network protocols
–	8	System administration commands

OSF Although it is generally BSD-ish, OSF/1 uses the ATT organization.

Many systems further subdivide the man pages in each section. For example, section 3m often contains man pages about the system's math library. There is also considerable variation in the exact distribution of pages; some systems leave section eight empty and lump the system administration commands into section one. A lot of systems have discontinued games and demos, leaving nothing in section six.

Most systems allow you to create a section of the manuals called "l" for local man pages. Another common convention is section "n" for software

4. But this is not always the case. HP has done an excellent job of editing the man pages.

that isn't strictly local but isn't standard, either (such as many of the software packages on the CD-ROM).

`troff` input for the man pages is traditionally kept in the directories `/usr/man/man`X, where X is a digit 1 through 8, or 1 or n. Formatted versions of the manuals are kept in `/usr/man/cat`X. The `man` command will format man pages on the fly; if the `cat` directories are writable, it will also deposit the formatted pages as they are created, generating a cache of commonly-read man pages. All man pages can be preformatted at once with the `catman` command if space permits. On many systems, the man pages have been moved to `/usr/share/man`.

 IRIX's formatted man pages live under `/usr/catman`. Local man pages should be added to `/usr/man` as usual.

A recent trend in UNIX systems is the elimination of source files for man pages. `nroff` and `troff` (the commands with which man pages are usually formatted) belong to AT&T; some systems have dropped them to avoid paying additional royalties. This doesn't affect the `man` command, but it may limit your options in some other ways. For example, you can't format the man pages for a high-resolution output device such as a laser printer without the source files.

 IRIX is the only one of our example systems that does not include the source for man pages. Under BSDI, installation of the source is optional.

 BSDI's `man` command supports about a zillion silly options that can be set from `/etc/man.conf`. This is a perfect example of going to a lot of trouble to solve nonexistent problems.

man: Read Manual Pages

`man` *title* formats a specific manual page and sends it to your terminal via `more` (or whatever program is specified in your PAGER environment variable). *title* is usually a command, device, or filename. The sections of the manual are searched in roughly numeric order, although sections that describe commands (sections 1, 8, and 6) are usually searched first. On ATT-ish systems, you can set the search order by installing a `man.cf` file at the root of the manual hierarchy.

The form `man` *section title* gets you a man page from a particular section. Thus, on a BSD system, `man tty` gets you the man page for the `tty` command and `man 4 tty` gets you the man page for the serial driver. Some ATT systems require the section to be prefaced with `-s`.

Almost all versions of `man` check to see if you have defined the MANPATH environment variable, which should contain a colon-separated list of directories if it exists. MANPATH overrides or extends the list of directories that `man` searches. For example, the command

```
setenv MANPATH /home/share/localman:/usr/man
```

in your `.login` file would cause **man** to search a hierarchy of local man pages before `/usr/man`. The **sh** version would be

```
MANPATH=/home/share/localman:/usr/man
export MANPATH
```

On some systems, MANPATH completely overrides the default search path, so you must explicitly include the default directory if you want to continue to see the vendor-supplied man pages.

man -k *keyword* prints a list of man pages that have *keyword* in their one-line synopsis. For example:

```
% man -k translate
gftype (1L)   - translate a font file for humans to read
pktype (1L)   - translate a packed font file
tr (1)        - translate characters
```

The keywords database is normally kept in a file called **whatis** in the root of the man page hierarchy (`/usr/man` or `/usr/share/man`). If you add additional man pages to your system, you may need to rebuild this file with **catman -w**.

1.5 ESSENTIAL TASKS OF THE SYSTEM ADMINISTRATOR

The sections below give an overview of some tasks that system administrators are typically expected to perform. These duties do not necessarily have to be performed by one person, and at many sites the work is distributed among several people. However, there needs to be at least one person who understands all of the chores and makes sure that someone is doing them.

Adding and Removing Users

See Chapter 6 for more information about adding new users.

It is the system administrator's responsibility to add accounts for new users and to remove the accounts of users that are no longer active. The process of adding and removing users can be automated, but there are still decisions that must be made before a new user can be added.

When a user should no longer have access to the system, the user's account must be disabled. All of the files owned by the account must be disposed of so that they do not consume valuable disk space.

Adding and Removing Hardware

When new hardware is purchased, or when hardware is moved from one machine to another, the system must be configured to recognize and use that hardware. This may range from the simple task of adding a printer to the more complex job of adding a disk drive.

Performing Backups

See Chapter 11 for more information about backups.

Performing backups is one of the most important jobs of the system administrator, and also the job that is most often ignored or sloppily done. Backups are time-consuming and boring, but they are absolutely necessary. Backups can be automated and delegated to an underling, but it is still the system administrator's job to make sure that they are executed correctly and on schedule.

Installing New Software

When new software is acquired, it must be installed and tested. Once the software is working correctly, users must be informed of its availability and location. Local software should be installed in a place that makes it easy to differentiate from the software included with UNIX. This makes the task of upgrading the operating system much simpler, since the software won't be overwritten by the upgrade procedure.

Monitoring the System

There are numerous daily activities that must be performed. These include making sure that email and news are working correctly, watching log files for early signs of trouble, ensuring that local networks are all properly connected, and keeping an eye on the availability of system resources such as disk space.

Troubleshooting

UNIX systems and the hardware they run on occasionally break down. It is the administrator's job to play mechanic by diagnosing problems and calling in experts if needed. Finding the problem is often harder than fixing it.

Maintaining Local Documentation

See Chapter 32 for suggestions about documentation.

As your system is changed to suit your needs, it begins to differ from the plain-vanilla system that your documentation describes. It is the system administrator's duty to document all aspects of the system that are specific to the local environment. This includes documenting any software that is installed but did not come with the operating system, documenting where cables are run and how they are constructed, keeping maintenance records for all hardware, recording the status of backups, and documenting local procedures and policies.

Auditing Security

The system administrator must implement a security policy and periodically check to be sure that the security of the system has not been violated. On low-security systems, this might only involve only a few cursory checks for unauthorized access. On a high-security system, it can include an elaborate network of traps and auditing programs.

Helping Users

Although helping users with their various problems is rarely included in a system administrator's job description, it claims a significant portion of most administrators' workdays. System administrators are bombarded with problems ranging from "My program worked yesterday and now it doesn't! What did you change?" to "I spilled coffee on my keyboard! Should I pour water on it to wash it out?"

1.6 SYSTEM ADMINISTRATION UNDER DURESS

System administrators wear many hats. In the real world, they are often people with other jobs who have been asked to look after a few computers on the side. If you are in this situation, you may want to think a bit about where it might eventually lead.

The more you learn about UNIX, the more the user community will come to depend on you. Networks invariably grow, and there may be pressure to spend an ever-increasing portion of your time on administration. You will soon find that you are the only person in your organization that knows how to perform a variety of important tasks.

Once coworkers come to think of you as the local system administrator, it is difficult to extricate yourself from this role. We know several people that have changed jobs to escape it. Since many administrative tasks are intangible, you may also find that you're expected to be both a full-time administrator and a full-time engineer, writer, or secretary.

Some unwilling administrators try to fend off requests by adopting an ornery attitude and providing poor service. We do not recommend this approach; it makes you look bad and creates additional problems.

Instead, we suggest that you document the time you spend on system administration. Your goal should be to keep the work at a manageable level and to assemble evidence that you can use when you ask to be relieved of administrative duties. In most organizations, you will need to lobby the management from six months to a year to get yourself replaced, so plan ahead.

On the other hand, you may find that you enjoy system administration and that you yearn to be a full-time administrator. You will have no problem finding a job. Unfortunately, your political problems will probably intensify. Refer to Chapter 32, *Policy and Politics*, for a preview of the horrors in store.

1.7 RECOMMENDED SUPPLEMENTAL READING

ANDERSON, GAIL AND PAUL ANDERSON. *The UNIX C Shell Field Guide*. Englewood Cliffs, NJ: Prentice Hall. 1986.

HEWLETT PACKARD COMPANY. *The Ultimate Guide to the VI and EX Text Editors*. Redwood City, CA: Benjamin/Cummings. 1990.

ABRAHAMS, PAUL W. AND BRUCE A. LARSON. *UNIX for the Impatient*. Reading, MA: Addison-Wesley. 1992.

REICHARD, KEVIN AND ERIC F. JOHNSON. *teach yourself... UNIX, Second Edition*. MIS:Press. 1992.

PEEK, JERRY, TIM O'REILLY, AND MIKE LOUKIDES. *UNIX Power Tools*. Sebastopol, CA: O'Reilly & Associates/Random House. 1993.

2 *Booting and Shutting Down*

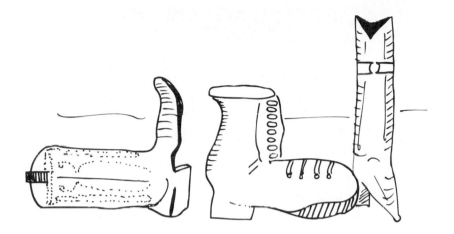

2.1 INTRODUCTION

UNIX is a complex operating system, and turning UNIX systems on and off is more complicated than just flipping a power switch. Both operations must be performed correctly if the system is to stay healthy.

2.2 BOOTSTRAPPING

Bootstrapping is the nerd word for "starting up a computer." The normal facilities of the operating system are not available during the startup process, so the computer must "pull itself up by its own bootstraps." During bootstrapping, the kernel is loaded into memory and begins to execute. A variety of initialization tasks are performed, and the system is then made available to users. Bootstrapping is often abbreviated to "booting."

Boot time is a period of special vulnerability. Errors in configuration files, missing or unreliable equipment, and damaged filesystems can all prevent a computer from coming up. Boot configuration is often one of the first tasks an administrator must perform on a new system. Unfortunately, it is also one of the most difficult, and it requires some familiarity with many other aspects of UNIX.

Although this chapter appears early in the book, it refers to material that is not discussed in detail until many hundreds of pages later. In particular, familiarity with the material in Chapter 4, *The Filesystem*,

Chapter 13, *Configuring the Kernel*, and Chapter 31, *Daemons*, will prove helpful. If your system already boots without any problem, you may want to skip this chapter and come back to it later.

An additional caveat: the booting process is very hardware-dependent. The information that follows is generically true, but may differ from reality for your particular system.

We will first present an overview of the bootstrapping procedure, and then we'll examine two sample initialization sequences in more detail. Troubleshooting hints for extreme situations start on page 42.

Automatic and Manual Booting

Most UNIX systems can boot in either automatic mode or manual mode. In automatic mode, the system performs the complete boot procedure on its own, without any external assistance. In manual mode, the system follows the automatic procedure up to a point, but then turns control over to an operator before most initialization scripts have been run. The computer is in "single-user mode" at this time. Most system processes are not running, and other users cannot log in.

In day-to-day operation, automatic booting is used almost exclusively. A typical boot procedure for a modern machine is to turn on the power and wait for the system to come on-line. Nevertheless, it's important to understand your automatic boot procedure and to know how to perform a manual boot. You'll usually have to boot manually when there is some problem that breaks automatic booting, such as a corrupted filesystem or an improperly configured network interface.

Steps in the Boot Process

A typical bootstrapping process consists of six distinct phases:

- Loading and initialization of the kernel
- Device detection and configuration
- Creation of spontaneous system processes
- Operator intervention (single-user boot only)
- Execution of system startup scripts
- Multi-user operation

An administrator has little control over most of these steps. Most bootstrap configuration is achieved by editing the system startup scripts.

Kernel Initialization

See Chapter 13 for more information about the kernel.

The UNIX kernel is itself a program, and the first bootstrapping task is to get this program into memory so that it can be executed. The pathname of the kernel is vendor-dependent, but is usually something like `/unix` or `/vmunix`.

Manual __single user__

SunOS
Solaris   ok boot -s

IRIX   >> boot -f sash __stand alone shell__

See Chapter 9 for information about installing a boot program.

Most systems implement a two-stage loading process. During the first stage, a small boot program is read into memory from a disk or tape. This program arranges for the kernel to be loaded. All of this occurs outside the domain of UNIX, so there is no standardization whatsoever between systems.

See page 220 for more information about the sizes of kernel tables.

The kernel performs tests to find out how much memory is available. Most kernels run in a fixed amount of memory,[1] and they know right from the start how much memory to reserve for their internal storage areas and I/O buffers. On most systems, the kernel prints a message on the console that reports the total amount of physical memory and the amount remaining after the kernel has extracted its share.

Hardware Configuration

One of the kernel's first chores is to check out the machine's environment to see what hardware is present. When you construct a kernel for your system, you tell it what hardware devices it should expect to find; when the kernel begins to execute, it tries to locate and initialize each device that you have told it about. Most kernels will print out a line of cryptic information about each device they find.

See Chapter 7 for more information about devices and their drivers.

The device information provided at kernel configuration time is often underspecified. In these cases, the kernel tries to determine the other information it needs by probing the bus for devices and asking the appropriate drivers for information. The drivers for devices that are missing or that do not respond to a probe will be disabled. Even if a device is later connected to the system, it will not be accessible to UNIX processes until the machine has been rebooted.

System Processes

Once basic initialization is complete, the kernel creates some "spontaneous" processes in user space.[2] The number and nature of these processes varies from system to system. On BSD systems, there are three:

- `swapper` – process 0
- `init` – process 1
- `pagedaemon` – process 2

The exact number of spontaneous processes varies on ATT systems:

- `sched` – process 0
- `init` – process 1
- Various memory handlers (except on Solaris)

---

1. Loadable drivers excepted; see Chapter 7.
2. They are called spontaneous processes because they are not created via the normal UNIX `fork` mechanism. See page 70 for more details.

Of these processes, only `init` is a full-fledged user process; the others are actually portions of the kernel that have been dressed up to look like processes for scheduling reasons.

At this point, the kernel's role in bootstrapping is complete. However, none of the processes that handle basic operations (such as accepting logins on terminals) have been created, nor have most of the UNIX daemons been started. All of these tasks are taken care of (indirectly, in some cases) by `init`.

Operator Intervention (Manual Boot Only)

See Chapter 3 for more information about the root account.

If the system is to be brought up in single-user mode, `init` is notified of this as it starts up via a command-line flag passed in by the kernel. During a single-user boot, `init` simply creates a shell on the system console and waits for it to terminate (via <Control-D> or `exit`) before continuing with the rest of the startup procedure. The single-user shell is always the Bourne shell, `sh`, not the C shell, `csh`. It runs as root, UNIX's privileged user.

See Chapter 4 for more information about filesystems and mounting.

From the single-user shell, the operator can execute commands in much the same way as when logged in on a fully booted system. However, only the root partition is usually mounted; the operator must mount other filesystems by hand in order to use programs that do not live in `/bin`, `/sbin`, or `/etc`.[3] Daemons do not normally run in single-user mode, so commands that depend on server processes (for example, `mail`) will not work correctly.

The `fsck` command, which checks and repairs filesystems, is normally run during an automatic boot. When the system is brought up in single-user mode, `fsck` must be run by hand. See page 146 for more information about `fsck`.

Startup Scripts

The next step in the bootstrap procedure is the execution of startup scripts. These scripts are actually just garden-variety shell scripts, and `init` runs `sh` to interpret them. The exact location, content, and organization of the scripts vary from system to system.

There are two prevailing ways to organize startup scripts. On BSD systems, the scripts are kept in the `/etc` directory and have names starting with the letters `rc`. On ATT systems, the startup scripts are kept in `/etc/init.d`, and links are made into the directories `/etc/rc0.d`, `/etc/rc1.d`, and so on. ATT's organization is cleaner, and it also allows the system to be shut down in an orderly manner.

---

3. Some systems will also have `/usr` mounted.

Some tasks that are often performed in the initialization scripts are:

- Setting the name of the computer
- Setting the time zone
- Checking the disks with **fsck** (only in automatic mode)
- Mounting the system's disks
- Removing files from the **/tmp** directory
- Configuring network interfaces
- Starting up daemons and network services
- Turning on accounting and quotas

Most startup scripts are quite verbose and print out a description of everything they are doing. This is a tremendous help if the system hangs midway through booting or if you are trying to locate an error in one of the scripts.

Multi-User Operation

See page 119 for more information about the login process.

After the initialization scripts have been run, the system is fully operational, except for the fact that no one can log in. In order for logins to be accepted on a particular terminal, there must be a **getty** process listening on it.[4] After the startup scripts have been run, **init** spawns these **getty** processes, completing the boot process. UNIX's handling of terminals is described in Chapter 8, *Serial Devices*, so we will not go into more detail at this point. Just keep in mind that **init** continues to perform an important role even after bootstrapping is complete.

On BSD systems, **init** has only two states: single-user and multi-user. On modern ATT systems, **init** has one single-user and several multi-user "run levels" that determine which of the system's resources are enabled. Run levels are described later in this chapter, on page 31.

2.3 A STROLL THROUGH THE BSD STARTUP SCRIPTS

In this section, we will pick through some sample BSD-style **/etc/rc*** files from a machine running SunOS. If your machine has a directory called **/etc/init.d**, skip ahead to the next section, where we will look at the startup process on an ATT-ish machine.

If your system is BSD-ish, this example will be interesting but not exactly like your system. On older BSD systems, a lot of changes had to be made by editing the **/etc/rc*** files directly. On newer systems (like the one in this example), scripts commonly read site-specific configuration information (such as the system's hostname) from small text files.

While we've taken out some lines that were unduly site-specific, we will go through the files below in essentially their native state. Since

---

4. Except under Solaris, which uses a more complex system.

startup scripts vary so much from one system to another, we want to stress that there is not necessarily anything wrong with your system's **rc** files if they don't look like these. **man rc** will usually give you a vague description of the startup process on your machine.

A Sample /etc/rc.boot

Under SunOS, the first **rc** script to be run is **/etc/rc.boot**.

```
PATH=/sbin:/single:/usr/bin:/usr/etc; export PATH
HOME=/; export HOME
```

The first two lines set the HOME and PATH environment variables to appropriate values. The commands executed during boot are for the most part basic system commands, so the command search path is not complicated. There are no spaces around the equal signs or the colons in the first line.

```
# Set hostname from /etc/hostname.xx0 file
hostname="`shcat /etc/hostname.??0 2>/dev/null`"
if [ ! -f /etc/.UNCONFIGURED -a ! -z "$hostname" -a
  "$hostname" != "noname" ]; then
      hostname $hostname
fi
```

Here, the system sets its hostname to the contents of the first file called **/etc/hostname.??0**. There is generally a hostname file in **/etc** for each network interface. For example, **/etc/hostname.le0** would contain the name by which the machine is known on the network connected to the **le0** interface.

```
# Break /etc/hostname.* into separate args  using "." as a
# shell separator char, then ifconfig every other arg.
interface_names="`shcat /etc/hostname.* 2>/dev/null`"
if test -n "$interface_names"
then
    (
        IFS="$IFS."
        set `echo /etc/hostname\.*`
        while test $# -ge 2
        do
            shift
            if [ "$1" != "xx0" ]; then
                ifconfig $1 "`shcat /etc/hostname\.$1`"
                    netmask+ -trailers up
            fi
            shift
        done
    )
fi
```

The system next tries to enable IP networking on each interface for which there is a **hostname** file.

```
# configure other interfaces automatically.
ifconfig -ad auto-revarp up
```

See page 262 for more information about **ifconfig***.*

Here, interfaces that were not assigned a specific hostname try to determine their addresses using the RARP protocol. This feature exists mainly to support diskless machines, which do not have any place to store their own address information. RARP is described on page 251.

```
# set host info from bootparams if not locally configured
if [ -z "`hostname`" ]; then
    hostconfig -p bootparams
fi
```

If the system still does not have a hostname, it tries to find it from another machine on the network using the **hostconfig** program. See page 721 for a description of **bootparamd**, which **hostconfig** uses.

```
# If local and network configuration failed, re-try
# forever in an interuptable sub-shell.  We want this
# sub-shell to be interuptable so that the machine can
# still be brought up manually when the servers are not
# cooperating.
if [ -z "`hostname`" -a ! -f /etc/.UNCONFIGURED ]; then
    echo "host configuration failed - re-trying..."
    intr sh /etc/rc.ip
fi
```

The boot process goes into a loop if the hostname still cannot be determined. At this point, a system administrator would have to intervene and fix the problem.

```
if [  f /sbin/route -a -f /etc/defaultrouter ]; then
    route -f add default `cat /etc/defaultrouter` 1
fi
```

If **/etc/defaultrouter** exists, the IP address or hostname of the default Internet gateway is read from it. This allows non-local network connections to work before more complicated routing schemes are brought into play later in the boot process. See *Routing*, starting on page 252, for more information about the default route.

```
intr mount -n -r /usr
```

This line mounts the **/usr** filesystem read-only.

```
if [ -r /fastboot ]; then
    echo "Fast boot ... skipping disk checks"
    error=0
else
```

```
            if [ $1x = singleuserx ]; then
                echo "checking / and /usr filesystems"
                intr fsck -p -w / /usr
                error=$?
                what="Fsck"
            else
                echo "checking filesystems"
                intr fsck -p -w
                error=$?
                what="Reboot"
            fi
        fi
```

See page 146 for more information about fsck.

Here, the system checks to see if the file **/fastboot** exists. If it does, the system was shut down cleanly and the filesystems should be in a consistent state. If the **/fastboot** file does not exist, all filesystems listed in **/etc/fstab** will be checked with **fsck**.[5]

```
case $error in

0|2)
    # Everything looks good.
    sh /etc/rc.single
    # Check whether rc.single successfully completed.
    nerr=$?
    case $nerr in
    0)
        error=$nerr
        ;;
    1)
        echo "Remount of / failed - check /etc/fstab"
        error=$nerr
        ;;
    2)
        echo "Remount of /usr failed - check /etc/fstab"
        error=$nerr
        ;;
    *)
        echo "Unknown error in /etc/rc.single - help!"
        error=$nerr
        ;;
    esac
    ;;

4)
    if [ $1x = singleuserx ]; then
        echo "Mounted FS fixed - rebooting single-user."
        reboot -q -n -- -s
```

5. On some systems, only filesystems that are "dirty" will be checked with **fsck**.

```
        else
            echo "Mounted FS fixed - rebooting."
            reboot -q -n
        fi
        ;;

8)
        echo "$what failed...help!"
        noremount
        ;;

12)
        echo "$what interrupted."
        noremount
        ;;

*)
        echo "Unknown error in reboot fsck."
        noremount
        ;;

esac
# exit with error status from fsck
exit $error
```

See page 143 for a discussion of file-system superblocks.

If the disks check cleanly, **rc.boot** runs **/etc/rc.single**, which is the next script we will examine. Finally, **rc.boot** exits with an error code that indicates whether the **fscks** were successful. If the root file-system was repaired, the system reboots without synchronizing the file-systems. This precaution prevents the fixed superblocks from being overwritten by older copies cached in memory by the kernel.

A Sample /etc/rc.single

Commands in **/etc/rc.single** are executed at boot time whether the system is planning to enter single-user mode or not. The **rc.single** script starts much like **rc.boot**, by setting its PATH and HOME variables (we will not repeat that code here).

```
intr mount -o remount /
if [ $? -ne 0 ]; then exit 1 ; fi
intr mount -o remount /usr
if [ $? -ne 0 ]; then exit 2 ; fi
```

Here, the system tries to remount the / and /usr filesystems read write. If these filesystems can't be remounted, the system will not be able to come up.

```
intr umount -at nfs
> /etc/mtab
intr mount -f /
intr mount -f /usr
```

These bizarre commands clean out the `/etc/mtab` file (where a list of mounted filesystems is stored) and add entries for `/` and `/usr`. Even though they were previously mounted, these filesystems were not listed in the `mtab` file because the root filesystem was not writable.

```
intr mount /usr/kvm  2>/dev/null
```

`/usr/kvm` is mounted next if it exists. This is another entry that is most often used on diskless systems.

```
mv /etc/ld.so.cache /etc/ld.so.cache-
rm -f /etc/ld.so.cache-
```

These commands clean up the shared library cache used by SunOS commands. If the file is in use, it cannot be removed; therefore, it is moved aside to ensure that a clean cache can be created. The `-f` option to `rm` prevents it from complaining if the file can't be deleted.

```
> /etc/utmp
```

This line cleans out the `/etc/utmp` file, which contains a list of users that are currently logged in. Since the system just booted, this file should be empty.

```
if [ ! -d /usr/share/lib ]; then
    intr mount /usr/share
fi
```

These lines mount yet another filesystem for diskless workstations.

```
tzsetup
```

The `tzsetup` command sets the time based on your local time zone and the status of daylight savings time. The kernel always keeps its internal clock running in Greenwich Mean Time. Library routines then determine the offset from GMT to the local time.

It would be very painful for the system administrator to have to change every machine's clock when daylight savings time came into effect. On older systems, there were a set of pre-defined time zone values. If one of them did not match your local conditions, the system failed. Modern systems provide the `zic` command, which allows time zone information to be specified in a data file. `zic` takes the data file and compiles it into a database format that can be accessed quickly by library routines. Most areas of the world where UNIX systems are found are covered by standard time zone files, so you will probably never have to use `zic`.

```
loadkeys -e
sync
exit 0
```

The `loadkeys` command sets the keyboard mapping to one appropriate for the current keyboard. Finally, `rc.single` exits and returns back to `rc.boot`, which also exits. If no problems were encountered and the system is in autoboot mode, `init` continues on to process `/etc/rc`. If the system is being booted single-user, an `sh` process is spawned on the system console.

A Sample /etc/rc

`/etc/rc` is the main system startup script. During automatic booting, it's executed immediately after `rc.boot`. If the system boots into single-user mode, the `rc` script is executed after the single-user shell is terminated. The `rc` script starts off like other startup scripts by setting its PATH and HOME variables (not shown).

```
touch /

if [ $? -ne 0 ]; then
    echo "Remounting file systems"
    sh /etc/rc.single
fi
```

If the root filesystem is not writable, `rc.single` must not have been run, so `rc` tries to rerun that script.

```
# Clean up shared library cache
if [ -f /etc/ld.so.cache ]; then
    mv /etc/ld.so.cache /etc/ld.so.cache-
    rm /etc/ld.so.cache-
fi
```

These commands clean up the shared library cache. A very similar set of commands appeared in `rc.boot`. The reason they are repeated here is that if the system were brought down to single-user mode, then brought back up to multi-user mode without a reboot, the cache would become corrupt. To avoid this, the cache is cleared again in the `rc` script. If it were not deleted in `rc.boot` as well, the cache might be corrupt in single-user mode. This convoluted logic is a good example of the reasons why you should not change the `rc*` scripts randomly, even if you think you understand them.

```
# Check for quick bootstrap
if [ -r /fastboot ]; then
    rm -f /fastboot
elif [ $1x = autobootx ]; then
    echo Automatic reboot in progress...
else
    echo Multiuser startup in progress...
fi
```

Here, the system removes the `/fastboot` file, which was used in `rc.boot` to decide if the filesystems needed to be checked with `fsck`.

```
    # attempt to rationally recover the passwd file if needed
    if [ -s /etc/ptmp ]; then
        if [ -s /etc/passwd ]; then
            ls -l /etc/passwd /etc/ptmp
            rm -f /etc/ptmp # should really remove the shorter
        else
            echo 'passwd file recovered from ptmp'
            mv /etc/ptmp /etc/passwd
        fi
    elif [ -r /etc/ptmp ]; then
        echo 'removing passwd lock file'
        rm -f /etc/ptmp
    fi
```

*See Chapter 6 for information about the **passwd** file.*

These lines deal with the case in which a machine crashes while its **/etc/passwd** file is being edited. The password file is very important to the system because it contains information needed to allow users to log in. Many systems provide the **vipw** command, which "checks out" a copy of the file as **/etc/ptmp** before allowing you to edit it. **vipw** and the **/etc/rc** script cooperate to make sure that the **passwd** file is not destroyed during a crash. See page 86 for more information about **vipw**.

```
    intr mount -at 4.2
```

This line mounts all local filesystems.

```
    echo -n 'checking quotas: '
    intr quotacheck -a -p
    echo 'done.'
    quotaon -a
```

*See page 143 for a description of **/etc/fstab***

These lines enable quotas if they are in use. The second line validates and updates disk quota information for each partition. The last line then enables quotas on partitions where they are appropriate, as specified in **/etc/fstab**. Quotas are discussed starting on page 624.

```
    /bin/ps -U
```

/bin/ps -U cleans out the **ps** database. **ps**, which displays the status of processes, is discussed on page 78.

```
    rm -f /etc/nologin
```

The file **/etc/nologin** is created by **shutdown** (see page 46) to prevent users from logging in as the system is shutting down. Even though the file is removed here, users won't be able to log in to the system immediately because **init** is still busy processing the **rc** file; it has not yet created any **gettys**.[6]

---

6. Actually, it may be possible to log in over the network before the startup scripts have finished running; **init** is not involved in that kind of login.

```
# Clean up ptys
if [ -f /dev/ttyp0 ]; then
    chown 0 /dev/tty[pqrs]*
    chmod 666 /dev/tty[pqrs]*
fi

/usr/etc/ttysoftcar -a  > /dev/null 2>&1
```

See page 116 for more information about soft carrier.
The first four lines set the correct modes on pseudo-terminals, which are used for remote logins on a network, among other things. See page 234 for a description of pseudo-terminals. The last line sets the serial ports' "soft carrier" flags based on the contents of **/etc/ttytab**.

```
sh /etc/rc.local
```

This line executes the **rc.local** script. The original purpose of **rc.local** was to hold site-specific startup commands. Unfortunately, most systems have allowed some generic OS commands to migrate into this script. We will parse through a sample **rc.local** in the next section; for now, we continue with the **rc** file.

```
swapon -a
```

swapon -a tells the system to make use of all swap partitions listed in **/etc/fstab**. See Chapter 9 for more information about swapping and the **fstab** file.

```
echo preserving editor files
(cd /tmp; /usr/lib/expreserve -a)
echo clearing /tmp
(cd /tmp; rm -f - *)
```

The **expreserve** command looks in **/tmp** to find files that were being edited when the system went down. **expreserve** sends mail to the owner of each editor file explaining how to recover most of the changes that were made, but not saved, when the system died. Of course, only users of the One True Editor (**vi**) ever edit anything worth saving, so it only works for them.

After editor files are saved, the **/tmp** directory is sterilized. Note that **/usr/tmp** is not normally cleaned out at reboot.

```
echo -n 'standard daemons:'
update;  echo -n ' update'
rm -f /var/spool/cron/FIFO
cron;  echo -n ' cron'
# accounting, off by default
#/usr/lib/acct/startup
```

The next step is to start the standard system daemons. Each daemon's name is echoed to the screen as it starts to give the operator some feedback about what's going on.

The **update** daemon is described on page 712. **cron** is discussed in Chapter 10, *Periodic Processes*. Accounting is covered in more detail than it deserves in Chapter 28.

```
# Do UUCP chores
if [ -d /var/spool/uucp ]; then
    (cd /var/spool/uucp
    >LCK.0
    rm -f LCK.*
    if [ -d /usr/lib/uucp ]; then
        su uucp -c /usr/lib/uucp/uusched & \
            echo -n ' uucp'
    fi)
fi
echo '.'
```

These lines clean up the UUCP system and start the **uusched** daemon. UUCP is described in Chapter 30.

```
echo -n 'starting network daemons:'
# rwhod is a performance pig
# if [ -f /usr/etc/in.rwhod ]; then
#   in.rwhod;  echo -n ' rwhod'
# fi
```

Here we see that someone wisely decided that **rwhod** was not worth running and commented out the lines that start it. See page 715 for more information about **rwhod**.

```
if [ -f /usr/etc/inetd ]; then
    inetd;  echo -n ' inetd'
fi
```

inetd, the system's superdaemon, is described in detail starting on page 708. **inetd** is an extremely important daemon; it is responsible for managing other daemons that run only when they are needed.

```
if [ -f /usr/lib/lpd ]; then
    # Clean up after previous lpds
    rm -f /dev/printer /var/spool/lpd.lock
    /usr/lib/lpd;  echo -n ' printer'
fi
echo '.'
```

The **lpd** daemon, in charge of print spooling, is started next. The UNIX printing system is discussed in Chapter 25, *Printing and Imaging*.

```
date
exit 0
```

The script prints the date and time, and then exits. The bootstrap process is complete.

A Sample /etc/rc.local

Theoretically, the `rc.local` script should only contain commands that vary between systems. However, most vendors have tainted `rc.local` with some boilerplate code.

We will look through a sample file, tossing out uninteresting cruft and leaving only a few localized examples to give you a taste of what the `rc.local` script should be used for.

Our example begins by starting up a very non-local system daemon:

```
# Start the RPC portmapper.
if [ -f /usr/etc/portmap ]; then
    portmap;  echo 'starting rpc port mapper.'
fi
```

The **portmap** daemon maps RPC (Remote Procedure Call) service numbers to the network ports of their appropriate servers. **portmap** is described on page 710.

Next, the NIS (Network Information Service) domain name[7] is set from the file **/etc/defaultdomain**, if it exists. If there is an NIS domain name, the rest of the NIS system is started up:

```
if [ -f /etc/defaultdomain ]; then
    domainname `cat /etc/defaultdomain`
fi
# Run NIS only if we have a set domainname.
dname=`domainname`
if [ "$dname" -a -d /var/yp ]; then
    echo "NIS domainname is $dname"
    echo -n "starting NIS services:"
    if [ -f /usr/etc/ypserv -a -d /var/yp/$dname ]; then
        ypserv;  echo -n ' ypserv'
    fi
    if [ -f /etc/security/passwd.adjunct ]; then
        ypbind -s;  echo -n ' ypbind'
    else
        ypbind;  echo -n ' ypbind'
    fi
    if [ -f /usr/etc/rpc.ypupdated -a -d /var/yp/$dname ];
    then
        rpc.ypupdated;  echo -n ' ypupdated'
    fi
    echo '.'
fi
```

The Network Information Service, also known as the Yellow Pages, is described starting on page 392.

---

7. Note that this is independent of the DNS domain name discussed in Chapter 16.

```
ifconfig -a netmask 255.255.255.0 broadcast 131.106.1.255
```

This line sets the subnet mask of all the machine's interfaces. This line is in **rc.local** because the netmask and broadcast address depend on your network address. See Chapter 14 for a description of IP addressing.

```
if [ ! -f /sbin/route -a -f /etc/defaultrouter ]; then
    route -f add default `cat /etc/defaultrouter` 1
fi
```

The default route (already defined in **rc.boot**) is reset. This is done because the hostname specified in **/etc/defaultrouter** may not have been in the local **/etc/hosts** file; it may only now be resolvable via NIS. We suggest that you specify the default gateway by address rather than by hostname; this sidesteps the name resolution problem.

```
echo "network interface configuration:"
ifconfig -a
```

These lines list the current configuration of all network interfaces to the console, allowing an operator to verify that everything is OK.

```
defroute="`netstat -n -r | grep default`"
if [ -z "$defroute" ]; then
    if [ -f /usr/etc/in.routed ]; then
        in.routed;  echo 'running routing daemon.'
    fi
fi
```

These commands start up a routing daemon if there is no default route. The system administrator might choose to always start the routing daemon, or to start a different routing daemon (such as **gated**) here. See *Routing*, starting on page 252, for a complete discussion of IP routing.

```
intr -a mount -vat nfs
```

Here, all NFS filesystems listed in **/etc/fstab** are mounted. See Chapter 17, *The Network File System*, for a complete description of file sharing facilities under UNIX.

```
if [ -f /usr/etc/in.named -a -f /etc/named.boot ]; then
    in.named;  echo -n ' named'
fi
```

named is the server for the Domain Name System, which maps between hostnames and Internet addresses. Chapter 16 describes the DNS system in detail.

```
if [ -f /usr/etc/biod ]; then
    biod 4;  echo -n ' biod'
fi
```

biod is a client-side NFS daemon. Here, it is asked to fork four copies of itself. See page 373 for more information.

```
# Put kernel description string in message of the day
rm -f /tmp/t1
dmesg | grep SunOS | tail -1 |
    sed -e "s/^.*SunOS/SunOS/" >/tmp/t1
tail +2 /etc/motd >>/tmp/t1
mv /tmp/t1 /etc/motd
chmod 666 /etc/motd
```

These commands replace the first line of the **/etc/motd** file (which is shown to users as they log in) with a description of the current kernel. This example shows that the default **rc** files are not always perfect. On this system, any user could sneak a nasty message into the **motd**.

```
if [ -f /usr/etc/syslogd ]; then
    echo 'starting system logger'
    rm -f /dev/log
    syslogd
fi
```

These lines start **syslogd**, which is responsible for managing the log messages produced by other pieces of software. Most of Chapter 12 deals with issues related to **syslogd**.

```
mkdir -p /var/crash/`hostname`
echo -n 'checking for crash dump... '
intr savecore /var/crash/`hostname`
echo ''
```

These lines save a kernel core dump in **/var/crash/**hostname, if necessary. When the kernel crashes, it saves an image of its current state on a swap partition. The **savecore** command copies this image from the swap partition back to a real filesystem where it can be examined later with a debugger.

```
if [ -f /usr/lib/sendmail -a -f /etc/sendmail.cf ]; then
    (cd /var/spool/mqueue; rm -f nf* lf*)
    /usr/lib/sendmail -bd -q1h; echo -n ' sendmail'
fi
```

These lines clean up temporary mail lock files and start **sendmail**, the daemon responsible for delivering mail. See Chapter 21 for more information about electronic mail.

```
if [ -f /etc/exports ]; then
    > /etc/xtab
    exportfs -a
    nfsd 8 &   echo -n ' nfsd'
fi
```

These lines make the machine an NFS server if there are filesystems to be exported. See Chapter 17 for a description of NFS.

```
# Diskless client support
if [ -d /tftpboot ]; then
    rarpd -a;          echo -n ' rarpd'
    rpc.bootparamd;    echo -n ' bootparamd'
fi
```

These lines start up some server daemons needed to support diskless clients. Chapter 31, *Daemons*, gives an expanded description of them.

```
# NFS locking daemons
if [ -f /usr/etc/rpc.statd ]; then
    rpc.statd &   echo -n ' statd'
fi
if [ -f /usr/etc/rpc.lockd ]; then
    rpc.lockd &   echo -n ' lockd'
fi
```

rpc.statd and **rpc.lockd** manage advisory locks on NFS filesystems. See page 713 for more information.

```
if [ -f /usr/etc/automount ]; then
    automount &&  echo -n ' automount'
fi
```

These lines start Sun's **automount** daemon, which is supposed to automatically mount remote filesystems when they are needed. See page 377 for a description of **automount**, and see page 379 for a description of its vastly superior replacement, **amd**.

```
# Start license manager
if [ -f /usr/openwin/lib/builderXcessory/bin/lmgrd ]; then
    echo "Starting Highland Flexible License Manager..."
    /usr/openwin/lib/builderXcessory/bin/lmgrd -c
        /usr/local/flexlm/licenses/license.dat 2>&1 >
        /usr/local/flexlm/licenses/flexlm.log &
fi

# Start Xinet AppleTalk Stack
if [ -f /usr/etc/appletalk/atinit ] ; then          #K-Talk
    /usr/etc/appletalk/atinit START >/dev/console    #K-Talk
fi
```

At the end of the file, we find some actual localizations. The first starts a license manager for a Motif tool kit. On a machine with lots of add-on software, it is not unusual to find several different license managers running to make sure you are being a good citizen and not stealing software. Then, an AppleTalk protocol stack is started.

It is normal for third-party vendors' installation scripts to tack additional lines onto the end of **rc.local**. When you upgrade the OS, be sure to reintegrate any local commands that are overwritten.

2.4 A STROLL THROUGH THE ATT STARTUP SCRIPTS

The startup process on ATT systems is considerably different from that of BSD. We will use IRIX 5.2 as an example of a modern ATT-style system. Old ATT systems (based on V3) used a very different startup process, but since these systems are not in common use, we will not describe them.

Run Levels and the inittab File

The `init` daemon on ATT systems supports various "run levels" that enable different sets of system resources. The startup scripts are broken into small, manageable pieces that are invoked as `init` moves among run levels.

The exact definition of each run level is governed by `/etc/inittab`. If the `inittab` file does not exist or is corrupted, only single-user operation is possible. The format of a line in the `inittab` file is

> *id*:*rstate*:*action*:*process*

The *id* field is the name of the `inittab` entry. The *rstate* field specifies which level or levels the entry should apply to. The *process* (an **sh** command line) will be started when `init` switches to one of the run levels specified in *rstate* and sent a hangup signal when it moves to any run level that is not listed.

action tells whether `init` should wait for the process to finish (wait), should run the process only once (once), should restart the process whenever it dies (respawn), or should ignore the entry (off). There are several special action categories. The most important is sysinit, which identifies actions needed to bring the system to a state where `init` can query the operator for information.[8]

`inittab` not only controls how the startup scripts are run, but also contains a list of **getty** processes to be run on terminals. On BSD systems, this list is kept in its own file. The use of `inittab` for terminal configuration is discussed in Chapter 8, *Serial Devices*.

While `inittab` allows you to change the meaning of all the run levels, this is not normally done in practice; it confuses other users and the system software. In general, you should accept the meaning of the run levels as distributed with your OS. However, you can add or remove commands at appropriate run levels as you see fit. Here are some example snippets from an `inittab` file:

```
fs::sysinit:/etc/bcheckrc </dev/console >/dev/console 2>&1
mt::sysinit:/etc/brc </dev/console >/dev/console 2>&1
...
```

8. There are actually some more legal values for the *action* field on most systems. See page 121 for more information about the `inittab` file.

```
s0:06s:wait:/etc/rc0 >/dev/console 2>&1 </dev/console
s1:1:wait:/etc/shutdown -y -iS -g0 >/dev/console 2>&1
   </dev/console
s2:23:wait:/etc/rc2 >/dev/console 2>&1 </dev/console
s3:3:wait:/etc/rc3 >/dev/console 2>&1 </dev/console
...
```

The line beginning with s1 has been folded to fit on the page; entries in the **inittab** file should normally be on one line.

The first two lines identify scripts that are run before **init** tries to enter any run level (this is specified with the sysinit action). The next four lines are some of those used to control the definitions of the run levels. Note that all of the scripts' I/O must be redirected to the console if the operator is to see the output and respond to any queries.

The line that begins with s0 specifies that **/etc/rc0** should run when **init** enters run levels zero, six, or s.[9] **init** will wait for this script to finish before continuing. The line that starts with s1 tells **init** to run **shutdown** with a particular set of arguments when entering level one; on this system, level one means to shut down and then come back up again in single-user mode.

Full multi-user mode with networking is run level three. According to the configuration shown here, **init** will run the **/etc/bcheckrc** and **/etc/brc** scripts at boot time, and will run **/etc/rc2** and **/etc/rc3** as the system goes multi-user. We will take a look at these scripts (and the other scripts they call), and then describe **/etc/rc0**, which is a shutdown script.

A Sample /etc/bcheckrc

On our example system, **bcheckrc** is the first script to be executed. The names of the startup scripts vary between systems, so look in your **inittab** file to see what will actually be executed first. In this example, **bcheckrc** is responsible for setting up the root filesystem to allow single-user operation.

```
# Make symlink "/usr/bin -> ../../sbin".  Must be done
# *before* /usr is mounted, so programs executed as
# /bin/* will work in single user mode.  Do not use the
# same algorithm as libc.so.1 since /usr/bin may be a
# real directory if root and usr are merged.

/sbin/ls /usr/bin > /dev/null 2>&1
if [ $? != 0 ]; then
    /sbin/ln -s ../sbin /usr/bin <&- > /dev/null 2>&1
fi
```

9. S and s are interchangeable names for the single-user run level.

These first lines set up the system so it can run without a **/usr** partition. Essential commands are kept in **/usr/sbin** and are compiled without shared libraries so that they will work correctly even when **/usr** isn't available.

```
# Make devices if we are diskless
if [ "`/sbin/nvram diskless 2> /dev/null`" -eq 1 ] ; then
    if [ -f /var/boot/makedev ] ; then
    echo "Making client's devices..."
    cd /dev; ./MAKEDEV > /dev/null
    rm -f /var/boot/makedev
    fi
else
```

If the system is diskless, devices entries are made. Otherwise, the root filesystem needs to be checked:

```
set `/sbin/devnm /`
rootfs=$1
/sbin/fsstat ${rootfs}  >/dev/null 2>&1

if [ $? -eq 1 ] ; then
    echo "The root, ${rootfs}, is being checked."
    /sbin/fsck -y ${rootfs}
fi

set `ls -Lid /dev/root $rootfs`
if [ ! -b /dev/root -o "$1" -ne "$3" -o ! -c
  /dev/rroot ] ; then
    rm -rf /dev/root
    ln $rootfs /dev/root
    rm -rf /dev/rroot
    ln /dev/rdsk/`basename $rootfs` /dev/rroot
fi

if [ -f /etc/lvtab ] ; then
    if /sbin/chkconfig verbose
    then
        echo "Starting LV:"
    fi
    /sbin/lvinit
fi
fi
```

This system makes links called **/dev/root** and **/dev/rroot** for the root filesystems. It uses a program called **chkconfig** to see if the system is configured for verbose output, and if so, it prints out more information about what it is doing.

lvinit initializes the logical volume system, which allows you to spread filesystems across multiple disks.

```
# Make symlink /usr/lib/libc.so.1 -> ../../lib/libc.so.1
# Must be done *before* /usr is mounted, so dynamic linked
# programs can be run in single user mode.
if [ ! -s /usr/lib/libc.so.1 ]
then
    mkdir -p /usr/lib > /dev/null 2>&1
    rm -rf /usr/lib/libc.so.1 > /dev/null 2>&1
    ln -s ../../lib/libc.so.1 /usr/lib/libc.so.1 <&- >
        /dev/null 2>&1
fi
```

These commands set up shared libraries. Most modern UNIX systems use shared libraries to reduce the size of executable programs. Unfortunately, when there is problem with the libraries themselves (especially with the shared version of **libc**), it causes most programs to break. Typically, a group of "essential" commands are linked statically (without shared libraries) so that you can bring the system up and attempt to fix the problem. Each vendor seems to have a different idea of which commands are essential.

A Sample /etc/brc

On this system, the **brc** script tries to check and mount the rest of the local filesystems (the root filesystem is handled in **bcheckrc**).

```
#!/sbin/sh

# This script is responsible for initializing the mounted
# filesystem table kept in /etc/mtab. It also creates
# /etc/fstab if it does not exist.

if [ "`/sbin/nvram diskless 2> /dev/null`" -eq 1 ] ; then
    > /etc/mtab
    /sbin/mount -f /
    if [ -d /sbin ]; then
        /sbin/mount -f /sbin
    fi
    if [ -d /swap ]; then
        /sbin/mount -f /swap
    fi
else
    rootdev=/dev/root
    usrdev=/dev/usr
    if [ ! -f /etc/fstab ] ; then
        /sbin/fsstat /dev/usr  >/dev/null 2>&1
        if [ $? -eq 3 ] ; then
            echo "$rootdev /" | setmnt -f /etc/fstab
        else
            echo "$rootdev /\n$usrdev /usr" | setmnt -f \
                /etc/fstab
```

```
            fi
       fi
       if [ ! -f /etc/mtab ] ; then rm -f /etc/mtab; fi
       echo "$rootdev /" | setmnt
  fi
```

This set of commands mounts the filesystems on a diskless system. On a diskful system, it cleans out the **mtab** file (which contains a list of mounted filesystems) and then uses the **setmnt** command to fake an entry for the root filesystem. The root filesystem must be treated as a special case since that is the filesystem where the **mtab** file lives.

```
if test -n "`grep '[    ]/var[/]*[   ]' /etc/fstab`"; then
     if /sbin/mount -c /var > /etc/fscklogs/rvar 2>&1
     then
          cat /etc/fscklogs/rvar
     else
          cat /etc/fscklogs/rvar
          echo "Unable to Mount /var\n"
          sleep 5
     fi
else
```

*See page 146 for more information about **fsck**.*

If **/var** is a separate filesystem, it is mounted early in the boot procedure because it probably contains the system's log files. The **-c** option to **mount** tells it to **fsck** the filesystem before mounting, if it is believed to be "dirty." Log files are kept in **/etc** for now, because only the root filesystem has been mounted.

```
if test -n "`grep '[    ]/usr[/]*[   ]' /etc/fstab`"; then
     deflvl="`/sbin/nvram initstate 2>/dev/null`"
     if [ "$deflvl" = "s" -o "$deflvl" = "1" ]; then
          if /sbin/mount /usr
          then :
          else
               echo "Unable to Mount /usr\n"
               sleep 5
          fi
     else
          if /sbin/mount -c /usr  > /etc/fscklogs/rusr 2>&1
          then
               cat /etc/fscklogs/rusr
          else
               cat /etc/fscklogs/rusr
               echo "Unable to Mount /usr\n"
               sleep 5
          fi
     fi
fi
```

Next, **/usr** is mounted. If the system is coming up single-user, **fsck** is not run. On this particular system, a program called **nvram** is used to check the non-volatile RAM for a default run level. The way that this information is stored is completely system-dependent.

```
if [ ! -d /var/adm ]
then
    if [ -l /var ]
    then
        mkdir /usr/var > /dev/null 2>&1
    fi
    mkdir /var/adm
fi
```

The system expects to place log files in **/var/adm**. If that directory does not exist by now, it must be created.

```
/etc/mntproc
```

This command mounts the **/proc** filesystem, a fake filesystem that contains images of running processes. It's used for debugging, and is called **/debug** on some systems.

```
if [ ! -d /dev/fd ]; then
    /bin/rm -rf /dev/fd  > /dev/null 2>&1
    mkdir /dev/fd
fi
/sbin/mount -t fd /dev/fd /dev/fd
```

This code makes device entries for file descriptors, another debugging tool. This is the end of the script; the system is now ready to enter single-user mode (if the system is being booted manually).

Task-Specific Scripts

Thus far, the ATT-style startup scripts have differed only slightly from their BSD counterparts; both versions contain vendor-specific commands executed from a few monolithic scripts. But once we get to **/etc/rc2**, we can start to see the hygienic advantages of the ATT system.

```
# Pick up packages for mounts, daemons, services, etc.
set `who -r`
if [ $9 = "S" ]
then
    # Coming from single-user
    BOOT=yes
    if [ -f /etc/rc.d/PRESERVE ] # historical  for vi/ex
    then
        mv /etc/rc.d/PRESERVE /etc/init.d
        ln /etc/init.d/PRESERVE /etc/rc2.d/S02PRESERVE
    fi
```

The system uses **who** with the **-r** option to determine from which state the system is arriving. If the system is coming up from single-user mode, the script does some incantations to preserve **vi** and **ex** buffers. Then the real work begins:

```
elif [ $7 = "2" ]
then
        # Coming from some other state (ie: not single user)
        # Shut down any services available in the other state.
        echo 'Changing to state 2.'
        if [ -d /etc/rc2.d ]
        then
            for f in /etc/rc2.d/K*
            {
                if [ -s ${f} ]
                then
                    /sbin/sh ${f} stop
                fi
            }
        fi
    fi
```

The directory **/etc/rc*N*.d** contains all the scripts associated with run level *N*. In reality, the scripts are symbolic links that point back to files in **/etc/init.d**. These scripts are expected to take one argument, either **start** or **stop**. When called with **start**, the scripts should start the service in question, and when called with **stop**, they should kill it. This setup makes it easy for a piece of software to be configured to start and stop at specific points in the boot or shutdown sequence. This particular script deals with the transition to run level two, so the script looks in **/etc/rc2.d**.

In the example above, each script in **/etc/rc2.d** that starts with a **K** is called with the argument **stop**. Kill links are named **K***N*command where *N* is a number and *command* is, by convention, the name of the original script in **/etc/init.d**. Scripts are run in alphanumeric order.

After running killing scripts, **rc2** runs the startup scripts for the level:

```
# Run package init scripts (mounts, daemons, etc.)
if [ -d /etc/rc2.d ]
then
    for f in /etc/rc2.d/S*
    {
        if [ -s ${f} ]
        then
            /sbin/sh ${f} start
        fi
    }
fi
```

The startup scripts are named *SNcommand*, much like the kill scripts. The scripts are run in order of *N*. Lets take a look at one of the scripts, **/etc/rc2.d/S60lp** (which is a symbolic link to **/etc/init.d/lp**):

```
case "$1" in
    'start')
    if test -x /usr/lib/lpshut -a -x /usr/lib/lpsched; then
        /usr/lib/lpshut > /dev/null 2>&1
        rm -f /var/spool/lp/SCHEDLOCK /var/spool/lp/FIFO
        /usr/lib/lpsched
    fi
    ;;
    'stop')
    if test -x /usr/lib/lpshut; then
        /usr/lib/lpshut > /dev/null 2>&1
    fi
    ;;
    *)
    echo "usage: $0 {start|stop}"
    ;;
esac
```

See Chapter 25 for more information about **lp**.

This script is responsible for controlling the **lp** printing system. Since at run level two the service is being started, the script turns off the **lpsched** daemon (the print scheduler) with **lpshut**, removes lock files, and then starts the scheduler again.

We have now seen the meat of an **rc** script on an ATT system. The structure of all scripts in **init.d** will be similar, with a `case` statement and a few different commands that get run depending on whether the argument is **start** or **stop**.

The nice thing about this whole arrangement is that it lends itself to an orderly shutdown process. The **/etc/rc0** script is essentially the same as **rc3** and **rc2**; however, its function is quite different. **/etc/rc0.d** contains only killing scripts (with filenames beginning with **K**), so **rc0** acts as a shutdown procedure. For example, the **rc0.d** directory would contain a link to the **/etc/init.d/lp** script we examined above, but this link would be called **/etc/rc0.d/K25lp** and it would be called with the argument **stop**.

Rather than tediously parsing through the other scripts in **init.d**, we will just list their names and a brief description of what each script does (when called with **start**) in Table 2.1. The exact population of scripts will vary between systems, but this table should give you the general flavor of the ATT startup procedure. If more information about a topic is available in this book, the "Info" column tells which chapter to refer to. Some rows have been shaded to improve readability.

Table 2.1   Some typical startup scripts from /etc/init.d

Script	Function	Info
acct	Starts accounting	28
announce	Displays startup and shutdown announcements	2
audio	Enables audio functionality	–
autoconfig	Rebuilds the kernel to match current configuration	13
bsdlpr	Starts the BSD-style line printer daemons	25
chkdev	Checks for the existence of devices on the system	7
configmsg	Notifies operator if config files need to be checked	–
cron	Starts the cron daemon	10
filesystems	Runs fsck and mounts filesystems	9
fontserver	Starts the X Windows font server	–
lp	Starts the ATT-style line printer daemons	25
mail	Starts the sendmail daemon	21
netls	Starts a network licensing daemon	–
network	Configures network interfaces	14
quotas	Starts quotas and runs quotacheck	26
rmtmpfiles	Cleans out files from /tmp	2
savecore	Saves a copy of a kernel core dump from swap space	13
swap	Starts swapping on filesystems listed in /etc/fstab	9
sysetup	Starts the system logging daemon (syslogd)	12
usr	Mounts the /usr filesystem	9
uucp	Enables the UUCP system	30
xdm	Starts the X Windows display manager	–

2.5 SPECIFICS FOR VARIOUS OPERATING SYSTEMS

The tables below list each system's main startup scripts and, where appropriate, the configuration files they use.

 Solaris's organization is of the ATT variety. Table 2.2 shows the main boot scripts. The "Files" column lists the configuration files (and supplemental scripts) that each script consults.

Table 2.2   Major boot scripts in Solaris

Script	Purpose	Files
/sbin/autopush	Loads STREAMS modules	/etc/iu.ap
/sbin/rcS	Single-user startup	/etc/rcS.d/*
/sbin/rc2	Multi-user startup	/etc/rc2.d/*
/sbin/rc3	Exports network resources	/etc/rc3.d/*
/sbin/rc0	Brings the system down	/etc/rc0.d/*

Some other important files used at boot time are shown in Table 2.3 (on the next page).

Table 2.3   Boot-time configuration files in Solaris

File	Purpose
`/etc/defaultrouter`	Contains the address of the default IP gateway
`/etc/defaultdomain`	Contains the machine's NIS domain name
`/etc/nodename`	Contains the machine's primary hostname
`/etc/hostname.`*XXX*	Contains the hostname for interface *XXX*

 HP-UX uses an old version of the ATT startup system. The system does have `inittab` and multiple levels of `init`. However, the actual startup scripts are in `/etc` rather than in `/etc/init.d`. Many files in `/etc` that contain the string `rc` in their names are startup scripts. There are a lot of them, and there is no consistent naming scheme.

Most configuration changes are made by editing the actual startup scripts. Services spawned from startup scripts may be sent a hangup signal (HUP) sometime soon after they are started; this is a recurring bug in the operating system. There is a provision for putting shutdown scripts in `/etc/shutdown.d`, but it does not appear to be used.

Almost every release of HP-UX uses a slightly different startup sequence, and some releases have two completely independent startup tracks, one using `csh` and one using `ksh`. Table 2.4 lists the files for an HP 9000/700 running HP-UX 9.03.

Table 2.4   HP-UX startup scripts

Script	Purpose
`/etc/bcheckrc`	Checks and mounts local filesystems
`/etc/recoversl`	Cleans up shared libraries
`/etc/brc`	Configures the console
`/etc/rc`	The main `rc` script, calls many other scripts
`/etc/netlinkrc`	Sets up networking
`/etc/netnfsrc`	Sets up NFS and NIS
`/etc/netbsdrc`	Sets up BSD services (`named`, `gated`, `sendmail`, etc.)
`/etc/vuerc`	Starts the Visual User Environment (X plus Motif)

The file `/etc/src.sh` contains the system name and timezone.

IRIX is organized in the ATT-ish manner. We used IRIX 5.2 as the ATT example in this chapter; see the commented scripts starting on page 31 for a complete exposition.

Optional services can be enabled or disabled by creating files in the `/etc/config` directory. The `chkconfig` command shows the state of these files and lets you turn services on and off. Some files that play an important role in the startup procedure are shown in Table 2.5.

Table 2.5   Boot-time configuration files in IRIX

File	Contents
`/etc/sys_id`	The system's hostname
`/etc/config/netif.options`	Addresses of network interfaces
`/etc/config/ifconfig`*XXX*`-options`	`ifconfig` opts for interface *XXX*
`/var/yp/ypdomain`	The system's NIS domain name

 SunOS uses the BSD-style `rc` scripts (as detailed in this chapter, starting on page 17). The scripts are named `rc.boot`, `rc.single`, `rc`, and `rc.local`. The important configuration files are shown in Table 2.6.

Table 2.6   Boot-time configuration files in SunOS

File	Purpose
`/etc/hostname.`*XXX*	Sets the IP address for interface *XXX*
`/etc/defaultrouter`	Sets the IP address of the default IP gateway
`/etc/defaultdomain`	Sets the NIS domain name

OSF OSF/1's organization is of the ATT variety, except that the `rc` directories are in `/sbin` instead of `/etc`. The most important scripts are listed in Table 2.7. Config files and sub-scripts are shown in the Files column.

Table 2.7   Major boot scripts in OSF/1

Script	Purpose	Files
`/sbin/bcheckrc`	Mounts local filesystems	`/etc/fstab`
`/sbin/it`	Basic system configuration	`/sbin/it.d/`*runlev*
`/sbin/rc2`	Multi-user operation	`/sbin/rc2.d/*`
`/sbin/kmknod`	`mknod`s for kernel devices	`conf/.product.list`[a]
`/sbin/rc3`	Starts network file sharing	`/sbin/rc3.d/*`

a. In `/usr/sys`.

All of the options and variables are set in the `/etc/rc.config` and `/etc/rc.config.site` files. `rc.config.site` is for site-wide information (subnet mask, etc) while `rc.config` can be customized for each host. These files are normally read and written with the `rcmg` command. They are just text files and can be edited by hand if you are careful. After making manual changes, check that `rcmg` can still read the entries you modified.

 BSDI uses BSD-style `rc` scripts (surprise!) with names `rc`, `netstart`, and `rc.local`, all in the `/etc` directory. Configuration changes are made by editing the scripts directly.

2.6 WHAT IF THE SYSTEM WON'T BOOT?

Some problems that can keep a UNIX system from booting are:

- Hardware problems
- Defective boot blocks
- Damaged filesystems
- An improperly configured kernel
- Errors in the startup scripts

These pathologies are discussed in the following sections.

Hardware Problems

Before you call a technician or dig out your own tool kit, be sure that the problem is really hardware-related. If when booting you consistently receive a message complaining about a memory defect or some other specific ailment, it is a good bet that the problem is with the hardware. But if the machine simply does nothing or hangs up halfway through the boot sequence, there are a couple of things to try before calling the hardware squad.

- Check the power supply to each piece of equipment. This may seem too obvious to mention, but it is surprising how often this step is overlooked, even by folks who should know better.

- Look for any kind of problem that could impair communication between components of the system. Check cables to be sure they are firmly connected. Some old disk drives have a switch that takes them on and off-line, just like a printer. Don't forget to check Ethernet connections, especially on machines that boot from the network rather than a disk drive.

- Check the fault lights on each piece of equipment that has them. Some computers (Suns, for example) have several lights that can identify problems with a high degree of specificity.

- Try turning everything off. Wait ten seconds or so, then restore power and try to bootstrap the system again. This superstitious little ritual is effective in many cases (it resets all hardware to a known state).

- If the boot procedure gets as far as the kernel's initial probing of devices before encountering problems, make sure each device appears in the kernel's diagnostic printouts. If the kernel doesn't see a device that it should be seeing, the device is broken or it's not connected properly.

- Most systems come with a set of stand-alone diagnostic utilities. The diagnostics are often built into the bare hardware so that they are available even when UNIX can't be booted. Depth of coverage varies from machine to machine, but most diagnostics include at least memory, CPU, and bus tests. Consult your manuals. If the built-in diagnostics won't run at all, it is a pretty good indication that you have a hardware problem.

The best defense against hardware problems is to take good care of your hardware in the first place. Chapter 27, *Hardware Maintenance*, describes the options available to you.

Defective Boot Blocks

Usually, there is some intelligence built into a machine's PROM monitor about how to boot the system. On some workstations, the firmware knows enough about UNIX to read a filesystem and find the kernel. On other systems (especially systems that run more than one operating system), the firmware will load a small boot program which is in turn responsible for loading the kernel. If the boot program is damaged, the system may not boot, even though your disk and operating system might themselves be intact.

Try to boot from your distribution media (floppy disk, tape, or CD-ROM) and ask for a shell rather than performing the software installation. If you can mount your filesystems from this state, you might just need to reinstall the boot blocks. If that isn't possible, try to use the distribution media to boot through to your own root partition. Once you are up and running, you can reinstall the boot blocks in the usual way. See the vendor-specific sections in Chapter 9, *Adding a Disk*, for help with installing boot blocks.

Damaged Filesystems

A damaged disk is one of the scariest types of failure, since it is possible that the system's files (or even, in rare cases, a disk drive itself) may be damaged beyond recovery. The symptoms vary depending on whether the damage is soft (e.g. scrambled information on the disk) or hard (e.g. a head crash), and on which partitions are affected. If you believe that your disks have problems, you should read and understand the material in Chapter 9 before taking any action.

See Chapter 11 for more information about backups.

If the root partition cannot be read, it will not be possible to load the kernel, and the system may behave as if a hardware problem were at fault. Unless you have had the foresight to prepare an alternative root partition (preferably on a different disk drive), this kind of situation can be almost hopeless. In the worst-case scenario, you will have to go back to the original CD-ROM and reinitialize the entire system to its distributed state. If you have recent backups, the loss of data from this operation will be minimized.

If your system allows you to boot from the distribution media, you may be able to boot from that, mount and dump your other filesystems, and then reload the operating system. If you have user files on auxiliary disks, disconnect them from the system while you fix the original problem to minimize the risk of causing additional damage.

See Chapter 10 for more information about cron.

If your system has a backup root partition, you must occasionally duplicate the master root onto the slave root to keep the two partitions synchronized. This can be done most easily by running a script out of **cron**. Usually, the **dump** and **restore** commands are used to copy the root partition's contents. You must also make whatever other preparations are necessary to allow you to boot off the alternate partition. All systems allow you to use an alternate root, but you may need to prepare a special boot disk or use a magic incantation from the PROM monitor to do so. It's a good idea to test the alternate root before you need it.

In less severe instances of root partition damage, the boot procedure may proceed part way but crash before the **fsck** checks are reached. Pay close attention to the message printed by the kernel as it panics, as it can be a clear indicator of the source of the problem. Any kind of message about inodes, superblocks, maps, or filesystems probably indicates a disk problem. Here are a few representative messages:

```
clrblock         namei:null cache ino      getfs:bad magic
bread:size 0     namei:duplicating cache   ialloc:dup alloc
free:bad size    free:freeing free block   free inode isn't
mkdir:dquot      ifree:freeing free inode
```

If you suspect filesystem corruption, try to boot into single-user mode. If this is impossible, the system has real problems. You may be able to boot from your distribution media and **fsck** the root partition. If essential files are lost, you can restore them from the distribution.

See page 146 for more information about fsck.

If the system does come up single-user, use the **fsck** command before doing anything else. This will fix many problems and will inform you about others even if they cannot be automatically fixed. **fsck** the root partition first, and if any problems are uncovered, reboot and repeat the process until the root comes up clean. Then use **fsck** to check the remaining filesystems. If at any point an unfixable error becomes evident, stop messing around and find someone that knows what they are doing to help you. Repeat the **fsck** until you do not get any errors.

Improperly Configured Kernels

Chapter 13 describes the process of building a new kernel. Every time you rebuild and replace your kernel, you run the risk that it won't work and that you'll be left in a difficult situation. Be sure to make arrangements for booting an old kernel in case of problems. It's a good idea to keep an old kernel around even during day-to-day operation.

Errors in Startup Scripts

Script errors are the most common impediment to successful booting, and they are also the easiest to fix. You need to identify the problem and fix it as you would when debugging any other shell script, but from single-user mode.

Often, the only editor available in single-user mode is **ed**, but you can mount the **/usr** partition by hand to get to **vi**. You will need to adjust your terminal type and environment by hand before screen editors will work properly. Remember to either modify your search path or to refer to programs in **/usr** by their full pathnames.

Commands in startup scripts may fail if run more than once, so you should reboot from scratch after each change rather than trying to repeatedly run the script from the single-user shell. Unless you present the script with the environment it expects, it may fail for odd reasons, thus masking the original problem and tricking you into "fixing" sections of the code that are actually OK.

2.7 REBOOTING AND SHUTTING DOWN

On a PC, rebooting the operating system is an appropriate first course of treatment for almost any problem. On a UNIX system, it's better to think first and reboot second. UNIX problems tend to be subtler and more complex, so blindly rebooting is effective in a smaller percentage of cases. UNIX systems also take a long time to boot, and multiple users may be inconvenienced.

You must reboot when you add a new piece of hardware, or when existing hardware becomes so confused that it cannot be reset. If you modify a configuration file that's used only at boot time, you must reboot to make your changes take effect. And obviously, if the system is so wedged that you cannot log in to make a proper diagnosis of the problem, you have no alternative but to reboot.

Unlike bootstrapping, which can be done in essentially only one way, there are a number of ways to shut down or reboot. They are:

- Turning off the power
- Using the **shutdown** command
- Using the **halt** and **reboot** commands (BSD)
- Sending **init** a TERM signal
- Using **telinit** to change **init**'s run level (ATT)
- Killing **init**

Turning Off the Power

Even on a small-scale UNIX system, this is not an acceptable way to shut down. Not only will you potentially lose data and leave the system's files in an inconsistent state, but you may also damage certain kinds of disk drives that expect to have a protect switch activated or to have their heads parked before being powered off.

However, in the event of a flood or fire, it is probably advisable to turn off the power if you can't afford the time to bring machines down gracefully. Old-style machine rooms often have a panic button that turns everything off at once.

shutdown: The Genteel Way to Halt the System

shutdown is the safest, most considerate, and most thorough way to initiate a halt or reboot, or to return to single-user mode. Unfortunately, almost every vendor has decided to tamper with its arguments. We will discuss the command in general, then provide a table listing the syntax and arguments you will need on each platform.

You can ask shutdown to wait a while before bringing down the system. During the waiting period, shutdown sends messages (a la wall) to logged-in users at progressively shorter intervals, warning them of the impending down time. By default, the warnings simply say that the system is being shut down and give the time remaining until the event; you can also supply a short message of your own. Your message should tell why the system is being brought down and should estimate how long it will be before users can log in again. On most systems, users cannot log in when a shutdown is imminent.

Most versions of shutdown let you specify if the machine should halt, go to single-user mode, or reboot. Sometimes, you can also specify if you want to fsck the disks after a reboot. On modern systems with large disks, a complete fsck can take a long time; you can generally skip the checks if you shut the system down cleanly. At the appropriate time, shutdown carefully brings the system down to the requested state.

Table 2.8 outlines shutdown's command-line arguments on our six example systems. Dashes indicate the default behaviors.

Table 2.8   The many faces of shutdown

System	Pathname	Time	R[a]	H	S	No fsck
Solaris	/usr/sbin/shutdown	-g*secs*	-i6	-i0	-iS	–
HP-UX	/etc/shutdown	*secs*	-r	-h	–	–
IRIX	/etc/shutdown	-g*secs*	-i6	-i0	-iS	–
SunOS	/usr/etc/shutdown	+*mins*	-r	-h	–	-f
OSF	/usr/sbin/shutdown	+*mins*	-r	-h	–	-f
BSDI	/sbin/shutdown	+*mins*	-r	-h	–	-f

a. R = Reboot, H = Halt, S = Enter single-user mode.

halt: A Simpler Way to Shut Down

The `halt` command performs the essential duties required to bring the system down. It is called by `shutdown -h`, but can also be used by itself. `halt` logs the shutdown, kills non-essential processes, executes the `sync` system call (called by and equivalent to the `sync` command), waits for filesystem writes to complete, and then halts the kernel.

`halt -n` prevents the `sync` call; it's used after repairing the root partition with `fsck` to prevent the kernel from overwriting repairs with old versions of the superblock. `halt -q` instigates an almost immediate halt, without synchronization, killing of processes, or writing of logs. This flag is rarely appropriate.

reboot: Quick and Dirty Restart

`reboot` is almost identical to halt, but it causes the machine to reboot from scratch rather than halting. `reboot` is called by `shutdown -r`. Like `halt`, it supports the `-n` and `-q` flags.

In addition to `halt` and `reboot`, some BSD systems provide commands called `fasthalt` and `fastboot`. These commands create a file called `/fastboot` before executing `halt` or `reboot`, respectively. The existence of this file tells the startup scripts to skip `fsck` checks, making the restart much quicker.

Sending init a TERM Signal

The results of killing `init` are unpredictable and often nasty. Consult your documentation before sending any signals. When the BSD version of `init` receives a TERM signal, it usually kills all user processes, daemons, and `gettys` and returns the system to single-user mode. This facility is used by `shutdown`.

See page 76 for more information about `kill`.

To send a signal to a process, you normally need to discover its process ID number using `ps`; however, `init` is always process number one. To send a signal, the `kill` command is used:

```
# sync
# kill -TERM 1
```

More information about signals is given in Chapter 5.

telinit: Change init's Run Level

On systems with the beefy multi-level `init`, you can use the `telinit` command to direct `init` to go to a specific run level. For example,

```
telinit S
```

takes the system to single-user mode. You do not get the nice warning messages or grace period that you get with `shutdown`. The command

```
shutdown -iS
```

brings the system to the same state with more grace. `telinit` is most useful for testing changes to the `inittab` file. The `-q` option makes `init` reread `inittab`.

Killing init

`init` is so important to the operation of the system that if it is killed, most computers will reboot automatically (some kernels just panic). This is a rough way to reboot; use **shutdown** or **reboot** instead.

3 *Rootly Powers*

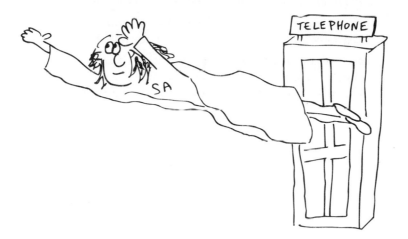

3.1 INTRODUCTION

As in any wholesome operating system (i.e., not MS-DOS or Macintosh), administrative control of a UNIX system is separated from general user access. The superuser is the UNIX demigod who can perform privileged tasks such as controlling processes and adding devices.

This chapter introduces the basics of superuser access. Chapter 23, *Security*, describes how to avoid unwanted superuser access by others.

3.2 THE UNIX MODEL OF OWNERSHIP

UNIX processes and files have an associated concept of ownership. The owner of a file or process has primary control over it. The owner's rights can only be overridden by the superuser.

Ownership of Files

chmod is used to modify the permissions of a file. See page 64.

Every UNIX file has both an owner and a group owner. The owner of the file enjoys only one privilege that is not shared with everyone on the system: the ability to modify the permissions of the file. In particular, the owner can set the permissions on a file so restrictively that no one else can access it.

See page 92 for more information about groups.

While the owner of a file is always a single person, many people may be group owners of the file, so long as they are all part of a single UNIX group. Groups are defined in the /etc/group file.

The owner and group of a file can be changed with chown *and* chgrp.

The owner of a file specifies which operations the group owners may perform on it. This scheme permits files to be shared among members of the same project. For example, we used a UNIX group to control access to the source files for the first edition of this book.

See page 65 for more about ls.

Both ownerships of a file can be determined with `ls -lg` *filename* under BSD and `ls -l` *filename* under ATT. For example, under BSD:

```
% ls -lg /staff/scott/ToDo
-rw------- 1 scott staff 1258 Jun 4 18:15 /staff/scott/ToDo
```

This file is owned by "scott" and has a group ownership of "staff." The ATT output is identical.

UNIX keeps track of owners and groups as numbers rather than as text names. User numbers (UIDs for short) are mapped to user names in the `/etc/passwd` file, and group numbers (GIDs) are mapped to group names in `/etc/group`.[1]

The text names that correspond to UIDs and GIDs are defined only for the convenience of the system's human users. When commands such as `ls` want to display ownership information in a human-readable format, they have to look up each name in the appropriate file.

Ownership of Processes

Process management is described in Chapter 5.

The kernel associates four numbers with each process: a real and effective UID, and a real and effective GID. The "real" numbers are used for accounting, and the "effective" numbers are used for the purpose of determining access permissions. Normally, the real and effective numbers are the same. The owner of a process can send the process *signals* and can also reduce the process's scheduling priority.

While it is not normally possible for a process to alter its four ownership credentials, there is a special situation in which its effective user and group IDs may be changed. A process that wishes to start executing a different program file calls one of the **exec** family of system calls. When this occurs, the effective UID and GID of the process may be set to the UID and GID of the file containing the new program image if the file has its "setuid" or "setgid" permission bits set. **exec** is the mechanism used by programs such as **/bin/passwd** to temporarily gain superuser privileges (**passwd** needs these privileges in order to modify **/etc/passwd**).

3.3 THE SUPERUSER

System administrators need to override UNIX's protection mechanisms in a variety of situations. To make this possible, UNIX treats one UID

---

1. Some systems no longer store this information in text files. See Chapter 18, *Sharing System Files*, for more information.

differently from all others: UID zero, the superuser. By convention, UNIX systems define a user account named "root" with this UID.[2]

UNIX allows the superuser to perform any valid operation on a file or process. In addition, some system calls (requests to the kernel) may be executed only by the superuser. A few system calls are available to all users, but have special options for root. Some examples of restricted operations are:

- Mounting and unmounting filesystems
- Changing the root directory of a process with `chroot`
- Creating device files
- Setting the system clock
- Changing ownership of files (on BSD systems)
- Raising resource usage limits and setting process priorities
- Setting the system's hostname
- Configuring network interfaces
- Shutting down the system

An example of superuser powers is the ability of a process owned by root to change its ownership credentials at will. The `login` program is a case in point; the process that prompts you for your password when you log in to the system initially runs as root. If the password and user name that you enter are legitimate, `login` changes its UIDs and GIDs to those of the specified user and executes the user's shell. Once a root process changes its ownerships to become a normal user process, it can't recover its former privileged state.

3.4 CHOOSING A ROOT PASSWORD

It is important that the root password be selected so as not to be easily guessed or discovered by trial and error. In theory, the most secure type of password consists of a random sequence of letters, punctuation, and digits. But because this type of password is hard to remember and usually difficult to type, it may not be optimally secure if the system administrator writes it down or types it slowly.

See Chapter 23, Security, for further information about password choice.

A password that consists of two randomly-selected words separated by a punctuation mark, or the first letters of a favorite phrase (in mixed case) is usually secure enough. Passwords of this form also comply with some systems' requirement that all passwords contain mixed case or at least one number or special character. The root password should be eight characters in length, as seven-character passwords are substantially less secure. It doesn't help to use a password longer than eight characters; only the first eight are significant.

2. The name is arbitrary and could just as well be "fred." Only the UID matters. Chapter 23, *Security*, explains why this feature opens the door to a number of security problems.

You should change the root password

- At least every three months or so
- Every time someone who knows the password leaves your site
- Whenever you think security may have been compromised
- On a day you're not planning to party so hard in the evening that you will have forgotten the password the next morning

3.5 BECOMING ROOT

There are several ways that you can access the superuser account. The simplest is to just log in as root. Unfortunately, logging out of your own account and logging in as root is often inconvenient. A better way is to use the **su** command. If invoked without any arguments, **su** will prompt you for the root password and then start up a root shell. The privileges of this shell remain in effect until the shell terminates.

The **su** command is also capable of substituting identities other than root. If you know someone's password, you can substitute directly to their account by executing **su** *username*. As with an **su** to root, you will be prompted for the password for *username*. On some systems, the root password will allow an **su** or **login** to any account; on others, you must first **su** explicitly to root before **su**ing to another account.

It's a good idea to get in the habit of typing **/bin/su** rather than just **su**. This will give you some protection against programs called **su** that may have been slipped into your search path with the intention of harvesting passwords.

On many systems, you must be a member of the group "wheel" in order to use the **su** command. Another common hedge on the use of **su** and the root account is to restrict their use to certain terminals. See page 119 for more details.

sudo: A Limited su

Superuser access has three problems: its power is all-encompassing, there is no record of the operations performed, and "root" may be a group login. Since the privileges of the superuser account cannot be subdivided, it is hard to give someone the ability to do backups (which must be done as root) without giving them free run of the system. And if root is a group account, you really have no idea who's using it or what they've done.

sudo is included on the CD-ROM.

Our solution to these problems is a program called **sudo**. **sudo** takes as its argument a command line to be executed as root. **sudo** consults the file **/etc/sudoers**, which is a list of people authorized to use **sudo** and the commands they are allowed to run on each host. If the proposed command is permitted, **sudo** prompts for the user's own password and executes the command as root.

Additional **sudo** commands may be executed without having to type a password until a five-minute period has elapsed with no further **sudo** activity. This password check serves as a modest protection against users with **sudo** privileges who leave terminals unattended.

An **/etc/sudoers** file looks like this:

```
# Define aliases for machines in CS & Physics departments
Host_Alias   CS=tigger,anchor,piper,moet,sigi
Host_Alias   PHYSICS=eprince,pprince,icarus
# Define an alias for all dump/restore commands
Cmnd_Alias   DUMP=/usr/etc/dump, /usr/etc/rdump,
   /usr/etc/restore, /usr/etc/rrestore
#
mark   CS=ALL, PHYSICS=DUMP
herb   CS=/usr/local/bin/tcpdump
randy  ALL=ALL
```

In this example, user mark is allowed to execute any command as root on the CS machines (tigger, anchor, piper, moet, and sigi), but only the commands needed to do dumps on the Physics machines (eprince, pprince, and icarus). Herb can execute **tcpdump** on CS machines in order to gather data for his network experiments. And user randy is allowed to run any command on any machine.

To modify **/etc/sudoers**, you use a special **visudo** command which lets you edit the file and then constructs a database file in the format understood by **sudo**.

See Chapter 12 for more information about ***syslog****.* In addition to running the requested command, **sudo** also keeps a log of the command lines that were executed, the people who requested them, the directory from which they were run, and the times at which they were invoked. This information is logged via **syslog** and can be placed in the file of your choice. Likewise, it can be forwarded to a "secure" host for hardcopy logging.

A log entry for randy executing **sudo /bin/cat /etc/sudoers** might look like this:

```
Dec 7 10:57:19 tigger sudo: randy:
   PWD=/tigger/users/randy; COMMAND=/bin/cat /etc/sudoers
```

Suppose that the user mark wants to look up information about icarus's telephone connection with colossus in the **/etc/uucp/Systems** file, which is not world-readable. Since he knows that as himself he cannot access the file, he tries

```
% sudo grep colossus /etc/uucp/Systems
```

Unfortunately, mark's entry in `/etc/sudoers` only allows him to execute dump-related commands, so he gets the message

```
Sorry, user mark is not allowed to execute grep.
```

If mark were to use **sudo** to invoke `/usr/etc/dump`, then **sudo** would be transparent except for asking for a password, and his request would be honored. Note that commands in `/etc/sudoers` are specified using full pathnames to prevent people from executing their own programs and scripts as root. (Of course, mark could simply **dump** the filesystem which contained `/etc/uucp/Systems` and then use **restore** to obtain a readable copy of the file. Security is never absolute.)

The use of **sudo** has the following advantages:

- Accountability is higher due to command logging.
- Operators can do chores without unlimited root privileges.
- The root password can be known by only one or two people.
- It's faster to use **sudo** than to **su** or to log in as root.
- Privileges may be revoked without changing the root password.
- A canonical list of all users with root privileges is maintained.
- There is less chance of a root shell being left unattended.
- Since access restrictions are host-dependent, a single file can be used to control access for an entire network.

There are a couple of disadvantages as well. The worst of these is that any breach in the security of a user's account can be equivalent to breaching the root account itself. There is not much you can do to counter this threat other than cautioning your sudoers to protect their accounts like they would the root account. In addition, **sudo**'s command logging can be subverted by tricks such as shell escapes from within an allowed program, or by **sudo csh** and **sudo su** if you allow them.

3.6 OTHER IMPORTANT USERS

Root is the only user that has special status in the eyes of the UNIX kernel, but there are several other nonhuman logins that are used for system purposes. It is customary to replace the passwords of these special users in the `/etc/passwd` file with a star so that their accounts cannot be logged in to.

daemon: Owner of Unprivileged Software

The daemon account usually has UID one. Files that should properly belong to UNIX rather than to a particular user are often given to daemon rather than to root to avoid the security hazards associated with ownership by root. There is also a UNIX group called "daemon," created for similar reasons.

bin: Owner of System Commands

The bin user often owns directories that contain the system's commands, and most of the executable files as well.

sys: Owner of the Kernel and Memory Images

On some systems, the user sys owns special files such as `/dev/kmem`, `/dev/mem`, and `/dev/drum` or `/dev/swap`, which are, respectively, the kernel's address space, the physical memory of the system, and an image of the system's swap space. Few programs access these files, but those that do run setuid to sys if this ownership convention is in use. On some systems, the group "kmem" is used rather than sys.

nobody: Owner of Nothing

See Chapter 6 for more information about adding users.

Most versions of UNIX define a user called "nobody" with UID -1 or -2. UIDs are short integers and thus -1 might appear as 32,767. This can thwart the scheme for determining the next available UID used by many `adduser` programs.

See Chapter 17 for more information about NFS.

"nobody" is the owner of software that doesn't need or shouldn't have special permissions. NFS uses it to secure file servers on networks where diskless clients can be rebooted in single-user mode by anyone with physical access. Some daemons, such as `fingerd`, run as nobody.

4 *The Filesystem*

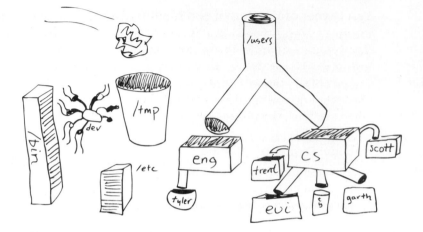

4.1 INTRODUCTION

The filesystem is the abstraction used by the kernel to represent and organize the system's storage resources. Storage resources can include different kinds of media (for example, hard disks, floppy disks, and CD-ROM drives) in various sizes and quantities. The kernel integrates these resources together under a single hierarchy that starts at the directory / and continues downwards through an arbitrary number of subdirectories. The top-level directory is called the root directory.

The directories that must be crossed to locate a particular file combine with the file's own name to form a *pathname*. Pathnames can be either absolute (for example, **/tmp/afile**) or relative (**bin/emacs**). Relative pathnames are interpreted starting at the current directory.[1]

The terms *file*, *filename*, *pathname*, and *path* are more or less interchangeable. *Filename* and *path* can be used for both absolute and relative paths; *pathname* generally suggests an absolute path. *File* is often used to focus attention on a file's contents rather than its name.

The UNIX file tree can be arbitrarily deep. However, each directory must have a name less than 256 characters long, and you can't use more than 1,023 characters in a single path. To access a file whose absolute path-

---

1. You might be accustomed to thinking of the current directory as a feature of the shell. In fact, every UNIX process has a current directory.

name is longer than this, you must `cd` to an intermediate directory and then use a relative pathname.

4.2 Deconstructing the Filesystem

The file tree is composed of chunks called filesystems, each of which consists of one directory and its subdirectories and files. Filesystems are attached to the file tree with the `mount` command. `mount` maps a directory within the existing file tree, called the mount point, to the root of the new filesystem. The previous contents of the mount point become inaccessible as long as a filesystem is mounted there. Mount points are usually empty directories, however. For example,

```
mount /dev/sd0a /users
```

would install the filesystem stored on the device `/dev/sd0a` under the path `/users`. You could then use `ls /users` to see what the filesystem contained. Instructions for configuring a device to hold a filesystem are given in Chapter 9, *Adding a Disk*.

Filesystems are detached with the `umount` command. On most systems, you cannot unmount a filesystem that is busy; there mustn't be any open files or processes `cd`'ed there. If the filesystem contains executable programs, they cannot be running. BSDI and OSF/1 allow `umount -f`, which forces a busy filesystem to be unmounted. This is not usually a good idea, as the programs that are using it may become quite confused. Use the `-f` option at your own risk.

There is a nifty program called `lsof` ("list of open files") that catalogs open file descriptors by process and filename. This information makes it much easier to figure out why you can't unmount a filesystem. `lsof` was written by Victor A. Abell of Purdue University, with support from a cast of thousands. It works on all six of our example systems and is available via anonymous `ftp` from vic.cc.purdue.edu

The word "filesystem" actually has two separate meanings. As used in the preceding paragraphs, "filesystem" means a subsection of the file tree. As used in the title of this chapter, "filesystem" denotes the entire file tree and the algorithms UNIX uses to manage it. It's normally apparent from context which meaning is intended.

See Chapter 13 for more information about configuring the kernel.

The root filesystem includes the root directory and a minimal set of files and subdirectories. The kernel lives in the root filesystem; it's usually called `/unix`, `/vmunix`, or `/kernel/unix`. Also part of the root filesystem are `/dev` for device files, `/etc` for critical system files, `/sbin` and `/bin` for important utilities, and often `/tmp` for temporary files.

The filesystems `/usr` and `/var` are also of great importance. `/usr` is where most standard programs are kept, along with various other booty such as on-line manuals and libraries. It is not strictly necessary that /usr be a separate filesystem, but for convenience in administration it almost always is.

/var provides a home for spool directories, log files, accounting information, and various other items that grow or change rapidly and vary on each host. The contents of /var originally lived in /usr; on your system, you may still find symbolic link fossils from the usrzoic era. /var was created as a place to put host-specific files so that /usr could be shared among several machines.

Home directories of users should be kept on a separate filesystem, usually mounted in the root directory or occasionally beneath /usr. Separate filesystems can also be used to store bulky items such as source code libraries and databases.

UNIX allows filesystems to be shared over a network using NFS, the Network File System. See Chapter 17, *The Network File System*, for more information about NFS.

4.3 ORGANIZATION OF THE FILESYSTEM

The UNIX filesystem has never been very well organized. Various incompatible naming conventions are used simultaneously, and different types of files are scattered randomly around the namespace. In many cases, files are divided up by function and not by how likely they are to change, making it difficult to upgrade the operating system. The /etc directory, for example, contains some files that are never customized and some that are entirely local.

Innovations such as /var have helped to solve a few problems, but most systems are still a mess. Nevertheless, there's a culturally correct place for everything. Most UNIX software can be installed with little reconfiguration if your system is set up in a standard way. If you try to improve upon the default structure, you're asking for trouble. Some of the more important standard directories are listed in Table 4.1.

4.4 TYPES OF FILES

There are eight kinds of UNIX files:

- Regular files
- Directories
- Character device files
- Block device files
- UNIX domain sockets
- Named pipes (FIFOs)
- Hard links
- Symbolic links

Table 4.1   Standard directories and their contents[a]

Pathname	Contents
/	The root directory
/bin or /sbin	Commands needed for minimal system operability[b]
/dev	Device entries for terminals, disks, modems, etc.
/etc	Critical startup and configuration files
/lib	Libraries for the C compiler
/tmp	Temporary files that disappear between reboots
/sys	Kernel-building work area, configuration files (BSD)
/proc	Images of all running processes (some newer systems)
/stand	Stand-alone utilities, disk formatters, etc.
/usr/bin	Executable files
/usr/games	Games and diversions (most are not much fun)
/usr/include	Header files for C programs
/usr/5bin	System V compatibility commands on BSD systems
/usr/etc	System maintenance commands
/usr/sbin	Even more system maintenance commands
/usr/lib	Support files for standard UNIX programs
/usr/man	On-line manual pages
/var/adm	Accounting files, records of resource usage
/var/spool	Spooling directories for printers, UUCP, mail, etc.
/var/tmp	Temporary space (files don't disappear after reboots)
/usr/ucb	Berkeley utilities and programs
/usr/local	Local software (stuff you install)
/usr/local/adm	Local accounting and log files
/usr/local/bin	Local executables
/usr/local/etc	Local system configuration files and commands
/usr/local/lib	Local support files
/usr/local/sbin	Local system maintenance commands
/usr/local/src	Source code for /usr/local/*
/kernel	Files needed to load the kernel (Solaris)

a. Some rows have been shaded to improve readability.
b. Where /sbin is present, /bin is usually a symbolic link to /usr/bin.

Hard links are not really a distinct type of file, as we shall soon see. A few systems do not support UNIX domain sockets and/or named pipes.

Regular Files

A regular file is just a bag o' bytes. It is the most common type of file. A regular file can hold an executable program, a chapter of a book, a pornographic GIF image, source code for a C program, or anything else that has to be stored for later retrieval. UNIX provides no kernel-level support for structuring the contents of a file. However, both sequential and random access are supported.

Directories

A directory can contain any kind of files, in any combination. The special entries "." and ".." refer to the directory itself and its parent directory. Directories can be created with **mkdir** and deleted with **rmdir** if empty. Non-empty directories can be deleted with **rm -r**.

Character and Block Device Files

For more information about devices and drivers, see Chapter 7.

Device files allow UNIX programs to communicate with the system's hardware and peripherals. When the kernel is configured, modules that know how to communicate with each of the system's devices are linked in.[2] The module for a particular device, called a device driver, takes care of the messy details of managing it.

Device drivers present a standard communication interface that looks like a regular file. When the kernel is given a request that refers to a character or block device file, it simply passes the request to the appropriate device driver.

Character device files allow their associated drivers to perform their own input and output buffering. Block device files are used by drivers that handle I/O in large chunks and want the kernel to perform buffering for them. Some types of hardware, such as hard disks and tape drives, can be represented by both block and character device files.

There can be more than one instance of each type of device. Accordingly, device files are characterized by two numbers, called the major and minor device numbers. The major device number tells the kernel which driver the file refers to, while the minor device number tells the driver which physical unit to address. For example, major device number 12 on a SunOS system indicates the terminal driver. The second terminal (**ttyb**) would have major device number 12 and minor device number 1. (In standard nerd fashion, UNIX numbering always starts at zero.)

Some device drivers use the minor device number in a nonstandard way. For example, tape drivers often use the minor device number to select a density at which to write tapes, and to determine whether or not the tape should be rewound when the device file is closed. On some systems, the "terminal driver" (which actually handles all serial devices) uses minor device numbers to distinguish modems used as outgoing dialers from modems used on dial-in ports.

Device files can be created with **mknod** and removed with **rm**.

UNIX Domain Sockets (BSD)

Sockets are connections between processes that allow them to communicate in a hygienic manner. UNIX provides several different kinds of

---

2. On some systems, these modules can also be loaded dynamically by the kernel.

sockets, most of which involve the use of a network. UNIX domain sockets are local to a particular host and are referenced through a filesystem object rather than a network port.

See Chapter 12 for more information about syslog.

Although socket files are visible to other processes as directory entries, they cannot be read or written by processes not involved in the connection. Some standard facilities that use UNIX domain sockets are the printing system, the X Windows system, and `syslog`.

UNIX domain sockets are created with the `socket` system call and can be removed with the `rm` command or the `unlink` system call when the socket no longer has any users.

Named Pipes (ATT)

Like UNIX domain sockets, named pipes allow communication between two unrelated processes running on the same host. Named pipes may be created with the `mknod` command and removed with `rm`.

Hard Links

A link is not really a file type, but rather an additional name for a file. Each file has at least one link, usually the name under which it was first created. Adding a link creates an alias for the file.

A link is indistinguishable from the file it is linked to; as far as UNIX is concerned, they are identical. UNIX maintains a count of the number of links that point to each file and does not release the file's data blocks until its last link has been deleted. Since a link is a direct connection between files, hard links cannot exist across filesystem boundaries.

Links are usually called "hard links" these days to distinguish them from symbolic links. Links are created with `ln` and removed with `rm`.

Symbolic Links

A symbolic or "soft" link points to a file by name. When the kernel needs to open or pass through a symbolic link, it evaluates the pathname stored as the contents of the link. The difference between hard links and symbolic links is that a hard link is a direct reference, while a symbolic link is a reference by name; symbolic links are distinct from the files they point to.

Symbolic links are created with `ln -s` and removed with `rm`. Since they contain an arbitrary path, they can refer to files on other filesystems or to nonexistent files. Several symbolic links can also form a loop.

A symbolic link can contain either an absolute or a relative path. For example, the command

```
ln -s ../../ufs /usr/include/bsd/sys/ufs
```

links /usr/include/bsd/sys/ufs to /usr/include/ufs using a relative path. The entire /usr/include directory could be moved somewhere else without causing the symbolic link to stop working.

Beware of using ".." in pathnames that travel through symbolic links, since symbolic links can't be followed in reverse. ".." always refers to a directory's true parent. For example, with the link above, the path

```
/usr/include/bsd/sys/ufs/../param.h
```

resolves to

```
/usr/include/param.h
```

not to

```
/usr/include/bsd/sys/param.h
```

4.5 FILE PERMISSIONS

Every file has a set of nine permission bits that control who can read, write, and execute the contents of the file. Together with three other bits that affect the operation of executable programs, these bits constitute the file's *mode*. The twelve mode bits are stored together with four bits of file-type information in a 16-bit word.

The four file-type bits are set when the file is created and can't be changed, but the twelve mode bits can be modified by the file's owner or the superuser using the **chmod** (change mode) command. **ls** is used to inspect the values of these bits. An example is given on page 65.

The Setuid and Setgid Bits

The bits with octal values 4000 and 2000 are the setuid and setgid bits. These bits allow programs to access files and processes that would otherwise be off limits to the user that runs them.

Although all files can have these bits set, most versions of UNIX only pay attention to them when they are set on executable files. On some systems, such as SunOS, the setgid bit may be set on a directory to control the default group ownership of newly-created files within it.

The Sticky Bit

The bit with octal value 1000 is called the sticky bit. The sticky bit is an example of UNIX outgrowing something but not being able to keep it from tagging along anyway. Small-memory systems like the PDP-11/70s where UNIX spent its pre-teen years needed some programs to stay in memory continuously. The sticky bit was very important then. In today's world of $25 SIMMs and fast disk drives, the sticky bit on an executable is obsolete, and modern kernels silently ignore it.

If the sticky bit is set on a directory, some versions of UNIX don't allow you to delete or rename a file unless you are the owner of the directory, the owner of the file, or the superuser. Having write permission on the directory is not enough. This is an attempt to make directories like /tmp a little more private.

The Permission Bits

The nine permission bits are used to determine what operations may be performed on a file, and by whom. UNIX does not allow permissions to be set on a per-user basis. Instead, there are sets of permissions for the owner of the file, the group owners of the file, and everyone else. Each set has three bits: a read bit, a write bit, and an execute bit (called the "search" bit on a directory).

The topmost three bits (with octal values of 400, 200, and 100) control access for the owner. The second three (40, 20, and 10) control access for the group. The last three (4, 2, and 1) control access for everyone else ("the world"). In each triplet, the high bit is the read bit, the middle bit is the write bit, and the low bit is the execute bit.

Each user fits into only one of the three permission sets. The permissions used are those that are classwise most restrictive. For example, the owner of a file always has access determined by the owner permission bits and never the group permission bits. It is possible for the "other" and "group" categories to have more access than the owner, although this configuration is rarely used.

On a regular file, the read bit allows the file to be opened and read. The write bit allows the contents of the file to be modified or truncated; however, the ability to delete or rename the file is controlled by the permissions on its parent directory.

The execute bit allows the file to be executed. There are two types of executable files: binaries, which the CPU runs directly, and scripts, which must be interpreted by a shell or some other program. By convention, scripts begin with a line of the form

```
#!/bin/csh -f
```

that specifies an appropriate interpreter. Non-binary files that do not specify an interpreter are assumed (by your shell) to be **sh** scripts.

For a directory, the execute bit (often called the "search" bit in this context) allows the directory to be entered, but not to have its contents listed. The combination of read and execute bits allows the contents of the directory to be listed. The combination of write and execute bits allows files to be created, deleted, and renamed within the directory.

Changing Permissions

The chmod command changes the permissions on a file. Only the owner of the file and the superuser can change its permissions. To use the command on early UNIX systems you had to learn a bit of binary or octal notation, but current versions accept either octal notation or an even more cryptic mnemonic syntax. We will describe the octal syntax here; it is generally more convenient for system administrators.

The first argument to chmod is an octal number that represents the permissions to be assigned, and the second and subsequent arguments are names of files on which permissions should be changed. In the usual case, the first octal digit is for the owner, the second is for the group, and the third is for everyone else. If you want to turn on the setuid, setgid, or sticky bits, you use four octal digits rather than three, with the three special bits forming the first digit.

Table 4.2 illustrates the eight possible combinations for each set of three bits, where r, w, and x stand for read, write, and execute.

Table 4.2   Permission encoding for chmod

Octal	Binary	Perms	Octal	Binary	Perms
0	000	---	4	100	r--
1	001	--x	5	101	r-x
2	010	-w-	6	110	rw-
3	011	-wx	7	111	rwx

For example, chmod 711 myprog gives all permissions to the owner and execute-only permission to everyone else.

Assigning Default Permissions

The built-in shell command umask may be used to set default permissions on the files you create. umask is specified as a three-digit octal value that represents the permissions to take away. When a file is created, its permissions are set to whatever the creating program asks for minus whatever the umask forbids. The digits allow the permissions shown in Table 4.3.

For example, umask 027 would allow all permissions for the owner but would forbid write permission to the group and allow no permissions for anyone else. The default umask value is 022, which gives write permission only to the owner.

Table 4.3   Permission encoding for umask

Octal	Binary	Perms	Octal	Binary	Perms
0	000	rwx	4	100	-wx
1	001	rw-	5	101	-w-
2	010	r-x	6	110	--x
3	011	r--	7	111	---

See Chapter 6 for more information about default startup files.

There is no way you can force users to have a particular `umask` value, since they can always reset it to whatever they want. However, you can provide a suitable default in the sample `.cshrc` and `.profile` files you give to new users.

4.6 INODES

The kernel maintains information about each file in a structure called an *inode*. Inode tables for a filesystem are laid out when the filesystem is created, and their size and location on the disk never change. Each inode contains about forty separate pieces of information, but most of these are useful only to the kernel. As a system administrator you will be concerned mostly with the link count, owner, group, mode, size, last access time, last modification time, and type.

All of these can be found using the `ls` command with various options. Under BSD, `ls -lg` gives a listing showing mode, size, last modification time, owner, group, link count, and type. Under ATT, `ls -l` shows a similar display.

Consider the following line, produced by `ls -lg /bin/sh`:

```
-rwxr-xr-x   1 root   bin    85924 Sep 27  1994 /bin/sh
```

The first field specifies the file type and its mode. Since the first character is a dash, the file is just a regular file. The one-character codes shown in Table 4.4 are used to represent the various types of files.

Table 4.4   File-type encoding used by ls

File type	Symbol	Created by	Removed by
Regular file	-	editors, cp, etc.	rm
Directory	d	mkdir	rmdir, rm -r
Character device file	c	mknod	rm
Block device file	b	mknod	rm
UNIX domain socket	s	socket(2)	rm
Named pipe	p	mknod	rm
Symbolic link	l	ln -s	rm

The next nine characters in this field are the three sets of permission bits. Although these bits have only binary values, `ls` shows them symbolically with the letters `r`, `w`, and `x` for read, write, and execute. In this case, the owner has all permissions on the file and everyone else has only read and execute permission.

If the setuid bit had been set, the `x` representing the owner's execute permission would have been replaced with an `s`, and if the setgid bit had been set, the `x` for the group would also have been replaced with an `s`. The last character of the permissions (execute permission for "other") is shown as `t` if the sticky bit of the file is turned on. If either the setuid bit or the sticky bit is set but the corresponding execute bit is not, these bits appear as `S` or `T`.

The next field in the listing is the link count for the file. In this case it is one, indicating that **/bin/sh** is the only name by which this file is known. Every time a hard link is made to a file this count is incremented by one.

All directories will have at least two links: the link from the parent directory and the link from the special file "." inside the directory itself. Symbolic links do not affect the link count.

The next two fields are the owner and group owner of the file. The file's owner is root, and the file belongs to the group bin. The kernel actually stores these as the user and group ID numbers rather than strings. If the text versions can't be determined, these fields will contain numbers.

The next field is the size of the file in bytes. This file is 85,924 bytes long, almost 84K.[3] Next comes the date of last modification: September 27, 1994. The last field in the listing is the name of the file, **/bin/sh**.

`ls` output is slightly different for a device file. The following line was produced with `ls -lg /dev/ttya`:

```
crw-rw-rw-  1 root daemon   12, 0 Dec 20  1993 /dev/ttya
```

Most fields are the same, but instead of a size in bytes, the major and minor device numbers are shown. **/dev/ttya** is the first unit controlled by device driver 12 (on this system, the terminal driver).

The system keeps track of modification time, link count, and file size information automatically. The permission bits, ownership, and group ownership change only when they are specifically altered.

---

3. K stands for kilo, a metric prefix meaning 1,000; however, computer types have bastardized it into meaning 2^{10} or 1,024. Similarly, a megabyte is not really a million bytes but rather 2^{20} or 1,048,576 bytes. Sneaky hard disk manufacturers sometimes quote disk sizes in million-byte megabytes.

The **chown** command is used to change the ownership of a file, and the **chgrp** command to change the group ownership. On some systems, **chown** can change both the owner and group of a file at once.

The syntax of **chown** and **chgrp** mirrors that of **chmod**, except that the first argument is the new owner or group, respectively. To use **chgrp**, you must either be the owner of the file and belong to the group you're changing to, or be the superuser.

Most versions of **chown** and **chgrp** offer the recursive **-R** flag, which changes the owner or group of a directory and all the files underneath it. For example, the sequence

```
# chmod 755 ~matt
# chown -R matt ~matt
# chgrp -R staff ~matt
```

might be used to set up the home directory of a new user after you have copied in the default startup files. (~matt is shorthand for "the home directory of matt" in most shells.)

5 *Controlling Processes*

a.out

5.1 INTRODUCTION

A "process" is the UNIX abstraction that manages the memory, CPU, and I/O resources that comprise a running program. Although UNIX gives the impression that many things are happening at once, only one process is actually executing at any particular moment.[1] The illusion of concurrent execution is maintained by a technique called time-slicing, in which UNIX changes the process that is executing at regular, short intervals (usually at least every 20 milliseconds). Processes rotate so quickly that it appears that everything is running at once, when in fact each process is executing only a small percentage of the time.

The system administrator has the ability to monitor the status of processes, control how much of the CPU's time a process gets, send signals to a process, and suspend or halt its execution.

5.2 COMPONENTS OF A PROCESS

A process consists of an address space and a set of data structures inside the kernel. The address space is a set of memory pages[2] that the kernel has marked for the use of the process; it contains segments for

---

1. Some machines have more than one processor, but the concept remains the same, since each CPU can only execute a single process at a time.
2. Pages are small chunks of memory, usually 1K to 4K in size.

the program code that the process is executing, the variables used by the process, the process's stack, and various extra information needed by the kernel while the process is running.

Saying that the address space is a section of memory is actually a slight lie, because in a virtual memory system the address space may be all, partially, or not at all in physical memory at any given time.

The kernel's internal data structures record various pieces of information about each process. Some of the more important of these are:

- The process's address space map
- The current status of the process
- The execution priority of the process
- Information about the resources the process has used
- The process's signal mask
- The owner of the process

Many of the parameters associated with a process directly affect its execution: the amount of processor time it gets, the files it can access, and so on. In the following sections, we discuss the meaning and significance of the parameters that are most interesting from a system administrator's point of view.

PID

Each new process created by the kernel is assigned a unique process identification number. Like a Social Security number, the actual value of the PID has little significance. PIDs are assigned in order as processes are created; when the kernel runs out of PIDs, it starts again at zero, skipping over PIDs that are still in use.

PPID

UNIX does not supply a system call that creates a new process running a particular program. Instead, an existing process must clone itself to create a new process. The clone can then exchange its text[3] for that of another program.

The original process is called the "parent" process, and the clone is called the "child." The PPID attribute of a process is the PID of its parent.

UID and EUID

The UID is the user identification number of the person who created the process. Only the creator and the superuser can make changes to a process. The creator is charged by the accounting system for any resources that the process uses.

3. "Text" is the geek word for the series of machine instructions that the CPU executes.

The EUID is the "effective" UID of the process. This number is used to determine what resources and files the process has permission to access. For most processes, the UID and EUID will be the same, the usual exception being programs that are setuid.

GID and EGID

The GID is the group identification number for the process. Valid group numbers are enumerated in **/etc/group**, and in the GID field of the **/etc/passwd** file. When a process is started, its GID is set to the GID of its parent process.

The EGID is related to the GID in the same way that the EUID is related to the UID. If a process tries to access a file on which it does not have owner permission, the kernel will automatically check to see if permission may be granted on the basis of the EGID.

On some systems, a process can be in more than one group at a time. In this case the GID is actually a list of group numbers, and when you attempt to access a resource, the entire list is checked to see if you belong to the appropriate group.

Priority and Nice Value

A process's priority determines how much CPU time it will receive. When the kernel selects a process to run, it chooses the process with the highest "internal priority."

Instructions for setting the nice value of a process are given on page 77. It isn't possible to set the internal priority directly, but it's possible to set a process's "nice value," which has a substantial influence on the internal priority. Other factors that influence the internal priority are the amount of CPU time that the process has recently consumed and the length of time it has been waiting to run.

Control Terminal

Most processes have a control terminal associated with them. The control terminal determines default linkages for the standard input, standard output, and standard error channels. When you start a command from the shell, your terminal normally becomes the process's control terminal. The concept of a control terminal also affects the distribution of signals, which are discussed starting on page 72.

5.3 THE LIFE CYCLE OF A PROCESS

Processes do not just magically appear on the system, nor are they created spontaneously by the kernel. New processes are created by other processes, just like new humans.[4]

---

4. New humans are normally created by other humans, not by UNIX processes.

To create a new process, a process copies itself using the **fork** system call. **fork** creates a copy of the original process that is identical to the parent except for the following differences:

- The new process has a distinct PID.
- The new process's PPID refers to the original process.
- The new process's accounting information is reset.
- The new process has its own copy of file descriptors.

The last of these differences can be somewhat tricky. Descriptors are reference numbers that the kernel gives out to processes when a file or socket is opened. These numbers are actually indexes into a small table that contains pointers back to the kernel's own data structures. When a **fork** occurs, it is the table that is copied, not the underlying kernel structures. The child's manipulation of these structures can have a direct effect on the parent.

For example, suppose the child process reads some data from a file descriptor. The next time the parent tries to read from this descriptor, it will start reading at the place where the child left off, not from where it would have started reading before the **fork**.

fork has the unique property of returning two values. From the child's point of view, **fork** always returns zero. The parent, on the other hand, is returned the PID of the newly-created child. This is how the two processes can tell themselves apart. In C, it looks like this:

```
int     kidpid;

kidpid = fork();

if (kidpid == 0) {
    /* This is the child process, act childish. */
} else {
    /* This is the parent. */
}
```

After a **fork**, a new process will often use one of the **exec** family of system calls to begin execution of a new program.[5]

All calls in the **exec** family perform roughly the same function; they change the program text that the process is executing and reset the data and stack segments to a predefined initial state. When one of the **exec** routines is called, it overwrites the address space of the process with the contents of the new program file, and then resumes execution at the new text's designated entry point. The various forms of **exec** differ only in the ways that they specify the command-line arguments and environment to be given to the new program text.

5. Actually, they're not all system calls. Under BSD, all but one are library routines.

For a simple example of how **fork** and **exec** are used to spawn a new process, consider the following C code:

```
if (fork() == 0) {
    /* I'm the child... */
    execl("/bin/ls", "ls", "/usr/bin", (char *)0);
}
```

In this example, the program that is running starts a new process that becomes an invocation of the **ls** command. The effect is identical to typing **ls /usr/bin** from the shell. By convention, the name of the program is the first argument supplied to the new text. The shell normally enforces this rule for you, but you must do it yourself when coding.

See Chapter 2 for more information about booting and the **init** *daemon.*

When the system boots, the kernel creates and installs several processes autonomously. The most notable of these is **init**, which always has PID 1. **init** is responsible for forking a shell to execute the **rc** startup scripts, if your system uses them. All processes other than the ones the kernel creates are descendants of **init**.

init also plays another important role in process management. When a process completes, it calls a routine named **_exit** to notify the kernel that it is ready to die. It supplies as a parameter to **_exit** an *exit code*, an integer that tells why the process is exiting. By convention, an exit code of zero means that the process was "successful."

The exit code is supplied for the benefit of the process's parent, so the kernel must store it until it is requested by the parent with the **wait** system call.[6] The address space of the exiting process is released and the process is given no CPU time, but it does retain its identity. A process in the exiting state is called a zombie.

This scheme works OK if the parent outlives its children and is conscientious about calling **wait** so that zombie processes don't stay alive. If the parent dies first, however, the kernel recognizes that no **wait** will be forthcoming and donates the zombie to **init**. **init** is supposed to accept these orphaned zombies and perform the **wait** needed to "reap" (exorcise) them. **init** occasionally does not do its job properly and zombies are left on the system, but they do not cause any real problems.

5.4 SIGNALS

A signal is a way of telling a process, "Something interesting has happened, so you'd better drop whatever you're doing and handle it." More

---

6. The exit code is actually only one of several pieces of information the kernel preserves for processes that have exited. If a process was terminated externally (with a signal), the parent can find out what that signal was and whether or not a core dump was performed. A summary of the resources used by the child is also available.

than thirty different kinds of signals are defined. Signals can be sent to a process with the `kill` command.

A core dump is a memory image of a process that can be used for debugging.

When a signal is delivered, one of two things can happen. If the process has designated a handler routine for that particular signal, this routine is called with information about the context in which the signal was delivered. Otherwise, the kernel takes some default action on behalf of the process. The default action varies from signal to signal; many signals terminate the process, and some also generate a core dump.

Specifying a handler routine for a signal is referred to as *catching* the signal. When the handler completes, execution restarts at the point where the signal was received.

To prevent signals from arriving, programs can request that they be either ignored or blocked. A signal that is ignored is simply discarded and has no effect on the process. A blocked signal gets queued for delivery, but the kernel doesn't require the process to act on it until it is explicitly unblocked. The handler for a newly-unblocked signal is called only once, even if multiple instances of the signal were received while the signal was blocked.

Originally, ATT and BSD systems differed greatly in the signals they provided and their meanings. Over time, however, the lines have become blurred. As far as an administrator is concerned, modern systems are virtually indistinguishable in this area.[7]

Table 5.1 (on the next page) lists the UNIX signals. The "Name" column shows the name by which each signal is known in the `/usr/include` header files. These names are only used when writing C programs. Most shell commands use an abbreviated form of the name that drops the SIG prefix; for example, HUP rather than SIGHUP.

The signals named KILL and STOP cannot be caught, blocked, or ignored. The KILL signal destroys the receiving process, while the STOP signal suspends its execution until a CONT signal is received. CONT may be caught or ignored, but not blocked.

Signals are used in many ways. Signals can be sent among processes as a means of communication, by the control terminal of a process as a way of letting the user interrupt or suspend it, by the kernel in any number of situations (many signals indicate an execution fault of one sort or another), or even by the process to itself.

As a simple example of signals in action, consider what happens when a <Control-C> character is typed on the keyboard. The terminal driver

---

7. Some differences remain at the programming level, particularly with regard to the handling of signals that interrupt system calls.

Table 5.1   UNIX signals

ID	Name	Description	Default action	Can catch	Can block	Dump core
1	SIGHUP	Hangup	Terminate	Yes	Yes	No
2	SIGINT	Interrupt	Terminate	Yes	Yes	No
3	SIGQUIT	Quit	Terminate	Yes	Yes	Yes
a	SIGILL	Illegal instruction	Terminate	Yes	Yes	Yes
a	SIGTRAP	Trace trap	Terminate	Yes	Yes	Yes
a	SIGIOT	IOT trap	Terminate	Yes	Yes	Yes
a	SIGEMT	EMT trap	Terminate	Yes	Yes	Yes
a	SIGFPE	Arithmetic exception	Terminate	Yes	Yes	Yes
9	SIGKILL	Kill	Terminate	No	No	No
a	SIGBUS	Bus error	Terminate	Yes	Yes	Yes
a	SIGSEGV	Segmentation fault[b]	Terminate	Yes	Yes	Yes
a	SIGSYS	Bad syscall argument	Terminate	Yes	Yes	Yes
a	SIGPIPE	Broken pipe	Terminate	Yes	Yes	No
a	SIGALRM	Alarm clock	Terminate	Yes	Yes	No
15	SIGTERM	Software termination	Terminate	Yes	Yes	No
a	SIGURG	Socket in extremis	Ignore	Yes	Yes	No
a	SIGSTOP	Stop	Stop	No	No	No
a	SIGTSTP	Keyboard stop	Stop	Yes	Yes	No
a	SIGCONT	Continue after stop	Ignore	Yes	No	No
a	SIGCHLD	Child status changed	Ignore	Yes	Yes	No
a	SIGTTIN	Invalid read	Stop	Yes	Yes	No
a	SIGTTOU	Invalid write	Stop	Yes	Yes	No
a	SIGIO	I/O possible on fd	Ignore	Yes	Yes	No
a	SIGXCPU	CPU time limit up	Terminate	Yes	Yes	No
a	SIGXFSZ	File size limit up	Terminate	Yes	Yes	No
a	SIGVTALRM	Virtual time alarm	Terminate	Yes	Yes	No
a	SIGPROF	Profiling timer alarm	Terminate	Yes	Yes	No
a	SIGWINCH	Window changed	Ignore	Yes	Yes	No
a	SIGLOST	Resource lost	Terminate	Yes	Yes	Yes
a	SIGUSR1	User-defined	Terminate	Yes	Yes	No
a	SIGUSR2	User-defined	Terminate	Yes	Yes	No

a. Varies among systems.
b. Sent when a process attempts to access an undefined region of its address space.

receives the character and sends out an INT (interrupt) signal to the active process group. Since the default handler for INT specifies termination, most programs abort when they receive this signal.

5.5   PROCESS STATES

A process is not automatically eligible to receive CPU time just because it exists. There are essentially five execution states that you need to be aware of; they are listed in Table 5.2.

Table 5.2   Process states

State	Meaning
Runnable	The process can be executed.
Sleeping	The process is waiting for some resource.
Swapped	The process is not in memory.
Zombie	The process is trying to die.
Stopped	The process is suspended (not allowed to execute).

A runnable process is ready to execute whenever there is CPU time available. It has acquired all the resources it needs and is waiting for CPU time to process its data. As soon as the process makes a system call that cannot be immediately completed (such as reading part of a file), UNIX will put it to sleep.

A sleeping process is waiting for a specific event to occur. Interactive shells and system daemons spend most of their time sleeping, waiting for terminal input or network connections. Since a sleeping process is effectively blocked until its request has been satisfied, it will get no CPU time unless it receives a signal.

A sleep can last anywhere from microseconds to days, but most sleeps last a few tens of milliseconds. A process that has been sleeping much longer than this is assumed to be interactive and is accorded special considerations by the kernel. When the sleep finally ends, the kernel will ensure that the process gets to run immediately. This makes programs that depend on input from a terminal more responsive than they would otherwise be.

A swapped process is one that has been written out to disk and removed from the computer's main memory. Most systems swap out processes when contention for memory is so intense that paging bogs down and an unreasonable amount of time is spent on processing page faults rather than doing useful work.

Strictly speaking, being swapped is not a true process state. A swapped process can also be sleeping, stopped, or even nominally runnable; it remains frozen in whatever state it was in when it was swapped out, until it is brought back into memory.

A stopped process is forbidden to run. Processes are stopped by receiving a STOP or TSTP signal, and are restarted by being sent a CONT signal. Being stopped is similar to sleeping, but there's no way to get out of the stopped state other than having some other process wake you up.

Processes generally get stopped in three situations:

- When a <Control-Z> (or the "suspend" character declared with stty) is typed to an interactive process

- At the specific request of a user or program
- When a process that has been put in the background tries to access its control terminal

If you use a modern shell, you're probably familiar with this first case. Here's how it works: When the terminal driver receives the <Control-Z> that you've typed, it figures out what the active foreground processes attached to the terminal are and sends them a TSTP signal. The default handler for TSTP simply stops the process, but because TSTP can be caught, the process has the option of doing cleanup operations before stopping. For example, **vi** makes sure that the cursor goes to the bottom of the screen before it stops so that you don't get stuck with the cursor in some strange place.

The second case is the most general. Since the STOP signal cannot be caught, it's the signal you use when you want to reliably stop a process. The STOP signal is the only sure way to halt processes that catch TSTP; the TSTP handler for a well-behaved program like **vi** must actually send itself a STOP signal as the last step in its cleanup routine.

The last of these cases is used to prevent the coexistence of two or more programs that both believe themselves to be interactive foreground processes. The discipline imposed by the terminal driver prevents background processes from accessing the terminal. As soon as a background process tries to act interactive, it gets sent a TTIN or a TTOU signal, the default handler for which puts the process to sleep.

5.6 KILL: SEND SIGNALS

As the name implies, **kill** is most often used to stop the execution of a process. **kill** can send any signal to a process, but by default it sends the TERM signal, which is the "software termination" signal. **kill** can be used by normal users on their own processes, or by the superuser on any process. The syntax for a **kill** is

kill [*-signal*] *pid*

Where *signal* is the number or symbolic name of the signal to be sent and *pid* is the process identification number of the target process. On some systems, a *pid* of -1 broadcasts the signal to all processes except system processes and the current shell. A **kill** without a signal number does not guarantee that the process will die, because the TERM signal can be caught, blocked, or ignored. The command

kill -9 *pid*

will "guarantee" that the process will die because signal 9, KILL, cannot be caught by any process. Sending a KILL signal is often necessary when the process you are trying to kill is a system or hung process. Sometimes processes get into states in which they cannot be killed, even with a KILL signal. `reboot` is an effective method of killing such processes.

See Chapter 16 for more information about named.
Another signal that is commonly used with `kill` is the hangup (HUP) signal, signal 1. Many system daemons catch this signal and interpret it as a command. Many programs reread their configuration files when they receive it. It's a good idea to send a HUP before sending a KILL to any process—many programs interpret a HUP to mean, "You might soon be killed, so get yourself into a reasonable state."

5.7 NICE AND RENICE: INFLUENCE SCHEDULING PRIORITY

The "nice value" of a process is a hint to the kernel about how the process should be treated in relationship to other processes contending for the CPU. The strange name is derived from the practice of referring to priority as "niceness," because it determines how nice you are going to be to other users of the system. The *lower* the nice value of a process, the *higher* the priority. On BSD systems, nice values range from -19 to +19; on ATT systems nice values range from 0 to 39.[8]

Except for the different numbering schemes, BSD and ATT handle nice values in much the same way. Unless the user takes special action, a newly-created process inherits the nice value of its parent process. The owner of the process can increase its nice value but cannot lower it, even to return the process to the default nice value. This prevents processes with low priority from bearing high-priority children.

A process can change its own nice value, but only in the same way that the owner can. The superuser has complete freedom in setting nice values and may even set the priority on a process so high that no other process can run. On some systems, the kernel will automatically boost the nice value of processes that have accumulated "excessive" CPU time or that have been put in the background.

A process's nice value can be set at the time of creation using the `nice` command, and, on BSD systems, can be changed during execution with the `renice` command.

See Chapter 29 for more information about performance.
Manually setting process priorities is quickly becoming a thing of the past. When UNIX ran mostly on one-MIPS VAX 11/780s, performance was most significantly affected by which process was on the CPU. Today, with 100+ MIPS on many desktops, the UNIX scheduler usually does a more than adequate job of servicing all processes. Unfortunately, I/O performance has not kept up with increasingly fast CPUs, and the major bottleneck on most systems has become the disk drives.

---

8. Most modern ATT system's `nice` commands accept -19 to +19, too.

The most commonly **niced** process in the modern world is **xntpd**, the clock synchronization daemon. Since CPU promptness is critical to its mission, it usually runs at a nice value of -12. If a process goes berserk and drives the system's load average to 65, you may need to use **nice** to start a high-priority shell before you can run commands to investigate the problem. Otherwise, your commands may never get a chance to run.

5.8 PS: MONITOR PROCESSES

ps is the system administrator's main tool for monitoring processes. While the ATT and BSD versions of **ps** differ in their arguments and display, they both provide essentially the same information. Solaris uses the ATT **ps** by default, but also provides the BSD **ps** in /usr/ucb.

ps can be used to show the PID, UID, priority, and control terminal of processes. **ps** also gives information about how much memory a process is using, how much CPU time it has consumed, and its current status (running, stopped, sleeping, idle, etc.). Zombies can be readily spotted because they show up in a **ps** listing as <exiting> or <defunct>.

Understanding **ps** output is an important administrative skill. Looking at a **ps** listing, you can determine (among other things) what processes are running on your system, how much CPU time and memory they're using, and who owns each one. **ps** usually supports a couple of dozen options, many of them system-specific.

ps can be an important tool in diagnosing problems on your system. If you notice that your system is sluggish and **ps** shows that dozens of **talkd**s are running but that no one is using **talk**, you know that the cause of the problem may be that **talkd** has gone berserk.

On a BSD system, a good overview of all the processes running on the system can be found with **ps -aux**.[9] Here is an example of a **ps -aux** on a machine running BSDI:

```
% ps -aux
USER    PID %CPU %MEM VSZ   RSS TT  STAT START   TIME    COMMAND
root    137 5.5  0.0  3832 2140 co  S    8:38PM 5:38.12 X :0
karels  155 3.0  0.0  172    16 p0  S    8:38PM 0:00.00 (xterm)
root      0 0.0  0.0     0    0 ??  DLs  8:35PM 0:00.06 (swapper)
root      1 0.0  0.0   208  120 ??  Ss   8:35PM 0:00.20 init -s
root      2 0.0  0.0     0   12 ??  DL   8:35PM 0:00.03 (pagedaemon)
root     46 0.0  0.0   160  112 ??  Ss   8:37PM 0:01.45 syslogd
root     64 0.0  0.0    72   28 ??  Ss   8:37PM 0:00.80 update
root     66 0.0  0.0   228  152 ??  I    8:37PM 0:00.23 cron
root     71 0.0  0.0   356  272 ??  Is   8:37PM 0:01.58 name
root     75 0.0  0.0   236  104 ??  IWs  8:37PM 0:00.02 lpd
root     77 0.0  0.0   160   88 ??  IWs  8:37PM 0:00.07 portmap
```

9. On BSD systems, the - of **-aux** is optional for historical reasons.

```
USER     PID  %CPU %MEM VSZ   RSS  TT STAT START   TIME    COMMAND
root      84  0.0  0.0  260   204  ?? IWs  8:37PM 0:00.23 mountd
root      86  0.0  0.0  132    64  ?? IWs  8:37PM 0:00.04 nfsd-listen
root      90  0.0  0.0  132    44  ?? IW   8:37PM 0:00.53 nfsd-udp
root     100  0.0  0.0  204    92  ?? Is   8:37PM 0:00.19 inetd
karels   120  0.0  0.0  320   232  co IWs  8:37PM 0:00.68 -csh (csh)
karels   135  0.0  0.0  160    92  co IW+  8:38PM 0:00.03 /bin/sh -
karels   147  0.0  0.0  844   636  co S    8:38PM 0:03.15 twm
karels   190  0.0  0.0  336   248  p0 IWs  8:38PM 0:01.05 -csh (csh)
karels  1101  0.0  0.0  4516 3884  p0 TW   12:14PM 0:03.16 gdb -k bsdg
evi     1251  0.0  0.0  320   256  p8 Is+  1:50PM 0:00.47 -csh (csh)
evi     1264  0.0  0.0  210   256  p8 Ss   1:52PM 0:00.02 vi bondage
trent   1485  0.0  0.0  292   184  pa Ss   3:14PM 0:00.18 -csh (csh)
evi     1517  0.0  0.0  128    64  p8 S+   3:17PM 0:00.03 man logger
trent   1520  0.0  0.0  332   224  pa R+   3:17PM 0:00.04 ps -aux
```

We put in an extra set of headings after the page break; normally, there's only one. The meaning of each field is explained in Table 5.3.

Table 5.3   Explanation of ps -aux output (BSD)

Field	Contents
USER	User name of the process's owner
PID	Process ID
%CPU	Percentage of the CPU this process is using
%MEM	Percentage of real memory this process is using
VSZ	Virtual size of the process, in kilobytes
RSS	Resident set size (number of 1K pages in memory)
TT	Control terminal ID
STAT	Current process status:
	R = Runnable D = In disk (or short-term) wait
	I = Sleeping (< 20 sec) S = Sleeping (> 20 sec)
	T = Stopped Z = Zombie
	Additional Flags:
	L = Some pages are locked in core (for rawio)
	s = Process is a session leader (head of control terminal)
	W = Process is swapped out
	+ = Process is in the foreground of its control terminal
START	Time the process was started
TIME	CPU time the process has consumed[a]
COMMAND	Command name and arguments

a. No surprise that the X Windows server is at the top of the list!

Another useful set of arguments in BSD is **-axl**, which provides more technical information. It is also faster to run; this can be very important if the system is already bogged down by some other process. **ps** is generally quite expensive to run.

```
% ps -axl
UID PID PPID CPU PRI NI VSZ RSS WCHAN STAT TT   TIME    COMMAND
  0   0    0   0 -18  0   0   0 a5e6c DLs  ??  0:00.06 (swapper)
  0   1    0   0  10  0 208 120 wait  Is   ??  0:00.20 init -s
  0   2    0   0 -18  0   0  12 a203c DL   ??  0:00.06 pagedaemon
  0  46    1   0   2  0 160 112 select Ss  ??  0:01.47 syslogd
  0  64    1   0  18  0  72  28 pause Ss   ??  0:00.91 update
  0  66    1   0  18  0 228 152 pause S    ??  0:00.23 cron
  0  71    1   0   2  0 360 276 select Is  ??  0:01.62 named
  0  75    1   0   2  0 236 104 select IWs ??  0:00.02 lpd
  0  77    1   0   2  0 160  88 select IWs ??  0:00.07 portmap
  0  84    1   0   2  0 260 204 select IWs ??  0:00.23 mountd
```

Shown here in an abbreviated example, **ps -axl** includes information such as the parent process ID (PPID), nice value (NI), and resource the process is waiting for (WCHAN).

On ATT systems, **ps -ef** is a good place to start:

```
% ps -ef
  UID   PID  PPID  C   STIME TTY     TIME COMD
 root     0     0 80  Dec 21 ?      0:02 sched
 root     1     0  2  Dec 21 ?      4:32 /etc/init -
 root     2     0  8  Dec 21 ?      0:00 pageout
 root     3     0 80  Dec 21 ?     31:54 fsflush
 root  7138     1 80 14:25:19 ?     0:29 /usr/lib/lpsched
 root   101     1 80  Dec 21 ?      0:17 /usr/sbin/rpcbind
 root   117     1 56  Dec 21 ?      0:01 /usr/sbin/inetd -s
 root   128     1 34  Dec 21 ?      0:00 /usr/lib/nfs/statd
 root   130     1 80  Dec 21 ?      0:01 /usr/lib/nfs/lockd
 root   142     1 41  Dec 21 ?      0:00 /usr/sbin/syslogd
 root   152  1253     Dec 21 ?      0:08 /usr/sbin/cron
 root   171     1 80  Dec 21 ?      0:02 /usr/lib/sendmail -bd
 root   178     1 80  Dec 21 ?      0:01 /usr/sbin/vold
 root   198   195 80  Dec 21 ?      0:03 /usr/lib/saf/ttymon
  evi  4388  4386 80 13:41:09 pts/5 0:01 -csh
scott  4402  4400 80 13:54:39 pts/6 0:02 -csh
trent  8482  8444 35 14:34:10 pts/7 0:00 ps -ef
trent  8444  8442203 14:32:50 pts/7 0:01 -csh
```

The columns are explained in Table 5.4.

Table 5.4 Explanation of ps -ef output (ATT)

Field	Content	Field	Content
UID	User name of the owner	STIME	Time the process was started
PID	Process ID	TTY	Control terminal
PPID	PID of the parent process	TIME	CPU time consumed
C	CPU use/scheduling info	COMD	Command and arguments

Like **ps -axl** in the BSD world, **ps -elf** on ATT systems shows additional gory details.

```
% ps -elf
 F S   UID PID PPID C  P NI    ADDR  SZ    WCHAN TIME COMD
19 T  root   0    0 80 0 SY f00c2fd8   0         0:02 sched
 8 S  root   1    0 65 1 20 ff26a800  88 ff2632c8 4:32 init -
19 S  root   2    0  8 0 SY ff260200   0 f00ca398 0:00 pageout
19 S  root   3    0 80 0 SY ff258000   0  f00ca50 9:55 fsflush
 8 S  root 142    1 41 1 20 ff2e8000 176  f00cb69 0:00 syslogd
 8 S trent 444  442 63 1 20 ff480000 118 ff4830c8 0:01 -csh
 8 O trent 500  444 13 1 20 ffae2000 305         2:03 crack
 8 O trent 523  444 37 1 20 ff1c5000  85         0:00 ps -elf
```

STIME and TTY columns have been omitted to fit the page; they are identical to those produced with **ps -ef**. Fields are described in Table 5.5.

Table 5.5   Explanation of ps -elf output (ATT)

Field	Contents
F	Process flags: 00 = Terminated 01 = System process 02 = Being traced 04 = Stopped while being traced 10 = In primary memory
S	Process status: O = Currently running S = Sleeping (waiting for event) R = Eligible to run I = Being created Z = Zombie
UID	User name of the process's owner
PID	Process ID
PPID	Process ID of the parent process
C	Process CPU utilization/scheduling info
PRI	Scheduling priority
NI	Nice value or SY for system processes
ADDR	Memory address of the process
SZ	Size (in pages) of the process in main memory
WCHAN	Address of the object the process is waiting for

5.9 TOP: MONITOR PROCESSES EVEN BETTER

top is included on the CD-ROM.

Since commands like **ps** offer only a one-time snapshot of your system, it is often difficult to grasp the "big picture" of what's really happening. **top** is a freely-available program that compiles on many systems and provides a regularly-updated summary of active processes and their use of resources.

For example:

```
last pid: 21314; load averages: 2.97, 2.95, 2.89  15:51:51
75 processes:  71 sleeping, 3 running, 1 zombie
cpu states: 44.5% user, 0% nice, 23.9% system, 31.6% idle
Memory: 113M avail, 108M in use, 4972K free, 6232K locked
```

PID	USER	PRI	NICE	SIZE	RES	STATE	TIME	WCPU	CPU	COMMAND
1313	root	1	-19	292K	148K	sleep	0:00	9.3%	0.7%	erpcd
2858	root	1	0	1564K	676K	sleep	0:20	5.4%	0.7%	sendma
1310	root	27	0	812K	488K	run	0:00	7.6%	0.3%	sendma
981	root	29	0	2152K	2324K	run	0:03	0.0%	0.0%	top
192	root	1	0	44K	276K	sleep	0:48	0.0%	0.0%	in.rlo
5791	root	1	0	44K	276K	sleep	0:22	0.0%	0.0%	in.rlo
776	root	1	0	44K	276K	sleep	0:00	0.0%	0.0%	in.rlo
778	uucp	27	0	244K	508K	run	0:04	0.0%	0.0%	uucico
5298	randy	15	0	228K	176K	sleep	0:00	0.0%	0.0%	csh
151	root	15	0	12K	8K	sleep	54:40	0.0%	0.0%	update
0962	trent	15	0	212K	0K	sleep	0:00	0.0%	0.0%	csh
5843	beth	15	0	208K	0K	sleep	0:00	0.0%	0.0%	csh
167	root	15	0	100K	0K	sleep	0:00	0.0%	0.0%	lpd
1311	randy	5	0	224K	408K	sleep	0:00	0.0%	0.0%	prev

By default, the display is updated every ten seconds. The most active processes appear at the top. **top** also accepts input from the keyboard and allows you to send signals and **renice** processes, so that you can observe how your actions affect the overall condition of the machine.

top must consume a significant portion of the CPU to show an update every ten seconds. It should only be used for debugging purposes, not as a "Hey, look what neat tools I run in my spare windows" toy.

5.10 NOHUP: PROTECT BACKGROUND PROCESSES

When a primitive shell such as **sh** is terminated, it sends a hangup signal to all of its descendants. If a process is running in the background, it will often be killed by this signal, which is not usually what you want. If you intend to run a program in the background that continues to execute after you log out, it should be started with the **nohup** command. The format of this command is:

    nohup *command* **&**

This makes the specified *command* ignore the hangup signal. It also has the side effect of increasing the niceness by five. Any output the process generates will be placed in the file **nohup.out** if standard output and standard error are not redirected.

Users of **csh** and other modern shells have little need for **nohup**.

5.11 ERRANT PROCESSES

There are occasionally processes on the system that for some reason or another need to be managed by the system administrator.

The most common type of problematic process is a hung process. A hung process is no longer executing properly, does not respond to its control terminal, and generally just hangs around doing nothing, hence the name. Hung processes often show up on a **ps** listing as <exiting>.

See page 669 for more information about handling runaway processes.

A more unpleasant type of errant process is a runaway process. Runaways come in two flavors: user processes that use up excessive amounts of a system resource such as CPU time or disk space, and system processes that suddenly go berserk and exhibit wild behavior. The first type of runaway is simply a resource hog and is not necessarily malfunctioning.

Processes using excessive CPU time can be identified by looking at the output of **ps**. If it is obvious that a user process is consuming more CPU than can be reasonably expected, the process should be investigated. The easiest way to handle the situation is to contact the process's owner and ask what is going on, but if this can't be done you will have to do some poking around of your own. Although you should not normally look into users' home directories, it is acceptable to track down the source code of a runaway process to find out what it's doing.

There are two reasons to find out what the process is trying to do before tampering with it. First, the process may be both legitimate and important to the user. It isn't a great idea to go around randomly killing processes just because they happen to use a lot of CPU. Second, the process may be malicious or destructive. In this case, you've got to know exactly what the process was doing so you can fix the damage.

If the reason for a runaway process's existence can't be determined, suspend the process with a STOP signal and send email to the owner explaining what has happened. The process can be restarted later with a CONT signal. If a process is using an excessive amount of CPU but appears to be doing something reasonable and working correctly, you should **renice** it to a lower priority and ask the owner to do the nicing in the future.

See page 629 for more information about handling disk overflows.

On systems that do not implement quotas (see Chapter 26), runaway processes can fill up an entire filesystem, causing numerous problems. When a filesystem fills up, lots of messages will be logged to the console, and attempts to write to the filesystem will produce error messages.

The first thing to do in this situation is to stop the process that was filling up the disk. If you have been keeping a reasonable amount of breathing room on the disk, you can be fairly sure that something is amiss when it suddenly fills up. You'll have to use some sleuthing skills to find a disk-eating runaway, since there's no tool analogous to **ps** that will tell you who's consuming disk space at the fastest rate. By the time you get to looking for the culprit, it may no longer be active.

You may want to suspend all suspicious-looking processes until you find the one that's causing the problem, but remember to restart the innocents when you are done. When you find the offending process, remove the files it was creating; your filesystem should be back to normal.

An old and well-known "prank" is to start an infinite loop from the shell that does:

```
while 1
    mkdir adir
    cd adir
    touch afile
end
```

This occasionally shows up originating from an unprotected login or from a terminal that was left logged in. There is nothing you can do except clean up the aftermath and warn users about protecting their accounts. Because the directory tree that is left behind by this little jewel may be too large for **rm -r** to handle, you will have to write a script that descends to the bottom of the tree and then removes directories as it backs out.

If the problem occurs in **/tmp** and you have set up **/tmp** as a separate filesystem, you can reinitialize **/tmp** with **newfs** instead of attempting to delete individual files. See Chapter 9 for more information about the management of filesystems.

6 *Adding New Users*

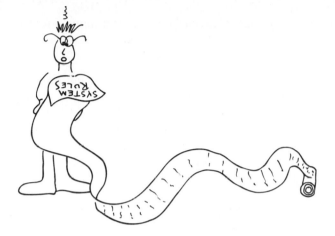

6.1 INTRODUCTION

Adding and removing users is a routine chore on most systems. These tasks are simple, but they are also boring; most administrators build tools to automate the process and then delegate the actual work to an assistant or operator.

This chapter discusses the gritty details of account management, along with some pointers for automation. Our own tool for adding and removing users (**adduser**) is included on the CD-ROM.

6.2 ADDING USERS

The process of adding a new user consists of three steps required by the system, two steps that establish a useful environment for the new user, and several extra steps for your own convenience as an administrator.

Required:

- Edit the `/etc/passwd` file to define the user's account.
- Set an initial password.
- Create the user's home directory.

For the user:

- Copy default startup files to the user's home directory.
- Set the user's mail home and establish mail aliases.

For you:

- Add the user to the /etc/group file.
- Record accounting information.
- Enter the user in the site-wide user database.
- Enter contact information in the local phone book.
- Configure disk quotas.
- Verify that the account is set up correctly.

The **adduser** program on the CD-ROM performs most of these operations for you (although you'll probably need to customize it for your site). A cookbook-style recipe for manually adding a new user follows. These steps must all be performed as root.

Editing the /etc/passwd File

The **passwd** file is a list of users recognized by the system. It is consulted at login time to determine the user's UID and, on most systems, to verify the login password. Each line in /etc/passwd represents one user and contains seven fields separated by colons:

- Login name
- Encrypted password
- UID number
- Default GID number
- "GECOS" information – full name, office, extension, home phone
- Home directory
- Login shell

The following lines are all valid /etc/passwd entries:

```
root:Ig764L2qjvdrT:0:0:The System,,x6096,:/:/bin/csh
jl:JJ4hER3.w3gf6:100:0:Jim Lane,ECT8-3,,:/staff/jl:/bin/sh
dotty:ntkYob4A1f3ci:101:20::/home/korbel/dotty:/bin/csh
```

The /etc/passwd file is often managed by a database system such as NIS. See Chapter 18, *Sharing System Files*, for more information.

On BSD systems, you use the **vipw** command to edit the **passwd** file so that your editing session and a user's change of password cannot collide. **vipw** locks the file and then invokes the text editor specified by the environment variable EDITOR, or **vi** if EDITOR is not defined.

For example, adding the following line to /etc/passwd would define an account called "tyler":

```
tyler:*:103:10:Tyler Stevens, ECEE 3-27, x7919,:
    /home/staff/tyler:/bin/csh
```

This line has been wrapped to fit the page; in real life, each entry in /etc/passwd must be on a single line.

Login name

Login names must be unique and no more than eight characters long. They may include numbers (except as the first character), but should not contain punctuation. Login names may contain both upper- and lowercase letters; however, they are case-sensitive. Uppercase-only login names cause UNIX to think you have a terminal that does not support lowercase letters, so it is best to avoid these.

Login names should be relatively easy to remember, so random sequences of letters do not make good login names. Avoid "handles" and cutesy nicknames. Since login names are often used as email addresses, it's useful to establish a standard way of forming them. It should be possible for your users to make educated guesses about each other's login names. First names, last names, initials, or some combination of these all make reasonable naming schemes.

See page 449 for more information about mail aliases. Any fixed scheme eventually results in duplicates or login names that are too long, so you will sometimes have to make exceptions. In the case of a long name, the **/etc/aliases** file can be used to equate two versions of the name, at least as far as mail is concerned.

For example, you might use an employee's first initial and last name as a paradigm. Brent Browning would therefore be "bbrowning," which is nine characters and thus too long. Instead, you can assign the user the login "brentb," leaving bbrowning as an **alias** file entry:

```
bbrowning: brentb
```

If your site has a global mail aliases file, each new login name must be distinct from any alias in this file. If it is not, mail will be delivered to the alias rather than the new user.

If you have more than one machine, login names should be unique in two senses. First, a user should have the same login on every machine. This is mostly for convenience, both yours and the user's.

See page 548 for a discussion of login equivalence issues. Second, a particular login name should always refer to the same person. Large security holes are created if the same name refers to two different users in a networked environment. For example, if scott@boulder was Scott Seebass and scott@refuge (on the same physical network) was Scott Hudson, then either Scott could access the other's files under certain circumstances.

Encrypted password

/etc/passwd stores passwords in an encrypted form. Unless you can perform DES encryption in your head (we want to meet you), you must either set the contents of this field using **passwd** (**yppasswd** if you use

NIS; see Chapter 18 for details) or copy an encrypted password string from another account.

When you edit **/etc/passwd** to create a new account, you should put a star ("*") in the encrypted password field. The star prohibits unauthorized use of the account until you have set a real password. Never leave this field empty; that introduces a jumbo-sized security hole because no password is required to access the account.

With the advent of faster computing hardware and more efficient encryption algorithms, it has become increasingly important to obscure the encrypted passwords by placing them in a separate file that is not world-readable. This is known as a shadow password mechanism. See page 543 for a complete discussion of shadow passwords.

On two of our example systems, shadow passwords are required. On these systems, you must modify the shadow password file when adding and removing users to keep it consistent with **/etc/passwd**. Unfortunately, the syntax and location of the shadow password file vary from platform to platform.

 /etc/shadow contains the encrypted password string, as well as password aging and account-life information. However, it does not contain most of the other information from **/etc/passwd**. Sun suggests that you use the **useradd**, **usermod**, and **userdel** commands to add, modify, and delete accounts; they understand the **/etc/shadow** dependencies. **vipw** allows you to edit **/etc/shadow** by hand. See the man page on **shadow** for details.

BSD **/etc/master.passwd** contains the complete version of the **passwd** file (with three bonus fields), including encrypted password strings. **/etc/passwd** contains regular seven-field entries in which the password has been replaced with a star. **vipw** edits the **master.passwd** file, then generates the stripped-down version automatically (in addition to running **pwd_mkdb**, which creates a hashed copy of the file).

UID number

See Chapter 17 for more information about NFS.

UIDs must be distinct integers between 0 and 32,767. In a networked environment using NFS, they must be unique across the entire network. That is, a particular UID must refer to the same login name and the same person throughout the network.

By definition, root has UID 0. Most systems also have pseudo-users bin (UID 1) and daemon (UID 2). It is customary to put UUCP logins and other fake logins at the beginning of the **/etc/passwd** file, with low UIDs. To give yourself plenty of room for non-human users, we recommend that you assign UIDs to real users starting at 100.

Avoid recycling UIDs, even those of users that have left your organization and had their accounts removed. This precaution avoids confusion if files are later restored from backups, where users are identified by UID rather than by login name.

In the example on page 86, Tyler's UID is 103. Here is that same example again, so you don't have to keep turning pages:

```
tyler:*:103:10:Tyler Stevens, ECEE 3-27, x7919,:
    /home/staff/tyler:/bin/csh
```

Default GID number

"wheel" was analogous to the root account in TOPS-20.

A group ID number must also be an integer between 0 and 32,767. Tyler's default GID in the example above is 10. GID 0 is reserved for the group called "root" or, in recent distributions, "wheel." GID 1 is usually used for the group "daemon."

Groups are defined in the `/etc/group` file. On some older versions of UNIX, a user could only be in one group at a time. The `newgrp` command was used to change the current working group, and the default GID field in `/etc/passwd` was used to specify the login-time default.

Most modern versions of UNIX allow a user to be in up to eight or sixteen groups at a time. The `newgrp` command is obsolete, and the GID field in `/etc/passwd` is essentially vestigial. However, this GID is still included in the user's group list.

GECOS field[1]

This field has no well-defined syntax. It was originally used to hold the login information needed to submit batch jobs to a mainframe running GECOS from UNIX systems at Bell Labs; now only the name remains. It is commonly used to record personal information for each user. An & in the GECOS field expands to the user's login name under BSD and saves a bit of typing.

Although you can use any formatting conventions you like, `finger` interprets comma-separated entries in the following order:

- Full name (often the only field used)
- Office number and building
- Office telephone extension
- Home phone number

Since "tyler" has not provided a home phone number, there is a trailing comma after his extension to indicate that the next field is empty. See the `/etc/passwd` examples on page 86 for more comma magic.

---

1. When Honeywell took over the computer division of GE, GECOS was changed to GCOS; both spellings survive today.

The **chfn** command allows users to change their GECOS information. **chfn** is useful for keeping things like phone numbers up to date, but it can be misused; a user can change the information to be either obscene or incorrect. Our academic computing center, which caters to hordes of undergraduates, has disabled **chfn**.

Home directory

Users are placed in their home directories when they log in. If a user's home directory is missing at login time, a message such as "no home directory" is printed. Some systems allow the login to proceed and put the user in the root directory. Other systems do not allow logins without a home directory.

If home directories are shared via NFS, they may be unavailable in the event of server or network problems.

Home directories are usually named with their owners' login names; for example, the home directory for tyler is **/home/staff/tyler**.

Shell

We recommend csh as the default shell for new users.

The login shell is normally a command interpreter such as the Bourne shell or the C shell (**/bin/sh** or **/bin/csh**), but it can be any program. **sh** is the default on most systems and is used if **/etc/passwd** does not specify a login shell. Other common shells include **ksh** (the Korn shell) and **tcsh** (a fancy C shell with command editing).

On BSD systems, users can change their shells with the **chsh** command. The file **/etc/shells** contains a list of shells that **chsh** will permit users to select; root may use **chsh** without restrictions. Be sure the entries in **/etc/shells** are absolute paths.

Setting an Initial Password

Root can change any user's password with the command

```
passwd user
```

Rules for selecting good passwords are given on page 542.

passwd will prompt you for new password and will ask you to repeat it. If you choose a short, all-lowercase password, **passwd** will complain and ask you to use something longer. If you insist on the same password about three times, BSD will grudgingly accept it, but most versions of ATT UNIX will force you to use a password that contains mixed case or more characters. **passwd** might let you know what the rules are for your particular UNIX if it doesn't like your initial attempt.

Never leave a new account, or any account with access to a shell, without a password.

Creating the Home Directory

Any directory you create will initially be owned by root, so you must change its owner and group with the **chown** and **chgrp** commands. The following sequence of commands would create a home directory appropriate for our example user:

```
# mkdir /home/staff/tyler
# chown tyler /home/staff/tyler
# chgrp staff /home/staff/tyler
# chmod 700 /home/staff/tyler
```

Copying in the Startup Files

Some commands and utilities can be customized by placing configuration files in your home directory. Startup files traditionally begin with a dot and end with the letters **rc**, short for "run command," a relic of the CTSS operating system. The initial dot causes **ls** to elide these files from directory listings unless the **-a** option is used; they are considered "uninteresting." Some common startup files are listed in Table 6.1.

Table 6.1 Startup files and their uses

Command	Filename	Typical uses
csh	.login	Sets the terminal type Sets up environment variables Sets **biff** and **mesg** switches
	.cshrc	Sets command aliases Sets path for command searches Sets **umask** value to control permissions Sets cdpath for filename searches Sets variables prompt, history, savehist
	.logout	Prints "to do" reminders Runs the **fortune** command Clears the screen
sh	.profile	Similar to .login and .cshrc for **sh**
vi	.exrc	Sets **vi** editor options
emacs	.emacs_pro	Sets **emacs** editor options Sets **emacs** key bindings
mail[a]	.mailrc	Defines personal mail aliases Sets parameters for mail reader
rn	.newsrc	Specifies newsgroups of interest
xrdb	.Xdefaults	Specifies X11 configuration: fonts, color, etc.
startx	.xinitrc	Specifies initial X11 environment

a. The BSD version.

If you don't already have a set of good, general startup files, make a directory `/usr/local/lib/skel` and create them with a text editor. Make sure the startup files contain defaults that are reasonable for unsophisticated users. However, don't confuse users by "protecting" them from UNIX; entries such as

```
alias dir ls -l
alias rm rm -i
```

are considered poor form.[2]

The command sequence for installing startup files for the new user tyler would look like this:

```
# cp /usr/local/lib/skel/.[a-zA-Z]* /home/staff/tyler
# chmod 644 /home/staff/tyler/.[a-zA-Z]*
# chown tyler /home/staff/tyler/.[a-zA-Z]*
# chgrp staff /home/staff/tyler/.[a-zA-Z]*
```

Notice that we cannot use

```
# chown tyler /home/staff/tyler/.*
```

because tyler would then own not only his own files but also the parent directory ".." (**/home/staff**) as well. Be careful not to make this mistake; it is a very common and dangerous one.

Setting the Mail Home

See page 449 for more information about mail aliases.

It is convenient for each user to receive electronic mail on only one machine. This is often implemented with an entry in the global aliases file **/etc/aliases** (or the userDB in **sendmail** V8; see Chapter 21) that forwards all mail to a particular machine. For example, the lines:

```
tyler: tyler@tigger
tstevens: tyler
```

would route all of tyler's mail to the machine tigger and would establish "tstevens" as an alias for "tyler."

Editing the /etc/group File

/etc/group contains the names of UNIX groups and a list of each group's members. For example:

```
wheel:*:0:root,evi,garth,scott,trent
staff:*:10:lloyd,evi
student:*:20:dotty
```

Each line represents one group and contains four fields:

- Group name
- Encrypted password (vestigial and never used)
- GID number
- List of members (separated by commas)

2. One of our reviewers wrote, "Not quite cricket, eh?"

As in **/etc/passwd**, fields are separated by colons. The group name must be eight or fewer characters on some systems. Standard UNIX distributions do not provide for group passwords, although the field is allocated in the **/etc/group** file. Most sites put stars in this field.

To continue the processing of the new user "tyler," we should add his login name to the list of users in group 10, since that was the default group to which we assigned him in the **/etc/passwd** file. Strictly speaking, tyler will be in group 10 whether he's listed in **/etc/group** or not, because his **passwd** entry has already given him this membership. However, this information should be entered in **/etc/group** so that you always know exactly which users belong to which groups.[3]

Suppose we also wanted to put tyler in the group "wheel." (On some systems, users must be in this group to use the **su** command.) We would simply make the following changes to **/etc/group**:

```
wheel:*:0:root,evi,garth,scott,trent,tyler
staff::10:lloyd,evi,tyler
```

Recording Accounting Information

An industrial-strength accounting system needs information about the user's full name, billing address, account number, and fee schedule. If your site intends to do real accounting, this information should be entered when each user is added.

In our opinion, usage-based accounting is not a good way to charge for computer services. See Chapter 28, *Accounting*, for more information about the accounting system, and refer to Chapter 32, *Policy and Politics* for a discussion of various billing options.

Updating the User Database and Phone Book

An on-line user database and phone book can easily be created from the GECOS fields of the **passwd** file, especially if the comma conventions of the **finger** program are observed. A simple **phone** script can be written to search for items in the database. Our local version first searches a private file (**.phonelist**) in the user's home directory and then looks in the system-wide database.

Under **csh**, this is simply:

```
#!/bin/csh -f
grep -i $1 ~/.phonelist /usr/local/pub/phonelist
```

3. The kernel doesn't actually care what's in **/etc/passwd** or **/etc/group**; it only cares about raw UID and GID numbers. **passwd** and **group** store account information for use by high-level software such as **login**. See page 119 for details about the login process.

Setting Quotas

See Chapter 26 for more information about disk quotas.

If your site uses disk quotas, you should set them for each new account with the **edquota** command. **edquota** can be used to interactively specify various limits, but it is more commonly used in "prototype" mode to model the quotas of the new user after those of someone else. For example, the command

```
edquota -p proto-user new-user
```

sets *new-user*'s quotas to be the same as *proto-user*'s. This way of using **edquota** is especially useful in **adduser** scripts.

Verifying the New Login

To verify that a new account is properly configured, first log out, then log in as the new user and execute the following commands:

```
% pwd          /* To verify the home directory */
% ls -lag      /* BSD: check owner/group of startup files */
% ls -la       /* ATT: check owner/group of startup files */
```

You will need to notify new users of their login names and initial passwords. This is also a good time to supply documentation on local customs and expected behavior as a good citizen of the user community.

See page 725 for more information about written user contracts.

If your site requires users to sign a written contract, be sure this step has been completed before releasing the account. This will prevent oversights and strengthen the legal basis of any sanctions you might later need to impose. Also, be sure to remind new users to change their passwords immediately.

6.3 REMOVING USERS

When a user leaves, that user's login and files must be removed from the system. This procedure involves removing all references to the login name that were added by the **adduser** program, including those in user databases, phone lists, and accounting databases. Before you remove a user's home directory, you should relocate any files that are needed by other users.

Accounting is typically done on a monthly basis, so sites that use accounting must implement a two-stage removal process. The login should at first be disabled, but still available to the accounting programs. After accounting has been run, all traces of the login should be extirpated. (But remember, avoid recycling UIDs.)

6.4 DISABLING LOGINS

Occasionally, a user's login must be temporarily disabled. Before networking invaded the UNIX world, we would just put a star in front of the encrypted password, making it impossible for the user to log in. However, the user could still log in across the network. These days, we replace the user's shell with a program that prints a message explaining why the login has been disabled and provides instructions for rectifying the situation.

6.5 PASSWORD AGING

Password aging is a feature of many modern UNIX implementations. It forces users to change their passwords on a regular basis. We find that in our environment it is unnecessary and in fact is a bit of a security hole. A complete discussion of password aging is given on page 544.

6.6 PSEUDO-LOGINS

A pseudo-login is one that does not correspond to a real person. The "bin" and "daemon" pseudo-logins are distributed with the system. It is often convenient to create additional pseudo-logins.

For example, pseudo-logins called "who," "tty," and "hostname" that execute the corresponding commands as their shells often come in very handy. Pseudo-logins such as "diskhog," "nolimit," or "tiny" can be used as prototypes for disk quotas.

7 Devices and Drivers

BUS DRIVER

7.1 INTRODUCTION

A device driver is a program that manages the system's interaction with a particular piece of hardware.[1] The driver translates between the hardware commands understood by the device and the stylized programming interface used by the kernel. The existence of the driver layer helps to keep UNIX reasonably device-independent.

Device drivers are part of the kernel; they are not user processes. However, a driver can be accessed both from within the kernel and from user space. User-level access to devices is provided through special device files that live in the **/dev** directory. The kernel transforms operations on these special files into calls to the code of the driver.

In the olden days (the 1980s), most pieces of hardware required an interface board and a custom driver that was compiled into the kernel. Several things have happened to change this:

- The adoption of the SCSI standard for most disk and tape drives has eliminated the need for manufacturers to make up their own proprietary interface specifications.

- The implementation of loadable kernel modules has allowed drivers to be added to the kernel without relinking.

---

1. Or more accurately, with a particular *type* of hardware. One driver can support several devices of the same type.

- Workstation manufacturers now include many devices that used to be optional (such as Ethernet interfaces) in their standard configurations.

- The UNIX market has become larger and more naïve, and hardware vendors have discovered that they can no longer sell and support hardware that is difficult to install.

Most devices you add to your system will fall into three categories:

SCSI   Devices that attach to a SCSI bus are easy to configure. See Chapter 9, *Adding a Disk*, for a description of SCSI. Most systems have one driver that allows direct access to the SCSI bus, plus additional drivers for special types of devices such as disks and tapes.

Vendor   Most devices you can buy from your hardware vendor will already be supported by the operating system. Unless you have explicitly removed drivers, the kernel will usually recognize a new device as soon as you install it. In addition, the appropriate device files in **/dev** will already have been created for you, or the OS will create them on the fly.

Some vendors (for example, Sun) publish such thorough documentation that third-party hardware can configure itself in the same way as the vendor's. You will probably not have to perform any configuration chores when you add additional Ethernet boards, graphics boards, and SCSI controllers.[2]

Third-party   When you purchase a piece of hardware from a third party (someone other than your hardware vendor), it will usually come with an installation script that installs the device, reconfigures the kernel (if necessary), and makes device entries. At the very least, step-by-step instructions will be provided. On systems with loadable drivers, kernel reconfiguration may not be necessary.

You may never need to add a device driver by hand, but there is still quite a bit of useful information in this chapter. We will discuss the relationship between device drivers and files in the **/dev** directory, a relationship that every administrator will eventually need to understand. We'll also give some pointers on the handling of loadable device drivers on our example platforms. If you are planning to add a device

---

2. Of course, you will have to configure high-level software to take advantage of the new devices, but that is a different layer of abstraction.

driver to the system by hand, be sure to read Chapter 13, *Configuring the Kernel*, as well.

7.2 DEVICE NUMBERS AND JUMP TABLES

See page 65 for more information about inodes.

Device files are mapped to devices via their "major and minor device numbers," values that are stored in the file's inode structure. The major device number identifies the driver that the file is associated with. The minor device number identifies which particular device of a given type is to be addressed. The minor device number is often called the unit number or "instance" of the device.

The minor device number is sometimes used by the driver to select particular characteristic of a device. For example, a single tape drive may have several files in /**dev** representing it in various configurations of recording density and rewind characteristics.

There are actually two types of device files: block device files and character device files. A block device is read or written a block (a group of bytes, usually a multiple of 512) at a time, while a character device can be read or written one byte at a time. Some devices support access via both block and character device files. Disks and tapes lead dual lives; terminals and printers do not.

Device drivers present a standard interface to the kernel. Each driver has routines for performing some or all of the following functions:

```
probe    attach    open    close    read    reset      stop
select   strategy  dump    psize    write   timeout

process a transmit interrupt
process a receive interrupt
ioctl (input/output control)
```

Inside the kernel, the addresses of these functions for each driver are stored in a structure called a jump table. There are actually two tables: one for character devices and one for block devices. The jump tables are indexed by major device number.

It is sometimes convenient to implement an abstraction as a device driver even when there is no actual device for it to control. Such phantom devices are known as pseudo-devices. For example, a user who logs in over the network is assigned a PTY (pseudo-TTY) that looks, feels, and smells like a serial port from the perspective of high-level software. This trick allows programs written in the days when everyone used a TTY to continue to work without modification.

When a program performs an operation on a device file, the kernel automatically catches the reference, looks up the appropriate function name in the jump table, and transfers control to it. To perform an unusual operation that doesn't have a direct analog in the filesystem model (for example, ejecting a floppy disk), the `ioctl` system call is used to pass a message directly from user space into the driver.

All UNIX systems provide some way to add entries to the jump tables. On old systems where source code for the kernel was provided, you just edited the C code and made changes. Most vendors have now developed a system for building a jump table from one or more text files. There is usually an additional file or set of files that determine which modules will be linked into the kernel.

Table 7.1 lists the driver-related configuration files for each of our six example systems. The Man column lists the man pages you should refer to on each system for more information.

Table 7.1   Driver configuration files

System	Device table	Included files	Man[a]
Solaris	`/usr/kernel/drv/*conf`	`/usr/kernel/drv/*`	DP
HP-UX	`/etc/master`	`/etc/conf/dfile`	MCU
IRIX	`/var/sysgen/master.d/*`	`/var/sysgen/system/*`	MA
SunOS	`/sys/sun`*X*`/conf/`*KERNEL*	`/sys/sun`*X*`/conf/files*`	C
OSF/1	`/sys/conf/`*KERNEL*	`/sys/conf/files*`	C
BSDI	`/sys/`*X*`/conf/devices.`*X*	`/sys/conf/files.`*X*	C

a. A = `autoconfig`, C = `config`, D = `driver.conf`, M = `master`, P = `prtconf`, U = `uxgen`

In the sections below, we will show three examples of adding a new driver to the kernel: one BSD-style system (SunOS) and two ATT-style systems (HP-UX and IRIX). Most systems will be similar to one of these, or will use loadable drivers and will therefore not require you to modify the kernel to add a new driver.

Adding a BSD Device Driver

Adding a completely new device driver to a BSD machine involves adding it to a couple of configuration files and editing the kernel source code to include references to the driver's routines. The procedure is not for the faint of heart. We will use a SunOS system as our example. All BSD systems (including OSF/1 and BSDI) are similar, except that the locations of files may differ. We will add a WINDY device (a wind speed indicator) as our example.

The first step is to add the object files for the new driver to the list of files that are linked into the kernel. To do this, add an entry for the object files in `files.`*kernel* in the kernel configuration directory. On our example system, the kernel is called **RA** and the configuration directory is **/sys/sun4c/conf**. There is no **files.RA** by default, so we create one that contains the following line:

```
local/windy.o  optional  windy  device-driver
```

If there was already a **files.RA**, we'd just append this line to it. Our new device requires only one object file, **windy.o**. The optional keyword indicates that the driver should not be included in all kernels, but only ones that list the device in their configuration files. The next field, windy, specifies the name of the device. The last field identifies the entry as pertaining to a device driver.

Pathnames in the **files.**_kernel_ file are relative to the **sys** directory (in this case **/sys**), so we must create the **local** directory and copy in the new device driver:

```
# mkdir /sys/local
# cp ~scott/windy.o /sys/local/windy.o
```

The next step is to locate **conf.c** and add the driver to the system's jump tables (which are also known as "device switches"). Under SunOS, **conf.c** is in **/sys/sun/conf.c**. There are two device switches: one for character devices, called cdevsw, and one for block devices, called bdevsw. If your new device uses a character device file, modify the character device switch; if it uses a block device file, modify the block device switch. Some devices need entries in both switches.

Each of these device switches is a C struct that contains the names of all the appropriate control routines for a given device. Each slot in the switch holds a fixed number of names.

The character device switch looks something like this:

```
struct cdevsw cdevsw[] =
{
    {
        cnopen,     cnclose,   cnread,    cnwrite,   /*0*/
        cnioctl,    nulldev,   nulldev,   &cons,
        cnselect,   0,         0,
    },
    ...
    {
        nodev,      nodev,     nodev,     nodev,     /*52*/
        nodev,      nodev,     nodev,     0,
        nodev,      0,         0,
    },
    ...
```

The first two lines start the declaration of the entire switch, and each subsequent group of five lines gives information about one driver.

Notice the numbers in the comments; they tell you the major device number of the set being declared. Major device numbers are determined by offsets into the switch, so the numbering is actually implicit.

Next, you need to find a set that contains only null declarations (that is, a set of nodevs). Something like the second set in the example above is what you are looking for. Once you've found an empty entry, replace the nodevs with the names of your device driver's routines. If there are no unused slots, you can create a new entry at the end of the switch.

You must put the routines into the switch in the correct order; look at other entries to determine what this is. Our example driver has only the **open**, **read**, and **close** routines, so we edit the entry to look like this:

```
    {
        windy_open, windy_close, windy_read, nodev, /*52*/
        nodev,      nodev,       nodev,      0,
        nodev,      0,           0,
    },
```

Near the top of the **conf.c** file, you'll have to declare these routines so that the C compiler recognizes them as the names of functions:

```
    extern int   windy_open(), windy_close(), windy_read();
```

After adding the entry to the device switch, you need to add it to the kernel configuration file. We put the following entry in the **RA** file:

```
    device-driver windy      # WINDY wind speed indicator
```

This instructs the **config** program to include the files needed for the driver in the kernel. The next steps include:

- Running **config** and building a new kernel
- Copying the old kernel aside and installing the new kernel
- Rebooting and testing the new kernel.

These steps are all covered in Chapter 13, *Configuring the Kernel*. Finally, you will need to create device files (see page 105) and test the device itself.

Adding an HP-UX Device Driver

 On HP-UX systems, the jump tables are constructed from specifications in a text file called **master**. On our example system (HP-UX 9.03 on an HP 9000/700) the **master** file is in /etc and looks like this:

* name	handle	type	mask	block	char
scsi	sdisk	3	3FB	7	47
sctl	sctl	1	1FB	-1	105
autox	schgr	1	1FB	-1	33
autoch	autoch	3	10FB	10	55

```
opal            opal            3       10FB    14      104
scsitape        stape           1       1FB     -1      121
...

* Reserved for Third Party and User Drivers.
*               ---             -       -       -1      38
*               ---             -       -       -1      39

...
*               ---             -       -       8       -1
*               ---             -       -       15      -1

...
```

The first field specifies the device name. This is the name used in the configuration file (`/etc/conf/dfile` on this system) to indicate that the device should be included in the kernel. If the device is listed in the **master** file but does not appear in the kernel configuration file, it will not be compiled into the kernel.

The second field is the name by which the device is known inside the kernel. The kernel will expect the various device routines to be called *name_routine* (for example, **sdisk_open**). The third field is a bit mask that specifies some information about the type of the driver. Included in this mask are bits that specify whether it is a block driver, a character driver, or both. In the man page for **master**, the bits are defined as shown in Table 7.2.

Table 7.2 Driver description bits in HP-UX

Bit	Meaning (when turned on)	Value
Bit 1	The device has an interface card.	16
Bit 2	Only one copy of the driver is allowed.	8
Bit 3	This is a required driver.	4
Bit 4	This driver supports block device files.	2
Bit 5	This driver supports character device files.	1

After a quick glance at the man page, you might jump to the conclusion that a value of 1 indicates device with an interface card. But in HP's ultra-perverse nomenclature, "bit five" is actually the least-significant bit. For example, to specify that a device is a block and character device, we would use a binary mask of 00011. (However, the mask must be specified in hex in the **master** file.)

The fourth field is another bit mask that indicates which of the standard routines (**open**, **close**, **read**, etc.) are supported by the driver. The numbering conventions are equally bizarre. We refer you to the man page itself for the exact definitions of the bits. The fifth field indicates the major device number of the block device (-1 if there isn't one), and the last field gives the major device number for the character device (again, -1 if there isn't one).

Further down in the **master** file, some entries are marked for third-party use. As in the BSD example, we will add an entry for a WINDY, a character device that returns the wind speed from an anemometer. We steal the first available entry and change it to:

```
windy           wind            1       EO      -1      38
```

This line indicates that if we want to build the driver into the kernel, we need to add the specification windy to the **dfile**. The routines in the driver are called **wind_***routine*. The hex value 1 indicates that the driver may only be accessed through a character device file. The mask EO specifies that the device only supports the **open**, **read**, and **close** operations. There is no block device number, but the device can be accessed through character device number 38.

Later in the **master** file, library dependencies are specified:

```
* Driver handle    <libraries>
*
* subsystems first
lan01           liblan.a
fddi            liblan5.a libfddi.a
 ...
```

These entries specify which libraries are required to support various devices; for example, the FDDI driver requires both **liblan5.a** and **libfddi.a**. Our WINDY device has its own library, **libwind.a**:

```
windy           libwind.a
```

The first field is the same as the first field of the device entry. Note that unless we specify windy in the **dfile** for the kernel, **libwind.a** will not be linked in unless it was also needed by another device. Our changes to the **master** file for the WINDY device are now complete.

If you wrote your own driver and had only a **.o** file, you would need to archive it into a library with the **ar** command before you could include it in the kernel. The kernel build procedures only look in the **conf** directory for the libraries, so each file must be copied or linked there.

After copying the library, you would still need to:

- Add windy to the **dfile** for the system
- Build a new kernel
- Copy the old kernel aside and install the new one
- Reboot and test the new kernel

These tiresome chores are covered in Chapter 13, *Configuring the Kernel*. The last step is to create device files using **mknod**.

Adding an IRIX Device Driver

IRIX uses a directory of files (`/var/sysgen/master.d`) to perform the same function as the single `master` file in HP-UX. An IRIX master file would look something like this:

```
* IP6 Multichannel I/O Parallel Port Driver
*FLAG    PREFIX  SOFT    #DEV    DEPENDENCIES
c        plp     38      -
                                 plpintr(){true}
$$$
```

The name of the file is the name of the device; in this case, it is `plp`. The lines starting with a star ("*") are comments, and a $$$ indicates the end of the entry.

The first non-comment line contains five fields. The first of these indicates the type of device, in this case c for "character." See the man page for `master` for a complete list. The second field lists the naming prefix for the service routines. In this example, the routines would be called `plp_open`, `plp_close`, and so on. The third field specifies the major device number. If you duplicate a device number or exceed the table size, you'll be notified when you try to build the kernel. Field four indicates the number of subdevices, in this case, none. The last field identifies any other drivers that this module depends on (none).

The second line defines routines that might be referred to from other places in the kernel. These definitions are used only when the driver is not compiled into the kernel. In this example, the `plpintr` routine would be stubbed out to return true if the driver were omitted.

For the WINDY device, we'd create a file called `windy` that contained the following lines:

```
*FLAG    PREFIX  SOFT    #DEV    DEPENDENCIES
c        wind    60      -

$$$
```

The major device number (60) was selected by `grep`ping through the files in `master.d` and finding a device number that was not in use. After creating the `windy` file, we put the driver code in a file called `windy.a` in `/var/sysgen/boot`. The next few steps include:

- Adding the device to a file in `/var/sysgen/system.dl`
- Rebuilding the kernel
- Copying the old kernel aside and installing the new kernel
- Rebooting and testing the new kernel

All of this is covered Chapter 13, starting on page 239. The last steps are to create device entries using `mknod` and to test the device.

7.3 DEVICE FILES

By convention, device files are kept in the `/dev` directory.[3] On large systems, especially those with networking and pseudo-terminals, there may be hundreds of devices. ATT systems handle this quite nicely by using a separate subdirectory of `/dev` for each type of device: `disk`, `tape`, `terminal`, etc.

Device files are created with the `mknod` command, which has the syntax

`mknod` *filename type major minor*

where *filename* is the device file to be created, *type* is `c` for a character device or `b` for a block device, and *major* and *minor* are the major and minor device numbers. If you are creating a device file that refers to a driver that's already present in your kernel, check the man page for the driver (in section four on BSD systems, section seven for ATT) to find the appropriate major and minor device numbers.

A shell script called `MAKEDEV` is sometimes provided (in `/dev`) to automatically supply default values to `mknod`. Scan through the script to find the arguments needed for your device. For example, to make PTY entries on a SunOS system, you would use the following commands:

```
# cd /dev
# ./MAKEDEV pty
```

7.4 NAMING CONVENTIONS FOR DEVICES

Naming conventions for devices are somewhat random. They are often holdovers from the way things were done on a DEC PDP-11.

Devices that have both block and character identities usually preface the character device name with the letter `r` for "raw" (e.g., `/dev/sd0` and `/dev/rsd0`), or place it in a subdirectory with a name that starts with `r` (e.g., `/dev/dsk/dks0d3s0` vs. `/dev/rdsk/dks0d3s0`). However, an `r` does not always imply a raw device file.

See Chapter 8 for more information about serial ports.

Serial devices are usually named `tty` followed by a sequence of letters that identify the interface the port is attached to. There is sometimes more than one device file for a TTY; the extra files usually support alternate flow control methods or locking protocols.

BSD disk names often begin with a two-letter abbreviation for either the drive or the controller, followed by the drive number and partition name. For example, `sd0a` is the block device representing the `a` partition of the first disk drive on a SCSI controller; `rsd0a` is the corresponding character device.

---

3. The primary device files in Solaris are kept in `/devices`, but links to `/dev` are maintained automatically.

The names of tape devices often include not only a reference to the drive itself, but also an indication of whether the device rewinds after each tape operation and the density at which it reads and writes. Each vendor has a different scheme.

Table 7.3 lists some typical names for common devices (disk and tape drives) on our example systems. N indicates a unit number, P indicates a partition, and B indicates a unit and partition number ORed together.

Table 7.3   Device naming conventions for disks and tapes

System	SCSI Disk	Tape	NR Tape[a]
Solaris	/dev/[r]dsk/c201dNsP	/dev/rmt/N	/dev/rmt/Nn
HP-UX	/dev/[r]dsk/c201dNsP	/dev/rmt/Nm	/dev/rmt/Nmn
IRIX	/dev/[r]dsk/dks0dNsP	/dev/tape	/dev/nrtape
SunOS	/dev/[r]sdNP	/dev/rmtN	/dev/nrmtN
OSF/1	/dev/[r]rzB	/dev/rmtN{lmh}	/dev/nrmtN{lmh}
BSDI	/dev/sdNP	/dev/rmtN	/dev/nrmtN

a. Non-rewinding.

7.5 LOADABLE KERNEL MODULES

Most of our reference systems support loadable kernel modules. Loadable modules allow device drivers (among other things) to be linked into and removed from the kernel while it is running. This makes the installation of drivers much easier, since the kernel binary does not have to be changed. It also allows the kernel to be smaller, because drivers are not loaded unless they are needed.

Loadable modules are implemented by providing one or more documented "hooks" into the kernel where additional device drivers can grab on. A user-level command communicates with the kernel and tells it to load new modules into memory and to make entries for them in the system's jump tables. There is usually a user-level command that unloads drivers as well.

Although loadable drivers are convenient, they are not entirely safe. Any time you load or unload a module, you risk causing a kernel panic. We do not recommend loading or unloading an untested module when you are not willing to crash the machine.

Like other aspects of device and driver management, the implementation of loadable modules is operating system dependent. The sections below outline the commands and caveats appropriate for the four of our example systems that support loadable modules: Solaris, HP-UX, IRIX, and SunOS.

In Solaris, virtually everything is a loadable module. The **modinfo** command lists the currently-loaded modules. The output looks like this:

```
# modinfo
Id Loadaddr   Size Info Rev Module Name
 1 ff07e000   3ba0   1   1  specfs (filesystem for specfs)
 2 ff086000   1340   -   1  swapgeneric (root/swap config)
 3 ff082000   1a56   1   1  TS (time sharing sched class)
 4 ff084000    49c       1  TS_DPTBL (Timesharing dispatch)
 5 ff095000  15248   2   1  ufs (filesystem for ufs)
 6 ff0b8000    20e0   1   1  rootnex (sun4c root nexus)
 7 ff084a00    170  57   1  options (options driver)
 8 ff08dc00    2f4  62   1  dma (Direct Memory Access)
 9 ff08c000    968  59   1  sbus (SBus nexus driver)
 ...
```

On our Solaris system, the list continued for seventy-odd lines. Many elements that are hard-wired into the kernel on other versions of UNIX (such as UFS, the local filesystem) are loadable drivers in Solaris. This organization should make it much easier for third-parties to write add-on software packages that integrate easily and seamlessly into the kernel, at least in theory.

You can add a driver with the **add_drv** command. This command loads the driver into the kernel and makes the appropriate device links. All links are rebuilt each time the kernel reboots. Once you **add_drv** a driver, it will remain a part of the system until you actively remove it.

Modules can be unloaded by hand with **rem_drv**. Loadable modules that are not accessed through device files can be loaded and unloaded with **modload** and **modunload**. See Chapter 13, *Configuring the Kernel*, for more information about Solaris devices.

 Generic HP-UX does not support loadable modules, but there is an option that allows the loading of STREAMS modules. This option is supposed to become standard in HP-UX 10.0.

 IRIX 5.2 supports loadable modules; earlier versions did not. Modules are manipulated with the **ml** command. An active module can exist in two states: registered or loaded. If a module is registered, the kernel creates device entries for it but does not actually integrate its code. The first time the device files are accessed, the module is loaded. This convention allows the kernel to remain small but still provide access to numerous obscure devices. Some modules are always loaded.

ml with the **list** option catalogs the modules that the kernel is currently aware of.

For example:

```
# ml list
Loaded Modules:
Id: 264110088  Character device driver: prefix atalk,
   filename /usr/etc/appletalk/atalk.o
Registered Modules:
Id: 1016  Streams module: prefix kbd, fmodsw name kbd,
   filename /var/sysgen/boot/kbd.o
Id: 38  Character device driver: prefix plp, major 38,
   filename /var/sysgen/boot/hpcplp.o
Id: 1017  Streams module: prefix calcomp, fmodsw name
   calcomp, filename /var/sysgen/boot/calcomp.o
...
```

In this example, only one module is loaded (**atalk**), but numerous modules are registered and ready to be loaded if they are needed. For example, the **plp** (parallel line printer) driver is ready to be loaded if any device with major device number 38 is opened. Some modules will automatically unload themselves when they are no longer in use.

Various arguments to **ml** allow you to register, unregister, load, and unload modules. Currently, no major parts of IRIX are implemented as loadable modules, but this will probably change in future releases.

 SunOS versions 4.1.2 and later contain support for loadable modules. Currently-loaded modules can be listed with **modstat**. For example:

```
# modstat
Id  Type  Loadaddr  Size  B-major C-major Sysnum  Mod Name
 1  Pdrv  ff04c000  d000                          K-Talk
```

No standard parts of the OS are loadable modules, but many third parties make use of the facility, especially for S-BUS boards. Modules are loaded with **modload** and unloaded with **modunload**. If you want to use loadable modules, the VDDRV option must be included in your kernel configuration file and **/dev/vd** must exist.

8 *Serial Devices*

Child left to
its own
serial devices

8.1 INTRODUCTION

Serial ports are perhaps the handiest I/O facility available on UNIX systems. Although they are not especially fast, they are quite flexible and can be found on everything from PCs to mainframes.

Serial ports can be used with a variety of devices, including printers, terminals, and other computers. A device can be attached to the system either directly (with a cable) or via a telephone line with modems at each end to modulate and demodulate the serial signals.

This chapter describes how to attach serial devices to your system and how to configure your software to take advantage of them. We will often use terminals and modems as specific examples, but other serial devices are essentially similar.

8.2 STANDARDS FOR SIGNALS AND CONNECTORS

Most serial ports obey some variant of the standard known as RS-232. This standard specifies the electrical characteristics and meaning of each signal wire, as well as pin assignments on the traditional 25-pin (DB-25) serial connector.

Full RS-232 is overkill for many situations, as it defines signals that are unnecessary for basic communication. DB-25 connectors are also unpleasantly large for applications such as patch panels and laptop computers. As a result, a number of alternative connectors have come into widespread use. These are described in *Alternative Connectors* starting on page 112.

Traditional RS-232 uses twisted-pair cable, usually stranded 22-gauge wire. The original RS-232 signal voltages were ±12 volts DC, but ±5 volts is more common these days. Sometimes, ±3 volts is used.

DB-25 connectors are either male (with pins sticking out, called DB25P) or female (with matching holes, DB25S). There are tiny invisible numbers near the pins or holes which label them from 1 to 25. You can see them best by holding the connector up to the light and viewing it at an angle. Sometimes only pins 1, 13, 14, and 25 are numbered.

There was originally no standardization with regard to the sex of connectors. Both terminals and computers could be either male or female. Eventually, hardware designers realized that male hardware is much more fragile and subject to injury from sudden impact. Expensive computing hardware now usually has female connectors, and most cables are male on both ends.[1]

Exhibit A shows a male DB-25. As with most serial connectors, the pin numbers on a female connector are a mirror image of those on a male connector, so that like-numbered pins mate.

Exhibit A   A DB-25 connector

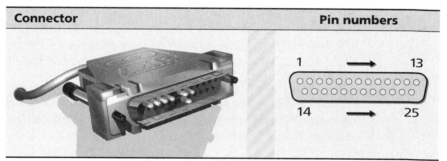

Note that in this picture, only seven pins are actually installed. This is typical for the real world. Most applications you will encounter use fewer than ten of the defined signals. Serial cables simply leave the unused pins disconnected.

The RS-232 signals and their pin assignments on a DB-25 connector are shown in Table 8.1.

---

1. At USWest, the words "male" and "female" are considered offensive. Employees are encouraged to use the politically correct terms "plug" and "receptacle."

Table 8.1   RS-232 signals and pin assignments

Pin	Name	Function	Pin	Name	Function
1	FG	Frame ground	14	STD	Secondary TD
2	TD	Transmitted data	15	TC	Transmit clock
3	RD	Received data	16	SRD	Secondary RD
4	RTS	Request to send	17	RC	Receive clock
5	CTS	Clear to send	18	–	Not assigned
6	DSR	Data set ready	19	SRTS	Secondary RTS
7	SG	Signal ground	20	DTR	Data terminal ready
8	DCD	Data carrier detect	21	SQ	Signal quality detector
9	–	Positive voltage	22	RI	Ring indicator
10	–	Negative voltage	23	DRS	Data rate selector
11	–	Not assigned	24	SCTE	Clock transmit external
12	SDCD	Secondary DCD	25	BUSY	Busy
13	SCTS	Secondary CTS			

There are two cabling configurations for serial equipment: DTE (Data Terminal Equipment) and DCE (Data Communications Equipment). These configurations determine which signals a device expects on which connector pins. Every device is configured as either DTE or DCE; some support both (but not at once). Computers, terminals, and printers are generally DTE, while most modems use DCE. This means that cables for hard-wired terminals are different from those for modems.

There is no sensible reason for both DTE and DCE to exist; all equipment could use the same wiring scheme. The existence of two conventions is merely one of the many pointless historical legacies of RS-232. Future serial systems, such as Apple's FireWire, promise to eliminate some of the silliness of the RS-232 standard.

Exhibit B shows pin assignments and connections for both null-modem and straight-through cables. Only "useful" signals are shown.

Exhibit B   Pin assignments and connections for DB-25 cables

Legend		Straight	Nulled
Frame ground	FG	1 —— 1	1 —— 1
Transmitted data	TD	2 —— 2	2 ✕ 2
Received data	RD	3 —— 3	3 ✕ 3
Request to send	RTS	4 —— 4	4 ✕ 4
Clear to send	CTS	5 —— 5	5 ✕ 5
Data set ready	DSR	6 —— 6	6 ✕ 6
Signal ground	SG	7 —— 7	7 —— 7
Data carrier detect	DCD	8 —— 8	8 ✕ 8
Data terminal ready	DTR	20 —— 20	20 ✕ 20

8.3 ALTERNATIVE CONNECTORS

The following sections describe the most common alternative connector systems: DB-9, DIN-8, and RJ-45. Despite their physical differences, these connectors all provide access to the same electrical signals as a DB-25. Devices that use different connectors are always compatible if the right kind of converter cable is used.

The DIN-8 Variant

DIN-8s are found on Macs and on some laptops and workstations. This almost circular and extremely compact connector provides pins for the seven most common serial signals. It is illustrated in Exhibit C.

Exhibit C A DIN-8 Connector

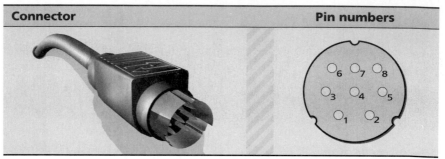

Neighborhood computer dealers usually carry injection-molded DB-25 to DIN-8 converter cables. Don't try to make them yourself because a DIN-8 is so tiny that it defies attempts to secure connections with human fingers. Pin assignments for a DIN-8 are shown in Table 8.2.

Table 8.2 Pins for a DIN-8 to DB-25 straight cable

DIN-8	DB-25	Signal	Function
3	2	TD	Transmitted data
5	3	RD	Received data
6	4	RTS	Request to send
2	5	CTS	Clear to send
4,8	7	SG	Signal ground
7	8	DCD	Data carrier detect
1	20	DTR	Data terminal ready

The DB-9 Variant

Commonly found on PCs, this nine-pin connector (which looks like a DB-25 "junior") provides the eight most commonly-used signals.

Exhibit D   A DB-9 Connector

Connector	Pin numbers

PC dealers in your area should carry prefab DB-9 to DB-25 converter cables. Table 8.3 shows the pin assignments.

Table 8.3   Pins for a DB-9 to DB-25 straight cable

DB-9	DB-25	Signal	Function
2	2	TD	Transmitted data
3	3	RD	Received data
8	4	RTS	Request to send
7	5	CTS	Clear to send
6	6	DSR	Data set ready
5	7	SG	Signal ground
4	8	DCD	Data carrier detect
1	20	DTR	Data terminal ready

The RJ-45 Variant

An RJ-45 is essentially an eight-wire modular telephone connector.

Exhibit E   An RJ-45 Connector

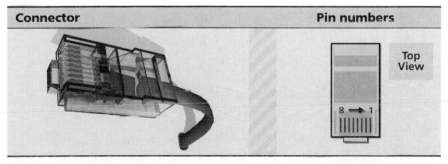

Connector	Pin numbers

RJ-45 jacks are almost never found on computers or garden-variety serial equipment, but they are often used as intermediate connectors when routing serial lines through patch panels. They can sometimes be found on devices that have many ports in close proximity, such as terminal servers. RJ-45s are used with flat telephone cable rather than stranded twisted-pair.

There are a number of standards for mapping the pins on an RJ-45 connector to a DB-25 connector. The best is Dave Yost's system, which wires all RJ-45-to-DB-25 connections in the same way while using the symmetric properties of the flat RJ-45 cable to allow connections to either DCE or DTE equipment. Dave's standard is presented in the next section.

The Yost Standard for RJ-45 Wiring

This specification was written by Dave Yost (email Dave@Yost.com) in June, 1987. He updated it for this book.

Here is a scheme that offers solutions to several RS-232 hassles:

- All cable connectors are of the same sex.
- There is no distinction between DTE and DCE.
- You can mass-terminate connector cables.

One consequence of #1 and #2 is that you only need one kind of cable.

Theory of operation

Each serial port on every piece of equipment at your site gets its own appropriately-wired DB-25 to RJ-45 adaptor. This adaptor is permanently screwed onto the port. The port now presents the same connector interface, female RJ-45, regardless of whether its underlying DB-25 connector was DTE or DCE or male or female.

Once you have put these adaptors on your RS-232 ports, you can connect anything to anything without

- Using null-modems or null-terminals
- Changing pins on cable connectors
- Building special cables

You can connect

- Modem to computer
- Modem to terminal
- Terminal to computer
- Terminal to terminal
- Computer to computer

etc., all with one kind of cable.

The cables are jacketed, eight-wire ribbon cable. The connectors on each end are squeezed onto the cable with a crimping tool, so there is no soldering or messing with pins. The cables are *not* wired normally (i.e. with each connector pin connected to the corresponding pin at the other end of the cable). They are wired "with a twist," or "mirror image," or "side-to-side reversed," or whatever you want to call it. Because of the way the adaptors are wired, the twist in the cable connects each transmit pin to its corresponding receive pin at the other end of the cable.

This scheme works because the layout of the signals on the ribbon cable is symmetrical. That is, each transmit pin has its corresponding receive pin at the mirror-image wire position across the flat cable.

Many vendors make DB-25 to RJ-45 adaptors. Their internal color coding does not match the cable colors, which I believe are standard. The adaptors, wire connectors, and wire have become available at electronics stores, sadly without any help on using them for RS-232.

Inside an adaptor there is an RJ-45 socket with 8 wires coming out of it. These wires have RS-232 pins (or pin sockets, as appropriate) crimped onto them. You simply push these pins into the holes in the RS-232 connector and then snap the adaptor housing on.

Table 8.4   How to wire a Yost RJ-45 to DB-25 adaptor

RJ-45 Cable		Adaptor	DCE pin		DTE pin	
Gray	(to Brown)	White	5	CTS	4	RTS
Orange	(to Blue)	Brown	8	DCD	20	DTR
Black	(to Yellow)	Yellow	3	RD	2	TD
Red	(to Green)	Green	7	GND	7	GND
Green	(to Red)	Red	7	GND	7	GND
Yellow	(to Black)	Black	2	TD	3	RD
Blue	(to Orange)	Orange	20	DTR	8	DCD
Brown	(to Gray)	Blue	4	RTS	5	CTS

There is one problem, however: both ground pins have to go into the same DB-25 hole (pin 7). You can solder and tape these wires together so they come out to one pin, or you can crimp them together with a tiny plastic thingy made by AMP called a "Tel-splice connector 1/2 tap dry," part number 553017-4. So far, this part seems to only be available in quantity 1,000 for $80 or so. Believe me, you want them if you're going to wire more than a few adaptors.

The best cable crimp tool is AMP part number 1-231666-1, which costs $185. You will probably have to order it from an industrial telephone equipment distributor. (Many industrial electronics houses will not even recognize the AMP part number as valid). There are cheaper crimp tools on the market, but you get what you pay for in this case.

Thanks to folks at Berkeley for this idea. Their wiring is slightly different, I gather for historical reasons, but the basic idea was there. If I can find out who really originated this scheme, I'd like to credit him or her by name.

Historical note

Dave Yost
Los Altos, CA
April, 1994

When I first published this scheme in 1987, I wrote "Maybe one day before the year 2000, the world will have a new, simple, high-speed, flow-controlled type of connection for point-to-point applications that currently use RS-232, with an adaptor available to talk to old RS-232 equipment." As I write this in 1994, Apple has come out with GeoPort, a 2 Mb/s technology that seems to be what I was wishing for, and even better, FireWire, a superb 100 Mb/s technology for point-to-point connections, with 200 and 400 Mb/s on the way. Add to this the fact that Fire-Wire equipment is "plug and play" and can be connected or disconnected while the system is running, and you can see that we have come a long way, at least in technology if not yet in deployment.

8.4 HARD AND SOFT CARRIER

UNIX expects to see the DCD signal, carrier detect, go high (+5 volts) when a device is attached and turned on. This signal is carried on pin 8 of the standard DB-25 connector. If your serial cable has a DCD line and your computer really pays attention to it, you are using what is known as *hard carrier*. Most systems also allow *soft carrier*, where the computer pretends that DCD is always asserted.

For certain devices (particularly terminals), soft carrier is a great blessing. It allows you to get away with using only three lines for each serial connection: transmit, receive, and signal ground. However, modem connections really need the DCD signal. If a terminal is connected through a modem and the carrier signal is lost, the modem should hang up, especially on a long distance connection. There are numerous war stories about astronomical phone bills incurred when a modem became wedged and did not drop carrier for days.

Different versions of UNIX deal with soft carrier in different ways. Early versions required a patch to the terminal driver, but that was cumbersome and silly. Most modern systems have solved this problem by setting a default carrier mode for serial ports in the system configuration files. In addition, `stty -CLOCAL` can be used to force a terminal to assume soft carrier on a running system. For example,

```
stty -CLOCAL < /dev/tty03
```

would enable soft carrier for the port `tty03`.

 SunOS doesn't support the `-CLOCAL` flag in the usual way. Instead, the `ttysoftcar` command is used. For example,

```
ttysoftcar -y /dev/ttya
```

would place `ttya` in soft carrier mode.

8.5 HARDWARE FLOW CONTROL

The CTS and RTS pins are used to make sure that a device does not send data faster than the receiver can process it. For example, if a modem is in danger of running out of buffer space (perhaps because the connection to the remote site is slower than the serial link between the local machine and the modem), it can tell the computer to shut up until the buffer drains.

Flow control is essential for high-speed modems and is also very useful for printers. On systems that do not support hardware flow control (either because the serial ports do not understand it, or because the serial cable leaves CTS and RTS disconnected), flow control can sometimes be simulated in software using the ASCII characters XON and XOFF. However, software flow control must be explicitly supported by high-level software, and even then it does not work very well.

Most terminals ignore the CTS and RTS signals. The few terminals that require a handshake across these pins before they will communicate can be fooled by jumpering pins 4 and 5 together at the terminal end of the cable. When the terminal sends out a signal on pin 4 saying "I'm ready," it gets the same signal back on pin 5 saying "Go ahead." The DTR/DSR/DCD handshake can also be jumpered in this way.

8.6 CABLE LENGTH

The RS-232 standard specifies a maximum cable length of 75 feet at 9,600 bps. Standards are usually very conservative, and RS-232 is no exception. We routinely run RS-232 cables much greater distances, up to about 1,000 feet. We have hit the limit somewhere between 800 and 1,000 feet, but have found that the particular brand of terminal and computer make quite a difference.

8.7 SOFTWARE CONFIGURATION FOR SERIAL DEVICES

Once a device has been connected with the proper cable, software on the host machine must be configured to take advantage of it. Unlike devices that connect directly to the host's bus, serial devices do not require configuration at the kernel level.[2] High-level software must still be told about the new devices, however.

Serial ports are represented by device files in /dev. Most workstations have one or two serial ports built in; these are usually /dev/ttya and /dev/ttyb. On systems that have serial ports on a separate card, the names will be different.

---

2. Actually, the serial ports themselves do require kernel-level configuration, but this is always done for you by the vendor.

See page 130 for information about modems with more than one device file.

Sometimes, more than one device file refers to the same serial port. For example, `/dev/cua0` on a SunOS system is another name for the port `/dev/ttya`. However, use of the `cua0` file turns on certain behaviors that are only appropriate when using a modem. As always, the names of the device files do not matter; behavior is determined by the major and minor device numbers.

The configuration chores for a new device depend on the type of device and the uses to which it will be put:

- For a hard-wired terminal, you must tell the system to listen for logins at the terminal's port. You specify the speed and parameters of the serial connection. Configuration for terminals is described in the next section.

- Dial-in modems are configured similarly to hard-wired terminals. However, the exact files and procedures may be slightly different on some systems.

- To configure a dial-out modem for use by humans, you must describe the modem in the `/etc/remote` file for the `tip` and `cu` commands. This procedure is described on page 129.

- To set up a modem for use with UUCP, refer to the configuration instructions on page 681. UUCP can also make use of a direct serial connection between computers; however, that configuration is not described in this book. Refer to your manuals.

- To use a modem for a remote network connection, see Chapter 19. You may need additional software.

- See Chapter 25, *Printing and Imaging*, for information about how to set up a serial printer. Some printers only receive data; others are bidirectional and can return status information to the host computer.

- From UNIX's perspective, a plotter is just another kind of printer. Refer to Chapter 25.

- A custom serial device that you will use only from your own software needs no special configuration. You can simply open the device file to access the device. Refer to the manual page for the `tty` driver to learn about the `ioctl` calls that set the speed, flag bits, and buffering mode of the serial port.

8.8 CONFIGURATION OF HARD-WIRED TERMINALS

Over the last decade, workstations and X terminals have nibbled away at the terrain where ASCII terminals once reigned supreme. However, even the "terminal" windows on a graphical display use the same drivers and configuration files as real terminals.

Terminal configuration involves two main tasks: making sure that a process is attached to a terminal to accept logins, and making sure that information about the terminal is available once a user has logged in.

The Login Process

The login process involves several programs whose actions are controlled by configuration files described in subsequent sections.

The `init` daemon is started at boot time. One of its jobs is to spawn a process, usually `getty`, on each terminal port that is turned on in the `/etc/ttys` or `/etc/inittab` file (depending on the system). `getty` sets the port's initial characteristics (such as speed and parity) and prints a login prompt.

The sequence of events in a complete login is as follows:

- A user enters a login name at `getty`'s prompt.
- `getty` executes the `login` program with the specified account name as an argument.
- `login` requests a password and validates the name and password against those stored in `/etc/passwd`.[3]
- `login` prints the message of the day from `/etc/motd`.
- `login` runs a shell and sets up the TERM environment variable.
- The shell executes the appropriate startup files (`.profile` for the Bourne shell, `.login` and `.cshrc` for the C shell).
- The shell prints the UNIX prompt and waits for input.

When the user logs out, control returns to `init`, which wakes up and spawns a new `getty` on the terminal port.

Files in `/etc` control the characteristics associated with each terminal port. These characteristics include the presence of a login prompt and `getty` process on the port, the baud rate to expect, and the terminal type (among other things).

Unfortunately, terminal configuration is one area where there is little agreement among vendors. Table 8.5 lists files used by each system.

The /etc/ttytab and /etc/ttys Files

Systems based on 4.3BSD or later have both the port and terminal type information merged into a single file, sometimes called `ttytab` (SunOS) and sometimes called `ttys` (BSDI). The format is:

```
device program termtype {on|off} [secure]
```

---

3. On some systems, `/etc/passwd` is superseded or complemented by an administrative database system such as NIS. See Chapter 18 for more information.

Table 8.5 Terminal configuration files

System	On/off	Term type	Parameters	Monitor
Solaris[a]	_sactab	_sactab	zsmon/_pmtab	ttymon
HP-UX	/etc/inittab	/etc/ttytype	/etc/gettydefs	getty
IRIX	/etc/inittab	/etc/ttytype	/etc/gettydefs	getty
SunOS	/etc/ttytab	/etc/ttytab	/etc/gettytab	getty
OSF/1	/etc/inittab	/etc/inittab	/etc/gettydefs	getty
BSDI	/etc/ttys	/etc/ttys	/etc/gettytab	getty

a. Solaris configuration files are in /etc/saf and should be managed using sacadm.

Fields are separated by whitespace. *program* is the monitor process that **init** should start if the port is turned on. **getty**, the usual entry in this field, takes an argument that indicates the speed and configuration parameters of the serial port.

termtype is the terminal type; it names an entry in **/etc/termcap** or **/etc/terminfo** (see page 124). When you log in, the TERM environment variable is set to the value of this field.

The keywords on and off enable or disable logins on the port. If the secure keyword is present, root may log in on this terminal. Many sites do not allow root logins from public terminal rooms or dial-ins.

 SunOS allows a local keyword to be added after on or off. It turns on soft carrier for the port.

Here are some sample entries from an **/etc/ttys** file:

```
console   "/usr/etc/getty std.9600"    sun       on secure
ttya      "/usr/etc/getty std.38400"   dialup    on
ttyb      "/usr/etc/getty std.9600"    unknown   off
```

The argument to **getty** refers to an entry in the **inittab**, **gettytab**, or **gettydefs** file, depending on the system.

init reads the **ttys** or **ttytab** file only once. If you change the configuration file, you must explicitly tell **init** to reread the file by sending it a hangup signal. **init** is always process #1, so the command

```
kill -1 1
```

will usually work.

The /etc/ttytype File

On some systems, terminal type information is separated out from **/etc/ttys** and kept in a file called **/etc/ttytype**. The format of an entry in **ttytype** is:

termtype device

device is the short name of the device file representing the port, and
termtype is as described above for the new-style **/etc/ttys**. Here is a
sample **ttytype** file:

```
wyse     console
dialup   ttyi0
dialup   ttyi1
vt320    ttyi2
h19      ttyi3
dialout  ttyi4
```

The /etc/gettytab File

The **gettytab** file associates symbolic names (such as std.9600, used
in the examples above) with port configuration information such as
speed, parity, and desired login prompt. Here is a sample:

```
# The default entry, used to set defaults for other
# entries, and in cases where getty is called with no
# specific entry name.

default:\
    :ap:lm-\r\n%h login\72 :sp#9600:

# Fixed-speed entries

2|std.9600|9600-baud:\
    :sp#9600:
h|std.38400|38400-baud:\
    :sp#38400:
```

The format is the same as **/etc/printcap** and **/etc/termcap**. The
lines with names separated by a vertical bar ("|") list the names by
which each configuration is known. The other fields in an entry set the
options to be used with the serial port.

Most systems come with preset **gettytab** entries appropriate for a
variety of terminals. See page 585 for a description of the general file
format; refer to you manuals for information about specific variables.

The /etc/inittab File

The ATT version of **init** supports various "run levels" that determine
which system resources are enabled. There are eight run levels: 0 to 6,
plus "s" for single-user operation. When you leave single-user mode,
init prompts you to enter a run level unless an initdefault field
exists in **/etc/inittab** as described below. **init** then scans the
inittab file for all lines that match the specified run level.

Run levels are usually set up so that you have one level where only the
console is enabled and another level that enables all terminals. You can

define the run levels in whatever way is appropriate for your system; however, we recommend that you not stray too far from the defaults.

Entries in **inittab** are of the form

> *id*:*run-levels*:*action*:*process*

A complete example looks like this:

```
::sysinit:/etc/setclk </dev/console >/dev/console 2>&1
co:234:respawn:/etc/getty console console
11:234:respawn:/etc/getty tty11 9600
12:234:off:/etc/getty tty12 9600
```

In this format, *id* is a one- or two-character string used to identify the entry. *id* may be null, as in the first line. For terminal entries, it is customary to use the terminal number as the *id*.

run-levels enumerates the run levels to which the entry pertains. If no levels are specified (as in the first line) the entry is valid for all run levels. The *action* field tells how to handle the *process* field; permissible values are listed in Table 8.6.

Table 8.6   Possible values for the /etc/inittab action field

Value	Wait?	Meaning
initdefault	–	Sets initial run level
boot	No	Runs when **inittab** is read for the first time
bootwait	Yes	Runs when **inittab** is read for the first time
once	No	Starts the process once
wait	Yes	Starts the process once
respawn	No	Always keeps the process running
ondemand	No	Same as respawn
powerfail	No	Runs when **init** receives a power fail signal
powerwait	Yes	Runs when **init** receives a power fail signal
sysinit	Yes	Runs before accessing console
off	–	Terminates the process if it is running

If one of the *run-levels* matches the current run level and the *action* field indicates that the entry is relevant, **init** uses **sh** to execute (or terminate) the command specified in the *process* field. The "Wait?" column in Table 8.6 tells whether **init** waits for the command to complete before continuing.

In the example **inittab** file above, the first line sets the clock, the middle lines spawn **getty** processes, and the last line ensures that there is no **getty** on **tty12**.

The command **telinit -q** makes **init** reread the **inittab** file.

The /etc/gettydefs File

Like the `gettytab` file, `gettydefs` defines port configurations used by `getty`. A system will usually have one or the other, never both. The `gettydefs` file looks like this:

```
console# B9600 HUPCL # B9600 SANE IXANY #login: #console
19200# B19200 HUPCL # B19200 SANE IXANY #login: #9600
9600# B9600 HUPCL # B9600 SANE IXANY HUPCL #login: #4800
4800# B4800 HUPCL # B4800 SANE IXANY HUPCL #login: #2400
2400# B2400 HUPCL # B2400 SANE IXANY HUPCL #login: #1200
1200# B1200 HUPCL # B1200 SANE IXANY HUPCL #login: #300
300# B300 HUPCL # B300 SANE IXANY TAB3 HUPCL #login: #9600
```

The format of an entry is

label#*initflags*#*finalflags*#*prompt*#*next*

`getty` tries to match its second argument with a *label* entry. If it is called without a second argument, the first entry in the file is used. The *initflags* field lists `ioctl` flags that should be set on a port until **login** is executed. The *finalflags* field sets flags that should be used thereafter. An entry that sets the speed of the connection is required in both *initflags* and *finalflags*.

The *prompt* field defines the login prompt, which may include tabs and newlines in backslash notation. The *next* field gives the label of an **inittab** entry that should be substituted for the current one if a break is received. This is useful for dial-up lines where you might want to cycle through various baud rates, as in the preceding example. For a hard-wired terminal, *next* should refer to the label of the current entry.

Each time you change the **gettydefs** file, you should run **getty -c gettydefs**, which checks the syntax of the file to make sure that all entries are valid.

Solaris and sacadm

 Terminal management under Solaris has no basis in the rational universe. Rather than traditional UNIX **getty**s that watch each port for activity and provide a login prompt, Solaris has a convoluted hierarchy called the Service Access Facility that is used to control TTY monitors, port monitors, and many other things that provide a lot of complexity but little added functionality.

To set up a serial port to provide a login prompt, you must first configure a "monitor" that watches the status of the port (`ttymon`). You then configure a port monitor that watches that status of the TTY monitor. For example, to set up a 9,600 baud monitor on `ttyb` to print a login prompt with terminal type VT100, you'd use the following commands.

```
sacadm -a -p myttymon -t ttymon -c /usr/lib/saf/ttymon -v 1
pmadm -a -p myttymon -s b -i root -fu -v 1 -m "`ttyadm -d
    /dev/term/b -l 9600 -T vt100 -s /usr/bin/login`"
```

The `/etc/ttydefs` file is used much like `gettydefs` on other systems to set speed and parity parameters.

See the manual pages for `pacadm`, `pmadm`, `ttyadm`, and `ttymon` as well as the terminals chapter in the Solaris AnswerBook for more information about setting up these monitors. Have fun.

Terminal Support: The termcap and terminfo Databases

UNIX supports many different terminal types, as opposed to some large vendors (with three-letter acronyms) whose software only supports their own brand of terminals. UNIX provides this support via a database of terminal capabilities that specifies the features and programming quirks of each brand of terminal.

BSD-ish systems call this database `/etc/termcap`, while some ATT-ish systems use `/etc/terminfo`. As shipped, the database usually contains entries for over 500 different terminals. You almost never have to write your own terminal descriptions.

See page 126 for more information about configuring the environment at login time.

UNIX programs look at the TERM environment variable to determine what kind of terminal you are using. The terminal can then be looked up in `termcap` or `terminfo`. Alternatively, the terminal's `termcap` entry can be placed directly in the environment under the TERMCAP environment variable. Usually, the user arranges for the TERMCAP and TERM variables to be set up at login time.

8.9 SPECIAL CHARACTERS AND THE TERMINAL DRIVER

The terminal driver supports several special functions that are accessed by typing particular keys (usually control keys) on the keyboard. The exact binding of functions to keys can be set using the `tset` and `stty` commands. Table 8.7 lists some of these special functions, along with their default key bindings.

8.10 STTY: SET TERMINAL OPTIONS

`stty` lets you directly change and query the various settings of the terminal driver. There are about a zillion options; these are documented in the man page for `tty`. In most cases, the option names used in the `tty` man page are the same names used by `stty`, but sometimes there are slight differences. Many options are the same for ATT and BSD, but there are enough discrepancies, even among related variants, that you should consult the man page for your local system.

Table 8.7   **Special characters for the terminal driver**

Name	Default	Function
ERASE	^H	Erases one character of input
WERASE	^W	Erases one word of input
KILL	^U	Erases entire line
EOF	^D	Sends end of file
INTR	^C	Interrupts currently running process
QUIT	^\	Kills current process with core dump
STOP	^S	Stops output to screen
START	^Q	Restarts output to screen
DISCARD	^O	Throws away pending output
SUSPEND	^Z	Suspends current process
LNEXT	^V	Interprets next character literally

Options to `stty` can be placed on the command line in any order and in any combination. A dash before an option negates it. For example, to configure a terminal for 9,600 bps operation with even parity and without hardware tabs, the command

```
stty 9600 even -tabs
```

can be used. A good combination of options to use for a plain-vanilla terminal is:

```
stty intr ^C kill ^U erase ^H -tabs
```

Here, `-tabs` prevents the terminal driver from taking advantage of the terminal's built-in tabulation mechanism (useful because many terminals are stupid about tabs), and the other options set the interrupt, kill, and erase characters to <Control-C>, <Control-U>, and <Control-H> (backspace), respectively.

`stty` can be used to examine the current modes of the terminal driver as well as to set them. `stty` with no arguments produces output like:

```
speed 9600 baud; -parity hupcl
rows = 24; columns = 80
erase = ^h; swtch = <undef>;
brkint -inpck -istrip icrnl -ixany imaxbel onlcr
echo echoe echok echoctl echoke iexten
```

A more verbose status report can be obtained with `stty everything`, `stty -a`, or `stty all`, depending on your system. The output in this case is something like:

```
speed 9600 baud;
rows = 24; columns = 80; ypixels = 364; xpixels = 739;
eucw 1:0:0:0, scrw 1:0:0:0
intr = ^c; quit = ^|; erase = ^h; kill = ^u;
```

```
eof = ^d; eol = <undef>; eol2 = <undef>; swtch = <undef>;
start = ^q; stop = ^s; susp = ^z; dsusp = ^y;
rprnt = ^r; flush = ^o; werase = ^w; lnext = ^v;
-parenb -parodd cs8 -cstopb hupcl cread -clocal -loblk
-crtscts -parext -ignbrk brkint ignpar -parmrk -inpck
-istrip -inlcr -igncr icrnl -iuclc ixon -ixany -ixoff
imaxbel isig icanon -xcase echo echoe echok -echonl
-noflsh -tostop echoctl -echoprt echoke -defecho -flusho
-pendin iexten opost -olcuc onlcr -ocrnl -onocr -onlret
-ofill -ofdel
```

The format of the output is similar, but lists all available information.
The meaning of the output should be intuitively obvious.

stty operates on the file descriptor of its standard input or standard
output (depending on your system), so it is possible to set and query the
modes of a terminal other than the current one using the shell redirec-
tion characters ">" and "<". On some systems, you must be the superuser to change the modes on someone else's terminal.

8.11 TSET: SET OPTIONS AUTOMATICALLY

tset initializes the terminal driver to a mode appropriate for a given
terminal type. The type can be specified on the command line; if it is left
out, the value of the TERM environment variable is used.

tset supports a syntax for mapping certain values of the TERM environment variable into other values. This is useful if you often log in
through a modem or data switch and would like to have the terminal
driver configured correctly for the terminal you are really using on the
other end of the connection rather than something generic and unhelp-
ful such as "dialup."

For example, suppose that you have a DEC VT320 at home and that the
/etc/ttytab or /etc/ttys file is configured to think that the terminal type of a modem is "dialup." If you put the command

```
tset -m dialup:vt320
```

in your .login or .profile file, the terminal driver will be set appropriately for a VT320 whenever you dial in.

If there are several terminals that you are likely to use when coming in
through a modem, you can have **tset** ask you what you're using each
time you log in, with a suitable default provided if you just hit return.
For example, the line

```
tset -m dialup:?vt320
```

produces the question:

```
TERM = (vt320)?
```

At this prompt you can either hit return to accept a VT320 configuration or enter a different type of terminal.

Unfortunately, the **tset** command is not really as simple as it pretends to be. To have **tset** adjust your environment variables TERM and TERM-CAP in addition to setting your terminal modes, you will need lines something like this:

```
set noglob
eval `tset -s -Q -m dialup:?v320 -m annex:z29`
unset noglob
```

This incantation suppresses the messages that **tset** normally prints (the **-Q** flag), and asks that shell commands to set the environment be output instead (the **-s** flag). In addition, it says that if the user logs in on a dialup, **tset** should prompt for the terminal type with a default of VT320, and if the user logs in through the local terminal server (type "annex") then the terminal is really a Zenith Z29.

The shell commands printed by **tset** are captured by the backquotes and fed to the shell as input using the built-in command **eval**, causing them to have the same effect as if they had been typed by the user.

set noglob prevents the shell from expanding any metacharacters such as "*" and "?" that are included in **tset**'s output. These commands are not needed by Bourne shell users, since **sh** does not normally expand special characters within backquotes. The **tset** command itself is the same whether you use the C shell or the Bourne shell; **tset** looks at the environment variable SHELL to determine what kind of commands to print out.

8.12 How to Unwedge a Terminal

Some programs (such as **vi**) make drastic changes to the state of the terminal driver while they are running. This meddling is normally invisible to the user, since the terminal state is carefully restored when the program exits or is suspended. However, it is possible for a program to crash or be killed without performing this cleanup. When this happens, your terminal will start to behave very strangely; it will fail to handle newlines correctly, to echo characters that you type, or to execute commands properly.

To fix this situation, you can use **reset** on BSD systems or **stty sane** on ATT systems. **reset** is actually just a link to **tset** on most systems, and it can accept most of **tset**'s arguments. However, it is usually run without arguments. Both **reset** and **stty sane** restore the sanity of the terminal driver and output an appropriate reset code from **termcap** or **terminfo**, if one is available.

In many cases where a reset is appropriate, the terminal has been left in a special mode in which no processing is done on the characters you type. Most terminals generate carriage returns rather than newlines when the return or enter key is pressed; without input processing, this key generates <Control-M> characters instead of sending the current command off to be executed. To enter newlines directly, use <Control-J> or the line feed key (if there is one) instead of the return key.

8.13 MODEMS

A modem converts the digital serial signal produced by a computer into an analog signal suitable for transmission on a standard phone line. Modems usually have an RJ-11 jack on the analog side and an RS-232 interface on the digital side. Modems are used for a variety of applications. See Chapter 30 and Chapter 19 for some typical examples.

Modems come in many different shapes, sizes, and price ranges. When evaluating the capabilities of a particular modem, the following characteristics should be examined:

- Modulation protocol
- Error correction protocol
- Data compression protocol

Modems also vary in general robustness, but this characteristic is hard to judge without direct experience. We have found some modems to be significantly more tolerant of line noise than others. Also, high-speed modems require complex firmware, and this firmware is occasionally buggy. Manufacturers share firmware among their models when possible, so good or bad firmware tends to run in product lines.

Modulation Protocols

A modem's modulation protocol determines the characteristics of the analog signal, and as a result, its base transmission rate. Table 8.8 shows some popular modulation protocols and their base data rates.

Table 8.8 Basic speeds (in bps) of modulation protocols

Protocol	Speed	Protocol	Speed
Bell 103	300	CCITT V.21	300
Bell 212A	1,200	CCITT V.22	1,200
CCITT V.22bis	2,400	CCITT V.32	9,600
CCITT V.32bis	14,400	CCITT V.34	28,800

A protocol's baud rate is the rate at which the carrier signal is modulated. If there are more than two signal levels, then more than one bit of information can be sent per transition, and the speed in bits per second will be higher than the baud rate. Historically, the data speed and signaling speed of modems were the same, leading to a casual conflation of the terms "baud" and "bps."

You should generally purchase the fastest modem you can afford. In today's market, even fast modems are quickly outdated.

Error Correction Protocols

Line noise can introduce a significant number of errors into a modem connection. At 300 bps, a half-second glitch might produce 15 characters of junk data. But at 14,400 bps, that same half second of noise could easily fill your screen. As a result, various error correction protocols have been developed to packetize the transmitted data and provide checksum-based correction for errors, insulating the user or application from line faults.

The two most popular error correction protocols are MNP-4 and CCITT V.42 LAP-M. Usually, the error correction protocol you use is determined by the data compression protocol.

Data Compression Protocols

See page 621 for more information about non-modem data compression.

Data compression algorithms can be used to shrink the number of bits that must be transmitted between analog endpoints. There are two popular compression protocols for modems: MNP-5, with a theoretical maximum compression ratio of 2 to 1, and CCITT V.42bis, with a maximum ratio of 4 to 1.

On a good day when the moon is full and you're transmitting a set of 1,000 A's, V.42bis will give you four times the throughput of your base modulation rate. This turns a 2,400 bps modem into a 9,600 bps modem, or a 14,400 bps modem into a 57,600 bps modem.[4]

In general, the average user does better with one of these compression algorithms turned on. Keep in mind, however, that it is possible to get worse throughput than the base data rate, such as when transmitting data that are already compressed. Your milage may vary.

Dial-Out Configuration: /etc/phones and /etc/remote

The `tip` and `cu` commands provide a basic keyboard interface to serial devices. They're most often used with modems, but can also be used to talk to printers and terminals. `tip` and `cu` use two configuration files

---

4. Be careful! There are companies marketing cheapo "9,600 baud" modems that are really 2,400 baud modems with compression.

that record phone numbers (`/etc/phones`) and serial port information (`/etc/remote`).[5]

The `/etc/remote` file looks like this:

```
# /etc/remote:  Dialer definitions

dial2400|2400 Baud hayes:dv=/dev/cul0:br#2400:\
    cu=/dev/cul0:at=hayes:du:
dial1200|dialer|1200 Baud hayes:dv=/dev/cul0:br#1200:\
    cu=/dev/cul0:at=hayes:du:

# Commonly-dialed hosts

ucc:pn=3338118:tc=dial2400
cc:pn=@:tc=UNIX-1200
dca:dv=/dev/ttyh1,/dev/ttyh2:br#9600:pa=none
```

The first three entries describe dialer configurations. The next section, commonly-dialed hosts, provides shortcuts for dialing particular hosts. Note that in the "cc" entry, the phone number is written as `pn=@`, which means to look for the phone number(s) in `/etc/phones`.

```
# /etc/phones: This file can contain long distance
# billing numbers and unpublished telephone numbers,
# so it's not usually world-readable.

cc      5552530
monet   8,,510,555-4567,,,,xxxx-xxx
```

The **phones** file contains symbolic definitions of phone numbers. In this example, xxxx-xxx could represent a long distance billing number. Punctuation is used to signify delays, or to wait for a second dial tone. The characters depend on the brand of modem: commas, equal signs, and asterisks all commonly have special meanings.

Bidirectional Modems

It is often handy to use a single modem for both dial-in and dial-out services. This requires special treatment of the serial port, since `getty` normally takes full control of serial ports at boot time. Other processes that want to use the modem are left out in the cold, unable to open the port even when the modem is not actually in use. Unfortunately, there is little standardization among systems for the management of bidirectional modems.

 Wacky as ever, Solaris requires you to take the following steps to make a port bidirectional.

5. `tip` behaves strangely when run inside a Sun `cmdtool` window. Always run `tip` from a `shelltool` in the Sun environment.

- Include the **-b** flag to **ttyadm** when attaching the port monitor.
- Use **/dev/cua/a** (not **/dev/term/a**) as the argument to **ttyadm**.
- Edit **/etc/uucp/Devices** to list the bidirectional service name.

See *How to Set Up Bidirectional Modem Service* in the Solaris Answer-Book for explicit examples and details.

 Under HP-UX, IRIX, and OSF/1, a special **getty** called **uugetty** can be used on bidirectional ports. **uugetty** shares lock files with programs like **cu**, **tip**, and **uucico** in order to avoid conflicts.

 Under SunOS, bidirectional use of a port is enabled by creating a second device file that has the high bit of its minor device number set. **getty** continues to run on the original device, but **cu**, **tip**, and **uucico** can all be told to use the new device file.

Normally, the dial-out device is called **/dev/cua0** (for "the calling unit attached to **ttya**"). If the original device for **/dev/ttya** looks like this:

```
# ls -l /dev/ttya
crw--w--w-  1 root       12,    0 Dec  9 09:17 /dev/ttya
```

The calling unit device could be created with:

```
# mknod /dev/cua0 c 12 128
# chown uucp /dev/cua0
# chmod 666 /dev/cua0
# ls -l /dev/cua0
crw-rw-rw-  1 uucp       12, 128 May 23 15:05 /dev/cua0
```

The device driver for the serial port automatically locks out the **getty** while the modem is being used as a dial-out.

 Under BSDI, The **gettytab** bi option makes **getty** behave in a more social, sharing, and caring manner. And it gets you twice as many dates on the weekend. See the manual page for **getty** for more details.

8.14 Debugging a Serial Line

Debugging serial lines is not difficult. Some typical errors are:

- Forgetting to tell **init** to reread its configuration files
- Forgetting to set soft carrier when using three-wire cables
- Using a cable with the wrong nullness
- Soldering or crimping DB-25 connectors upside down
- Connecting a device to the wrong wire due to bad wire maps
- Setting the terminal options incorrectly

Using a Breakout Box

A breakout box is an indispensable tool for debugging cabling problems. It is patched into the serial line and shows the signals on each pin as they pass through the cable. The better breakout boxes have both male and female connectors on each side and so are totally flexible and bisexual in their positioning. LEDs associated with each "interesting" pin (pins 2, 3, 4, 5, 6, 8, and 20) show when it is active.

Some breakout boxes are read-only and just allow you to monitor the signals; others let you rewire the connection and assert a voltage on a particular pin. For example, if you suspected that a cable needed to be nulled (crossed) you could use the breakout box to override the actual cable wiring and swap pins 2 and 3 and also pins 6 and 20.

See page 312 for more information about Black Box.
A cheap breakout box can be worse than no breakout box at all. Our favorite is the BOB-CAT-B made by Black Box. It is an easy-to-use box that costs around $250. You can reach them at (412) 746-5500.

9 *Adding a Disk*

9.1 INTRODUCTION

See Chapter 26 for some hints on keeping disk usage in check.

There is never enough disk space. The minute a new disk is added to the system, it is half full; or so it seems. Getting users to clean up their disk space is as difficult as getting a teenager to clean his room. Therefore, an administrator will occasionally have to install new disk drives.

Most systems accept new disks on a standard peripheral bus called SCSI (Small Computer Systems Interface, pronounced "scuzzy"). We begin this chapter with a general discussion of the SCSI standard and the structure of modern hard disks. We then discuss the general mechanisms by which disks are formatted and partitioned, and the procedure for initializing filesystems.

Although most vendors have standardized on SCSI interfaces, they seem to have made a point of using proprietary commands to set up new disks; accordingly, there are a lot of vendor-specific details in this chapter. We try to cover each system in enough detail that you can at least understand the commands that are used and can locate the necessary documentation. We also illustrate each system's installation procedure for one particular disk.

9.2 THE SCSI STANDARD

In the beginning, computer manufacturers all had proprietary interfaces to their peripherals. This was due in part to the immature state of interface technology. However, vendors were also eager to control the peripheral market for their machines. Eventually, third-party vendors started to make add-on disk systems that were very cost effective and totally compatible, and that often yielded better performance.

Computer vendors didn't much care for this turn of events. There were several highly publicized lawsuits that attempted to protect interface specifications as trade secrets or as patented technology. Ultimately, the question became moot as the industry migrated to standard interfacing technologies.

SCSI won the battle for UNIX systems. However, there are three other standards you might occasionally come across:

SMD   SMD (Storage Module Disk) is an older standard that used to be somewhat popular on UNIX machines. An SMD controller could handle up to four drives. There were two cables attached to each drive: one was a 60-pin command cable that was daisy-chained to each drive, and the other was a 26-pin data cable. Both were usually ribbon cables.

IPI   IPI was developed as a high-speed replacement for SMD. But SCSI proved to be a more popular system.

IDE   IDE is standard on PCs, but is almost unheard of on UNIX systems (except for those based on PC hardware).

In this chapter, we will discuss only SCSI.

There are several chip sets that implement the SCSI standard, so vendors often put SCSI support right on the CPU or peripherals board. SCSI defines a generic data pipe that can be used by all kinds of peripherals. Most commonly, it's used for disks, tape drives, scanners, and printers. The SCSI standard does not specify how a disk is constructed or laid out, only how it communicates with other devices.

The SCSI standard specifies a 50-pin Centronics connector. That is the most common kind of connector these days, but vendors have used several other standards in the past. Sun previously used DB-50 connectors, and Apple uses DB-25s to this day. Another common connector allowed by SCSI-2 is the "mini-micro," which looks like a shrunken DB-25 packed with 50 pins. These connectors are illustrated in Exhibit A.

SCSI cables are usually male-to-male, and SCSI devices are almost always female. The SCSI bus uses a daisy-chain configuration, so most devices have two SCSI ports. The two ports on a device are identical and interchangeable, so either one can be the input. For some reason, scanner vendors seem to consider themselves exempt from the normal laws of physics and sometimes provide only one SCSI port (if not internally terminated, these devices require a special type of terminator).

Exhibit A   Common SCSI connectors (front view)

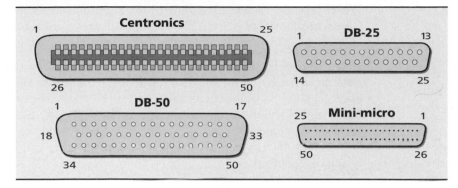

There must be a terminator at each end of the SCSI bus. Terminators take several forms, from small external plugs that you snap onto a regular port to sets of teensy resistor packs that install on a device's circuit boards. One end of the bus will usually terminate inside the host computer (either on the SCSI interface or after an internal SCSI drive), so you should only have to worry about terminating the external end. We strongly recommend that you strip peripherals of all internal termination devices and use an external terminator. It will save time in the long run and is well worth the extra cost ($5 to $20).

Each device has a SCSI address or "target number" that distinguishes it from the other devices on the bus. Target numbers go from zero to seven, so there can never be more than eight SCSI devices connected to one system.[1] The SCSI controller itself counts as a device and is usually target seven. All other devices must have their target numbers set to unique values. A SCSI address is arbitrary and does not determine a device's priority on the bus.[2]

If you're lucky, a device will have an external thumbwheel with which the target number can be set. Other common ways of setting the target number are DIP switches and jumpers. If it is not obvious how to set the unit number on a device, consult the hardware manual.

Setting a device to the same target number as the controller is a common problem. A device's target number may or may not be related to its UNIX device name; more on this later.

The SCSI standard supports a form of sub-addressing called a "logical unit number." Each target may have several logical units inside it. A plausible example might be a drive array with several disks but only

---

1. More accurately, to one bus; some systems let you install multiple SCSI controllers.

2. However, some systems pick the disk with the lowest target number to be the boot disk.

one SCSI controller. However, logical units are seldom used in real life. When you hear "SCSI unit number," you should assume that it is really a target number that's being discussed until proven otherwise.

There are two major versions of the SCSI specification: SCSI and SCSI-2. SCSI-2 allows faster transmission speeds, but requires that the bus be no longer than two meters in total length (including the cables inside devices). It is perfectly acceptable to put SCSI devices on a SCSI-2 bus, but they will run at the slower speed. Some SCSI-2 buses require an "active" terminator, so you should not use old SCSI terminators on a SCSI-2 device. Unfortunately, there is no easy way to tell if a terminator is active. Terminators with LEDs on them are generally active.

SCSI-2's high-speed transfers are achieved using two new protocol features. "Fast" SCSI allows up to ten megatransfers per second, as opposed to SCSI, which is limited to five. Each transfer can handle one, two, or four bytes; if more than one byte is handled per transfer, this is known as "wide" SCSI. Fastness and wideness are independent, so you can have a SCSI connection that is wide but not fast, or vice versa.

Both of these embellishments have their price. Wide SCSI requires a bus with more than 50 pins. This is usually simulated by running multiple cables. Fast SCSI is difficult to run over standard SCSI cables because of electrical noise. It's sometimes used with an alternate signaling system known as "differential SCSI," which uses two pins per signal rather than one. This configuration also requires you to run extra cables.

At the moment, fast and wide SCSI is an expensive option found only on specialized hardware. While it may become cheaper and more common in the future, we expect that workstations will not support it out of the box for another few years.

While SCSI buses are generally quite easy to configure, a variety of things can go wrong. The following are some of the mistakes we have made in the past:

- Many workstations have internal SCSI devices. Check the listing of current devices before you reboot to add a new device. Remember that most tape systems are SCSI. Some vendors' floppy drives (most notably, HP's) are SCSI.

- After you have added a new SCSI device, check the listing of devices discovered by the OS when it reboots to make sure that everything you expect is there. Most SCSI drivers will not detect multiple units at the same SCSI address (this configuration will cause many other problems, too).

- Devices that claim to be "auto-terminating" usually are not. It never hurts to put on a terminator at the end of the chain.

- Some disk drives have a series of resistor packs installed on their controller board as a terminator. Remove and discard these resistors to avoid future headaches.

- Some expansion boxes (enclosures with a power supply and one or more SCSI devices) terminate the bus inside the box. This will keep you from seeing any devices further along the bus. Old-style Sun boxes are infamous for this trick.

- Sometimes, the thumbwheel used to set the SCSI address is connected backwards. When this happens, the thumbwheel will change the SCSI address, but not to the displayed value.

- When figuring the length of your SCSI-2 bus, make sure you count the cables inside of devices and expansion boxes (they can be quite long).

- Don't forget that your SCSI controller has a SCSI address.

9.3 DISK GEOMETRY

The geometry of a modern Winchester disk and the terminology used to refer to its various parts are shown in Exhibit B.[3] This information is provided mainly to improve your general knowledge. Thanks to SCSI, you don't really need to understand the details of how a particular disk is laid out.

Exhibit B   Disk geometry lesson

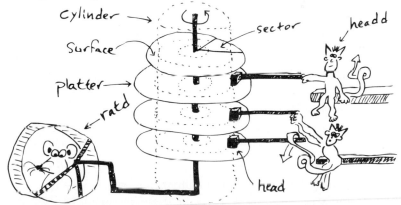

The data platters of a Winchester disk are completely sealed so that no dust or dirt can get in. This feature makes Winchester disks far more reliable than removable media.

3. Winchester disks are named after the Winchester Mystery House, a favorite Silicon Valley attraction.

In the very early days of computer hardware, disk drives usually had one platter. An increase in storage capacity was provided by increasing the diameter of the platter. On the wall of one of our user areas is an ancient disk over four feet in diameter that held approximately 280K of data. That's less than 10% of the capacity of a modern extended density floppy. Today, hard disks usually have several small platters stacked on top of one another rather than a single large platter. Both sides of the platters are used to store data.

Platters rotate at a constant speed. They are read and written by little skating heads that move back and forth like the needle on a record player. The heads float very close to the surface of the platters but do not actually touch them. If a head does touch a platter, this is called a head crash; it can be very destructive.

At least one head is required for each surface. The heads on early drives had to move huge distances, but the modern geometry of small, stacked platters is more efficient. The diameter of disks continues to decrease, from a standard of 14 inches ten years ago, to 5 1/4 inches a few years ago, to 3 1/2 inches and smaller today.

In a stacked-platter system, it is possible for the armatures to be independent of one another, although adjacent surfaces usually share an arm. Moving the head into the correct position to read a particular piece of data is called seeking.

Each position that a head can occupy is called a track. Tracks are further divided into sectors, which are then mapped to the basic data block size in software. Data blocks are usually 512 or 1,024 bytes long.

A set of tracks on different platters that have the same distance from the spindle is called a cylinder. If all the heads move together, the data stored in a single cylinder can be read without any additional movement. Although heads move amazingly fast, they still move much slower than the disks spin around. Therefore, any disk access that does not require the heads to seek to a new position will be faster.

The UNIX filesystem attempts to exploit this fact to improve efficiency. Unfortunately, the original BSD filesystem code is thwarted by a now-universal practice known as "zone sectoring," in which tracks on the outside of a platter contain more sectors than inner tracks.[4] To really take advantage of disk geometry, the filesystem needs to know and understand the zone sectoring plan for each hard disk; most vendors' filesystems do not.

4. If you are familiar with LaserDisc systems, zone sectoring is analogous to the CLV format. Like CLV, it allows a lot more data to be packed on a disk.

9.4 AN OVERVIEW OF THE INSTALLATION PROCEDURE

The process of adding a new disk involves the following steps:

- Connecting the disk to the computer
- Creating device files through which the disk can be accessed
- Formatting the disk
- Labeling and partitioning the disk
- Creating UNIX filesystems within disk partitions
- Verifying the integrity of new filesystems
- Setting up automatic mounting
- Setting up swapping on swap partitions

The following sections describe the process in general, without reference to any particular vendor's peculiarities. Starting on page 148, we describe the exact procedure for our six example systems.

Creating Device Entries

See Chapter 7 for more information about device files. Before you can access a new disk, you need device files in **/dev** that point to it. You will need both block devices (generally used for mounting filesystems) and character devices (used for backing up and checking the integrity of filesystems). Many versions of UNIX automatically create files for all possible SCSI devices; details are given in the vendor specifics section starting on page 148.

It is possible to completely destroy a filesystem in seconds by writing randomly on the disk, so disk device files should have their permissions set quite restrictively. We allow read and write access for the owner (root) and read access for "operator," the group owner; this allows **dump** to be run by operators without superuser privileges.

Formatting a Disk Drive

Overeager vendors often quote disk capacities in terms of the number of unformatted bytes. Typically, about 10% of the capacity is used up in marking the disk surfaces so that the hardware and software can find the data written there. When purchasing disks, always think in terms of formatted size and compare prices accordingly.

Another sneaky but common trick is to quote disk sizes in "megabytes" that are really millions of bytes. A megabyte is actually 2^{10} or 1,048,576 bytes, so this funky math ends up overstating the capacity of a disk drive by almost 5%.

The formatting process writes address information and timing marks on the platters to delineate each sector. It also identifies "bad blocks," imperfections in the media that result in areas that cannot be reliably read or written. On older disks (including SMD disks) the UNIX driver is responsible for understanding bad blocks and mapping them to different blocks elsewhere on the disk. SCSI disks have bad-block management built in, so neither you nor the driver has to worry about it.[5]

SCSI disks are usually pre-formatted, so you don't really have to bother with formatting them yourself on most machines. However, we recommend it, as additional defects may have been uncovered by vibrations and thermal shock during transportation and storage. Depending on the host operating system and the disk drive, it can take a long time to format a disk (up to an hour or so per gigabyte).

Some systems allow you to verify the integrity of the disk by writing random patterns onto the disk and reading them back. This is usually a very time-consuming process, so unless you suspect the disk is bad or you bill by the hour, you may want to skip it. Barring that, let the tests run overnight.[6]

Partitions and Labels

After a disk has been formatted and the bad sectors remapped, the disk must be divided into chunks called partitions. Partitioning allows the disk to be treated as a group of independent data areas rather than one vast expanse of blocks. Partitioning also allows "bonus" items on the disk (such as the boot blocks and the partition table itself) to be hidden from high-level software (e.g. the filesystem). Only the device driver knows about the layout of the entire disk; other software works through the cleaned-up abstraction of partitions.

Partitions make dumping easier, prevent users from poaching each other's disk space, improve performance, and confine potential damage from runaway programs. On most operating systems, the partition table (as well as other information about the disk) is kept on the disk in a record called the label. The label usually occupies the first few blocks of the disk. Its contents vary among systems, but it generally contains enough information to allow the machine to find the kernel at boot time.

Partitions are, in concept, distinct and separate from one another. However, almost all systems define one partition to be an image of the entire disk. That way, user-level commands can access the disk "directly" through a normal device file. For example, a user-level process could write the disk's label or duplicate its contents to a backup disk using the dd command. Of course, this special partition must be used carefully, since it allows every partition on the disk to be screwed up at once.

5. However, any bad blocks that appear after a disk has been formatted will not be "handled"; they can manifest themselves in the form of read and write errors and lost data.

6. Don't be concerned about "wearing out" a disk with overuse or aggressive testing. Disks are designed to withstand constant, round-the-clock activity.

Some systems go even farther down this treacherous path and define multiple, overlapping sets of partitions. For example, partitions 0, 1, and 2 might divide up the disk one way, while partitions 3 and 4 do it another way. You're expected to use one set of self-consistent partitions and simply ignore the others. In real life, such configurations invite operator errors.

Modern systems tend to use fewer partitions than their predecessors, but on most systems you will have at least three:

- The root partition – This is the partition where everything needed to bring the system up to single-user mode is kept. A second copy of this partition is often stored on another disk for emergency purposes.

- The swap partition – A swap area stores pages of virtual memory when there is not enough physical memory to hold them. Every system should have at least one swap partition. See page 660 for more information about virtual memory.

- The user partition – Generic space for home directories, data files, source code libraries, etc.

There are some widely differing opinions on the best way to split your disks into partitions. Here are some hints:

- If you have multiple disks, make a copy of the root filesystem on one of them and verify that you can boot from it.

- As you add memory to your machine, you should also add swap space. For normal use, you should have from two to four times as much swap space as real memory.

- Splitting swap space among several disks will increase performance. This works for filesystems, too; put the busy ones on different disks. See page 667 for notes on this subject.

- If you intend to back up a partition, don't make it bigger than the capacity of your backup device. See page 191.

- Try to cluster information that changes quickly on a few partitions that are backed up frequently.

- It's a good idea to create a separate filesystem for temporary files (/tmp), as it limits them to a finite size and prevents you from having to back them up.

- If your system keeps log files in /var, it's a good idea for /var to be a separate disk partition. Many systems ship with /var as part of a very small root partition, making it easy to fill the root and bring the machine to a grinding halt.

- If you run news, isolate it on its own partition (or set of partitions) to avoid affecting essential system activities when news gets out of control. See Chapter 24 for more tips on controlling the Usenet monster.

Filesystems

Even after a hard disk has been conceptually divided into partitions, it is still not ready to hold UNIX files. The filesystem needs to add a little of its own overhead before the disk is ready for use.

To install a filesystem within a disk partition, you use either `mkfs` or `newfs`. The `newfs` command is actually just a friendly front end for `mkfs`. Under old versions of UNIX you needed to know a lot about the characteristics of the disk, but this is no longer the case. Unless you are doing something strange, you should be able to build the filesystem by specifying nothing but the correct command (`mkfs` or `newfs`) and the partition name.

We will cover the exact procedure in more detail later. The rest of this section discusses how files are placed on the disk when you build the filesystem. If you are not interested, just skip ahead to the next section and revel in blissful ignorance.

Here, we describe the fast filesystem implemented by McKusick, Joy, and Leffler for 4.2BSD. It's used by most modern versions of UNIX. A BSD filesystem consists of five structural components:

- A set of inode storage cells
- A set of scattered "superblocks"
- A map of the disk blocks in the filesystem
- A block usage summary
- A set of data blocks

Each filesystem partition is divided into cylinder groups of from one to 32 cylinders each. Structures such as inode tables are allocated among the cylinder groups so that blocks that are accessed together can be stored close to each other on the disk.

The role of inodes is discussed in Chapter 4, *The Filesystem*. Since space for inodes must be set aside when UNIX does its initial structuring of the filesystem, it is necessary to decide in advance how many of them to create. It is impossible to predict exactly how many files (inodes) will someday be needed; UNIX uses an empirical formula to guesstimate an appropriate number based on the size of the partition.

You can adjust the number of inodes either up or down when you create the filesystem: more inodes for filesystems with lots of small files, and fewer inodes for filesystems with a few large files. We recommend that, unless your needs are unusual, you accept the default value.[7]

See page 146 for more information about fsck.
A superblock is a record that describes the characteristics of the filesystem. It contains information about the length of a disk block, the size and location of the inode tables, the disk block map and usage information, the size of the cylinder groups, and a few other important parameters of the filesystem. Because damage to the superblock would erase some extremely crucial information, several copies of it are maintained in scattered locations. This was not always true: early filesystems were totally destroyed if the superblock became corrupted. If necessary, you can tell **fsck** to use an alternative superblock when rebuilding a damaged filesystem. **newfs -N** will show the locations of backup superblocks. There is always one at block 32.

For each mounted filesystem, UNIX keeps both an in-memory copy of the superblock and several on-disk copies. The **sync** system call flushes the cached superblocks to their permanent homes on disk, making the filesystem consistent for a split second. This minimizes the amount of damage that would occur if the machine were to crash when the filesystem had not updated the superblocks. **sync** also flushes modified inodes and cached data blocks.

The **update** daemon calls **sync** every thirty seconds; additional calls may be made by executing the **sync** command. A single **sync** does not guarantee that all flushing operations have been completed by the time it returns, but a second **sync** will not start until the previous **sync** has finished. For this reason, always run **sync** twice if you really want to flush the caches.

The disk block map for a partition is simply a map of the free blocks within it. When new files are written, this map is examined to devise an efficient layout scheme. The block usage summary records basic information about the blocks that are already in use.

Mounts and the fstab File

A filesystem must be mounted before it becomes available to UNIX processes. The mount point for a filesystem can be any directory, but the files and subdirectories beneath the mount point will not be accessible while a filesystem is mounted there. More information about mounting filesystems is given on page 57.

After installing a new disk, you should mount new filesystems by hand to test that everything is working correctly. For example,

```
mount /dev/sd1a /mnt
```

7. You may need extra inodes on a filesystem devoted to storing news. Refer to Chapter 24.

would mount the filesystem in the partition represented by the device file **/dev/sd1a** (device names will vary between systems) on the directory **/mnt**. If the filesystem is brand new, its contents should look something like this:

```
# ls /mnt
lost+found
```

The **lost+found** directory is automatically created when you build a filesystem. It is used by **fsck** in emergencies; do not delete it.

You can verify the size of the filesystem with the **df** command. Here's an example from a BSD system:

```
# df /mnt
Filesystem     kbytes    used    avail capacity  Mounted on
/dev/sd1a        7508       9     6749      0%   /mnt
```

 You will generally want to configure the system to mount local filesystems at boot time. A configuration file in **/etc** lists the device names and mount points of all the system's disks (among other things). On most systems this file is called **fstab**, but under HP-UX it has been renamed **checklist**, and on Solaris it has been renamed **vfstab** (and reformatted). For the rest of this section, we will refer to the file as "the **fstab** file" even though it might actually be named something different on your system.

An **fstab** file that includes the filesystem above might look something like this:[8]

```
/dev/sd0a    /            4.2 rw              0 1
/dev/sd0d    /usr         4.2 rw              0 2
/dev/sd1a    /mnt         4.2 rw              0 1
/dev/sd1f    /foo         4.2 rw              0 2
rem:/files   /remfiles    nfs rw,intr,soft,bg 0 0
```

There are six fields per line, separated by whitespace. Each line describes a single filesystem. The fields are traditionally aligned for readability, but this is not required.

See Chapter 17 for more information about NFS.

The first field gives the device name. The **fstab** file can include mounts from remote systems, in which case the first field contains an NFS path, as in the last line. The notation rem:/files indicates the **/files** directory on the machine rem.

The second field specifies the mount point, and the third field indicates the type of filesystem. The exact type name used to identify local filesystems varies among machines: Solaris, OSF/1, and BSDI use ufs; HP-UX

8. This entry is from SunOS. All but Solaris will be very similar.

uses hfs; IRIX uses efs, and SunOS uses 4.2. We have also seen systems that use 4.3.

The fourth field lists the mount options (rw for read/write, the default). The fifth field specifies the "dump frequency," which as far as we know is used only by Sun's new backup product.

fsck is described   The sixth field specifies the pass in which **fsck** should check the filesys-
on page 146.   tems. Filesystems with the same value in this field are checked concurrently, if possible.

The **fstab** file is read by the **mount**, **umount**, **swapon**, and **fsck** commands, so it is important that the data presented there be correct and complete. **mount** and **umount** use the **fstab** file to figure out what you want done if you specify only a partition name or a mount point on the command line. For example, using the **fstab** just shown, the command

    mount /mnt

would be interpreted to mean

    mount /dev/sd1a /mnt

The command **mount -a** mounts all filesystems listed in **/etc/fstab**; it is usually executed from the startup scripts at boot time. The **-t** flag constrains this to filesystems of a certain type. For example,

    mount -at ufs

would mount all local filesystems on a BSDI system. The **mount** command reads **/etc/fstab** sequentially; therefore, filesystems that are mounted beneath other filesystems must follow their parent partitions in the **fstab** file. For example, the line for **/usr/local** must follow the line for **/usr**, if **/usr** is a separate filesystem.

The **umount** command for unmounting filesystems accepts a similar syntax. On most systems, you cannot unmount a filesystem that a process is using as its current directory, or on which files are open.

Enabling Swapping

One of the early advantages of UNIX was its implementation of a concept called virtual memory. This feature allows the operating system to pretend that the machine has more memory than it actually does. If processes try to use the "extra" memory, the system's disks are brought into use as a kind of ultra-slow RAM. Juggling the contents of memory to and from disk is known as swapping or paging.[9]

---

9. Swapping and paging are technically distinct. For now, we will group them together and call the combination "swapping," as the UNIX manuals do. For a more detailed description of virtual memory under UNIX, see page 660.

To make swapping efficient, raw partitions (without filesystems) are normally used as the backing store. Instead of using a filesystem structure to keep track of the swap area's contents, the kernel maintains its own simplified mapping from memory blocks to disk blocks.

See page 667 for more information about splitting swap areas.

The more swap space you have, the more virtual memory can be allocated by processes. The best swapping performance is achieved when the swap area is split among several drives (or better yet, among several SCSI buses).

You can enable swapping to a particular device by hand, but you will generally want to have this function performed automatically at boot time. On most systems, swap areas can be listed in the **fstab** file, the same file that's used to enumerate mountable filesystems. A swap entry looks something like:[10]

```
/dev/sd3b      -                swap
```

During startup, a command (often **swapon** or **swap**) is run to enable swapping on all partitions listed in the **fstab** file. The vendor-specific sections starting on page 148 identify the particular command and syntax used on each system.

9.5 FSCK: CHECK AND REPAIR FILESYSTEMS

The UNIX filesystem is surprisingly reliable, and it does a remarkable job of coping with unexpected system crashes and flaky hardware. However, there are a number of ways that filesystems can become damaged or inconsistent.

Any time the kernel panics or the power fails, small inconsistencies will be introduced into filesystems that were active immediately preceding the crash. Since the kernel buffers both data blocks and summary information, the most recent image of the filesystem is split between disk and memory. During a crash, the memory portion of the image is lost. The buffered blocks are effectively "overwritten" with the versions that were most recently saved to disk.

Minor damage can usually be fixed with the **fsck** (file system consistency check, spelled aloud or pronounced "fs check" or "fisk") command. The five most common types of damage are:

- Unreferenced inodes
- Inexplicably large link counts
- Unused data blocks not recorded in the block maps
- Data blocks listed as free that are also used in a file
- Incorrect summary information in the superblock

10. From SunOS; other systems will vary.

These five problems can be fixed safely and automatically with **fsck**.

Disks are normally checked at boot time with **fsck -p**, which examines the local filesystems in **/etc/fstab** and corrects the five errors listed above. Recent operating systems (including SunOS 4.1.3, Solaris, and IRIX) remember which filesystems had blocks buffered in memory before a crash, and they only check these "dirty" filesystems.

fsck -p can also be run on a particular filesystem. For example:

```
fsck -p /dev/rsd0g
```

fsck accepts both block and character devices; it usually runs faster on the character ("raw") device.

When **fsck** reads the **fstab** file to find out which filesystems to check, it obeys the sequence indicated by the last field of each entry. Filesystems are checked in increasing numeric order. If two filesystems are on different disks, they may be given the same sequence number; this will cause **fsck** to check them simultaneously, minimizing the time spent waiting for disk I/O.[11] The root partition should always be checked first.

Errors that do not fall into one of the five categories above are potentially serious; they cause **fsck -p** to print a call for help and then quit. In this case, you must run **fsck** without the **-p** option. When run in manual mode, **fsck** will ask you to confirm each of the repairs that it wants to make. Some errors that **fsck** considers dangerous are:

- Blocks claimed by more than one file
- Blocks claimed outside the range of the filesystem
- Link counts that are too small
- Blocks that are not accounted for
- Directories that refer to unallocated inodes
- Various format errors

Unfortunately, it is impossible to patch a disk by hand without extensive knowledge of the implementation of the filesystem. Unless you are attempting to establish yourself as a cult leader in a small town in Texas, you should never attempt to write directly to the filesystem through the device files. As long as you stick to reading the filesystem and do not try to modify it, there is no risk of compounding the corruption; mount the filesystem read-only for extra security

In practice, this means that you have little choice but to accept the fixes proposed by **fsck**. You can minimize problems by carefully recording the messages that **fsck** produces, since they will sometimes provide a

11. Conversely, if you accidentally assign the same pass number to two filesystems on the same disk, **fsck** performance will suffer because the heads must constantly jump from partition to partition.

clue about the file or files that are causing problems. If **fsck** asks for permission to delete a file, you should try to copy it to a different filesystem before allowing **fsck** to proceed. Be aware that any time you attempt to access a damaged filesystem, you risk panicking the system.

If **fsck** knows only the inode number of a file, the **ncheck** command can be used on some systems to discover its pathname. The **clri** command can be used to clear a bad inode that **fsck** is unable to fix (the data will of course be lost).

If **fsck** finds a file whose parent directory cannot be determined, it will place the file into the **lost+found** directory in the top level of the filesystem. Since the name given to a file is recorded only in the file's parent directory, names for orphan files will not be available and the files placed in **lost+found** will be named with their inode numbers.

9.6 SPECIFICS FOR VARIOUS OPERATING SYSTEMS

Unfortunately, the installation of new disks is a task that every UNIX vendor has decided to handle differently. For each vendor, we will list the commands needed to add a disk and then present a bloody, blow-by-blow example of the procedure. Each example will show the addition of a SCSI disk with three partitions: one partition will be a backup root partition (mounted on **/bkroot**), one will be a swap partition, and one will store user files (mounted on **/new**). Note that even a single vendor's commands may vary between hardware architectures and OS releases.

In many cases, seemingly arbitrary values will be passed to the formatting programs. This is because many of the arguments are not meaningful for SCSI disks.[12] In the olden days, you really had to know the exact layout of each disk.

Solaris

 Device names under Solaris are of the SVR4 ilk, with entries in the directories **/dev/dsk** and **/dev/rdsk**. Device names are tied to the SCSI address of each disk. **man sd** gives a detailed description of the naming conventions. Essentially, the devices are named

```
/dev/[r]dsk/cCtAd0sP
```

where C is the controller number, A is the SCSI target number, and P is the partition number.

In a characteristically perverse twist of nomenclature, Solaris insists on calling partitions "slices." However, the transition to the new, improved

---

12. While it is still sometimes possible to adjust geometry specifications to improve the performance of your disk, that topic is beyond the scope of this book.

word has not been consistently implemented, so you will see both terms in Sun's documentation.

When you add a disk, you run the **disks** command to create its device files. The **format** command is used to write the label and partitioning information on the disk. **prtvtoc**[13] will display the disk's current label.

Either **newfs** or **mkfs** can be used to install a filesystem within a partition. The **swap** command configures and audits swap areas. Swap partitions and mount points are listed in **/etc/vfstab**. Read the man page for **vfstab** carefully; not only is its format alien, but its parser is also quite picky. If you are installing Solaris from scratch, do not allow the installer to pick your disk partitions for you. It will want to partition your disk with **/usr** and **/opt** too small for a real system.

After you install a new disk, use the PROM monitor's **probe-scsi** command to check the target numbers of all SCSI devices.[14] If your system continuously auto-reboots with no message but

```
rebooting...
```

this indicates that you have an address conflict or a termination problem. If the system boots, you can look at the console messages to be sure the disk was found.

For our sample disk at SCSI target three, we look in the output of **dmesg** to find the output below. The kernel complains because we have not yet written a Solaris label on the disk.

```
...
sd3 is /sbus@1,f8000000/esp@0,800000/sd@3,0
WARNING: /sbus@1,f8000000/esp@0,800000/sd@3,0 (sd3):
    corrupt label - wrong magic number
    Vendor 'FUJITSU', product 'M2624F-512', 1015812
    512 byte blocks
...
```

This disk will be accessed through files called **/dev/[r]dsk/c0t3d0s**X, where X is the partition number. The **disks** command creates the appropriate device files for all disks that the kernel is aware of. It doesn't require any arguments:

```
# disks
```

Under Solaris, partition two refers to the entire disk. We use that partition when formatting and installing a label. The Solaris **format** program is menu-driven.

---

13. **prtvtoc** stands for "print volume table of contents."
14. If your PROM monitor does not seem to understand **probe-scsi**, try typing **n** to get to the new-style monitor.

```
# format /dev/rdsk/c0t3d0s2
/dev/rdsk/c0t3d0s2: configured with capacity of 482.87MB
selecting /dev/rdsk/c0t3d0s2
[disk formatted]
FORMAT MENU:
...
```

Just starting up **format** does not really do anything. Try placing a default label on the disk and see if the partitions are reasonable:

```
format> label
Ready to label disk, continue? y
format> partition
PARTITION MENU:
...
partition> print
Current partition table (default):
Part   Tag          Flag   Cylinders   Size       Blocks
   0   root         wm     0-94        32.15MB    (95/0/0)
   1   swap         wu     95-189      32.15MB    (95/0/0)
   2   backup       wu     0-1426      482.87MB   (1427/0/0)
   3   unassigned   wm     0           0          (0/0/0)
   4   unassigned   wm     0           0          (0/0/0)
   5   unassigned   wm     0           0          (0/0/0)
   6   usr          wm     190-1426    418.57MB   (1237/0/0)
   7   unassigned   wm     0           0          (0/0/0)
```

The label looks reasonable for our needs (it has a root on partition zero, swap on partition one, and a general area on partition six). Exit **format** with the **quit** command (twice: once to get out of partition mode, and once to leave **format**):

```
partition> quit
...
format> quit
```

Now let's check the label using **prtvtoc**:

```
# prtvtoc /dev/rdsk/c0t3d0s2
* /dev/rdsk/c0t3d0s2 partition map
*
* Dimensions:
*     512 bytes/sector
*      63 sectors/track
*      11 tracks/cylinder
*     693 sectors/cylinder
*    1429 cylinders
*    1427 accessible cylinders
*
* Flags:
*   1: unmountable
```

```
*   10: read-only
*
*                        First   Sector     Last
* Part   Tag  Flags  Sector     Count   Sector   Mount
   0      2    00         0     65835    65834
   1      3    01     65835     65835   131669
   2      5    01         0    988911   988910
   6      4    00    131670    857241   988910
```

It looks fine. Now we're ready to create filesystems for the backup root and user filesystems. For some strange reason, newfs in Solaris 2.3 does not use a reasonable default value for the platter rotation speed.[15] We'll specify 3,600 RPM (the standard speed) by hand:

```
# newfs -r 3600 /dev/rdsk/c0t3d0s0
newfs: construct file system /dev/rdsk/c0t3d0s0: (y/n)? y
Warning: 1 sector(s) in last cylinder unallocated
/dev/rdsk/c0t3d0s0:  65834 sectors in 95 cylinders of
   11 tracks, 63 sectors
32.1MB in 6 cyl groups (16 c/g, 5.41MB/g, 2624 i/g)
super-block backups (for fsck -F ufs -o b=#) at:
   32, 11184, 22336, 33488, 44640, 55792

# newfs -r 3600 /dev/rdsk/c0t3d0s6
newfs: construct file system /dev/rdsk/c0t3d0s6: (y/n)? y
Warning: 1 sector(s) in last cylinder unallocated
/dev/rdsk/c0t3d0s6:  857240 sectors in 1237 cylinders of
   11 tracks, 63 sectors
418.6MB in 78 cyl groups (16 c/g, 5.41MB/g, 2624 i/g)
super-block backups (for fsck -F ufs -o b=#) at:
   32, 11184, 22336, 33488, 44640, 55792, 66944, 78096,
   89248
...
```

After creating the filesystems, check them immediately with **fsck**:

```
# fsck /dev/rdsk/c0t3d0s0
** /dev/rdsk/c0t3d0s0
** Last Mounted on
** Phase 1 - Check Blocks and Sizes
** Phase 2 - Check Pathnames
** Phase 3 - Check Connectivity
** Phase 4 - Check Reference Counts
** Phase 5 - Check Cyl groups
2 files, 9 used, 30827 free (19 frags, 3851 blocks, 0.1%
   fragmentation)
```

The **fsck** should be repeated for each new filesystem.

15. This is fixed in Solaris 2.4.

Once the filesystems have been created, we can go ahead and mount them. **mount** uses block device files (in **/dev/dsk**) rather than character device files (in **/dev/rdsk**) to access the partition.

```
# mkdir /bkroot
# mkdir /new
# mount /dev/dsk/c0t3d0s0 /bkroot
# mount /dev/dsk/c0t3d0s6 /new
# df
/bkroot   (/dev/dsk/c0t3d0s0):    41806 blocks    14806 files
/new      (/dev/dsk/c0t3d0s6):   803522 blocks   204668 files
...
```

df shows that the filesystems are now correctly mounted. We next enable swapping on partition one, then make sure that the new swap area is being used with **swap -1**:

```
# swap -a /dev/dsk/c0t3d0s1
# swap -1
swapfile               dev   swaplo blocks    free
...
/dev/dsk/c0t3d0s1   32,25      8  65824   65824
```

Entries must be added to **/etc/vfstab** so that the new filesystems will be mounted automatically when the system boots. Here are the new lines we would add:

```
/dev/dsk/c0t3d0s0 /dev/rdsk/c0t3d0s0 /bkroot ufs 1 yes -
/dev/dsk/c0t3d0s6 /dev/rdsk/c0t3d0s6 /new    ufs 2 yes -
/dev/dsk/c0t3d0s1 -                  -        swap - no -
...
```

We want to make **/bkroot** be a backup of the root partition. **ufsdump** and **ufsrestore** are used to copy the filesystem:

```
# cd /bkroot
# ufsdump 0uf - / | ufsrestore -rf -
DUMP: Date of this level 0 dump: Tue Jun  7 19:11:44 1994
...
```

The **bkroot** partition will not be bootable until **installboot** is run on the new disk. **installboot** copies a small boot program to the beginning of the disk. When the system is powered on, the PROM monitor loads the boot program, and the boot program then loads the kernel from the root filesystem. **installboot** needs to be pointed at the disk and at a file that contains the boot block to be written:

```
# /usr/sbin/installboot /usr/lib/fs/ufs/bootblk
    /dev/rdsk/c0t3d0s0
```

The last step is to reboot and verify that all filesystems mount correctly and that swapping is enabled on the new swap partition. You must also ensure that you can boot from the `/bkroot` partition; don't wait until your main root partition is blown to find out that there's a problem.

HP-UX

The authors of HP-UX decided that users don't really need partitions. All disks have one giant partition, and the space not allocated to that partition is assumed to be swap.[16]

The `/etc/disktab` file contains entries for various "common" disks. It is usually several years out of date. If you don't find your disk listed, you can use `diskinfo` to determine the disk's characteristics and then make an entry of your own. Be very careful, as there is no error checking. If you make the size slightly too big, you will not discover the mistake until you start swapping on the disk.

Device files are found in `/dev/dsk` and `/dev/rdsk`. They are created automatically for SCSI devices. Before you can use a new disk, you must `mediainit` it to format the device. To make a new disk bootable, run `mkboot`. There is no specific command that labels the disk—you just specify the `/etc/disktab` entry you want when you run `newfs` on the one and only partition.

If you specify a `disktab` entry that contains swap space, you will need to add an entry to `/etc/checklist` for it. The current swap partitions can be checked with `swapinfo`. HP does allow you to group multiple disks together into logical volumes; see the man pages for `lvdisplay` and `lvcreate` for details.

Before you boot UNIX, you can get a listing of the SCSI devices from the PROM monitor. The way in which this is done varies quite a bit among machines. After you have booted, you need to know the SCSI target number of the device and the select code (HP's word for "major device number") of the SCSI interface (which you can get from `dmesg`).

Device files are basically of the form

```
/dev/[r]dsk/cSldAsP
```

where S is the select code of the interface, A is the disk's SCSI address, and P is the partition number. See the man page for `disk` in section seven of the manual for the complete scoop on naming.

The `diskinfo` command lets you to check and see if you have the correct device name. For purposes of this example, we will assume that the SCSI controller is at select code 20 and that our new disk is set to SCSI address three.

---

16. Some HP workstations (notably, the 9000/800 series) do allow partitions. The procedure for adding a disk on those systems is very different from the one described here.

```
# diskinfo /dev/rdsk/c201d3s0
SCSI describe of /dev/rdsk/c201d3s0:
  vendor: FUJITSU
  product id: M2624F-512
  type: direct access
  size: 507906 Kbytes
  bytes per sector: 512
```

The disk should be initialized with **mediainit**:

```
# mediainit /dev/rdsk/c201d3s0
```

This command took about 20 minutes and provided no feedback.

Our disk, like most modern disks, does not appear in **/etc/disktab**. Since there is no other entry for a disk of this size, we have to create an entry of our own. We will use the generic values for ns (number of sectors per track) and nt (number of tracks), and adjust nc (number of cylinders) to reflect the disk size according to the formula

```
ns * nt * nc * 1,024 = size in bytes
```

The size of the first (and only) partition is specified with s0; we'll accept the defaults for b0 (block size) and f0 (fragment size). The man page for **disktab** alludes to being able to specify multiple "sections" on the disk, but we do not recommend trying this at home. About 10% of the disk should be reserved for swap. The final entry looks like this:

```
FUJITSUM252F:\
 :ns#28:nt#16:nc#1020:\
 :s0#456960:b0#8192:f0#1024:\
 :se#512:rm#4002:
```

We picked a name for the entry based on our disk's manufacturer and model number. Note that

```
ns * nt * nc * 1024 = s0 * 1024 = 467927040
```

That's about 90% of the disk. The rest of the parameters were stolen from another entry. Now that there is a **disktab** entry, a filesystem can be created with **newfs**:

```
# newfs /dev/rdsk/c201d3s0 FUJITSUM252F
/dev/rdsk/c201d3s0:  456960 sectors in 1020 cylinders of
   16 tracks, 28 sectors
467.9Mb in 64 cyl groups (16 c/g, 7.34Mb/g, 2048 i/g)
super-block backups (for fsck -b#) at:
    16, 7216, 14416, 21616, 28816, 36016, 43216, 50416,
    57616, 64816, 72016, 79216, 86416, 93616, 100816,
    108016, 114704, 121904, 129104, 136304, 143504,
    150704,157904, 165104, 172304, 179504, 186704,
    193904, 201104, 208304, 215504, 222704, 229392,
```

```
    236592, 243792, 250992, 258192, 265392, 272592,
    279792,
```

We checked that the size calculated by **newfs** was roughly correct. Then we used **fsck** to make sure the filesystem was OK:

```
# fsck /dev/rdsk/c201d3s0
** /dev/rdsk/c201d3s0
** Last Mounted on
** Phase 1 - Check Blocks and Sizes
** Phase 2 - Check Pathnames
** Phase 3 - Check Connectivity
** Phase 4 - Check Reference Counts
** Phase 5 - Check Cyl groups
2 files, 0 icont, 9 used, 439526 free (14 frag, 54939 blk)
```

If you do your **disktab** calculations incorrectly and make the filesystem bigger than the disk, **fsck** will complain. After checking the filesystem, we can mount it:

```
# mkdir /new
# mount /dev/dsk/c201d3s0 /new
# df /new
/new  (/dev/dsk/c201d3s0):  791144 blocks 131068 i-nodes
```

As always, **mount** requires a block device. We did the **df** just to verify that the **mount** worked correctly. Next, we add an entry for the disk to the **/etc/checklist** file:

```
/dev/dsk/c201d3s0 /new hfs defaults 0 1
```

hfs is the type specifier for a local filesystem. Since we left space on the end of the disk for swapping, we can enable swapping with the **swapon** command. The **-e** argument tells **swapon** to use up whatever space is available outside the filesystem partition:

```
# swapon -e /dev/dsk/c201d3s0
# swapinfo
        Kb    Kb    Kb    PCT   START/
TYPE  AVAIL USED  FREE   USED  LIMIT PRI NAME
dev   76559 12891 63668  17%   948480 0   /dev/dsk/c201d6s0
dev   50946 1794  49152   4%   456960 1   /dev/dsk/c201d3s0
hold  0     28080 -28080
```

swapinfo's output shows that the disk is indeed being swapped on. To make swapping automatic, add another **/etc/checklist** entry for the disk as follows:

```
/dev/dsk/c201d3s0 -    swap end       - -
```

After doing all this, it is time to reboot and verify that the automatic mounts happen correctly and that swapping is properly configured.

IRIX

On IRIX systems, the **fx** command is used to specify partitioning information. In its normal mode, it only allows you to select between two partitioning schemes: one for a root disk (with root, swap, and user), and another with a single giant partition. If you want to define a new partitioning scheme, you must use the **-x** option (expert mode) and divide up the disk by hand. If you create a custom partition map and you want the disk to be bootable, you must also run **dvhtool** to install the boot blocks.

Device files for disk partitions are in **/dev/dsk** and **/dev/rdsk**. If you use the standard SGI partition numbers—0, 1, 6, 7, 8 (**vh**, the label) and 10 (**vol**, the whole disk)—then device entries will be created automatically; otherwise, use **mknod** to create the files by hand.

prtvtoc prints a disk's current label. Filesystems are created with **mkfs**, which acts much like **newfs** does on other systems. To add a swap device, you simply add an entry to **/etc/fstab**. The current swap information can be listed with **swap -l**.

IRIX allows you to create filesystems that span multiple partitions, even if the partitions are on different physical disks. This is definitely the coolest thing since sliced bread. See the man pages for **mklv** and **growfs** for details.

When you install a new disk, you should verify that it appears in the output of **hinv** ("hardware inventory"):

```
# hinv
...
Disk drive: unit 5 on SCSI controller 0
Disk drive: unit 3 on SCSI controller 0
...
```

Our example drive is unit three. The naming convention for device files is **/dev/[r]dsk/dks**N**d**U**P** where N is the controller number (usually zero), U is the SCSI address, and P is a partition: **s0**, **s1**, etc., or **vh** for the volume header, or **vol** for the entire disk.

The device files for our example disk are called **/dev/[r]dsk/dks0d3**P. Here's how we initialized the disk with the **fx** command:

```
# fx
fx version , Feb 14, 1994
fx: "device-name" = (dksc)
fx: ctlr# = (0)
fx: drive# = (1) 3
...opening dksc(0,3,)
...controller test...
...creating default volume directory
```

```
----- please choose one (? for help, .. to quit)-----
[exi]t          [d]ebug/        [l]abel/
[b]adblock/     [exe]rcise/     [r]epartition/
fx> r
... /* display of current partition */
----- please choose one (? for help, .. to quit)-----
[ro]otdrive     [u]srrootdrive    [o]ptiondrive     [re]size
```

Since we wanted a disk with a backup root, a user partition, and a swap area, we choose **u**. If we wanted just a user partition, we'd use **o**.

```
fx/repartition> u
Warning: you will need to re-install all software and
restore user data from backups after changing the
partition layout. Changing partitions will cause all data
on the drive to be lost. Be sure you have the drive
backed up if it contains any user data. Continue? y
----- partitions-----
part type      cyls        blocks          MB (base+size)
   0: efs       4 + 73     2760 + 50370    1 + 25
   1: rawdata  77 + 118    53130 + 81420   26 + 40
   6: efs      195 + 1277  134550 + 881130 66 + 430
   8: volhdr   0 + 4       0 + 2760        0 + 1
  10: entire   0 + 1472    0 + 1015680     0 + 496
capacity is 1015812 blocks
----- please choose one (? for help, .. to quit)-----
[ro]otdrive     [u]srrootdrive    [o]ptiondrive     [re]size
fx/repartition>..
----- please choose one (? for help, .. to quit)-----
[exi]t          [d]ebug/        [l]abel/
[b]adblock/     [exe]rcise/     [r]epartition/
fx> exit
```

The disk now has a backup root on partition zero and a swap area on partition one. The rest of the disk is partition six. To actually verify the disk, chose the **exercise** option before exiting **fx**.

The label can be inspected with **prtvtoc** (the volume header device is specified as an argument):

```
# prtvtoc /dev/rdsk/dks0d3vh
* /dev/rdsk/dks0d3vh (bootfile "/unix")
*      512 bytes/sector
*       63 sectors/track
*       11 tracks/cylinder
*        3 spare blocks/cylinder
*     1472 cylinders
*        4 cylinders occupied by header
*     1468 accessible cylinders
*
```

```
* No space unallocated to partitions
Part  Type     Start: sec (cyl)    Size: sec    (cyl)  Mount
   0  efs         2760   (    4)       50370   (   73)
   1  raw        53130   (   77)       81420   (  118)
   6  efs       134550   (  195)      881130   ( 1277)
   8  volhdr         0   (    0)        2760   (    4)
  10  volume         0   (    0)     1015680   ( 1472)
```

Since the partition map we selected in **fx** contains a root partition, **fx** automatically made the disk bootable. The boot file (**/unix**) is displayed on the first line of **prtvtoc**'s output.

The next step is to build filesystems with **mkfs**. In most situations, SGI's **mkfs** needs no arguments other than the partition name.

```
# mkfs /dev/rdsk/dks0d3s0
mkfs: /dev/rdsk/dks0d3s0: blocks=50370 inodes=10600
mkfs: /dev/rdsk/dks0d3s0: sectors=63 cgfsize=25177
mkfs: /dev/rdsk/dks0d3s0: cgalign=1 ialign=1 ncg=2
mkfs: /dev/rdsk/dks0d3s0: firstcg=15 cgisize=1325
mkfs: /dev/rdsk/dks0d3s0: bitmap blocks=13

# mkfs /dev/rdsk/dks0d3s6
mkfs: /dev/rdsk/dks0d3s6: blocks=881130 inodes=90240
mkfs: /dev/rdsk/dks0d3s6: sectors=63 cgfsize=29363
mkfs: /dev/rdsk/dks0d3s6: cgalign=1 ialign=1 ncg=30
mkfs: /dev/rdsk/dks0d3s6: firstcg=218 cgisize=752
mkfs: /dev/rdsk/dks0d3s6: bitmap blocks=216
```

As always, new partitions should be checked with **fsck**:

```
# fsck /dev/rdsk/dks0d3s0
fsck: checking /dev/rdsk/dks0d3s0
** Phase 1 - Check Blocks and Sizes
** Phase 2 - Check Pathnames
** Phase 3 - Check Connectivity
** Phase 4 - Check Reference Counts
** Phase 5 - Check Free List
2 files 22 blocks 47682 free
```

The **fsck** should be repeated for each new filesystem. To mount the filesystems, use the following commands:

```
# mkdir /bkroot
# mkdir /new
# mount /dev/dsk/dks0d3s0 /bkroot
# mount /dev/dsk/dks0d3s6 /new
# df
Filesystem           Type  blocks use    avail %use  Mounted
...
/dev/dsk/dks0d3s0    efs   47704  22     47682  0%   /bkroot
/dev/dsk/dks0d3s6    efs   858330 22     858308 0%   /new
```

df is used to verify that the disks are mounted and have the expected sizes. Note that it is necessary to specify block devices (**/dev/dsk** files) for mounts.

To enable swapping on the new disk, use the **swap** command:

```
# swap -a /dev/dsk/dks0d3s1
```

swap -l can be used to verify that the new partition is being used.

To activate all the partitions at boot time, make the following entries in the **/etc/fstab** file:

```
/dev/dsk/dks0d3s0 /bkroot efs rw,raw=/dev/rdsk/dks0d3s0 0 2
/dev/dsk/dks0d3s6 /new    efs rw,raw=/dev/rdsk/dks0d3s6 0 1
/dev/dsk/dks0d3s1 swap    swap pri=1                     0 0
```

The filesystem type for a garden-variety local filesystem is efs. The raw entry in the options field is a bit unusual; it specifies the character device for **fsck**. The pri=1 clause specifies the priority of the swap partition. It is only necessary if you want to specify the order in which your swap partitions get used (lower numbers are used first).

To make a copy of your existing root partition on the new backup partition you'd use **dump** and **restore**:

```
# cd /bkroot
# dump 0f - / | restore -rf -
```

As a final step, reboot and verify that all filesystems mount correctly and that the new swap partition is being utilized. Check to be sure you can boot off the backup root partition.

SunOS

SunOS uses the **format** command to format and label disks. It reads device and partitioning information from /etc/format.dat. If the disk you are adding does not have a standard entry in that file, you can create one for it by copying the entry for another disk and modifying the sizes. You can check a disk's current label with **dkinfo**.

SunOS device files for SCSI disks have the form **/dev/sd**XC, where X is a unit number and C is the partition name. Partitions are named **a** through **f**. The **c** partition is usually the entire disk. The **a** partition is traditionally a small root area, and **b** is the swap partition.

Under SunOS, unit numbers are *not* the same as SCSI target numbers, although there is a one-to-one correspondence between the two. When the first SPARCs with internal disks came out, Sun mapped SCSI address three to logical unit zero and SCSI address zero to logical unit three. This allowed customers with Sun3 hardware to connect "shoebox" drives without changing their SCSI addresses.

If you want a disk to be bootable, use **installboot** to write the boot code appropriate for that type of disk. To create filesystems, use the **newfs** command, which will generally pick reasonable parameter values if you specify only the raw device name. To make a partition available as swap space, add an entry for it in **/etc/fstab**.

The best way to test your SCSI addresses and cabling is to run the **probe-scsi** command from the PROM monitor.[17] After you're sure the bus is okay, boot the machine and figure out what unit number has been assigned to the new drive. This can be determined with **dmesg**:

```
# dmesg
...
sd0 at esp0 target 3 lun 0
sd0: corrupt label - wrong magic number
sd0: Vendor 'FUJITSU', product 'M2624F-512', 1015812
    512 byte blocks
```

Our disk is SCSI target three, but it appears as logical unit zero; maybe "illogical unit number" would be a better term for Sun to adopt. In fact, if we had not picked SCSI ID three or zero for our disk, the target number and logical unit numbers would match.

If you try to check the status of a new disk with **dkinfo**, it gives the following non-intuitive response:

```
# dkinfo sd0
sd0: no such disk
```

That's because there is no label on the disk. To install a label, use the **format** command:

```
# format sd0
... /* a bunch of help menus */
format> type
AVAILABLE DISK SELECTIONS:
0. sd0 at esp0 slave 24
    sd0: <drive type unknown>
Specify disk (enter its number) [0]:
AVAILABLE DRIVE TYPES:
0. Quantum ProDrive 80S
1. CDC Wren IV 94171-344
...
14. other
```

We picked the "other" option because our Fujitsu is not on the list. Most of the geometry information that **format** asks for is not important on SCSI disks; however, that doesn't stop **format** from demanding it.

17. If your PROM monitor does not seem to understand **probe-scsi**, try typing **n** to get to the new-style monitor.

If you know the actual number of cylinders, heads, and tracks on your disk, you can use these numbers. If not, you can placate `format` by factoring the disk size in blocks (displayed by `dmesg`) into three pieces. In this case, 1,015,812 factors into 252, 29, and 139. On some systems, you can use `/usr/games/factor` to figure this out.

Once the factors have been determined, you must lie to `format`. Subtract two from the greatest factor (or the actual number of cylinders, if you know it) because `format` will insist on allocating two alternates:

```
Enter number of data cylinders: 250
Enter number of alternate cylinders [2]:
Enter number of physical cylinders [252]:
```

Use the second factor as the number of heads:

```
Enter number of heads: 29
```

Use the third factor as the number of sectors per track:

```
Enter number of data sectors/track: 139
Enter rpm of drive [3600]:
Enter disk type (remember quotes): "FUJITSU M2624F-512"
selecting sd0: <FUJITSU M2624F-512>
[disk formatted, no defect list found]
No defined partition tables.
format>
```

Now the disk is "formatted" (actually, no formatting was really done), but it still needs to be partitioned. The disk is set up to have 250 usable cylinders, with 4,031 (129 * 29) blocks per cylinder (again, these numbers are mostly arbitrary for SCSI disks). For this example, let's suppose we want 50 cylinders for a backup root partition, 40 cylinders for swap, and the remaining 160 cylinders for user files. The sizes of the partitions are computed by multiplying the number of cylinders by the number of blocks per cylinder. The size of the whole disk must also be calculated.

After navigating to the partitioning menu of the `format` command, we will define the **a** partition as the backup root. This partition needs to be at least as big as the primary root partition.

```
partition> a
partition a - starting cyl    0, # blocks     0 (0/0/0)
Enter new starting cyl [0]: 0
Enter new # blocks [50, 0/0/0]: 201550
```

Next, we'll do the **b** partition, which is traditionally used for swap.

```
partition> b
partition b - starting cyl    0, # blocks     0 (0/0/0)
Enter new starting cyl [0]: 50
Enter new # blocks [40, 0/0/0]: 161240
```

The **c** partition is traditionally the whole disk:

```
partition> c
partition c - starting cyl   0, # blocks        0 (0/0/0)
Enter new starting cyl [0]: 0
Enter new # blocks [40, 0/0/40]: 1007750
```

Finally, the **d** partition, where user files will be placed:

```
partition> d
partition d - starting cyl   0, # blocks        0 (0/0/0)
Enter new starting cyl [0]: 90
Enter new # blocks [0, 0/0/0]: 644960
```

We can now display the partition table with the **print** command:

```
partition> print
Current partition table (unnamed):
partition a - starting cyl   0, # blocks  201550 (50/0/0)
partition b - starting cyl  50, # blocks  161240 (40/0/0)
partition c - starting cyl   0, # blocks 1007750 (250/0/0)
partition d - starting cyl  90, # blocks  644960 (160/0/0)
partition e - starting cyl   0, # blocks       0 (0/0/0)
partition f - starting cyl   0, # blocks       0 (0/0/0)
partition g - starting cyl   0, # blocks       0 (0/0/0)
partition h - starting cyl   0, # blocks       0 (0/0/0)
```

As expected, the right-hand column shows the cylinder sizes we selected above. When the partition table looks correct, we write it to disk with the **label** command:

```
partition> label
Ready to label disk, continue? y
```

If the partitioning process worked correctly, **dkinfo** should now give better results:

```
# dkinfo sd0
sd0: SCSI CCS controller at addr f8800000, unit # 24
250 cylinders 29 heads 139 sectors/track
a: 201550 sectors (50 cyls)
   starting cylinder 0
b: 161240 sectors (40 cyls)
   starting cylinder 50
c: 1007750 sectors (250 cyls)
   starting cylinder 0
d: 644960 sectors (160 cyls)
   starting cylinder 90
e: No such device or address
f: No such device or address
g: No such device or address
h: No such device or address
```

Once the mathematical gyrations needed for labeling and partitioning have taken their toll, the remaining steps are more logical. To make filesystems, just use **newfs** with the simple name of the device:

```
# newfs sd0a
/dev/rsd0a:  201550 sectors in 50 cylinders of 29 tracks,
   139 sectors
103.2MB in 4 cyl groups (16 c/g, 33.02MB/g, 15104 i/g)
     32, 64672, 129312, 193952,

# newfs sd0d
/dev/rsd0d:  644960 sectors in 160 cylinders of 29
   tracks, 139 sectors
330.2MB in 10 cyl groups (16 c/g, 33.02MB/g, 15104 i/g)
super-block backups (for fsck -b #) at:
     32, 64672, 129312, 193952, 258592, 323232, 387872,
     452512, 517152, 581792,
```

Test the filesystems with **fsck**:

```
# fsck /dev/sd0a
** /dev/sd0a
** Last Mounted on
** Phase 1 - Check Blocks and Sizes
** Phase 2 - Check Pathnames
** Phase 3 - Check Connectivity
** Phase 4 - Check Reference Counts
** Phase 5 - Check Cyl groups
2 files, 9 used, 93133 free (21 frags, 11639 blocks, 0.0%
   fragmentation)
...
```

Try to mount them:

```
# mkdir /bkroot
# mkdir /new
# mount /dev/sd0a /bkroot
# mount /dev/sd0d /new
# df
Filesystem kbytes  used   avail  capacity  Mounted on
...
/dev/sd0a    93142     9   83819        0%  /bkroot
/dev/sd0d   303423     9  273072        0%  /new
```

The output of **df** shows that the filesystems are indeed mounted. To make them mount automatically at boot time, we add the following entries to **/etc/fstab**:

```
# sd0 - the Fujitsu disk next to the machine
/dev/sd0a    /bkroot    4.2    rw   0 1
/dev/sd0b    -          swap   -
/dev/sd0d    /new       4.2    rw   0 2
```

The second entry shows that we want to swap on the **b** partition. The comment on the first line is not necessary, but it makes it a lot easier for someone else to figure out what is going on.

To copy the contents of the root partition to the new backup root, use **dump** and **restore**:

```
# cd /bkroot
# dump 0f - / | restore -rf -
```

This will make an exact copy of the root partition on **/bkroot**. The disk also needs to be made bootable with **installboot**:

```
# /usr/kvm/mdec/installboot /bkroot/boot
    /usr/kvm/mdec/bootsd /dev/rsd0a
```

This puts a copy of **bootsd** (the SCSI disk booting program) on the device, and tells it to load **/bkroot/boot** (a higher-level boot program) when it starts.

Once all the configuration work is complete, reboot and make sure that the filesystems mount correctly. Also, test the backup root partition to be sure that you can boot from it.

OSF/1

Under OSF/1, device files for SCSI disks are named **/dev/[r]rz**U P, where U is eight times the SCSI controller number plus the device's SCSI target number, and P is a letter representing the partition (with **c** being the entire disk). Files for disks on the first two controllers are pre-installed.

Disks are labeled with the **disklabel** command, which gets its information from **/etc/disktab**. The **disktab** file that DEC gives you contains entries for DEC peripherals only; for other disks, you will have to copy an existing entry and modify it. Filesystems are created with **newfs**. Swapping is enabled with **swapon**.

In the following scenario, we will install a DEC RZ55 that is set to SCSI target one and lives on the second SCSI bus. The disk's device files are therefore **/dev/[r]rz9**P.

The first step is to label the partition. Since it is a DEC disk, it is already included in the **disktab** file:

```
# disklabel -r -w /dev/rrz9c rz55
```

The **disklabel** command can then be used to check the new label:

```
# disklabel -r /dev/rrz9c
/dev/rrz9c:
type: SCSI
disk: rz55
```

```
label:
flags:
bytes/sector: 512
sectors/track: 36
tracks/cylinder: 15
sectors/cylinder: 540
cylinders: 1224
sectors/unit: 649040
rpm: 3600
interleave: 1
trackskew: 0
cylinderskew: 0
headswitch: 0              # milliseconds
track-to-track seek: 0   # milliseconds
drivedata: 0
8 partitions:
#      size   offset   fstype   fsize bsize
a: 131072        0   unused   1024  8192   # (0 - 242)
b: 262144   131072   unused   1024  8192   # (242 - 728)
c: 649040        0   unused   1024  8192   # (0 - 1201)
d:      0        0   unused   1024  8192   # (0 - -1)
e:      0        0   unused   1024  8192   # (0 - -1)
f:      0        0   unused   1024  8192   # (0 - -1)
g: 255824   393216   unused   1024  8192   # (728 - 1201)
h:      0        0   unused   1024  8192   # (0 - -1)
```

The partition table looks appropriate for our example, where the **a** partition will be used for a backup root partition, **b** will be a swap area, and **g** will hold user files. If the partition sizes were not acceptable, you would need to adjust the sizes specified in **/etc/disktab**, then run the **disklabel** command again.

The next step is to make filesystems on the **a** and **g** partitions:

```
# newfs /dev/rrz9a
Warning: 148 sector(s) in last cylinder unallocated
/dev/rrz9a:     131072 sectors in 243 cylinders of 15
   tracks, 36 sectors
67.1MB in 16 cyl groups (16 c/g, 4.42MB/g, 1024 i/g)
super-block backups (for fsck -b #) at:
    32, 8720, 17408, 26096, 34784, 43472, 52160, 60848,
    69536, 78224, 86912, 95600, 104288, 112976, 121664,
    130352,

# newfs /dev/rrz9g
Warning: 136 sector(s) in last cylinder unallocated
/dev/rrz9g:     255824 sectors in 474 cylinders of 15
   tracks, 36 sectors
131.0MB in 30 cyl groups (16 c/g, 4.42MB/g, 1024 i/g)
super-block backups (for fsck -b #) at:
```

```
32, 8720, 17408, 26096, 34784, 43472, 52160, 60848,
69536, 78224, 86912, 95600, 104288, 112976, 121664,
130352, 138272, 146960, 155648, 164336, 173024,
181712, 190400, 199088, 207776, 216464, 225152,
233840, 242528, 251216,
```

After creating the filesystems, we check them with **fsck** and then mount them:

```
# mkdir /bkroot
# mkdir /new
# mount /dev/rz9a /bkroot
# mount /dev/rz9g /new
```

Swapping is enabled on the **b** partition with the **swapon** command:

```
# swapon /dev/rz9b
```

To make the mounts and swapping configuration permanent, some new entries must be added to **/etc/fstab**:

```
/dev/rz9a      /bkroot   ufs rw 1 2
/dev/rz9b      swap2     ufs sw 0 0
/dev/rz9g      /new      ufs rw 1 3
```

For swap partitions, you must lie and claim that the partition type is ufs. The partition is identified as a swap area by a mount point of swap1 or swap2 and the value sw in the options field. These are highly unusual conventions, to say the least.

To finish the installation, reboot and verify that all partitions are correctly activated.

BSDI

BSDI has one grand command, **disksetup**, which takes care of all disk-related operations. Because many sickos want to run DOS on the same machine they use for BSDI, there are provisions for maintaining a DOS-style **fdisk** partition table as well as the normal UNIX partition table.

BSDI is the only one of our example systems on which non-SCSI disks are commonly seen (you might see IDE and ESDI disks). Information about disk sizes and geometry is kept in **/etc/disktab**.

SCSI device names are **/dev/sd[0-6][a-h]** with **a** through **h** being the UNIX partitions. In the BSD style, partition **c** represents the entire disk, and partition **a** must be the root partition on the primary disk. Filesystems are built with **newfs**, and configuration information for mounts is kept in **/etc/fstab**. The standard filesystem type is ufs.

The first step in installing a new SCSI disk on a BSDI system is to run the **disksetup** command. It's responsible for labeling and partitioning the disk, and for installing the boot block. In this example, we will install a Maxtor disk drive at SCSI target zero. **disksetup -i** guides you through the configuration process interactively:

```
# disksetup -i sd0
Do you intend to share this disk between BSD/386 and
another operating system? [no]:

Disk geometries can be entered in several ways.
Your choices are:

'scsi'       Queries the scsi disk itself to build a label
             (use this for all scsi disks unless you know
             of some problem).
'internal'   Queries the kernel for the current label info.
'st506'      Queries an IDE/ESDI controller for parameters
'prompt'     Queries you for the parameters directly.
'file'       Queries you for a saved label file (of the
             form created by disksetup or disklabel with
             only a disk argument or by 'scsicmd -l').

Any other string is assumed to be a disk type name for
an entry in the /etc/disktab file.
```

The **disksetup** program is used for all of the disk types supported by BSDI. For this example, scsi is the appropriate choice:

```
Enter choice ['scsi', 'internal', 'st506', 'prompt',
   'file', or type]: scsi
Executing scsicmd to build a label:
Scanning for logical cylinder sizes...
Zone 1: 1626 cylinders, 427 sectors per cylinder
Total number of logical cylinders found in scan (1626)
differs from reported drive parameters (1629+3);
assuming 1626+6 cylinders for disk label.
Current geometry:
     Type:             SCSI
     Vendor/Type:      MAXTOR XT-8380S
     Bytes/Sector:     512
     Cylinders:        1626
     Heads:            8
     Sectors/track:    54
     Total Sectors:    694302

Is this information correct? [yes]:
```

disksetup queries the disk using the SCSI "mode sense" command and figures out the appropriate information. If the layout info looks kosher, **disksetup** will try to make up a reasonable partition table based on the size of the disk.

```
BSD Partition Sizing
BSD Type              Size    MB      Start      End  Warnings
     a   4.2         16653  (   8)        0    16652
     b   swap        65758  (  32)    16653    82410
     c   Unused     694302  ( 339)        0   694301
     d   <unused>
     e   <unused>
     f   <unused>
     g   <unused>
     h   4.2        611891  ( 298)    82411   694301
Last Data Sector:    694301
```

These partitions look just fine for our use, with a small partition to use as the backup root (**a**), a swap partition (**b**), and another data partition filling up the rest of the disk (**h**). The **c** partition refers to the entire disk. If the partitions were not acceptable, we could use additional **disksetup** commands to adjust them.

The program next installs boot blocks:

```
Commands:  [T]ype  [S]tart  [L]ength  [N]ext phase
Command> N
Which boot blocks do you wish to install?
    1: wd    (IDE, ESDI, ST506)
    2: aha   (ISA SCSI -- AHA154[02][BC[F]], BT542, BT445S)
    3: eaha  (EISA SCSI -- AHA174[02])
Boot block type: 2
```

This is a slightly confusing part of the installation. You need to know what kind of SCSI adaptor board you have in order to select the correct book block. If you are not sure, you will need to consult your hardware manual or look at the board itself.

Next, it is time to actually write the label and boot blocks to the disk:

```
Ready to write BSD label and boot blocks.
Proceed? [yes]:
BSD boot blocks written successfully.
#
```

The next step is to create filesystems on our data partitions with **newfs**. Character device files must be used for this:

```
# newfs /dev/rsd0a
Warning: 1 sector(s) in last cylinder unallocated
/dev/rsd0a:  16652 sectors in 39 cylinders of 8 tracks,
   54 sectors
8.1MB in 3 cyl groups (16 c/g, 3.34MB/g, 832 i/g)
super-block backups (for fsck -b #) at:
   32, 6928, 13824,
```

```
# newfs /dev/rsd0h
Warning: 1 sector(s) in last cylinder unallocated
/dev/rsd0h:  611890 sectors in 1433 cylinders of 8
   tracks, 54 sectors
298.8MB in 90 cyl groups (16 c/g, 3.34MB/g, 832 i/g)
super-block backups (for fsck -b #) at:
     32, 6928, 13824, 20720, 27616, 34512, 41408, 48304,
     54688, 61584, 68480, 75376, 82272, 89168, 96064,
     102960, 109344, 116240,
 . . .
```

After the filesystems have been created, check them with **fsck**:

```
# fsck /dev/rsd0a
** /dev/rsd0a
** Last Mounted on
** Phase 1 - Check Blocks and Sizes
 . . .
** Phase 5 - Check Cyl groups
1 files, 1 used, 7948 free (20 frags, 991 blocks, 0.3%
   fragmentation)

# fsck /dev/rsd0h
** /dev/rsd0h
** Last Mounted on
** Phase 1 - Check Blocks and Sizes
 . . .
** Phase 5 - Check Cyl groups
1 files, 1 used, 295126 free (14 frags, 36889 blocks,
   0.0% fragmentation)
```

The next step is to create mount points and mount the filesystems:

```
# mkdir /bkroot
# mount /dev/sd0a /bkroot
# mkdir /new
# mount /dev/sd0h /new
```

mount and **df** can be used to verify that the filesystems are mounted and are the right size:

```
# mount
 . . .
/dev/sd0a on /bkroot (local)
/dev/sd0h on /new (local)

# df
Filesystem    1K-blocks    Used    Avail Capacity  Mounted on
 . . .
/dev/sd0a         7949       1     7153      0%     /bkroot
/dev/sd0h       295127       1   265613      0%     /new
```

Since the **a** partition is going to be used as a backup of the root, we can use **dump** and **restore** to copy the contents over:

```
# cd /bkroot
# dump 0f - / | restore -rf -
    DUMP: Date of this level 0 dump: Tue Jul 19 12:12 1994
    DUMP: Date of last level 0 dump: the epoch
    DUMP: Dumping /dev/rsd1a (/) to standard output
    DUMP: mapping (Pass I) [regular files]
    DUMP: mapping (Pass II) [directories]
    DUMP: estimated 9466 tape blocks.
    DUMP: dumping (Pass III) [directories]
    DUMP: dumping (Pass IV) [regular files]
...
```

Next, entries must be added to **/etc/fstab** for the new partitions. Note that the swap partition must have the option sw.

```
/dev/sd0a    /bkroot    ufs     rw    0 1
/dev/sd0b    swap       swap    sw    0 0
/dev/sd0h    /new       ufs     rw    0 2
```

The final step is to reboot and verify that the partitions mount correctly. Also, be sure that you can boot from the backup root partition.

10 *Periodic Processes*

10.1 INTRODUCTION

The key to staying in control of your system is to automate as many tasks as possible. For example, an **adduser** program can add new users faster than you can, with a smaller chance of making mistakes. Almost any task can be encoded in a shell, **expect**, or **perl** script.

See page 525 for more information about automatic network checks.

Sometimes, it's useful to have a script or command executed without any human intervention. For example, you might want to have a script verify (say, every half an hour) that your network routers and bridges are working correctly, and have it send you electronic mail when problems are discovered.[1]

10.2 CRON: SCHEDULE COMMANDS

Under UNIX, periodic execution is handled by the **cron** daemon. **cron** starts when the system boots and remains running as long as the system is up. **cron** reads one or more configuration files containing lists of command lines, times at which they are to be invoked, and (on some systems) login names under which they are to run. The command lines are executed by **sh**, so almost anything you can do by hand from the shell can be done using **cron**.

---

1. Many sites go further than this and dial a pager with a modem so that the administrator can be summoned even when out of email range.

A `cron` configuration file is called a "crontab," short for "cron table." BSD systems have one file, usually `/usr/lib/crontab` or `/etc/crontab`. Some BSD systems have a bonus crontab called `crontab.local`; you can distribute the main crontab network-wide and keep the local crontab for commands specific to a particular machine. BSD crontabs can only be modified by root, and they include information about what user name to use when running each command. Since ordinary users cannot modify the crontab file, BSD `cron` is primarily an administrator's tool.

ATT systems use a more open model; instead of a single crontab file, they have a crontab directory. A command called `crontab` is used to submit crontab files to this directory, and `cron` reads the contents of every file. Typically, there is one crontab file per user: one for root, one for jsmith, and so on. The file is named with the login name of the user that it belongs to, and `cron` uses this filename to figure out which UID to use when running the commands it contains. There is no login name field in ATT crontabs.

vixie-cron is included on the CD-ROM. The ATT `cron` is clearly the more flexible of the two, and it is used by many otherwise-BSD-ish systems, such as SunOS. If you have a BSD `cron` and are feeling ambitious, you can install `vixie-cron` (written by Paul Vixie of DEC), which provides ATT functionality for BSD systems.

Old versions of `cron` scan their crontabs periodically and execute all commands that should have been run since the last scan. Modern versions parse the crontabs, figure out which of the listed commands needs to be run soonest, and go to sleep until the command's execution time has arrived. On some systems, sending `cron` a hangup signal forces it to reread the crontabs; you may have to do this after editing the crontab files to make `cron` aware of any changes. On ATT-ish systems, the `crontab` command tells `cron` to reread the configuration files, so `cron` is automatically kept in sync.

`cron` normally does its work silently, but some versions can keep a log file (usually `/var/cron/log` or `/usr/lib/cron/log`) that lists the commands that were executed, and when. On some systems, creating the log file enables logging and removing the log file turns logging off. On other systems, the log is turned on or off in a configuration file. The log file grows quickly and is rarely useful; leave logging turned off unless you're debugging a specific problem.

Most `cron`s do not compensate for commands that are missed while the system is down. In addition, many versions of `cron` do not understand daylight savings time, causing commands to be skipped or run twice when time changes occur. If you use `cron` for important tasks such as accounting, keep an eye open for these situations.

10.3 FORMAT OF CRONTAB FILES

Different versions of UNIX have a different number of crontabs, but all the configuration files on a system share a common format. As far as `cron` is concerned, there might as well be one giant file containing lines from all crontabs merged together.[2]

Comments in a crontab file are introduced with a pound sign in the first column of a line. Each non-comment line in a configuration file contains either six or seven fields, and represents one command.

The seven-field format is:

```
minute hour day month weekday username command
```

The six-field format omits *username*. Fields are separated by whitespace, but within the *command* field whitespace is taken literally.

minute, hour, day, month, and *weekday* give information about the times at which the command should be run. Their interpretations are shown in Table 10.1.

Table 10.1 **Crontab time specifications**

Field	Description	Range
minute	Minute of the hour	0 to 59
hour	Hour of the day	0 to 23
day	Day of the month	1 to 31
month	Month of the year	1 to 12
weekday	Day of the week	1 to 7

All systems interpret a *weekday* value of 1 as Monday. Most number the days from 1 to 7, but there are a few which start the week on Sunday and use the range 0 to 6.

Each of the time-related fields may contain

- A star, which matches anything
- A single integer, which matches exactly
- Integers separated by commas, matching any listed value
- Two integers separated by a dash, matching a range of values

For example, the time specification

```
45 10 * * 1-5
```

means "10:45 a.m., Monday through Friday."

2. Except for the determination of UID in ATT systems.

There is a potential ambiguity to watch out for with the *weekday* and *day* fields. Every day is both a day of the week and a day of the month. If both *weekday* and *day* are specified, a day need satisfy only one of the two conditions in order to be selected. For example,

```
0,30  *  13  *  5
```

means "every half hour on Friday, and every half hour on the 13th of the month," not "every half hour on Friday the 13th."

*See page 52 for more information about **su**.*

The *username* field specifies the account name (and indirectly, the UID) under which the command should be run. On ATT systems, which use the six-field format, the name of the configuration file is the user name. The superuser's crontab can run commands as an arbitrary user by prefacing them with **/bin/su** *username* **-c**.

command is the **sh** command line to be executed. It can be any valid shell command, and should not be quoted. *command* is considered to continue to the end of the line, and may contain blanks or tabs.

Most versions of **cron** allow the use of percentage marks ("%") to indicate newlines within the *command* field. Only the text up to the first percentage mark is included in the actual command; the remaining lines are given to the command as standard input.

Here are some examples of legal crontab commands:

```
echo The time is now `date` > /dev/console
write garth % Hi Garth. % Remember to get a job.
cd /etc; cat passwd | /usr/ucb/mail -s "Passwords" evi
```

And here are some complete examples:

```
30  2  *  *  1    joe   (cd /users/joe/project; make)
```

This (BSD-style) line will be activated at 2:30 each Monday morning. It will run **make** in the directory **/users/joe/project**. This might be used to start a long compilation at a time when other users would not be using the system. Usually, any output produced by a **cron** command is mailed to the "owner" of the command (in this case, Joe).

```
20  1  *  *  *    find /tmp -atime +3 -exec rm -f {} ';'
```

This command, which is in the ATT format and would presumably be in root's crontab, will be run at 1:20 each morning. It removes all files in the **/tmp** directory that have not been accessed in 72 hours.

```
55  23  *  *  1,2,3,4,7   /staff/trent/bin/acct-script
```

This line starts up **acct-script** at 11:55 p.m. on Monday, Tuesday, Wednesday, Thursday, and Sunday. The notation "1,2,3,4,7" is unfortunately required, since "1-4,7" would not be understood.

10.4 CHANGING CRONTABS

On BSD systems, you edit the crontab files directly, then notify `cron` of the changes by sending it a hangup signal. On ATT systems, you use the `crontab` command to submit and retrieve crontab files.

`crontab` *filename* installs *filename* as your crontab. `crontab -e` checks out a copy of your crontab, invokes your editor on it (as specified by the EDITOR environment variable), and then resubmits it to the crontab directory. `crontab -l` lists the contents of your crontab to standard output, and `crontab -r` removes your crontab file.

Most systems allow root to supply a *username* argument so that other users' crontabs can be viewed or edited. If no *filename* argument is supplied, `crontab` will try to read a crontab from its standard input. If you enter this mode by accident, don't try to exit by typing <Control-D>; this will erase your entire crontab. Use <Control-C> instead. Before editing your crontab, it's best to back it up with `crontab -l`. For various reasons, it seems easy to make mistakes when using `crontab`.

See Chapter 23 for information about auditing programs that can check for crontab problems.

Since crontabs cause commands to be executed, they have implications for security. On ATT systems, the `crontab` command takes care of managing crontab file permissions for you, but on BSD systems you must keep things under control by hand. When you create or edit a crontab file, be sure that only authorized users can modify it.

On ATT systems, the system administrator can specify who may and may not use `cron`. This is done using two configuration files called `cron.allow` and `cron.deny`. These files can be rather hard to find: check the directories `/etc/cron.d`, `/usr/lib`, `/usr/lib/cron`, and `/var/spool/cron`.

If `cron.allow` exists, then it contains a list of all users that can use `cron`, one per line. Anyone not listed can't invoke the `crontab` command. If `cron.allow` doesn't exist, then `cron.deny` is checked. Like `cron.allow`, it is just a list of users, but here the meaning is reversed: everyone *except* the listed users is allowed access.

10.5 SOME COMMON USES FOR CRON

A number of standard tasks are especially suited for invocation by `cron`, and these usually make up the bulk of the material in a site's crontab files. In this section we'll look at a variety of such tasks and the crontab lines used to implement them.

UNIX systems often come with some crontab entries preinstalled for you. If you want to deactivate them, comment them out by inserting a pound sign at the beginning of each line. Don't delete them completely; you might want to refer to them later.

Processing Appointment Calendars

Several files of interesting dates in `calendar` *format are included on the CD-ROM.*

Some systems have a facility that allows users to be automatically reminded of important dates. To use this service, you create a file called `calendar` in your home directory that contains a list of all the events you want to be reminded about. You can then run the `calendar` program to see a list of reminders for the current and following day.

When the superuser runs `calendar` with a dash as the only argument, `calendar` peeks into the calendar file of each user on the system, extracts the relevant reminders, and mails the results directly to the user rather than sending them to standard output. This operation should be performed early in the morning (not late at night) because `calendar` processes entries for the current day.

A crontab line to implement this might be

```
30  1  *  *  *   /usr/bin/calendar -
```

If the filesystems containing user accounts are widely cross-mounted at your site, make sure that only one machine is responsible for running `calendar`, or that your `calendar` only checks calendar files on local disks. Otherwise, users may receive duplicate notifications.

 If you use NIS, be warned that some versions of the SunOS `calendar` program concatenate the NIS password map with the contents of `/etc/passwd`. Duplicate messages may result.

Cleaning the Filesystem

Some of the files on any UNIX system are worthless junk (no, not the system files). For example, whenever a program crashes, the kernel writes out a file called `core` that contains an image of the program's address space.[3] Core files are useful for software developers, but for mere mortals they are usually a waste of space. Users often don't know about core files, so they tend not to delete them on their own.

NFS, the Network File System, is described in Chapter 17.

NFS is another source of extra files. Because NFS servers are stateless, they have to use a special convention to preserve files that have been deleted locally but are still in use by a remote machine. Most implementations rename such files to `.nfs`*xxx* where *xxx* is a number. There are various situations which result in these files being forgotten and left around after they are supposed to have been deleted.

Many programs create temporary files in `/tmp` or `/var/tmp` that don't get erased for one reason or another, and some programs, especially editors, like to make backup copies of each file they work with.

---

3. The word "core" means "memory." This term originated on early computer systems, which used little ferrite donuts mounted on a woven mesh as memory elements.

A partial solution to the junk file problem is to institute some sort of nightly disk space reclamation out of **cron**. The following examples all use the **find** command to delete junk files.

```
find / -xdev -name core -atime +7 -exec rm -f {} ';'
```

This command removes core images that have not been accessed in a week. The **-xdev** argument makes sure that **find** won't cross over to filesystems other than the root, which is important on networks where many filesystems may be cross-mounted.[4] If you want to clean up more than one filesystem, use a separate command for each.

```
find / -xdev -atime +3 '(' -name '#*' -o -name '.#*' -o
    -name '*.CKP' -o -name '.nfs*' ')' -exec rm -f {} ';'
```

This command deletes files that begin with # or .# or .nfs, or end with .CKP, and have not been accessed in three days. These are often backup files created by **emacs**, but other programs use a similar naming convention for temporary files.

```
find /var/preserve -mtime +14 -exec rm -f {} ';'
```

This command removes files in **/var/preserve** two weeks after they were last modified. This directory is used by **vi** to store copies of files that users were editing when the system crashed. The files are deposited and never removed unless claimed by their owners.

```
cd /tmp; find . ! -name . ! -name lost+found -type d
    -mtime +3 -exec /bin/rm -rf {} ';'
```

See page 148 for more information about lost+found.

This command recursively removes all subdirectories of **/tmp** not modified in 72 hours. Plain files in **/tmp** are removed at boot time by the system startup scripts, but some systems do not remove directories. If a directory named **lost+found** exists, it is treated specially and is not removed. This is important if **/tmp** is a separate filesystem.

If you use any of these commands, you should make sure that users are aware of your cleanup policies.

UUCP Polling

UUCP relies heavily upon **cron**. It is primarily used to initiate calls to other sites at specific times; however, it can also be used for other tasks such as summarizing logs and cleaning the UUCP spool area. The use of **cron** with UUCP is covered in Chapter 30.

Accounting

CPU accounting information has to be summarized and archived at least once a day, and summaries can be reviewed every month to compute

---

4. Not all versions of **find** support the **-xdev** argument. On some systems, it's called **-x**.

usage totals for each account. Chapter 28, *Accounting*, describes the use of **cron** for accounting purposes.

Network Distribution of Configuration Files

See Chapter 18 for more information about distributing configuration files on a network.

If you are administrating a network of machines, it's often convenient to maintain a single, distributed version of configuration files such as the mail aliases database (**/usr/lib/aliases** or **/etc/aliases**). Master versions of these files can be distributed every night using **rdist** or an **expect** script.

Sometimes, post-processing is required. For example, many systems require you to run **newaliases** to convert a text file of mail aliases to the hashed format used by **sendmail**. You might also need to load files into an administrative database such as NIS or NIS+.

10.6 SPECIFICS FOR VARIOUS OPERATING SYSTEMS

Solaris systems use the ATT-style **cron**. Crontab files are located in **/var/spool/cron/crontabs**. Config files such as **cron.allow** and **cron.deny** are in **/etc/cron.d**. To turn on logging for **cron**, edit **/etc/default/cron** and set CRONLOG=YES; this will cause logging information to be written to **/var/cron/log**.

HP-UX uses the ATT-style **cron**. Crontab files are kept in the directory **/usr/spool/cron/crontabs**. Other config files are in **/usr/lib**.

IRIX uses the ATT **cron**. IRIX 4.0 config files are in **/usr/lib/cron**, and crontab files are in the **/usr/spool/cron/crontabs** directory. IRIX 5.2 uses **/var/spool/cron/crontabs** and **/etc/cron.d**.

SunOS uses an ATT-style **cron** similar to that of Solaris. Crontab files are in **/var/spool/cron/crontabs**. **cron.allow** and **cron.deny** are in **/var/spool/cron**. Logging is done through **syslog**.

OSF/1 is mostly like ATT, but not completely. Crontab files are stored in **/var/spool/cron/crontabs**. Other files, including **cron.deny** and **cron.allow**, are located in **/var/adm/cron**. Logging is automatic. OSF/1's **crontab** command does not understand the **-e** or *username* options. This is a clue that you can easily wipe out your crontab file—see page 175.

BSDI uses **vixie-cron**. It's mostly ATT-ish, with several enhancements. Refer to the CD-ROM for more information.

 Backups

11.1 INTRODUCTION

At most sites, the information stored on computers is worth more than the computers themselves. It is also much harder to replace. Protecting this information is one of the system administrator's most important (and unfortunately, most tedious) tasks.

There are hundreds of creative ways to lose data. Software bugs routinely corrupt data files. Users accidentally delete their life's work. Hackers and disgruntled employees erase disks. Hardware problems and natural disasters take out entire machine rooms. No system should be operated without backups.

If executed correctly, backups allow the administrator to restore a filesystem (or any portion of it) to the condition it was in at the time of the last backup. Backups must be done carefully and on a strict schedule.

11.2 BACKUP DEVICES AND MEDIA

Since many types of failure can damage several pieces of hardware at once, backups must be written to some sort of removable media. For example, backing up one disk to another (although better than no backup at all) provides little protection against a controller failure. Most organizations keep backups off-site so that a disaster such as a fire cannot destroy both the original data and the backups.

179

Many kinds of media use magnetic particles to store their data. These media are subject to damage by electrical and magnetic fields. Here are some specific hazards to avoid:

- Audio speakers contain large electromagnets; don't store tapes on or near them. Even small speakers designed for use with computers can be hazardous.

- Transformers are basically electromagnets. They're usually found in wall adapters and power supplies.

- Hard disks and tape drives have motors and magnetic heads, and their cases are often unshielded. Drives in metal cases are probably safe.

- Monitors use transformers and high voltages. Many monitors retain an electrical charge even after being turned off. Color monitors are the worst. Never store tapes on top of a monitor.

- Metal detectors, especially those found at airports, can do a very effective job of destroying data. If you have to transport tapes on a plane, carry them with you and pass them to a guard for hand inspection.

- Prolonged exposure to the Earth's background radiation affects the data on magnetic media, limiting its lifespan. All tapes will become unreadable over a period of years. Most media will keep for three years, but if you plan to store data longer than that, you should either use optical media or re-record the data.

The following sections describe some of the media that can be used for backups. They are listed in order of increasing capacity.

Floppy Disks

Floppies are the most inconvenient way to store backups. They are slow and do not hold much data (up to 2.8MB, currently). They are also more expensive than other storage media on a cost per megabyte basis. Floppy disks only last for a couple of years; *never* use them for long-term storage.

On the other hand, floppy drives are inexpensive and often come with the system. Floppy drives are cleaned with a special cleaning disk.

Flopticals

Flopticals are written magnetically but read optically. They are the same physical size as a 3.5" floppy but hold anywhere from 60 to 200MB, depending on the device. Many floptical drives can read regular floppies, too. These devices are quite new and it is unclear how long the data will last, or how reliable the media and drives will be.

Cartridge Tapes

Cartridge tapes are often found on workstations. They are faster and hold more information than floppies. QIC (Quarter Inch Cartridge) tapes are quite expensive and are not particularly suited for backups, as even a small filesystem will take multiple tapes. However, QIC tapes are often used for distributing software, and they are a good format for exchanging small amounts of data among different platforms.

The most common cartridge tapes are QIC-11, QIC-24, and QIC-150.[1] The numbers specify the approximate capacity in megabytes. QIC drives can generally read (but not always write) tapes written in a less-dense format. For example, a normal QIC-150 drive can read QIC-11, QIC-24, and QIC-150, but can only write QIC-150.

See page 198 for more information about dd.

Not all vendors use the same byte order for QIC tapes. If you have problems reading a tape written on a different machine, you may need to swap bytes or perform an even more heroic incantation with **dd**.

You can clean a QIC drive by opening the door by hand (if there is one) and activating the tape insertion lever (if there is one) to expose the heads. A long Q-Tip covered with tape drive cleaning solution can then be swabbed over the heads and rollers.

hp   HP produces a line of tape drives that are identified on the front as "16 track." These drives use the same physical cartridges as QIC drives, but the tapes must be pre-formatted. The drives and the tapes they produce are completely incompatible with QIC; if you place an HP tape in a QIC drive, the tape may be destroyed. You can identify these tapes by their HP label and the by the markings "16 track" or "32 track."

Nine-Track Magnetic Tapes

Nine-track tape was once the most commonly used backup medium on UNIX systems. Most minicomputers had nine-track drives, and the tapes were the cheapest removable media. However, that day is past.

The only real use for a nine-track drive these days is to read tapes produced on a mainframe (there are still quite a few of these around), or to read old backup tapes. Nine-track tapes are large and heavy, and the drives are quite expensive. However, they do look very cool.

There are three standard densities of nine-track tape: 800 bpi (bits per inch), which is found only on older systems, 1,600 bpi, which is the most common density, and 6,250 bpi, which is a more recent (1982) format. One holdover from the nine-track days is the format of arguments to

---

1. There are numerous other QIC formats, but unless you are unfortunate enough to own a PC, you will not have to deal with them.

many tape-related commands, which expect tape sizes to be specified as a density in bits per inch and a length in feet. Default values are often appropriate for a 1,600 bpi nine-track tape that is 2,400 feet long.

Nine-track drives are cleaned by wiping the heads and numerous rollers with tape drive cleaning solution.

Write-Once CD-ROM

Write-once CD-ROM is a member of a class known as WORM (Write Once Read Many) devices. There have been numerous attempts to produce a WORM drive that would gain consumer acceptance, but WCD-ROM is the first to see any sort of widespread use. It is popular mainly because the disks that the system creates are readable by regular CD players and CD-ROM drives.

Write-once CDs are "burned" rather than pressed, and the resulting disks are not quite as durable as normal CDs. They will last much longer than magnetic media, however. The capacity is currently only 600 megabytes, and the blank disks are relatively expensive. The drives are quite slow for writing.

These drives are not a particularly good choice for normal backups, but they are good for archiving data you might want to recover a long time in the future.

8mm Cartridge Tapes

There are several brands of tape drive that record to standard 8mm (small-format) videotapes. The drives are often referred to as "Exabytes," after the first company that produced them. The original format holds about 2GB, and a newer format holds 5GB. Hardware compression on some drives pushes the effective capacity to 10GB.

These systems are relatively fast and allow a complete backup to be performed without operator intervention because of their large capacity. 8mm tapes are compact, reducing the need for storage space and making off-site storage easy.

The main disadvantage of 8mm tapes is that the drive mechanisms are somewhat temperamental. They tend to wander out of alignment every few years, requiring a costly trip back to the manufacturer. To clean these drives, you use a special cleaning cassette that is good for a limited number of cleanings.

The drive manufacturers tell you to use only "data quality" tapes, as opposed to normal "video quality" tapes. In our experience, there is little difference; however, we have heard reports of problems with some newer video-grade tapes.

4mm DAT Tapes

Many manufacturers supply drives that use DAT tapes. Technically, the DAT standard for data storage is called DDS (Digital Data Storage), but both the drives and media are similar to audio DAT. DAT tapes are currently the smallest magnetic media available (a little bigger than a box of matches). Tapes hold about two gigabytes of data, but some drives contain hardware data compression that pushes the effective capacity to around eight gigabytes. Access to data (seeking) is much quicker than on 8mm tapes, and the drives are more reliable. Currently, these are the best choice for backups, with 8mm tapes a close second. As with 8mm tapes, a special cartridge is used to clean the drive.

Jukeboxes and Stackers

Many sites have so much disk space that a full backup requires multiple tapes, even at eight gigabytes per tape. One solution for these sites is a stacker or jukebox.

A stacker is a simple tape changer that's used with a standard tape drive. It has a hopper that you load with tapes; it unloads full tapes as they are ejected from the drive and replaces them with blank tapes from the hopper. Most stackers hold about ten tapes.

A jukebox is a hardware device that can automatically change removable media in a limited number of drives, much like an old-style jukebox changed records on a single turntable. Jukeboxes are available for several types of media, including WORM, 8mm, and DAT. Often, jukeboxes are bundled with special backup software that understands how to manipulate the changer.

Summary of Media Types

Table 11.1 gives the best-case numbers for the media discussed above.

Table 11.1   Comparison of Backup Media

Medium	Capacity	Cost	Cost/MB	Type[a]	Reuse?	Random?
Floppy disk	2.8 MB	50¢	17.6¢	M	Yes	Yes
QIC	150 MB	$20	13.3¢	M	Yes	No
Nine-track	160 MB	$10	6.25¢	M	Yes	No
Floptical	200 MB	$15	7.50¢	M/O	Yes	Yes
WCD-ROM	600 MB	$10	1.67¢	B/O	No	Yes
Exabyte (8mm)	5.1 GB	$9	0.18¢	M	Yes	No
DAT (4mm)	5.5 GB	$7	0.13¢	M	Yes	No

a. M = Magnetic, B = Burn, O = Optical

In the following discussions, we will use the generic term "tape" to refer to the media chosen for backups. Examples of backup commands will be phrased in terms of tape devices.

11.3 Setting Up an Incremental Backup Regime

The **dump** and **restore** commands are the most common way to create and restore from backups. These programs have been part of UNIX for a very long time, and their behavior is well known. For most sites, **dump** and **restore** are the backup method of choice.

Dumping Filesystems

The **dump** command builds a list of files that have been modified since a previous dump, then packs those files into a single large file to archive to an external device. **dump** has several advantages over other utilities described later in this chapter:

- Backups can span multiple tapes.
- Files of any type (even devices) can be backed up and restored.
- Permissions, ownerships, and modify times can be restored.
- Files with holes are handled correctly.[2]
- Backups can be performed incrementally.

The **dump** command understands the layout of raw filesystems, and it reads a filesystem's inode tables directly to decide which files need to be backed up. This knowledge of the filesystem allows **dump** to be very efficient, but it also imposes several limitations.[3]

See Chapter 17 for more information about NFS. The first limitation is that every filesystem must be dumped individually. If you have a disk that is partitioned, you must dump each section of the disk separately. The other limitation is that only filesystems on the local machine can be dumped; you cannot dump an NFS filesystem. However, you can dump a local filesystem to a remote tape drive using **dump**'s evil twin, **rdump**.

The most important feature of **dump** is the concept of incremental backups. While it is possible to back up the entire system each day, it is usually not practical. Incremental dumps make it possible to back up only files that have changed since the last backup.

When you do a dump, you assign it a backup level, which is an integer from 0 to 9. A level N dump backs up all files that have changed since

---

2. Holes are blocks that have never contained data. If you open a file, write one byte, seek 1MB into the file, then write another byte, the resulting file will be only two blocks long. Files created by **dbm** or **ndbm** contain many holes.

3. **dump** requires access to raw disk partitions. Anyone allowed to do dumps can read all the files on the system with a little work.

the last dump of level less than N. A level zero backup places the entire filesystem on the tape. With an incremental backup system, you may have to restore files from several sets of backup tapes to reset a filesystem to its exact state during the last backup.[4]

Another nice feature of **dump** is that it does not care about the length of filenames. Hierarchies can be arbitrarily deep, and long component names are handled with aplomb.

dump accepts many arguments, but they do not vary too much from platform to platform. We will give a short description of the flags you will probably need to dump a network of machines. However, you *must* check these flags against the manual pages on the machine where you are dumping, as most vendors have mucked with the meaning of at least one flag.

dump parses its arguments differently from most other UNIX commands. It expects the flags to be contained in the first argument, and the flags' arguments to follow in order.

The first argument to **dump** must be the incremental dump level. **dump** uses the /etc/dumpdates file to determine how far back an incremental dump must go. The **u** flag causes **dump** to update /etc/dumpdates automatically when the dump completes. The date, dump level, and filesystem name are recorded. If you never specify the **u** flag, all dumps become level zeros, as there will never be a record of having previously dumped the filesystem. If a filesystem's name is changed, you can edit the /etc/dumpdates file by hand.

dump sends its output to some default device, usually the primary tape drive on a large system or the first floppy drive on a small system. Many vendors default to a nine-track or QIC device. **dump** must be instructed to send its output elsewhere if you want to use a different device. This is done with the **f** flag.

See page 60 for information about device numbers. If you are placing multiple dumps on a single tape, make sure you specify a non-rewinding tape device (a device file that does not cause the tape to be rewound when it is closed). Most tape drives have both a standard and a non-rewinding device entry. Read the manual page for the tape device in section 4 (BSD) or 7 (ATT) to determine the exact name of the appropriate device file.[5]

If you choose the rewinding device by accident, you will end up saving only the last filesystem dumped. Since **dump** does not have any idea

---

4. Actually, most versions of **dump** do not keep track of files that are deleted. If you restore from incremental backups, deleted files will be re-created.

5. The entries for a tape unit all use the same major device number. The minor device number tells the driver about special behaviors (rewinding, byte-swapping, etc.).

where the tape is positioned, this mistake will not cause any errors and will only become apparent when you try to restore files.

If you are dumping to a remote system using **rdump**, you specify the remote system as *hostname*:*device*, for example:

```
rdump 0uf anchor:/dev/nrtape /spare
```

dump makes some assumptions about the length and density of the tape you are using. Consult the manual for your version of **dump** to determine if these assumptions are reasonable, and if not, to see how to set these parameters correctly.

If you specify the wrong tape length and **dump** reaches the end-of-tape marker (EOT), the dump is ruined. If you are placing multiple volumes on a single tape, the length parameters cannot protect you from hitting EOT because the dump of each filesystem is independent.

For a discussion of data compression, see page 621.

On drives that provide data compression, the length of the "virtual tape" is somewhat indeterminate, since not all data compresses equally well. Compression ratios tend to be fairly stable when averaged over many gigabytes, but there are no guarantees.

For example, to do a level five dump of **/work** to a 1,000 bpi, 1,700 foot cartridge tape drive for which the device file is called **/dev/rst0**, you would use the command

```
dump 5usdf 1700 1000 /dev/rst0 /work
```

The flags **5usdf** are followed by the parameters to **s** (size: 1,700), **d** (density: 1,000), and **f** (device file: **/dev/rst0**). Finally, the filesystem name (**/work**), which is always present, is given. Most versions of **dump** allow you to specify the filesystem by its mount point, as in the example above. Some require you to specify the raw device file.

 Under Solaris, the standard version of the UNIX **dump** program is available as **/usr/lib/fs/ufs/ufsdump**. **ufsdump** accepts the same flags and arguments as traditional **dump**, except that you must specify Solaris-style device names. For example, the command

```
ufsdump 0uf /dev/rmt/2 /dev/rdsk/c0t3d0s2
```

dumps partition two of the drive at SCSI target three onto tape drive two.

Dump Sequences

Because dump levels are arbitrary (they only have meaning in relation to other levels), there are various schedules by which dumps can be done. The schedule that is right for you depends on:

- The activity of your filesystems
- The capacity of your dump device

- The amount of redundancy you want
- The number of tapes you want to buy

We will describe several possible sequences and give the motivation behind them. One of them might be right for your site, but your needs may require a different schedule altogether.

A *simple schedule*

If your total amount of disk space is smaller than the capacity of your tape device, you can use a completely trivial dump schedule. Do level zero dumps of every filesystem each day. Reuse a group of the tapes, but every N days (where N is determined your site's needs), keep the tape forever. This will cost you

```
(365/N) * (price of tape)
```

per year. This schedule provides massive redundancy and makes data recovery very easy. This is a good solution for a site with lots of money but limited operator time (or skill).

A *moderate schedule*

A more reasonable schedule is to assign a tape to each day of the week, each week of the month (you'll need five), and each month of the year. Every day, do a level nine dump to the daily tape. Every week, do a level five dump to the weekly tape. And every month, do a level three dump to the monthly tape. A level zero dump should be done whenever the incrementals get too big to fit on one tape. This is most likely to happen on a monthly tape. Do a level zero dump at least once a year.

The choice of levels three, five, and nine is arbitrary. You could use levels one, two, and three with the same effect. However, the gaps between dump levels give you some breathing room if you decide you want to add another level of dumps later.

This schedule requires 24 tapes plus however many tapes are needed for level zero dumps. While it does not require too many tapes, it also does not provide much redundancy.

The *Towers of Hanoi sequence*

A more complicated sequence based on a mathematical puzzle called the Towers of Hanoi provides extensive redundancy. The connection between the sequence and the puzzle is limited and unimportant.

The Hanoi sequence is designed to balance the desire to save as much information for as long as possible against practical limitations, such as the amount of time you want to spend doing dumps and the number of tapes you want to buy. The sequence is illustrated in Exhibit A.

Exhibit A   The Towers of Hanoi Dump Sequence

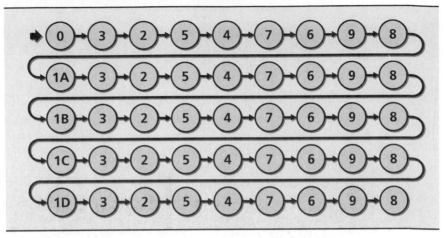

When this sequence is finished, it is repeated; however, new tapes are used for each level zero dump. Tapes for levels two through nine are reused every nine dumps. There are four sets of level one tapes for each filesystem, labeled 1A, 1B, 1C, and 1D; these are reused every 45 dumps. Dumps should be done often enough (or the filesystems should be made small enough) that the level two through nine dumps fit on one tape.

This system is probably overkill for most sites, but it does provide excellent redundancy. One disadvantage is that restoring files can be quite tedious, since you must often spin several sets of tapes.

You can modify the Hanoi sequence in various ways to make it simpler, for example, by having only one set of level one tapes or by doing level nines for an entire week. Use your imagination, but make sure you clearly document the sequence you choose.

Selecting a Dump Sequence

In the days when it took many tapes to back up a filesystem, complicated dump sequences were very useful for minimizing the number of tapes consumed by each day's backups. As tape capacities have grown, it has become less useful to make fine distinctions among dump levels.

Because most files never change, even the simplest incremental schedule eliminates a high proportion of files from the daily dumps. As you add additional levels to your dump schedule, you divide the relatively few active files into smaller and smaller segments.

A complex dump schedule provides the following three benefits.

- You can back up data more often, limiting the potential loss.
- You can use fewer daily tapes (or fit everything on one tape).
- You can keep multiple copies of each file, in case of tape errors.

In general, the way to select a sequence is to determine your needs in each of these areas. Given these constraints, you can design a schedule at the appropriate level of sophistication.

11.4   MOTHERHOOD AND APPLE PIE

Now that we have explained the use of the dump program and the idea of incremental backups, we will try to pass on some general hints for backups that we have learned over time (usually, the hard way). None of these suggestions is an absolute rule, but you will find that the more of them you follow, the smoother your dump process will be.

Perform All Dumps from One Machine

rdump allows you to perform dumps over the network. While there is some performance penalty for doing this, the ease of administration makes it worthwhile. We have found that the best method is to run a script from a central location that executes rdump (via rsh) on each machine that needs to be dumped. All dumps should go to the same (non-rewinding) tape device.

If you have a large network and need multiple tape drives, it is still best to centralize the control of dumps on one machine. Centralized control makes administration easier and allows you to verify that all machines were dumped correctly.

 Dumps created with rdump can only be restored on machines with the same byte order (and in some cases, only on machines running the same OS). You can sometimes use dd to take care of byte-swapping problems, but this won't help resolve differences between incompatible versions of rdump. Some operating systems provide a device file that swaps bytes for you automatically. For example, under IRIX, a tape drive is normally referred to as /dev/tape; it can be accessed without byte swapping through the device /dev/tapens.

Label your Tapes

It is essential that you label each dump tape clearly and completely. The tapes themselves should be labeled to uniquely identify their contents. Detailed information such as the list of filesystems and the dump dates can be written on the tape case. An unlabeled tape is a scratch tape.

It is important that the root and /usr filesystems can be restored without looking at dump scripts. The dump tapes for these filesystems should be labeled with the format, the exact syntax of the dump command used, and any other information you would need to restore from them without referring to on-line documentation.

The **exalabel** program included on the CD-ROM can be used to label Exabyte tapes easily and painlessly. This is especially important when dozens of filesystems are dumped to the same tape.

Pick a Reasonable Backup Interval

The more often backups are done, the smaller the amount of data that can be lost in a crash. However, backups use system resources and an operator's time. The system administrator must provide adequate security at a reasonable cost of time and materials.

On busy systems, it is generally appropriate to back up filesystems with home directories every workday. On systems that are used less heavily, or on which the data is less volatile, you might decide that performing backups several times a week is sufficient. On a small system with only one user, performing backups once a week is probably adequate.

Choose Filesystems Carefully

Filesystems that are rarely modified do not need to be backed up as frequently as users' home directories. If there are a few files that change on an otherwise static filesystem (such as **/etc/passwd** in the root filesystem), these files can be copied every day to another partition that is backed up regularly.

If **/tmp** is a separate filesystem, it should not be backed up. The **/tmp** directory should not contain anything essential, so there is no reason to preserve it. In case this seems obvious, we know of one large site that does daily backups on **/tmp**.

Make Daily Dumps Fit on One Tape

See Chapter 10 for information about scheduling backups with **cron**.

With large-capacity devices such as 8mm and DAT, you should be able to do daily dumps of all your user filesystems onto one tape. You can mount a tape each night before you leave and run the dumps automatically from **cron**. This scheme allows the dump to happen at a time when files are less likely to be changing, with minimal impact on users. If you can't fit your daily backups on one tape, either buy a higher-capacity backup device, change your dump sequence, or use multiple backup devices.

Your automated dump system should always record the name of each filesystem it has dumped. This allows you to quickly skip forward to the correct filesystem when you want to restore something. It is also a good idea to record the order of the filesystems on the outside of the tape. Use the non-rewinding tape device on tapes with multiple dumps.

Make Filesystems Smaller than your Dump Device

dump is perfectly capable of dumping filesystems to multiple tapes. But if a dump spans multiple tapes, an operator must be present to change tapes,[6] and the tapes must be carefully labeled to allow restores to be performed easily. Unless you have a good reason to create a really large filesystem, don't do it.

Keep Tapes Off-Site

See page 556 for a more complete discussion of off-site backups.

You should store your low-level dump tapes off-site to prevent damage in the case of a fire or natural disaster. Backup media are so small now that it is reasonable to have a trusted operator carry the tapes home, if your security policy permits this. How soon tapes are moved off-site will depend on how often you need to restore files and how much latency you can accept. Some sites avoid making this decision by performing two dumps a day (to different tape devices): one that stays on-site and one that is moved immediately.[7]

Limit Activity During Dumps

Filesystem activity should be limited during dumps, because changes can cause dump to make mistakes. Activity can be limited either by doing the dumps when there are few users (at night or on weekends) or by making the filesystem accessible only to dump.

If dumps are performed at night, they should not be scheduled at the same time as other programs that modify the filesystem, such as accounting programs. An inconsistency in a level zero dump can make it impossible to restore the filesystem; therefore, the filesystem should be absolutely stationary while a level zero dump is being done. It is not as important to limit filesystem activity during higher-level dumps because mistakes on these tapes will usually affect only files that were modified during the dump.

Some vendors have picked up modifications from Purdue University that provide better assurance that level zero dumps performed on live filesystems will be coherent. Other vendors (including Sun) have developed their own methods for avoiding constipated dumps. Keep this in mind: when you absolutely, positively must have the file there in the morning (such as before and after an upgrade), start the night off right with a level zero dump in single-user mode, and a beer.[8]

---

6. Unless you have a stacker or a jukebox.

7. A large financial institution located in the World Trade Center kept their "off-site" backups in the basement of the building. When the building was bombed, the backup tapes (as well as the computers) were destroyed. Make sure "off--site" really is.

8. We suggest a "40" of Pabst Blue Ribbon for this project.

Check your Tapes

There are many horror stories about system administrators that did not discover problems with their dump regime until after a serious system failure. It is essential that you continually monitor your backup procedure and verify that it is functioning correctly. Operator error causes more dumps to be ruined than any other problem.

The first step is to have your dump procedure attempt to re-read every tape after it is finishing dumping. Scanning the tape to verify that it contains the expected number of files is a good check.

More information about restore is given on page 192.

It is often useful to run **restore t** to generate a table of contents for each filesystem and to store the results on disk. These catalogs should be named in a way that relates them to the appropriate tape; for example, **host:usr.Jan.13**. A week's worth of these records make it easy to discover what tape a lost file is on; you just **grep** for the filename and pick the newest instance. In addition to providing a catalog for the tapes, a successful **restore t** indicates that the dump is OK and that you will probably be able to read the tape when you need to.

You should periodically attempt to restore from various tapes to make sure that it is possible. Every so often, try to restore from an old (months or years) dump tape, as drives have been known to wander out of alignment and become unable to read tapes they have written.

A related check is to verify that you can read the tapes on hardware other than your own. If your machine room burns, it does not do much good to know that the dump could have been read on a tape drive that has now been slagged.

Prepare for the Worst

After you have established a backup procedure, explore the worst-case scenario: your site is completely destroyed. Determine how much data would be lost and how long it would take you to get your system back to life (including time for acquiring new hardware). Then determine if you feel comfortable with the answers you get.

Secure your backup tapes; they contain all of your organization's data and can be read by anyone who has physical access to them.

11.5 RESTORING FROM DUMPS

There are many variations of the program that extracts data from dump tapes. Some old versions are called **restor**, but most are called **restore**. We will first discuss restoring individual files (or a small set of files), then explain how to restore entire filesystems.

Restoring Individual Files

The first step to take when you are notified of a lost file is to determine which tapes contain versions of the file. Users often want the most recent version of a file, but that is not always the case. For example, a user who loses a file by inadvertently copying another file on top of it would want the version that existed before the incident occurred.

If you do not keep on-line catalogs, you must mount tapes and attempt to restore the missing files until you find the correct tape. If the user remembers when the file was last changed, you may be able to make an educated guess about which tape it might be on.

After determining which tape the desired file is on, **cd** to a place such as **/tmp** or **/usr/tmp** where a large directory hierarchy can be created; most versions of **restore** must create all of the directories leading to a particular file before that file can be restored. Use

```
restore x filename
```

to restore the file, where *filename* is the complete path to the file relative to the root of the dump.

If you used **rdump** to make the backup, we recommend that you use its counterpart **rrestore** to extract files. To minimize the chance of problems, use the same host to read the tape as was used to write it.

See page 198 for a description of **mt***.* If you placed multiple files on a single tape, you must use **mt** to position the tape at the correct dump file before running **restore**.

For example, to restore the file **/users/janet/iamlost** on a BSD system using a remote tape drive, the following sequence of commands might be used:

```
/* First, mount the right tape on tapehost:/dev/nrtape */
# cd /tmp
/* Skip to 4th tape file */
# rsh tapehost mt -f /dev/nrtape fsf 3
# rrestore xf tapehost:/dev/nrtape /users/janet/iamlost
/* the command prints out various messages */
# ls /tmp/users/janet
iamlost
# ls /users/janet
afile bfile cfile
# cp /tmp/users/janet/iamlost /users/janet/iamlost
# chown janet /users/janet/iamlost
# chgrp student /users/janet/iamlost
# mail janet
Your file iamlost has been restored as requested and has
been placed in /users/janet/iamlost.

Your Name, Humble System Administrator
```

This sequence doesn't preserve the modification time or permissions of the file; if these are important, use **tar** to copy the restored file from /tmp to the user's home directory as shown on page 197.

If there were already a file **/users/janet/iamlost** in existence, the restored version should be installed under a different name (for example, **iamlost.restored**) and the mail message altered to reflect this change. *Under no circumstances* should you delete an existing file.

Some administrators prefer to restore files into a special directory, allowing users to copy their files out by hand. If you choose to do this, remember to clean out that directory every so often.

Interactive Restore

Most versions of **restore** support the i flag, which allows the restore to seem more interactive. This option reads the catalog from the tape and then lets you step through the files as you would a normal directory tree using commands called **ls**, **cd**, and **pwd**. Files that you want to restore are marked with the **add** command; when you have selected all of the files you want, the **extract** command will pull them off the tape.

If your version of **restore** supports the i option, we suggest that you use it. It makes restoring much easier. Here is part of the previous example repeated with **restore i**:

```
# rrestore if tapehost:/dev/nrtape
restore> ls
.:
janet/  garth/  lost+found/  scott/
restore> cd janet
restore> ls
core  iamlost  mbox  src/
restore> add iamlost
/* This doesn't cause the extraction to start. Adding
   directories recursively adds their contents */
restore> ls⁹
core  iamlost*  mbox  src/
restore> extract
You have not read any volumes yet.
Unless you know which volume your files are on you should
start with the last volume and work towards the first.
Specify next volume #: 1
/* You wait while the restore actually happens. */
set owner/mode for '.'? [yn] n
#
```

9. The star next to **iamlost** indicates that it has been marked for extraction.

Volumes (tapes) are enumerated starting at 1, not 0, so for a dump that fits on a single tape, you specify 1. When **restore** asks if you want to set the owner and mode for ".", it's asking if it should set the current directory to match the root of the tape. Unless you are restoring an entire filesystem, you probably don't want to do this.

In general, **restore i** is the easiest way to restore a few files or directories from a dump. However, it will not work if the tape device cannot be moved backwards a record at a time (a problem with some 8mm drives). If it fails, try **restore x** before jumping out the window.

Restoring Entire Filesystems

With luck, you will never have to restore an entire filesystem due to a system failure. However, the situation does occasionally arise. Before attempting to restore the filesystem, you must make sure that whatever problem caused the filesystem to be destroyed has been solved. It is pointless to spend numerous hours spinning tapes only to lose the filesystem once again.

Before beginning a full restore, the filesystem must be created and mounted. See Chapter 9, *Adding a Disk*, for more information about how to do this. **cd** to the mount point of the new filesystem, mount the first tape of the most recent level zero dump, and type **restore r**.

restore will prompt for each tape in the dump. After the level zero dump has been restored, mount and restore each dump up to the last dump done, in the same order they were performed.

For example, if the last dump was a level five using the Towers of Hanoi sequence, the commands to restore the filesystem **/usr**, residing on the physical device **/dev/dsk/c201d6s0**, would look like this (the device names and **newfs** command are OS-dependent):

```
# /etc/newfs /dev/dsk/c201d6s0 QUANTUM_PD1050S
# /etc/mount /dev/dsk/c201d6s0 /usr
# cd /usr
/* Mount first tape of level 0 dump of /usr. */
# restore r
/* Mount the tapes requested by restore. */
/* Mount first tape of level 1 dump. */
# restore r
/* Mount the tapes requested by restore. */
/* Mount the level 3 tape for /usr. */
# restore r
/* Mount the level 2 tape for /usr. */
# restore r
/* Mount the level 5 tape for /usr. */
# restore r
```

If you had multiple filesystems on one dump tape, you would have to use the mt command to skip forward to the correct filesystem before running restore. See page 198 for a description of mt.

This sequence would restore the filesystem to the state it was in when the level five dump was done, except that all deleted files would be ghoulishly resurrected.[10]

11.6 DUMPING AND RESTORING FOR UPGRADES

When you perform an OS upgrade (or perhaps a "rightgrade" from Solaris to SunOS), all filesystems must be backed up with a level zero dump and possibly restored. The restore is needed only if the new OS uses a different filesystem format, or if you change the partitioning of your disk. However, you must do backups as insurance against any problems that might occur during the upgrade. A complete set of back-ups also gives you the option of re-installing the old OS if the new version does not prove satisfactory.

Be sure to back up and restore any system-specific files that are in / or /usr, such as /etc/passwd, /usr/local, etc. UNIX's brain-dead directory organization mixes local files with vendor-distributed files, making this quite a difficult task.

You should do a complete set of level zero dumps immediately after an upgrade, too. Most vendors' upgrade procedures set the modification dates of system files to the time when they were mastered rather than the current time. This means that incremental dumps made relative to the pre-upgrade level zero will not be sufficient to restore your system to its post-upgrade state in the event of a crash.

11.7 OTHER ARCHIVING PROGRAMS

dump is not the only program you can use to archive files to tapes; how-ever, it is usually the most efficient way to back up an entire system. tar, cpio, and dd can also move files from one medium to another.

tar: Package Files

tar takes multiple files or directories and stores them as one file, often a tape file. tar is a useful way to back up files that you anticipate need-ing to recover. For instance, if a user is leaving for six months and the system is short of disk space, the system administrator can use tar to put the user's files on a tape and then remove them from the disk.

tar is also very useful as a way of moving directory trees from place to place, especially if your system's cp doesn't support recursive copying or

---

10. Some versions of dump and restore are rumored to keep track of deletions.

you are copying files as root (since **tar** will preserve ownerships). For example, the command

```
tar cf - fromdir | ( cd todir ; tar xfp - )
```

would create a copy of the directory tree *fromdir* in *todir*. A note of caution: do not put ".." in the arguments for **cd** in this command, or things may get confused on some systems.

Most versions of **tar** do not follow symbolic links by default, but they can be instructed to do so. Consult your **tar** manual for the correct flag, as it varies from system to system. The biggest drawback of **tar** is that most versions do not allow multiple tape volumes; if the data you want to archive will not fit on one tape, **tar** cannot be used. If your **tar** does claim to support multiple volumes, be very skeptical. Most multi-volume implementations of **tar** are broken.

gnutar is included on the CD-ROM.   Another problem with many versions of **tar** is that pathnames are limited to 100 characters, which prevents it from being used to archive deep hierarchies. If your version of **tar** supports an option to use longer pathnames (as GNU's version does), and you use it, remember that people with standard **tar** will not be able to read the tapes you write.

tar's **b** option lets you specify a block size to use when writing a tape. The block size is specified in bytes; it determines how much data **tar** buffers internally before performing a write operation. Some DAT devices don't work correctly unless the block size is set to a special value, but other drives do not require this. However, certain block sizes may yield better performance. Optimal block sizes can vary from 126 bytes on some QIC drives to 40K on an Exabyte drive. This will all depend on your particular computer and tape drive. In many cases, you won't notice any difference in speed.

tar cannot read or write device files, and it expands holes. It is also intolerant of tape errors.

cpio: ATT-ish Archiving

cpio is another archiving program that it is similar to **tar** in functionality. All ATT versions of UNIX have **cpio**, but some of them do not have **tar**. **cpio** is therefore a good method for archiving files for transfer between systems using ATT UNIX. **cpio** can also be used to move directory trees. The command

```
find fromdir -depth -print | cpio -pdm todir
```

would make a copy of the directory tree *fromdir* in *todir*. Like **tar**, most versions of **cpio** do not allow multiple tape volumes. Some versions of **cpio** do not handle pipes gracefully, and only the superuser can copy special files.

dd: Twiddle Bits

dd is a file copying and conversion program. Unless it is told to do some sort of conversion, dd just copies from its input file to its output file. If a user brings you a tape that was written on some non-UNIX system, dd may be the only way to read it.

See Chapter 9 for more information about newfs.

One historical use for dd was to create a copy of an entire filesystem. However, a better option these days is to newfs the destination filesystem and then run dump piped to restore. dd can sometimes clobber partitioning information if used incorrectly.

dd can also be used to make a copy of a magnetic tape. With two tape drives (/dev/rmt8 and /dev/rmt9), use the command

```
dd if=/dev/rmt8 of=/dev/rmt9 cbs=16b
```

With one drive (/dev/rmt8), use the following sequence:

```
% dd if=/dev/rmt8 of=tfile cbs=16b
/* Change tapes. */
% dd if=tfile of=/dev/rmt8 cbs=16b
% rm tfile
```

Of course, if you only have one tape drive, you must have enough disk space to store an image of the tape.

Another use of dd is to convert between various flavors of QIC tape that differ only in their byte order. For example, to read a tar tape written on an SGI machine on a Sun, you could use

```
dd if=/dev/rst8 conv=swab | tar xf -
```

The name of the tape device is system-dependent.

volcopy: Duplicate Filesystems

volcopy makes an exact copy of a filesystem to another device, changing the block size as appropriate. It is available on most ATT versions of UNIX. volcopy can be used to back up a filesystem to a removable disk pack or to make a complete copy of a filesystem on tape.

11.8 USING MULTIPLE FILES ON A SINGLE TAPE

The mt command can be used to position a tape at a particular place. mt is very useful if you put multiple files (for example, multiple dumps) on a single tape. It also has some of the most interesting error messages of any UNIX utility. The basic format of the command is

```
mt [-f tapename] command [count]
```

 tapename is the device name of the tape (non-rewinding if you want to do any sort of file operations). HP-UX and IRIX use -t instead of -f.

There are numerous choices for *command*. They vary from platform to platform, so we will discuss only the ones that are essential for doing backups and restores:

rew   Rewind the tape to the beginning.

offl   Put the tape off-line. On some tape drives, this causes the tape to pop out of the drive. Most dump scripts use this command to eject the tape when they are done, giving a clear indication that everything finished correctly.

status   Prints information about the current state of the tape drive (whether there is a tape loaded, etc.).

fsf [*count*]   This command fast-forwards the tape. If no *count* is given, it skips forward one file. With a numeric argument, it skips the specified number of files. This command can be used to skip forward to the correct filesystem on a tape with multiple dumps.

bsf [*count*]   Should backspace *count* files. On some systems the current file is counted. On others, it is not. On some systems it does nothing (silently). If you go too far forward on a tape, your best bet is to **rew** it and start again from the beginning.

Consult your manuals for an exact list of commands supported by **mt**.

12 *Syslog and Log Files*

12.1 INTRODUCTION

The accounting system, the kernel, and various utilities all produce data that is logged and eventually ends up on your finite-sized disks. Most of that data has a limited useful lifetime and needs to be summarized, compressed, archived, and eventually thrown away.

Logging policies vary from site to site. Common schemes include:

- Throw away all data immediately.
- Reset log files at periodic intervals.
- Rotate log files, keeping data for a fixed time.
- Compress and archive to tape or other permanent media.

The correct choice for your site depends on how much disk space you have and how security-conscious you are. Even sites with an abundance of disk space must deal with the cancerous growth of log files.

Whatever scheme you select, regular maintenance of log files should be automated using `cron`. See Chapter 10, *Periodic Processes*, for general information about this daemon.

Throwing Away Log Files

We do not recommend throwing away all logging information. Sites that are subject to security problems routinely find that accounting data and log files provide important evidence of break-ins. Log files are also helpful for alerting you to hardware and software problems. In general, given a comfortable amount of disk space, data should be kept for one or two months and then discarded. In the real world, it may take a week or two for you to realize that your site has been compromised by a hacker and that you need to review the logs.

Some administrators allow log files to grow until they become bothersome, then restart them from zero. This is better than keeping no data at all, but does not guarantee that log entries will be retained for any particular length of time. Average disk usage may also be higher than with other management schemes.

Rotating Log Files

Most sites do not archive log files to tape, but rather store each day's log information on disk, sometimes in a compressed format. These daily files are kept for a specific period of time and then deleted. If you have sufficient disk space, it is handy to keep the log files uncompressed so that they can be easily searched with **grep**.

One common way of implementing this policy is called "rotation." In a rotation system, you keep backup files that are one day old, two days old, and so on. Each day you rename the files to push older data toward the end of the chain. If a file is called **logfile**, for example, the backup copies might be called **logfile.1**, **logfile.2**, and so on. If you keep a week's worth of data, there will be a **logfile.7** but no **logfile.8**. Every day, the data in **logfile.7** is lost as **logfile.6** overwrites it.

Suppose a file needs daily attention and you want to archive its contents for three days (to keep the example short). The following script would implement an appropriate rotation policy:

```
#!/bin/sh
cd /var/log
mv logfile.2 logfile.3
mv logfile.1 logfile.2
mv logfile logfile.1
cat /dev/null > logfile
```

See page 621 for more information about compression.

If you choose to compress the log files, their names would have a suffix indicating the compression program you used. After creating the new **logfile**, you would compress **logfile.1**. The **compress** program is the most common compression utility found on UNIX systems, but better compression algorithms exist.

Ownership information is important for some log files. You may need to run your rotation script from **cron** as the log files' owner rather than as root, or add a **chown** command to the sequence.

Some sites identify log files by date rather than by sequence number; for example, **logfile.tues** or **logfile.aug26**. This naming system is a little harder to implement, but it can be worth the effort if you frequently refer to old log files.

Some daemons keep their log files open all the time. Because of the way the filesystem works, this script cannot be used with such daemons. Instead of flowing to the re-created **logfile**, log data will start to mysteriously disappear.[1] To install a new log file, you must either signal the daemon or kill and restart it.

Here is an example with both compression and signals:

```
#!/bin/sh
cd /var/log
mv logfile.2.Z logfile.3.Z
mv logfile.1.Z logfile.2.Z
mv logfile logfile.1
cat /dev/null > logfile
kill -signal pid
compress logfile.1
```

signal represents the appropriate signal for the program writing the log file; *pid* is its process ID. Each program behaves differently with respect to logging. Consult the chapter that describes it (or your manuals) to determine what procedures are necessary in each case.

At our site we dedicate a disk partition (**/var/log**) on a central logging host to log files. Data are kept for 30 days. The most recent week's data is kept uncompressed, and the rest is compressed using **gzip**.

Archiving Log Files

Some sites must archive all accounting data and log files as a matter of policy, perhaps to provide data for a potential audit. In this situation, log files should be first rotated on disk and then written to tape or other permanent media. This scheme reduces the frequency of tape backups and gives you fast access to recent data.

See Chapter 11, Backups, for more information about keeping permanent records.

Archival records can be kept as part of regular backups, or as a separate tape series. Separate tapes are more cumbersome, but they impose less of a documentation burden and won't interfere with your ability to recycle dump tapes. If you use separate tapes, use **tar** format and write a script to automate your backup scheme.

---

1. The active reference to the original file keeps it alive even after you delete the directory entry and create a new file with the same name. The file doesn't disappear (and its disk space is not reclaimed) until every reference has been closed.

12.2 FINDING LOG FILES

UNIX is often criticized for being inconsistent, and indeed it is. Just take a look at a directory of log files and you're sure to find some with names like `maillog`, some like `ftp.log`, and maybe even some like `lpNet`, `lpd-errs`, or `console_log`. In addition to having random names, log files are often scattered across directories and filesystems.

This section attempts to help you find all the files that are quietly taking over your disk, and to suggest a granularity for dealing with each. We also note the "usual place" for log files on our six example systems.

The format of the
`syslog.conf` file
is described on
page 207.

To locate your log files, read the system startup scripts (`/etc/rc*` or `/etc/init.d/*`) to see if logging is turned on when daemons are run, and if so, where messages are sent. Some programs handle logging via `syslog`, described later in this chapter. Check `syslog`'s configuration file, `/etc/syslog.conf`, to find out where this data goes.

Table 12.1 (on the next page) compiles some information about log files on our example systems. Specifically, it lists

- The log files to archive, summarize, or truncate
- The program that creates each
- An indication of how each filename is specified
- The frequency of attention that we consider reasonable
- The required owner and group of the log file
- A description of the file's contents

If you use `syslog` with a central logging machine, you will only have to manage log files on that machine.

Table 12.1 lists the logs under their generic names; vendor-specific deviations begin on page 205. This table combines files from both BSD and ATT, so not all files will appear on all systems.

Filenames are relative to `/var/adm` unless otherwise noted (however, files in the group called "Extras" are locally installed and would follow your local conventions).

The character in the "Where" column tells how the log file is specified: S for programs that use `syslog`, C if logging options are set on the command line at boot time, F for programs that use a configuration file, and H if the filename is hard-wired in code.

The "Freq" column indicates our suggested cleanup frequency.

Log files usually have mode 644. Some sites reduce permissions to 640 or to 600; never give write permission to anyone but the owner. `sulog`, `authlog`, and `sudo.log` should have mode 600. `mqueue/syslog` and `pacct` are also good candidates for restrictive permissions.

Table 12.1   Log files

	File	Program	Where[a]	Freq	Owner	Contents
Accounting Files	acct	kernel	C	D	R	BSD process accounting
	pacct	kernel	C	D	R	ATT process accounting
	wtmp	login	H	M	R	Connect-time accounting
	lpacct	lpd	F	M	D	BSD printer accounting
	lpd-errs	lpd	F	W	D	BSD printer errors
	aculog	tip, uucp	H	M	U	Dial-out accounting
	fd2log	runacct	F	M	R	ATT accounting errors
Vendor-Supplied Files	messages	various	S	M	R	Console messages
	shutdownlog	shutdown	S	M	R	Reasons for shutdown
	sulog	su	H	M	R	Root access via su
	authlog	su[b]	S	M	R	Authorizations
	mqueue/syslog	sendmail	F	W	R	Email handling log
	timed.log	settime	F	M	R	Time daemon log
	uucp/LOGFILE	uucico	H	M	U	UUCP contact log (BSD)
	uucp/SYSLOG	uucico	H	M	U	UUCP transfer log (BSD)
	uucp/.Log/*	uucico	H	M	U	UUCP logs (HDB)
	ftp.log	ftpd	S	W	R	ftp connection log
	gatedlog	gated	CS[c]	W	R	Network routing log
Extras	news/news	innd	H	D	N	News transactions
	news/*log	nnrpd	S	W	N	News readers' activity
	majordomo.log	majordomo	F	M	R	Mailing list manager log
	sudo.log	sudo	S	M	R	su via sudo log
	tcp.log	tcpd	S	W	R	TCP connections
	X0msgs	X11	H	M	R	X server log
	xdm-errors	xdm	F	M	R	X display manager errors
	httpd/*_log	httpd	F	W	R	WWW server logs

a. Where: S = Syslog, H = Hardwired, F = Configuration file, C = Command line
   Freq: D = Daily, W = Weekly, M = Monthly
   Owner: R = root/system, U = uucp/daemon, N = news/news, D = daemon/daemon

b. passwd, login and shutdown also write to the authorization log.

c. Specified on the command line in version 2.1; later versions use syslog.

12.3 Files NOT to Manage

You might be tempted to manage all log-like files with a rotation and archiving scheme. But there are two log files that you should not touch: /usr/adm/lastlog and /etc/utmp.

lastlog records each user's last login and is a sparse file indexed by UID. It stays smaller if you have all your UIDs in a fixed range, but this is impossible to do with root at 0 and nobody at -2 (=65,534). Don't copy lastlog or it will really use all the disk space that ls -l reports. See *Hog Detection* on page 620 for the complete scoop on sparse files.

utmp attempts to keep a record of each user who is currently logged in. It is sometimes wrong, usually because a user's shell was killed with an inappropriate signal and the parent of the shell did not clean up properly. utmp is often world-writable.

12.4 SPECIFICS FOR VARIOUS OPERATING SYSTEMS

Vendors seem to have hidden log files all over the disk. Careful detective work with your startup files and your syslog configuration file will find many of them. This section details some of the more obscure nooks and crannies in which log files have been hidden.

 Solaris has the most disorganized collection of log files ever. With a directory called /var/log it shouldn't be so hard. A few pointers:

- /var/log/*
- /var/cron/log
- /var/lp/logs/*
- /var/saf/_log
- /var/saf/zsmon/log
- /var/adm/{messages,aculog,sulog,vold.log,wtmp}
- /var/adm/log/asppp.log

See Chapter 19 for more information about PPP.

This last file is for the PPP protocol for dialup network connections. Solaris 2.4 seems to ship with logging to it turned on, even if you do not have the PPP software installed or in use. It fills with messages about the lack of connection paths.

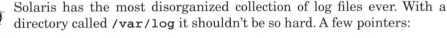 Log files are in /usr/adm. The file nettl.LOG00 is a network control and statistics file. The diag directory contains many log files in binary form. Do not touch them.

 Most log files are in /usr/adm in IRIX 4.0 or /var/adm in IRIX 5.2. Logs for the ATT printing system are in the directory /usr/spool/lp.

 Most log files are in /var/adm. Accounting data files are stored there as well, in the acct subdirectory. /var/log exists but contains only two files: authlog and syslog.

Most log files are in /var/adm or beneath it. DEC's OSF/1 keeps kernel error messages in a binary file and provides a utility (uerf) that dumps them as text. The log is /var/adm/binary.errlog by default, but this can be changed in /etc/binlog.conf.

The **sialog** file is part of DEC's Security Integration Architecture and contains a record of each execution of security-related commands such as **su**, **passwd**, and **login**. The **smlogs** directory contains logs from the latest operating system installation. As shipped, **syslog** data is put in **/var/adm/syslog.dated/**_date_/_facility_**.log**.

 All log files are in the **/var/log** directory. Accounting data files are kept in **/var/account**.

12.5   SYSLOG: THE SYSTEM EVENT LOGGER

*The **syslog** system is included on the CD-ROM.*

syslog, written by Eric Allman of Berkeley, is a comprehensive logging system. Many vendors use **syslog** to manage information generated by the kernel and system utilities.

syslog has two important functions: to liberate programmers from the tedious mechanics of writing log files, and to put administrators in control of logging. Before **syslog**, every program was free to make up its own logging policy; system administrators had no control over what information was kept or where it was stored.

syslog is quite flexible. It allows messages to be sorted by their source and importance ("severity level") and routed to a variety of destinations: log files, users' terminals, or even other machines. **syslog**'s ability to centralize the logging for a network is one of its most valuable features.

syslog consists of three parts:

- **syslogd** and **/etc/syslog.conf** – the daemon that does the actual logging and its configuration file

- **openlog**, **syslog**, **closelog** – library routines that programmers use to send data to **syslogd**

- **logger** – a user-level command for submitting log entries

syslogd is usually in **/etc**, **/usr/etc**, or **/usr/sbin**. The **logger** program is in **/usr/ucb**. The **syslog** library routines are part of the standard C library. In the following discussion, we first cover the configuration of **syslogd** and then briefly show how to use **syslog** from C programs and **perl** scripts.

syslogd is started at boot time and runs continuously. Programs that are **syslog**-aware write log entries (using the **syslog** library routine) to the special file **/dev/log**, which is either a UNIX domain socket, a named pipe, or a STREAMS module, depending on the system. **syslogd** reads messages from this file, consults its configuration file, and dispatches each message to the appropriate destinations. On many systems, **syslogd** also reads kernel messages from the device **/dev/klog**.

A hangup signal (HUP, signal 1) causes **syslogd** to close its log files, reread its configuration file, and start logging again. If you modify the **syslog.conf** file, you must HUP **syslogd** to make your changes take effect. A TERM signal causes **syslogd** to exit.

syslogd writes its process ID (PID) to the file **/etc/syslog.pid** (or on some systems, **/var/run/syslog.pid**). This makes it easy to send signals to **syslogd** from a script. For example, the following command sends a hangup signal:

```
kill -1 '/bin/cat /etc/syslog.pid'
```

Trying to compress or rotate a log file that **syslogd** has open for writing is not healthy and has unpredictable results. Some vendors provide you with a skeletal script, often in **/usr/lib/newsyslog**, that purports to rotate log files. A better one, **rotz**, is included on the CD-ROM.

Configuring syslogd

The configuration file **/etc/syslog.conf** controls **syslogd**'s behavior. It is a text file with a relatively simple format. Blank lines and lines with a pound sign ("#") in column one are ignored. The basic format is:[2]

```
selector <Tab> action
```

For example, the line

```
mail.info        /var/log/maillog
```

would cause messages from the electronic mail system to be saved in the file **/var/log/maillog**. The *selector* and *action* fields must be separated by one or more tabs; spaces don't work and become invisible errors that can be very hard to track down. Cutting and pasting with your window system is one way to introduce such errors.

Selectors identify the program ("facility") that is sending a log message and the message's severity level using the syntax

```
facility.level
```

Both facility names and severity levels must be chosen from a short list of defined values; programs can't make up their own. There are facilities defined for the kernel, for common groups of utilities, and for locally-written programs. Everything else is classified under the generic facility "user."

Selectors can contain the special keywords "*" and "none," meaning all or nothing. A selector can include multiple facilities separated with commas. Multiple selectors can be combined with semicolons.

---

2. Very old versions of **syslog** use a different syntax that we will not describe here.

In general, selectors are ORed together; a message matching any selector will be subject to the line's *action*. However, a selector with a level of none excludes the listed facilities regardless of what other selectors on the same line may say.

Here are some legal ways to format and combine selectors:

```
facility.level                          action
facility1,facility2.level               action
facility1.level1;facility2.level2       action
*.level                                 action
*.level;badfacility.none                action
```

Table 12.2 lists the valid facility names (some rows have been shaded to improve readability). 24 facilities are provided for, of which 18 are defined in most versions of **syslog** (21 in the latest release). The extra slots are reserved for future use.

Table 12.2 Syslog facility names

Facility	Programs that use it
kern	The kernel
user	User processes (the default if not specified)
mail	The mail system
daemon	System daemons
auth (security[a])	Security- and authorization-related commands
lpr	The BSD line printer spooling system
news	The Usenet news system
uucp	Reserved for UUCP, which doesn't use it (yet?)
cron	The cron daemon
mark	Timestamps generated at regular intervals
local0-7	Eight flavors of local message
syslog[b]	syslogd internal messages
authpriv[b]	Private (not system) authorization messages
ftp[b]	The ftp daemon, ftpd
*	All facilities except "mark"

a. The security facility is being retired in favor of auth.
b. New facilities in version 8.1 from Berkeley.

syslogd itself produces timestamp messages which are logged if the mark facility is specified. If your system is quite busy, other log messages often provide adequate timestamp information. But in the wee hours of the morning, that is not always the case.

Timestamps can be used to log the time at regular intervals (by default, every 20 minutes) so you can figure out that your machine crashed between 3:00 and 3:20 a.m., not just "sometime last night." This can be a big help when debugging problems that seem to occur on a regular basis. For example, many sites have experienced mysterious crashes when the housekeeping staff plugged in vacuum cleaners late at night, tripping the circuit breakers.

syslog's severity levels are listed in order of descending importance in Table 12.3. They are represented internally by small integers: 0 is emerg, 1 is alert, and so on.

Table 12.3   Syslog severity levels

Level	Approximate meaning
emerg (panic[a])	Panic situations
alert	Urgent situations
crit	Critical conditions
err (error[a])	Other error conditions
warning (warn[a])	Warning messages
notice	Unusual things that may need investigation
info	Informational messages
debug	For debugging

a. Being retired; don't use.

The level of a message specifies its importance. In the **syslog.conf** file, levels indicate the minimum importance that a message must have in order to be logged. A message logged to a particular facility and level, say *facx.levx*, matches **syslog.conf** lines of the form *facx.level* or **.level* as long as *levx* is a level equal to or higher than *level*.

For example, a message from the mail system at level warning would match mail.warning as well as mail.notice, mail.info, mail.debug, *.warning, *.notice, *.info, and *.debug. If **syslog.conf** specifies that mail.info messages be logged to a file, then mail.warning messages will go there also.

The *action* field tells what to do with a message. The choices are listed in Table 12.4.

Table 12.4   Syslog actions

Action	Meaning
filename	Write message to a file on the local machine
@*hostname*	Forward message to the **syslogd** on *hostname*
@*ipaddress*	Forward message to the host at IP address *ipaddress*
user1,user2,...	Write message to users' screens if they are logged in
*	Write message to all users logged in

*See Chapter 18 for
more information
about name resolu-
tion systems.*

If a *filename* action is used, the filename should be an absolute path. The file must exist; **syslogd** will not create it. If a *hostname* is used rather than an IP address, it must be resolvable via a translation mechanism such as DNS or NIS.

Some versions of **syslog** use the **m4** macro preprocessor on the configuration file. Check your manual pages and use quotes liberally so that your configuration means what you intend. For example, you must quote anything that is an **m4** keyword or contains a comma. Here is a typical **m4**-style entry:

```
auth.notice  ifdef('LOGHOST', /var/log/authlog, @loghost)
```

It directs messages to be logged (at facility auth, level notice) to the file **/var/log/authlog** if LOGHOST is defined. Otherwise, messages are forwarded to the machine loghost. ifdef statements are very powerful in **m4**; they allow sysadmins to create a single **syslog.conf** which is used on all machines. LOGHOST is defined by the **m4** macro

```
define('LOGHOST', hostname)
```

Note that the quotes used are the back-tick and the single apostrophe.

While multiple facilities and levels are allowed in a selector, there is no provision for multiple actions. To send a message to two places (such as to a local file and to a central logging host), two lines with the same selectors are needed in the configuration file.

Config File Examples

Below are three sample **syslog.conf** files which correspond to a stand-alone machine on a small network, a client machine on a larger network, and a central logging host on the same large network. The central logging host is called "netloghost."[3]

Stand-alone machine

A basic configuration for a stand-alone machine is shown below:

```
# Small network or stand-alone syslog.conf file
# emergencies: tell everyone who is logged on
*.emerg                              *

#   important messages
*.warning;daemon,auth.info       /var/adm/messages

#   printer errors
lpr.debug                        /var/adm/lpd-errs
```

3. More accurately, it uses "netloghost" as one of its hostname aliases. This allows the log host to be changed with little reconfiguration. An alias can be added in **/etc/hosts** or set up with a CNAME record in DNS. For more information about DNS, see Chapter 16.

The first non-comment line writes emergency messages to the screens of all current users. An example of emergency-level messages are those generated by **shutdown** when the system is being turned off.

The second line writes important messages to **/var/adm/messages**. The info level is below warning, so the "daemon,auth.info" clause includes additional logging from **passwd**, **su**, and daemon programs. The third line writes printer error messages to **/var/adm/lpd-errs**.

Network client

A network client typically forwards serious messages to a central logging machine.

```
# CS Department syslog.conf file: non-master machines

# emergencies: tell everyone who is logged on
*.emerg;user.none                       *

# important messages, forward to central logger
*.warning;lpr,local1.none               @netloghost
daemon,auth.info                        @netloghost

# local stuff to central logger too
local0,local2,local7.debug              @netloghost

# cardd syslogs to local1 -  to boulder
local1.debug                            @boulder.colorado.edu

#  printer errors, keep them local
lpr.debug                               /var/adm/lpd-errs

#  sudo logs to local2 - keep a copy here
local2.info                             /var/adm/sudolog
```

At a site with extensive local software installed, lots of messages can be logged incorrectly to user.emerg. In this example, it has been specifically excluded with the user.none clause in the first line.

For more information about **sudo**, see page 52.

The second and third lines forward all important messages to the central logging host; messages from the printing system and the campus-wide card access system are explicitly excluded. The fourth line forwards local logging information to netloghost as well. The fifth line forwards the card access logging information to the campus-wide logging host, boulder. The last two entries keep local copies of printer errors and **sudo** log messages.

Central logging host

This example is for netloghost, the central, secure logging host for a moderate sized network of 400 to 500 hosts.

```
# CS Department syslog.conf file, master logging host

# emergencies to the console  and log file, w/timing marks
*.emerg                              /dev/console
*.err;kern,mark.debug;auth.notice    /dev/console
*.err;kern,mark.debug;user.none      /var/adm/console.log
auth.notice                          /var/adm/console.log

# non-emergencies to usual log files
*.err;user.none;kern.debug           /var/adm/messages
daemon,auth.notice;mail.crit         /var/adm/messages
lpr.debug                            /var/adm/lpd-errs
mail.debug                           /var/adm/mail.log

# local authorization stuff like sudo and npasswd
local2.debug                         /var/adm/sudo.log
local2.alert                         /var/adm/sudo-errs.log
auth.info                            /var/adm/auth.log

# other local stuff
local0.info                          /var/adm/netblazer.log
local4.notice                        /var/adm/da.log

local6.debug                         /var/adm/annex-isn.log
local7.debug                         /var/adm/tcp.log

# main logging facility via pseudo-user "netlog"
*.notice;kern,lpr.debug;auth.info  netlog
local3,local4,local7,mail.none       netlog

# user stuff, default if no facility is specified
user.info                            /var/adm/user.log
```

Logging data arriving from local programs and from **syslogd**s on the network is written to files. In some cases, output from each facility is put into its own file. The pseudo-user netlog receives a copy of all important messages (see page 213).

Sample syslog Output

Below is a snippet from one of the log files on the master **syslog** host at the University of Colorado's Computer Science Department. About 200 hosts log to this machine.

```
Dec 27 02:45:00 x-wing netinfod[71]: cannot lookup child
Dec 27 02:50:00 bruno ftpd[27876]: open of pid file
   failed: Not a directory
Dec 27 02:50:47 anchor vmunix: spurious VME interrupt at
   processor level 5
Dec 27 02:50:47 anchor vmunix: VME lvl 3, vector 0xffffff
Dec 27 02:52:17 bruno pingem[107]: moose.cs.colorado.edu
   has not answered 34 times
```

```
Dec 27 02:55:33 bruno sendmail[28040]: host name/address
    mismatch: 192.93.110.26 != bull.bull.fr⁴
Dec 27 02:09:17 moet vmunix: NFS server amd:124 not
    responding
```

This example contains entries from several hosts (x-wing, bruno, moet, and anchor) and from several programs: **netinfod**, **pingem**, **ftpd**, the kernel (**vmunix**), and **sendmail**. Both vendor-supplied and locally-written programs can use **syslog**.

It's a good idea to peruse your log files regularly. Determine what is normal so that when an anomaly occurs, you can recognize it.

Designing a Logging Scheme for your Site

At a small site it is adequate to configure logging so that important system errors and warnings are kept in a file on each machine, much as was done before we had **syslog**. The **syslog.conf** file can be customized for each host.

On a large network, central logging is essential. It keeps the flood of information manageable, and with luck, makes auditing data unavailable to a person who violates the security of a machine on the network. Hackers often edit system logs to cover their tracks; if log information is whisked away as soon as it is generated, it is much harder to fake. But be aware that anyone can call **syslog** and fake log entries from any daemon or utility. **syslog** also uses the UDP protocol, which is not guaranteed to be reliable; messages can get lost.

For information about distributing files on a network, see Chapter 18.

Choose a stable machine as your logging server, preferably one that is physically secure and does not have many logins. Other machines can use a generic configuration file which is maintained in a central place. Thus, only two versions of the **syslog.conf** file need be maintained. This allows logging to be complete, but at the same time not a nightmare to administer.

Some very large sites may want to add more levels to the logging hierarchy. Unfortunately the current version of **syslog** only retains the name of the originating host for one hop. If host "client" sends some log entries to host "server," which sends them on to host "master," master will see the data as coming from server, not from client.

syslog's ability to write to a user's screen can be used as an early warning system for administrators. Rather than hear about a problem from an irate user, an administrator can sometimes anticipate the problem by seeing messages from **syslog**. One way to do this is to create a

---

4. This error message is reporting a misconfiguration in the DNS database at Groupe Bull in France. See Chapter 16 for complete information about DNS.

13 *Configuring the Kernel*

13.1 INTRODUCTION

A UNIX system has essentially three main layers:

- The hardware
- The operating system kernel
- The user-level programs

The kernel hides the system's hardware underneath an abstract, high-level programming interface. It is responsible for implementing many of the facilities that users and user-level programs take for granted. For example, the kernel assembles all of the following UNIX concepts from lower-level hardware features:

- Processes (time-sharing, protected address spaces)
- Signals and semaphores
- Virtual memory (swapping, paging, mapping)
- The filesystem (files, directories, namespace)
- Pipes and network connections (inter-process communication)

For more information about drivers, see Chapter 7.

The kernel contains *device drivers* which manage specific pieces of hardware; the rest of the kernel is to a large degree device-independent. The relationship between the kernel and its device drivers is similar to the relationship between user-level processes and the kernel. When a process asks the kernel to "Read the first 64 bytes of /etc/passwd," the kernel might translate this into a device driver instruction such as

"Fetch block 3,348 from device 3." The driver would further break this command down into sequences of bit patterns to be presented to the device's control registers.

The kernel is written mostly in C, with a little assembly language for low-level processing. Many years ago, a compiled UNIX kernel was quite modest in size, usually well under half a megabyte. Today, with fancy networking, network file systems, multi-threading, and inexpensive memory, kernel sizes range from 700K to well over 2MB.

13.2 DIFFERENCES BETWEEN ATT AND BSD

It is essential that the kernel be aware of and communicate with the system's hardware. On both BSD and ATT systems, you can provide the kernel with explicit information about the hardware it should expect to find (or pretend not to find, as the case may be).

It is a popular myth (propagated widely by marketeers) that ATT kernels "configure themselves" while BSD kernels do not. A more accurate representation is that BSD kernels ask for guidance in advance, while ATT kernels forge blindly ahead and then beg for forgiveness after something has gone horribly wrong.

This philosophical split leads to substantial differences in the configuration process. In this chapter, we'll explicitly cover the procedures for configuring a BSD-style kernel (HP-UX, SunOS, OSF/1 and BSDI), an ATT-style kernel (Solaris), and one fairly random variant (IRIX).

There was a time when only individuals sporting pocket protectors built kernels. But now, configuring and building a kernel is an administrator's rite of passage. It usually involves tweaking a few of the kernel's operational parameters and telling it about the hardware you are using.

13.3 WHEN TO CONFIGURE THE KERNEL

There are only a few situations in which kernel reconfiguration is necessary. The following sections describe them.

Installing a New System

You should reconfigure the kernel every time you bring up a new machine and every time you upgrade the operating system. Most versions of UNIX come with a "generic" kernel already configured. You will usually be supplied with both a generic configuration file and the corresponding executable kernel.

The generic kernel probably works just fine, but you should reconfigure it for reasons of efficiency. Generic kernels are designed to cope with any kind of hardware you might care to attach to your system. They often include all of the commonly used device drivers, all the pseudo-devices, and most of the kernel options. This makes them flexible, but bloated.[1] Initial reconfiguration is mostly a process of shedding drivers for devices you don't have and eliminating options that you don't use.

Adding Device Drivers

Instructions for adding a new driver are given in Chapter 7.

To add a new type of device to your system, you must include its driver in your kernel. The driver code can't just be mooshed onto the kernel like a gob of Play-Doh; it has to be integrated into the kernel's data structures and tables.

On some systems, this may require that you go back to the configuration files for the kernel and add in the new device, rebuilding the kernel from scratch. On other systems, it may require the execution of a program designed to make these configuration changes for you.

Some systems include the concept of a "loadable" device driver, in most cases implying that new code can be loaded into the kernel while it is running. A good human analogy might be having brain surgery while operating heavy machinery.

Tuning Table Sizes

The kernel runs in constant space. When you boot the system, the kernel figures out the number of process table slots, filesystem buffers, and file table entries to allocate, then goes out and scarfs up the appropriate amount of memory.

You cannot start more processes or open more files than the kernel is configured to support. When you operate with too few table entries, the system will behave inconsistently. Some commands will be unable to run, and attempts to open files will fail at random times.

On many systems, you can run out of table space because there are too many simultaneous users, or even because of a few high-activity processes. Increasing the kernel's table sizes will solve some problems but will also divert more memory to the kernel. Since the amount of memory available to user processes has a significant effect on performance, you might want to consider buying more memory.

Conversely, there is no point in wasting memory on table slots that are not used. Having extras does reduce the amount of time the kernel spends searching for free slots, but the first few make the most difference, and the law of diminishing returns soon comes into play. The solution is the same: reconfigure.

---

1. Remember that physical memory used by the kernel is not available to user programs.

13.4 BUILDING A BSD KERNEL

Both BSD and ATT kernels are fairly easy to configure. The processes are completely different, but the ideas behind them are much the same. Although the examples in this section are specifically from a SunOS machine, configuration for HP-UX, OSF/1, and BSDI is very similar. The ATT construction process is described later in this chapter.

The files for building a BSD kernel are all in **/usr/sys**, which is usually symbolically linked to **/sys**. In the following discussion, we will use the uppercase name **SYS** to refer to this directory, just to emphasize that it doesn't really matter where it is located. If you cannot find the configuration directory for your machine, consult your manuals.

Here is an **ls -F** of the **SYS** directory for a Sun SPARC:

```
conf.common/    net/        sbusdev/     sun4m/          sys/
debug/          netinet/    scsi/        sundev/         ufs/
krpc/           nfs/        sparc/       sunif/          vm/
lofs/           os/         spects/      sunwindow/
mon/            rpc/        sun/         sunwindowdev/
```

The **sun4m** directory is architecture-specific. **ls -F sun4m** yields:

```
CHIMCHIM/       conf/          intreg.h      psl.h      trap.h
GENERIC/        cpu.h          machine@      pte.h      vm_hat.h
OBJ/            dbx_machdep.c  memerr.h      reg.h      vmparam.h
asm_linkage.h   devr.h         mmu.h         romvec.h
auxio.h         eeprom.h       openprom.c    scb.h
buserr.h        cnable.h       param.h       seg_kmem.h
clock.h         frame.h        pcb.h         setjmp.h
```

In many operating systems, these two directories are merged together under **SYS**. SunOS separates them because of the many architectures it supports (**sun3**, **sun4c**, and **sun4m**, among others).

Note that some directories have uppercase names. This convention identifies directories that are compilation areas for particular kernels. Each kernel configuration has a name, and the name of the kernel is the same as the name of its compilation directory. The most common scheme is to name kernels after the machines they run on, but any system will work as long as it helps you keep things straight. The **GENERIC** directory was provided with the operating system and contains control information for a generic kernel.

Another important directory in the **SYS** area is **conf** (on some systems, **SYS/**_arch_**/conf**). This directory holds text files that describe each configuration. Each file corresponds to one kernel; the **config** command is used to read a configuration file from **SYS/conf** and generate files in the corresponding compilation directory.

The rest of the directories in **SYS** contain various parts of the kernel that are assembled to create the executable image. The exact files and subdirectories vary widely from system to system.

Building a new kernel is a nine-step process:

- Audit the system's hardware.
- Create and edit the kernel's configuration file in **SYS/conf**.
- Create the kernel's compilation directory in **SYS**.
- Run the **config** program from the **conf** directory.
- Run **make depend** to build dependencies for the **Makefile**.
- Build the kernel with **make**.
- Archive the old kernel and install the new one.
- Test and debug the new kernel.
- Document the new kernel.

Auditing the System's Hardware

Before you can configure a kernel, you need to know what devices it must handle. Take a hardware inventory of your system. Make a list of all the devices connected to the computer, including:

- Terminal interfaces
- Disk drives and their controllers
- Tape drives and their controllers
- Network interfaces
- Coprocessors (encryption chips, graphics processors, etc.)
- Frame buffers
- Keyboard and mouse

Creating a Configuration File in SYS/conf

Once you know how you want your kernel configured, you must put this information into a form that **config** can understand. To do this, you create a configuration file in **SYS/conf**. The configuration file should have the same name as the kernel you are configuring. The name can be any valid filename, but it should be descriptive enough that a stranger to your **SYS** directory can tell what each kernel is for.

Don't create the configuration file from scratch. Instead, copy the **GENERIC** configuration and delete the parts you don't want. If you get stuck on something related to the configuration file and can't figure it out from the material here, refer to your documentation for **config**.

The format of a kernel configuration file requires quite a few pages to describe, so instead of interrupting our overview of the kernel-building process with a complete discussion, we refer you to *Creating a BSD Configuration File* starting on page 225.

Creating the Kernel's Compilation Directory

This part is easy; just cd to your **SYS** area and run the command `mkdir kernel`. Some versions of `config` will do this for you, but it never hurts to do it yourself.

Running config

You must cd to the **SYS/conf** directory before running `config`; it expects to find the configuration file specified on the command line in the current directory. Simple versions of `config` take the name of the configuration file as their only argument. Fancier versions support a number of options. `config` is very quiet, so don't be alarmed if nothing seems to be happening. It has a lot of work to do and may take a minute to run. To set up the compilation directory for the kernel described in **SYS/conf/EXAMPLE**, we'd use the following commands:

```
# cd conf
# config EXAMPLE
```

If you see a message that says "Doing a make depend," it is probably safe to skip the next step. It will not hurt anything to repeat it, though.

If `config` produces error messages, you must go back and fix your configuration file before continuing. If you get through `config` without any errors, you can assume that your configuration was at least syntactically valid and that the kernel compilation can proceed.

Running make depend

After `config` finishes, cd to the compilation directory for the new kernel and do an `ls`. You should see lots and lots of files. Don't worry about their contents; `config` knows what it's doing.

Now run **make depend** inside the compilation directory. This will initialize the file dependency information used by **make**. This command may produce voluminous output. (As mentioned above, `config` may already have done this step for you.)

Building the Kernel

See page 229 for specific information about the config *keyword.*

In the compilation directory, type **make** *kernel*, where *kernel* is the name of one of the configurations you specified with a `config` keyword inside the configuration file. This will usually be **vmunix**. If you want to make the kernel that was specified in the first `config` line, you can simply run **make**.

You must watch carefully for error messages during the kernel compilation. **make** will usually detect errors and abort the compilation, but it always helps to be alert. For extra protection, have `make` keep a record of everything that gets sent to your terminal with the `tee` command.

```
make vmunix |& tee ERRS.LOG
```

The `&` behind the pipe mark ensures that both error messages and status messages will be directed through the pipe. Bourne shell users should use

```
make vmunix 2>&1 | tee ERRS.LOG
```

to achieve a similar effect.

If there is an error during compilation, you should first suspect your configuration file. If you get messages about missing files or undefined routines, you have probably left something out. If you get messages complaining about syntax errors, the fault may be with your configuration file or with the system, although the latter is not likely. Consult your system's manuals or contact your service representative.

Installing the Kernel

Before you boot a new kernel, make sure that you can recover your system if it doesn't work. Never replace the old kernel directly with a new one, as this will leave you with nothing to boot from in the event of a catastrophe. If your system supports booting an arbitrary program, you can move your old `/vmunix` to `/vmunix.works` and copy or rename your new kernel to `/vmunix`.

`/vmunix` can be a link to some other filename, so you can actually put the real kernel anywhere within the root filesystem. If the kernel is not called `/vmunix` and you don't make this link, programs like `ps` and `w` that need to access the kernel's list of symbols will not work.

All systems provide some way to keep an old kernel bootable while you test a new one. See your manuals for specifics.

Don't rush the installation of a new kernel. Send mail to users explaining what is going to happen (and when) before taking the machine down, preferably a few days in advance. The `/etc/motd` file is a good place to put warnings like this, though it is often ignored by users.

Testing and Debugging the Kernel

Before you reboot the machine, bring it down to single-user mode and use `fsck -p` to clean the root partition of the disk. This may save time later if you have problems with the new kernel. Then reboot.

If the system comes up, you are probably in good shape. But there are a few checks you can try just to make sure. First, do a `ps`. If you get a message that says "no namelist," either the kernel has the wrong name, the permissions on it are set incorrectly, or something important didn't get compiled in.[2]

Try to **ls** at least one directory in each filesystem. Success indicates that the correct partition tables are in the kernel and that the filesystem is functioning correctly.

Documenting the Kernel

Before washing your hands of this whole sordid kernel business, you should go back to your original **SYS/conf/***kernel* file and put in copious comments so that you will understand what you have done when you come back to read it six months or a year later. If you have lots of free space, you can preserve the **SYS/***kernel* directory to speed up subsequent alterations. If you're tight on space, just delete it; everything it contains can be regenerated with **config**.

Finally, send mail to the users of your system describing the changes that have been made.

13.5 CREATING A BSD CONFIGURATION FILE

Creating a configuration file in **SYS/conf** is the hardest part of building a BSD kernel; the rest of the process is quite mechanical.

A configuration file is a list of control phrases, one per line. Any line beginning with a tab character is considered a continuation of the previous line. Anything between a pound sign ("#") and the end of a line is considered a comment, and blank lines are ignored. Keywords must be separated by whitespace, but except for this and the special meaning of tabs as continuation characters, spaces and tabs are ignored.

Integers in the configuration file may be entered in hexadecimal, octal, or decimal form. Octal numbers are identified by a leading zero, and hexadecimal numbers by a leading 0x. Strings must be double-quoted if they contain numbers used as text.

A control phrase begins with a single keyword that indicates how the remainder of the line is to be interpreted. The rest of the line provides the keyword's arguments. Some keywords can accept a list of arguments separated by spaces or commas, but it is wise to use only one argument per line. Most keywords that can accept multiple arguments can also have arbitrarily many control lines.

The order in which control phrases appear is usually not important, but the traditional order is shown in Table 13.1 (on the next page).

---

2. Never use **strip** on the kernel, as this will remove symbolic information needed by **ps**.

Table 13.1   Keywords used in BSD configuration files

Keyword	Function
machine	Sets the machine type
cpu	Sets the CPU type
ident	Sets the name of the kernel
maxusers	Sets the kernel's table sizes
options	Sets various compile-time options
config	Assigns the root and swap areas
controller	Declares a disk or tape controller
disk	Declares a disk connected to a controller
tape	Declares a tape connected to a controller
device[a]	Declares devices without controllers
pseudo-device	Declares pseudo-devices

a. Called device-driver under SunOS.

See page 22 for more information about modern time zone configuration.

Ages ago, a timezone keyword was used to set the time zone in which the computer lived. Modern kernels keep track of time using Greenwich Mean Time, and time zone determination is performed in user-level code. This makes the timezone keyword obsolete.

The machine Keyword

The machine keyword sets the type of machine on which the kernel will be run. Only one machine type may be specified. The argument is a text string, and it must be enclosed in double quotes if it contains any numbers. Machine types generally map to processor architectures rather than model numbers.

On a SunOS 4.1.3 IPX, the machine declaration is as follows:

```
machine    "sun4c"
```

The cpu Keyword

The cpu keyword enumerates the CPU types that the kernel will be run on. Unlike machine, cpu can accept many arguments. This syntax is somewhat misleading, since it implies that a kernel can be built to run on two different CPUs. This is untrue; only CPUs that are binary-compatible can run the same kernel.

We recommend specifying a single CPU type. Other binary-compatible machines should have their own kernels. A typical cpu declaration looks like this:

```
cpu      "SUN4C_60"  # Sun-4/60 (all the Sun-4c's, really)
```

To determine the code for your CPU, look in the **GENERIC** configuration file or your system's manual page for **config**.

The ident Keyword

The `ident` keyword sets the name of the kernel. This should be the same as the name of the configuration file. The name is compiled into the kernel, so it can prove useful for identifying UFKs.[3]

The maxusers Keyword

The `maxusers` keyword sets the sizes of several important system tables. As its name suggests, the argument to `maxusers` is roughly the maximum number of simultaneous users that the system is expected to support (though most versions of UNIX don't actually enforce a limit on the number of users per se). In general, you should boost this parameter by one for each real user you expect to be simultaneously logged on, and, if you are configuring the kernel for a network disk server, by one for each client machine. Add eight for each frame buffer on which a window system can be run.

Table 13.2 shows some formulas used to determine table sizes for a given value of `maxusers`.

Table 13.2   Formulas for system table sizes

Item to be sized	SunOS formula
Maximum number of processes	10 + 16 * MAXUSERS
Number of system file table entries	64 + (16/5) * (26 + 16 * MAXUSERS)
Number of buffers for terminal I/O	100 + 16 * MAXUSERS

These calculations are enumerated in **SYS/conf/param.c**, which the **config** command makes a copy of for each kernel. If you want to modify the formulas, use the kernel's private copy of **param.c** after running **config**; never modify the master copy.

The formulas have been boosted on some systems to accommodate the heavy loads imposed by window systems or large databases. This should be taken into account when selecting a value of `maxusers`.

The options Keyword

Clauses asserted in an `options` directive become variables that are defined for the C preprocessor during compilation of the kernel. There are two forms of `options` statement.

In the first form, tokens are defined but given no particular value. These tokens are used to specify whether an option is on or off using the preprocessor directives `#ifdef` and `#ifndef`. If a token is supplied as

---

3. Unidentified Flying Kernels, of course.

an argument to `options`, then the corresponding preprocessor symbol is defined and the option is enabled. For example, the phrase to include quotas in the kernel is

```
options   QUOTA
```

The second form not only defines a symbol but also gives it a specific value. The kernel code uses the symbol as if it were a constant, and the C preprocessor makes an appropriate substitution wherever it appears. This type of symbol is declared with the syntax

```
options   symbol="value"
```

For example, to modify the default value of MAXDSIZ, the maximum amount of virtual memory that may be allocated to the data segment of a single process, a line such as

```
options   MAXDSIZ="(64*1024*1024)"
```

would be used. This example sets a value of 64 megabytes.

A complete list of options should be provided by your vendor, but the most common ones are listed below. None of these options take a value.

QUOTA   QUOTA asks that code to limit each user's disk space be included in the kernel. Compiling quota support into the kernel is just the beginning of a successful quota regime. See *Disk Quotas* on page 624 for tips on setting up a quote regime.

INET   If you plan to operate a local area network, you must include the INET option. Binary-only distributions may require that the INET option be used even if no network is installed. When you enable INET, you should also include the pseudo-devices `loop` and `ether`. See page 233 for information about pseudo-devices and the `pseudo-device` keyword.

The INET option asks for software-side networking support. The declaration of networking hardware comes later in the configuration file.

UFS   This option allows local disks to be attached to the machine. This is always used except when setting up an extremely lean kernel for a diskless client.

NFSCLIENT   The NFSCLIENT option should be used on machines that mount filesystems from other machines via NFS. See Chapter 17, *The Network File System*, for more details about sharing files with NFS.

NFSSERVER   The NFSSERVER option is mandatory for machines that export filesystems via NFS.

GATEWAY   The GATEWAY option should be used on machines
that have more than one network interface and are
supposed to perform Internet routing and forwarding
functions. This option currently has only minor rami-
fications: it increases the sizes of some kernel data
structures to cope with the expected load and provides for special network behavior if one of the interfaces becomes nonfunctional. The GATEWAY option is
now obsolete in some systems.

The config Keyword

The config keyword is used to specify the locations of the root partition, crash dump area, and swapping areas on the system's disks.

*See page 143 for
more information
about fstab*
The root partition is the topmost component of the filesystem. It contains the directory / and several other important files and subdirectories. Information about how to mount filesystems is normally kept in
the /etc/fstab file, but UNIX can't get to this file until the root partition is already mounted.

To bootstrap the filesystem, information about the partition that holds
the root must either be compiled into the kernel, or, on some systems,
passed to the kernel by the bootstrap loader. The situation for swapping
is not as dire, since it is unlikely that any swapping will occur until the
/etc/rc* scripts run the **swapon** command.

When a process encounters some kind of fault, the kernel dumps an
image of the process's address space into a file named **core** in the current directory. A human can then inspect the remains with a debugger
to figure out what went wrong. Similarly, when the kernel crashes, it
dumps its state to one of the swap partitions.

The kernel core image is put at the end of the partition so that it is less
likely to be overwritten by data swapped out before the image can be
harvested with the **savecore** command (after a reboot). The place to
put crash dumps is set at kernel configuration time.

We said earlier that each configuration file in **SYS/conf** represents one
kernel. This is slightly inaccurate; there may be any number of config
lines in the configuration file, and each line defines a kernel that can be
built within the compilation directory. However, these kernels differ
only in the locations of their root, swap, and dump areas.

The ability to build variant kernels is useful for disaster planning. An
alternate root partition equipped with its own kernel can be of great
help when your main root partition is damaged. If the alternate root is
on the same disk drive or controller as the one that got trashed, be sure

to verify the stability of the hardware before rebooting. You run the risk of destroying it in the same way as the original root.

On some systems, a floppy disk or cartridge tape controls the boot procedure. This floppy disk knows the location of the kernel and is able to control its invocation. If you maintain an alternate root partition, you may have to build a new boot floppy that makes use of it.

A `config` line takes the following form:

```
config name rootspec swapspec crashspec
```

The `name` parameter sets the filename under which the compiled kernel will be stored. Most BSD kernels are named **vmunix**; alternates should be named to identify the disk they use for the root partition, for example, **sdvmunix**. The `rootspec`, `swapspec`, and `crashspec` clauses all take the form

```
keyword on partition
```

where `keyword` is `root`, `swap`, or `dumps`, and `partition` is a standard UNIX partition such as `sd0a` or `xy1a`. There may be any number of swap partitions; if there is more than one, they should be separated with the word `and`. For example, to request swapping on both `sd0b` and `sd1b`, you would use the clause

```
swap on sd0b and sd1b
```

If `crashspec` is omitted, the kernel dump device is assumed to be the first swap partition.

Every time you mention a disk partition in a `config` phrase, it is possible to underspecify to some extent. If you give a complete disk name without a partition (e.g., `sd0`), **config** will fill in a default partition. The default is to have the root partition on **a** and swap partitions on **b**. If you do not specify a unit number (e.g., `sd`), unit zero is assumed.

The **config** program takes all of the partition names and looks up the devices they refer to in the file **SYS/conf/devices**. This file maps device names to the major device numbers of their drivers. Here is part of a **devices** file from a Sun IPX:

```
xy     3
sd     7
st     11
ns     12
rd     13
```

The **devices** file should already be set up for you, but if you do some weird reorganization of your drivers or you add a new driver type, you may have to modify it.

A complete `config` phrase looks like this:

```
config vmunix root on sd0a swap on sd0b dumps on sd0b
```

Many modern systems use the weasel-words `swap generic` instead of actually specifying partitions in the configuration file:

```
config vmunix swap generic
```

This is a special notation that means "Figure it out at boot time." On systems that support it, information about the root partition is provided by the bootstrap loader. The **b** partition on the root disk is assumed to be swap space, and is also used for crash dumps. Additional swap partitions are added later with the **swapon** command.

The controller, tape, disk, and device Keywords

These keywords tell the kernel about the devices present on the system. Every device must be declared before it can be used. Declaring a nonexistent device is not harmful, but it does cause a useless driver to be compiled into the kernel.

The `controller` keyword declares:

- Disk and tape drive controllers
- Bus interfaces or bus adaptors

The `device` (`device-driver` under SunOS) keyword declares:

- Terminal interfaces
- Network interfaces
- Frame buffers and graphics accelerators
- Other devices that do not interface through a controller

The `tape` keyword declares tape drives connected through a controller, and the `disk` keyword is used similarly for disk drives.

The syntax for declaring devices is confusing, and the basic entries required to make the system run vary from machine to machine. Take the following instructions with a grain of salt. We will discuss the general syntax, but since we expect that you will mostly be paring down your system's generic configuration, we won't talk about how to write your own device specifications from scratch.

The basic form of a declaration is:

```
keyword device-name at connection-info csr address
    drive drive-number flags flags priority priority-level
    vector vector-info
```

Not all clauses are applicable to all devices. Furthermore, the drive numbers of disks (and sometimes parts of *connection-info*) may be replaced with a question mark, indicating that the system is to be investigated at boot time to determine what values are appropriate.

device-name is the standard name for the device, plus the logical unit number. For example, the name for the first SCSI adaptor on a Sun is scsibus0. As you wade through the generic configuration, you can look up each device in section 4 or section 7 of the manuals (depending on the system) to find out what it is and whether it applies to you. Note that the logical unit number has *no* relationship to any hardware-specified selection number of the device.

The *connection-info* for a device tells the kernel where to find it. For disk and tape drives, this is usually the name of a controller. For controllers and devices, it is usually the name of a bus or bus controller, or a token to indicate that the device is located on I/O circuitry inside the machine itself.

Bus interfaces are configured as controllers, and their connection information is usually the token nexus plus a question mark to indicate that the exact connection point of the bus is to be determined at boot time. The term "nexus" only has a literal meaning on DEC Vaxes; when this descriptor is used on other systems, it is merely a dusty remnant of a time long gone by.

It is usually sufficient to state that a device is connected to a particular type of controller without specifying which one. For example, indicating that a disk controller is connected to one of the SCSI adaptors on a Sun by giving its *connection-info* as scsibus? will work fine.

The *address* parameter, the argument to the csr keyword, represents the location of the device's command and status registers in the address space of the bus or backplane to which it is connected. Controllers and devices connected directly to a bus often have this parameter filled in. (On many systems, the address can be configured with DIP switches on the board itself. The switches and configuration file must agree.) Each kind of device has a certain number of address locations that it takes up in the bus address space.

drive-number specifies the logical unit number of a disk or tape drive. If this field is filled in with a question mark, the drive number is determined at boot time. This wild card function can be useful only if you swap disk drives around frequently; you should fill in actual drive numbers unless there is a specific reason not to.

The *flags* for a device are passed on to its driver at boot time without being interpreted by the kernel. This allows simple configuration information to be provided in a generic way.

See page 116 for more information about soft carrier.

The `flags` are just a simple integer, which is usually interpreted bit by bit. For example, some terminal drivers use the flags on an interface to distinguish between serial ports that must supply soft carrier and those that can expect hard carrier, with one bit being dedicated to each port.

The `priority-level` of a device gives an indication of how urgent the interrupts generated by the device should be considered. Device types have standard priorities that should not be readjusted at whim. Some systems do not use the `priority` keyword.

Some hardware systems use a single channel to handle hardware interrupts. Since interrupts cannot be distinguished by the channels on which they arrive, each device must be able to identify itself to the kernel when it signals a hardware exception. This is done using a hardware interrupt vector described in the `vector-info` field. Some devices have a single vector and others use two: one for transmit and one for receive. Look in the hardware manual that came with your peripheral device to determine the value of the interrupt vector.

The most effective way to organize your declarations is to identify the control phrases that declare devices to which nothing else is connected. These outer-level devices include disk and tape drives (but not controllers), terminal interfaces, and networking interfaces. Once the control lines for these devices are found, you can see what other devices they depend on and follow the configurations back to the root of the device hierarchy, the "nexus."

The pseudo-device Keyword

Theoretically, pseudo-device drivers are programs that act like device drivers but don't have any real hardware to back them up. We say "theoretically" because some kernel options that masquerade as pseudo-devices do not act like device drivers at all, at least from the user's point of view. The syntax for `pseudo-device` lines is

```
pseudo-device device-name number-of-instances
```

`device-name` is the name of the pseudo-device and `number-of-instances` is an optional integer telling how many of the imaginary devices the driver should pretend are present. Many drivers do not use the instance count.

There are only a few pseudo-devices, but most of them are obligatory for correct operation of the system. Some systems have a number of non-standard pseudo-devices that support windowing systems, extra keyboards, or auxiliary displays. Consult the manuals of your system to learn how to deal with these, or just include all the pseudo-devices from your generic configuration file for a more festive atmosphere.

Some common pseudo-devices are:

*See page 390 for
more information
about **expect**.*

pty   PTYs are pseudo-terminals. They mimic terminals, but instead of having an actual terminal on one end, they are connected to a UNIX process. PTYs are heavily used by networking programs such as `rlogin` and `rsh`, and they are also used by a few standard utilities such as `script` to do input processing. **expect** is an interactive scripting language that exploits the power of PTYs by simulating human keyboard input.

The `pty` driver can accept an instance count that indicates how many pseudo-terminals may be active at one time. The default is usually 32, more than enough in most circumstances.

*See Chapter 14 for
more information
about interfaces
and addressing.*

loop   The `loop` driver simulates an interface to a network that contains only the local host. It allows stand-alone machines to use network-based software, and it also provides a standard way for a machine to address packets to itself. It is required if you specify the INET option.

ether   This pseudo-device includes various Ethernet-related material in the kernel. It is required with INET.

A Sample Configuration File

Let's look at a sample configuration file for a simple kernel. Let's call this kernel EXAMPLE, and set it up appropriately for a Sun SPARCserver 690 running SunOS.

```
# A configuration file for an example kernel.
machine         "sun4m"
cpu             "SUN4M_690" # Sun-4M/6[379]0
ident           "EXAMPLE"
maxusers        32
```

The first two lines of the file set the machine type to be a Sun-4M (SPARCstation 10, SPARCserver 690, etc.). The name of the kernel is EXAMPLE. This kernel is configured for at most 32 simultaneous users.

```
options         INET            # basic networking support
options         UFS             # for local disks
options         HSFS            # High-Sierra CDROM
options         NFSCLIENT       # NFS client side code
options         NFSSERVER       # NFS server side code
options         QUOTA           # UFS quota code
options         MULTIPROCESSOR  # Multi-Processor support
```

Our sample kernel is configured with support for Internet (IP) networking, local filesystems, the ISO-9660 filesystem (used most commonly on

CD-ROMs), NFS client and server operations, and quotas. All Sun-4M kernels require the `MULTIPROCESSOR` option.

```
config vmunix swap generic
```

The locations of the root and swap partitions are passed along from the bootstrap process. The root will be located on the **a** partition of the boot drive, and the kernel will swap on the **b** partition of that same drive.

```
# connections for machine type 1 (SUN4M_690)

controller     obmem 1 at nexus ?
controller     obio 1 at nexus ?
controller     vme16d16 1 at nexus ?
controller     vme24d16 1 at nexus ?
controller     vme32d16 1 at nexus ?
controller     vme16d32 1 at nexus ?
controller     vme24d32 1 at nexus ?
controller     vme32d32 1 at nexus ?
controller     ipi 1 at nexus ?
```

These lines declare the bus adaptors available on the machine.

```
# Support for 2 IPI-2 Channel adaptors.
# Declares the channel driver of the VME IPI-2 controller.

controller isc0 at vme32d32 ? csr 0x01080000 priority 2
    vector isintr 0x4c
channel is0 at isc0 ipi_addr 0x00000 # channel 0 slave 0
controller isc1 at vme32d32 ? csr 0x01080400 priority 2
    vector isintr 0x4d
channel is1 at isc1 ipi_addr 0x00100 # channel 0 slave 1
```

These lines declare the IPI "channel adaptors" which connect to the VME bus (which is in turn connected to the "nexus," or backplane). The `csr` and `vector` addresses listed here are configured on the IPI cards with DIP switches.

```
# Support for 2 VME IPI 2 Controllers with 4 drives each.
# Declares the disk driver of the VME IPI-2 controller.

# channel 0 slave 0
controller idc0 at ipi ? csr 0x0000ff priority 2
disk id 0 at idc0 drive 0 # facility 0
disk id 1 at idc0 drive 1
disk id 2 at idc0 drive 2
disk id 3 at idc0 drive 3

# channel 0 slave 1
controller idc1 at ipi ? csr 0x0001ff priority 2
disk id 0x10 at idc1 drive 0 # facility 0
disk id 0x11 at idc1 drive 1
```

```
disk id 0x12 at idc1 drive 2
disk id 0x13 at idc1 drive 3
```

These lines declare the IPI controllers and their associated drives.

```
device-driver   sbus        # 'driver' for sbus interface
device-driver   bwtwo       # monochrome frame buffer
device-driver   cgsix       # 8-bit color frame buffer
device-driver   dma         # DMA engine on sbus interface
device-driver   esp         # Emulex SCSI interface
device-driver   le          # LANCE ethernet
device-driver   zs          # UARTs
device-driver   vme         # VME interface
device-driver   pn          # VME/IPI pseudo driver
device-driver   idpseudo    # IPI Disk pseudo device driver
```

These lines declare other devices that are available for the kernel to talk to. The sbus is the primary I/O bus of this machine; thus, this driver (along with its helpmate, the dma driver) allows the kernel to talk to external devices. bwtwo and cgsix are used for local framebuffers, such as might be used to run X11 on an unlucky day. esp is the onboard SCSI adaptor, le is the on-board Ethernet adaptor, and zs is the serial circuitry that communicates with the keyboard, mouse, and external RS-232 ports. vme is for the VME-bus controller, and idpseudo and pn are both used by the IPI disk drivers.

```
scsibus0 at esp                            # first scsi bus
disk sd0 at scsibus0 target 3 lun 0 # first SCSI disk
disk sd1 at scsibus0 target 1 lun 0 # second SCSI disk
tape st0 at scsibus0 target 4 lun 0 # first SCSI tape
```

These lines "attach" the SCSI bus to the esp adaptor, and then instruct the kernel to search this bus for disks at SCSI target addresses 1 and 3 (target addresses are usually set with DIP switches or thumbwheels on the drives themselves). A SCSI tape drive at target 4 is also configured.

```
pseudo-device   pty         # pseudo-tty's
pseudo-device   ether       # basic Ethernet support
pseudo-device   loop        # loopback network - mandatory
pseudo-device   win128      # window devices, 128 windows
pseudo-device   dtop4       # desktops (screens), allow 4
pseudo-device   ms          # mouse support
pseudo-device   kb          # keyboard support
pseudo-device   openeepr    # onboard configuration NVRAM
pseudo-device   clone       # clone device
```

These pseudo-devices are necessary for a Sun system that is on a network, uses the Sun-supplied windowing system, and has luxuries such as a keyboard.

13.6 CONFIGURING A SOLARIS (ATT) KERNEL

After you've added a new device, it is sometimes necessary to reboot using boot -r.

Out of the box, a Solaris kernel acts much like a generic SunOS kernel. It probes the machine looking for devices, initializing the driver for each device found. However, there is one fundamental difference: unlike a traditional BSD kernel, which leaves drivers for non-existent hardware in memory, a Solaris kernel only loads code for devices that are actually found (unless forced to do otherwise).

Depending on your point of view, this automatic configuration makes building a custom kernel more or less of a necessity on a Solaris machine. In an ideal world, the Solaris kernel would correctly identify its hardware environment 100% of the time. Unfortunately, flaky, non-standard, or just plain buggy hardware (or Solaris drivers) can make this "creature comfort" more of a torment.

That having been said, let's look at how to custom-configure a Solaris kernel, should you ever need to do so.

The Solaris Kernel-Building Area

Solaris kernel files are stashed in the `/kernel` directory. An `ls -F` of this directory produces:

```
drv/  exec/  fs/  misc/  sched/  strmod/  sys/  unix*
```

These files and directories are described in Table 13.3.

Table 13.3   Subdirectories of /kernel in Solaris

Subdir	What it contains
drv	Loadable objects for device drivers and configuration files listing probe addresses for each device
exec	Loadable objects that understand object files (a.out, ELF, etc.)
fs	Loadable objects that manage filesystems (UFS, NFS, RFS, etc.)
misc	ELF loadable objects for miscellaneous kernel routines
sched	Directory containing process scheduling modules
strmod	Directory containing STREAMS modules
sys	Directory containing various optional kernel systems
unix	The base kernel itself

See Chapter 7 for information about installing drivers.

You shouldn't normally have to change files in these directories unless you install a new device driver. The one exception to this rule may be the files in the `/kernel/drv` directory that specify the hardware addresses for each possible device. For example, `le.conf` contains entries such as

```
name="le" parent="obio" on_cpu=0x23
    reg=0x210,0xf9000000,0x4 interrupts=6;
```

You may run into cases where your hardware configuration isn't specifically described. In that case, you'd need to add the configuration to its proper configuration file.

Configuring the Kernel via /etc/system

Solaris's **/etc/system** file serves much the same purpose as the configuration files in **SYS/conf** on a BSD system. The directives that can appear in this file are shown in Table 13.4.

Table 13.4   Directives used in /etc/system

Directive	Purpose
rootfs, rootdev	Specify type and location of root partition
forceload	Specifies drivers ("modules") that should be loaded
exclude	Specifies modules that should NOT be loaded
moddir	Specifies alternate location of modules
set	Sets kernel tuning variables (such as MAXUSERS)

/etc/system is consulted at boot time, and you can mutilate it so badly that the system no longer boots. **boot -a** lets you specify the path to a backup copy of **/etc/system**, if you made one.

An Example /etc/system File

Let's look at a sample **/etc/system** file for a simple kernel.

```
rootfs:ufs
rootdev:/sbus@1,f8000000/esp@0,800000/sd@3,0:a
```

These lines specify that the root filesystem will be of type UFS and that it will reside on the **sd3a** partition. The syntax used to specify the root device is identical to that used by Sun's **openprom** monitor. It varies from platform to platform, so consult your hardware manual.

```
exclude: sys/shmsys
forceload: drv/superplotter
```

The first line excludes the shared memory system from the kernel, making it slightly leaner. The second forces the "superplotter" driver to be loaded. Oh yeah.

```
set maxusers=64
```

This would size the kernel's tables to support 64 simultaneous users.

Debugging a Solaris Configuration

Since Solaris makes up its view of the world on the fly, debugging a troubled machine can be frustrating. Fortunately, Solaris provides several tools that display the machine's current configuration.

The `prtconf` command prints out the machine's general configuration, including the machine type, model number, amount of memory, and information about configured hardware devices. Lines that describe devices (drivers, really) are indented to show the dependencies among them. `sysdef` is `prtconf` on steroids; in addition to the information given by `prtconf`, it lists pseudo-device drivers, tunable kernel parameters, and the filenames of loaded modules.

Information about dynamically loaded modules can be obtained with the `modinfo` command. Solaris dynamically loads device drivers, filesystem drivers, and STREAMS modules, among other things. Don't be surprised if `modinfo`'s output contains upwards of fifty entries.

13.7 CONFIGURING AN IRIX KERNEL

The IRIX kernel is a beast all its own, visionary in some senses and archaic in others. IRIX conveniently provides an interactive tool for tuning kernel parameters, and the system's configuration files are well-commented. The files and directories listed in Table 13.5 are the major inputs to the IRIX configuration process.[4]

Table 13.5 IRIX kernel files

File	What it is
`/var/sysgen`	Home of modules and config files used to create a kernel
`/var/sysgen/system/*.sm`	Files used by `lboot` to obtain configuration hints. `lboot` concatenates all files in this directory when making a kernel.
`/usr/sbin/lboot`	Command to configure a bootable kernel (called by `autoconfig` at boot time)
`/usr/sbin/autoconfig`	User interface to `lboot`, called at boot time by `init`
`/usr/sbin/systune`	Interactive tool that allows examination and tuning of kernel variables

The `lboot` command reads the files in `/var/sysgen/system/*.sm` at boot time and loads the appropriate kernel modules. Thus, the process of manually tuning an IRIX kernel involves editing the files in the `/var/sysgen/system` directory to reflect your desired configuration. For example, to include support for multicast routing (as used on the Internet multicast backbone), you would add the following lines to the `/var/sysgen/system/irix.sm` file.

4. This information is for IRIX 5.2. IRIX 4.0 is quite different; the files are in `/usr/sysgen` and they take a somewhat different form.

```
* IP Multicast routing (see mrouted(1M))
*
USE: ip_mroute
```

To disable multicast routing, the line

```
* IP Multicast routing (see mrouted(1M))
*
EXCLUDE: ip_mroute
```

would be used. The ***.sm** files are verbosely self-documented. Consult the manual pages for **system** (section 4) and **systune** (section 1M) for detailed help with configuring an IRIX kernel.

SECTION TWO

NETWORKING

14 *TCP/IP and Routing*

14.1 INTRODUCTION

The TCP/IP protocol suite is the low-level networking software most commonly used with UNIX. It includes several components:

- Internet Protocol (IP), which transports raw data from one machine to another

- Internet Control Message Protocol (ICMP), which provides several kinds of low-level support for IP, including error messages, routing assistance, and echo requests.

- Address Resolution Protocol (ARP), which translates logical network addresses to hardware addresses

- User Datagram Protocol (UDP) and Transmission Control Protocol (TCP), which send data from one program to another using IP. UDP provides unverified transportation for individual messages, while TCP is reliable and connection-based.

This chapter discusses the TCP/IP suite and several related software packages with which it is often supported. Low-level network debugging is also covered. For additional information about managing a network, see Chapter 22, *Network Management*, and Chapter 32, *Policy and Politics*. Since networks are one of the main breeding grounds for security problems, you may also want to refer to Chapter 23, *Security*.

TCP/IP provides a uniform programming interface to different types of network hardware and guarantees that systems can exchange data ("interoperate") despite their many differences. TCP/IP also permits separate physical networks to be joined together in software, forming a larger and more flexible "logical network."

14.2 NETWORKING ROAD MAP

Network systems are often described in terms of a model called the Open Systems Interconnection (OSI) Reference Model used by the International Organization for Standardization (ISO). The OSI model consists of seven layers of software and/or hardware, each of which represents a level of abstraction.[1]

The structure of the OSI model is shown in Table 14.1. At the lowest layer, the model specifies how the hardware passes bits of information across the network. At higher layers, concerns such as reliability, security, and machine-independent data representation are addressed.

Table 14.1   ISO/OSI network model

Layer	Name	Function
1	Physical layer	The cable or physical medium itself
2	Data link layer	Transmit/receive packets, identify H/W addresses
3	Network layer	Determine routing and keep accounting
4	Transport layer	Guarantee end-to-end correct data transfer
5	Session layer	Handle authentication and authorization
6	Presentation layer	Deal with data problems and data compression
7	Application layer	Provide end-user services: mail, login, etc.

Some think a financial layer and a political layer should be added to these. There is no magic about the number seven; seven committees were involved in the specification, and one layer was created for each.

The OSI scheme is more than just an abstract model—there is actually a set of "standard" protocols that go along with it. The construction of the OSI system began in the early 1980s and dragged on for many years. While the committees were arguing over the standards, the whole concept of networking was changing underneath them, and TCP/IP was being deployed on networks around the world.

Despite the fact that the standards had never been implemented or tested, the US Government decided they were such a good idea that all government computers should use them. This little plan was outlined in

---

1. You will sometimes hear the OSI model referred to as the ISO model; both are correct.

the GOSIP (Government Open Systems Interconnection Profile) specification, which set off a flurry of implementations by vendors.

But lo and behold, when the OSI protocols were finally implemented, several problems came to light:

- They relied on concepts that made no sense in modern networks.
- The specifications for them were, in some cases, incomplete.
- They were functionally inferior to existing protocols.
- The numerous layers made them slow and hard to implement.

Vendors quickly discovered that none of their non-government customers were willing to give up existing TCP/IP networks in exchange for an untested and poorly-designed alternative.

Vendors were stuck with a choice between supporting two sets of protocols, abandoning the commercial market, or abandoning the government market.[2] Enough vendors decided not to play along with GOSIP that the government was limited in its ability to buy modern systems. In 1993, the government finally relented and decided that TCP/IP might be an acceptable set of network protocols after all.

That was the death knell for OSI. Even the protocols' biggest promoters now admit that OSI is on its way to becoming a footnote in computer history. The main thing that can be learned from the OSI story is that computer systems should not be designed by committees.

Although the divisions among layers in the OSI model are somewhat arbitrary and do not match real-world protocol stacks,[3] the model is still widely used and cited. This is done primarily to humiliate the members of ISO standards committees. TCP/IP is actually designed around a simpler four-level layering scheme, shown in Table 14.2.

Table 14.2   TCP/IP network model

Layer	Function
Link layer	Network hardware and device drivers
Network layer	Basic communication, addressing, and routing
Transport layer	Communication among programs on a net
Application layer	End-user application programs

Some reference books attempt to map between the layers of TCP/IP and the layers of OSI, but in our opinion the analogy is somewhat strained and only ends up obscuring the actual structure of TCP/IP.

2. The government actually granted exceptions to the GOSIP requirement to anyone that asked. But the purchaser had to request the waiver, not the vendor.

3. In fact, they don't fit the OSI protocols that well either, but that is another matter.

As you can see, TCP/IP is (in theory) missing some of the features provided for in the OSI model; it also combines features of some adjacent OSI layers and splits other layers apart. Exhibit A shows how various components and clients of TCP/IP fit into the general architecture.

Exhibit A   One big happy TCP/IP family

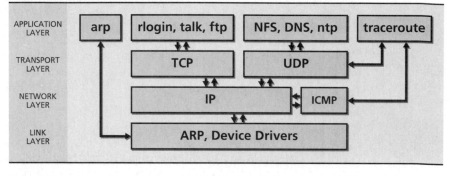

The protocols at each layer build upon those beneath them. Data travel down the protocol stack on the originating machine, across the physical network, and up the protocol stack on the destination machine. For example, an application that thinks it's only using UDP is really invoking protocols for UDP, IP, and the physical network all at once.

14.3 PACKETS AND SEGMENTATION

UNIX can support a variety of physical networks, including Ethernet, token ring, and modem-based systems. Hardware is managed within the link layer of the TCP/IP architecture, and higher-level protocols do not know or care about the specific hardware being used.

Each of a machine's connections to a network is called a network interface. A machine that has more than one interface may transfer data among networks by receiving it on one interface and retransmitting it on another. This function is known as routing, and a machine that performs it is called a router or gateway.[4] Most of the complexity of low-level network management arises from routing issues.

Data travels on a network in the form of *packets*, each of which consists of a header and a payload. The header tells where the packet came from and where it's going. It can also include checksums, protocol-specific information, or other handling instructions. The payload is the data to be transferred. In the context of low-level network hardware, packets are often called *frames*.

---

4. Many people argue that the word "gateway" should be reserved for routers that perform protocol conversion. Unfortunately, the distinction between the terms seems to be fading.

As a packet travels down the protocol stack in preparation for being sent, each protocol adds its own header information. Each protocol's finished packet becomes the payload part of the packet generated by the next protocol. This is known as nesting or encapsulation. On the receiving machine, the nested frames are unwrapped in reverse order.

For example, a UDP packet being transmitted via Ethernet contains three different wrappers. On the Ethernet wire, it is wrapped with a simple header that lists the source and destination hardware addresses, the length of the frame, and the frame's checksum. The payload of the Ethernet frame is an IP packet; the IP packet's payload is a UDP packet, and the UDP packet's payload is the actual data being transmitted. Exhibit B shows such the components of such a frame.

Exhibit B   A typical network packet

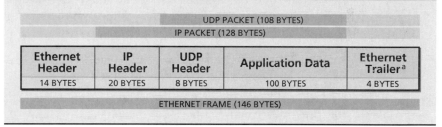

a. A trailer is a wrapper that's put at the end of a packet instead of the front.

The size of packets may be limited by both hardware specifications and by protocol conventions. For example, the payload of an Ethernet packet can be no longer than 1,500 bytes. Some modern networks use packet sizes of less than 100 bytes. The size limit for a network or protocol is called the Maximum Transfer Unit or MTU.

On some systems, an interface's MTU can be set using `ifconfig`*. See page 262.*

In the TCP/IP suite, the IP layer is responsible for splitting packets to conform to the MTU of a particular network. If a packet is routed through several networks, one of the intermediate networks may have a smaller MTU than the network of origin. In this case, the gateway to the small-MTU network will further subdivide the packet. Other protocol layers may also perform a segmentation function. For example, modern versions of TCP tune their packet sizes in an attempt to improve throughput on specific media.

14.4 PACKET ADDRESSING

Like letters or email messages, network packets must be properly addressed in order to reach their destinations. TCP/IP uses several addressing schemes in combination.

The lowest level of addressing is dictated by network hardware. For example, Ethernet devices are assigned a unique six-byte hardware address at the time of manufacture. Token ring interfaces have a similar two, four, or six-byte address. Some point-to-point networks (such as SLIP and PPP, described in Chapter 19) need no hardware addresses at all; the identity of the destination is specified as a link is established.

See page 249 for more information about IP addresses.

At the next level up, Internet addressing (more commonly known as IP addressing) is used. One four-byte IP address is assigned to each networked device. IP addresses are globally unique and hardware-independent. They are designed to facilitate the process of routing packets from one network to another so that machines on different physical networks can communicate with each other.

See page 251 for more information about the ARP and RARP protocols.

The mapping between IP addresses and hardware addresses is implemented at the link layer of the TCP/IP model. On networks that allow broadcasting, a protocol called ARP allows mappings to be discovered automatically, without assistance from a system administrator.

Since IP addresses are long, seemingly random numbers, they are hard for people to remember. UNIX systems allow text names to be associated with an IP address so that users can type **telnet anchor** instead of **telnet 128.138.242.1**.

There are several ways to set up this mapping, ranging from use of the **/etc/hosts** file on simple networks to the complex-but-nifty Domain Name System described in Chapter 16. Keep in mind that names are just a shorthand way of writing IP addresses; they are translated to IP addresses by applications and are not understood directly by low-level networking software.

IP addresses identify machines; they are not specific enough to address particular processes or services. The TCP and UDP protocols extend IP addresses with a concept called ports. A port is a two-byte number that supplements an IP address to specify a particular protocol "mailbox." Standard UNIX services such as email, **ftp**, and the remote login server all associate themselves with "well-known" ports defined in the file **/etc/services**. To help prevent impersonation of these services, port numbers under 1,024 may only be accessed by root.

See Chapter 20 for more information about the Internet.

IP is currently being extended to handle multicast addressing, which allows packets to be sent to more than one machine at a time. In the version of multicasting currently supported on the Internet's multicast backbone (MBONE), IGMP (Internet Group Management Protocol) is used to construct and manage sets of hosts that are treated as one destination. Multicasting is still in the experimental stage.

14.5 INTERNET ADDRESSES

An Internet address is four bytes long and is divided into a network part and a host part. The network part identifies a logical network to which the address refers; routing decisions are made based on this information. The host part identifies a machine on that network.

By convention, IP addresses are written as decimal numbers (one for each byte) separated by periods. For example, the IP address for our machine boulder is written as "128.138.240.1". The leftmost byte is the most significant and is always part of the network portion.

There are several "classes" of IP address; they differ in the way that bytes are allocated between the host and network parts. The commonly used addresses are in classes A, B, and C; classes D and E also exist and are used for multicasting and research purposes.

The class of an address can be determined by examining its first byte. Table 14.3 describes the characteristics of each address class; the network portion of an address is denoted by N, and the host portion by H.

Table 14.3 **Internet address classes**

Class	1st Byte[a]	Format	Comments
A	1-126	N.H.H.H	Major networks, almost never assigned now
B	128-191	N.N.H.H	For large sites; usually subnetted, hard to get
C	192-223	N.N.N.H	Easy to get, often obtained in sets
D	224-239	–	Multicast addressing (still in development)
E	240-254	–	Experimental addresses

a. The values 0, 127, and 255 are special and are not used for regular IP addresses.

For example, we can tell from the first byte that 130.95.100.5 is a class B address. 130.95 is the network part, and 100.5 is the host part.

See Chapter 20 for more information about the Internet and the NIC.

The allocation of IP addresses is centrally managed by InterNIC Registration Services, under contract to the National Science Foundation. The InterNIC distributes network numbers, and local administrators are responsible for assigning host numbers. The growth of the Internet (the world-wide TCP/IP backbone network) and the advent of CIDR (see page 257) have pushed the address assignment process in the direction of increasing decentralization. Soon, you may have to obtain IP addresses from a regional authority or network provider. This is a Real Good Thing.™

Specific instructions for obtaining network numbers are given in *Obtaining and Assigning Internet Addresses* starting on page 260.

Since the number of bits of network address varies from class to class, there are more networks in some classes than in others. For example, there can be at most 126 class A networks. These network addresses are essentially impossible to get now unless you are a major national or international network.

Class B addresses interpret the bytes as N.N.H.H, allowing for many networks and many hosts per network (actually, more hosts than is reasonable to put on a single network). Class A and B addresses are usually subdivided in a special way; see *Subnetting* on page 256 for more details. Because the number of class B addresses is fairly limited, they are doled out very carefully. Only sites with tens of thousands of machines in a single geographic location should consider trying to obtain a class B address.

Class C addresses interpret the bytes as N.N.N.H, which allows for only 254 hosts (since 0 and 255 are reserved). Class C addresses are easy to obtain. Large or growing sites can apply for a block of several class C network numbers at once.

There are a total of only slightly more than two million class A, B, and C network addresses. At the rate that UNIX and TCP/IP are metastasizing, the current address space could be exhausted some time in the next several years. To forestall this problem, the IP protocols are in the process of being revised. In late 1994, the IETF selected SIPP (Simple Internet Protocol Plus) as the successor to the current version of IP. You may also hear this protocol referred to as IPng (for "next-generation IP").

IPng enlarges the IP address space to 128 bits and simplifies the basic IP protocol. It removes several features of IP that experience has shown to be of little value, making the protocol potentially faster and easier to implement. It also provides for embedding special options in a variable-length header, allowing them to be implemented without a performance penalty for simple packets.

The numbers 0, 127, and 255 have special meanings in an Internet address. In general, a 0 in any part of an address indicates "this host" or "this network" and usually means that the sending host does not know that part of its own address. 255 is a broadcast address that all hosts must listen for. The 255 may be used in all four bytes of a broadcast address, or it may appear only in the host part, with the network part identifying a real network.

See page 263 for more information about the loopback interface.

When 127 is the first byte of an address, it denotes the "loopback network," a fictitious network that has no real hardware interface and includes only the local host. The loopback address 127.0.0.1 always refers to the current host; its symbolic name is "localhost".

Broadcast addresses had not been standardized when 4.2BSD was released, and 0 was used instead of 255. Most descendants of 4.2BSD have been adjusted to use the new standards. Compatibility problems may occur if hosts on a network disagree about broadcast conventions.

An interface's broadcast address is set with the `ifconfig` command. See page 262 for a complete description of `ifconfig`.

14.6 ARP 'N' RARP: ADDRESS TRANSLATION

Even though IP packets are addressed using IP addresses, hardware addresses must be used to actually transport data from one computer to another.[5] ARP, the Address Resolution Protocol, is used to discover what hardware address is associated with a particular IP address. It can be used on any kind of network that supports broadcasting, but is most commonly described in terms of Ethernet.

ARP can only be used on a network to which the destination host is actually connected. A packet that crosses several networks on the way to its destination is routed according to its destination IP address; however, the packet is physically transferred only between routers that are on the same networks. ARP may be used at every hop: several times along the path to look up hardware addresses of routers, and once at the last hop to find the hardware address of the final destination.

Every machine maintains an ARP cache that contains the result of recent ARP queries. Under normal circumstances, many of the addresses a host needs are discovered soon after booting, so ARP does not generally have a dramatic effect on network congestion.

ARP functions by broadcasting[6] a packet of the form, "Does anyone know the hardware address for 128.138.116.4?" The machine being searched for recognizes its own address and sends back a reply of the form, "Yup, that's me. My Ethernet address is 8:0:20:0:fb:6a."

The original query includes the IP and Ethernet addresses of the requestor; since it is likely that the requestor and target will soon be communicating, the target records the requestor's information in its ARP cache in addition to returning its own. Thus, the two machines learn each other's ARP mapping with only one exchange of packets.

Other machines that hear the requestor's initial broadcast can record its address mapping, too. However, most systems will not do this unless they already have an out-of-date ARP cache entry for that host.

5. Except on certain types of point-to-point link.
6. Using the underlying hardware's broadcasting conventions, not IP broadcasting.

Most systems include a command called **arp** that can be used to examine and manipulate the ARP cache. It is generally useful only for debugging and for situations that involve special hardware. See page 281 for more information about the **arp** command.

Sometimes, hardware addresses need to be translated into IP addresses. This is most commonly done at boot time; instead of having an IP address hard-wired into a configuration file, a machine can query a central server to discover its own address. The near-obsolete RARP protocol (Reverse ARP) extends ARP to cover reverse translations.

Unlike ARP, RARP requires a central server process to be installed on each network. RARP is not self-configuring; you must supply an explicit mapping between Ethernet addresses and IP addresses. On most systems that support RARP, the server is called **rarpd** and configuration data is drawn from **/etc/ethers** and **/etc/hosts**.

See page 720 for more information about BOOTP.

RARP has been superseded by a newer protocol known as BOOTP. BOOTP provides the address-mapping function of RARP, plus a number of other features designed to help client machines bootstrap on a network. Like **rarpd**, the BOOTP server must be explicitly configured.

14.7 ROUTING

Routing is the process of directing a packet through the maze of networks that stand between its source and destination. In the TCP/IP system, it is similar to asking for directions in an unfamiliar country. The first person you talk to might point you toward the right city. Once you were a bit closer to your destination, the next person might be able to tell you how to get to the right street. Eventually, you get close enough that someone can identify the building you're looking for.

TCP/IP routing information takes the form of rules ("routes") such as, "To reach network A, send packets through machine C. The cost is one hop." There can also be a default route that tells what to do with packets bound for a network to which there is no explicit route.

Routing information is stored in a table in the kernel. Each table entry has several parameters, including a reliability field that prioritizes routes when the table contains conflicting information. To route a packet to a particular address, the kernel picks the most specific of the available rules. If there is no relevant route and no default, a "network unreachable" error is returned to the sender.

As far as TCP/IP is concerned, that's all there is to routing. Packets come in on one interface and are either delivered locally or compared to the routing table to determine where they should be forwarded. The hard part is to make sure that the routing table contains the right data.

A machine's routing table can be examined with the `netstat` command. We will discuss `netstat` in detail starting on page 274, but here's a short example to give you a better idea of what routes look like:

```
% netstat -r -n
Routing tables
Destination     Gateway         Flags  Refs     Use  If
...
128.138.238.0  128.138.238.18  U         5  2845294  il1
128.138.240.0  128.138.240.1   U         1   168589  il0
130.118.0.0    128.138.238.36  UG        0        0  il1
...
```

For example, the third route says that to reach the network 130.118, packets must be sent through the gateway 128.138.238.36.

Maintenance of routing tables can be done statically, dynamically, or with a combination of the two approaches. A static route is one that you enter explicitly using the `route` command. Static routes should stay in the routing table forever; they are often set up at boot time from one of the system startup scripts. For example, the command

```
route add net 202.87.240.0 202.87.242.23 1
```

A complete description of the **route** *command is given on page 264.*

adds a route to the class C network 202.87.240 via the router machine 202.87.242.23. In a relatively stable local network, static routing is an efficient solution. It is easy to manage and reliable. However, it requires that the system administrator know the topology of the network accurately at boot time, and that the topology not change between boots.

Dynamic routing is performed by a daemon process that maintains and modifies the routing table. Routing daemons on different hosts communicate to discover the topology of the network and to figure out how to reach distant destinations. Several routing daemons are available. In this chapter, we will describe the standard UNIX daemon, `routed` ("route dee"), and a more full-featured daemon called `gated` ("gate dee"). Specifics about these daemons begin on page 266.

Routing protocols

Routing protocols are used by routing daemons to exchange information about the network. Each protocol is usually classified as either an interior gateway protocol (IGP) or an exterior gateway protocol (EGP).

An interior protocol manages routing information within what is called an "autonomous system," a collection of networks under the control of a single central authority. In general, autonomous systems are fairly large. It's rare for an organization to have more than one unless there are several geographically separate sites.

Exterior gateway protocols manage routing among autonomous systems. The details of routing within each autonomous system are not propagated, although lists of each system's networks are. Autonomous systems are usually connected at only a few points; the separation of EGPs from IGPs exploits this natural bottleneck to reduce the complexity of the global routing problem. EGPs are typically "dumber" than IGPs. They worry less about optimizing paths through complicated network mazes and more about distributing large quantities of routing data.

To participate in an EGP, you must register as an autonomous system with the InterNIC. The registration form is available via `ftp` from the host internic.net or via email from HOSTMASTER@internic.net. After registering, you will be assigned an autonomous system number to give to your routing daemon; routing information originating at your site will be stamped with this number.

The more sophisticated routing protocols assign a cost metric to each potential route which reflects its usability. The protocols try to distinguish between good and bad routes using this cost metric. Only a subset of the collected information is entered into the kernel's routing table. Most protocols use the best route from their point of view, but some will split network traffic among several equally good routes.

Routing protocols use various metrics to measure cost. Some use complicated heuristics to estimate the time delay for each potential link, while others consider only the number of links in a path. EGPs usually don't worry too much about path costs and for this reason are sometimes referred to as reachability protocols.

There are several routing protocols in common use:

- Routing Information Protocol (RIP)
- Open Shortest Path First (OSPF)
- Interior Gateway Routing Protocol (IGRP)
- Exterior Gateway Protocol (EGP)
- Border Gateway Protocol (BGP)
- Distance Vector Multicast Routing Protocol (DVMRP)

RIP, OSPF, and IGRP are interior protocols; EGP (a specific implementation of the generic "EGP" category) and BGP are exterior protocols. DVMRP is a routing protocol used for the current (experimental) implementation of IP multicasting. It has a voracious appetite for bandwidth. A few more routing protocols exist, but we do not discuss them here, either because they are obsolete or because they are not widely deployed.

RIP is an old XNS protocol that has been adapted for IP networks. It is the protocol used by the standard UNIX `routed` daemon. The cost metric is the hop count, with each machine that a packet flows through counted as one hop. Because the RIP protocol becomes unstable if long paths are permitted, RIP considers any host sixteen or more hops away to be unreachable. Therefore, large local networks with more than sixteen routers along a single path cannot use RIP.

Although RIP is a resource hog due to its profligate use of broadcasting, it does a good job when a network is changing often or when the topology of remote networks is not known. However, it can be slow to stabilize after a link goes down.

OSPF is documented in RFCs 1245, 1246, 1247, and 1583.

OSPF is a relatively new protocol which has only recently become widely available. It is an industrial-strength protocol that works well for large, complicated topologies. It offers several advantages over RIP, including the ability to manage several paths to a single destination and the ability to subdivide the network into segments that share only high-level routing information. OSPF uses a more centralized control model than RIP and is also more complicated to administrate.

IGRP is a proprietary protocol spoken by Cisco routers. It was created to address some of the shortcomings of early protocols before robust standards like OSPF existed. In the long run it will probably fade away, but it is still very popular now.

EGP is documented in RFCs 827, 911, and 904.

EGP is the old protocol spoken by ARPANET gateways. It uses a cost metric with only three values and infinity (there are actually eight values, but only four are distinguishable). EGP assumes a certain network topology (specifically, a group of autonomous systems connected to a central hub) and is therefore somewhat limited in applicability. It has been largely replaced by BGP.

BGP is documented in RFC1267.

BGP, the Border Gateway Protocol, expands upon the EGP protocol to add support for an arbitrarily complex topology of autonomous systems. Under BGP, systems need not be arranged in a strict hierarchy, and it is possible for packets to be transported by non-hub networks. BGP allows routing policy to be based on political factors as well as reachability.

ICMP Redirects

Although IP generally does not concern itself with the management of routing information, it does have a small damage-control feature which you can use to simplify your routing setup.

When a router forwards a packet to a machine on the same network from which the packet was originally received, there is clearly something wrong. Since the sender, the router, and the next-hop router are all on the same network, the packet could have been forwarded in one hop rather than two. The router can conclude that the sender's routing tables are inaccurate or incomplete.

In this situation, the router can notify the sender of its problem with an ICMP redirect packet. In effect, a redirect says, "You should not be sending packets for host *xxx* to me; you should send them to host *yyy* instead." The ICMP protocol allows redirects to be sent for both individual host addresses and entire networks. However, many implementations generate only host redirects.

Upon receiving a redirect, a well-behaved sender updates its routing table so that future packets bound for that destination will take the more direct path. This feature allows you to use default static routes even on networks that have more than one outbound gateway. As long as gateway machines have an accurate picture of the network topology, they will gently correct hosts that try to use the wrong router.

Since each host will have to be corrected for each remote host address it refers to, redirects can be a very inefficient way of distributing routing information. However, a redirect-based scheme is sometimes a workable compromise between administrative complexity and performance. In general, redirects are most useful when the default route is appropriate for most traffic, with only a few packets being routed via redirects.

Subnetting

It is rare for a single network to have more than a couple of hundred computers attached to it. The utility of class A and class B addresses (which allow for 16,387,064 and 64,516 hosts per network, respectively) is therefore somewhat limited.

Most sites that have these addresses use a refinement of the addressing scheme called subnetting, in which part of the host portion of an address is "borrowed" to extend the network portion. For example, the four bytes of a class B address would normally be interpreted as N.N.H.H. If subnetting is used to assign the third byte to the network number rather than the host number, the address would be interpreted as N.N.N.H. This turns a single class B network address into 254 distinct class-C-like networks.

The division between network part and host part need not fall on a byte boundary, but that is the most common arrangement. The network bits should be contiguous. Configurations such as N.N.H.N are technically OK but are silly and might not be supported in the future.

Even a class C network address can be subnetted, although this is relatively uncommon. For example, by borrowing two bits of the host number, you could divide a class C network into four networks of 62 hosts each (host numbers of all zeros and all ones retain their special meanings, so it costs you six additional host numbers to subnet).

*See page 262 for
more information
about* ifconfig.

Subnetting is specified using a "subnet mask" that has the network bits
turned on and the host bits turned off. You specify the subnet mask at
boot time when you configure a network interface using the ifconfig
command. The kernel normally uses the inherent class of an IP
addresses to figure out which bits are part of the network; when you set
an explicit mask, you simply override this behavior.

While the hosts on a network may share the delusion that they are
using class C addresses, the rest of the world isn't fooled and continues
to treat the addresses as class B. Rather than advertising every network to the outside world, you need only advertise the single class B
network; once a packet arrives within the subnetted area, the full network address will be seen and the packet routed to its exact destination.

You must be particularly aware of subnet issues if your organization
has more than one connection to the Internet. If the outside world can't
distinguish your subnets from each other, it will not be able to figure out
which connection point a packet should be sent to.

CIDR: Classless Inter-Domain Routing

Although it's possible for a route to apply to only a single host (a complete IP address), routing is usually done on a network-by-network
basis, using only part of the destination address. For this reason, routing software needs to be able to figure out which bits of an IP address
refer to the network, and which refer to the host. In fact, this is the only
reason why the host and network are distinguished at all. Without routing, there would be no need for address classes or subnetting.

In the past, non-local routing was done on the basis of address classes.
Subnetting was used strictly within autonomous systems. However, the
rapid growth of the Internet and the proliferation of class C addresses
have created a crisis of routing on the Internet backbone.

The problem is that a separate route is required for each class C
address. A site that has twenty class C networks needs twenty routes
propagated everywhere on the Internet backbone. The backbone currently supports tens of thousands of routes, but it can't be loaded too
much further without performance penalties.

The solution is to define aggregate routes that handle more than one
network at a time. The CIDR scheme, defined in RFC1519 (9/93), effectively extends the idea of subnetting to the Internet backbone. But
instead of adding bits to the network portion of an address, CIDR uses
masking to *hide* the low-order bits of the network number, effectively
grouping several networks together in one route. CIDR is sometimes
referred to as *supernetting*.

In order to be grouped, addresses must be numerically adjacent. For example, the networks 199.128.0, 199.128.1, 199.128.2, and 199.128.3 could be supernetted together with the mask 0xFFFFFC00. Because supernetting can only be performed at a bit boundary, the number of networks combined must be a power of two.

In addition to reducing the total number of routes, supernetting allows address assignment and routing to be performed hierarchically. For example, each Internet service provider could be assigned a large supernet to divide among its clients. The backbone need only look for the single supernet address to know that a packet is bound somewhere within that provider's domain.

Although CIDR is only an interim solution, it is strong enough to handle the Internet's growth problems until the next generation of the IP protocol has been deployed. It is now supported by both the Internet backbone and by major manufacturers of routing equipment. CIDR will have little impact on routing within autonomous systems.

Selecting a Routing Strategy

There are essentially four levels of complexity at which routing for a network can be managed:

- No routing
- Static routes only
- Mostly static routes, but clients listen for RIP updates
- Dynamic routing everywhere

The topology of the overall network has a dramatic effect on each individual segment's routing requirements. Different nets may need very different levels of routing support. The following rules of thumb can help you choose a strategy:

- A stand-alone network requires no routing.

- If there is only one way out of a network, clients (non-gateway machines) on that network should have a default route to the lone gateway. No other configuration is necessary, except on the gateway itself.

- A gateway with a small number of networks on one side and a gateway to "the world" on the other side can have explicit static routes pointing to the former and a default route to the latter. However, dynamic routing is advisable if there is more than one routing choice on both sides.

- Even if you use RIP, avoid using `routed` in active mode, as it broadcasts everything it knows (correct or not) at short intervals. `gated` allows you to specify what routes may be sent out ("advertised"), thus reducing the flood of routing information. gated can also send RIP updates to particular gateways rather than broadcasting them everywhere.

- To have clients listen passively for routing updates without sending out their own information, use routed -q. Clients can also listen passively with gated.

- If RIP is not your primary routing protocol, you can have gated translate and broadcast its routing information as RIP purely for the benefit of passive clients.

- routed listens to everyone and believes everything it hears. gated gives you much more control over updates. Even if your site uses RIP, you may want to manage the exchange of routing data with gated and run routed only on client machines.

- Dynamic routing should be used at points where networks cross political or administrative boundaries.

- On dynamically-routed networks that contain loops or redundant paths, use OSPF if possible.

- If you need to run an EGP, ask your Internet provider and neighboring autonomous systems what to do; you must use a routing protocol that's compatible with your neighbors'.

A good routing strategy for a medium-sized site with a relatively stable local structure and a connection to someone else's net is to use a combination of static and dynamic routing. Machines within the local structure that do not gateway to external networks can use static routing, forwarding all unknown packets to a default machine that understands the outside world and does dynamic routing.

A network that is too complicated to be managed with this scheme should rely on dynamic routing. Default static routes can still be used on leaf networks, but machines on networks with more than one router should run routed in passive mode. All machines with more than one network interface should run gated in active mode.

14.8 SETTING UP A NETWORK

Only a few steps are involved in setting up a network:

- Plan the physical and logical structure of the network.
- Assign IP addresses.
- Install the network hardware.
- Set up each host to configure network interfaces at boot time.
- Set up routing daemons and/or static routes.

Of course, you could add a debugging step to this sequence as well. In the discussion below, we will describe the process of network configuration in terms of Ethernet, but many other systems (for example, token ring) are essentially similar. Point-to-point links are rather special; refer to Chapter 19 or your manuals for more information.

One fact worth mentioning is that some systems are smart enough to distinguish whether they are connected to a network or not. The boot sequence may be quite different in the networked and non-networked cases; a machine that works fine on its own can inexplicably hang at boot time when a network cable is plugged in, even if no configuration changes have been made. Don't assume that you can take care of all the hardware work first and then do the software configuration; you may be better off attacking the problem machine by machine.

The process of designing and installing a physical network is lovingly described in Chapter 15, *Network Hardware*. If you are dealing with an existing network and have a general idea of how it is set up, it may not be necessary for you to read too much more about the physical aspects of networking unless you plan to extend the existing network.

The sections below cover the non-hardware network setup topics: dealing with IP addresses, using the `ifconfig` command to configure network interfaces, and using the `route` command and the `gated` and `routed` daemons to manage routing.

Obtaining and Assigning Internet Addresses

See Chapter 20 for more information about the Internet.

IP addresses must be unique on the Internet, the global TCP/IP network that is a conglomeration of MILNET, NSFNET, regional networks, campus/organizational networks, and networks served by commercial providers. Network numbers are assigned by a central authority, InterNIC Registration Services.

The IP address request form is included on the CD-ROM.

The application for an Internet address is available via anonymous `ftp` from internic.net; it's located in the `templates` directory and is called `internet-number-template.txt`. If you don't have Internet access, you can email HOSTMASTER@internic.net and ask for the form. IP addresses assigned by the InterNIC are guaranteed to be unique from all others blessed by the InterNIC, but not necessarily from rogue sites that assign network numbers randomly.

You can subdivide the address space assigned to you by the InterNIC however you like. If you're using class C addresses, you are responsible for assigning a host number to each machine on your network; the NIC doesn't want to hear about it. If you choose to subnet your addresses, that's fine and is entirely up to you.

It is common to speak of assigning an IP address to a particular host. Actually, addresses are assigned to *network interfaces*, not machines. If a machine has more than one interface, it will have more than one address. Each address will have a different network number, reflecting the fact that the interfaces connect to different physical nets.

When you assign an IP address to a machine, you should normally enter the mapping between the address and the machine's name into the `/etc/hosts` file, the Domain Naming System, or a network administrative database. This mapping allows you and your users to refer to machines by their hostnames.

The `/etc/hosts` file is the oldest and simplest way to map names to IP addresses. Each line starts with an IP address and continues with the various symbolic names by which that address is known. For example, the entries

```
128.138.197.10    rupertsberg dwim
128.138.197.1     circuit
128.138.240.56    circuit-gw
128.138.197.2     snake

...
```

define IP addresses for the machines circuit, snake, and rupertsberg. circuit has two network interfaces: one on the 197 subnet known as "circuit," and one on the 240 subnet known as "circuit-gw," short for "circuit gateway." Due to the magic of routing, the machine can be referred to as "circuit" from anywhere on the network.

A major disadvantage of the `/etc/hosts` file is that the data it contains must be replicated on every machine that wants to use symbolic names. There are various schemes that allow a single version of the hosts file to be kept in a central location; see Chapter 18, *Sharing System Files*, for more information.

Due to the complexity and importance of the name-to-address mapping problem, a special scheme called the Domain Naming System has been invented to manage the problem on a world-wide scale. DNS is really the "correct" way to manage the mapping, but it is unfortunately somewhat complex. Chapter 16 describes this scheme and the software used to implement it.

At a small site, you can easily dole out IP addresses by hand. But when many networks and many different administrative groups are involved, it helps to have some central coordination. Our home-grown `addhost` system is a set of distributed tools that solve several of the problems of host management. It's included on the CD-ROM and is described in more detail on page 359.

ifconfig: Configure Network Interfaces

`ifconfig` is used to enable or disable a network interface, to set the IP address, broadcast address, and subnet mask associated with it, and to set various other options and parameters. It is usually run at boot time, but can also be used to make changes on the fly.

An `ifconfig` command most commonly has the form

   `ifconfig` *interface* [*family*] *address* **up** *option* ...

For example:

```
ifconfig en0 128.138.240.1 up netmask 255.255.255.0
  broadcast 128.138.240.255
```

interface identifies the hardware interface to which the command applies. It is usually a two or three-character device name followed by a number. Some common names are `ie0`, `le0`, `ln0`, `en0`, `we0`, `qe0`, and `lan0`. The interface name is derived from the name of the device driver used to run it; it usually corresponds to the chip set used by the interface. For Ethernet, the most common sets are made by Intel (`ie`) and AMD (`le`). `netstat -i` can be used to find out what interfaces are present on the system; see page 274.

 Under Solaris, network interfaces must be "attached" with `ifconfig` `plumb` before they become configurable and visible to `netstat -i`.

Because of the layered architecture of networking software, more than one protocol may be associated with each interface. The *family* argument tells which protocol layer you want to configure with the subsequent arguments. For example, an interface could be configured at the hardware level (perhaps setting the hardware address, though not for Ethernet), at the IP level, or maybe at the level of some other protocol such as XNS or AppleTalk.

In real life, you almost never want to deal with anything but IP configuration, for which *family* should be set to `inet`. Some versions of the `ifconfig` command assume `inet` if the *family* argument is left out, but HP-UX and BSDI require you to say it explicitly.

The *address* parameter specifies the interface's IP address. It's usually given in the traditional Internet dot notation, but can also be specified as a hostname on most systems. If it is given as a hostname, the address is discovered by looking up the name in `/etc/hosts` or DNS. We strongly recommend the use of numeric dot notation; if there's a problem resolving the hostname, the machine won't boot, or will boot into a state in which it cannot be accessed from the network, requiring you to physically go to the machine in order to debug the problem.

The loopback interface is usually called lo0. It's a fictitious piece of hardware through which packets bound for the local host can be routed, allowing network protocols and services to function correctly even on a stand-alone machine. The loopback interface needs to be configured just like any other network interface; it should be assigned the IP address 127.0.0.1 (aka "localhost").

The keyword up turns the interface on; down turns it off. Other options, of which there may be several, follow. ifconfig options all have symbolic names. Listing the option selects it. Some options require an argument, which should be placed immediately after the option name.

The most common options are:

netmask   This option sets the subnet mask for the interface. The mask is given as an argument; it may be specified in dot notation or as a four-byte hexadecimal number beginning with 0x. In either case, bits set to 1 are part of the network number and bits set to 0 are part of the host number.

On some systems, a logical name may be used instead of an explicit number. Logical names usually refer to the /etc/networks file, but under Solaris, /etc/netmasks is used. Both SunOS and Solaris allow a + to indicate that the subnet mask should be derived from the IP address using the NIS versions of these files. Refer to Chapter 18 for more information about NIS.

broadcast   This option specifies the IP broadcast address for the interface, in hex or dot notation. The correct broadcast address is one in which the host part is set to all 1s, and most systems default to this value.

Some systems, including SunOS, default to a host part of all 0s for broadcasts. Solaris and SunOS allow the address to be specified as +, which recomputes the default broadcast address based on the new values of other options you may have set, such as the subnet mask. But under SunOS, this will still give you an incorrect host part of all 0s.

metric   The metric option affects routing. Usually, it costs one "hop" to transfer a packet from one network to another (no hops for a directly-connected network). The argument to the metric option is the hop count to be associated with the interface. You might set the hop count artificially high to reflect some real-life inefficiency of the actual hardware, or simply to make the gateway appear less tasty than it really is so as to avoid carrying extra traffic.

 Solaris allows the option `auto-revarp` to be used instead of an explicit address. It causes the IP address to be discovered using RARP.

Let's look at some complete examples:

```
ifconfig lo0 127.0.0.1 up
```

This command configures the loopback interface, which doesn't usually require any options to be set.

```
ifconfig en0 128.138.240.1 up netmask 255.255.255.0
    broadcast 128.138.240.255
```

This is a typical example for an Ethernet interface. The IP and broadcast addresses are set to 128.138.240.1 and 128.138.240.255, respectively. The network is class B (you can tell from the first byte of the address), but it has been subnetted by an additional byte.

`ifconfig` *interface* prints the current settings for *interface*. Many systems understand `-a` to mean "all interfaces."

 Solaris also supports the options `-au` and `-ad`, meaning all interfaces that are up or down, respectively.

HP-UX requires the `lanconfig` command to be used in conjunction with `ifconfig`. See page 270 for more information.

route: Configure Static Routes

The `route` command defines static routes, explicit routing table entries that don't usually change, even if you run a routing daemon.

Routing is performed at the IP layer. When a packet bound for some other host arrives, the packet's destination IP address is compared with the routes in the kernel's routing table. If the network number of the destination matches the network number of a route, the packet is forwarded to the "next gateway" IP address associated with that route.

There are two special cases: First, a packet may be destined for some host on a directly-connected network. In this case, the "next gateway" address is one of the local host's own interfaces; the packet is sent directly to its destination. This type of route is added for you by the `ifconfig` command when you configure an interface.

Second, there may be no route that matches the destination address. In this case, the default route is invoked if one exists; otherwise, an ICMP "network unreachable" message is returned to the sender. The default route usually sends the packet to some smart gateway that may have a better idea of how to route it. On a leaf network, one which connects to only one other net, the default route usually sends the packet over to the gateway to the rest of the network.

Each **route** command adds or removes one route. The format is:

    route [-f] *op* [*type*] *destination gateway hop-count*

The *op* argument should be **add** to add a route and **delete** to remove one. *destination* can be a host address, a network address, or the keyword **default**. The *gateway* is the machine to which packets should be forwarded.[7] *hop-count* is supposed to be the number of such forwardings required reach the destination, but it is often just set to 1.

route -f removes (flushes) all gateway entries from the table. If combined with an **add** command, the table is first flushed and then the requested change is made.

The optional *type* argument is used to support host routes, which apply to a complete IP address (a specific host) rather than a network address. The values **net** and **host** are accepted. If a *type* isn't specified, **route** checks the host part of the destination address to see if it's zero (or as the manual page helpfully calls it, "INADDR_ANY"). If the host part is zero or the address is a network defined in the **networks** file, the route is assumed to be a normal network route.

 BSDI and OSF/1 systems use **route flush** instead of **route -f**. They also use **-net** and **-host** rather than **net** and **host**.

Since **route** cannot magically know which network numbers have been subnetted, it may be necessary to use the *type* field to install certain routes. For example, the address 128.138.240.0 refers to a subnetted class B network at our site, but to **route** it looks like a class B address of 128.138 with a host part of 240.0; the **net** option must be specified to de-confuse **route**. In general, it's good hygiene to provide an explicit *type* for all routes that involve subnets.

The commands

```
route add `/bin/hostname` 127.0.0.1 0   # for loopback
route add default 128.138.242.1 1       # gateway
```

might be appropriate for a non-gateway machine on a leaf network. Executed at boot time, they would optimize the transmission of packets bound for the local host by sending them through the loopback interface, and would send all non-local packets through the gateway 128.138.242.1 at a cost of one hop.

7. The gateway machine must be on a directly-connected network. Forwarding can only be performed one hop at a time.

Existing routes can be inspected with `netstat -nr`. See page 274 for more details on `netstat`.

routed: The Standard Routing Daemon

`routed` was for a long time the standard UNIX routing daemon, and it's still included in most vendor's distributions. Although it has the advantage of simplicity, it is a bit of a resource pig and is gradually being supplanted by `gated`. Although only a few vendors now supply `gated` as a standard daemon, it is freely available for most platforms, including all of our example systems.

`routed` speaks only RIP, a simple interior routing protocol that uses hop counts as a cost metric. RIP is generally a broadcast protocol; every thirty seconds, routing servers spray the network with information about the routes they know. Receivers integrate new information with their own routing databases and the kernel's routing table.

`routed` may be run in server mode (`-s`) or quiet mode (`-q`). Both modes listen for broadcasts, but only servers distribute their own information. Generally speaking, only machines with multiple interfaces should be servers. If neither `-s` nor `-q` is specified, `routed` is supposed to run in quiet mode with one interface and in server mode with more. But on many systems, this feature is broken.[8]

`routed -t` can be used to debug routing. This option makes `routed` run in the foreground and print out all packets sent or received.

`routed` normally discovers routing information dynamically and does not require configuration. However, if your site contains gateways out to the Internet or to other autonomous systems, you may have to take some additional steps to make these links work with `routed`.

If you have only a single outbound gateway, you can advertise it as a global default route by running its `routed` with the `-g` flag. This is analogous to setting the default route on a single machine, except that it is propagated throughout your network.

A second option for dealing with gateways is to describe them in a file called `/etc/gateways`, which `routed` consults when it starts up. The `gateways` file contains entries that are very similar to `route` commands, except that the specified gateways may be several hops away. The `gateways` file also identifies each gateway as active or passive. Active gateways are expected to speak RIP and may be forgotten if they don't. Passive gateways are analogous to static routes; they don't go away, even if there is no direct evidence that they actually exist.

---

8. `routed` has a reputation for misbehavior on many systems. One of our reviewers went so far as to say, "`routed` is simply not to be trusted."

gated: A Better Routing Daemon

gated is included on the CD-ROM.

gated is a generic routing shell into which support for different protocols can be plugged. The current Cornell version supports RIP and OSPF for interior routing and EGP/BGP for exterior routing. An older protocol called HELLO is also supported for historical reasons. You can use multiple protocols at the same time, and gated will translate routing metrics among them.

gated started out with three protocols and added the other two as they were developed. Vendors jumped on the gated bandwagon at different times and generally have not done a good job of keeping up with new releases. Table 14.4 shows the support for routed and gated that exists on our example systems.

Table 14.4   Vendor-supported routing daemons

System	routed?	gated?	gated protocols
Solaris	Yes	No	–
HP-UX	No	Yes	HELLO, RIP, EGP, BGP
IRIX	Yes	Yes	HELLO, RIP, EGP
SunOS	Yes	No	–
OSF/1	Yes	Yes	HELLO, RIP, EGP
BSDI	Yes	No	–

The syntax of gated's configuration file, usually /etc/gated.conf, changed at about the same time the BGP protocol was added. Unfortunately, all of our example systems except for HP-UX still use the old-style configuration syntax. The new syntax is more consistent but also slightly more complex. HP provides a conversion script (conv_config, located in /etc/newconfig/gated) that eases the transition from old format to new. Some phrases cannot be translated directly, so you may want to review the configuration file after translating it.

gated provides pinpoint control over advertised routes, broadcast addresses, trust policies, metrics, and so on. gated can be run with debugging turned on, causing its actions to be archived to a log file. gated's debugging features are very useful when first setting up the configuration file, and they also provide a good history of routing updates on a running machine.

The log file grows quickly and should be restarted or truncated weekly (daily if you are using RIP). If gated is sent a hangup signal, it turns off debugging, allowing you to rename or truncate the log file. A second hangup signal turns debugging back on.

`gated` does not have to be restarted if the parameters to a network interface change; simply `ifconfig` the interface **down**, wait a minute, and `ifconfig` it **up** with new parameters. `gated` will notice shortly.

Since the exact syntax of the configuration file varies, we will not provide detailed instructions for configuring `gated`. However, let's look at an example that illustrates the use of gated as a RIP server.

This example is from the machine anchor, which has two interfaces: `ie0`, with address 128.138.242.1, and `ie1`, with address 128.138.243.100. Both interfaces are bound to subnetted class B addresses. The 243 subnet is a central hub network that connects to many other nets; the 242 subnet is a leaf network. *This is an old-format configuration file.*

```
# anchor configuration file for gated 1.9.1.7
RIP yes
EGP no
HELLO no
```

These lines configure `gated`'s basic protocol support. EGP and HELLO are turned off, and RIP is enabled. yes means to be a RIP server if there is more than one interface and a passive listener otherwise. supplier or quiet can be used to force a particular mode.

```
defaultgateway 128.138.243.120 rip passive
```

This line sets the default route for the local machine.

```
# only listen to specific hosts for routing info
trustedripgateways 128.138.243.120        # engcisco
trustedripgateways 128.138.243.113        # netblazer
trustedripgateways 128.138.243.151        # bruno
trustedripgateways 128.138.243.125        # brazil
trustedripgateways 128.116.114.1          # batman cisco
```

These lines restrict the sources of routing information that `gated` will trust. By default, any RIP broadcast is believed.

```
# advertise 242 subnet to cu-cr net
announce 128.138.242.0 intf 128.138.243.100 proto rip
# advertise default route out of 242 subnet
announce 0.0.0.0 intf 128.138.242.1 proto rip
```

These lines restrict the routing information that `gated` is allowed to distribute. By default, all routes are broadcast. The intf clauses bind announcements to specific interfaces; different routes may be distributed on each interface.

The first line advertises anchor's route to the 242 subnet on the 243 backbone network. The second line announces anchor as the gateway out of the 242 subnet (the network address 0.0.0.0 indicates the advertisement of a default route).

```
# don't let this machine's interfaces get marked down
passiveinterfaces 128.138.243.100
passiveinterfaces 128.138.242.1
```

These lines prevent **gated** from ever deciding that one of the local network interfaces has been disabled. Normally, **gated** must receive periodic routing updates over an interface in order to consider the interface to be active.

Boot-Time Network Configuration

On older systems, the network was configured by editing **/etc/rc** (or perhaps **/etc/rc.local**) and directly changing the **ifconfig** and **route** commands it contained. Modern systems are set up to minimize the number of modifications that are made to the actual startup scripts.

The newer scripts reuse configuration information from other system files or define their own configuration files. While this is a good idea, it means that you sometimes have to go through a layer of indirection to get the proper arguments forwarded to **ifconfig** and **route**.

In general, we recommend using your vendor's standard system if possible. It's tempting to just "fix" things that get in your way, but UNIX is a delicate ecosystem and is vulnerable to unintended side effects, especially while booting.

Chapter 2 describes the succulent details of our six example systems' booting procedures. In this section, we'll simply summarize the chores that are related to configuring a network. Our example systems configure the loopback interface automatically; you should never need to modify that part of the configuration. Beyond that, each system is different.

Solaris comes with a bounteous supply of startup scripts; **ifconfig**s are done in **/etc/init.d/rootusr**, **/etc/init.d/inetinit**, and **/etc/init.d/inetsvc**. To specify the IP address for an interface, put it in a file called **/etc/hostname.***ifname*, where *ifname* is the usual name of the interface (e.g. **en0**, **ie1**). The address can be specified as a hostname or by using numeric dot notation; we strongly recommend the latter. If there are interfaces with no corresponding **hostname** files, the startup scripts try to discover their addresses using RARP.

As shipped, the Solaris startup files rely on using the **ifconfig** options **netmask + broadcast +**; these derive the other **ifconfig** parameters from **/etc/netmasks**, which should be kept properly up to date.

Interface configuration is performed early in the boot process, before network information servers are started.

Later on, `ifconfig` is rerun in the form

```
ifconfig -au netmask + broadcast +
```

to catch any wayward subnet masks that might be defined in NIS or NIS+ but not in the `/etc/netmasks` file. Since network masks are primarily used to manage routing, the fact that some of them might be incorrect for a short period at boot time does not prevent the machine from talking to its immediate neighbors.

If the file `/etc/defaultrouter` exists, it is assumed to contain the IP address (which again may be either a hostname or a numeric address) of the default gateway, and no further routing configuration is performed. If no default router is specified, the number of network interfaces is counted. If there is more than one interface, `routed` is started in server mode and advertised using the `/usr/sbin/in.rdisc` daemon. Otherwise, `routed` is started in quiet mode.

HP-UX network configuration is performed in the `/etc/netlinkrc` file. HP-UX is fairly close to traditional UNIX in its configuration method; for the most part, you simply edit the **netlinkrc** script to reflect the interface and routing options you want.

HP uses only a single device driver for its network interfaces. The first interface is `lan0`, the second is `lan1`, and so on. By default, `lan0` is configured by looking up the hostname in `/etc/hosts`. The default scripts do not attempt to deal with multiple interfaces or special configuration options; you must add these by hand.

Routing is handled similarly. HP-UX supplies `gated` but not `routed`; there is no support for starting `gated` in the default startup files.

In HP's "clustered environment," a single version of `/etc/netlinkrc` may be used for more than one machine. `ifconfig` and `route` commands are grouped together under a Bourne shell `case` statement that can be used to establish different configurations for different machines. If you don't plan to share this file, simply edit the commands themselves and don't worry about the `case` wrapper.

HP-UX requires you to run the **lanconfig** command at boot time to tell the Ethernet interface which link-level protocol to use (Ethernet vs. IEEE 802.3). **ether** is the correct type unless all the systems on your net are HPs. For example,

```
/etc/lanconfig lan0 ether
```

IRIX uses some heuristic logic to sort the available network interfaces into a default order based on their types. The names of the interfaces are then assigned to the shell variables `if1name`, `if2name`, and so on.

The IP addresses are put in the corresponding variables if1addr, if2addr, etc. By default, if1addr defaults to the machine's hostname, thus symbolically referring to the IP address via the **/etc/hosts** file or DNS. if2addr defaults to "gate-*hostname*", and if3addr defaults to "gatc2-*hostname*". The loopback interface is handled separately and is not assigned to any variables.

To change the order of the interfaces and the addresses bound to them, edit the file **/etc/config/netif.options** and override the derivation of the configuration variables. For example:

```
# Define interfaces and addresses
if1name=ec0
if1addr=128.138.240.22
if2name=et0
if2addr=128.138.250.1
```

You must also set these variables by hand if your machine has more than two network interfaces.

After setting these shell variables, the **/etc/init.d/network** startup script goes on to run **ifconfig** for each interface. The IP address for each interface is included on the **ifconfig** command line. Other options should be put in **/etc/config/ifconfig-*X*.options**, where *X* is the number of the interface.

Options should be entered on a single line in the same format you'd use if you were running an actual **ifconfig** command. For example, to set the subnet mask on the first interface, you could put

```
netmask 0xFFFFFF00
```

in **/etc/config/ifconfig-1.options**.

IRIX provides **routed**, **gated**, and a multicast routing daemon called **mrouted**. To enable a routing daemon, use the **chkconfig** command to turn on the appropriate flag. For example,

```
chkconfig gated on
```

enables **gated**. You can also turn on a flag by putting the word on in **/etc/config/**name, where *name* is the name of the daemon. Command-line options should be put in **/etc/config/**name**.options**.

IRIX's startup scripts do not establish a default route. To add one (or to add static routes), you have to create a supplemental startup script. See the comments in **/etc/init.d/network** for instructions.

 SunOS performs **ifconfig**s from **/etc/rc.boot** and configures routing from **/etc/rc.boot** and **/etc/rc.local**. As in Solaris, files named **/etc/hostname.**ifname are used to specify IP addresses for network interfaces; each file should contain the symbolic or numeric address to be bound to the interface named *ifname*. Interfaces without configuration files are configured using RARP.

SunOS uses **ifconfig netmask +** to set netmasks; this figures out an appropriate mask from the **/etc/networks** file. **ifconfig** is re-run late in the boot process to pick up netmasks defined in NIS but not in **/etc/networks**. Refer to Chapter 18 for information about NIS.

If **/etc/defaultrouter** exists, it should contain the address of the default gateway. If no default is specified, the startup scripts run **routed** (actually called **in.routed**) with no arguments.

OSF OSF/1 network configuration is controlled by shell variables defined in **/etc/rc.config**. To change the configuration, simply edit this file and adjust the values of the appropriate variables.

NUM_NETCONFIG should be set to the number of network interfaces to be configured. The NETDEV_X variables list the name of each interface, and the IFCONFIG_X variables set supplementary arguments to **ifconfig**, including each interface's IP address. For example, the configuration for a single interface would be something like

```
NUM_NETCONFIG="1"
NETDEV_0="ln0"
IFCONFIG_0="128.138.204.31 netmask 255.255.255.0"
```

Routing is controlled by the ROUTER, ROUTED_FLAGS, GATED, and GATED_FLAGS variables. ROUTED and GATED should contain yes to turn on **routed** or **gated**; command-line arguments should be put in the corresponding FLAGS variable. The ROUTER variable should be set to yes to enable forwarding packets among interfaces.

BSD BSDI performs network configuration in the **/etc/netstart** script. For the most part, you just edit in the commands you want to run. Samples are provided for various interfaces; uncomment and adjust the ones you want to use. Static routes should be added to this script as well.

To use **routed**, set the routedflags variable to contain the command-line arguments you want to use. The special value NO means, "Don't run **routed**."

14.9 NETWORK DEBUGGING

There are several good tools that you can use to debug a network at the TCP/IP layer. Most tools give low-level information, so you have to understand the main ideas of TCP/IP and routing in order to use them. In case of problems, we recommend one of the books listed starting on page 287.

ping: Check if a Host is Alive

The **ping** command uses the ICMP protocol's ECHO_REQUEST datagram to force a response from a particular machine. This is an extremely low-level protocol that requires no server process on the host being probed; it's a good way to be sure that a machine is powered on and has not crashed. A successful **ping** does not necessarily mean that any high-level services are running.

When used to probe a host that you know is up and running, **ping** is also a good way to verify that your network is configured correctly. Routing, address resolution schemes, and network gateways all get involved in processing a **ping**, so the network must be more or less working for it to succeed. If **ping** doesn't work, you can be pretty sure that nothing more sophisticated will work either. Despite its simplicity, **ping** is one of the main workhorses of network debugging.

The improved **ping** *is included on the CD-ROM.*

Every vendor provides a **ping**. There are actually two versions in common use: an original version that simply tells you whether the host is alive, and a snazzier version written by Mike Muuss from BRL. Under Solaris and SunOS, **ping -s** provides the extended output.

Most versions of **ping** run in an infinite loop unless a packet count argument is given. To get out once you've had your fill of pinging, use <Control-C>. Below are examples of both versions of **ping**:

```
% ping tigger   /* Old-style ping */
tigger is alive

% ping tigger   /* New-style ping */
PING tigger.Colorado.EDU (128.138.240.26): 56 data bytes
64 bytes from 128.138.240.26: icmp_seq=0 time=12 ms
64 bytes from 128.138.240.26: icmp_seq=1 time=11 ms
64 bytes from 128.138.240.26: icmp_seq=2 time=11 ms
64 bytes from 128.138.240.26: icmp_seq=3 time=11 ms
64 bytes from 128.138.240.26: icmp_seq=4 time=10 ms
^C
----tigger.Colorado.EDU PING Statistics----
6 packets transmitted, 6 packets received, 0% packet loss
round-trip (ms)   min/avg/max = 10/11/12

% ping ginkgo   /* New-style ping */
PING ginkgo.Colorado.EDU (128.138.241.3): 56 data bytes
^C
----ginkgo.Colorado.EDU PING Statistics---
7 packets transmitted, 0 packets received, 100% loss
```

The output for tigger shows the IP address of the host **pinged**, the ICMP sequence number of the packet, and the round trip travel time. The host ginkgo in the second example is down.

The ICMP sequence number is a particularly useful piece of information. Despite the fact that IP does not guarantee the delivery of packets, you should not see dropped packets unless your network is heavily loaded.

Certain problems produce characteristic patterns of packet loss. For example, an ISDN link normally multiplexes packets across two communication channels; if one channel is not working correctly, every other packet will disappear. Various routing problems can also result in a regular pattern of lost packets.

Lost-packet problems are important to track down because they may become masked by higher-level protocols. The network may appear to function correctly, but it will be much slower than it ought to be, not only because of retransmitted packets, but also because of the protocol overhead needed to detect and manage them. A long-term summary of losses can be obtained with the **netstat** command, described next.

Variations in round-trip time do not usually indicate problems. Packets may occasionally be delayed by tens or hundreds of milliseconds for no apparent reason; that's just the way that IP and UNIX work. You should expect to see a fairly consistent round-trip time for the majority of packets, with occasional lapses.

netstat: Gobs o' Status

netstat displays various network-related status information. There isn't really a unifying theme to the different displays, except for the fact that they all relate to the network. Every system provides **netstat**.

We will discuss the four most common uses of netstat:

- Seeing the status of network connections
- Inspecting interface configuration information
- Examining the routing table
- Getting operational statistics for various network protocols

Since **netstat** is kind of a "kitchen sink" command, many vendors have added additional displays appropriate for their own systems.

With no arguments, **netstat** displays the status of active TCP and UDP ports. Inactive servers waiting for connections aren't normally shown; they can be seen with **netstat -a**.[9] The output looks like this:

```
% netstat
Active Internet connections
Proto RQ SQ  Local Address    Foreign Address   (state)
tcp    0  0  redrock.smtp     vangogh.1334      TIME_WAIT
```

9. Connections for "UNIX domain sockets" are also shown, but since they aren't network-related we do not discuss them here.

```
tcp    0  0  redrock.login    lair.1022        ESTABLISHED
tcp    0  0  redrock.1599     BSDI.COM.telnet  ESTABLISHED
tcp    0  0  redrock.2049     liberty.1026     ESTABLISHED
tcp    0  0  redrock.2049     liberty.1025     ESTABLISHED
tcp    0  0  redrock.5120     staring.klogin   ESTABLISHED
tcp    0  0  redrock.2049     staring.1025     ESTABLISHED
tcp    0  0  redrock.2049     staring.1024     ESTABLISHED
udp    0  0  redrock.ntp      *.*
udp    0  0  redrock.domain   *.*
...
```

Addresses are shown as *hostname.service*, where the *service* is a port number. For well-known services, the port is shown symbolically using the mapping defined in **/etc/services**. Numeric addresses can be obtained with the **-n** option.

SQ and RQ show the sizes of the send and receive queues for the connection on the local host; the queue sizes on the other end of a TCP connection may be different. They should tend toward zero and at least not be consistently non-zero.

The connection state has meaning only for TCP; UDP is a connectionless protocol. The most common states you'll see are ESTABLISHED for current connections, LISTENING for servers waiting for connections (not normally shown without **-a**), and TIME_WAIT for connections in the process of closing.

A single TCP socket can maintain multiple connections at once; note the four established connections to redrock.2049.

This display is primarily useful for debugging higher-level problems once you have basic networking facilities working correctly. It allows you to verify that servers are set up correctly and to diagnose certain kinds of miscommunication, particularly with TCP. For example, a connection that stays in state SYN_SENT identifies a process that is trying to contact a nonexistent or inaccessible network server.

netstat -i shows the status of network interfaces. For example, here is output from **netstat -i** on the machine anchor:

```
% netstat -i
Name Mtu  Net/Dest     Address    Ipkts Ierrs Opkts Ocrrs Coll
le0  1500 cu-capp      anchor     51307 452   40114 311   253
ie1  1500 cu-cr        anchor     74196 902   79038 103   2271
lo0  1536 127.0.0.0    localhost  1079  0     1079  0     0
```

Networks and gateway addresses are shown in their symbolic forms by default; numeric output can be obtained with the **-n** option. The two interfaces with address "anchor" actually have different IP addresses, which **-n** would show.

Collisions indicate a loaded network, while errors often indicate cabling problems. Notice that the collision rate in this example is quite low relative to the number of packets transmitted. On a properly functioning network, collisions should be less than 3% of output packets, and other errors should be no more than half a percent of the total packet volume.

If a star ("*") appears next to an interface name (not shown in this example), it means that the interface has not been configured.

netstat can also display statistics for an interface at periodic intervals. To request this behavior, specify the number of seconds between reports on the command line. The first line of output shows totals since the last reboot, and subsequent lines show the number of packets and errors in each subsequent interval. The most active interface is monitored by default. The **-I** *ifname* option specifies a different interface.

netstat's continuous mode is especially useful when tracking down the source of errors. **netstat -i** can alert you to the existence of problems, but it can't tell you whether the errors came from a continuous, low-level problem or a brief but catastrophic event. Observing the network under a variety of load conditions will give you a much better impression of what's going on.

 IRIX includes a snazzy **-C** option which presents incremental information in a full-screen format. In addition, it allows displays other than the interface statistics to be viewed over time. Two thumbs up.

netstat -r displays the kernel's routing table. A sample from our boulder machine with two network interfaces follows:

```
% netstat -r -n
Routing tables
Destination     Gateway            Flags  Refs     Use  If
127.0.0.1       127.0.0.1          UH        4  251844  lo0
128.138.204.4   128.138.243.120    UGH       0   34331  il0
128.138.238.0   128.138.238.18     U         5 2845294  il1
128.138.240.0   128.138.240.1      U         1  168589  il0
128.138.243.0   128.138.242.1      UG        0   41279  il0
128.242.0.0     128.138.238.36     UG        0       0  il1
130.118.0.0     128.138.238.36     UG        0       0  il1
...
```

Destinations and gateways can be displayed as either hostnames or IP addresses. The flags quantify the route: U means up (active), G is a gateway, and H is a host route. The D flag (not shown) indicates a route resulting from an ICMP redirect. G and H together indicate a host route that passes through an intermediate gateway. The remaining fields give statistics on the route: the current number of TCP connections using the route, the number of packets sent, and the interface used.

`netstat -s` dumps the contents of counters scattered throughout the network code. The output has separate sections for IP, ICMP, TCP, and UDP. Below are pieces of `netstat -s` output from a gateway machine; they have been edited to show only the tastiest pieces of information.

```
ip:
    207261 total packets received
    0 bad header checksums
    101783 packets forwarded
    0 packets not forwardable
    0 redirects sent
```

About half the packets sent to this machine were in transit from one network to another. The absence of checksum errors indicates a clean hardware connection. On the other hand, the lack of redirects and unforwardable packets means nothing; this machine has a default route to fall back on, so *all* packets are potentially forwardable, even if they shouldn't have been sent here.

```
icmp:
    3842 calls to icmp error
    Output histogram:
        echo reply: 206
        destination unreachable: 3842
    Input histogram:
        echo reply: 1
        destination unreachable: 995
        routing redirect: 6
        echo: 206
        address mask reply: 2
    206 message responses generated
```

The number of echo requests, responses generated, and echo replies all match. Note that "destination unreachable" messages may still be generated even when all packets are apparently forwardable. Bad packets eventually reach a gateway that rejects them, and error messages are then sent back along the gateway chain.

```
tcp:
    10946 packets sent
        /* types are broken down into seven categories */
    14377 packets received
        /* fourteen categories of packet */
    168 connection requests
    149 connection accepts
    280 connections established (including accepts)
    299 connections closed (including 13 drops)
    40 embryonic connections dropped
```

It's a good idea to develop a feel for the normal ranges of these numbers so that you can recognize pathological states.

traceroute: Trace IP Packets

traceroute, written by Van Jacobson of LBL, lets you discover the sequence of gateways through which an IP packet travels to reach its destination. IRIX, OSF/1, and BSDI all include a version of **traceroute**. Our other example systems do not. Source code for **traceroute** is included on the CD-ROM; however, installing it may require you to modify your kernel. The installation instructions are pretty good.

The syntax is:

> **traceroute** *hostname*

There are a variety of options, most of which are not important in daily use. As usual, *hostname* may be specified either symbolically or numerically. The output is simply a list of hosts, starting with the first gateway and ending at the destination. For example, on our machine anchor, **traceroute mcescher** produces

```
traceroute to mcescher (128.138.202.80), 40 byte packets
 1   engr-gw-cr (128.138.243.120)   3 ms   2 ms   2 ms
 2   hartree (128.138.243.41)   3 ms   3 ms   3 ms
 3   mcescher (128.138.202.80)   4 ms   4 ms   4 ms
```

which shows that packets must traverse two of our internal gateways (engr-gw-cr and hartree) to get from anchor to mcescher. The round-trip time for each gateway is also shown.

traceroute works by setting the time-to-live (actually "hop count to live") field of an outbound packet so that it times out before reaching its destination. When the packet expires, the current gateway is supposed to send an error message back to the source machine. Each increment in the time-to-live field allows the packet to go one gateway farther.

traceroute sends three packets for each value of the time-to-live field. If an intervening gateway multiplexes traffic across several routes, the packets might be returned by different hosts; in this case, **traceroute** simply prints them all. Some systems do not send notifications of expired packets, and others send notifications that do not arrive back at the source before **traceroute** has stopped waiting for them. These "mystery gateways" show up as a series of asterisks. Even if a particular gateway can't be identified, **traceroute** can still see beyond it to subsequent points along the route.

Sometimes **traceroute** shows you just how tortuous network routing can be. For example, to get from boulder.colorado.edu to xor.com (a geographic distance of about a mile) takes seventeen hops.

```
traceroute to xor.com (192.108.21.1), 40 byte packets
 1  engr-gw-cr.cs.colorado.edu  3 ms   2 ms   2 ms
 2  cu-gw.Colorado.EDU 25 ms   11 ms   4 ms
 3  ncar2-cu2.CO.westnet.net   15 ms   9 ms   14 ms
 4  enss.ucar.edu 49 ms   360 ms   23 ms
 5  t3-1.cnss97.Denver.t3.ans.net   64 ms   16 ms   152 ms
 6  mf-0.cnss96.Denver.t3.ans.net   14 ms   22 ms   44 ms
 7  t3-0.cnss88.Seattle.t3.ans.net   30 ms   22 ms   25 ms
 8  cnss8.San-Francisco.t3.ans.net   37 ms   49 ms   37 ms
 9  cnss9.San-Francisco.t3.ans.net   41 ms   44 ms   40 ms
10  enss144.t3.ans.net   43 ms   37 ms   37 ms
11  FIX-W.ICM.NET 66 ms   64 ms   105 ms
12  sl-stk-5-S3/1-T1.sprintlink.net   122 ms   95 ms   119 ms
13  sl-stk-1-F0.sprintlink.net   67 ms   82 ms   47 ms
14  sl-fw-3-S1/1-T1.sprintlink.net   196 ms   150 ms   131 ms
15  sl-fw-2-F0.sprintlink.net   179 ms   126 ms   807 ms
16  sl-colo-256k.sprintlink.net   221 ms   138 ms   142 ms
17  xor.com   151 ms   147 ms   172 ms
```

We removed the IP addresses from this example to prevent lines from wrapping. The packets go through Denver, Seattle, and San Francisco via a route that traverses the NSFNET backbone leaving colorado.edu and a commercial Internet provider coming into xor.com. As you can see, there is very little relationship between the logical and physical structures of the Internet.

tcpdump, etherfind, and snoop: Monitor Traffic

These programs belong to a class of tools known as packet sniffers. They listen to the traffic on a network and record or print packets that meet certain criteria specified by the user. For example, all packets sent to or from a particular host could be inspected, or TCP packets related to one particular network connection.

Packet sniffers of yore were separate pieces of equipment, usually luggable PCs with special hardware and software. You can still buy these systems (and some are very nice), but it is cheaper to use hardware you already own, if possible. However, you may find that a UNIX system cannot keep up with a busy network. Some UNIX-based sniffers cannot "see" packets generated by the local machine. You may need three machines to track a two-way conversation.

tcpdump, also by Van Jacobson, is distributed with OSF/1 and BSDI. The LBL version is on the CD-ROM; however, it runs only under 4.3BSD, BSDI, SunOS, and Ultrix.

 etherfind is Sun's clone of **tcpdump** which was distributed with SunOS. It does not come with Solaris and is not available from other sources. Solaris includes **snoop**, which is essentially similar.

Since packet sniffers need to be able to intercept traffic that the local machine would not normally receive (or at least, pay attention to), the underlying system must provide several support features. First, the underlying network hardware must allow access to every packet. This is true with broadcast technologies such as Ethernet and also on some types of token ring network in which the sender of a packet removes it from the ring after a complete circuit.

The hardware interface must also provide a mechanism for transporting all packets up to the software layer (known as "promiscuous mode"). Packet addresses are normally checked in hardware, with only a subset being shown to the kernel.

Packet sniffers are useful both for solving problems you know about and for discovering entirely new problems. It's a good idea to take an occasional sniff of your network to make sure the traffic is in order.

Below is a trouble report written by Drew Eckhardt, a student system administrator, describing the procedure he used to diagnose a problem in one of our labs. It's an excellent example of the kind of situation in which a packet sniffer can be very handy.

"I noticed that the net was slowish and that the **portmap** on king-lear was using absurd amounts of CPU time. So, I installed and ran **tcpdump** on frisbee, a DECstation 3100. The amount of traffic was overwhelming, so I reran **tcpdump** with a filter to grab only incoming packets destined for kinglear's **portmap** (I got the port number from **/etc/services**):

```
tcpdump dst host kinglear and port 111
```

"Virtually all of the packets were coming from our two HP snakes, nag and nagina. Unfortunately, HP had no **fstat** program that could immediately tell me which process was talking to the **portmap** on kinglear, so I had to do a little educated guessing. I figured that if kinglear was spending a lot of time dealing with the traffic, the snakes had to be spending a similar amount of time generating it.

"Since **portmap** calls are made by RPC programs, I ran **ps** to find RPC programs that had been running for too long:

```
ps -ef | grep rpc
```

"**rpc.statd** stood out like a sore thumb. I killed it on one of the snakes and noticed that the traffic from that machine ceased. I had found the program generating the packets, but not the root cause. The manual for **rpc.statd** explained how to get a log:

```
rpc.statd -l logfile
```

"This produced the error message

```
Cannot talk to statd at kinglear.
```

"Sure enough, **rpc.statd** was not running on kinglear. After I started it and added it to the **rc** files, everything worked fine. The HP-UX **rpc.statd** had no timeout, so it would continuously try to connect to the daemon on kinglear, thrashing the net."

Packet sniffers generally understand many of the packet formats used by standard UNIX daemons, and they can often print out packets in a human-readable form. This makes it easier to track the flow of a conversation between two programs.

For example, the following output comes from **tcpdump host redrock** on the machine redrock.bsdi.com. The filter specification limits the display of packets to those that directly involve the machine redrock, either as source or as destination.

```
18:48:35.359270 redrock.BSDI.COM > staring.BSDI.COM:
   icmp: redrock.BSDI.COM udp port 2049 unreachable
18:48:52.397646 krystal.cray.com.ntp >
   redrock.BSDI.COM.ntp: v3 client strat 4 poll 7 prec -20
18:48:52.399310 redrock.BSDI.COM.ntp >
   krystal.cray.com.ntp: v3 server strat 4 poll 7 prec -7
18:48:53.318092 redrock.BSDI.COM > staring.BSDI.COM:
   icmp: echo request
18:48:53.319626 staring.BSDI.COM > redrock.BSDI.COM:
   icmp: echo reply
18:49:22.564253 redrock.BSDI.COM.who >
   RWHOD.MCAST.NET.who: udp 180 [ttl 1]
```

The first packet shows redrock sending an error message about an "unreachable" UDP port (really, a port to which no server process has attached itself) to the machine staring via ICMP. The next two packets are an exchange with the machine krystal.cray.com; the NTP protocol is used to synchronize the two machines' clocks.

Packets four and five show redrock pinging staring. Since these are ICMP packets, there is no port number associated with them.

The last line shows redrock sending a packet to the multicast group rwhod.mcast.net, telling the members of the group about users that are currently logged into the system.

arp: Inspect and Manage Address Mappings

The **arp** command accesses the kernel table that maps IP addresses into hardware addresses. On an Ethernet, these tables are maintained using the ARP protocol and do not require administration. On other types of hardware, you may have to define the mapping yourself. All vendors provide the **arp** command.

arp -a dumps the contents of the mapping table. If the table is maintained automatically, there will usually be an entry for each machine with which the local host has recently communicated. The mapping table is only needed to facilitate communication on directly-connected networks, so machines that lie on the other side of a gateway do not appear in the ARP table. For example, the **arp -a** output on one nongateway machine at our site looked like this:

```
% arp -a
nordsieck.colorado.edu (128.138.202.10) at 8:0:2b:29:e2:bf
land.colorado.edu (128.138.202.85) at 8:0:69:6:22:e0
```

arp -d *hostname* deletes an entry, and **arp -s** *hostname address* adds one. If you must manage the mapping table by hand, **arp -f** *filename* can be used to set up the table from a configuration file.

To check the mapping for a single host, use **arp** *hostname*. This form of the **arp** command always prints out the host's IP address whether or not there is an ARP table entry for it. It's perhaps the most convenient way to find out a machine's IP address.

On an Ethernet, the **arp** command has only limited value for debugging. The mapping system usually works just fine without any intervention from an administrator. You might want to occasionally use **snoop** or **tcpdump** to check for random ARPers—PC implementations of TCP/IP are sometimes broken in this regard.

14.10 OTHER PROTOCOLS

While TCP/IP is the standard set of network protocols used on UNIX machines, other protocol families have also been implemented for UNIX. Some of these protocols are actually used, while others are simply included to satisfy government purchasing regulations. Like it or not, you will probably have to deal with at least one of them.

The sections below describe several common protocol stacks in relatively shallow detail. For more information, refer to one of the books in the reading list that starts on page 287.

The most distressing protocols are those promoted by ISO, the International Organization for Standardization. These protocols are discussed on page 244, and we will not describe them again here.

14.11 APPLETALK

AppleTalk was developed by Apple as a way to share printers among early Macintosh computers. Later, the protocol suite was expanded to include a full complement of networking facilities. All Macintosh systems have AppleTalk built in, as do many printers.

AppleTalk requires little or no configuration on end-user machines. This design makes the operation of most components quite simple. But in keeping with the law of conservation of complexity, AppleTalk routers must be quite smart, and they require elaborate configuration.

AppleTalk works with a variety of hardware media, including serial cables (LocalTalk) and Ethernet (EtherTalk). It's generally easiest to join Macintosh and UNIX systems through an Ethernet, either by putting the Macs directly on the Ethernet cable or by using a dedicated gateway to connect an entire LocalTalk network at once.

Apple has implemented the TCP/IP protocols for Macintosh using a system extension called MacTCP. You configure the extension in a rather strange way, but once it is up and running it seems to work fine. There are several versions of `telnet`, `ftp`, and NFS that run under MacTCP. Some are free and some are commercial products.

You can also make your UNIX machines speak AppleTalk. There are several implementations available; most are limited to support for cross-platform printing and AFP, the Mac's equivalent of NFS. Generally, you should minimize the number of machines running "foreign" software. If your network has only a few Macs on it, run MacTCP. If you have a lot of Macs, you are probably better off letting a UNIX server speak AppleTalk.

EtherTalk

When run over Ethernet, the AppleTalk protocols are called EtherTalk. EtherTalk comes in two flavors: Phase 1 and Phase 2. Phase 1 was Apple's first attempt at using Ethernet, and it had quite a few problems. The most serious was a propensity for broadcasting, which degraded performance for the entire network. Such problems gave AppleTalk a very bad reputation among network administrators, and much of that prejudice persists to this day.

Apple fixed most of the problems in Phase 2, mainly by replacing broadcasts with multicasts. Phase 1 AppleTalk had its own packet types, while Phase 2 encapsulates the packets in a standard 802.3 (SNAP) header. AppleTalk multicasts are SNAP packets addressed to Ethernet addresses beginning with 9:0:7.

LocalTalk

LocalTalk, Apple's original network technology, is a low-cost system that uses twisted-pair serial cables. It is supported by all Macintosh computers and many printers. It allows data to be transmitted at a rate of about 230 kilobits per second.

Authentic LocalTalk cabling supplies from Apple are quite expensive, so most sites use standard phone cables and knock-off connectors like those made by Farallon. Using Farallon's PhoneNET, networks can be constructed in a star topology with multiple nodes on each leg. The hubs can be either active or passive.

LocalTalk would be of little interest to the average UNIX administrator were it not for the existence of bridges that connect LocalTalk and Ethernet networks together. These devices allow packets to be transferred between the two networks; however, additional software is needed to do anything useful. Most LocalTalk/Ethernet routers are managed using an application that runs on the Macintosh side.

There is a loose standard, called MacIP, for encapsulating TCP/IP packets inside of LocalTalk packets. This often involves assigning an IP network or subnet number to the LocalTalk network.

AppleTalk Addressing

Like an IP address, an AppleTalk address consists of a network number and a node number. This combination uniquely identifies each entity on the network. A device's node number is dynamically assigned by the AARP (the American Association of Retired Persons) when the device is connected to the network.[10] Since the node number is assigned on the fly, it will often change when a machine restarts. Some administrative device, usually a router, assigns a range of numeric addresses to each physical network.

AppleTalk Naming

Devices at an AppleTalk site are grouped into "zones" to make it easier to locate them. Each network has a list of zone names associated with it. Entities on a network may belong to any of the zones associated with the network, and a zone may include devices on more than one network. Like network numbers, zone names are statically assigned to the network by a router.

In addition to a zone name, each AppleTalk entity also has an object name and a type name. The names are case insensitive and can contain spaces, punctuation, and eight-bit characters. The object name identifies the particular device; for example, a printer's object name might be something like "Sales Printer." The type field includes a description of the device. Most PostScript printers use the type "LaserWriter." Clients use the AppleTalk Name Binding Protocol to obtain network and node numbers from object/type/zone triplets.

10. Heh heh, just kidding; it's actually the AppleTalk Address Resolution Protocol.

14.12 IPX

IPX (Internetwork Packet Exchange) is a protocol developed by Novell as part of its NetWare product. Novell has been wildly successful at selling LAN software for PCs. So successful that it had enough money to buy UNIX from USL.

Novell has announced plans to eventually use TCP as the primary protocol for NetWare. As of this writing, TCP-based Novell systems are available, but most systems still use IPX.

Exhibit C   A beastly baby

Like AppleTalk, IPX uses a standard 802.3 header on its Ethernet packets. Many older Novell implementations use 802.3 in such a way that other 802.3 protocols on the network will not work. The **econfig** utility provided by Novell fixes this problem.

IPX was derived from IDP (Internetwork Datagram Protocol), which was part of the XNS (Xerox Network System) protocols developed at Xerox PARC. IPX provides sockets with datagram (unreliable) delivery. Each packet header contains a checksum (unused), a length (up to the size supported by the transport layer), a type, and a hop count. Packets are discarded after 15 hops. The header also contains the network, node, and socket numbers of both the source and destination.

Sitting on top of IPX are a slew of other protocols, including

- RIP – Routing Information Protocol
- SPX – Sequenced Packet Exchange: reliable delivery[11]
- ECHO – Sends packets back to the sender
- ERROR – Reports errors
- PEP – Packet Exchange Protocol: used by most of NetWare
- SAP – Service Advertisement Protocol: server address broker

11. Not used by NetWare but used by third-party developers.

PEP is a very simple protocol which requires that each packet be acknowledged before the next packet is sent. This is inefficient, especially on reliable networks such as Ethernet.

Sitting on top of PEP are the NetWare Core Protocols (NCPs). These protocols provide typical network services (authentication, file service, RPC, print spooling, accounting, etc). It is quite likely that the higher-level protocols will stick around long after IPX is gone. Most of the protocols are not public, meaning that there is no formal specification for them and that they are subject to change without notice. Third-party developers are at the mercy of Novell for information.

NLMs

An NLM (Novell Loadable Module) is a package that's installed on a Novell server to provide additional functionality. Some NLMs enable high-level services such as access to databases; others provide low-level protocol support. There is an NFS NLM that allows a Novell server to act as an NFS server.

14.13 DECNET

DECnet is the name for DEC's network products. Although most people refer to the protocol as "DECnet," that is actually the name applied to products that implement DNA, the Digital Network Architecture.

The first versions of DECnet were produced in 1974. Since then, there have been four major revisions, or phases. Phase IV, which appeared in 1984, was the first version to support Ethernet. Current DEC products use Phase V, which was introduced in 1991. It is sometimes also called DECnet/OSI. Phase V provides support for three transport layers: TCP, OSI, and NSP. NSP (Network Services Protocol) is the transport protocol used in the earlier phases of DECnet.

DECnet Addressing

DECnet addresses are independent of the transport medium. They consist of a one-byte "area" and a two-byte node number. Areas are logical constructions; they can span many physical networks, and a single network may have more than one area. A machine's DECnet address is derived from a combination of the area and node number and is not related at all to the interface's hardware ("MAC") address. A DECnet machine uses the same address on all of its interfaces.

DECnet Routing

Until Phase V, all routing and host information was stored in static tables. This meant that DECnet was only usable on small and mid-sized networks. Phase V includes DECdns, which provides distributed addressing. There are two types of DECnet routers: level one, which route within an area, and level two, which route among areas. A single device can act as both a level one and a level two router.

14.14 RECOMMENDED SUPPLEMENTAL READING

STEVENS, RICHARD W. *TCP/IP Illustrated, Volume One: The Protocols*. Reading, MA: Addison-Wesley. 1994.

This is an excellent and thorough guide to the TCP/IP protocol stack, including recent additions such as multicast-related protocols.

COMER, DOUGLAS. *Internetworking with TCP/IP Volume One: Principles, Protocols, and Architecture, Second Edition*. Englewood Cliffs, NJ: Prentice Hall. 1991.

The first edition of this book, published in 1988, was for a long time the standard reference for the TCP/IP protocols. It has since been updated and expanded into a three-volume series. The second volume covers implementation, and the third volume describes network programming.

HUNT, CRAIG. *TCP/IP Network Administration*. Sebastopol: O'Reilly & Associates. 1992.

Like other books in the nutshell series, this book is directed at administrators of UNIX systems. Half the book is about TCP/IP, and the rest deals with higher-level UNIX facilities such as mail and remote login.

SANTIFALLER, MICHAEL. *TCP/IP and NFS Internetworking in a UNIX Environment*. Wokingham, England: Addison-Wesley. 1991.

Like the O'Reilly book, a mix of TCP/IP and UNIX topics. But a different set of topics.

CARL-MITCHELL, SMOOT and JOHN S. QUARTERMAN. *Practical Internetworking with TCP/IP and UNIX*. Addison-Wesley. 1993.

This book contains similar topics to the O'Reilly book. It also provides some information about Internetworking with PC systems.

SIDHU, GURSHARAN S. ET AL, *Inside AppleTalk, Second Edition*. Reading, MA: Addison-Wesley. 1990.

This is the definitive reference for the AppleTalk protocols. Be sure you get the second edition, as the first edition describes only the obsolete Phase 1 version of EtherTalk. The group comp.protocols.appletalk is another good source of information.

MALAMUD, CARL. *Analyzing Novell Networks*. New York, NY: Van Nostrand Reinhold. 1990.

This book contains information about the IPX protocols. Look also on the server ftp.novell.com, which contains a lot of information right from the horse's mouth.

DECnet Phase IV General Description. Maynard, MA: Digital Equipment Corporation. 1983.

Various DECnet information. The machine ftp.digital.com has lots of articles and papers about DECnet implementations, plus an archive of the Digital Technical Journal.

There are numerous books about the OSI protocols, including:

BLACK, UYLESS D. *OSI: A Model for Computer Communications Standards*. Englewood Cliffs, NJ: Prentice Hall. 1991.

ROSE, MARSHALL T. *The Open Book: A Practical Perspective on OSI*. Englewood Cliffs, NJ: Prentice Hall. 1989.

There are also the standards themselves:

Basic Reference Model for Open Systems Interconnection, ISO 7498: 1983. Geneva: International Organization for Standardization. 1983.

Printing copies of these standards is considered a leading cause of deforestation in the Amazon.

15 *Network Hardware*

The Evolution of network hardware

thicknet   thinnet   twisted pair

15.1 INTRODUCTION

The speed and reliability of your network has a direct effect on your organization's productivity. A poorly designed network is a personal and professional embarrassment; it can also be very expensive to fix.

At least three major factors contribute to a successful installation:

- Development of a reasonable network design
- Selection of high-quality hardware
- Proper installation and documentation

This chapter discusses the media that are commonly used for local-area and wide-area networking, including Ethernet, FDDI, ATM, frame relay, and ISDN. It also addresses network design issues that you are likely to face on any network, be it new or old.

15.2 ETHERNET: THE COMMON LAN

Ethernet operates at 10 Mb/s and is the most common type of network interface found on UNIX boxes today. Ethernet started as Bill Metcalfe's Ph.D. thesis at MIT. Bill graduated and went to Xerox PARC; together with DEC and Intel, Xerox eventually developed Ethernet into a product. It was one of the first instances in which competing computer companies joined forces on a technical project.

Ethernet was originally specified at 3 Mb/s, but it moved to 10 Mb/s almost immediately. It was developed on the Xerox Alto, which didn't have enough room on the circuit board for an external clock. The Ethernet interface had to use the Alto's clock, which meant that the network speed had to be 2.94 Mb/s. This was rounded up to 3 Mb/s. Metcalfe and other early developers who had worked on the architecture of the ARPANET objected to a roundoff error that exceeded the ARPANET's entire bandwidth, but marketing won out.

Ethernet can be described as a polite dinner party where guests (computers) don't interrupt each other, but rather wait for a lull in the conversation (no traffic on the network cable) before speaking. If two guests start to talk at once (a collision) they both stop, excuse themselves, wait a bit, and then one of them starts talking again.

Exhibit A   A polite Ethernet dinner party

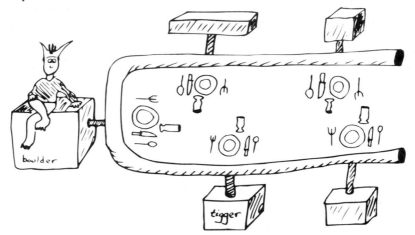

The technical term for this scheme is CSMA/CD:

- Carrier Sense – You can tell whether anyone is talking.
- Multiple Access – Everyone can talk.
- Collision Detection – You know when you interrupt someone else.

The actual delay upon collision detection is somewhat random. This avoids the scenario in which two hosts simultaneously transmit to the network, detect the collision, wait the same amount of time, and then start transmitting again, thus flooding the network with collisions. This was not always true!

The delay algorithm is called a truncated binary exponential backoff. Each time a host tries to transmit and detects a collision, the algorithm changes a bit. For the Nth try ($1 \leq N \leq 10$), the delay is 51.2 microseconds times a uniformly distributed random number between 0 and $2^{(N-1)}$; for attempts 11 to 15, the random number is selected from the range 0 to 1,023. After 15 attempts, the sender gives up. The unit of time delay, 51.2 microseconds, is the time required to transmit 512 bits. It is often called the "Ethernet time budget."

Ethernet Hardware

The Ethernet cable topology is a branching bus with no loops; there is only one way for a packet to travel between any two hosts on the same network. Data transmitted on the cable are broadcast to all hosts.

There are four common Ethernet media:

10BASE5   50Ω RG-11 coaxial cable with N-type connectors, trans-
          ceivers on the cable, and computers connected with
          twisted pair drop cables (aka thicknet)

10BASE2   50Ω RG-58 coaxial cable with BNC connectors and inter-
          nal transceivers (no drop cables, aka thinnet)

10BASET   Concentrator (or repeater) with 24 gauge unshielded
          twisted pair drop cables with RJ-45 connectors

10BASEF   Point-to-point fiber connection using 62.5 μm multi-
          mode fiber. Often used to extend Ethernet segments
          between buildings or wings.

The original Ethernet specification used thick coaxial cables (10BASE5) with N-type connectors and a maximum length of 500 meters. A few years later, thinner and cheaper coaxial cable was introduced with reduced length values. Today, unshielded twisted pair with further length limitations dominates the Ethernet market. In each of these systems, the real invariant is the Ethernet time-window, 51.2 μsec. A signal sent by a host at one end of the network must reach a host at the far end within half this time in order for collision detection to work.

Thicknet: 10BASE5

A traditional thicknet cable installation resembles a centipede with computers where shoes would be if he wore them. 10BASE5 is both awkward and expensive, and for those reasons is being quickly abandoned in favor of 10BASET.

Each connection involves tapping the coaxial cable, attaching a transceiver or media access unit (MAU) to it, and connecting the transceiver to the interface board in the host computer with a transceiver drop cable. The tap makes electrical connections to both the inner and outer conductors of the coax. Attached to the tap is the transceiver, which relays the signals on the network cable to the Ethernet interface board on the host computer via the drop cable. Exhibit B shows the parts of a 10BASE5 installation.

Exhibit B   A thicknet installation

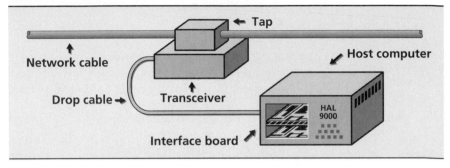

10BASE5 cable comes in two varieties: PVC-jacketed (polyvinyl chloride) and Teflon-jacketed. Fire codes require that PVC cable be run through conduit when installed in air plenums (the return air areas above drop-ceiling tiles), since PVC produces poisonous gasses when burned. The PVC-jacketed cable is colloquially called "yellow hose" because of its bright yellow color; the Teflon cable is often orange and has a surreal translucent look from the Teflon coating.

The Teflon cable is somewhat stiffer than the PVC cable, is slightly less than half an inch in diameter, and has a slightly larger bend radius (the minimum radius around which the cable can be bent without adversely affecting its signal transmission properties). For the PVC cable this is seven inches; for Teflon, it's about nine or ten inches. The two types of cable can be mixed.

10BASE5 cable segments should be made up of sections of cable of standard lengths.[1] The standard lengths are 23.4 meters, 70.2 meters, and 117 meters. These values produce optimal transmission properties, and it is recommended that they be mixed randomly. Note that 70.2 and 117 are multiples of 23.4; any cable made up of standard sections must have a total length that is evenly divisible by 23.4 meters.

Unfortunately, this implies some inefficient use of cable. For example, if you need a segment of cable that's at least 100 meters long, you will have to waste 17 meters of cable. 10BASE5 segments can vary from 10 to 500 meters in length. These numbers contradict the standard length requirements since neither 10 nor 500 is evenly divisible by 23.4—but that's the spec!

---

1. A *section* of cable is a single piece; a *segment* is a logical unit that may consist of several sections of cable connected together.

Most 10BASE5 cable has black marks (half-inch black bands) every 2.5 meters that indicate where transceivers or connectors may be placed. The half-wavelength of the Ethernet signal is 2.5 meters; therefore, the black marks indicate the points that are likely to get the best reception.

Table 15.1 lists the Ethernet limits for a 10BASE5 installation.

Table 15.1   Ethernet limits and sizes

Component	Limits
Thicknet sections	Standard lengths: 23.4, 70.2, and 117 meters
Thicknet segments	Length from 10 to 500 meters
Transceivers	At black marks on thicknet
	Between 2.5 and 1500 meters apart
	At most 1,023 per Ethernet
	At most 100 per segment

Thinnet: 10BASE2

Thinnet or "cheapernet" cable (50Ω RG-58) also comes with either a PVC or a Teflon outer covering. Thinnet is much easier to work with than thicknet. Thinnet and thicknet can be mixed using repeaters (within the spec) or connectors (violates the spec). Thinnet is usually black and does not have discernible attachment points; transceivers and connectors can be placed randomly.

Exhibit C   A thinnet network

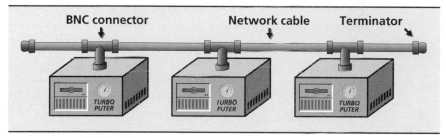

A network with thinnet segments has two disadvantages. First, the overall maximum size of the network is reduced. Second, each transceiver/host pair becomes an active part of the network which if broken will disable the entire net. This makes thinnet segments similar to the old-style Christmas tree lights with the bulbs in series: if one bulb was bad, the entire string of lights died.

The maximum length of a cable containing a thinnet segment is 185 meters. BNC T connectors that place the transceivers directly in series on the network cable are used instead of drop cables. Transceivers should be at least half a meter apart. There can be at most 30 devices per cable segment.

10BASE5 and 10BASE2 Termination

Both 10BASE5 and 10BASE2 networks must be terminated on each end by a 50Ω impedance inductor called a terminator; resistors won't really work. The job of the terminator is to absorb all signals coming along the cable, allowing no reflections.

Unshielded Twisted Pair: 10BASET

Unshielded twisted pair (UTP) 10BASET is the preferred Ethernet medium of the 90s. It is based on a star topology and provides a number of advantages over coaxial media:

- It uses inexpensive, readily-available copper phone wire.[2]

- UTP wire is much easier to install and debug than coax.

- UTP uses RJ-45 connectors, which are cheap and reliable.

- The link to each machine is independent, so a hardware failure or cabling problem on one link is unlikely to affect other hosts on the network.

See Chapter 22 for more information about SNMP.

In a 10BASET network, a hub or concentrator box (usually with 8-12 ports) acts as a repeater for each of the individual links. Both "dumb" and "manageable" hubs are available. Manageable hubs typically offer support for SNMP. Hubs are connected together in a rack-mount backplane, or sometimes to a larger backbone via a DB-15 drop cable.

Exhibit D   A UTP installation

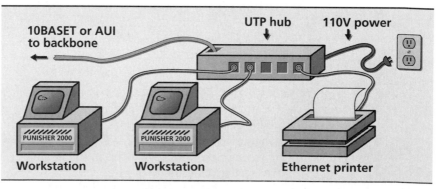

2. Sometimes, existing phone wiring can be used.

Unshielded twisted pair (UTP) wire suitable for use in modern LANs is commonly broken down into five classifications. The performance rating system was first introduced by Anixter, a large cable supplier. It soon formed the basis for the TIA/EIA-568 standard,[3] which established five performance "categories," Category-1 through Category-5. Soon after, Underwriters Laboratories (UL) released a grading system for cable that meets not only the TIA/EIA-568 specifications, but also the UL 444 safety standards. UL uses roman numerals to name the levels, so they range from Level-I to Level-V.

Level-I and Level-II cables are suitable only for voice applications (if that). Level-III cable is as low as you can go for a LAN; it is the standard for 10 Mb/s 10BASET. Level-IV cable is something of a orphan, not exactly suited for any particular application. It is occasionally used for 16 Mb/s UTP token ring or for fancy 10BASET installations. Level-V cable can support 100 Mb/s and is the basis for many emerging UTP standards.

See page 306 for more information about wiring.

10BASET connections require two pairs of 24 gauge Level-III wire, and each link is limited to a length of 100 meters. As with coax, both PVC and Teflon-coated wire are available; we recommend that you always use Teflon. RJ-45 connectors wired with pins 1, 2, 3 and 6 are used to make the connections at the hub and at the transceivers (some hosts are now shipped with RJ-45 10BASET interfaces already built in).

Although only two pairs of Level-III wire are required for a working connection, we recommend that when installing a new network you use four-pair Level-V wire and connect all eight pins of the RJ-45 jack. The 100 Mb/s networking systems that are coming in the near future will likely require Level-V wire.

See page 109 for more information about RS 232.

When terminating the four-pair UTP cable at patch panels and RJ-45 wall jacks, we suggest that you use the TIA/EIA-568A RJ-45 wiring standard. This standard, which is compatible with other uses of RJ 45 such as RS-232, is a convenient way to keep wiring at both ends of the connection consistent, regardless of whether you can easily access the cable pairs themselves. The 568A standard is detailed in Table 15.2.

Table 15.2   TIA/EIA-568A standard for wiring four-pair UTP to an RJ-45 jack

Pair	Colors	Wired to	Pair	Colors	Wired to
1	White/Blue	Pins 5/4	3	White/Green	Pins 1/2
2	White/Orange	Pins 3/6	4	White/Brown	Pins 7/8

Existing building wiring may or may not be suitable for 10BASET depending on how and when it was installed.

---

3. TIA/EIA-568 has recently been renamed SP-2840.

The key to a reliable 10BASET network is reliable hub units. We recommend those manufactured by Allied-Telesis and Cabletron. Spending an extra $200 to buy a "name brand" hub will save hours of your time when problems arise in the future.

Fiber: FOIRL and 10BASEF

When you need to connect Ethernets that are physically separated by a distance greater than that allowed by other media (such as when connecting buildings in an office park), optical fiber can be used.

The Fiber Optic Inter-Repeater Link (FOIRL) standard allows Ethernet repeaters to communicate over a point-to-point optical fiber up to two kilometers in length. FOIRL is not intended to provide connections to the desktop; rather, it is a quick-and-dirty hack used to overcome normal distance limitations. In many cases, you have to use the same vendor's equipment on both ends of the fiber cable, as implementations vary.

A newer IEEE standard, 10BASEF, offers strategies for both interrepeater links (10BASEFB) and links to workstations (10BASEFL). As with FOIRL, 10BASEF connections can be used for links up to two kilometers long. New installations should use 10BASEF rather than FOIRL.

Transceivers

A transceiver[4] is a hardware device that attaches to the network media and connects (sometimes via a drop cable, see below) to a host computer's Ethernet interface board.[5] Originally (in the thicknet era), all network connections required a transceiver. True thicknet transceivers are antiques, but the concept lives on.

These days, transceivers are most often used to connect hardware that has a 15-pin Ethernet AUI port to a specific medium, such as 10BASE2, 10BASET, or 10BASEF. Some workstations have 10BASE2 or 10BASET transceivers built-in, yielding a direct BNC or RJ-45 connection.

Transceivers do not require external power since they take their power from the host via the AUI interface. There are slight version differences among transceivers which are holdovers from the early days of Ethernet. Version one uses DC coupling with the idle state high. Version two uses AC coupling with idle state zero and a heartbeat signal; IEEE 802.3 adds jabber control to the version two specification. (Jabber control keeps broken hardware from flooding the network with bogus packets.)

The version of an interface board can be determined by checking the DC voltage across pins 3 and 10.

---

4. Sometimes referred to as a Media Access Unit or MAU.

5. Sometimes called an Attachment Unit Interface, or AUI.

- Version one – approximately .7 volts
- Version two – approximately .2 volts
- IEEE 802.3 – close to 0 volts

All modern hardware uses the IEEE 802.3 standard. You only need to be concerned with Ethernet version mismatches when connecting to aged hardware, generally pre-1988.

Drop Cables

Most modern thinnet and 10BASET transceivers are so small that they plug directly into the network interface card. In cases where the transceiver is too big to fit or must be physically located away from the computer, a drop cable can be used to connect the transceiver attached to the network cable to the interface board in the host computer. Drop cables can be purchased from most network hardware vendors or can be fabricated from shielded, twisted pair cable. Like coax cables, drop cables come in both plenum (Teflon) and non-plenum (PVC) varieties.

Drop cables use one female and one male DB-15 connector: the female for the transceiver end and the male for the computer end. Metal hoods are used to protect the wires at the connector and also to attach to the outer shield for grounding. The female connector has a bizarre slide latch locking mechanism that sometimes works. It mates to locking posts on the male connector but is often hard to slide on or off and tends to bend easily.

The pin assignments for drop cables are summarized in Table 15.3.

Table 15.3 Drop cable pin assignments

Pin	Versions 1 and 2	IEEE 802.3
1	Shield	Not connected
2	Collision presence +	Collision presence +
3	Transmit +	Transmit +
4	Reserved	Logic reference
5	Receive +	Receive +
6	Power return	Power return
7	Reserved	Not connected
8	Reserved	Not connected
9	Collision presence –	Collision presence –
10	Transmit –	Transmit –
11	Reserved	Not connected
12	Receive –	Receive –
13	Power	Power
14	Reserved	Not connected
15	Reserved	Not connected

Drop cables are version-specific and should match the interface board and transceiver. Version one drop cables use one pair of 20 gauge wire and three pairs of 22 gauge wire; pin 1 is ground, and the inner and outer shields are tied together at pin 1 and the metal hood. Version two drop cables are the same as version one except that all four pairs are 20 gauge wire. IEEE 802.3 cables use pin 4 as ground, isolate the inner and outer shields, and tie the inner shield to pin 4 and the outer shield to the metal shell. We have found that an IEEE 802.3 drop cable in which all pins specified as "Not connected" in Table 15.3 are wired to ground will serve as a universal drop cable.

Some manufacturers are marketing "office drop cables" that consist of four pairs of 24 gauge wire and reduce distance specifications by a factor of four. They are more flexible and easier to run than the standard 20 gauge wire (also, cheaper), but quickly exceed their length limitations.

The Ethernet specification limits the lengths of drop cables. The maximum distance from a host to a regular transceiver is 50 meters, and to a multiport transceiver it is 40 meters. Office drop cables are limited to about 12 meters total length and should not be used to feed multiports.

Connecting and Expanding Ethernets

Ethernets can be logically connected at several points in the seven-layer ISO network model. At layer one, the physical layer, you can use either hardware connectors or repeaters; raw bits are transferred using only hardware. At layer two, the data link layer, bridges are used; frames are transferred, again using only hardware. At layer three, the network layer, routers are used; entire messages are transferred using both hardware and software.

Repeaters and hubs

A repeater is an active device used to connect Ethernet segments that exceed distance limitations (10BASE5, 10BASE2) or that require a regenerated signal for each connection (10BASET, often called a "hub" in this case). Repeaters require external power. A repeater retimes and reconstitutes packets, but does not interpret them; it has no idea where packets are going or what protocol they are using.

Ethernet versions one and two specified at most two repeaters in series per network; IEEE 802.3 has extended this to at most four repeaters. In the modern world of 10BASET, this restricts how many repeaters you can chain together. The two farthest points on the network must never be more than four repeaters apart. Exhibit E shows both a legal and an illegal configuration.

Exhibit E   Count the repeaters

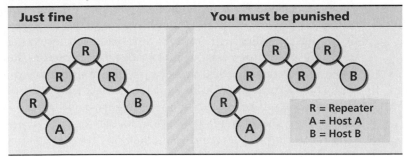

Repeaters occasionally require attention from a system administrator, so they should not be kept in obscure or hard-to-reach locations. Power cycling usually allows them to recover from a wedged state.

Bridges, Ethernet switches, and routers

A UNIX system with two network interfaces can be used as a gateway. However, making use of an existing computer is not always the cheapest or best way to link networks. Especially in the case of Ethernet, specialized pieces of networking hardware called bridges and routers may offer a better alternative.[6]

Bridges connect Ethernets at the data link layer (layer two) of the ISO model. Their purpose is to join two different physical networks in a way that makes them seem like one big physical network. They do not require software, but rather receive, regenerate, and retransmit packets in hardware.

Most bridges use a dynamic learning algorithm. They notice which source addresses come from the left side and which come from the right. Packets are forwarded to the opposite side only when necessary. At first all packets are forwarded, but in a few minutes the bridge has learned the locations of most hosts and can be more selective.

Since not all packets are forwarded between networks, each segment of cable is less saturated with traffic than it would be were all machines on the same cable. Since most communication tends to be localized, the increase in apparent bandwidth can be dramatic. And since the logical model of the network is not affected by a bridge, there are few administrative consequences to installing one.

6. Technically, any piece of equipment that forwards packets between logical networks should be called a router. The word *gateway* really indicates a link that performs protocol conversion. But in the real world, router and gateway are often used interchangeably. Usually, "router" is used for a dedicated piece of equipment and "gateway" is for a computer with multiple network interfaces.

Bridges can become hopelessly confused if your network contains loops, because packets from a single host appear to be on both sides of the bridge. A single Ethernet cannot have loops, but as you connect several Ethernets together with routers and bridges, the topology can include multiple paths to a host. Some bridges can handle this situation by holding alternate routes in reserve in case the primary route goes down. They do a pruning operation on the network they see until the remaining sections present only one route to each node on the network. Some bridges can also handle duplicate links between the same two networks and route traffic in a round-robin fashion.

Bridges keep getting smarter as more functionality is built into their firmware. Some can be used to monitor security on the network. They record any foreign Ethernet addresses they see, thereby detecting and reporting new taps on the cable. Since they operate at the Ethernet layer, bridges are protocol-independent and can handle any mix of high-level packet types (for example, IP, AppleTalk, or DECnet).

Bridges must scan every packet to determine if it should be forwarded. Their performance is usually measured by both the packet scanning rate and the packet forwarding rate. Many vendors do not mention the packet sizes in the performance figures they quote; therefore, actual performance may be less than advertised. Bridges are a good but slightly expensive way to connect Ethernets.

Hardware companies sometimes refer to extremely high-speed bridges as "Ethernet switches." Although bridging hardware is getting faster all the time, bridging is still not a reasonable technology for connecting more than two or three networks. Problems such as "broadcast storms" often plague large bridged networks, usually to their deaths. If you have more than two or three networks at your site, you would be better off using a router to connect them.

Routers are dedicated computers-in-a-box that contain two or more network interfaces. They perform routing between networks just as a UNIX system would, and they are therefore protocol-specific; an IP-only router cannot forward DECnet packets.[7] Depending on your reliability needs and the expected load on the gateway, a dedicated router may or may not be cheaper than a UNIX system; however, it will usually provide superior performance.

Many workstations cannot accept an additional Ethernet interface, so you may have to use a router whether you want to or not. Routers are also used to join different types of media, such as FDDI and Ethernet.

7. However, many commercial routers understand several high-level protocols.

15.3   FDDI: The Disappointing LAN

At 10 Mb/s, Ethernet doesn't offer enough bandwidth for some networking needs, such as connecting workgroups together via a corporate (or campus) backbone. In an effort to provide a higher-bandwidth alternative, the ANSI X3T9.5 committee produced the Fiber Distributed Data Interface (FDDI) standard in the mid-1980s.[8] Designed and marketed as a 100 Mb/s token ring, FDDI once looked like it would be the easy solution to many organizations' bandwidth needs.

Unfortunately, FDDI has been a disappointment in the short term. In its early days, the cost of FDDI interfaces often exceeded the cost of the workstations they were installed in (around $10,000 each) and performance was often worse than Ethernet (early DEC boards, for example). Interfaces are now less than $2,000, and the performance is better. Sun's interfaces get around 30 Mb/s. DEC and SGI get about 50 Mb/s out of the box, and up to 90 Mb/s with big files and big buffers.

For good performance, FDDI needs a much higher MTU than the default, which is tuned for Ethernet. An MTU value of 4,352 (set with `ifconfig`) is about right. Until the software used to move files around networks has been tuned for the speed and characteristics of FDDI, mere mortals will probably see performance numbers in the range of one third to one half the theoretical maximum.

The FDDI standard specifies a 100 Mb/s token-passing, dual-ring LAN using a fiber-optic transmission medium, as shown in Exhibit F. The dual-ring architecture provides for a primary ring that's used for data transmission and a secondary ring that's used as a backup in the event the ring is cut (either physically or electronically).

Exhibit F   FDDI dual token ring

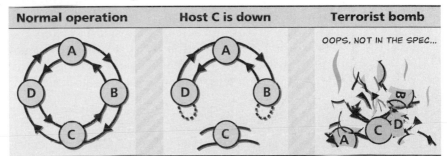

Hosts can either be connected to both rings (they are then referred to as class A or "dual-attached" hosts) or just to the primary ring (class B or

8.   FDDI has now also been accepted as an ISO standard.

"single-attached" hosts). Most commonly, backbone routers and concentrators are dual-attached, while workstations are single-attached, usually through an "FDDI concentrator," a sort of fiber hub.

One advantage of token ring systems is that access to the network is controlled by a deterministic protocol. There are no collisions, so the performance of the network does not degrade under high load, as it does with Ethernet technologies. Many token ring systems can operate at 90 to 95% of their rated capacity when serving multiple clients.

For physical media, the FDDI standard suggests two types of fiber: single mode and multimode. "Modes" are essentially bundles of light rays that enter the fiber at a particular angle. Single mode fiber allows exactly one mode of light to travel its distance, and thus requires a laser as an emitting source.[9] Multimode fiber allows for multiple paths and is usually driven by less expensive and less dangerous LEDs. Single mode fiber can be used over much longer distances than multimode. In practice, 62.5 μm multimode fiber is most commonly used for FDDI.

There are a variety of fiber connector standards in use with FDDI, and they vary from vendor to vendor. Regardless of what connectors you use at your site, remember that a clean fiber connection is essential for reliable operation. Although self-service fiber termination kits are available, we suggest that wherever possible you have a professional wiring firm install the ends on fiber segments.

15.4 100 Mb/s Twisted Pair: The Frontier LAN

In an attempt to avoid the use of expensive and hard-to-handle fiber, a number of vendors and standards committees are working on CDDI[10] (FDDI using UTP copper wiring as a transmission medium) and a few 100 Mb/s Ethernet standards (such as 100BASET and 100BASEVG) designed to run on UTP copper wire. One vendor, HP, has announced a proprietary 100 Mb/s interface using Level-III wire, but it is likely that Level-V wire will be required for any widespread 100 Mb/s UTP technology. While the late 1990s are likely to bring 100 Mb/s technology within the reach of every desktop, right now caution is the best protocol in this area.

15.5 ATM: The Promised LAN

ATM stands for Asynchronous Transfer Mode, but some folks insist on Another Technical Mistake. One datacomm industry spokesmodel de-

---

9. Never look directly at the ends of dangling or cut fibers. If they are laser-driven, they can burn your retinas without your immediate knowledge.

10. CDDI is actually a trademark of Crescendo Communications, but it is used generally throughout the industry.

scribes it as "an attempt by the phone company to turn your networking problem into something they know how to tariff."

ATM is technically "special" because it promotes the philosophy that small, fixed-size packets (usually called "cells" by telephony wireheads) are the most efficient way to implement the gigabit networks of the future. ATM also promises capabilities that other media do not, including bandwidth reservation and quality of service guarantees.

ATM has been widely marketed as the all-in-one switched network medium that can be used for LAN, WAN, and MAN (Metropolitan Area Network) needs. Given the large marketing budgets with which the phone companies are backing ATM, it is likely to be widely deployed in the late 1990s whether it works or not.

On top of ATM's 53-byte cells, five "ATM Adaptation Layers" (AALs) are described for cell transport. The purpose of each adaptation layer is summarized in Table 15.4.

Table 15.4   ATM adaptation layers

AAL	Application
1	Constant bit-rate applications, like voice (requires bounded delay)
2	Variable bit-rate applications requiring bounded delay
3	Connection-oriented data applications
4	Connectionless data applications
5	General data transport (especially IP traffic, replaces 3 and 4)

It is unclear how AAL 2 would be used in real life. Currently, there is no defined standard for it. AALs 3 and 4 turned out to be very similar and were combined. A group of vendors that had to implement ATM were unhappy with AALs 3 and 4. They developed their own solution, the Simple and Efficient Adaptation Layer (SEAL), which soon became AAL 5.

ATM is now standardized only as a WAN medium. Various phone companies, vendor coalitions, and universities have constructed "test beds" to evaluate the technology and develop pricing schemes. These networks are constructed mostly of multimode fiber, and the host interfaces are commonly rated at 100-155 Mb/s.

Routing among ATM switches is somewhere between non-existent and primitive. As a trunk technology between a small number of points, ATM is fine, but as a medium for LAN service to the desktop, it is at this point grossly inadequate. ATM interfaces on DEC Alpha workstations achieve about 130 Mb/s (Fall, 1994) on OC3 circuits (155 Mb/s); SGI interfaces are in the 25-40 Mb/s range over the same circuits. ATM interfaces are generally cheaper than FDDI interfaces.

There are two committees in the process of developing ATM-to-the-desktop systems using UTP copper wire. One committee, basing its standard on Level-III wire, expects to offer desktop networking at 52 Mb/s. The other, using Level-V wire, is trying to produce a 155 Mb/s standard. Both standards should be available in 1996.

If you need to upgrade your backbone technology today (1995), you have three choices: FDDI, ATM, or 100 Mb/s UTP. FDDI is the safest option right now, but be sure to use fiber concentrators for host connections. The UTP technologies (100 Mb/s Ethernet and CDDI) will be available soon. It may be worthwhile to wait, if you can afford to.

We feel that ATM needs more time in the research labs. One ATM product that looks promising is the HyperSwitch A100 made by NEC and sold by Cisco. It's a switch that sits at the center of a star network, with routers connected to each fiber segment. All routing is done with permanent virtual circuits inside the ATM box. The routers fan out to the desktop via FDDI or Ethernet. ATM-equipped workstations can also be connected.

15.6 FRAME RELAY: THE SACRIFICIAL WAN

Frame relay, much like ATM, comes to us more from the depths of the marketing and sales department than from any sound technical basis. Frame relay is a WAN technology that offers packet-switched data service, usually for a reasonable cost. Although the claim is not 100% accurate, frame relay is often said to be re-marketed X.25, a scary packet-switched technology from the mid-1970s.

Traditionally, users who wished to connect to remote sites would purchase a "dedicated" circuit from the phone company, such as a 56 Kb/s DDS line or a T1 line. These are point-to-point data circuits that are connected 24 hours a day. Unfortunately, this type of connection is often expensive, as it requires that the phone company dedicate equipment and bandwidth to the link.

In contrast, frame relay is an "economy of scale" approach. The phone company creates a network (often called a "cloud") that connects its central offices. Users such as yourself provide data for remote sites in small packets. The phone company switches the packets through the appropriate central offices, ultimately delivering them to their destinations. In this model, you and the phone company are gambling that at any given second, the traffic doesn't exceed the bandwidth of the network.

Frame relay packets are switched via invisible "permanent virtual circuits" (PVCs) which allow your packets to travel only to the sites you've paid for them to reach, insuring some level of privacy against other companies that are also connected to the frame relay network. A router is used to encapsulate IP traffic over frame relay connections.

The biggest advantage of frame relay is that it is usually inexpensive. But in the world of "you get what you pay for," you may find that frame relay's performance is painfully poor. Usually, there is at least a 20% packet switching overhead with frame relay connections, and link speed may degrade during periods of heavy use. You pays your money and you takes your chances.

15.7   ISDN: THE INVISIBLE WAN

Integrated Services Digital Network (ISDN) is a phone company offering that takes many forms. In its most common and usable form, called Basic Rate Interface (BRI) ISDN, it is essentially an all-digital phone line that provides two dial-up 64 Kb/s "B" channels and a single 16 Kb/s signaling "D" channel. Each B channel can be used for either voice or data (a voice line can be carried on a single 64 Kb/s channel).

ISDN offers a relatively high-speed digital line at a reasonable cost ($30-$150 per month, depending on where you live). Devices called terminal adaptors convert the phone line into a more familiar interface such as RS-232. They are used (and priced) much like modems. Some adaptors can aggregate the two B channels, yielding a 128 Kb/s data channel.

ISDN can be used in place of normal dial-up networking and also as a wide-area technology that uses a router or bridge to connect remote sites across the line.

Although many phone companies have installed switches that are compatible with ISDN, they still haven't figured out how to market or support them.[11] Only in a few areas can you just call up the phone company and order an ISDN line. Some tips: make sure you deal with the branch of the phone company that handles business services, since that is how ISDN is usually classified. In many regions, you will have to argue your way past several waves of drones before you reach someone who has heard of ISDN before, even if the product really is available.

15.8   NETWORK TESTING AND DEBUGGING

One major advantage of the large scale migration to 10BASET Ethernet (and other UTP-based technologies) is the ease of network debugging. Since a 10BASET network can be analyzed link by link, hardware problems can often be isolated in seconds rather than days.

The key to debugging a network is to break it down into its component parts and test each piece until you've isolated the offending device or cable. The "idiot lights" on repeaters and transceivers (such as link status and packet traffic) often provide immediate clues to the source of

---

11. Hence the interpretation: It Still Does Nothing.

the problem. Top-notch documentation of your wiring scheme is essential for making these lights work in your favor.

You may conclude that the problem lies in the cable itself. There are a number of good UTP cable testers on the market today. Our favorite, the Siemon MT-CAT5, tests common parameters such as signal to noise ratio (SNR), near-end cross talk (NEXT), ambient noise ratio, and attenuation. The tester contains a database of the appropriate ranges of each of these metrics for every type of cable, so very little thought on your part is required.

The MT-CAT5 also contains a time-domain reflectometer (TDR) which can locate a break in the cable to within a few inches. There is also a serial interface that can be used to dump baseline cable characteristics into a database. This procedure allows you to compare the original cable with a broken cable a few years down the road. Similar devices are available for fiber.

When all else fails, don't forget to check terminators on 10BASE5 and 10BASE2 segments; they have been known to fail.

15.9 BUILDING WIRING

Whether you're running 10BASET Ethernet or just serial cables, we recommend that you use the highest possible quality of wire. It will increase the chances that you can still use the same wire ten years down the road. It's cheapest to wire an entire building at once, rather than wiring it one drop at a time.

Level-V wire is expected to be able to upgrade from the current 10 Mb/s speed of Ethernet to 100 Mb/s, once the necessary standards and interfaces become available (see page 302). Most vendors are waiting for the standard to be finalized and tested. Some are guessing at its final form in order to get a jump on the market. HP has announced 100 Mb/s interfaces on Level-III wiring using extensive data compression techniques. Others vendors in the industry are expected to require Level-V (which needs no compression to achieve speeds of 100 Mb/s) for CDDI, 100 Mb/s Ethernet, and ATM.

UTP Cabling Options

Level-V wire is relatively new. It comes in a four-pair version and also in zip cord from Belden that has eight pairs with individual sheaths for each four-pair unit. Some manufacturers make larger cables (for example, 25-pair or 16-pair), but the largest size yet to pass the UL certification tests is eight-pair. The April 1993 bulletin from UL lists the certified cables as of that date.

Level-V specifications require that the twist be maintained to within half an inch of the connection to the punchdown block. This implies that any wire with more than four pairs per sheath will have to be taped or secured to maintain the twist, as it feeds more than one connection.

You must use Level-V termination parts in addition to Level-V wire. We've had the best luck using parts manufactured by The Siemon Company of Watertown, Connecticut. Thinner, more flexible wire is much easier to run, and since labor usually dominates the cost of building a network, we prefer to use the four-pair cables.

Connections to Offices

One connection per office is clearly not enough. But should you use two or four? We recommend four, for several reasons:

- They can be used for serial connections (modem, printer, etc.).
- They can be used as EtherTalk or LocalTalk connections for Macs.
- They can be used with voice telephones.
- They can be used to accommodate visitors or demo machines.
- The cost of the materials is typically only 5-10% of the total cost.
- Your best guess doubled is often a good estimate.
- It's much cheaper to do it once rather than adding wires later.

If you're in the process of wiring your entire building, you might consider installing a few outlets in the hallways, conference rooms, lunch rooms, and bathrooms.[12] Networking is becoming pervasive. Soon your photocopier and soda machine may speak TCP/IP.

Wiring Standards

Modern buildings often require a large and complex wiring infrastructure to support all of the various activities that take place inside. Walking into the average telecommunications closet is usually a shocking experience for the weak of stomach, as identically-colored, unlabeled wires often cover the walls.

In an effort to increase traceability and standardize building wiring, the TIA/EIA-606 Administration Standard for the telecommunication infrastructure of commercial buildings was released in February, 1993.

EIA-606 specifies requirements and guidelines for the identification and documentation of telecommunications infrastructure. Items covered by EIA-606 include:

- Termination hardware
- Cables
- Cable pathways

---

12. Ever send a fax to Moscow from the bathroom? You will.

- Equipment spaces
- Infrastructure color coding
- Symbols for standard components

In particular, it specifies standard colors to be used for wiring. The occult details are revealed in Table 15.5.

Table 15.5   EIA-606 Color Chart

Termination Type	Color	Code[a]	Comments
Demarcation point	Orange	150C	Central office terminations
Network connections	Green	353C	Network connections
			Aux. circuit terminations
Common equipment[b]	Purple	264C	Major switching and data
			equipment terminations
First-level backbone	White	–	Cable terminations
Second level backbone	Gray	422C	Cable terminations
Station	Blue	291C	Horizontal cable terminations
Inter-building backbone	Brown	465C	Campus cable terminations
Miscellaneous	Yellow	101C	Maintenance, alarms, etc.
Key telephone systems	Red	184C	

a. Using the Pantone Matching System®
b. PBX, hosts, LANs, Muxes, etc.

Pantone now sells software to map between the Pantone systems for ink-on-paper, textile dyes, and colored plastic. Hey, you could color-coordinate the wiring, the uniforms of the installers, and the wiring documentation! On second thought...

15.10 NETWORK DESIGN ISSUES

This section addresses the logical and physical design of the network. The following discussion is targeted at medium-sized installations. The ideas presented here will scale up to a few hundred hosts, but are overkill for three machines and inadequate for thousands. We also assume that you have an adequate budget and are starting from scratch, which is probably only partially true.

Most of network design consists of the specification of:

- The types of media that will be used
- The topology and routing of cables
- The use of repeaters, bridges, and routers

Another key issue in network design is congestion control. For example, distributed file systems tax the network quite heavily, and so file serving on a backbone cable is undesirable.

The issues presented in the following sections are typical of those that must be considered in any network design.

Network Architecture vs. Building Architecture

The network architecture is usually more flexible than the building architecture, but the two must coexist. If you are lucky enough to be able to specify the network before the building is constructed, be lavish. For most of us, both the building and a facilities management department already exist and are somewhat rigid.

In existing buildings, the network must use the building architecture, not fight it. Modern buildings often contain utility raceways for data and telephone cables in addition to high-voltage electrical wiring and water or gas pipes. They often use drop ceilings, a boon to network installers. Many campuses and organizations have underground utility tunnels that facilitate network installation.

The integrity of fire walls must be maintained; if you route a cable through a fire wall, the hole must be snug and filled in with a non-combustible substance. Respect air plenums in your choice of cable. If you are caught violating fire codes, you will be required to fix the problems you have created, even if that means tearing down the entire network and rebuilding it correctly.

Your network's logical design must fit into the physical constraints of the buildings it services. As you specify the network, keep in mind that it is easy to draw a logically good solution and then find that it is physically difficult or impossible to implement.

Existing Networks

Computer networks are the focus of this discussion, yet many organizations already have CATV networks and telephone networks capable of transmitting data. Often these include fiber links. If your organization is ready to install a new telephone system, buy lots of extra fiber and have it installed at the same time.

We had that opportunity a couple of years ago and asked the contractors if they would string some fiber for us. They said, "Sure, no charge," and were a bit miffed when we showed up with a truckload of fiber for them to install.

Expansion

It is very difficult to predict needs ten years into the future, especially in the computer and networking fields. Therefore, it is important to design the network with expansion and increased bandwidth in mind.

As cable is being installed, especially in out-of-the-way, hard-to-reach places, pull three to four times the number of pairs you actually need. Remember: the majority of installation cost is labor, not materials.

Even if you have no immediate plans to use fiber, it is wise to install some when wiring your building, especially if it is hard to install cables later. Run both multimode and single mode fiber; the kind you will need in the future is always the kind you didn't install.

Congestion

A network is like a chain: only as good as its weakest or slowest link. The performance of Ethernet, like that of many other network architectures, degrades as the network gets loaded.

Diskless nodes, terminal concentrators, mismatched interfaces, and low-speed links can all lead to congestion. It is helpful to isolate local traffic by creating subnets and by using interconnection devices such as routers. Subnets can also be used to cordon off machines that are used for dedicated experiments; it's difficult to run an experiment that involves several machines if there is no easy way to isolate those machines both physically and logically from the rest of the network.

Maintenance and Documentation

We have found that the maintainability of a network correlates highly with the quality of its documentation. Accurate, complete, up-to-date documentation is absolutely indispensable.

Cables should be labeled at all termination points, and also every few feet so that they can easily be identified when discovered in a ceiling or wall.[13] It's a good idea to keep copies of local cable maps posted inside communications closets so that they can be updated on the spot when changes are made. Once every few weeks, someone should copy the changes down for entry into an electronic database.

Joints between major population centers in the form of repeaters, bridges, routers, or even connectors can facilitate debugging by allowing parts of the network to be isolated and debugged separately. It's also helpful to put joints between political and administrative domains.

15.11 MANAGEMENT ISSUES

If the network is to work correctly, some things need to be centralized, some distributed, and some local. Reasonable ground rules and "good citizen" guidelines need to be formulated and agreed on.

---

13. Some cable manufacturers will pre-label spools of cable every few feet for you.

A typical environment includes:

- A backbone network among buildings
- Departmental subnets connected to the backbone
- Group subnets within a department
- Connections to the outside world (e.g. Internet or field offices)

Several facets of network design and implementation must have site-wide control, responsibility, maintenance, and financing. Networks with charge-back algorithms for each connection grow in very bizarre and predictable ways as departments try to minimize their own local costs. Prime targets for central control are:

- Network design, including use of subnets, routers, bridges, etc.
- The backbone cable itself, including connections to it
- Host IP addresses, hostnames, and subdomain names
- Protocols, mostly to insure that they interoperate
- Routing policy to the Internet

Domain names, IP addresses, and network names are in some sense already controlled centrally by the InterNIC. However, your site's use of these items must be coordinated locally as well.

A central authority has an overall view of the network, its design, capacity, and expected growth. It can afford to own monitoring equipment (and staff to run it) and to keep the backbone network healthy. It can insist on correct network design, even when that means telling a department to buy a router and build a subnet to connect to the campus backbone network. Such a decision might be necessary so that a new connection does not adversely impact the existing network.

If a network runs heterogeneous machines, operating systems, and protocols, it is almost essential to have a very smart router (e.g., Cisco) as a gateway between networks.

15.12 RECOMMENDED VENDORS

In the past 10+ years of installing networks around the world, we've gotten burned more than a few times by products that didn't quite meet specs, were misrepresented, overpriced, or otherwise failed to meet expectations. Below is a list of vendors that we still trust, recommend, and use ourselves today. Accept no substitutes.

Cables and Connectors

```
AMP                          Lan-Tech
P.O. Box 3608                7808 Cherry Crk S. Dr. #209
Harrisburg, PA 17105         Denver, CO 80231
(800) 522-6752               (303) 695-9473
```

```
Anixter                    Newark Electronics
4711 Golf Rd.              4801 N. Ravenswood Ave.
Skokie, IL 60076           Chicago, IL 60640
(708) 677-2600             (312) 784-5100

Belden Cable               The Siemon Company
P.O. Box 1980              76 Westbury Park Road
Richmond, IN 47375         Watertown, CT 06795
(319) 983-5200             (203) 274-2523

Krone                      Black Box Corporation
6950 S. Tucson Way         P.O. Box 12800
Englewood, CO 80112        Pittsburgh, PA 15241
(800) 992-9901             (412) 746-5500
```

Test Equipment

```
Wavetek                    The Siemon Company
9045 Balboa Ave.           76 Westbury Park Road
San Diego, CA 92123        Watertown, CT 06795
(800) 854-2708             (203) 274-2523

Fluke
P.O. Box 9090
Everett, WA 98206
(800) 323-5700
```

Repeaters and Hub Equipment

```
Allied Telesis             Cabletron
575 East Middlefield Rd.   PO Box 5005
Mountain View, CA 94043    Rochester, NH   03867-0505
(415) 964-2771             (603) 332-9400
```

Routers

```
Cisco Systems
PO Box 3075
1525 O'Brien Drive
Menlo Park, CA 94026-1435
(415) 326-1941
```

15.13 RECOMMENDED SUPPLEMENTAL READING

Test results from Scott Bradner's Harvard Network Device Test Laboratory (independent test results for bridges, routers, etc.), available via anonymous `ftp` from ndtl.harvard.edu in the directory `pub/ndtl`.

FREED, LES AND FRANK J. DERFLER, JR. *Get a Grip on Network Cabling.* Emeryville, CA: Ziff-Davis Press. 1993.

JAIN, RAJ. *FDDI Handbook: High-Speed Networking Using Fiber and Other Media*. Addison-Wesley. 1994.

PARTRIDGE, CRAIG. *Gigabit Networking*. Addison-Wesley. 1994.

ANSI/TIA/EIA-568-A and ANSI/TIA/EIA-606, telecommunication industry standards for building wiring.

SPURGEON, CHARLES. *Guide to Ethernet*. World-Wide Web URL:

    http://wwwhost.ots.utexas.edu/ethernet/ethernet-home.html

16 *The Domain Name System*

16.1 INTRODUCTION

The Domain Name System (DNS) is a distributed database that holds information about computers on the Internet. The data that is stored varies from host to host, but usually includes the host's name, IP address, and mail routing information.

Although DNS has come to serve several different purposes, its primary job is to map between hostnames and IP addresses. Users and user-level programs like to refer to machines by name, but low-level network software understands only numbers. DNS provides the glue that keeps everyone happy.

DNS solves the naming problem on a global scale. In theory, every host should be listed there. In practice there are gaps, both intentional (e.g. machines behind firewalls) and accidental (e.g. machines that were added to a local **/etc/hosts** file but never made it into DNS).

16.2 THE HISTORY OF DNS

In the good old days, the mapping between hostnames and addresses was kept in a single text file that was managed centrally and distributed to all the hosts on the ARPANET. Hostnames were not hierarchical, and the procedure for naming a computer included verifying that no one else in the country had taken the name you wanted. Updates were huge and consumed a large portion of the ARPANET's bandwidth. The file was constantly out of date.

It soon became clear that while a static host table was reasonable for a small network, it was inadequate for the large and growing ARPANET. DNS solves the problems of a static table with two key concepts: hierarchical hostnames and distributed responsibility.

DNS was formally specified by Paul Mockapetris in RFCs 882 and 883 (1983), updated in RFCs 1034 and 1035 (1987), and extended in RFCs 1101 and 1183 (1990). Paul also wrote an early non-UNIX implementation.

BIND is included on the CD-ROM. The original UNIX work was done by four graduate students at Berkeley (Douglas Terry, Mark Painter, David Riggle, and Songnian Zhou) in 1984. It was then picked up by Ralph Campbell of Berkeley's Computer Systems Research Group, who started gluing it into BSD. In 1985, Kevin Dunlap, a DEC engineer on loan to Berkeley, took over the project and produced BIND, the Berkeley Internet Name Domain system. Mike Karels and Paul Vixie have maintained it over the years. Paul currently maintains it with help from isc.org and the bind-workers mailing list.

BIND is shipped with most vendors' UNIX systems and is also available from ftp.uu.net. BIND 4.8.3 is the basis for most implementations on our example systems. BIND 4.9.3 has just now become available and includes several new features. DNS has been implemented for other non-UNIX operating systems, but in this book we will discuss only BIND.

16.3 WHO NEEDS DNS?

DNS defines:

- A hierarchical namespace for hosts
- A host table implemented as a distributed database
- Library routines for querying this database (part of BIND, really)
- Improved routing for email
- A protocol for exchanging naming information

A site on the Internet needs DNS to participate fully. Maintaining a local `/etc/hosts` file with mappings for every host your users might ever want to contact is not generally feasible. All of your hosts should be DNS clients, but relatively few need to be DNS servers.

If your organization is small (a few hosts on a single network), run a server on one host or ask your Internet provider to supply DNS service. A medium-sized site with several subnets should run DNS servers on each subnet to reduce network load. A very large site can divide its domain into subdomains and run several servers for each subdomain.

We will first discuss the general anatomy of DNS (the specification) and then describe the specific configuration files used by BIND (the implementation). In the real world and elsewhere in this book, you will see the terms DNS and BIND used interchangeably. However, in this chapter we will preserve the distinction between them.

16.4 THE DNS NAMESPACE

The DNS namespace is a tree of *domains* with ascending authority.[1] Each domain represents a distinct chunk of the namespace and is managed by a single administrative entity. The root of the tree is called ".", and beneath it are the top-level (or "root-level") domains. The top-level domains are relatively fixed.

For historical reasons, there are two sorts of top-level domain names. In the US, top-level domains describe organizational and political structure and are usually given three-letter names. For domains outside the US, two-letter ISO (International Organization for Standardization) country codes are used. Note that both conventions coexist within the same global namespace. The current US domains are listed in Table 16.1.

Table 16.1 Top-level domains for the US

Domain	What it's for	Domain	What it's for
COM	Commercial companies	NET	Network providers
EDU	Educational institutions	ORG	Non-profit orgs
GOV	Government agencies	INT	International orgs
MIL	Military agencies	ARPA	A historical holdover

Most countries outside the US build an organizational hierarchy using second-level domains. Some countries use nonstandard naming conventions. For example, an academic institution is EDU in the United States and AC in Japan.

The top-level domain US is also used in the United States, primarily with locality domains; for example, bvsd.K12.CO.US, the Boulder Valley School District. The US domain is never combined with an organizational domain—there is no EDU.US (yet).

Some common country codes are shown in Table 16.2.

Domain names are case insensitive. "Colorado" is the same as "colorado" and "COLORADO" as far as DNS is concerned. DNS implementations should ignore case when making comparisons, but propagate case when it is supplied. You could theoretically use CoLoRaDo.EdU, but some

---

1. Parents have authority over children, unlike some families we know.

Table 16.2 Common country codes

Code	Country	Code	Country	Code	Country
AU	Australia	FI	Finland	HK	Hong Kong
CA	Canada	FR	France	CH	Switzerland
DK	Denmark	JP	Japan	MX	Mexico
DE	Germany	SE	Sweden	HU	Hungary

implementations (Ultrix, for example) might get confused. In the past it was common to use capital letters for top-level domains and an initial cap for second-level domains. These days, fingers are weary from typing and all-lowercase is the norm.

An Internet host is usually in one domain, but it can be in more than one or in none at all. Its fully qualified name is formed by appending the domain name to the hostname. For example, boulder.colorado.edu is the fully qualified name for the host boulder at the University of Colorado. Other sites can use the name "boulder" without asking because the fully qualified names will be different.

The structure of the naming tree is illustrated in Exhibit A.

Exhibit A   Sample entries from the DNS namespace

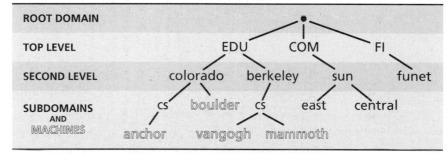

Second-level domains are managed centrally by the Network Information Center (NIC). When we were issued the name colorado.edu, we were guaranteed that "colorado" was unique within the "edu." domain.

We have further divided that domain into subdomains along department lines. For example, the host anchor in the Computer Science Department is called anchor.cs.colorado.edu on the Internet. The creation of each new subdomain must be coordinated with the administrators of the domain above to guarantee uniqueness.

Selecting a Domain Name

Certain names are taboo; for example, names that are already taken, the keyword AT, combinations of top-level domains such as edu.com, and repeating names like x.x.com.[2] Names should be short, easy to type, and should identify you or your organization.

RFC1032 recommends that the names of second-level domains be twelve characters or shorter, even though DNS actually allows up to 64 characters in each component.

A corporation with multiple sites should get one domain name for the entire company and use subdomains for branch offices. This maintains the corporate look and feel but delegates administrative responsibility to the local sites. It's not a good idea to obtain a separate second-level domain for each site or division of the company.

Registering a Second-Level Domain Name

See page 425 for more information about the NIC.

To obtain a second-level domain name, you must apply to the authority for the appropriate top-level domain. In the US, that authority is the Registration Services group of the Network Information Center.

The form for requesting a domain is included on the CD-ROM. You can also obtain the form via anonymous `ftp` from rs.internic.net. It is called **`domain-template.txt`** and lives in the **`templates`** directory. The US Mail contact address is

```
Network Solutions
InterNIC Registration Service
505 Huntmar Park Drive
Herndon, VA  22070
800-444-4345
```

The application form can be submitted electronically or via US Mail.

In Europe, contact RIPE (Reseaux IP Europeens) at mcsun.eu.net to apply for a domain name. Forms for European applications as well as for Japan and Asia are available from rs.internic.net.

In order to complete the domain registration forms, you must identify a technical contact person and at least two hosts that will be responsible for your domain. (The DNS jargon for being responsible is to be "authoritative.") You'll also have to choose a name that is not already taken. It takes about two weeks for the forms to be processed.

See page 260 for more information about obtaining an Internet address.

If you are new to the Internet, you can apply for an IP address at the same time. The form is **`internet-number-template.txt`** and is available from the same site. IP address assignment in the US is in the process of being localized. You might need to apply to your Internet provider or your regional network administrator.

2. You may have seen names that look like this. For example, xinet.xinet.com is a valid name, but the domain name is just xinet.com and there is a host called xinet in it.

Creating your Own Subdomains

The procedure for creating a subdomain is similar to that for creating a second-level domain, except that the central authority is now local (or more accurately, within your organization). Specifically, the steps are:

* Choose a name that is unique in the local context.
* Identify two or more hosts to be servers for your new domain.
* Coordinate with the administrator of the parent domain.

Each new domain defines a branch of the naming hierarchy. For example, the taxonomy of cs.colorado.edu is shown in Exhibit B.

Exhibit B   Components of a domain name

16.5 COMPONENTS OF **BIND**

There are three components of the BIND system:

* A daemon called **named** that answers queries
* Library routines that resolve host queries using DNS
* Command-line interfaces to DNS: **nslookup**, **dig**, and **host**

In DNS parlance, a daemon like **named** (or the machine on which it runs) is called a "name server," and the client code that contacts it is called a "resolver." We will briefly discuss the function of each component below, but the actual configuration of BIND is not covered until page 324.

named: The BIND Name Server

named answers queries about hostnames and IP addresses. If **named** doesn't know the answer to a query, it asks other servers and caches their responses. **named** is also responsible for performing "zone transfers" to copy data among the servers of a domain.

Name servers operate in one of three modes with respect to each domain: primary, secondary, and caching-only. The modes are distinguished by two characteristics: where the data comes from, and whether the server is authoritative for the domain.(A "zone" is a domain minus its subdomains. Name servers deal with zones, but "domain" is often used where "zone" is really meant.)

There is one primary name server for each domain or subdomain. The primary server keeps the master copy of the domain's data on disk.

See page 353 for more about zone transfers.

A secondary server copies its domain's data from the primary server via a "zone transfer" operation. There can be several secondary name servers for a domain; there *must* be at least one.

A caching-only name server loads the addresses of a few important machines (servers for the root domain) from a startup file and gets all the rest of its data by caching answers to the queries it resolves. Most primary and secondary servers also build their own caches.

An authoritative answer from a name server is "guaranteed" to be accurate; a non-authoritative answer may be out of date. However, a very high percentage of non-authoritative answers are perfectly correct. Primary and secondary servers are authoritative for their own domains, but not for cached information about other domains. Caching-only name servers are never authoritative.

Even "authoritative" answers can be inconsistent if a sysadmin changes the primary name server's data and forgets to tell the secondaries (or if the changes have not yet propagated to the secondaries).

The primary name server should be located on a machine that is stable, does not have many users, is relatively secure, and perhaps is on an uninterruptable power supply. There should be at least two secondaries, one of which is off-site. On-site secondaries should be on different networks and different power circuits.

Although they are not authoritative, caching-only servers can reduce the amount of DNS traffic on your networks. Consider putting a secondary or caching-only server on each network cable or subnet. It's fine for the same machine to be a primary server for your domains and a secondary server for other domains. Such cooperation usually makes for good DNS neighbors.

The Resolver Library

Before DNS, hostname mappings were looked up in **/etc/hosts** by the **gethostbyname** and **gethostbyaddr** library routines. In order for this information to be provided by DNS, these routines must change. New versions are usually integrated into your system's C library, **libc.a**, or put in their own library, **libresolv.a**.

When a library routine changes, application programs must be relinked unless your operating system supports shared libraries. In the case of **gethostbyname** and its ilk, only network-related programs are affected. If you are installing BIND from scratch, the instructions provide a list of programs that must be rebuilt. (However, modern systems almost always come with DNS support built in.)

BIND is shipped with each of our six example systems, along with versions of network programs that use the resolver library. However, as shipped, SunOS requires you to use NIS in order to use the BIND that is provided with the system. See page 403 for more information about using DNS on SunOS machines. BIND 4.9.3 includes a procedure for updating Sun's shared library routines so that DNS becomes "native," eliminating the need for NIS.

Shell Interface

The **nslookup** command allows you to access DNS from a shell. It can be used to query the database much as the **grep** command is used to look up a hostname in **/etc/hosts**. Details on **nslookup** and **dig**, another shell interface to DNS, are given on page 356.

16.6 How DNS Works

Each host using DNS is either a client of the system or simultaneously a client and a server. If you do not plan to run any DNS servers, it's not essential that you read the next few sections. However, they will help you develop a more solid understanding of the architecture of DNS.

Programs call the **gethostbyname** routine to map hostnames to IP addresses. When a host is configured to use DNS, **gethostbyname** uses the DNS resolver to query a name server for the address.

Name servers are either "recursive" or "non-recursive." A non-recursive server is a lazy, half-hearted server. If it has the answer cached from a previous query or is authoritative for the domain to which the name belongs, it will provide an appropriate response. Otherwise, instead of returning a real answer, it returns a referral to authoritative servers of another domain that are more likely to know the answer. A client of a non-recursive server must be prepared to accept and act on referrals.

A recursive server returns only real answers and error messages. It follows referrals itself, relieving the client of this responsibility. The basic procedure for resolving a query is essentially the same; the only difference is that the name server takes care of handling referrals rather than passing them back to the client.

One side effect of having a name server follow referrals is that its cache acquires information about intermediate domains. On a local network this is often what you want, since it allows subsequent lookups from any host on the network to benefit from the name server's previous work. On the other hand, the server for a high-level domain such as com or edu should not save up information requested by a host several domains below. Its cache would quickly bloat, and throughput would be reduced due to excessive time spent processing recursive queries.

For these reasons, low-level name servers are usually recursive while high-level servers (top-level and some second-level) are not. The resolver libraries that come with most versions of UNIX do not understand referrals; they expect the local name server to be recursive.

Recursion can permit intentional cache pollution. Root servers and secure primary servers should not do it. Versions of BIND earlier than 4.9.3 required patches to the source to control recursion. Version 4.9.3 introduced the -r command line option to turn it off.

Referrals are generated on a hierarchical basis. If a server can't supply an address for lair.cs.colorado.edu, for example, it will refer to the servers for cs.colorado.edu, colorado.edu, edu, or the root domain. A referral must include addresses for the servers of the referred-to domain, so the choice is not arbitrary; the server must refer to a domain that it already knows the servers for. The most complete known domain is generally returned. In this example, cs.colorado.edu would be returned if possible.

Name servers' caches are usually preloaded with servers for the root domain ("."), so some referral can always be made, even if it's just, "Go ask a root server."

Let's inspect a real example. Suppose we want to look up the address for mammoth.cs.berkeley.edu from the machine lair.cs.colorado.edu. The host lair asks its local name server, ns.cs.colorado.edu, to figure out the answer. Exhibit C illustrates the subsequent events. Relative names have been used to reduce clutter and to make the labels more readable. The order of events is shown.

We assume that none of the required information was cached before the query, except for the servers of the edu domain.

Exhibit C   DNS query process

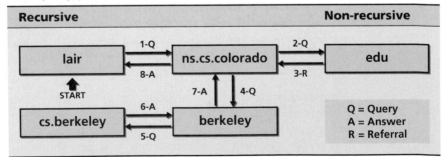

The local name server doesn't know the address; furthermore, it doesn't know anything about cs.berkeley.edu or berkeley.edu. It does know some servers for the edu domain, however, and since it is a recursive server it queries edu about mammoth.cs.berkeley.edu.

The edu domain is managed by non-recursive name servers, so instead of getting back an address, the local server is told, "Go ask the domain berkeley.edu; here are the servers' addresses." The local server sends a query about mammoth.cs.berkeley.edu to a server for berkeley.edu.

The Berkeley server doesn't know the answer offhand, but since it is a recursive server, it forwards the query to a server for cs.berkeley.edu. This server is authoritative for the requested information and returns mammoth's address. The server for berkeley.edu caches the address and returns it to ns.cs.colorado.edu.

When the dust settles, the following changes have occurred:

- ns.cs.colorado.edu has cached mammoth's address.
- ns.cs.colorado.edu has cached servers for berkeley.edu.
- A server for berkeley.edu has cached mammoth's address.

named queries use the UDP protocol and port 53. Responses come back via TCP if they are longer than 512 bytes. Zone transfers between servers also use TCP.

16.7 CACHING AND EFFICIENCY

Caching increases the efficiency of lookups; a cached answer is almost free and is usually correct because mappings change infrequently. Most queries are for local hosts and can be resolved quickly. Users also inadvertently help with efficiency since many queries are repeated. For example, a sequence such as

```
% finger egbert@eclipse.cs.colorado.edu
% talk egbert@eclipse.cs.colorado.edu
% mail egbert@eclipse.cs.colorado.edu
```

includes several references to the same host and is quite common.

Caching is usually only applied to positive answers. If a host's name or address can't be found, that fact is not saved. A study by Peter Danzig of the University of Southern California examined the effect of negative caching and found that its value was overshadowed by incorrect implementations in named.

However, in 1992, DNS accounted for 8% of the NFS backbone traffic. Now that the bugs have been worked out, negative caching should be reexamined. The version of BIND shipped with BSDI systems (4.9.1.2, March '94) includes negative caching.

16.8 BIND CLIENT ISSUES

See Chapter 18 for more information about distributing files on a network.

Before we dive into the configuration of BIND, let's outline the chores that are associated with using it on the Internet. Table 16.3 summarizes what must be done, for whom, and how often. An entry in the "How often" column that includes the word "distribute" means that you do it once per subnet or architecture and then copy the result to appropriate hosts using a tool like **rdist**.

Table 16.3 BIND installation and maintenance chores

Chore	For	How often
Obtain domain name	Site	Once
Choose name servers	Site	Once or more
Obtain BIND distribution	Site	Once, maybe
Configure resolver	Client	Once and distribute
Configure efficient resolver	Client	Each subnet and distribute
Configure services switch	Client	Each arch and distribute
Start **named** at boot time	Server	Each name server
Configure boot file	Server	Each type of server
Configure cache file	Server	Once and distribute to servers
Configure zone files	Primary	Once
Update **sendmail**	Mail hub	For your smart mail hub
	All hosts	Once and distribute
Update zone files	Primary	As needed
Review log files	Log host	At least weekly
Educate users	All hosts	Forever

We begin our detailed discussion with client-side chores, since each host using BIND is a client.

Configuring the Resolver

Each BIND client must have a file called **/etc/resolv.conf** that lists the name servers to query. The format of **resolv.conf** is

```
;  Comment³
search domainname ...
nameserver ipaddr
```

From one to three name servers can be listed. A complete example:

```
search cs.colorado.edu colorado.edu
; ns, piper, boulder
nameserver 128.138.243.151
nameserver 128.138.204.4
nameserver 128.138.240.1
```

3. Comments in **resolv.conf** must begin in column one.

If a host is itself a name server, it should be the first host listed. Use the actual IP address instead of the loopback address (127.0.0.1). A bug in the BSD networking code can cause problems if the loopback address is used. Each host listed must be running a recursive name server; the resolver doesn't follow referrals.

The first name server listed in `/etc/resolv.conf` is contacted first. If it does not respond to a query, the query times out and the next name server listed is tried. Each server is tried in turn, up to four times. The timeout interval increases with every failure.

Occasionally you will see a pound sign ("#") used for comments in name server files; administrators' habits are hard to break. It is incorrect but usually harmless, since BIND silently ignores lines it doesn't understand. BIND 4.9 allows either ";" or "#" to introduce a comment.

Earlier versions of BIND used the domain directive in **resolv.conf** instead of the search directive. RFC1535 strongly recommends replacing domain with search, and current resolvers try only the domains listed in the search list.

A small site should configure `/etc/resolv.conf` to point to its primary name server, or if there isn't one, perhaps to its Internet service provider. A larger site should have several name servers running throughout the site and should customize the **resolv.conf** file to spread the load among the servers, minimize network traffic, and reduce the vulnerability of machines to a single point of failure. If name service is broken, your whole site grinds to a halt.

If a user issues the command **telnet foo**, the resolver completes the name with the first domain in the search list (here, cs.colorado.edu) and looks for foo.cs.colorado.edu. If foo does not exist there, the resolver also tries foo.colorado.edu. If instead of a search directive, we had used

```
domain cs.colorado.edu
```

current resolvers (4.9.3 and later) would stop at foo.cs.colorado.edu. Earlier resolvers would (by default) continue to prune the domain until the name had only two parts. In this example, the forms foo.cs.colorado.edu and foo.colorado.edu would be checked, but foo.edu would not.

Users in our cs subdomain can use simple hostnames for any local host, but users in the parent domain must use *hostname*.cs to reach a host in the subdomain. If you create new subdomains, you will also have to reconfigure (educate) your users.

A search directive in the **resolv.conf** files of machines in the parent domain would allow simple hostnames to be used in both directions:

```
search  colorado.edu. cs.colorado.edu. ee.colorado.edu.
```

Of course, this assumes that hostnames are unique across the three domains. A `search` directive can specify up to six domains.

Testing the Resolver

On some systems, all you have to do to start using DNS is to add a *nameserver* line to `/etc/resolv.conf`. On others, you must explicitly tell the system to use DNS instead of the `/etc/hosts` file or NIS. Comments about using BIND on each of our example systems begin on page 361. For a more general discussion of the way to prioritize sources of administrative data, see page 403.

BIND and `dig` are included on the CD-ROM.

After configuring `/etc/resolv.conf`, test name lookups with either `nslookup` or `dig`. `nslookup` is included with BIND; `dig`, the Domain Information Groper, was written by Steve Hotz from ISI. `dig` gives more information than `nslookup` and has a zillion options. It also seems faster and more intuitive, especially for reverse domains. More details on both `nslookup` and `dig` are given on page 356.

In addition to direct tests with `nslookup` or `dig`, you should try network-related commands such as `telnet`, `rlogin`, `finger`, `talk`, and `who`. If commands that take hostnames as arguments work correctly, they are resolving names using DNS. Commands like `who` should display fully qualified names, not IP addresses.

Impact on the Rest of the System

Changing from static host tables to DNS creates some dependencies that you need to protect against. Three particular areas are affected: booting, configuration files, and mail delivery.

Booting

As a host boots, references to hostnames in the `/etc/rc*` or `init.d` startup files may be unresolvable if they are encountered before the network is up. The `rc` commands will unsuccessfully try to contact DNS. Thanks to the resolver's robustness, they will try multiple times on multiple servers, increasing their timeout period with each attempt. A couple of minutes later, the command needing the hostname will finally fail or hang.

To fix the problem, use only explicit IP addresses in the early stages of the boot process. Or, if your system supports the simultaneous use of both DNS and `/etc/hosts`, you can install a `hosts` file that contains the server addresses needed at boot time. Be sure the `hosts` file is checked first so you don't have to wait for DNS to time out.

Configuration files

See Chapter 17 for
more information
about NFS.

Now that your host is using DNS, there are several places where fully qualified domain names are required. One is the **/etc/exports** file, which controls NFS file sharing on some systems. The -access clauses that list the hosts allowed to mount a filesystem must contain the fully qualified names of those hosts. On some systems, each line in **exports** is limited to 1,024 characters; when hostnames change from "anchor" to "anchor.cs.colorado.edu", this limit comes awfully early.

Users' ~/.rhosts files will also need both fully qualified names and short names. Users that refer to hosts outside the local domain must use the fully qualified names.

These changes are really due to the fact that **rlogind** and NFS are pretty lame and do a simple string comparison when validating hostnames. But it's easier to make the data files bullet-proof than to teach all the **rlogind**s in the world to use a smarter string compare.

Mail delivery

See Chapter 21 for
more information
about **sendmail**.

sendmail must recognize its own fully qualified name as a local host. It must also make sure that any mail going off-site shows the sender's fully qualified address. If **sendmail** leaves the sender's address unqualified and a recipient replies to the mail, the remote domain will be added to the sender's hostname, creating a bogus address.

The local **sendmail** should either use DNS records correctly or forward mail to a smarter local hub. It should also use MX records.

16.9 SETTING UP A NAME SERVER

In this section, we assume that your political chores have been completed. That is, we assume that you have a domain name (possibly a subdomain) and have coordinated with the DNS administrator of the parent domain. You have chosen your primary name server and a couple of secondaries. And you have installed BIND.

The complete configuration for **named** consists of the boot file, the cache file, and, for primary servers, the data file or files containing address mappings for each zone.

/etc/named.boot: The Boot File

named is started at boot time and runs continuously. For example, to start **named** from **/etc/rc.local** on a SunOS system:

```
if [ -x /usr/etc/in.named -a -r /etc/named.boot ]; then
    /usr/etc/in.named; echo -n ' named' > /dev/console
fi
```

As **named** starts up, it writes its PID to the file **/etc/named.pid** (under BSDI, **/var/run/named.pid**). You can send a signal to **named** with:

```
kill -SIGNAL `cat /etc/named.pid`
```

 Under IRIX, the command **killall** -*SIGNAL* **named** serves the same purpose, so the **named.pid** file is not created.

See page 708 for more information about inetd.

named uses **syslog** and **syslogd** should therefore be started first. Do not use **inetd** to manage **named**; it will restart **named** every time it's needed, preventing any useful cache from being developed.

The **named.boot** file specifies the role (primary, secondary, or caching-only) of this host relative to each zone and the way in which it should get its copy of the resource records that make up the local part of the database. The format of the **named.boot** file is as follows:

```
directory    dirname
cache        .          filename
primary      zone       filename
secondary    zone       ipaddr [...] filename
```

Entries in **named.boot** are separated by whitespace. A semicolon introduces a comment.

The directory keyword specifies that all subsequent filenames are relative to the listed directory.

The cache keyword specifies the name of the file that contains root name servers and their addresses (called root name server hints). The hints are used to prime the cache to get the system started. The period in the middle is not a speck of dirt; it specifies the domain that the cache is for, namely, the root of the hierarchy. The cache file was originally called **/etc/named.ca**, but many sites have moved all BIND files into the **/var** directory.

The primary keyword indicates that this host is the primary server for the specified *zone* and that data for the zone is in *filename*.

The secondary keyword says that this host is a secondary server for *zone*. For secondaries, at least two parameters are specified: the IP addresses of the primary server from which to obtain the zone's data, and a *filename* where the data can be cached on disk.[4] When a secondary name server boots, it loads the data from its disk file and then contacts the primary server to determine if the data have changed and need to be downloaded.

If the primary server is down, the secondary will try an alternate IP address if one is listed in the boot file, or just use the data saved on disk

---

4. A secondary can also get its data from another secondary, but this is not recommended.

after its last update. Although multiple IP addresses can be specified, they are not intended to refer to different machines, but rather to multiple interfaces on the same primary server.

A single name server can provide service for several different zones. Accordingly, there may be multiple `primary` and `secondary` lines in the **named.boot** file.

As we have seen, **named.boot** specifies the names of the files containing the DNS database records. The cache file and the files associated with domains for which **named** is the primary server must be configured by hand. The files associated with `secondary` declarations are maintained by **named**.

named.boot can also contain a `domain` directive in the format:

```
domain        domainname
```

Any incomplete queries (that is, queries that do not end in a dot) will have this domain appended. While the use of `domain` in the boot file was standard in early versions of BIND, it is now considered harmful. Responsibility for specifying the local default domain has shifted from **named** to the resolver. If you use the `domain` directive, external clients who query with unqualified names will have your domain added instead of theirs.

Each time a name server queries another server, it adds the answer to its cache. Instead of having every name server perform its own external queries, you can designate one or more *forwarders*. A run-of-the-mill name server will look in its cache and at the records for which it is authoritative, and if it doesn't find the answer it's looking for, will send the query to a forwarder host. This way, forwarders build up caches that benefit the entire site. If a forwarder doesn't answer within a certain time, the original server will perform the query itself.

For example, the line

```
forwarders   128.138.243.151
```

at the end of the **named.boot** file will designate 128.138.243.151 as the site's forwarding host. It will also present the opportunity to misconfigure **named** and create a DNS forwarding loop. For example, if host A forwards to host B who forwards to host C who forwards to host A... In this infinite loop, infinity is about 20 thanks to BIND anticipating us.

If a name server wants to use forwarders exclusively, perhaps because it is a tired old Sun3 or is behind a firewall, it can add a `slave` directive after the `forwarders` line. A slave server will cache values and query forwarders but will not query anyone else. Dastardly forwarding loops can occur; e.g., forwarding to other slaves who forward back to you.

Many sites designate their more powerful and memory-rich servers as forwarders to reduce both overall network load and the CPU/memory load on weaker servers.

The boot file in earlier versions of BIND does not have a way to designate the class of a domain; it defaults to IN, the Internet class. BIND 4.9 allows multiple classes to be supported with a compile-time option and boot file syntax as follows:

```
primary/HS      zone   filename
secondary/IN    zone   filename
```

Only the Internet and Hesiod domains are supported. The /IN is not required to mix domains, but it makes things clearer.

Another new feature of BIND 4.9 is the ability to restrict zone transfers to particular networks or even individual hosts. As described in *Security Issues* on page 353, it has in the past been possible for any site to obtain your entire DNS database.

The xfrnets directive in the boot file allows you to specify an access list of networks and hosts that are allowed to receive zone transfers of your entire database. However, any user can still iterate through your database (requesting each possible PTR record) to obtain the same information. The syntax of the xfrnets directive is

```
xfrnets    ipaddr ...
```

For example, to restrict zone transfers to hosts on campus and our secondary server in Utah, the University of Colorado's primary name server would include the line

```
xfrnets    123.138.0.0 128.110.124.120
```

To include the xfrnets feature, BIND must be compiled with a special option. Early releases of BIND 4.9 called this option tcplist.

Version 4.9 also supports the bogusns directive. Name servers occasionally turn sour, and until their administrators rehabilitate them, they supply incorrect answers that fill log files with error messages, consume network bandwidth, and make wholesome, law-abiding name servers do lots of extra work.

The bogusns directive makes your name servers refuse to listen to or query a list of deviant name servers that you specify. This is another feature that must be enabled at compile time.

The format is like that of the forwarders directive:

```
bogusns 192.94.207.66 150.162.1.3 150.162.1.7
```

Sites can be secondary servers for many domains. To keep **named.boot** manageable, BIND 4.9 allows it to be divided up using the include directive. For example,

```
include utah.boot
include colostate.boot
```

would insert the files **utah.boot** and **colostate.boot** from the directory specified at the beginning of the boot file. These files could be maintained by the primary site and picked up regularly via **ftp**. For more information about automatically **ftp**ing files using the **expect** command, see page 390.

The **named.boot** file can also contain the keyword sortlist followed by a number of IP addresses. This keyword is now considered obsolete, and we do not recommend using it. It orders the addresses returned during querying when a host has multiple network interfaces. For example, you might know that the path to one interface is faster and should therefore be preferred. A sortlist directive specifying the preferred network address first would cause **named** to use it when contacting the host in question. For example,

```
sortlist  128.102.0.0 192.52.195.0
```

would cause the root server ns.nasa.gov to be contacted at its 128.102 address. If that interface was not reachable, the 192.52.195 address would be tried. All entries must be on the same line; you cannot have multiple sortlist directives.

16.10 THE DNS DATABASE

A domain's DNS database is a set of text files maintained by the system administrator on the domain's primary name server. Items stored in the database are called *resource records* and are sometimes referred to as RRs. The types and formats of resource records are defined in RFCs 882, 1035, and 1183.

The basic format of a resource record is

```
[name] [ttl] [class] type data
```

Fields are separated by whitespace (tabs or spaces) and may contain the special characters shown in Table 16.4 (next page).

The *name* field, which must begin in column one, identifies the entity (usually a host or domain) that the record describes. If there are several consecutive records about the same entity, the *name* field can be left out after the first record.

A name can be specified as either a relative name or a fully qualified name. The software deals internally with fully qualified names and

Table 16.4   Special characters used in RRs

Char	Meaning
;	Introduces a comment
#	Also introduces a comment (BIND 4.9 only)
@	The current domain name
( )	Allows data to span lines
*	Wild card[a] (*name* field only)

a. See page 339 for some cautionary statements.

appends the current domain to any name that does not end in a dot. This feature allows names to be shorter, but also invites mistakes.

For example, in the cs.colorado.edu domain, the name "anchor" would be interpreted as "anchor.cs.colorado.edu.". If the name were entered as "anchor.cs.colorado.edu", the absence of a final dot would imply a relative name and the domain would be appended, resulting in the name "anchor.cs.colorado.edu.cs.colorado.edu.". This kind of error is extremely common and can go undetected for a long time.

The ttl (time to live) field specifies the time, in seconds, that the data item can be cached and still be considered valid. It is often omitted, except in the cache startup file that contains the names and addresses of the root servers.

See Chapter 18 for more information about NIS and Hesiod.

$class$ specifies the network type. Three values are recognized: IN for the Internet, CH for ChaosNet, and HS for Hesiod. ChaosNet is an obsolete network formerly used by Symbolics Lisp Machines. Hesiod is a database service built on top of BIND; while not currently in common use, it is gaining popularity as a replacement for NIS. The default value for the class is IN.

We categorize the various types of resource records into three groups:

• Zone records – identify domains and their name servers
• Basic records – map names to addresses and route mail
• Optional records – provide extra information about hosts

The contents of the $data$ field depend on the record type. Record types are listed in Table 16.5.

There are some additional record types that are not widely used. MB, MG, and MINFO were designed to provide the same functionality as the mail aliases file. The DNS community has deprecated them. AFSDB, ISDN, X.25, and RT are new record types for wide area networks. They are not yet widely deployed.

The order of resource records is almost arbitrary. The SOA record for a zone must be first. The subsequent records can be in any order, but NS

Table 16.5 DNS record types

	Type	Name	Function
Zone	SOA	Start Of Authority	Defines a DNS zone of authority
	NS	Name Server	Identifies servers for a zone
Basic	A	Address	Name-to-address translation
	PTR	Pointer	Address-to-name translation
	MX	Mail Exchanger	Controls email routing
Optional	CNAME	Canonical Name	Nicknames for a host
	HINFO[a]	Host Info	Identifies hardware and OS
	RP	Responsible Person	Technical contact for a host
	WKS[b]	Well Known Services	Services provided by a host
	TXT	Text	Comments or untyped information

a. HINFO has been deprecated for security reasons.

b. WKS has been deprecated for performance reasons.

records usually come right after the SOA. The records for each host are usually kept together. It's a common practice to sort by the *name* field.

As we describe each type of resource record in detail, we will inspect sample records from cs.colorado.edu's data files. The default domain will be "cs.colorado.edu." throughout, so a host specified as "anchor" really means "anchor.cs.colorado.edu.".

The SOA Record

An SOA record marks the beginning of a *zone*, a group of resource records located at the same place within the DNS namespace. As we will discuss in greater detail on page 337, a DNS domain usually maps into at least two zones: one for translating hostnames to IP addresses, and others that map in the reverse direction.

There is only one SOA record for each zone; the zone continues until another SOA is encountered. The SOA record includes the name of the zone, a technical contact, and various timeout values. It must be the zone's first record. An example:

```
; Start of authority record for cs.colorado.edu

@   IN  SOA  ns.cs.colorado.edu.  admin.cs.colorado.edu. (
             1001      ; Serial
             21600     ; Refresh, 6 hours
             1800      ; Retry,   30 minutes
             1209600   ; Expire,  2 weeks
             432000 )  ; Minimum, 5 days
```

The *name* field contains the symbol @, which is shorthand for the name of the current zone. In this example, "cs.colorado.edu." could have been used instead. Don't worry about how @ was defined; we will explain later when we talk about **named**'s configuration files.

There is no *ttl* field. The class is IN for Internet, the type is SOA, and the remaining items form the *data* field.

"ns.cs.colorado.edu." is the zone's primary name server.

"admin.cs.colorado.edu." is the email address of the technical contact in the format "*user.host*." rather than *user@host*. Just replace that first dot with an @ and remove the final dot if you need to send mail to a domain's administrator. Sites often use an alias such as admin or hostmaster in place of an actual login name.

The parentheses continue the SOA record over several lines. Their placement is not arbitrary—we tried to shorten the first line by splitting it before the contact address, but then **named** (BIND 4.8.3) failed to recognize the SOA record. In some implementations, parentheses are only recognized in SOA and TXT records.

The first numeric parameter is the serial number of the zone's configuration data. It can be any integer and should be incremented every time the data file for the zone is changed.[5] Some sites encode the date the file was last modified in the serial number. For example, 1994040101 would be the first change to the zone on April 1, 1994. The serial number is used by secondary servers to determine when to get fresh data.

Serial numbers need not be continuous, but they must increase monotonically. If by accident you set a really large value on the primary server and it is transferred to the secondaries, then correcting the serial number on the primary will not work. The secondaries will only request new data if the primary's serial number is larger than theirs.

There are two ways to fix this. BIND 4.9 includes a hack that allows you to set the serial number to zero for one refresh interval and then restart the numbering. A sneaky but more tedious way to fix the problem is to change the serial number on the primary, then kill each secondary server, remove its backup data file, and restart it. This maneuver destroys the secondaries' caches, forcing them to reload.

It is a common mistake to change the data files but forget to update the serial number. **named** will punish you by ignoring your changes.

The next four entries are timeout values, in seconds, that control how long data can be cached at various points throughout the world-wide DNS database. These values represent a tradeoff between efficiency

5. Older versions of BIND accepted a serial number with a dot in it, such as 94.101 (which mapped to the integer 94000101); BIND 4.9 no longer allows this by default, but there is a compile-time option to reinstate it.

(using an old value is cheaper than fetching a new one) and accuracy (new values are more accurate).

The first is the *refresh* timeout, which specifies how often secondary servers should check with the primary to see if the serial number of the zone's configuration has changed. Whenever the zone changes, secondaries must make a new copy of the zone's data. Common values for this timeout range from one to six hours (3,600-21,600 seconds).

If a secondary server tries to check the primary's serial number but the primary does not respond, the secondary will try again after the *retry* timeout period has elapsed. Our experience suggests that 20-60 minutes (1,200-3,600 seconds) is a good value for this parameter.

If a primary server is down for a long time, secondaries will try to refresh their data many times but always fail. Each secondary should eventually decide that the primary is never coming back and that its data is surely out of date. The *expire* parameter determines how long the secondaries will continue to serve the domain's data in the absence of a primary. The system should be able to survive if the primary server is down for a week, so this parameter should have a longish value. We recommend a week to a month.

The *minimum* parameter sets the default time to live for resource records. It is cached with the records and used to expire them on non-authoritative servers. Each record can contain an explicit value in its *ttl* field; if none is set, the value from the SOA record is used. Experience suggests values between a few hours and several days. Increasing the value of this parameter to about a week reduces network traffic and DNS load substantially.

The *expire* and *minimum* parameters eventually force everyone using DNS to discard old data values. If a user's workstation is turned into an X terminal, a DNS record must be added to re-direct mail to another host. Sites that cache old values will not see the new mail exchanger record and will be unable to send mail to the user. But *minimum* seconds later, the cached record would have to be discarded. And *expire* seconds after that, all authoritative servers would either have the new record or would be providing no data at all. Fortunately, DNS data does not change too often.

NS Records

NS (name server) records identify the servers that are authoritative for a zone. NS records usually follow the SOA record. The format is

```
zone [ttl] [class] NS hostname
```

For example:

```
cs.colorado.edu.    IN   NS   ns.cs.colorado.edu.
cs.colorado.edu.    IN   NS   anchor.cs.colorado.edu.
cs.colorado.edu.    IN   NS   ns.cs.utah.edu.
```

Since the zone name is the same as the *name* field of the SOA record that precedes the NS records, it can be left blank. Thus the lines

```
IN   NS   ns.cs.colorado.edu.
IN   NS   anchor.cs.colorado.edu.
IN   NS   ns.cs.utah.edu.
```

are equivalent. Every authoritative name server should be listed. Caching-only servers cannot be authoritative; do not list them. There is no keyword that specifies which name server is the primary—that is determined in the boot file used by **named**.

To be totally honest, NS records are not really used by DNS when they refer to name servers for the *current* zone. They just make it clear to humans how the zone is organized and which machines are the key players in providing name service.

NS records do define subdomains and delegate authority to them. For example, the sample NS records given above, if present in the domain colorado.edu, would delegate authority for the cs subdomain to the three servers listed. Those same records in the cs.colorado.edu database would clarify the structure of the zone, but they are not essential.

Only name servers listed with the parent domain are accessible to the outside world. You may want to set up additional name servers that are used only within your organization. In general, you probably don't want to make all your departmental servers available to the Internet.

For example, a new server for cs.colorado.edu would not be queried by hosts outside that domain unless an additional NS record was added to the colorado.edu domain files.

See page 351 for more information about delegation.
A quick look at our own delegation information revealed a major server for colorado.edu that the edu domain knew nothing about. Do as we say and not as we do; check your delegations occasionally with **nslookup** or **dig** to be sure they specify an appropriate set of servers.

A Records

A (address) records are the heart of the DNS database. They provide the mapping from hostnames to IP addresses that was formerly specified in the **/etc/hosts** file. A host must have one A record for each of its network interfaces. The format is

```
hostname [ttl] [class] A ipaddr
```

For example:

```
anchor   IN   A   128.138.243.100
```

PTR Records

PTR (pointer) records perform the reverse mapping from IP addresses to hostnames. As with A records, a host must have one for each network interface. But before we describe PTR records, we need to digress and talk about a special top level domain called IN-ADDR.ARPA.

Fully qualified hostnames can be viewed as a notation where the "most significant bit" is on the right. For example, in the name

```
anchor.cs.colorado.edu
```

anchor is in cs, cs is in colorado, and colorado is in edu. IP addresses, on the other hand, have the "most significant bit" on the left:

```
128.138.243.100
```

Host 100 is on subnet 243 which is part of network 128.138.

The IN-ADDR.ARPA domain was created to allow one set of software modules to map from IP addresses to hostnames as well as from hostnames to IP addresses. Domains underneath it are named like IP addresses with their bytes reversed. For example, the zone for our 243 subnet is composed as shown in Exhibit D.

Exhibit D   Taxonomy of an IN-ADDR.ARPA zone

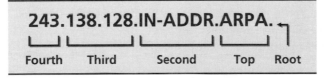

Note that in Exhibit D the component 138.128 (representing the class B network number 128.138) is marked as a single zone. There is in fact no zone named 128.IN-ADDR.ARPA. This contradicts common sense and what we've previously said in this chapter, but it's a very special case.

No one actually makes queries for "128.IN-ADDR.ARPA.". (Try it with **dig** or **nslookup**; it won't work.) The problem is to make sure that queries for addresses *underneath* 128.IN-ADDR.ARPA return meaningful results.

It turns out that as long as all servers of the IN-ADDR.ARPA zone are provided with NS records for 138.128.IN-ADDR.ARPA, the intermediate zone (128.IN-ADDR.ARPA) doesn't really need to exist. References to its subdomains will short-circuit directly to the longest component for which the server has an NS record.

This may sound a bit confusing in theory, but in practice it's an easy convention to use. Just pretend that the dot between 138 and 128 (or the components of whatever network you're creating a zone for) is a normal character such as a dash. Think of the address as one unit, and configure both the parent and subdomain exactly as usual.

The general format of a PTR record is

```
addr [ttl] [class] PTR hostname
```

The PTR record in the IN-ADDR.ARPA domain that corresponds to anchor's A record above is

```
100.243.138.128  IN  PTR  anchor.cs.colorado.edu.
```

The name 100.243.138.128 does not end in a dot and therefore is relative. But relative to what? Not "cs.colorado.edu." For this sample record to be accurate, the default domain has to be "IN-ADDR.ARPA.".

This can be accomplished by either putting the PTR records in their own file in which the default domain is "IN-ADDR.ARPA." (set in **named**'s boot file) or by using the $ORIGIN directive to change the domain.

If the default domain is defined as "243.138.128.IN-ADDR.ARPA.", the record can be written as

```
100  IN  PTR  anchor.cs.colorado.edu.
```

Since cs.colorado.edu and 243.138.128.IN-ADDR.ARPA are different regions of the DNS namespace, they constitute two separate zones. Each zone must have its own SOA record and RRs. In addition to defining an IN-ADDR.ARPA zone for each real network, you also need a zone that takes care of the loopback network, 127.0.0. Two ways of handling this are illustrated in the example configurations starting on page 344.

The reverse DNS files at larger sites are often organized by subnet, with the default domain including only the portion of the network address that is common to all subnets.[6] In this example, the default domain includes the complete subnet address. Note that the hostname anchor must be fully qualified to prevent the 243.138.128.IN-ADDR.ARPA domain from being appended to it.

The reverse mappings provided by PTR records within the IN-ADDR.ARPA domain are used by any program that authenticates inbound network traffic. For example, remote logins without a password are allowed when the machine of origin is listed, by name, in a user's ~/.rhosts file. When the destination host receives a connection request, it knows the source machine only by IP address. It uses DNS to convert the IP address to a hostname, which is then compared against the appropriate

---

6. This is possible only if subnets are split on a byte boundary.

file. `netstat`, `sendmail`, X Windows, `syslog`, `finger`, `ftp`, and `rlogind` all do reverse mappings to get hostnames from IP addresses.

It is important that A records match their corresponding PTR records. Mismatched and missing PTR records cause timeouts, slowing your system to a crawl.

MX Records

See Chapter 21 for more information about email.

Mail exchanger records are used by the mail system to route mail more efficiently. An MX record preempts the destination of a message, in most cases directing it to a mail hub at the recipient's site rather than the recipient's own workstation.

The format of an MX record is

```
name [ttl] [class] MX preference host ...
```

Two examples are below, one for a host that receives its own mail unless it is down, and one for a host that can't receive mail at all.

```
piper   IN  MX  10  piper
        IN  MX  20  mailhub
        IN  MX  50  boulder.colorado.edu.
xterm1  IN  MX  10  mailhub
        IN  MX  20  anchor
        IN  MX  50  boulder.colorado.edu.
```

Hosts with low preference values are tried first; 0 is the most desirable, and 65,535 the least. For example, mail addressed to bob@xterm1 would be sent to mailhub if it were accessible, to anchor as a second choice, and if both mailhub and anchor were down, to boulder. Note that boulder's name must be fully qualified since it is not a member of the default domain ("cs.colorado.edu." in this example).

The list of preferences and hosts can all be on the same line, but separate lines are easier to read. Leave numeric "space" between preference values; you might have to squeeze in a new destination.[7]

MX records are useful in many situations, for example:

* When you have a central mail hub
* When the destination host is down
* When the destination is not on Internet or isn't a UNIX system

In the first of these situations, mail is routed to the hub, perhaps the machine where most users read mail. In the second case, mail is routed to a nearby host and forwarded when the destination comes back up.

---

7. Perhaps this is why BASIC programmers make good DNS administrators.

If a host is not on the Internet, it cannot have an A record in DNS but can have MX records. **sendmail** cannot connect directly to the destination, but can get the mail closer by connecting to one of the destination's MX hosts. The MX host presumably has a direct connection to the destination host, perhaps via UUCP, DECNET, BITNET, or some other transport.

Every host should have MX records. For minor hosts, one or two alternates is enough. A major host should have several records:

- One for itself, as first choice
- Another nearby host as second choice
- A central mail hub for the domain or parent as a backup

The domain itself should have an MX record to a mail hub machine so that mail to *user@domain* will work. This does require unique user names across machines in the domain. For example, to be able to mail evi@cs.colorado.edu, we either need a machine called cs or an MX record in the colorado.edu domain:

```
cs      IN   MX   10   mailhub.cs.colorado.edu.
        IN   MX   20   anchor.cs.colorado.edu.
        IN   MX   50   boulder.colorado.edu.
```

Unfortunately, many sites do not use MX records. Sun ships a version of **sendmail** that is configured to ignore them. Often a version that understands MX records is provided, but is not installed as the default.

Wild card MX records are sometimes seen in the DNS database:

```
*       IN   MX   10   mailhub.cs.colorado.edu.
```

At first glance, this seems like it would save lots of typing and add a default MX record for all hosts. But wild card records don't quite work as you might expect. They will match anything in the *name* field of a resource record that is *not* already listed as an explicit name in another resource record.

Thus, you *cannot* use a star to set a default value for all your hosts. But, perversely, you can use it to set a default value for names that are not your hosts. This causes lots of mail to be sent to your hub only to be rejected there, because the hostname matching the star really does not belong to your domain.

See page 554 for more information about firewalls.

We do not recommend using wild cards. In fact we strongly recommend against them unless your network uses a firewall machine or is not directly connected to the Internet. A firewall machine needs to have a wild card record to accept mail for the domain and its invisible-to-the-Internet hosts. A wild card MX record is also appropriate for a machine that is a gateway to a non-Internet network and that accepts and reroutes mail for that network.

Wild card MX records can conflict. For example, the record above and this one for its parent domain

```
*        IN  MX  5  colorado.edu.
```

are in conflict. In such a situation, **sendmail** uses the most complete name ("cs.colorado.edu.", not "colorado.edu.") independent of the precedence value. This may or may not be what was intended.

CNAME Records

CNAME records allow you to assign nicknames to a host. Nicknames are commonly used either to associate a function with a host or to shorten a name. The real name is sometimes called the canonical name (hence, "CNAME"). Some examples:

```
ftp      IN  CNAME  anchor
kb       IN  CNAME  kibblesnbits
```

The format of a CNAME record is

```
nickname [ttl] [class] CNAME hostname
```

If there is a CNAME record nicknaming a host, other records for that host must refer to its real name, not its nickname. When the DNS software encounters a CNAME record, it stops its query for the nickname and switches to the real name.

HINFO Records

A host info record lists the manufacturer and model of a computer, and the operating system that it is running. Many sites do not use HINFO records, either for security reasons or because the sysadmins are lazy bums. If everyone with access to the Internet can find out what type of hardware you have and what version of the OS it is running, you are more vulnerable to a break-in. The format of a HINFO record is

```
name [ttl] [class] HINFO hosttype os
```

For example,

```
anchor  IN  HINFO  "sparc10"  "sunos 4.1.3"
```

indicates that anchor is a Sun Sparcstation 10 running SunOS 4.1.3. If a data value is one word, no quotes are needed; the quotes protect embedded blanks. You can use any strings you want, but some recommended values are listed in RFC1340.

WKS Records

A WKS record lists the well known services that a host supports. Again, for security reasons, most sites do not use it. We are not aware of any software that depends on WKS records; only Symbolics machines ever used them. The format is

```
name [ttl] [class] WKS [address] protocol services
```

For example,

```
anchor  IN  WKS  TCP  telnet smtp ftp
```

The *address* field (IP address) is usually omitted. In fact, we recommend that you omit the entire record.

Bonus Mail Handling Records

There are several mail handling records that were designed to assist with mail routing, especially to a group of recipients. MB specifies the host where a destination mailbox lives, MG defines a mail group, and MR specifies a new name for a mailbox. There were also MD and MF, which caused elusive race conditions and were replaced by MX records. MINFO records provide a way to manage mailing lists.

The only mail-related resource record in common use is the MX record. The functionality envisioned for MG, MR, and MINFO records can be accomplished using the **aliases** file.[8] See Chapter 21, *Electronic Mail*, for more information about aliases and mail handling.

TXT Records

A TXT record is used to add arbitrary text to a host's DNS records. For example, we have TXT records identifying our site:

```
IN  TXT  "University of CO, Boulder Campus, CS Dept"
IN  TXT  WP-PH://directory.colorado.edu/105
IN  TXT  WP-SMTP-EXPN-Finger://ns.cs.colorado.edu
```

The last two lines announce our support for white pages lookups (via **netfind**): phone numbers via a machine called directory at port 105, and login names via **sendmail**'s EXPN command and the **finger** command to the machine ns. These example records directly follow the SOA and NS records for the "cs.colorado.edu." domain and so inherit the *name* field from them.

The format of a TXT record is

```
name [ttl] [class] TXT info
```

BIND 4.9 includes a special TXT record called a secure_zone resource record. It is used to control exactly which hosts or networks may query your name server. See *Security Issues* on page 353 for more details. The format of a secure_zone TXT record is

---

8. Well, at least on UNIX systems running **sendmail**...

```
secure_zone [class] TXT net[:mask] or host:H
```

For example, the records

```
secure_zone   IN   TXT   128.138.0.0
secure_zone   IN   TXT   128.110.124.120:H
secure_zone   HS   TXT   128.138.243.0:255.255.255.0
```

would allow any host on the 128.138 network and the host with IP address 128.110.124.120 to query our name server for address information. Only the hosts on the 243 subnet could query Hesiod maps (**passwd** information, perhaps). Other hosts would be denied access. If no subnet mask is specified, a network is assumed to be un-subnetted.

New Resource Records

RFC1183 created several experimental record types designed to accommodate new wide-area network media, to glue in other types of databases, and to nail down the person responsible for a host or group of hosts. These are not yet in common use.

New record types include:

AFSDB   This is a name server record for either the Andrew Filesystem developed at Carnegie Mellon University (CMU) and now marketed by TransArc, or for the DCE (Distributed Computing Environment) authenticated database server. Its format is like that of an MX record, with the preference field used to specify AFS or DCE.

ISDN   An ISDN record contains an ISDN address, which is a phone number in disguise.

X.25   An X.25 record contains (you guessed it) an X.25 address.

RT   An RT or Route Through record is intended to give routing hints for reaching a host or domain via ISDN or X.25. They are like MX records for routing. RT records point to intermediate hosts that route packets to the destination host across non-Internet links.

RP   An RP record contains the email address (with the @ sign replaced by a dot) of a person who is responsible for a host or domain, plus the pseudo-name of a TXT record that can be used to provide additional information, such as a telephone number or full name.

RP records are an especially tasty addition, and we anticipate that they will become widely used. The DNS administrator listed in the SOA record is a contact for the whole domain; RP records allow a finer granularity and offer a way to include more information than just an email address.

For example, the records

```
nag         IN   RP   evi.cs.colorado.edu.   ugradops
ugradops    IN   TXT  "Evi Nemeth, Engineering 8-3"
            IN   TXT  "Undergraduate Operations Group"
            IN   TXT  "CS Dept, Univ. of Colorado"
            IN   TXT  "Lab: 303-555-1234, 303-555-5678"
```

would identify Evi as the responsible person for the host nag, give contact information for her, and identify ugradops, the group of administrators responsible for that machine. Subsequent hosts maintained by ugradops would need just the RP record, for example:

```
nagina      IN   RP   evi.cs.colorado.edu.   ugradops
```

Now that we have explored the contents of the DNS database, we will look at some complete configuration examples.

16.11 BIND CONFIGURATION EXAMPLES

In the following sections, we show three example configurations:

- A caching-only name server
- The primary server for a small company
- The primary server for the cs subdomain of colorado.edu

A Caching-Only Server

This configuration is appropriate for a subnet that wants a local server but does not want to soil its hands with data files. We need only configure the boot file and the cache file and start **named** at boot time. In the boot file there will be no primary or secondary lines:

```
; BIND boot file (caching-only for cs.Colorado.EDU)

directory   /var/domain
cache       .    root
```

The Cache File

The cache file here is called **/var/domain/root**; it is often called **/etc/named.ca** as well, but we prefer to put all the BIND configuration files beneath **/var/domain**. Although we call it a cache file, its real purpose is to hold name server and address records for the root servers, which are used to initialize (prime) **named**'s cache. The existence of these root servers in the cache bootstraps the query process.

The root name servers change from time to time, so the following examples should be used for reference only. The first edition of this book was published in 1988; of the root name servers listed there, only one (ns.nasa.gov) is still correct. If you already have a name server running, you can use it to verify the root servers by connecting to one of them with **nslookup** or **dig** and asking for NS records in the "." domain. For example, using the root server ns.nasa.gov, we get the following output:

```
% nslookup              /* Start nslookup */
Default Server: ns.cs.colorado.edu
Address:  128.138.243.151
> server ns.nasa.gov  /* Connect to the NASA server */
Default Server: ns.nasa.gov
Address:  128.102.16.10
> set type=ns           /* Set query type to nameserver */
> .
Server:  ns.nasa.gov
Address:  128.102.16.10
(root)   nameserver = NS.INTERNIC.NET
(root)   nameserver = TERP.UMD.EDU
(root)   nameserver = NS.NASA.GOV
...
NS.INTERNIC.NET  inet address = 198.41.0.4
TERP.UMD.EDU     inet address = 128.8.10.90
NS.NASA.COV      inet address = 128.102.16.10
NS.NASA.GOV      inet address = 192.52.195.10
...
```

This example has been truncated; there are currently eight root servers. From this list we can build the cache hints file. Its format is determined by the format of the NS and A resource records and is one of the only places you will see the ttl (time to live) field used. All eight root name servers are included in this sample cache file:

```
; Initial cache data for root domain servers.
.       99999999   IN   NS   NS.INTERNIC.NET.
        99999999   IN   NS   TERP.UMD.EDU.
        99999999   IN   NS   NS.NASA.GOV.
        99999999   IN   NS   AOS.ARL.ARMY.MIL.
        99999999   TN   NS   KAVA.NISC.SRI.COM.
        99999999   IN   NS   C.NYSER.NET.
        99999999   IN   NS   NIC.NORDU.NET.
        99999999   IN   NS   NS.NIC.DDN.MIL.
; Prime the cache, hotwire the addresses
NS.INTERNIC.NET.     99999999   IN   A   198.41.0.4
TERP.UMD.EDU.        99999999   IN   A   128.8.10.90
NS.NASA.COV.         99999999   IN   A   128.102.16.10
NS.NASA.GOV.         99999999   IN   A   192.52.195.10
AOS.ARL.ARMY.MIL.    99999999   IN   A   128.63.4.82
AOS.ARL.ARMY.MIL.    99999999   IN   A   192.5.25.82
KAVA.NISC.SRI.COM.   99999999   IN   A   192.33.33.24
C.NYSER.NET.         99999999   IN   A   192.33.4.12
NIC.NORDU.NET.       99999999   IN   A   192.36.148.17
```

Note the dot on the first non-comment line. It is another not-a-fly-speck and defines the domain (the root) to which the subsequent NS records apply. The dot after each root server's name is also significant. Without it, servers' hostnames would be expanded into monstrosities such as "ns.internic.net.cs.colorado.edu.".

A current cache file can also be obtained via anonymous `ftp` from the host rs.internic.net. It's called `/domain/named.cache`.

A Primary Server for a Small Company

Our next example is for a small company. Suppose the folks at xor.com have three machines and a laser printer on their net. They run their own primary name server but use two off-site hosts as secondaries: one at the University of Colorado and one at the University of Utah.

For the primary server, we must configure the boot and cache files as before. However, we must also add data files that contain resource records for the following three zones:

- The xor.com zone
- The 21.108.192.IN-ADDR.ARPA reverse-mapping zone
- The localhost reverse-mapping zone, 0.0.127.IN-ADDR.ARPA

Let's start by inspecting the `/etc/named.boot` file:

```
; BIND 4.9.3 boot file for xor.com

directory   /var/domain
cache       .                              root.cache
primary     xor.com                        xor.hosts
primary     21.108.192.IN-ADDR.ARPA   xor.rev
primary     0.0.127.IN-ADDR.ARPA      local.rev
```

The contents of the cache file are as before, except that in this configuration it is called `/var/domain/root.cache`. The domain's forward data are kept in `/var/domain/xor.hosts`:

```
; xor.com forward mappings, origin xor.com.

@           IN  SOA   xor.com.  trent.xor.com.  (
                      144         ; Serial
                      21600       ; Refresh
                      1200        ; Retry
                      3600000     ; Expire
                      432000 )    ; Minimum
            IN  NS    xor.COM.
            IN  NS    boulder.Colorado.EDU.
            IN  NS    cs.utah.edu.
            IN  A     192.108.21.1
            IN  MX    10 xor.com.
            IN  MX    50 boulder.colorado.edu.
```

```
localhost   IN   A       127.0.0.1
chimchim    IN   CNAME   xor.com.
ftp         IN   CNAME   xor.com.
bandicoot   IN   A       192.108.21.2
            IN   MX      10 xor.com.
mookie      IN   A       192.108.21.3
            IN   MX      10 xor.com.
chip-lw     IN   A       192.108.21.250
xor-gw      IN   A       192.108.21.254
```

The reverse mappings are in **xor.rev**:

```
; reverse mappings, origin 21.108.192.IN-ADDR.ARPA.

@           IN   SOA     xor.com.   trent.xor.com. (
                        21              ; serial number
                        7200            ; Refresh       2 hours
                        1800            ; retry         30 minutes
                        1209600         ; Expire        2 weeks
                        7200 )          ; Minimum       2 hours
            IN   NS      xor.com.
            IN   NS      boulder.colorado.edu.
            IN   NS      cs.utah.edu.
1           IN   PTR     xor.com.
2           IN   PTR     bandicoot.xor.com.
3           IN   PTR     mookie.xor.com.
250         IN   PTR     chip-lw.xor.com.
254         IN   PTR     xor-gw.xor.com.
```

And finally, the reverse localhost zone is in the file **local.rev**:

```
; reverse localhost, origin is 0.0.127.IN-ADDR.ARPA.

@           IN   SOA     xor.com.   trent.xor.com. (
                        3               ; serial number
                        1209600         ; refresh, 2 weeks
                        1800            ; retry, 30 minutes
                        1209600         ; expire, 2 weeks
                        1209600 )       ; minimum, 2 weeks
            IN   NS      xor.com.
            IN   NS      boulder.colorado.edu.
1           IN   PTR     localhost.xor.com.
```

The zone defined in **xor.hosts** includes the mail exchanger and address records for all hosts in the xor.com domain. The second file provides the reverse mappings with PTR records. The contents of the third file never change, so the timeouts are large.

A Primary Server for a Large Site

Our final example, cs.colorado.edu, is larger and more complex. It includes several hundred hosts and about 20 subnets. **named** runs on most subnets, so the majority of DNS traffic is local. A forwarder is used; most **named**s do not routinely perform remote queries. The primary server is a well-endowed workstation with plenty of memory and CPU cycles. Its user community consists of just the administrative staff and a few pushy faculty.

The DNS database is kept in several files. Reverse-mapping zones are organized by subnet number; each subnet (in our case, the third octet of a class B network address) has its own file. This is not strictly necessary, but it limits the files to a manageable size and makes updating quite straightforward. However, it does presuppose that subnets are divided on a byte boundary. If the campus goes to a nine-bit subnet field (as it is threatening to do), we will have to use a different scheme for managing our reverse zones.

If a single file were used for all reverse mappings, the records could be organized by network and the $ORIGIN directive used at the beginning of each section to reset the identity of the default domain.

Here is the boot file:[9]

```
; named.boot - primary for cs.colorado.edu
; contact: Lynda McGinley, mcginley@cs.colorado.edu
; last modified: apr 1, 1994

directory   /var/domain

;           domain                      filename
;           ------                      ---------
cache       .                           root
primary     0.0.127.in-addr.arpa        reverse/localhost
primary     cs.colorado.edu             forward/cs
primary     243.138.128.in-addr.arpa    reverse/243.138.128
primary     204.138.128.in-addr.arpa    reverse/204.138.128
... ; Several lines deleted
secondary ee.colorado.edu 128.138.200.1    forward/ee
secondary colorado.edu     128.138.240.1   forward/colo
secondary cs.utah.edu      128.110.124.120 forward/utah
secondary  138.128.in-addr.arpa   128.138.240.1
   reverse/138.128
secondary  110.128.in-addr.arpa   128.110.124.120
   reverse/110.128
```

The cache file, **/var/domain/root**, is the same as in earlier examples. Zone configuration files are supplied as specified in the primary directives: **/var/domain/forward/cs** for the forward zone, and various files under **/var/domain/reverse** for the reverse zones. No extra

9. Some lines have been wrapped to fit.

configuration is required to be a secondary for the EE Department, the parent domain (colorado.edu), and Utah's CS Department.

Below are some excerpts from **/var/domain/forward/cs**. This file is for a much larger domain than xor.com; however, it has been truncated mercilessly. More data is kept for each host, but the structure is the same for a three-host site as for 3,000-host site. Relative names in this file would have the default domain "cs.colorado.edu." appended.

```
; BIND forward maps for CS.Colorado.EDU

@   IN  SOA  ns.cs.colorado.edu. admin.cs.colorado.edu. (
                 9402100        ; Serial Number
                 21600          ; Refresh - 6 hours
                 1800           ; Retry   - 30 minutes
                 1209600        ; Expire  - 2 weeks
                 432000 )       ; Minimum - 5 days
       IN  NS   ns
       IN  NS   anchor
       IN  NS   boulder.colorado.edu.
       IN  NS   cs.utah.edu.
       IN  MX   10  mailhub
       IN  MX   50  anchor
       IN  MX   99  boulder.colorado.edu.
       IN  TXT  "University of Colorado, Boulder, CS Dept"
       IN  TXT  WP-PH://directory.colorado.edu/105
       IN  TXT  WP-SMTP-EXPN-Finger://ns.cs.colorado.edu

localhost.  IN  A      127.0.0.1
localhost   IN  CNAME  localhost.
adams       IN  A      128.138.202.31
            IN  MX     10 nordsieck
            IN  HINFO  "NCD 17c xterm" "3.2"
anchor      IN  A      128.138.242.1
            IN  A      128.138.243.100
            IN  MX     10 anchor
            IN  MX     50 mailhub
            IN  HINFO  "sparc10" "sunos 4.1.3"
anchor-gw   IN  A      128.138.243.100

...  ; 1675 lines deleted
```

The host anchor is functioning as a gateway (really a router) between a subnet of diskless clients and the CS Department backbone. It has diskless clients that must be served on each of its network segments. Because of this, there must be an actual host address record for the name anchor-gw, rather than just a CNAME record making it an nickname. Cheap hard disks have made diskless workstations obsolete; we expect that gateway machines will predominantly have a CNAME record for their additional interfaces and have all the A records associated with the real name of the host.

Below is part of the reverse file for one of the CS subnets; reverse files are usually sorted by the host digit of the IP address. The meaning of @ below is "243.138.128.IN-ADDR.ARPA.", which is set by the `primary` line for the 243 subnet reverse zone in the **/etc/named.boot** file listed earlier on page 348.

```
; BIND reverse maps for 128.138.243, cs-cr net

@   IN  SOA  ns.cs.colorado.edu. admin.cs.colorado.edu. (
                9402100     ; Serial Number
                21600       ; Refresh - 6 hours
                1800        ; Retry   - 30 minutes
                1209600     ; Expire  - 2 weeks
                432000 )    ; Minimum - 5 days
        IN  NS   ns.cs.colorado.edu.
        IN  NS   anchor.cs.colorado.edu.
        IN  NS   boulder.colorado.edu.
        IN  TXT  "University of Colorado, CS Dept"
1       IN  PTR  dumpster.cs.colorado.edu.
2       IN  PTR  tahiti.cs.colorado.edu.
4       IN  PTR  riker.cs.colorado.edu.
5       IN  PTR  watneys.cs.colorado.edu.
    ...
```

The reverse mapping for the localhost address (127.0.0.1) does not change, so the timeouts can be large. Note the serial number, which encodes the date; the file was last changed in 1992. Also note that off-site name servers are not listed for the localhost domain. The meaning of @ here is "0.0.127.IN-ADDR.ARPA.".

```
; Reverse file for the 127.in-addr.arpa zone:

@   IN  SOA  ns.cs.colorado.edu. admin.cs.colorado.edu. (
                9205301    ; serial number
                1209600    ; refresh, 2 weeks
                1800       ; retry, 30 minutes
                1209600    ; expire, 2 weeks
                1209600)   ; minimum, 2 weeks
        IN  NS   ns.cs.colorado.edu.
        IN  NS   anchor.cs.colorado.edu.
        IN  NS   boulder.colorado.edu.

1   IN   PTR   localhost.
```

Loose Ends

The case of the keywords in zone files is not important; some sites use uppercase and some use lowercase.

Many sites use the $INCLUDE directive in their zone database files to separate overhead records from data records. Its format is

```
$INCLUDE <filename>
```

The directive must begin in column one. The specified file is read into the database at the point of the $INCLUDE directive.

The origin is set initially to the domain specified in the boot file (the second argument of any primary or secondary directive). It can be modified within a zone file with the $ORIGIN directive (again, starting in column one). The use of relative names where fully qualified names are expected saves lots of typing and makes the files easier to read.

The address 127.0.0.1 refers to a host itself and is generally mapped to either "localhost." or "localhost.*domain*." In the xor.com example on page 346, "localhost.xor.com." is used; in the cs.colorado.edu example, the name "localhost.cs.colorado.edu." is mapped to "localhost." with a CNAME record so that both flavors are explicitly covered. Either form is fine, as long as the forward and reverse records match.

Glue Records

Each domain or zone stands alone with its own set of data files, name servers, and clients. But zones need to be connected together to form a coherent hierarchy; cs.colorado.edu is a part of colorado.edu, and we need some DNS linkage between them.

This linkage is effected by listing a subdomain's servers in the data for the parent zone. In fact, only the name servers listed in the parent zone can be returned as referrals in response to queries.

For example, the colorado.edu zone files contain records like these:

```
; subdomain information

cs          IN   NS   ns.cs.colorado.edu.
            IN   NS   piper.cs.colorado.edu.
            IN   NS   anchor.cs.colorado.edu.
ee          IN   NS   ee-gw.ee.colorado.edu.
            IN   NS   ns.cs.colorado.edu.

; glue records

ns.cs       IN   A    128.138.243.151
piper.cs    IN   A    128.138.204.4
anchor.cs   IN   A    128.138.243.100
ee-gw.ee    IN   A    128.138.200.1
```

There are glue records from the edu domain to the colorado.edu domain as well. When a new second-level domain is created, glue records for the two authoritative name servers supplied on the domain application form are added to the root servers' database. They connect the new domain to the Internet naming tree. Missing or incorrect glue records will leave part of your namespace inaccessible, and users trying to reach it will get "unknown host" errors.

Additional glue for mail is sometimes added to the parent domain's database as well. If you want your users to be able to receive mail as *user@domain* (for example, bob@cs.colorado.edu), you need to either have a machine named cs in the colorado.edu domain or have MX records that point into the cs.colorado.edu domain. For example, in the files for cs.colorado.edu, putting the record

```
IN   MX   10   mailhub.cs.colorado.edu.
```

immediately after the SOA and NS records for the zone would produce the desired effect.

16.12 UPDATING ZONE FILES

When you make a change to a domain (such as adding or deleting a host), the data files on the primary server must be updated. You must also increment the serial number in the SOA record for the zone and send a hangup signal to **named**. When **named** starts, it reads its database files into memory and does not look at them again until it receives this signal. You can also kill and restart **named**, but this will cause cached data from other domains to be discarded.

These steps will make the new data available immediately on the primary server and available after *refresh* seconds (one to six hours) on the secondaries. If you want a more timely update, a hangup signal sent to a secondary will cause it to check with the primary, see that the data has changed, and request a zone transfer.

Don't forget to modify both the forward and the reverse zones when you change a hostname or IP address. Forgetting the reverse files leaves sneaky errors—some commands will work and some won't.

Changing the data files but forgetting to send a hangup signal to **named** will make your changes invisible to all systems. Changing the primary data files but forgetting to change the serial number will make the changes take effect on the primary server (after a hangup signal) but not on the secondaries.

It is improper to edit data files belonging to secondary servers. These files are maintained by **named**; sysadmins should not meddle with them, as it makes them soggy and hard to light. It's fine to look at the data files as long as you don't make changes. They can often reveal hidden configuration errors.

For example, a pesky missing dot that's easy to overlook in the primary's config files can result in obviously bogus entries such as

```
foo.cs.colorado.edu.cs.colorado.edu
```

appearing in the data file of a secondary.

16.13 ZONE TRANSFERS

DNS servers are synchronized using a mechanism called a zone transfer. All the data for a zone is transferred at once; there are no incremental updates except as a side effect of specific queries.

The timeouts set in the SOA record determine how quickly secondary servers notice that their data is out of date. A secondary that wants to refresh its data requests a zone transfer from the primary server and makes a backup copy of the zone data on disk. If the data on the primary has not changed, no update occurs and the backup files are just touched (that is, their modification time is set to the current time).

Zone transfers use the TCP protocol on port 53 and log information via **syslog** with the tag "named-xfer."

Both the sending and receiving server remain available to answer queries during a zone transfer. Only after the transfer is complete does the secondary begin to use the new data. There were early problems with zone transfers, but both the BIND distributions from Berkeley and those shipped by most vendors now have it right.

16.14 SECURITY ISSUES

DNS is an inherently open system. Anyone on the Internet can investigate your domain with individual queries or, with **nslookup**'s **ls** command, dump your entire database. Some sites disable zone transfers to the outside world by changing the **named** code (**grep** for "xfr_disabled").

BIND 4.9 has added some important security features to address these vulnerabilities. Zone transfers can be controlled through the xfrnets directive in the **named.boot** file; see page 330.

Zones can be also secured with an access list of hosts and networks. To use this feature, you must compile **named** with the SECURE_ZONES symbol defined and then add special secure_zone TXT records to your zone database. These records are described on page 342.

Your network should still be protected at a lower level through router access control lists and normal security hygiene on each host. If this is not possible, you can refuse DNS packets except to a gateway machine that you monitor closely.

16.15 TESTING AND DEBUGGING

`named` has several built-in debugging aids. Command-line debug levels are supported. Signals can be used to tell `named` to adjust the debugging level or to dump its database or statistics. `nslookup` or `dig` can verify name lookups.

See Chapter 12 for more information about `syslog`.

`named` uses the `syslog` system to report error messages and anomalies. The messages are tagged with either "named" or "named-xfer" and are recorded with `syslog` facility "daemon" and `syslog` severity levels "debug" through "crit." Most messages are at level "err." Local configuration syntax errors do generate `syslog` messages; peruse your log files regularly, especially if you have just changed your configuration.

Log Messages

Table 16.6 shows some typical messages recorded by `syslog` and the severity levels of the incidents that generate them. You may want to capture most `syslog` messages when BIND is first set up, then reconfigure `syslog` to preserve only serious messages once `named` is stable.

Table 16.6   Syslog messages from named

Level	Approximate message or cause
crit	Serial number not monotonically increasing
	Permission problems on name server files
err	Lots of system errors: `malloc`, `open`, `close`, etc.
	Some database configuration errors including:
	Fewer than two root hints
	Domain name too long
	Unknown resource record type
	No SOA record
	Multiple SOA records
	Unknown directive
	CNAME has other data (illegal)
warning	More database configuration errors:
	HINFO CPU type too long (>255 chars)
	HINFO OS type too long (>255 chars)
	TXT record truncated at 255 chars
notice	Lame delegation to *xxx* received from *yyy*
	Attempted to query myself on *xxx* as server for *yyy*
	Maximum number of queries exceeded
	Reloading server, version #
info	Malformed response from *xxx*

Debug Levels

`named` debug levels are indicated by integers from 0 to 11. The higher the number, the more verbose the output. Level 0 turns debugging off.

Levels 1 and 2 are fine for debugging your configuration and database; levels beyond about 4 are appropriate for the maintainers of the code. Debugging can be invoked on the **named** command line with the **-d** flag. For example,

```
named -d2
```

would start **named** at debug level 2. Debugging information is written to the file **/var/tmp/named.run**. It will grow very fast, so don't go out for a beer while debugging or you will have bigger problems when you return. Debugging can also be turned on while **named** is running with the USR1 signal, which increments the debug level by one.

Watching the logs or the debugging output illustrates how often data is misconfigured. That pesky little dot at the end of names (or rather, the lack thereof) accounts for an alarming amount of DNS traffic. Theoretically, the dot is required at the end of each fully qualified domain name. Most applications know from context to add the dot for you and some (for example, mail) may break if you add it yourself.

Signals Understood by named

named listens for several signals, listed in Table 16.7. Signals that produce files put them in either **/var/tmp** or **/usr/tmp**.

Table 16.7   Signals understood by named

Signal	Function
USR1	Increments debug level by 1 (data goes to **named.run**)
USR2	Turns off debugging
INT	Dumps database to **named_dump.db**
IOT/ABRT	Dumps statistics to **named.stats**
HUP	Reloads boot file and database files
KILL	Kills **named**, must restart by hand (flushes cache)
WINCH	Toggles tracing of incoming queries (BIND 4.9)

To turn on debugging if **named** was started without the debug flag, type

```
kill -USR1 `cat /etc/named.pid`
```

as root a couple of times. And to turn it off, use

```
kill -USR2 `cat /etc/named.pid`
```

If your system does not support named signals, look in the header file **/usr/include/signal.h** to see the mapping from names to numbers. Ignore the SIG prefix (for example, USR1 appears as SIGUSR1).

An INT signal makes **named** dump its database to **named_dump.db**. The dump file is big and includes not only local data but also any cached data that the name server has accumulated. A recent dump of the database cache on our primary colorado.edu name server was over half a megabyte. One use of the database dump is to see if you are propagating old information. If so, kill and restart **named**.

 named keeps query statistics which can be accessed with an IOT or ABRT signal. IRIX uses ABRT, while our other example systems use IOT. Both are signal 6, but the names are in transition. On receipt of the signal, **named** writes statistics to **named.stats**. A sample from a secondary server that has been up for four days is shown below. This information is normally printed in one long column, but we've compressed it into two columns to save space.

```
### Sun Feb 13 02:02:11 1994
352788  time since boot (s)     5       Unknown query types
352788  time since reset (s)    192797  A queries
344829  input packets           412     NS queries
361642  output packets          5257    CNAME queries
249901  queries                 2       SOA queries
6       iqueries                11      MG queries
1163    duplicate queries       1       WKS queries
95031   responses               23178   PTR queries
3222    duplicate responses     286     HINFO queries
216200  OK answers              10616   MX queries
31489   FAIL answers            791     TXT queries
68      FORMERR answers         1       AXFR queries
1015    system queries          16543   ANY queries
2       prime cache calls
2       check_ns calls
3952    bad responses dropped
10      martian responses
```

The headings describe the types of queries and the problems with them. Any query that results in an error is logged to **syslog**, counted in one or more statistics buckets, and dropped. Duplicates represent a timeout occurring before an answer was received, causing a duplicate query to be sent. Martian responses are answers that arrive from an unexpected source. They are associated with the last query asked and so might just be delayed answers to previous questions.

Debugging with nslookup and dig

nslookup and BIND are included on the CD-ROM.

nslookup is a user-level command that queries the DNS database. It expects fully qualified names ending in a dot and will append the default domain if you forget the dot. For local names, this is often what you want. A short list of **nslookup** commands is given in Table 16.8.

dig is included on the CD-ROM.

dig, the Domain Information Groper, provides the same functionality as **nslookup**, but has more sensible defaults and a nicer user interface.

Table 16.8 Commands understood by nslookup

Command	Function
help	Shows a complete list of commands
exit	Quits
server *host*	Sets default server using current server
lserver *host*	Sets default server using initial server
set type=*xxx*	Sets query type[a]
set debug	Turns on debugging
set d2	Turns on lots of debugging
ls *domain*	Lists all host/address mappings

a. "any" is a good value that means "all."

For example, to ask for anchor's MX records, use

    dig anchor.cs.colorado.edu. mx

The command

    dig @berkeley.edu vangogh.berkeley.edu. any

obtains vangogh's complete records from a berkeley.edu server, and

    dig -x 128.32.130.2

performs a reverse query for vangogh.

dig is verbose. Its output includes not only the domain information, but also the number of queries sent and the answer's round-trip time. **dig** has also been known to lie about the host data. Bad **dig**.

While setting up BIND, be sure to test both local and off-site hosts in both the forward and reverse directions. **nslookup**'s default query is from name to address; you must set the query type to see other data. Here is a typical **nslookup** testing sequence:

```
% nslookup                      /* Start nslookup */
Default Server: piper.cs.colorado.edu
Address:   128.138.204.4
> anchor                        /* Local forward mapping */
Name:      anchor.cs.colorado.edu
Address:   128.138.242.1
> mammoth.cs.berkeley.edu.      /* Remote forward */
Non-authoritative answer:
Name:      mammoth.cs.berkeley.edu
Address:   128.32.149.78
> set type=PTR                  /* Default is type A */
> 1.242.138.128.in-addr.arpa.
1.242.138.128.in-addr.arpa  host name =
   anchor.cs.colorado.edu
```

The server and its address are echoed with each query, but these lines have been omitted to make the example more trenchant. **dig** can provide similar information:

```
% dig anchor                    /* Forward query */
; <<>> DiG 2.0 <<>> anchor
;; ->>HEADER<<- opcode: QUERY , status: NOERROR, id: 10
;; flags: qr aa rd ra ; Ques: 1, Ans: 2, Auth: 0, Addit: 0
;; QUESTIONS:
;;      anchor.cs.Colorado.EDU, type = A, class = IN
;; ANSWERS:
anchor.cs.Colorado.EDU. 7200    A       128.138.242.1
anchor.cs.Colorado.EDU. 7200    A       128.138.243.100
;; Sent 1 pkts, answer found in time: 13 msec
;; FROM: piper to SERVER: default  128.138.204.4
;; MSG SIZE  sent: 40  rcvd: 72
% dig -x 128.138.242.1          /* Reverse query */
; <<>> DiG 2.0 <<>> @piper -x
;; ->>HEADER<<- opcode: QUERY , status: NOERROR, id: 10
;; flags: qr aa rd ra ; Ques: 1, Ans: 1, Auth: 0, Addit: 0
;; QUESTIONS:
;;      1.242.138.128.in-addr.arpa, type = ANY, class = IN
;; ANSWERS:
1.242.138.128.in-addr.arpa.   7200    PTR
   anchor.cs.colorado.edu.
;; Sent 1 pkts, answer found in time: 36 msec
;; FROM: piper to SERVER: default  128.138.204.4
;; MSG SIZE  sent: 44  rcvd: 80
```

dig gives more information than **nslookup** and has a zillion options. It also seems faster and more intuitive, especially for reverse zones.

Lame Delegations

When you apply for a domain name, you are asking for a part of the naming tree to be delegated to your primary name server and your DNS administrator. If you never use the domain or you change the name servers without updating the parent domain's glue records, a "lame delegation" results.

The effects of a lame delegation can be very bad. If a user tries to contact a host in your lame domain, your name server will refuse the query. DNS will retry the query several hundred times, pummeling both your primary server and the root server.

Lame delegations are logged via **syslog**. For example:

```
Feb 27 01:22:41 boulder named[1478]: Lame delegation to
   'MINDVOX.com' received from 192.94.207.66 (purported
   server for 'MINDVOX.com') on query on name [mindvox.com]
```

mindvox.com uses an off-site secondary server (icm1.icp.net at IP address 192.94.207.66) that does not admit to being authoritative for the mindvox domain.

```
Feb 27 03:18:17 boulder named[1478]: Lame delegation to
   'uci.EDU' received from 128.200.9.5 (purported server
   for 'acs.UCI.edu') on query on name [vega.acs.uci.edu]
```

In this example, the machine csi2.ns.nts.uci.edu with IP address 128.200.9.5 is advertised to the Internet as authoritative for the name vega.acs.uci.edu, but denies being authoritative for the acs.uci.edu domain. This represents an error on the part of the administrators of uci.edu which accounted for many, many DNS queries. They must be lashed until they collapse.

For a 24 hour period, our syslog data shows 258 lame delegation entries, most of which are followed by the message

```
Feb 27 03:18:39 boulder last message repeated 3 times
```

Ergo, the actual number of lame delegation errors is higher. Many of the messages recorded in the file are for overseas sites. The worst offender, ufsc.br, accounted for 89 of the 258 entries, each repeated an average of 3 times. Where are the net police when you need them?

16.16 HOST MANAGEMENT TOOLS

DNS database files cover a whole naming domain but usually span local administrative and political domains. In many cases, tight central control is infeasible. This situation presents a common administration problem: How do you manage critical (but fragile) data files that many untrained people may need to edit at random times? It would also be nice if the Physics Department could not change the CS Department's records and vice versa.

If a political domain contains several hosts and has an administrative staff, then a subdomain is a good way to distribute control. But for a small department with only a few hosts, a subdomain is not necessary.

*addhost is
included on
the CD-ROM.*

Our **addhost** system, written by John Hardt while an undergraduate, is one way to solve this problem. The **addhost** database is a single campus-wide repository for host information, including

* Name server data
* Inventory data
* Responsible person/department

Each host record has associated with it an administrative domain (such as the Computer Science Department) and an administrative subdomain (such as the undergraduate lab). Write access to the database is controlled by a configuration file stating which users have authority over which administrative domains.

The **addhost** user interface can be run from any workstation on the network. It is **curses**-based (can be run from a terminal or PC) and uses the **ndbm** routines to manage its database files.

Using a tool to access host data has several advantages:

- It doesn't require users to memorize a file format.
- It prevents inadvertent errors.
- It avoids collisions between simultaneous updates.
- It allows records to be protected from other people's changes.
- It guarantees the uniqueness of hostnames and IP addresses.

Tools in the **addhost** system convert portions of the database to formats usable by other software. **dumphost** is a C program that, together with a configuration file, can dump any portion of the database. Another tool builds a file in **/etc/hosts** format from **dumphost** output, and a **perl** script called **named.perl** builds DNS data files.

addhost includes a daemon, **addhostd**, that manages connections to the hosts database from the **addhost** user interface, from **telnet** connections to port 711, or from programs like **dumphost**. **addhostd** is managed by **inetd**.

16.17 DNS FOR SYSTEMS NOT ON THE INTERNET

See page 554 for more information about firewalls.

If you are not part of the Internet but want to use DNS, you can declare your primary name server authoritative for the root domain. This configuration might be appropriate for either a small company that is not yet on the Internet or an organization that hides its local structure behind a firewall.

In this setup, your cache file should point to local name servers, not to the root servers of the Internet. You should still get a registered domain name and legitimate IP addresses; changing them later is a real nightmare at a large site.

Don't forget to change your DNS files before you connect to the Internet. If you screw up, **named**s everywhere will ferret you out and punish your poor name server and DNS administrator.

16.18 VERSIONS OF BIND

As we go to print, BIND 4.9.3 has just been released; BIND 4.8.3 accounts for the bulk of the installed base. A version based on 4.8.2 called UTBIND from the University of Toronto has many improvements and new features, including support for users' environment variables LOCALDOMAIN and DOMAINPATH.

Various patched versions for SunOS that coexist with NIS are available. The **contrib** directory of the 4.9.3 distribution also contains code for beating SunOS into submission.

16.19 SPECIFICS FOR VARIOUS OPERATING SYSTEMS

This section describes the atrocities committed on Berkeley's freely-distributed BIND code by our helpful vendors. We include pointers to the configuration files, the release of BIND that each vendor's software is based on, and information about how to integrate BIND with other sources of administrative data such as flat files or NIS.

A more complete discussion of this last topic is presented in Chapter 18. In particular, refer to the material beginning on page 403.

 Solaris's BIND is based on BIND version 4.8.3. Sun publishes a 360-page manual that describes NIS+ and BIND. Actually, about 40 pages are for BIND and the rest is for NIS+. A measure of complexity, perhaps. The copy we looked at was for Solaris 5.2.

The BIND section contains many errors in examples where whitespace has been misused. Some examples have no whitespace, yet need it to separate fields; others have so much whitespace that they span multiple lines when they shouldn't. Be very careful using any of the examples from the Solaris book as a model for your configuration files.

Solaris uses a service order file called **/etc/nsswitch.conf** to specify how BIND, NIS, NIS+ and the **/etc/hosts** file interact. Modifying the hosts line in that file to

```
hosts:  dns files
```

will cause name resolution to try DNS first and then try **/etc/hosts**. The Sun manual recommends that you add DNS as the second entry, behind NIS or NIS+:

```
hosts:  nisplus dns files
```

After modifying the **nsswitch.conf** file, the documentation says you must reboot the workstation (that's every workstation, folks) because not all library routines check to see if the switch file has changed. Our experience has been that this was not necessary with BIND.

Also, check the file **/etc/netconfig**; it must have **switch.so** listed as a name-to-address translation library for all three of the Internet transport protocols: UDP, TCP, and "rawip."

Filenames and locations are summarized in Table 16.9 (next page).

Table 16.9   **BIND files in Solaris**

File	Directory	Description
resolv.conf	/etc	Resolver library configuration
in.named	/etc	Name server daemon
named-xfer	/usr/sbin	Zone transfer code
named.boot	/etc	Boot file for name servers
named.pid	/etc	Process ID
named.run	/var/tmp	Output from debug mode
named.stats	/var/tmp	Statistics output
named_dump.db	/var/tmp	Dump of entire database

HP-UX's BIND is based on BIND 4.8.3. There is no service order file. DNS, if configured, is tried first. If that fails, NIS is tried, and if that fails or is not configured, then **/etc/hosts** is tried.

Several experimental resource records are supported, but not those outlined in RFC1183. Important filenames and locations are summarized in Table 16.10.

Table 16.10   **BIND files in HP-UX**

File	Directory	Description
resolv.conf	/etc	Resolver library configuration
in.named	/etc	Name server daemon
named-xfer	/etc	Zone transfer code
named.boot	/etc	Boot file for name servers
named.pid	/etc	Process ID
named.run	/usr/tmp	Output from debug mode
named.stats	/usr/tmp	Statistics output
named_dump.db	/usr/tmp	Dump of entire database
Zone files	/etc/newconfig[a]	Default location for zone files

a. In the bind directory.

HP-UX has well-commented sample files in **/etc/newconfig/bind**, including a **resolv.conf**, various boot files, a cache file, and forward and reverse zone files.

HP-UX provides some tools to help you transition to DNS files. The command **hosts_to_named** converts from **/etc/hosts** format to DNS resource record format. **sig_named** can be used to send signals to **named**; it is just a friendly front end to **kill**. **convert_rhosts** (in the directory **/etc/newconfig/bind**) is a shell script that converts a **.rhosts** file from relative names to fully qualified domain names. It can also leave in the relative names, which should satisfy most software.

SGI's BIND is based on BIND 4.8.3. IRIX uses files in `/etc/config` to indicate which services are configured rather than relying on the permissions and existence of configuration files.

Files in `/etc/config` can be manipulated by the **chkconfig** command or a text editor. A service in `/etc/config` (for example, **named**) is configured if the file called **named** contains the string on, and is not configured if it contains anything else.

A file in `/etc/config` called **named.options** can be used to pass command-line arguments to **named**. A popular option is **-L**, which suppresses **syslog** messages from lame delegations, incorrect root queries, or both. Since these errors are common, **-L lamedel,rootns** can be used to keep log files relevant and small.

The order in which services are consulted is set using the directive hostresorder in `/etc/resolv.conf`. For example, the line

```
hostresorder bind local
```

would try DNS first, and if that failed, try `/etc/hosts`. nis is also a possible value. A slash in the hostresorder line means that the preceding item is authoritative. For example,

```
hostresorder bind / local
```

means that DNS should be tried first and that `/etc/hosts` should be read only if DNS is unavailable (*not* if DNS simply didn't know the answer to the query).

Individual users can override the order set in `/etc/resolv.conf` by setting the HOSTRESORDER environment variable.

Filenames and locations are summarized in Table 16.11.

Table 16.11   BIND files in IRIX

File	Directory	Description
resolv.conf	/usr/etc	Resolver library configuration
in.named	/usr/etc	Name server daemon
named-xfer	/usr/etc	Zone transfer code
named.boot	/usr/etc/named.d	Boot file for name servers
named.run	/usr/tmp	Output from debug mode
named.stats	/usr/tmp	Statistics output
named_dump.db	/usr/tmp	Dump of entire database
Zone files	/usr/etc/named.d	Default location for zone files

IRIX provides some tools for manipulating **named**: **named.reload** sends **named** a hangup signal to make it reload its boot file and database, while **named.restart** kills and restarts it, flushing the cache.

The `domain` and `sortlist` directives have been demoted by IRIX. A smarter resolver library completes partial names rather than blindly appending the `domain`. The `sortlist` directive is honored only at startup; if a hangup signal is sent, causing **named** to reread its boot file, the `sortlist` is ignored.

SunOS's NIS and DNS have never peacefully coexisted. The problem is one of control. There are potentially three places where address mappings can be found: **/etc/hosts**, NIS, and DNS. NIS lives in its own little world and was not designed to share control with an upstart DNS.

See Chapter 18 for more information about NIS.

If you run NIS, the proper behavior is to ask NIS, and if NIS does not know the answer, to then ask DNS. If you do not run NIS, DNS followed or preceded by **/etc/hosts** is an adequate solution. But SunOS forces you to choose either static files or both NIS and DNS. The resolver is part of NIS's **ypserv** daemon, which makes separating NIS and DNS a bit like separating Siamese twins.

This inbreeding creates a problem for sites that have found NIS inadequate for their needs (usually large, heterogenous sites) and switched to other distribution mechanisms. Unless you run NIS, you cannot use the DNS software shipped with SunOS. Work-arounds exist; see the Usenet archive of comp.sys.sun.admin. BIND 4.9.3 comes with scripts and instructions (in the **contrib/sunlibc** directory) to bash a real resolver into the SunOS 4.1.3 shared library.

SunOS's official BIND is based on BIND 4.8.1; users have posted versions based on 4.8.3 that bypass NIS and work correctly. Filenames and locations are summarized in Table 16.12.

Table 16.12   BIND files in SunOS

File	Directory	Description
resolv.conf	/etc	Resolver library configuration
in.named	/usr/etc	Name server daemon
named-xfer	/usr/etc	Zone transfer code
named.boot	/etc	Boot file for name servers
named.pid	/etc	Process ID
named.run	/var/tmp	Output from debug mode
named.stats	/var/tmp	Statistics output
named_dump.db	/var/tmp	Dump of entire database
Zone files	/etc/named.*	Default location for zone files

 OSF/1's BIND is based on BIND 4.8.3. DEC first introduced the concept of sharing responsibility for hostname lookups with its service order file,

/etc/svcorder, under Ultrix. The file is now called /etc/svc.conf and contains lines of the form

```
hosts=local,bind
```

This example specifies that hostname lookups should first consult the /etc/hosts file and then the DNS system. If you hate your text editor or are afraid of making syntax mistakes, the /usr/sbin/svcsetup script can be used to modify the svc.conf file.

Filenames and locations are summarized in Table 16.13.

Table 16.13   BIND files in OSF/1

File	Directory	Description
resolv.conf	/etc	Resolver library configuration
in.named	/usr/sbin	Name server daemon
named-xfer	/usr/sbin	Zone transfer code
named.boot	/etc/namedb	Boot file for name servers
named.pid	/var/run	Process ID
named.run	/var/tmp	Output from debug mode
named.stats	/var/tmp	Statistics output
named_dump.db	/var/tmp	Dump of entire database
Zone files	/usr/local/domain	Default location for zone files

BSDI's BIND is based on BIND 4.9. There is no service ordering file; the library routines are hard-wired to try DNS, and if that fails, to then consult the /etc/hosts file.

BSDI's BIND includes negative caching, which should improve performance (especially in terms of network bandwidth).

Filenames and locations are summarized in Table 16.14.

Table 16.14   BIND files in BSDI

File	Directory	Description
resolv.conf	/etc	Resolver library configuration
in.named	/usr/sbin	Name server daemon
named-xfer	/usr/libexec	Zone transfer code
named.boot	/etc	Boot file for name servers
named.pid	/var/run	Process ID
named.run	/var/tmp	Output from debug mode
named.stats	/var/tmp	Statistics output
named_dump.db	/var/tmp	Dump of entire database
Zone files	/etc/namedb	Default location for zone files

16.20 RECOMMENDED SUPPLEMENTAL READING

There are a variety of references for DNS and BIND, ranging from chapters in several books on Internet topics to an entire book in the O'Reilly Nutshell series.

There is a public mailing list for DNS and BIND issues. To join, send mail to bind-request@uunet.uu.net. Before upgrading your version of BIND, it's a good idea to join and read the mailing list for a bit so you are familiar with the stability and bugs or features of the new release.

The RFCs that define the DNS system are included on the CD-ROM and are also available from ds.internic.net. They are listed in Table 16.15.

Table 16.15   DNS-related RFCs

RFC	Date	Contents
920	10/84	Domain Requirements
974	1/86	Mail Routing and the Domain System
1032	11/87	Domain Administrators Guide
1033	11/87	Domain Administrators Operations Guide
1034	11/87	Domain Names: Concepts and Facilities[a]
1035	11/87	Domain Names: Implementation and Specification[a]
1101	4/89	DNS Encoding of Network Names and Other Types[b]
1183	10/90	New DNS RR Definitions[b]
1535	10/93	Security Problems in DNS Software

a. These documents obsolete RFCs 973, 882, and 883.
b. These documents update RFCs 1034 and 1035.

Here are some other sources you may find useful:

> DUNLAP, KEVIN J., MIKE KARELS, and PAUL VIXIE. *"Name Server Operations Guide for BIND."* In *UNIX System Managers Manual* (SMM:10). Usenix Association, 1994.

This document outlines the management of BIND. It is quite complete and describes many of the new features in BIND 4.9. It's included with the BIND distribution and is also in both the BSD 4.3 and 4.4 system manager's manuals.

> CARL-MITCHELL, SMOOT and JOHN S. QUARTERMAN. *Practical Internetworking with TCP/IP and UNIX.* Addison Wesley, 1993.

DNS is a chapter in this book; it has wonderful diagrams.

> HUNT, CRAIG. *TCP/IP Network Administration.* O'Reilly, 1992.

DNS is a chapter with lots of examples.

ALBITZ, PAUL and CRICKET LIU. *DNS and BIND.* O'Reilly, 1992.

This book covers DNS in lots of detail, but it seemed to us to be poorly organized and a bit out of date (no coverage of BIND 4.9).

17 *The Network File System*

17.1 INTRODUCTION

The Network File System, commonly called NFS, allows you to share filesystems among computers. NFS is almost transparent to users and is "stateless," meaning that no information is lost when an NFS server crashes. Clients can simply wait until the server returns and then continue as if nothing had happened.

The NFS protocols are publicly documented in RFC1094.

NFS was introduced by Sun Microsystems in 1985. It was originally implemented as a surrogate filesystem for diskless clients, but has now been aggressively promoted as a file sharing panacea. In fact, it's difficult to remember what life was like before NFS. Most UNIX vendors provide a version of NFS; many use code licensed from Sun.

NFS consists of a number of components, including a mounting protocol and server, a file locking protocol and server, and daemons that coordinate basic file service. NFS is built on top of Sun's XDR and RPC facilities, which provide an architecture-independent way to represent data and a network remote procedure call interface, respectively.

17.2 SERVER-SIDE NFS

Under BSD, a server is said to "export" a filesystem when it makes the filesystem available for use by other machines. ATT has chosen to eliminate the use of the word "export"; instead, ATT servers "share" their filesystems. For clarity, we use "export" throughout this chapter.

An NFS client must explicitly mount a filesystem before using it. The server examines the mount request to be sure that the client has proper authorization, then tells the client a secret "magic cookie" (actually a random number) that the client can use later to obtain access.

The magic cookie scheme keeps the server stateless, since no permanent record of the clients that have been authenticated need be kept. Usually, unmounting and remounting a filesystem on the server changes its cookie.

As a special case, cookies persist across a reboot so that a server that crashes can return to its previous state. But don't try to boot single user, play with filesystems, then boot again; this will revoke cookies and make clients unable to access the filesystems they have mounted until they either reboot or remount.

Once a client has a magic cookie, it uses RPC to make requests for filesystem operations such as creating a file or reading a data block. Because NFS is stateless, the server doesn't care what requests the client has or hasn't made before. In particular, the client is responsible for making sure that the server acknowledges write requests before it deletes its own copy of the data to be written.

mountd: Respond to Mount Requests

Mount requests are handled by the **mountd** daemon.[1] On BSD systems, **mountd** reads the **/etc/exports** file to get information about which hosts should be allowed access and what restrictions, if any, should be enforced. The **exports** file consists of a list of exported directories in the leftmost column, followed by lists of associated options and attributes. For example, the **exports** file

```
/chimchim/users   -access=band:moonie,root=band
/usr/share/man    -access=xorasaurus:rastadon:moonie
```

permits **/chimchim/users** to be mounted by band and moonie, and allows root access to the filesystem from band.[2] In addition, it lets **/usr/share/man** be mounted by xorasaurus, rastadon, and moonie.

NFS deals with the logical layer of the filesystem, not the physical layer. Any directory can be exported; it doesn't have to be a mount point or the root directory of a physical filesystem. However, for security reasons, NFS knows about the boundaries between devices and requires each device to be exported separately. For example, on a machine with a partition mounted as **/users**, the root directory can be exported without giving away access to this partition.

---

1. Sometimes called rpc.mountd.

2. As well as from chimchim, the real owner of the filesystem.

The exact attributes that can be specified in /etc/exports vary from system to system. The most common attributes are listed in Tables 17.1 (for IRIX, HP-UX, and SunOS) and 17.2 (for BSDI and OSF/1).

Solaris uses the **share** command to export filesystems instead of the /etc/exports file; this brain damage will be described shortly.

Table 17.1   Common export attributes (IRIX, HP-UX, and SunOS)

Attribute	Description
-access=*list*	Lists hosts[a] that can mount the filesystem.
-ro	Export read-only; no clients may write on the filesystem.
-rw=*list*	Export read-mostly. *list* enumerates the hosts[a] allowed to mount for writing; all others must mount read-only.
-root=*list*	Lists hosts[a] permitted to access the filesystem as root. Without this option, root access from a client is equivalent to access by the user nobody (usually UID -2).
-anon=*n*	Specifies UID that should be used for requests coming from an unknown user. Defaults to nobody.

a. Colon-separated list that can include hostnames and netgroups; see Chapter 18.

Table 17.2   Common export attributes (BSDI and OSF/1)

Attribute	Description
hostname	Allow *hostname* to mount the filesystem.
-ro	Export read-only; no clients may write on the filesystem.
-root=*n*	Specifies UID that should be used for requests coming from a remote root user. If not specified, the user nobody (usually UID -2) is used by default.

Filesystems that are listed in the **exports** file without a specific set of hosts are usually mountable by *all* machines. This can be a sizable security hole. After changing /etc/exports, you must tell **mountd** to reread it. The procedure for doing so varies from system to system and is detailed in Table 17.3.

Table 17.3   What to do after editing /etc/exports

System	Required operation
Solaris	Not applicable (see below)
HP-UX	Run /usr/etc/exportfs -a
IRIX	Run /usr/etc/exportfs -a
SunOS	Run /usr/etc/exportfs -a
OSF/1	Send a SIGHUP to mountd with kill.
BSDI	Send a SIGHUP to mountd with kill.

Solaris has replaced `/etc/exports` with `/etc/dfs/dfstab`. This file is actually a shell script that executes the **share** command once for each exported filesystem. For example, on a server that shares the directory `/chimchim/users` with band and moonie (with band allowed root access), and shares `/usr/share/man` with xor, rastadon, and barkadon, `/etc/dfs/dfstab` would contain the following commands:

```
#!/bin/sh
share -F nfs -o rw=band:moonie,root=band /chimchim/users
share -F nfs -o rw=xor:rastadon:barkadon /usr/share/man
```

After editing `/etc/dfs/dfstab`, you must also execute any new or modified **share** commands in order for them to take effect. **share** notifies **mountd** of any changes when it is executed. Table 17.4 lists the options available for use with **share**.

Table 17.4   Options for the share command (Solaris)

Attribute	Description
-ro	Export read-only, or if used in the form -ro=*list*, restrict access only for the listed hosts.
-rw	Export read-write, or if used in the form -rw=*list*, allow writing only by the listed hosts.
-root=*list*	Lists hosts permitted to access this filesystem as root. Otherwise, root access from a client is equivalent to access by the user nobody (usually UID -2).
-anon=*n*	Specifies UID used for requests coming from an unknown user. If not specified, defaults to nobody.

nfsd: Serve Files

Once a client's mount request has been validated by **mountd**, it is allowed to request various filesystem operations. These requests are handled on the server side by **nfsd**, the NFS operations daemon.[3] **nfsd** need not be run on an NFS client machine unless the client also exports filesystems of its own.

nfsd takes one argument which specifies the number of copies of itself to fork. Selecting the appropriate number of **nfsd**s is important, and is unfortunately something of a black art. If the number is too low or too high, NFS performance can suffer.

You should run at least four **nfsd**s. Four is adequate for a server that is used infrequently, and is few enough that performance problems can't

---

3. In reality, **nfsd** is essentially a one-line program that makes a non-returning system call to NFS server code embedded in the kernel. It is disguised as a user process only because this makes the scheduling issues easier to implement.

really arise. In theory, you could start tens or hundreds of **nfsd**s. However, too many **nfsd**s will degrade performance because they will fight each other for the CPU.

The maximum number of **nfsd**s is closely tied to the number of hardware contexts supported by your computer's CPU chip. In today's RISC market the number of contexts on a chip may change with each version of the processor family, but it is usually in the range 8 to 32. If you can find out the exact number of contexts on your CPU (not always easy without the hardware manual for the chip), a good rule of thumb is to start no more than N-2 **nfsd**s, where N is the number of contexts.

If you cannot determine the exact number of on-board contexts, you can make a good guess by trial and error. Increase the number of **nfsd**s until the load average of the server (as reported by **uptime**) begins to increase significantly. When this happens, it's an indication that your system has more **nfsd**s than it knows what to do with. Back off a few from that number, and you should be safe. Remember, this is the *maximum* number of **nfsd**s, not the *best* number.

If you'd rather read a "probably good enough" answer out of a stupid book instead of doing your own experiments, use the following table:

Table 17.5   Maximum number of nfsds to use on a busy server

System	Processor	nfsds	System	Processor	nfsds
Solaris	SPARC	10	SunOS	SPARC	10
	SuperSPARC[a]	12		SuperSPARC[a]	12
HP-UX	PA-RISC	8	OSF/1	DEC Alpha	8
IRIX	MIPS R-4000[a]	10	BSDI	80486	8

a. Numbers quoted are for single-processor machines.

See Chapter 14 for more information about the UDP network protocol. On a loaded NFS server, UDP sockets can overflow if requests arrive while all **nfsd** "piers" are already in use. The number of overflows can be monitored with **netstat -s**. The first thing you should do when figuring out how many **nfsd**s to run is to add more **nfsd**s until UDP socket overflows drop to zero, or you reach the maximum number of **nfsd**s computed above.

17.3   CLIENT-SIDE NFS

On machines that support NFS, the **mount** command has been modified to understand the notation

    hostname:directory

as meaning the path *directory* interpreted by the host *hostname*.

The **mount** command and its associated NFS extensions represent the most significant concerns to a system administrator on an NFS client. On some systems, the optional but highly-recommended daemon **biod** (block I/O daemon) provides performance enhancements.

biod: Provide Client-Side Caching

In order to improve overall NFS performance, most systems include the **biod** daemon,[4] which does basic read-ahead and write-behind filesystem block caching. We strongly suggest that you run this daemon on all NFS clients, but it is not strictly required.

Like **nfsd**, **biod** takes as its argument the number of copies of itself to start. See page 371 for information about choosing this number; the rules for **nfsd** apply to **biod** as well. If both **nfsd** and **biod** run on the same machine, it may be wise to split the "optimal" number of process slots between them. This will depend on how your system is used; you'll have to experiment.

Mounting Remote Filesystems

See page 376 for more information about automount *and* amd.

The **mount** command can be used to establish temporary network mounts, but mounts that are part of a system's permanent configuration should be either listed in **/etc/fstab** (so that they are mounted automatically at boot time) or handled by an automatic mounting service such as **automount** or **amd**.

The following **fstab** entries mount the filesystems **/xor/users** and **/usr/man** from the hosts xor and chimchim:

```
# filesystem mountpoint tstype flags dump fsck
xor:/xor/users      /xor/users   nfs rw,bg,intr,hard 0 0
chimchim:/usr/man   /usr/man     nfs ro,bg,intr,soft 0 0
```

See page 143 for more information about fstab.

When you add entries to **/etc/fstab**, be sure to create the mount point directories with **mkdir**. You can make your changes take effect immediately by running

```
mount -a -t nfs
```

The *flags* field of **/etc/fstab** can be used to specify options for NFS mounts. Common flags are listed in Table 17.6 (on the next page).

 In Solaris, **/etc/fstab** has been gratuitously moved to **/etc/vfstab** in the style of System V, and the number of fields has changed slightly. Where NFS is concerned, the options are identical.

Filesystems mounted **hard** can cause processes to hang when their servers go down. This is particularly bothersome when the processes in

---

4. Called **nfsiod** on BSDI and OSF/1 systems.

Table 17.6   NFS mount flags

Flag	Description
rw	Mount the filesystem read-write (must be exported read-write by the server).
ro	Mount the filesystem read-only.
bg	If the mount fails (server doesn't respond), keep trying it in the background and continue with other mount requests.
hard	If a server goes down, make operations that try to access it block until the server comes back up.
soft	If a server goes down, make operations that try to access it fail and return an error. This is useful to avoid processes "hanging" on inessential mounts.
spongy[a]	Similar to a hard mount except for the stat, lookup, fsstat, readlink, and readdir operations, which behave like a soft mount. This keeps clients from tripping over dead server mount points.
retrans=n	Specifies the number of times to repeat a request before returning an error on a soft-mounted filesystem.
timeo=n	Sets the timeout period (in tenths of a second) for requests.
intr	Allows users to interrupt blocked operations (and make them return an error).
rsize=n	Sets read buffer size to n bytes.
wsize=n	Sets write buffer size to n bytes.

a. Currently available only on BSDI and OSF/1.

question are standard daemons. In general, the use of the soft and intr options will reduce the number of NFS-related headaches. However, these options can have their own undesirable side-effects, such as aborting a 20-hour simulation after it has run for 18 hours just because of a transient network glitch. **amd**, discussed starting on page 379, also provides some remedies for mounting ailments.

NFS partitions can be unmounted with the **umount** command.

17.4 ADMINISTRATIVE CONVENTIONS FOR NFS

See Chapter 6 for information about assigning unique UIDs and GIDs.

Running NFS forces some administrative decisions and suggests others. Any user who wants to access a file on the network should have a login on the machine where the file actually lives. There doesn't have to be a real shell associated with that login, but the login should be in the password file. Furthermore, both UIDs and GIDs must be unique across all machines that share filesystems. To forestall administrative headaches, it's best if UIDs and GIDs are unique across your entire site.

It is easier to manage NFS if you have a standard naming scheme. Names that include the server (such as **/anchor/tools** for a filesystem that lives on anchor) are useful, since they allow users to translate announcements such as "Anchor will be down all day Saturday for an upgrade" into "I won't be able to use `/anchor/tools/TeX` on Saturday to finish my thesis, so I should go skiing instead."

Unfortunately, this scheme requires the directory `/anchor` to exist in the root directory of all client machines. If a client gets filesystems from several other hosts, the root can get cluttered. Consider providing a deeper hierarchy; for example, `/home/anchor`, `/home/rastadon`, etc.

17.5 INTERACTIONS BETWEEN NFS AND NETWORKS

Traditional NFS uses UDP as its underlying transport protocol. Although NFS does its own packet sequence reassembly and error checking, UDP and NFS both lack the congestion control algorithms that are essential for good performance on a large IP network.

For this reason, you should avoid mounting traditional NFS partitions through a router, over long-haul (WAN) lines, or over the Internet. Although these are common (almost epidemic) practices at many sites, they are really bad ideas.

The solution is to use TCP as the underlying transport layer on mounts that cross a router or long-haul line. Some vendors (including BSDI and OSF/1) already ship "TCP-NFS" with their systems, which implements the usual NFS functionality on top of TCP instead of UDP.

17.6 DEDICATED NFS FILE SERVERS

NFS suffers its greatest performance troubles because of its stateless design. Since the client assumes a write operation is complete once it receives an acknowledgment from the server, servers must commit each modified block to disk before replying, to avoid discrepancies in the event of a crash. This introduces a significant delay in NFS writes, since modified blocks would normally be written only to the in-memory UNIX buffer cache.

In addition, NFS filesystems tend to be large (2GB+). By nature, filesystems of this size are plagued with backup and reliability problems.

Fueled by the popularity of NFS, a number of commercial solutions to these problems have appeared on the market. PrestoServe, an S-bus or VME card from Legato Systems, Inc. (also repackaged by Sun) is a board that you put in your existing NFS server to increase its write performance. This board uses non-volatile RAM to store modified blocks so that acknowledgments can be sent immediately. The blocks are then written to disk when convenient.

Auspex Systems, Inc. and Network Appliance Corporation (NAC) both make dedicated NFS servers. They include custom hardware and software to dramatically increase NFS performance and reliability. Both are outstanding products. Auspex offers extremely large-capacity servers and NAC offers smaller servers at inexpensive prices.

17.7 AUTOMATIC MOUNTING

Mounting filesystems one at a time by listing them in **/etc/fstab** introduces a number of problems in large networks. First, maintaining **/etc/fstab** on a few hundred machines can be tedious. Each one may be slightly different and thus require individual attention.

Second, if filesystems are mounted from a dozen or more hosts, chaos ensues when one of those servers crashes, since every command that **stats** the mount points will hang.

Third, when an important server crashes, it may cripple users by making important partitions like **/usr/share/man** unavailable. In this situation, it's best if a copy of the partition can be mounted temporarily from a backup server.

An automount daemon mounts filesystems when they are referenced and unmounts them when they are no longer needed. This minimizes the number of active mount points and is mostly transparent to users. With most automounters, it is also possible to supply a list of "replicated" (identical) filesystems so that the network can continue to function when a primary server becomes unavailable.

To implement this behind-the-scenes mounting and unmounting, the automounter poses as an NFS server. But instead of mirroring an actual filesystem onto the network, the automounter "makes up" a filesystem hierarchy according to the specifications you list in its configuration file.

When a user references a directory within the automounter's fake fantasy filesystem, the automounter intercepts the reference, mounts the actual filesystem the user is trying to reach, and forwards the operation along. There is usually a single directory where filesystems actually get mounted, and symbolic links are used to create the illusion of mounts occurring throughout the system.

The idea of an automounter originally comes from Sun. Sun's implementation, **automount**, is shipped with most Sun-derived NFS systems. Unfortunately, **automount** is plagued with bugs and design flaws and is an unworthy opponent to the freely-available alternative, **amd**.

amd is included on the CD-ROM.

amd, written by Jan-Simon Pendry of Imperial College in London, is the product of a doctoral thesis that expands upon Sun's idea. **amd** corrects many of **automount**'s serious flaws and can easily be installed on a wide variety of UNIX systems. Wherever possible, it's a good idea to use **amd** rather than **automount**.

If you must use **automount** instead of **amd**, be aware that it can "block" in a number of situations, causing all subsequent NFS accesses to hang and leaving you with an unusable system.

17.8 AUTOMOUNT: SUN'S AUTOMOUNTER

automount understands three different kinds of configuration files[5] (called "maps"): direct maps, indirect maps, and master maps. Direct and indirect maps provide information about filesystems that are to be automounted. A master map is a list of direct and indirect maps that **automount** should pay attention to. You can run **automount** without using a master map by specifying the direct and indirect maps on the command line.

Indirect Maps

Indirect maps are used to automount several filesystems underneath a common directory. The path of the directory is specified in the master map, not in the indirect map itself. For example, an indirect map for filesystems that get mounted under **/chimchim** might look like:

```
users   chimchim:/chimchim/users
devel   chimchim:/chimchim/devel
info    -ro chimchim:/chimchim/info
```

The first column names the subdirectory where each automount should be installed, and subsequent columns list the mount options and source path of the filesystem. This example (perhaps stored in a file such as **/etc/auto.chim**) tells **automount** that it can mount the directories **/chimchim/users**, **/chimchim/devel**, and **/chimchim/info** from host chimchim (with the **info** directory being mounted read-only). In this configuration the paths on chimchim and on the local host will be identical, but this is not required.

Direct Maps

Direct maps list filesystems that do not share a common prefix, such as **/usr/src** and **/cs/tools**. A direct map (e.g., **/etc/auto.direct**) that described both of these filesystems to **automount** might look like:

```
/usr/man    chimchim:/usr/man
/cs/tools   anchor:/cs/tools
```

In this case, each automount is actually implemented using a single symbolic link (and corresponding automount point) for each filesystem. This requires slightly more overhead, but has the added advantage that the mount point and actual directory structure are always accessible by

---

5. A direct map can also be managed as an NIS database, but don't try this at home.

commands such as `ls`. Using `ls` on a directory full of indirect mounts can often be confusing to users, because **automount** doesn't mount directories until their contents have been accessed. `ls` doesn't look inside the automounted directories, so it does not cause them to be mounted.

Master Maps

See Chapter 18 for more information about NIS.

A master map lists direct and indirect maps. For each indirect map, it also specifies the root directory used by the mounts defined in the map. **automount** uses the map in NIS by default.[6]

An master map that made use of the direct and indirect maps above would look something like this:

```
# Directory    Map
/chimchim      /etc/auto.chim
/-             /etc/auto.direct
```

The first column is a local directory name for an indirect map, or the special token `/-` for a direct map. The second column contains the filename in which the map is stored. If desired, there can be several maps of each type.

The **automount** daemon can be started in one of two ways. If your master map is called **/etc/auto.master** map, you can use the command

```
automount -f /etc/auto.master &
```

Direct and indirect maps can also be listed on the command line:

```
automount /- /etc/auto.direct /chimchim /etc/auto.chim &
```

Replicated Filesystems using automount

In some cases, a read-only filesystem such as **/usr/man** may be identical on several different servers. In this case, you can tell **automount** to choose a server for the filesystem based on which one responds most quickly. If you plan to do this, keep these four facts in mind:

• Replicated filesystems *must* be read-only filesystems such as **/usr/man** or **/usr/local/X11**. There is no way for the automount daemon to synchronize writes across a set of servers, and thus editable filesystems cannot be replicated.

• Despite popular belief, **automount** can *not* umount an active filesystem and replace it with a backup when a server crashes. Its abilities are limited to choosing a responsive server when the filesystem is first mounted.

---

6. **/etc/auto_master** under Solaris.

- You do not get to designate which servers are primaries and which are backups. `automount` selects a server based on its own idea of which ones are "closest" given network numbers and response times from an initial query.

- Replicated filesystems should be truly identical. Otherwise users will become agitated when a filesystem is replaced, and they may act in unpredictable ways.

An `auto.direct` file that defines `/usr/man` as a replicated filesystem served by both chimchim and band might look like this:

```
/usr/man    chimchim,band:/usr/man
/cs/tools   anchor:/cs/tools
```

Stopping automount

Since `automount` acts as an NFS server process, terminating it with a `kill -9` is poor strategy and can wedge your system. If you need to kill or restart `automount`, make sure you use a TERM signal (`kill -15`) so that `automount` has a chance to dislodge itself from your filesystem before it exits.

17.9 AMD: A BETTER AUTOMOUNTER

`amd` is a technically superior replacement for Sun's `automount` daemon. It offers the following advantages over `automount`:

- `amd` will never hang if a remote server goes down.

- `amd` sends "keep-alive" queries to remote servers at regular intervals and keeps a list of servers that are accessible. `amd` will mount, unmount, and replace filesystems based on this information. If a server crashes, future filesystem accesses return an "operation would block" error rather than hanging.

- `amd` contains no proprietary source code and has been ported to over 20 versions of UNIX. It is included with the standard BSDI and OSF/1 distributions.

- `amd` offers support for a number of mount types not supported by `automount`, such as the "union" mount.

- `amd` maps can be stored in a number of database formats, including NIS, Hesiod, `ndbm`, and the `/etc/passwd` file itself (for home directory mounts).

- The `amd` distribution includes a query-and-manipulation tool, `amq`, which allows you to monitor `amd`'s status and send it hints and commands (such as forced unmount requests).

- `amd`'s map syntax is more generic than `automount`'s. You can use a single file for all hosts at your site.

- **amd** is based on the concept that each server has one or more filesystems, with each filesystem containing one or more volumes (a coherent set of files). This makes the handling of subdirectories more straightforward than with **automount**.

- **amd** won't eat all the popcorn or send you out to get Milk Duds.

- **amd** sounds more like a hallucinogenic drug than **automount**, as in, "Hey dude, wanna drop some AMD?"

amd Maps

The **amd** map format is extremely flexible and allows a single configuration file to be used on many machines. Each filesystem listed in an **amd** map must have an associated mount type. The most common mount types are listed in Table 17.7.

Table 17.7   Commonly-used amd mount types

Type	Description
nfs	Basic access to an NFS server, no fancy tricks
ufs	Basic access to a local filesystem, no fancy tricks
host	Access to the entire export tree of an NFS server (the mountd on the server is queried to obtain its export list)
nfsx	Access to a group of filesystems on an NFS server with one map entry (for example: /usr/man, /usr/local/man)
program	Runs a program each time a mount or unmount is required, used to roll your own mount type
link	Creates a symbolic link that points to a physical mount point (allows any directory to be accessed via amd)
auto	Creates a new automount point beneath an existing one, sometimes used to replicate the mount tree of a server
direct	Almost identical to automount's direct map style
union	Allows merged contents of several directories to appear as a single directory (for example, to combine /tmp and /var/tmp)

Map entries may contain conditionals that allow them to be activated only in specific contexts (e.g. on a specific host or type of machine). Conditionals use built-in variables ("selectors") that are filled in with various pieces of information about the environment in which **amd** is running. The available selectors are listed in Table 17.8.

Here is an example map that expresses the same configuration as the direct **automount** map on page 377:

```
/default    opts:=rw,soft,timeo=10,retrans=5

usr/man     host==chimchim;type:=ufs;dev:=/dev/sd1f
            host!=chimchim;rhost=chimchim;rfs:=/${key};
            type=nfs;fs:=${autodir}/${key}
```

Table 17.8   amd selectors

Selector	Value
arch	Architecture of the current machine
autodir	Default directory under which to mount filesystems
byte	CPU byte sex (endian-ness: "little" or "big")
cluster	Name of local cluster of machines, defaults to domain
domain	Local NIS domain name
host	Local hostname
hostd	Hostname concatenated with local domain name
karch	Kernel architecture (defaults to value of arch selector)
key	Volume name being resolved
map	Name of mount map being used
os	Operating system
wire	Network name to which the primary interface is attached

```
cs/tools   host==anchor;type:=ufs;dev:=/dev/sd3c
           host!=anchor;rhost=anchor;rfs:=/${key};
           type=nfs;fs:=${autodir}/${key}
```

Elements of the form *name*:-*value* define various attributes of the mount. For example, the first line sets the default mount options to be the string "rw,soft,timeo=10,retrans=5". Elements of the form *name*==*value* or *name*!=*value* are conditionals; subsequent elements are only used if the conditional evaluates to true. Notations such as ${autodir} and ${key} insert the value of the appropriate selector.

This example **amd.master.map** file tells **amd** about two filesystems: **/usr/man** and **/cs/tools**. The /default clause specifies defaults that apply to all map entries unless they are explicitly overridden. The various options are described in Table 17.9.

Table 17.9   amd map options

Option	Description
rhost	The remote host on which the volume lives
rfs	The remote filesystem name
type	Mount type
fs	Local mount point

Starting amd

amd can be started with a script like this:

```
#!/bin/csh -f
cd /usr/local/etc/amd
exec /usr/local/bin/amd -x fatal,error,user -r -l syslog
  -a /tmp_mnt /amd amd.master.map >& /dev/console
```

The options used in this script are described in Table 17.10.

Table 17.10   amd command-line options

Option	Description
-x	Sets runtime logging options
-r	"Adopts" existing mounts
-1	Specifies log file or syslog for error messages
-a	Specifies alternate location for mount points[a]
/amd	Sets the directory map name
amd.master.map	Specifies the file containing the mount options

a. The default is /a.

When a user references one of the filesystems defined in **amd**'s map file, **amd** will mount the filesystem and monitor subsequent use of the mount. After it has been inactive for a period of time (usually 5-15 minutes), **amd** will umount the filesystem until it is referenced again.

The status of mounts can be obtained with the **amq** command.

Replicated Filesystems using amd

Like **automount**, **amd** allows multiple servers to be listed for a particular filesystem. However, **amd** has the added ability to disconnect active filesystems from crashed servers and mount replacements "on the fly" in most cases.

The following map defines **/usr/man** as a replicated filesystem available from both chimchim and band:

```
/default   opts:=rw,soft,timeo=10,retrans=5

usr/man    host==chimchim;type:=ufs;dev:=/dev/sd1f ||
           host==band;type:=ufs;dev:=/dev/sd3c ||
           rhost=chimchim rhost=band;rfs:=/${key};
           type=nfs;fs:=${autodir}/${key}

cs/tools   host==anchor;type:=ufs;dev:=/dev/sd3c
           host!=anchor;rhost=anchor;rfs:=/${key};
           type=nfs;fs:=${autodir}/${key}
```

Stopping amd

amd needs to be stopped gracefully so that it has a chance to untangle itself from the filesystem structure. Sending **amd** a SIGTERM is the polite way to ask it to leave.

17.10 SECURITY AND NFS

NFS provides a convenient way to access files on a network, and thus it is a significant source of security problems. For the average site, tight control on **/etc/exports** (or **/etc/dfs/dfstab**) is adequate protection from unwanted access. The greatest risk is presented by on-site machines that are legally allowed to mount a filesystem.

If a user can gain root access on a client machine, then there are several clandestine methods to access files owned by other users, even if root access is not enabled on export. If anyone that you don't fully trust has root access on a client host, don't export any filesystems to that host.

See page 552 for more information about Kerberos.

There have been two noteworthy attempts to make NFS more secure. The first, based on "secure RPC," is distributed with some vendor's systems. The second is based on the Kerberos system. While both may be worth investigating for a paranoid site, in reality they offer only a minimal increase in security over good common sense.

17.11 MONITORING AND TUNING NFS

Most systems provide a command called **nfsstat** that can display various statistics kept by the NFS system. **nfsstat -s** displays statistics for NFS server processes, and **nfsstat -c** shows information related to client-side operations. For example:

```
moet 64 % nfsstat -c

Client rpc:
calls badcalls retrans badxid timeout wait newcred timers
64235 1595      0       3      1592    0    0       886

Client nfs:
calls   badcalls  nclget   nclsleep
62613   3         62643    0
null    getattr   setattr  readlink  lookup  root  read
0%      34%       0%       21%       30%     0%    2%
write   wrcache   create   remove    rename  link  symlink
3%      0%        0%       0%        0%      0%    0%
mkdir   readdir   rmdir    fsstat
0%      6%        0%       0%
```

This example is from a relatively healthy NFS client. Two of the items are especially interesting from a performance-tuning standpoint. First, note the percentage of operations that are writes (in this example, 3%). If it is more than 10%, your network could probably benefit from a dedicated NFS server or cache board, such as a PrestoServe.

Second, if more than 3% of calls time out, there is likely a problem with your NFS server or network. You can usually discover the cause by checking the `badxid` field. If `badxid` is near 0 with timeouts greater than 3%, packets to and from the server are getting lost on the network. You may be able to solve this problem by lowering the `rsize` and `wsize` mount parameters (read and write block sizes). If `badxid` is nearly as high as `timeout`, then the server is responding, but too slowly. Either replace the server or increase the `timeo` parameter.

Running **nfsstat** regularly and becoming familiar with its output will help you to discover NFS problems before your users do.

17.12 OTHER FILE SHARING SYSTEMS

NFS is not the only way to share files on a network, but it is by far the most common. It is deeply entrenched and is not likely to face serious competition any time soon. But since you may occasionally encounter other systems, we mention two of them here as "cultural background."

RFS

The RFS system available under System V.3 and later releases provides similar functionality to NFS. RFS includes capabilities such as remote device mounting, but is not nearly as transportable or as widely used as NFS. As they say, "It's dead, Jim."

The Andrew Filesystem

AFS was developed at CMU and is commercially marketed by Transarc Corporation. It is currently in use among several East coast universities. In some cases, AFS scales better than NFS. Among other things, it provides client-side caching, which NFS does not. AFS also includes other progressive ideas such as a universal filesystem namespace.

AFS suffers from the fundamental problem of not being available as a standard part of most vendor's distributions. Thus, it is often difficult to integrate into a heterogeneous network.

Many sites have reported reliability and performance problems with current AFS implementations. If you are considering deployment of AFS at your site, take the time to speak with the system administrators from a site that is already using it.

17.13 RECOMMENDED SUPPLEMENTAL READING

STERN, HAL. *Managing NFS and NIS*. Sebastopol: O'Reilly & Associates, 1992.

PENDRY, JAN-SIMON AND NICK WILLIAMS. *"AMD: The 4.4BSD Automounter Reference Manual."* 4.4BSD System Manager's Manual, Usenix and O'Reilly. 1994.

18 *Sharing System Files*

18.1 INTRODUCTION

A properly functioning system depends on tens, perhaps hundreds of configuration files all containing the right pieces of information. When you multiply the number of configuration files on a host by the number of hosts on a network, the result can be thousands of files—too many to manage by hand.

In the real world, machines are often similar from an administrative point of view. Instead of editing the text files on each machine, it's more efficient to combine machines into groups that share configuration information. This can be done in several ways.

The simplest way is to keep a master copy of each configuration file in one place and distribute it to members of the group whenever it changes. This solution has the advantages of being simple and working on every UNIX system.

Another approach is to eliminate text files altogether and have each machine obtain its configuration information from a central server. This is more complicated than copying files, but it solves some other problems as well. For example, clients can't miss updates, even if they are down when a change is made. It may also be faster to obtain information from a server than from a file, depending on the speed of the local disk and the amount of caching performed by the server. On the other hand, the entire network can hang when the server goes down.

Several attempts have been made to develop administrative databases for large networks, and they are all interesting systems. However, none of the current products seems exactly right in its approach. Some are simple but not secure and not scalable; others are functional but unwieldy. All the systems seem to have limitations that can prevent you from setting up the network the way you want to.

In this chapter we'll discuss some basic techniques for keeping files synchronized on a network, and then we'll talk about the two most widely-used administrative database systems: NIS and NIS+.

18.2 WHAT TO SHARE

Of the many configuration files on a UNIX system, only a subset can be usefully shared among machines. The most commonly shared files are listed in Table 18.1.

Table 18.1   System files that are commonly shared

Filename	Function
/etc/passwd	User account information database
/etc/group	UNIX group definitions
/etc/hosts	Maps between hostnames and IP addresses
/etc/networks	Associates text names with IP network numbers
/etc/services	Lists port numbers for well-known network services
/etc/protocols	Maps text names to protocol numbers
/etc/ethers[a]	Maps between hostnames and Ethernet addresses
/etc/aliases	Electronic mail aliases
/etc/rpc	Lists ID numbers for RPC services
/etc/netgroup	Defines collections of hosts, users, and networks

a. Not used on all systems.

Most server-based systems are set up to work with only these and perhaps a few additional files. You can sometimes add more files, but since the standard system software won't automatically make use of them, that feature is most useful for sharing local files.

The files listed in Table 18.1 are usually accessed through routines defined in the standard C library. For example, the /etc/passwd file is searched with the getpwuid, getpwnam, and getpwent routines. These routines take care of opening, reading, and parsing the passwd file so that user-level programs don't have to.

Since few programs access these configuration files directly, it is relatively easy to convert a system to use a network database. Once the library routines are patched, most client programs become automatically "upgraded." Even software that you obtain from the public domain and from third-party vendors should work correctly if compiled against the new library.[1]

18.3 COPYING FILES AROUND

We use brute-force file copying to maintain the University of Colorado's Engineering network. It is not an elegant solution, but it works on every kind of machine and is easy to set up and maintain.

It's often assumed in manuals and in UNIX culture that you will use a system such as NIS or NIS+ if one is available. But if your needs aren't complex, you don't need a complex solution. Sometimes the dumbest, most straightforward solution is the best.

Our site consists of several connected but independent fiefdoms. Only a little bit of administrative data is shared everywhere. In our distribution scheme, each fiefdom has one or two servers that store master copies of its system files. This is the sort of environment in which file copying works well, since the task is simply to pump the data around, not to tailor it for particular machines or networks.

File copying systems can use either a "push" model or a "pull" model. With "push," the master server periodically distributes the freshest files to each client, whether the client wants them or not. Files may be pushed explicitly whenever a change is made, or may simply be distributed on a regular schedule (perhaps with some files being transferred more often than others).

The push model has the advantage of keeping the distribution system centralized on one machine. Files, lists of clients, update scripts, and timetables are all stored in one place, making the scheme easy to control. One disadvantage is that each client must allow the master to modify its system files, creating a possible security hazard.

In a pull system, each client is responsible for updating itself from the server. This is a less centralized way of distributing files, but it is also more adaptable and more secure. A pull system is especially attractive when sharing data across political boundaries, because the master and client machines need not be run by the same faction.

rdist: Push Files

In most cases, the **rdist** command is the best way to distribute files from a central server. It has something of the flavor of **make**: you create a specification of the files to be distributed using a text editor, and then

---

1. On systems that use shared libraries, even recompiling may not be necessary.

you use **rdist** to bring reality into line with your specification. **rdist** only copies files when they are out of date, so you can write your specification as if all files were to be copied and let **rdist** optimize out any unnecessary work.

rdist preserves the owner, group, mode, and modification time of files. When **rdist** updates an existing file, it deletes the old version before installing the new. This makes **rdist** suitable for transferring executables that might be in use during the update.[2]

Like **make**, **rdist** looks for a control file (**distfile** or **Distfile**) in the current directory. **rdist -f** *distfile* specifies the control file's pathname explicitly. Within the distfile, tabs, spaces, and newlines are used interchangeably as separators. Comments are introduced with a pound sign ("#").

The meat of a distfile consists of statements of the form

```
label: pathnames -> destinations commands
```

The *label* field associates a name to the statement. From the shell, you can say **rdist** *label* to distribute only the files described in a particular statement.

pathnames and *destinations* are a list of files to be copied and a list of hosts to copy them to, respectively. If there is more than one entry in a list, it must be surrounded with parentheses and the elements must be separated with whitespace. *pathnames* may include **csh**-style globbing characters (e.g. **/usr/lib/*** or **/usr/man/man[12345]**). The notation *~user* is also acceptable, but it is evaluated separately on the source and destination machines.

By default, **rdist** copies the files and directories listed in *pathnames* to the equivalent paths on each destination machine. This behavior may be modified by supplying a sequence of *commands*. Each command should be terminated with a semicolon.

The following commands are understood:

```
install options [destdir];
notify namelist;
except pathlist;
except_pat patternlist;
special [pathlist] string;
```

The install command sets options that affect the way **rdist** copies files. Options typically control the treatment of symbolic links, the cor-

---

2. Though the old version disappears from the filesystem namespace, it continues to exist until all references have been released. You must also be aware of this effect when managing log files. See page 202 for more information.

rectness of **rdist**'s difference-checking algorithm, and the way that files not present in the source tree are handled. Options are specified differently on different systems and are not explained here in detail.

The name "install" is somewhat misleading, since files are copied whether or not an install command is present. Options are specified as they would be on the **rdist** command line, but when included in the distfile they apply to only one set of files.

destdir specifies an installation directory on the destination hosts. It is optional; by default, **rdist** uses the original pathnames.

The notify command takes a list of email addresses as its argument. **rdist** sends mail to these addresses whenever a file is updated. Any addresses that do not contain an at sign ("@") are suffixed with the name of the destination host. For example, "pete" would expand to "pete@anchor" when reporting a list of files updated on host anchor.

except and except_pat remove pathnames from the list of files to be copied. except's arguments are matched literally, while those of except_pat are interpreted as regular expressions chez **ed**. These exception commands are useful because **rdist**, like **make**, allows macros to be defined at the beginning of its control file. You might want to use a similar list of files for several statements, specifying only the additions and deletions for each host.

The special command executes an **sh** command (the *string* argument, which should be quoted) on each remote host. If a *pathlist* is present, **rdist** executes the command once after copying each of the specified files. Without a *pathlist*, **rdist** executes the command after every file. There is unfortunately no way to execute a command after all files have been copied.

For example, the distfile

```
SYS_FILES = (/etc/passwd /etc/group /etc/aliases)
GET_ALL   = (julio batcomputer nynix)
GET_SOME  = (whammo spiff)

all: ${SYS_FILES} -> ${GET_ALL}
    notify barb;
    special /etc/aliases "/usr/ucb/newaliases";

some: ${SYS_FILES} -> ${GET_SOME}
    except /etc/aliases;
    notify eddie@spiff;
```

See page 454 for more info about newaliases.

replicates the three listed system files on julio, batcomputer, and nynix, and sends mail to barb@*destination* describing any updates or errors that occur. After **/etc/aliases** is copied, **rdist** runs **newaliases** on each destination. Only two files are copied to whammo and spiff, with a report being mailed to eddie@spiff. **newaliases** is not run.

expect: Pull Files

expect is included on the CD-ROM.

There are several ways to implement a pulling system. One way that we like, and which happens to be useful for other tasks, is to make system files available via **ftp** from a central server and to use **expect** to retrieve and install them. See page 427 for more information about **ftp**.

expect is a set of extensions to John Ousterhout's Tcl (Tool Command Language) that allow you to write control scripts for interactive programs. It was written by Don Libes at NIST. **expect** is different from a normal scripting language (such as that provided by most shells) in that it provides for incremental control of subprocesses. The output produced by each operation can be examined to determine what input should be sent next. **expect** is also immune to the unfriendly maneuvers a program may attempt because it thinks it is manipulating a real terminal.

Tcl is itself a complete scripting language. Technically, **expect** scripts are just Tcl scripts that happen to use the extra commands defined by the **expect** extensions. However, you don't need to know much Tcl to write simple **expect** scripts.

Tcl is syntactically simple. Most commands are invoked like shell commands, in that you simply separate the command and its arguments by spaces. Curly braces group elements into single Tcl "words" and extend statements over multiple lines. The command separator is a semicolon, but it is optional at the end of lines and before closing curly braces.

The fundamental **expect** commands are:

- spawn – start up a subprocess to control
- send – feed input to a subprocess
- expect – take action depending on a subprocess's output

A fourth command, interact, can also be useful if you want **expect** to do part of a task and then turn control over to you.

Before discussing the individual commands, let's look at a simple example. This script **ftps** the **/etc/passwd** file from the machine netserver:

```
spawn /usr/ucb/ftp netserver
while 1 { expect {
    "Name*: "   {send "netclient\r"}
    "Password:" {send "netclientpw\r"}
    "ftp> "     {break}
    "failed"    {send_user "Can't log in.\r"; exit 1}
    timeout     {send_user "Timeout problem.\r"; exit 2}
}}
```

```
send "lcd /etc\r"
expect "ftp> " {send "cd pub/sysfiles\r"}
expect "ftp> " {send "get passwd\r"}
expect "ftp> " {send "quit\r"; send_user "\r"}
exit 0
```

The general flow of control should be apparent. The script first starts the command **ftp netserver** and then waits to be prompted for a name and password inside a while loop (a generic Tcl construct). After arriving at the main ftp> prompt, the while loop is exited and a simple series of commands is spoon-fed to **ftp**. The script waits for each command to complete before sending the next; this is not strictly necessary, but it makes for tidy output.

Two kinds of problems are handled within the initial login loop. First, the check for the string "failed" traps the case in which the remote host rejects the given name and password, causing **ftp** to print "Login failed."[3] The timeout clause detects cases in which nothing interesting happens for ten seconds, perhaps because netserver is down. Either condition causes the script to print an error message and exit.

This script assumes that no errors can happen after a successful login; in the real world, you'd probably want to add more embellishments. In this example, the same error handling is applied to several exchanges through the use of a while loop. **expect** includes some special versions of the expect command that are designed to solve this problem in a less kludgey way.

spawn *command* creates an instance of the named *command*, which may include arguments. A magic cookie identifying the command is placed in the variable spawn_id. The expect and send commands deal with the process identified in this variable, so you can switch among multiple subprocesses by saving and restoring the value of spawn_id.

The send command places a string on a subprocess's standard input. You must include a carriage return explicitly (entered as \r) if you want one. A string without spaces or special characters need not be quoted. send_user is similar to send, except that the text is sent to the script's standard output.

The expect command accepts a series of *expect-pattern/action* pairs. If the pairs span multiple lines, as in the example above, they should be enclosed in curly braces. Actions should generally be enclosed in curly braces as well.

Each *expect-pattern* is something to watch for in the command's output; when a string is seen, its corresponding *action* is triggered.

---

3. The exact string may vary from system to system.

Patterns are normally matched using unanchored shell-style globbing, but regular expressions are also available. Actions for the special strings `timeout` and `eof` are triggered after a (settable) period of inactivity and at the end of the input stream, respectively.

expect comes with many example scripts that can be adapted for your own nefarious purposes. Another of our home-grown scripts is described on page 429.

18.4 NIS: THE NETWORK INFORMATION SERVICE

NIS, released by Sun in the 1980s, was the first "prime time" administrative database. It was originally called the Sun Yellow Pages, but eventually had to be renamed for legal reasons. NIS commands still begin with the letters **yp**, so it's hard to forget the original name. Many vendors have licensed Sun's code, making NIS the most widely-supported database system.

 Sun has lately come out with a new system called NIS+ and now provides only client-side support for NIS in Solaris.[4] Despite the similarity of the names, NIS+ and NIS are not related to one another; NIS+ is described starting on page 400.

Table 18.2 shows the current state of support for NIS and NIS+ on our example systems.

Table 18.2 Support for NIS and NIS+

System	Supports NIS?	Supports NIS+?
Solaris	Partially	Yes
HP-UX	Yes	No
IRIX	Yes	No
SunOS	Yes	No
OSF/1	Yes	No
BSDI	No	No

NIS provides about the same granularity of control as file copying. A master server maintains the authoritative copies of system files, which are kept in their original locations and formats and edited with a text editor just as before. A server process makes the contents of the files (or as NIS calls them, "maps") available over the network. A server and its clients comprise an NIS "domain."[5]

---

4. Actually, the NIS+ server daemon, **rpc.nisd**, can be configured to simulate an NIS server. However, you must abandon all hope of NIS+ security to make this work.

5. Do not confuse NIS domains with DNS domains. They are completely separate and have nothing to do with one another.

NIS maps are preprocessed by the **ndbm** extensible hashing routines to improve the efficiency of lookups. After editing system files on the master server, you tell NIS to convert them to **ndbm** format using either **make** or a script called **ypmake**, depending on your system.

ndbm allows only one "key" to be associated with each entry, so a system file may have to be translated into several NIS maps. For example, the **/etc/passwd** file is translated into two maps called **passwd.byname** and **passwd.byuid**; one is used to look up entries by user name, and the other to look up entries by UID. Either map can be used to enumerate all the entries in the **passwd** file.

NIS allows you to replicate the network maps on a set of "slave servers." Providing more than one server helps to relieve load on the master and to keep clients functioning even when some servers become unavailable. Whenever a file is changed on the master server, the corresponding NIS map must be pushed out to the slaves so that all servers provide the same data. Clients do not distinguish between the master server and the slaves.

You must place at least one NIS server on every physical network. Clients use IP broadcasting to locate servers, and broadcast packets are usually not forwarded by routers and gateways. The **ypset** command can be used to point a client at a particular server; however, at the first hint of trouble, the client will attempt to locate a new server using broadcasting. Unless there is a server on the client's network, this may cause the client to hang.

Magic NIS Cookies

On most systems, NIS defines a complicated scheme that allows clients to supplement the information obtained from NIS with their own local information. Some vendors have removed this function from NIS and created a separate configuration file that specifies the order in which sources of administrative information should be searched. A general overview of this topic is provided starting on page 403.

Under old-style NIS, merging is supported for some files but not for others. There are basically two kinds of files:

- Local priority – local machine's information overrides NIS copy
- Global priority – NIS copy supersedes local copy

/etc/passwd and **/etc/group** are usually the only local-priority files. NIS data must be "invited" into these files by including a special token (or "magic cookie") in the file itself. A plus on a line by itself includes the entire NIS map, while an entry of the form +*name* includes only the entry for the named account or group. A third form is used with netgroups, described below.

For example, the **/etc/passwd** file

```
dwight:EiOX1SKE:116:22:Dwight Melcher:/home/dwight:/bin/sh
paulm:eIkXPm7o:127:35:Paul Maybee:/home/paulm:/bin/csh
+
```

would add local accounts dwight and paulm to the accounts defined in the NIS passwd maps.

Local copies of global-priority files are completely ignored, with the exception of **/etc/hosts**, which may be consulted at boot time. The **/etc/hosts, /etc/networks, /etc/protocols, /etc/services**, and **/etc/netgroup** files are all global-priority.

Netgroups

NIS introduced a popular abstraction known as "netgroups." Netgroups are used to name sets of users, machines, and nets for easy reference in other system files. They are defined in **/etc/netgroup** but are also shared as a global-priority NIS map.

The format of a **netgroup** entry is

```
groupname list-of-members
```

Members are separated by whitespace. A member is either a netgroup name or a triplet of the form

```
(hostname, username, domainname)
```

Any empty field in a triplet is a wild card; thus the entry (boulder,,) refers to all users in all domains on the host boulder (or to the host boulder itself, depending on the context in which the netgroup is used). A "-" in a field indicates negation, so the entry (boulder,-,) refers to the machine boulder and no users. Group definitions can nest.

Here's a simple example of an **/etc/netgroup** file:

```
bobcats         (snake,,) (headrest,,)
servers         (anchor,,) (moet,,) (piper,,) (kirk,,)
anchorclients   (xx,,) (watneys,,) (molson,,)
beers           (anchor,,) (anchor-gateway,,) anchorclients
allhosts        beers bobcats servers
```

These netgroups are all defined in terms of hosts; that's typical for real-world use.

See Chapter 17 for more information about NFS.

Netgroups can be used in various files that define permissions. Used in **/etc/exports**, they can specify which hosts may mount filesystems. Used in **/etc/hosts.equiv** or in a user's **.rhosts** file, they can grant or revoke login permissions for groups of users or machines.

Netgroups can also be used in an NIS client's `/etc/passwd` file to import account information for the members of a particular netgroup. The syntax is *+@netgroup*.

 A security hole exists if the file `/etc/hosts.equiv` contains the NIS magic cookie "+": all hosts on your local Ethernet and the Internet are equivalenced. Versions of SunOS through 4.1.3 were shipped with `/etc/hosts.equiv` configured this way.

Netgroups are a nice idea. They simplify system files, making them more understandable. They also add a layer of indirection that permits the status of a user or machine to be changed in one file rather than fifteen. On some systems you *must* use them to export a filesystem to more than about forty hosts, because clauses in the **exports** file are limited to 1,024 characters.

Advantages and Disadvantages of NIS

One nice feature of NIS is that it can be understood by mere mortals. NIS is analogous to copying files around; in most cases, it's unnecessary for administrators to be aware of NIS's internal data formats. Administration is performed with the same old "flat" files, and only one or two new procedures need to be learned.

Since NIS doesn't provide any way to link domains, it's not suitable for managing a large network of machines unless a single configuration is to be applied to every machine. You can divide a large network into several NIS domains, but each domain must be administered separately.

NIS can also consume a fair amount of network bandwidth. NIS doesn't cache data on client machines, so every lookup causes an exchange of packets. And when a system file is updated on the NIS master server, every map derived from it is copied to every slave server.

See Chapter 10 for more information about cron. If a slave server is down or inaccessible when a map is changed, the slave's copy will not be updated. Slaves must periodically poll the master to be sure that they have the most recent version of every map. Although basic tools for doing this are provided with NIS, you must implement the polling scheme you want using **cron**. Even so, there is the possibility that two different versions of a map will be served simultaneously for a while, with clients randomly seeing one or the other.

NIS is not secure. Any host on a network can claim to serve a particular domain, thus feeding bogus administrative data to NIS clients. And anyone can read your NIS maps, perhaps feeding the encrypted passwords to a cracking program to look for poorly-protected accounts. If you are concerned about security or are connected to the Internet, you should not use NIS.

Technical Overview of NIS

NIS's data files and most of its commands are stored in one directory, usually **/var/yp**, **/usr/etc/yp**, or **/etc/yp**.[6] Hereafter, we will refer to this as "the NIS directory." Each NIS map is stored as a pair of **ndbm** files, one called *map*.**dir** and the other called *map*.**pag**, in a subdirectory of the NIS directory named for the NIS domain. For example, in the domain "cssuns," the **ndbm** files for the **/etc/passwd** maps might be

```
/usr/etc/yp/cssuns/passwd.byname.dir
/usr/etc/yp/cssuns/passwd.byname.pag
/usr/etc/yp/cssuns/passwd.byuid.dir
/usr/etc/yp/cssuns/passwd.byuid.pag
```

Remember that a separate map is required for each field by which the file can be searched. The **passwd** file is searchable by both name and uid, so two maps (four files) are derived from it.

ndbm files contain "holes" and are therefore apt to expand when copied. See Chapter 26 for more information about holey files.

The **makedbm** command generates NIS maps from flat files. However, you need never invoke this command directly. On most systems, a **Makefile** in the NIS directory is set up to generate all the common NIS maps; after you modify a system file, you **cd** to the NIS directory and run **make**. **make** checks the modification time of each file against the modification times of the maps derived from it and runs **makedbm** for each map that needs to be rebuilt. On HP-UX and IRIX systems, a command called **ypmake** is used instead of make.

Maps are copied from the master server to the slave servers using the **ypxfr** command. **ypxfr** is a "pull" command; it must be run on each slave server to make it import the map. A daemon called **ypxfrd** runs on the master server to respond to these requests. **ypxfr** is smart and does not transfer a map unless it is out of date. Slaves usually execute **ypxfr** every so often just to verify that they have the most recent maps; you can control how often this is done using **cron**.

yppush is a "push" version of **ypxfr** used on the master server. It actually does not transfer any data, but rather instructs each slave to execute a **ypxfr**. **yppush** is used by the **Makefile** in the NIS directory to ensure that newly-updated maps are propagated to slaves.

There is a special map called **ypservers** which does not correspond to any flat file. This map contains a list of all the servers of the domain; it's constructed for you automatically when the domain is set up. Its contents are examined whenever the master server needs to distribute maps to slaves.

6. Actually, some systems use two directories: one for commands and one for data files.

After initial configuration, the only active components of the NIS system are the **ypserv** and **ypbind** daemons. **ypserv** runs only on servers (both master and slave); it accepts queries from clients and answers them by looking up information in the **ndbm** maps.

ypbind runs on every machine in the NIS domain, including servers. The C library contacts the local **ypbind** daemon whenever it needs to answer an administrative query. **ypbind** locates a **ypserv** in the appropriate domain and returns its identity to the C library, which then contacts the server directly.

Once **ypbind** locates a server, it continues to rely on that server for all queries until the server goes down or some other communication problem occurs. A **ypbind** on a server machine does not give itself preferential treatment, so servers don't necessarily bind to themselves. The query mechanism is illustrated in Exhibit A.

Exhibit A   NIS query procedure

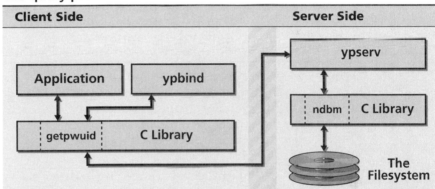

In some circumstances (for example, when all servers but one are simultaneously rebooted), clients can fixate on one server and refuse to let go even after other servers become available. This can slow response time considerably.

NIS includes a number of minor commands that are used to examine maps, find out which version of a map each server is using, and control the binding between clients and servers. A complete list of NIS commands and daemons is given in Table 18.3 (next page).

Setting Up an NIS Domain

NIS must be initialized on the master server, on the slave servers, and on each client. You do this in two steps. First, run **ypinit** on each server. Second, on every machine in the domain, set the domain name

Table 18.3 NIS commands and daemons

Program	Description
ypserv	NIS server daemon, started at boot time
ypbind	NIS client daemon, started at boot time
domainname	Sets the NIS domain a machine is in (run at boot time)
ypxfr	Downloads current version of a map from master server
ypxfrd	Serves requests from ypxfr (runs on master server)
yppush	Makes slave servers update their versions of a map
makedbm	Builds an ndbm map from a flat file
ypmake[a]	Rebuilds ndbm maps from flat files that have changed
ypinit	Configures a host as a master or slave server
ypset	Makes ypbind connect to a particular server
ypwhich	Finds out which server the current host is using
yppoll	Finds out what version of a map a server is using
ypcat	Prints the values contained in an NIS map
ypmatch	Prints map entries for a specified key
yppasswd	Changes a password on the NIS master server
ypchfn	Changes GECOS information on the NIS master server
ypchsh	Changes a login shell on NIS master server
yppasswdd	Server for yppasswd, ypchsh, and ypchfn
ypupdated	Server for updating NIS maps (managed by inetd)

a. Not used on all systems.

from one of the system startup files and configure **/etc/passwd** and **/etc/group** to import NIS data.

Configuring NIS servers

ypinit is used to initialize both the master and slave servers for a domain. On the master, the following commands are used:

```
cd /var/yp          /* The NIS directory, wherever it is */
domainname foo      /* Name the new domain. */
ypinit -m           /* Initialize as master server. */
/usr/etc/ypserv     /* Start the NIS server. */
```

The **-m** flag tells **ypinit** that it's configuring a master server; it will prompt you to enter a list of slave servers. Once the master is up and running, each slave server should be primed by running **ypinit** with the **-s** (slave) flag:

```
cd /var/yp
ypinit -s master    /* Argument is  master's hostname. */
/usr/etc/ypserv
```

ypinit -s makes a local copy of the master's current data; the presence of the domain's data files is enough to let **ypserv** know that it should serve the domain.

See Chapter 10 for
more information
about cron.

On each slave, you should set up crontab entries that pull fresh copies of all maps from the master. **ypxfr** *map*, where *map* is a name such as **passwd.byuid**, will transfer the specified map from the master server. You must run the command once for each map. Maps tend to change at different rates, and if network bandwidth is precious you may want to transfer some maps more often than others. In most circumstances, transferring all the maps once or twice a day (perhaps late at night) is good enough. The following script transfers every map:

```
#!/bin/csh -f
set mydomain = `/usr/bin/domainname`
cd /var/yp/$mydomain                    # the NIS directory
foreach map (`/usr/bin/ls`)
    /usr/etc/ypxfr $map
end
```

Some systems have scripts called **ypxfr_1perday**, **ypxfr_2perday**, and **ypxfr_1perhour** that transfer NIS maps at various frequencies.

Configuring NIS Clients

The second step is to inform each machine that it is a member of the new domain, and to configure it so that it pays attention to the network versions of **/etc/passwd** and **/etc/group**. The servers of a domain are generally clients as well. The **/etc/passwd** and **/etc/group** files on the master server are the files from which the NIS maps are built; don't put magic cookies in them.

See Chapter 2 for
more information
about the system
startup scripts.

The **domainname** command sets a machine's NIS domain. It's usually run at boot time from one of the startup scripts. Some systems check to see if **/etc/defaultdomain** exists, and if it does, the domain name is read from it. This convention allows you to set the domain name without editing the startup scripts.

Most systems that support NIS also check to see if the current host is an NIS server, and if so, they start the **ypserv** daemon automatically. The NIS-related startup commands generally look something like this:

```
# Tell the local machine what domain it's in
/usr/bin/domainname cssuns

# Check to see if local machine serves that domain
if [-f /etc/ypserv -a -d /var/yp/`domainname`]; then
    /etc/ypserv; (echo -n ' ypserv') > /dev/console
fi

# Start ypbind
if [ -f /etc/ypbind ]; then
    /etc/ypbind; (echo -n ' ypbind') > /dev/console
fi
```

Each client must have a minimal private version of the `passwd`, `group`, and `hosts` files. `passwd` and `group` are needed to allow root to log in when no NIS server is available. They should contain the standard system accounts and groups: root, bin, daemon, wheel, etc. The `hosts` file must be present to answer boot-time queries that occur before NIS is up and running. On most systems, `/etc/passwd` and `/etc/group` must contain the magic cookie "+" if they are to use NIS as an information source; see page 393.

18.5 NIS+: Son of NIS

NIS+, aka "NIS on Steroids whose Face Nobody is Ever Going to Kick Sand in Again," is designed to correct the deficiencies of NIS and introduce deficiencies of its own. It handles large networks of machines. It has security features built in. It permits multiple domains to be administrated from anywhere on a network. It transfers updates efficiently. It's a distributed database *and* a dessert topping; it sings, it dances, it leaps capital T in a single bound. But unfortunately, it is too complex to describe thoroughly here.

Although NIS+ servers can serve NIS clients (at some security expense), NIS+ is a new system that shares no code with NIS. As of mid-1994, NIS+ is supported only by Sun, but it will probably spread to other vendors' systems soon.

There are several significant differences between NIS and NIS+:

See Chapter 16 for more information about DNS.

- NIS+ domains are arranged in a site-wide hierarchy patterned after the one used by DNS (the Domain Name System). As with NIS, each domain includes various kinds of administrative information. You can subdivide domains to delegate administrative authority. Each machine belongs to a single domain, but domains can refer to each other's contents, allowing individual machines to obtain information from several domains.

- NIS+ is more database-like than NIS and allows maps (which are now called "tables") to be searched by any field. This removes the need to maintain several different maps for each system file; NIS+ equates each file with a single table. You can think of each table as having the field names written across the top, with each row being a separate entry in the file.

- NIS+ doesn't use flat files as NIS does. Although you can transfer data from a UNIX file (or an NIS map) into NIS+, NIS+ is then considered the authoritative source for the information; it won't automatically refresh itself if you later change the file. To make changes, you use a command that edits the information in NIS+'s tables directly.

- NIS+ is much better than NIS at maintaining slave servers (called "replicas" in NIS+). Only incremental changes are transferred, and a nifty logging scheme is used to accommodate replicas that come in and out of contact with the master server. The master is also able to transfer its entire NIS+ database to a replica if it decides that the replica is too far out of date to be updated incrementally.

- NIS+ is built on top of Sun's secure RPC system, which allows authentication based on public-key encryption as well as the standard "I claim to be fred" style non-authentication. NIS+ servers can be configured to require encrypted credentials or, for the more convenience-minded, to obey the usual UNIX conventions. Like a file, every NIS+ object (table, column, or entry) has an owner and a group owner; permissions on objects are set separately for the owner, the group, the world, and a special "nobody" category is applied to those who cannot supply credentials, such as NIS clients. Both users and machines can be secure RPC "principals" (entities capable of supplying credentials). When you access NIS+ as root, your machine's credentials are used instead of root's user credentials.

From a client's perspective, NIS+ looks much the same as any other administrative database system. Most data is accessed through the same library routines as always, and the complex world of domains, tables, permissions, and search paths is in the end rendered down to an analog of the original UNIX flat files.

NIS+ has nothing to do with DNS, but it borrows DNS's naming scheme. DNS and NIS+ use names that are the inverse of filesystem paths; as you read from left to right, you go up (towards the root) in the hierarchy. For example, cs.colorado.edu is a subdomain of colorado.edu. A machine in that domain might be named anchor.cs.colorado.edu.

By convention, the root of your NIS+ hierarchy is named the same as your site's top-level DNS domain. If your DNS domain is xor.com, then xor.com would also be your NIS+ root domain, and marketing.xor.com might be the NIS+ subdomain for your marketing department. Since DNS and NIS+ do not interact, you risk nothing but your sanity by using the same names for both.

Technically, NIS+ doesn't understand or enforce the idea of domains; it simply provides a generic way of creating NIS+ directories in a hierarchy, inserting various tables in those directories, and binding portions of the hierarchy to different master servers. But by convention, an NIS+ "domain" is a directory that contains subdirectories called org_dir and groups_dir. The domain's administrative data is put in tables inside org_dir, and the credentials for the domain's NIS+ principals are defined in groups_dir. Theoretically, a groups_dir or org_dir directory could have other subdirectories, but this isn't normally done.

For example, org_dir.marketing.xor.com would be the name of the directory containing system tables for the marketing.xor.com domain. Syntactically, tables are referred to as if they were directories: the string hosts.org_dir.marketing.xor.com refers to the NIS+ equivalent of the **/etc/hosts** file for this domain. To refer to a specific entry within a table, a different syntax (not described here) is used.

NIS+ commands accept both relative and fully-qualified names. Fully-qualified names are followed by a period, just as fully-qualified filesystem pathnames begin with a slash. Relative names are tested to see if they identify a legitimate NIS+ object in the machine's default domain; if not, each of the domain's parent directories is tried in turn.

For example, if you referred to hosts.org_dir on a host in the domain creative.marketing.xor.com, NIS+ would look for it in three places:

- hosts.org_dir.creative.marketing.xor.com
- hosts.org_dir.marketing.xor.com
- hosts.org_dir.xor.com

The domains would be searched in the order listed.

18.6 OTHER DATABASE SYSTEMS

Although NIS and NIS+ are not the only administrative database systems in the world, they are the big fish in a big pond. Two other systems, MIT's Hesiod and NeXT's NetInfo, have been around for several years without accumulating a substantial user base.

See Chapter 16 for more information about DNS.

Hesiod extends the protocols used by DNS for the distribution of administrative data. This gives Hesiod the benefits of DNS's tried-and-true protocols and implementations, and it avoids introducing yet another complicated system just for distributing configuration files. On the other hand, current implementations of DNS score low on the "ease of administration" scale and do not allow fine control of security. BIND 4.9 fixes many of the security concerns, however. To date, Hesiod has only been applied to certain subclasses of administrative data.

NetInfo is a lot like NIS+, only cleaner and simpler. It's included with the NEXTSTEP operating system and is available for other platforms as a commercial product. NetInfo uses a hierarchical domain structure similar to that of NIS+, but it stores data in a more uniform way and does not use explicit paths or links. Instead, a NetInfo client simply sees the information defined in all domains "above" it. Like NIS+, NetInfo considers itself an authoritative repository of information and requires conversions to and from flat files to be made explicitly.

18.7 PRIORITIZING SOURCES OF ADMINISTRATIVE INFORMATION

Most systems allow configuration information to be distributed in several ways. Every system understands flat files; most also understand NIS and know how to use DNS to look up hostnames and Internet addresses. Since there may be several potential sources for a given piece of information, vendors usually provide a way for you to specify which sources are to be checked, and the order in which the checks are to be made. Unfortunately, this is done differently on every system.

On some systems that support NIS, magic tokens are inserted into the **passwd** and **group** files to specify how their contents should be merged with the equivalent NIS maps; refer back to page 393 for more information about this brain damage. Other systems replace this behavior with a central switch.

Host and address lookups are unique in that they are the only operations that can refer to DNS (or any non-local information source, for that matter). Sometimes host lookups are configured in a different way from other kinds of lookups; on other systems, everything is set up in one place. Your mileage may vary.

For a long time, NIS and DNS did not coexist well at all. Eventually a hack was added to **ypserv**, the NIS server daemon, which causes it to refer to DNS when the NIS host maps don't contain the requested information. This featurette is still used on some systems and is enabled by the **-i** option to **ypserv** or the **-b** option to **makedbm**, depending on the system. Some systems cache responses from DNS and some do not; each behavior introduces its own problems.

18.8 SPECIFICS FOR VARIOUS OPERATING SYSTEMS

 Solaris uses the **/etc/nsswitch.conf** file to specify the sources of administrative data. It looks something like this:

```
passwd:   files nisplus
hosts:    nisplus dns
group:    files
...
```

Each line configures one type of information (usually, one flat-file equivalent). The potential sources are named nisplus, nis, files, dns, and compat; they refer to NIS+, NIS, vanilla flat files (ignoring tokens such as "+"), DNS, and NISified flat files (honoring "+"), respectively.

Sources are tried from left to right until one of them produces an answer for the query. In the example above, the **gethostbyname** routine would first check the NIS+ database, and if the host was not listed there, would then check DNS. Queries about UNIX groups, on the other hand, would check only the **/etc/group** file.

If necessary, you may define the "failure" of a source more specifically by putting bracketed expressions after it. For example, the line

```
hosts:   dns [NOTFOUND=return] nisplus
```

causes DNS to be used exclusively if it is available; a negative response from the name server makes queries return immediately (with a failure code) without checking NIS+. However, NIS+ will be used if no name server is available. The various types of failure are shown in Table 18.4; each may be set to `return` or `continue`, indicating whether the query should be aborted or forwarded to the next source.

Table 18.4   Solaris source failure modes

Condition	Meaning
UNAVAIL	The source doesn't exist or is down.
NOTFOUND	The source exists, but couldn't answer the query.
TRYAGAIN	The source exists, but is busy.
SUCCESS	The source was able to answer the query.

Several suggested **nsswitch.conf** configurations are provided in the files **nsswitch.files**, **nsswitch.nis**, and **nsswitch.nis+**. Check to see if one of these is appropriate for your site before rolling your own.

 HP-UX understands NIS and uses generic magic cookies in the **passwd** and **group** files. HP-UX's handling of host lookups is somewhat idiosyncratic, however. It uses DNS exclusively if it is available; if not, NIS is used exclusively. If neither DNS nor NIS is available, the **/etc/hosts** file is consulted.

 Under IRIX, source precedence for host lookups is set in the DNS resolver configuration file, **/etc/resolv.conf**. IRIX adds the nonstandard keyword `hostresorder`; its value is a list of sources separated by whitespace. The valid sources are `nis`, `bind`, and `local`, meaning NIS, DNS, and the **/etc/hosts** file, respectively. A slash may be placed between two sources to indicate that the source in front of the slash is "authoritative"; that is, if the source exists but cannot resolve the query, the search is terminated. For example, the line

```
hostresorder   nis bind / local
```

checks NIS, then DNS. **/etc/hosts** is checked only if a name server isn't available. Individual users can specify a different source order by setting the HOSTRESORDER environment variable. Legal values are the same as those used in **/etc/resolv.conf**.

IRIX also supports the -i option to **ypserv**, which makes it refer to DNS if a host-related NIS query cannot be answered. Both positive and negative responses from DNS are cached. This can cause stale data to get "stuck" in **ypserv**; send it a SIGHUP to flush the cache. The default timeout for cache entries is set with the -t option to **ypserv**.

Do not put DNS in the search path twice by using both **ypserv -i** and the hostresorder keyword in **/etc/resolv.conf**; this configuration will cause some queries to be needlessly repeated.

IRIX uses magic cookies to merge the contents of the **/etc/passwd** and **/etc/group** files with their respective NIS maps.

SunOS is a completely generic NIS system. It uses magic cookies to merge **/etc/passwd** and **/etc/group** with NIS data. According to the man page for **ypserv**, support for DNS is provided by **ypserv -d**. But in reality, this flag turns on debugging. To integrate NIS and DNS, change the B= at the top of **/var/yp/Makefile** to B=-b and then set up NIS as usual. This will pass the right flags to **makedbm**. **resolv.conf** files (see page 324) need to be installed on all NIS servers, even the slaves. Sun's version of **ypserv** does not cache DNS responses—this avoids the problem of stale cache entries, but slows response time.

DEC's version of OSF/1 is NIS-compatible, but doesn't use magic cookies. Instead, the search order is specified in **/etc/svc.conf**. DEC's original name for this file was **/etc/svcorder**; it addressed host lookups but not other kinds of information. **svc.conf** is more flexible. The current release of OSF/1 contains both **/etc/svcorder** and **/etc/svc.conf**, but the documentation denies the existence of the **svcorder** file. Caveat administrator.

Lines in **/etc/svc.conf** that deal with source order are of the form

```
passwd=local,yp
```

Sources are listed in the order they should be tried. Valid sources are local (flat files), yp (NIS), and bind (DNS). There is no way to declare a source authoritative. Whitespace is only allowed in certain places; it's best to avoid it altogether. The primary source for both **passwd** and **hosts** data must be local. Netgroups must come from NIS.

BSDI does not support NIS, and so little configuration is necessary or possible. For host lookups, a name server will be used if available. Otherwise, **/etc/hosts** is consulted.

19 SLIP and PPP

19.1 INTRODUCTION

A typical UNIX environment consists of hosts connected with some type of network hardware, such as Ethernet. On top of this hardware, hosts communicate using the TCP/IP protocols discussed in Chapter 14. These protocols facilitate file transfer among hosts (**rcp** and **ftp**), interactive logins (**rlogin** and **telnet**), and file sharing (NFS).

You may find yourself wanting these same network services in places where an Ethernet connection isn't readily available: an engineer's home, a remote office in Guam, or perhaps on a notebook computer that you carry when you travel. This chapter discusses the software that is available to help connect machines that are out of reach of your LAN. You might want to review Chapter 13, *Configuring the Kernel,* and Chapter 8, *Serial Devices,* before continuing.

Almost every UNIX machine, from mainframe to notebook, provides one or more serial ports. Because serial ports are so flexible and so widely supported, they provide the standard hardware interface used to connect "outlying" machines. Two machines' serial ports can be wired together directly or connected via telephone using inexpensive, high-speed modems.

SLIP (Serial Line Internet Protocol) and PPP (Point-to-Point Protocol) are protocols that allow the transmission of network packets over serial lines. SLIP and PPP are called "serial line encapsulation protocols" because they specify how packets must be encoded for transmission on a slow (and often unreliable) serial line. This chapter discusses how SLIP and PPP work, and how to use them to connect a machine to a network. We'll also discuss the differences between the two.

19.2   HOW SLIP AND PPP ARE DIFFERENT FROM UUCP

One of the first questions most people ask about SLIP and PPP is, "What do SLIP and PPP offer me that systems like UUCP do not?" The answer is full network connectivity, exactly like you'd get on an Ethernet. You can use `rlogin`, `rsh`, `ftp`, `rcp`, `telnet`, NFS, and even X Windows over a SLIP or PPP connection. Furthermore, multiple connections to (and from) remote hosts can be active simultaneously.

By comparison, UUCP is a batched, store-and-forward protocol that provides a relatively limited set of capabilities and commands. However, UUCP is a little easier to set up and is pre-installed on most systems.

19.3   PERFORMANCE ISSUES

SLIP and PPP provide all the functionality of Ethernet, but at *much* slower speeds. Normal office LANs operate at 10 Mb/s or 10,000 Kb/s. A dial-up connection operates at about 14 Kb/s.[1] To put this in perspective, it takes about 12.5 minutes to transfer a one-megabyte file across a SLIP line. This is usually suitable for home use, as well as for connections to remote offices that support only a handful of employees. A dial-up SLIP or PPP connection is *not* suitable as the only network connection for your 500-member engineering group based in Midwest City, Oklahoma.

19.4   SLIP AND PPP COMPARED

SLIP and PPP are different and independent serial line encapsulation protocols. But they are similar in spirit and function and thus fit nicely within a single chapter. As with `vi` and `emacs`, there are advantages and disadvantages to both. SLIP is usually the best choice if you are connecting a house or a small field office.

Both SLIP and PPP require you to add a driver to your kernel to manage communication between the serial interface and the network portion of the kernel. Both systems also provide user-level commands that set up and manage connections to remote hosts.

SLIP

SLIP is the hot-rod, "bare bones" encapsulation protocol. It can be traced back to TCP/IP implementations of the early 80s and was actually imple-

---

1. SLIP and PPP are normally used at speeds over 9,600 bps. Technically, they can be used on slower links, but they become insufferably slow.

mented and released to the world on 4.2BSD systems and Sun workstations by Rick Adams in 1984.[2] Today, SLIP is available on a large variety
of machines and operating systems, from UNIX and VMS to DOS, Macintosh, and even X terminals.

*See page 426 for
an explanation
of Internet RFCs.*

The original SLIP standard, RFC1055, defined the sequence of characters
used to frame IP packets for transmission across a serial line: nothing
more, nothing less. SLIP as defined in RFC1055 makes no effort to minimize the number of bytes sent across a low-speed serial line; whatever
would normally be contained in an IP packet is transmitted. Since IP
was designed to solve general network connectivity problems, it is not
as efficient as it could be for the case in which only one or a few hosts
are on the "remote" end of the link.

RFC1144 is a later SLIP standard (commonly referred to as "compressed
SLIP" or "CSLIP") which tries to minimize the number of bytes that are
actually transmitted over the serial line. CSLIP uses the following methods to reduce traffic and improve interactive response time:

- *TCP header compression* takes advantage of the small number
  of active connections over the link and the many fields of the
  header that can be predicted in the normal case (no dropped
  packets). To reduce the amount of data transmitted, the header
  for each connection is stored on both sides of the link, and only
  changes are sent. The header that normally accompanies each
  packet is reconstructed on the receiving side.

- *Type-of-service queueing* marks each packet coming from a user
  program to indicate whether it's "interactive." Modern versions
  of both `telnet` and `rlogin` request this option. Interactive
  packets are inserted at the front of the transmission queue,
  improving interactive response time when other programs
  (such as `ftp`) are contending for the serial line.

*See Chapter 14 for
more information
about ICMP.*

- *ICMP filtering* avoids the transfer of ICMP packets, which are
  used by `ping` to determine if a remote host is alive. Such
  inquiries, if done by many other sites, can consume a significant
  percentage of the bandwidth of a slow serial line.

Most implementations of CSLIP are backward-compatible with the original SLIP protocol.

Because SLIP is conceptually simpler than PPP, it is easier to debug
when problems arise. A pure CSLIP connection will usually perform
slightly better than an equivalent PPP connection.

---

2. The idea for SLIP debuted in a TCP/IP package called UNET by 3com and Ford Aerospace.

PPP

Designed by committee, PPP is the "everything *and* the kitchen sink" encapsulation protocol. PPP allows the transmission of "multi-protocol" packets over a single link. It is currently described in RFC1331. PPP is more flexible than SLIP, which only handles IP packets.

PPP has three main components:

- A method for encapsulating datagrams over serial links
- A Link Control Protocol (LCP) for establishing, configuring, and testing the data-link connection
- A family of Network Control Protocols (NCPs) for establishing and configuring different network-layer protocols

These components, complete with state tables that rival the best finite-state automata final exams, are explained in detail in the RFC; we won't discuss them further in this chapter. As with SLIP, there are a number of PPP implementations (both commercial and free) available for a wide variety of machines.

PPP does offer some interesting features beyond those of SLIP. In particular, PPP can encapsulate packets from many protocols simultaneously over a single serial line. Thus, PPP would be a good choice if you needed to exchange TCP/IP and DECnet packets between two sites. PPP also has built-in (but optional) error correction.

What PPP gains in bells and whistles, it loses in simplicity and performance over slow lines. That is why we make the general recommendation that, when possible, SLIP should be used on dial-up lines.

19.5 BASIC CONNECTION MODEL

In order to connect a remote host to a network with SLIP or PPP, you need to be concerned with three things:

- Your host's kernel must be able to send IP packets across a serial line as specified by the SLIP or PPP protocol standard.
- You must have a user-level program that allows you to establish and maintain SLIP or PPP connections.
- There must be a host on the other end of the serial line that understands the protocol you are using.

Making your Host Speak SLIP or PPP

See page 262 for more information about ifconfig.

The most fundamental requirement for a connection is that your host be capable of sending and receiving SLIP or PPP packets. In the case of a UNIX host, this generally involves adding a module to your kernel that takes network packets (normally stored in a chain of kernel data structures called *mbufs*) and places them in the serial device output queue, and vice-versa. This module is usually placed in the kernel so that it appears to be just another network interface and can be manipulated with standard tools such as **ifconfig**. Kernel modules that perform this task are discussed later in this chapter.

Controlling SLIP and PPP Links

There are three common ways to manage a serial IP link:

Static You configure a serial port as a network interface. This option can be used when the connection between the two machines is a serial cable or a dedicated link.

Dial-up You use a command to dial a modem, log in to a remote host, and start the remote SLIP or PPP protocol engine. If this procedure succeeds, the serial port is then configured as a network interface. This option normally leaves the link up for a long time, which makes it best suited for a phone line dedicated to this purpose.

Dynamic A daemon watches your serial "network" interfaces to see when traffic is queued for them. When someone tries to send a packet, the daemon automatically dials a modem to establish the connection, transmits the packet, and if the line goes back to being idle, disconnects the line after a reasonable amount of time.

Dynamic dial-up is often used if a phone line is shared between voice and data, or if the connection involves long distance or connect-time charges. It's a common myth that dynamic dial-up is only available with PPP.

Programs to implement all of these schemes are included with most versions of SLIP and PPP.

Finding a Host to Talk to

See Chapter 20 for more information about the Internet.

If you're setting up a link between two remote sites within your company, or between home and work, you can simply install the SLIP or PPP software on both ends. However, if your intent is to use SLIP or PPP to obtain an Internet connection, you'll probably need to talk to an Internet service provider. Many service providers offer dial-up connections to the public at a reasonable cost. See page 437 for a list of Internet providers in the United States.

19.6 NETWORK CONCERNS

Because a SLIP or PPP link is similar to an Ethernet connection, some of the administrative chores performed on a LAN must also be performed for a serial network connection. Since most links are similar to one another, sites often use boilerplate configurations that are modified only slightly for each connection.

On the other hand, since a SLIP or PPP link is not *really* an Ethernet connection, a few facilities should be used differently, or not at all. UNIX programs that assume the network is fast and reliable can easily run into trouble on a loaded 9,600 bps serial link.

Address Assignment

See page 260 for more information about assigning IP addresses.

Just as you assign an IP address to a new host on your Ethernet, you need to assign an IP address to each SLIP or PPP interface. There are a number of ways to assign addresses to these links (including assigning no addresses at all). We'll discuss only the simplest method here.

Think of a SLIP or PPP link as a network of its own. That is, a network of exactly two hosts, often called a "point-to-point" network. You need to assign a network number to the link just like you would assign a network number to a new Ethernet segment, according to whatever rules are used at your site. You can pick any two host addresses on that network, and assign one to each end of the link. Other local customs, such as the interface subnet mask, should be applied as well. Each host then becomes a "gateway" to the point-to-point network as far as the rest of the world is concerned.

This method is conceptually simple, but has the flaw of wasting a network number on each SLIP or PPP link. Check the documentation of the package you're using for other supported addressing conventions.

Routing

See page 252 for more information about routing.

Since SLIP and PPP turn the server into an IP router, you need to be concerned with IP routing just as you would on a "real" gateway, such as a machine that connects two Ethernets. The purpose of routing is to direct packets though gateways so that they can reach their ultimate destinations. There are a number of different ways to configure routing.

A run-of-the-mill SLIP or PPP client host should have a default route that forwards packets to its server. Likewise, the server needs to be known to the other hosts on its network as the gateway to the leaf machine.

Many SLIP and PPP packages handle these routing chores automatically.

Security

See Chapter 23 for more information about security.

Security concerns are introduced whenever you add a host to a network. Since a host connected via SLIP or PPP is a real member of the network, you need to treat it as such: verify that there are no accounts without passwords or with insecure passwords, that all appropriate vendor security fixes are installed, that `/.rhosts` and `/etc/hosts.equiv` files are not overly permissive, and so on.

NFS

See Chapter 17 for a general description of NFS.

One frequently-asked question is, "Can I use NFS with SLIP or PPP?" The answer is, "Maybe." Standard NFS uses the UDP protocol for packet transport. UDP does not guarantee reliable delivery and does not have TCP's congestion control algorithms. Congestion control becomes *extremely* important in the case of low-speed lines. Ergo, standard NFS performs poorly at best over SLIP and PPP. The solution is to use TCP-based NFS, which is now available from a few major vendors.

Perhaps the biggest problem with NFS over SLIP and PPP is that most vendors ship their machines with UDP checksums turned off (for backward compatibility with a time long past), and thus will accept packets that arrive corrupted. If you do not turn on UDP checksums in your kernel and an NFS packet arrives corrupted, it may corrupt your files. This is one case where PPP outshines SLIP, in that it is possible to have PPP do link-layer error checking. The solution, again, is to use TCP-based NFS, which doesn't have this problem.

X Windows

Since X Windows is based on TCP/IP, it is possible to run X applications over a SLIP or PPP connection. The X Windows protocol has a fairly high overhead, and therefore performance across SLIP/PPP is often less than stellar. Simple font-based applications such as **xterm** perform acceptably, but applications that use bitmap graphics do not. If you're looking into a serial connection for the sole purpose of remote X capability, your best bet is a protocol that is optimized for X over serial lines, such as XRemote from NCD.

19.7 FLAVORS OF SLIP

There are several freely-available implementations of SLIP. A collection of them is available via anonymous `ftp` from ftp.uu.net, in the directory `networking/ip/slip`. The `cslip-2.7.tar.Z` distribution is maintained by Craig Leres at Lawrence Berkeley Labs, and is the best reference copy of UNIX SLIP code. If you're interested in SLIP for DOS, look in the `networking/ip/ka9q` directory on ftp.uu.net.

19.8 FLAVORS OF PPP

Because of PPP's complexity, you may find that commercial implementations of PPP are more viable than any freely-available version. The best-supported package is the one sold by Morning Star Technologies in Columbus, Ohio. It is available for a variety of systems.

Fewer versions of free PPP are available than free SLIP, but there is still a decent selection. Look in the **networking/ip/ppp** directory at ftp.uu.net. We think **dp-3.0.tar.Z** by Kirk Smith at Purdue University is probably your best bet.

19.9 WALKTHROUGH: INSTALLING **SLIP** ON SUNOS

By now, you have a basic understanding of what SLIP and PPP are and what they can do for you. This section puts hand-waving aside and walks through an installation step by step. We will describe the installation of SLIP on a Sun IPX workstation that runs SunOS 4.1.3 and uses a Telebit T3000 V.32bis modem.

Before starting, collect the following items:

- Telebit T3000 modem
- Telebit T3000 modem manual
- RS-232 cable (male-to-male, straight through)
- Internet addresses you will use for the link
- Login name and password you will use for the link
- Phone number for the remote site

This package is also included on the CD-ROM.

Step 1: Obtain the **cslip-2.7** distribution. It's available via **ftp** from ftp.uu.net as **networking/ip/slip/cslip/cslip-2.7.tar.Z**. The package includes the kernel SLIP module for SunOS and the **tip**-with-SLIP program that we'll use to establish the connection.

Step 2: **uncompress** and un-**tar** the file. You may want to print out the **README** file for easy reference as you work.

Step 3: Following the instructions in the **README** under "Kernel Configuration," copy the SLIP include files to the appropriate directories:

```
% cp common/net/slcompress.h /sys/net
% cp common/net/slip.h /sys/net
% cp sunos4/net/if_slvar.h /sys/net
% cp common/net/slcompress.h /usr/include/net
% cp common/net/slip.h /usr/include/net
```

Step 4: Copy the source files for the SLIP kernel modules into the kernel source directory:

```
% cp common/net/slcompress.c /sys/net
% cp sunos4/net/if_sl.c /sys/net
```

These files will be compiled along with the rest of the kernel files when a new kernel containing SLIP is built.

Step 5: Edit **/sys/conf.common/files.cmn** to add the lines for the SLIP modules:

```
net/if_sl.c              optional sl INET
net/slcompress.c         optional sl INET
```

This file is used by **config** when generating a **Makefile** to control the compilation of a new kernel. These lines tell **config** to include the SLIP kernel modules.

Step 6: Edit **/sys/sun/str_conf.c** to include the lines that describe the streams used by SLIP. You'll see that the file is broken into three parts: include directives, external declarations, and an initialized structure. Add the three sets of additions to their appropriate sections:

```
#include "sl.h"

...

#if NSL > 0
extern struct streamtab if_slinfo;
#endif

...

#if NSL > 0
    { "slip", &if_slinfo },
#endif
```

These changes make SLIP a valid kernel module that can be used in association with a TTY stream to implement the SLIP protocol.

Step 7: Edit **/sys/sun4c/conf/***machine* (where *machine* is the name of your kernel configuration file) to add a line that declares the SLIP device within the kernel:

```
pseudo-device    slN  init slattach
```

N is the number of slip interfaces to add. Even if you're planning to use only one of your serial ports for a SLIP link, it's always a good idea to configure two SLIP devices in the kernel. In case of trouble, you can hook a cable between the two serial ports on the back of your system and try to get a SLIP connection running between them.

Step 8: Build a new kernel. This is done by first running **config** on your kernel configuration file (*machine*), to generate a **Makefile** in the directory **/sys/sun4c/***machine*. You can then use **make** in that directory to compile a new kernel.

Step 9: Install the new kernel. You'll need to copy the new kernel into the root directory, make a backup copy of the running kernel (in case something goes awry), and then name your new kernel **/vmunix** so it will be used the next time the system is booted. Be sure you know how to boot your old kernel before you reboot.

Step 10: Reboot the machine.

Step 11: **cd** to the **tip** directory of the **cslip-2.7** package. This directory contains a version of **tip** that Doug Kingston modified to know about login scripts and SLIP, hence the nickname **tip**-with-SLIP.

Step 12: Edit the **Makefile** in the **tip** directory to reflect the type of modem you'll be using. Since we're using a Telebit T3000 for this example, we'd edit the file to contain a line defining TELEBIT as a preprocessor constant. Many other modems are supported; they are described in the comment lines of the **Makefile**.

Step 13: Compile **tip**-with-SLIP using **make**.

Step 14: Install **tip**-with-SLIP. You may want to place it in a directory with other local executables, such as **/usr/local/bin**.

See Chapter 8 for more information about serial connectors.

Step 15: Connect the modem to your workstation. In this example, we'd use a 25-pin straight-through male-to-male RS-232 cable. Since the IPX really uses a DIN-9 connector for its serial ports, we'd also need a DIN-9 to DB-25 converter cable. We'll assume below that you connect the modem to the **ttya** port.

Step 16: Configure the machine to use hardware flow control on the serial port. Software flow control (XON/XOFF) interferes with the normal operation of SLIP, and so it should be avoided at all costs. Use the **eeprom** command to set the flow control parameter of the port:

```
eeprom ttya-mode=38400,8,n,1,h
```

The last argument, **h**, indicates hardware flow control.

See page 116 for more information about soft carrier.

Step 17: Turn off "soft carrier" on the port. Sun ships their machines configured to ignore loss of the carrier detect (CD) line from a modem. While this sometimes makes things work better "out of the box," it can cause disasters when a modem is connected. Add the word local after the on column for **ttya** in **/etc/ttytab**:

```
ttya      "/usr/etc/getty std.38400"    dialup     on local
```

See Chapter 8 for more about the /etc/remote file.

Step 18: Add an entry to **/etc/remote** so that you can use **tip** to connect to the modem and configure its onboard registers. Since you're just using the "standard" mode of **tip** to do this configuration, you can use either your system's original **tip** or the **tip** you just compiled. For this stage, you just need an entry that specifies the port and the baud rate at which you'll be talking to the modem:

```
telebit:dv=/dev/ttya:br#38400
```

We'll get to the fancy uses of **tip** a bit later.

Step 19: Use `tip` to connect to the modem and configure its registers. A good configuration for a T3000 would be

```
AT&F&C1&D2
ATS0=0S2=128S7=65S10=25S51=6S58=2S68=2S180=2S181=1S225=0
ATM0V1E0X0Q0&W&W1
```

A brief explanation of the meaning of each command code is given in Table 19.1. You'll have to adapt the settings to your particular modem. The ones that really matter are `S58` and `S68`, which set hardware flow control on the modem.

Table 19.1   Guide to command codes for example modem configuration[a]

Code	Meaning
AT	Tells the modem to listen to you
&F	Returns to factory default parameters, a sane baseline
&C1	Uses DCD (pin 8 of the RS-232 port) to indicate carrier detect
&D2	Disconnects when DTR (pin 20) is lost (`tip` dies or host crashes)
S0=0	Turns off auto-answer
S2=128	Disables the escape-to-command-mode sequence
S7=65	Waits 65 seconds for a connection, reasonable on many modems
S10=25	Waits 2.5 seconds before "loss of carrier," good on noisy lines
S51=6	Locks modem interface speed at 38,400 bits per second
S58=2	Uses RTS/CTS (hardware) flow control
S68=2	Uses RTS/CTS (hardware) flow control
S180=2	Uses V.42 error correction
S181=1	Requests error correction but doesn't require it
S255=0	Reloads profile A at power on or when reset
M0	Turns off the speaker
V1	Requests verbose result codes (required by `tip`)
E0	Turns off command echo (required by `tip`)
X0	Uses standard result codes
Q0	Returns result codes
&W	Writes to non-volatile profile A
&W1	Writes to non-volatile profile B

a. Some lines have been shaded to improve readability.

Step 20: Create an **/etc/remote** entry to be used by **tip**-with-SLIP to establish a SLIP connection. You'll need to know the phone number of the site that you'll be calling, your IP address on the SLIP link, and the IP address of the host on the other end of the link. If you're connecting to an Internet service provider, they can supply you with these addresses.

See page 256 for information about subnetting.

If you're connecting to another site that you administer, you'll need to allocate a pair of numbers on a network that you dedicate to the SLIP link. If you're going to install a lot of SLIP links, you can use subnetting to create network numbers that allow for only four hosts, thus reducing the number of class C network numbers you must apply for.

The definitions of the **/etc/remote** fields used by **tip**-with-SLIP are contained in the **README.SLIP** file in the **tip** directory. The ls parameter specifies a file that contains a login script, which we will discuss in the next step. Here's a complete sample configuration:

```
slip:\
  :ls=/usr/local/slip/etc/annex.login:\
  :sa=192.225.32.18:sm=255.255.255.252:da=192.225.32.17:\
  :st=slip:rt:at=telebit:dv=/dev/ttya:du:pn=5551000:\
  :br#38400:
```

Step 21: Create a login script for use by **tip**-with-SLIP. This file is also described in **README.SLIP** in the **tip** directory. It is basically an expect-send script that is used by **tip**-with-SLIP to log in to the remote host and start the SLIP server. In this example, the remote host will be a terminal server that asks for our user name and our password, and then expects us to send the command **slip**.

```
send \r
recv 10/again username:
goto login
label again
send \r
recv 10/error username:
label login
# your login name goes between the \d and the \r below
send \dSdemo\r
recv 10/error word:
# your password goes between the \d and the \r below
send \dour,pass\r
recv 10/error annex:
send \d\d\rslip\r\r
done
label error
fail
```

Step 22: Establish a SLIP connection and test. Use **tip**-with-SLIP with the **-s** flag to dial the modem, log in, and start the SLIP protocol.

```
% tip -s slip
[Logging In]
[SLIP Running]
% ping -s xor.com
PING xor.com: 56 data bytes
64 bytes from xor.com (192.108.21.1): seq=0. time=241ms
64 bytes from xor.com (192.108.21.1): seq=1. time=253ms
64 bytes from xor.com (192.108.21.1): seq=2. time=239ms
...
```

You can use tip-with-SLIP's -v flag to debug your script. Once the link is up, you should be able to connect to the host of your choice.

Now you are ready to being using your SLIP connection for day-to-day communication. Using commands like ping, you can easily write scripts that monitor the status of the SLIP line and restart tip-with-SLIP when necessary (if you did not turn on the CSLIP option that disables ping). Keep in mind that SLIP provides a real network connection and that the security of hosts attached via SLIP must be carefully monitored.

19.10 CONFIGURING PPP ON SOLARIS 2.4

Solaris 2.4 includes dial-up PPP as part of the standard distribution. Third-party versions of PPP for Solaris (such as the version from Morning Star Technologies) generally offer more features and are better supported. This section discusses the generic version as distributed by Sun.

The PPP package that is integrated into Solaris 2.4 is "asynchronous PPP," since it is designed to handle connections over standard serial lines (such as dial-up modems). It's an official part of the Solaris operating system, so you don't need to perform all the sticky steps of installing a kernel PPP module. You can verify that you have PPP available with the following command:

```
pkginfo | grep ppp
```

If PPP is installed, you should get a response similar to:

```
system    SUNWapppr    PPP/IP Async PPP configuration files
system    SUNWapppu    PPP/IP Async PPP login service
system    SUNWpppk     PPP/IP and IPdialup Device Drivers
```

If PPP is not already installed, you'll need to install it as a Solaris package. See the manual page for pkgadd for more details. Table 19.2 lists the files used to configure and manage Solaris PPP.

Table 19.2 Files Involved with PPP on Solaris 2.4

File	Purpose
/etc/init.d/asppp	Boot-time startup script for dial-up PPP
/usr/sbin/aspppd	Daemon that manages PPP links
/etc/asppp.cf	Config file containing list of connections
/usr/sbin/aspppls	Login shell for dial-in connections
/var/adm/log/asppp.log	PPP activity log file
/tmp/.asppp.fifo	Hook into aspppd for dial-in connections

Solaris PPP and UUCP cooperate to share dial-out modems. To set up a PPP connection to a remote site, you should first add the modem and the site to the `Systems`, `Dialers`, and `Devices` files in the `/etc/uucp` directory. Details on this procedure can be found in Chapter 30.

Once the modem and remote site have been set up in the UUCP files (including a login script for the remote site in `/etc/uucp/Systems`), you need to edit `/etc/asppp.cf` to configure the connection's IP address and associate it with a `Systems` entry.

Here's an example `/etc/asppp.cf` that illustrates a link to "sliphub" (192.225.32.1) from "myhost" (192.225.32.2):

```
# set IP addresses of the pseudo-interface
ifconfig ipdptp0 plumb 192.225.32.2 192.225.32.1 up

# dynamic dialup parameters for pseudo-interface
path
    interface ipdptp0
    peer_system_name sliphub # Same as in Systems file
    inactivity_timeout 600   # time out if idle 10 minutes
```

Once this is in place, you can start the PPP daemon manually with

```
/etc/init.d/asppp start
```

This step should only be necessary the first time. On subsequent reboots, the PPP daemon will be started by `init`. If all goes well (check `/var/adm/log/asppp.log`), you should be able to reach the remote site with commands such as `telnet` and `ftp`.

19.11 INSTALLING SLIP AND PPP ON OTHER ARCHITECTURES

SLIP and PPP are available for almost every major version of UNIX. Installation instructions and features vary widely. In some cases, the OS vendors ship SLIP or PPP either as "unsupported" software or as part of their "networking" distribution. In other cases, vendors sell them as separate products. Unfortunately, vendors' implementations are often poorly documented or just plain broken, which is why other companies also support a SLIP/PPP package for those machines.

19.12 DIAL-IN HUBS

You may find that once you begin offering SLIP or PPP connections to users at home, you have more requests than you have serial ports. A number of terminal servers offer SLIP/PPP capability, including the Telebit Netblazer, the Xylogics Annex, and the Livingston Portmaster. These products often provide a convenient and easily-maintainable source of serial ports complete with the SLIP or PPP software already installed. They allow you to establish a dial-in "pool" of modems that offer SLIP and PPP service to off-site users.

20 *The Internet*

20.1 INTRODUCTION

For years, dreamy PBS documentaries have promised that some day, all computers will be networked together. In fact, the age of universal networking is already here.

In previous chapters, we discussed various aspects of local area networking: the management of individual networks and the techniques used to connect them together with routing services. We also mentioned ways of tying local networks together into "wide area" networks which, while similar to local networks from a logical standpoint, connect using a different range of physical hardware.

Just as local networks combine to make wide area networks, wide area networks combine to form a bigger whole called the Internet. Logically, the Internet is like a large wide area network that happens to serve millions of computers. It uses the same communication protocols as a local network, and many of the services used on local networks are found on the Internet as well. The only real difference is that the connections between Internet sites are usually leased telephone lines rather than Ethernet or token ring cables.

As of 1994, at least two million computers have been connected to the Internet, and this number is doubling about every year. The number of Internet users isn't known for sure, but estimates range to the tens of millions. More than 120 countries are active on the Internet.

Exhibit A shows the state of computer networking in various countries around the world. Countries marked as having only email access may host FidoNet or UUCP nodes, but they do not have connections to a full-service network such as the Internet.

Exhibit A   World-Wide Network Connectivity as of July, 1994[a]

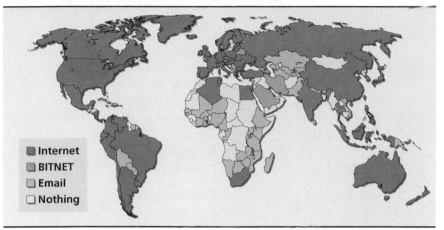

Internet
BITNET
Email
Nothing

a. Copyright © 1994 by Larry Landweber and the Internet Society. Used with permission.

20.2 THE INTERNET POPULACE

To a large degree, the Internet's population still reflects its origins. Most Internet sites are universities, businesses involved in the computer industry, or scientific research installations.

Scientific use of the Internet is haphazard. Computer scientists are usually heavy users, as are biologists. Unfortunately, some disciplines seem to remain forever marooned in the 1960s world of FORTRAN and punch cards.

More and more, Internet access is becoming available to people with no connection to its traditional roots. Companies outside the computer industry are discovering the benefits of worldwide networking, and technically-inclined individuals are finding that the Internet is a fun place to play and explore. Magazines like *Wired* and *Mondo 2000* promote the Internet as an avant-garde fashion accessory.

Currently, the two main factors limiting the expansion of the Internet are the price and convenience of connections. It costs at least $100 per month for a dedicated Internet link, and you have to understand a fair amount about networking and TCP/IP to make the link work. But the situation is improving, and we expect that Internet connections will be within the grasp of almost everyone within a few years.

20.3 INTERNET STRUCTURE AND POLITICS

The Internet isn't a service you connect to; it's something you (or more accurately, your computers) become a part of. A gateway machine at your site ties one of your local networks to a machine that is already on the Internet. From the standpoint of TCP/IP, the Internet is just another network that packets can come from or be sent to. Once the gateway is functioning correctly, IP routing allows any computer at your site to talk to any computer on the Internet.

Usually, the Internet gateway becomes the default route out of your site. Any packet with an address that isn't recognized as belonging to a computer on a local network can be sent to the Internet for delivery. This way, your site need not maintain any information about the topology of non-local networks; routing services further "upstream" take care of that for you.

The Internet Hierarchy

In theory, the networks of the Internet could be connected together with no particular organization. Even when network topology is complex, the Internet routing protocols are supposed to be able to provide a path between any two machines.

In reality, the Internet thrives on the centralization of resources, for three reasons. First, nobody likes to depend too much on other sites. If a packet has to pass through thirty sites to get to its destination, that's thirty opportunities for the packet to be misrouted, dropped, delayed, or corrupted. Short paths are faster and more reliable.

Second, administrators like to avoid getting involved with the details of Internet routing if they can. It's easy to classify packets as either local or non-local and to pass the non-local packets to a gateway machine. It's much harder to manage a network that has several outgoing connections, since routing knowledge must be brought into the local network rather than isolated on a gateway machine.

Third and most important, sites generally want to connect to the outside world with a cheap, slow network link. But they want their packets transferred along the intermediate networks at high speed.

All of these factors suggest an architecture that is roughly hierarchical, with a limited set of expensive, high-capacity lines feeding mid-capacity networks to which individual sites are connected. In the typical case, a site that wants to connect to the Internet will buy a network connection from a service provider that is only one or two hops from a main trunk (or "backbone," as they are called).

*See page 253 for
a discussion of
routing protocols.*
Backbone-level routing systems are different from those found on most workstations, since they must deal not only with thousands of packets per second, but also with hundreds of thousands of routes to tens of thousands of networks. Specialized hardware and software are used to perform this task efficiently. But from the outside, the backbones look exactly like any other IP network.

The Internet is expected to grow substantially in the future, and its structure is being adjusted to accommodate this. A new version of the IP protocol with 128-bit addresses has recently been adopted by the IETF. The larger address space will not only alleviate the address shortage, but will also allow addresses to be assigned hierarchically. This will greatly simplifying the routing chores that backbones sites must now perform. In the interim, some of these benefits can be obtained through supernetting, discussed on page 257.

Acceptable Use

In the United States, it is usually possible to talk to any machine in the country at interactive speeds, using about fifteen hops. However, since most Internet traffic must pass through one or more backbone links, use of the network becomes complicated by a number of political and financial issues.

Even though the Internet appears to be one large network, the owner of each individual component is responsible for setting the administrative policies that govern that portion of the network: who may use it, what types of information may be transmitted, and how packets will be gatewayed in and out.

The policies of networks run by the government and by academic institutions tend to be fairly similar. They usually state that the purpose of the network is to facilitate scientific and educational computing. Any network traffic that supports these goals is generally acceptable. Illegal use, commercial use, and use-for-profit are usually identified as not acceptable. Frivolous use and game-playing are sometimes forbidden or discouraged. Many policies contain escape clauses that permit reciprocal exchange of packets with other networks according to the other networks' acceptability policies.

The implementation of these policies is generally more permissive than the written rules would suggest. Enforcement is lax, and the prevailing attitude among network administrators is that reasonable uses that do not interfere with the functioning of the network should not be punished. On the other hand, blatant transgressions usually provoke a quick response.

The definition of "commercial use" is somewhat hazy. Use of the Internet to broadcast advertisements invariably brings swift retribution. On the other hand, private email of all types, including email sent in the conduct of business, is accepted. Many companies distribute software over the Internet, and this is almost universally accepted.

When businesses connect to the Internet, they usually do so through a commercial backbone rather than through a research net. This setup tends to enforce the usage guidelines automatically. If your backbone is commercial, there's no reason for your packets to be routed through a research net unless you're communicating with someone who lives on that net. If you're dealing with someone on that net, then your activities can probably be interpreted as supporting research or education.

Our advice is not to worry *too* much about the written policies. Use good judgement and avoid doing anything that's an obvious breach of etiquette. If caught, plead ignorance.

Internet History

The progenitor of the modern Internet was a network called ARPANET set up in the 1970s by the Department of Defense. The ARPANET was used mostly for military research, and connections to it were primarily limited to defense contractors and a few key universities. However, the ARPANET did serve to validate the TCP/IP protocols, which became widely used on local networks.

The National Science Foundation adopted the Internet protocols when it set up a group of backbone sites to facilitate the sharing of supercomputer time among researchers in the mid-1980s. The construction of this network, NSFNET, marked the beginning of the modern Internet era. Over time, a variety of governmental agencies, research groups, and commercial providers have added their own backbones. Modern backbones are constructed from leased "T3" telephone lines, which support speeds of up to 45 megabits per second.

In 1991, Congress passed a bill called the High-Performance Computing Act which provides for improvements to the Internet over a five-year period. One goal of the act is to bring the administration of various government-sponsored networks together into a National Research and Education Network, or NREN. In addition to allowing for a more uniform network structure, the NREN also proposes to upgrade the bandwidth of the Internet backbones by a factor of 50.

More recently, the Clinton administration has proposed an accelerated plan for development of the Internet (and other information and computer services) known as the National Information Infrastructure. The NII aims to promote the development of networking technology in the private sector, to remove legislative and regulatory obstacles to the deployment of this technology, and to make government data and services available on-line.

On the other hand, this is the same administration that brought us the Clipper initiative. The plans for the "information superhighway" sound good so far, but we'll believe it when we see it.

Internet Administration

A network of over two million computers can't function without some central administrative coordination. The tasks required to keep the Internet running generally fall into two categories: day-to-day chores and long-term planning.

See Chapter 16 for more information about the domain name hierarchy.

Day-to-day chores include assigning IP addresses to new (or growing) sites, managing the domain name hierarchy, managing routing information for backbones, monitoring the growth of the network, and distributing information about the Internet. These routine tasks are handled by three separate companies under contract to the National Science Foundation.

- Network Solutions, Inc., handles "registration services": the assignment of IP addresses and domain names, and the management of on-line services that access this information.

- AT&T provides "directory and database services," including lists of resources available on the Internet, searchable databases of Internet people and sites, and a "directory of directories" that can be used to find other sources of information.

- General Atomics provides "information services"; it acts as a clearing house for information about the Internet and assists sites that want to connect.

These three service providers operate together as the "InterNIC" (Network Information Center), and can be accessed at internic.net using most of the common Internet protocols.

Long-term strategic planning for the Internet involves the standardization of protocols, management of interoperability with foreign networks, projection of future needs, supervision of the physical structure of the network, and analysis of current patterns of use.

These concerns are addressed by the Internet Architecture Board (IAB), whose members are appointed by the Internet Society (ISOC), an open organization charged with providing for the general health and growth of the Internet.

Technical work is managed by the Internet Engineering Task Force (IETF), which operates under the aegis of the IAB. Subgroups of the IETF address the topic areas of applications, Internet services, network management, operational requirements, OSI integration, routing, transport and services, security, and user services.

Most of these organizations welcome the participation of outsiders. If you have an interest in working on the architecture of the Internet or just want to learn more, the IETF is a good place to start. To subscribe to the IETF mailing list, send mail to ietf-request@cnri.reston.va.us.

The technical activities of the ISOC are summarized in documents known as RFCs, short for Requests for Comment. Protocol standards, proposed changes, and informational bulletins all usually end up as RFCs. Sometimes the name is accurate and anyone who has comments on a proposal is encouraged to reply. Other times, the RFC mechanism simply documents or explains something about existing practice.

RFCs are available via anonymous **ftp** from numerous sources, including ds.internic.net and ftp.wustl.edu. The RFCs current at the time this book was published are included on the CD-ROM.

20.4 USING THE INTERNET

See Chapter 21 for more information about **sendmail**.

Anything you can do on a local network, you can also do on the Internet. This includes logging into other computers, distributing files, "talking" interactively with users at other sites, playing networked games, and connecting to network services such as **sendmail** and **xntpd**. But there are a few differences you should be aware of.

For more information about NFS, see Chapter 17.

Bandwidth on the Internet is precious, and there are some things you just shouldn't do. The use of NFS and X Windows across the Internet is especially frowned upon. Don't use the Internet as a substitute for buying your own resources. If you need more disk space, buy another disk— don't use the Internet to centralize scarce commodities.[1]

See Chapter 16 for more information about DNS.

The Internet uses a special way of naming machines called the Domain Name System (DNS). You may be used to referring to the machines on your local network by short names such as "venus" and "pluto." But with no coordination among sites, there's no way to prevent two people from giving their computers the same name. In fact, "venus" and "pluto" are two of the most common hostnames on the Internet, and there are more than six hundred machines with each of these names.

DNS defines a hierarchical scheme which guarantees that every system has a unique Internet name. For example, the Internet name of a local machine "venus" might be "venus.cs.colorado.edu". Chapter 16 describes the DNS system in luscious detail; for now, just be aware that you might see some odd names on the Internet.

---

1. In addition to being improper, such use of the Internet also invites security problems.

It's possible to use the Internet to transport data packets for protocols other than TCP/IP (for example, AppleTalk or SNA) using a technique called IP encapsulation or "tunneling." With encapsulation, each packet is "wrapped" into an IP packet at its point of origin, shipped across the Internet, and then unwrapped at the destination. The networks at each end don't know or care how the packet got from one place to the other.

Anonymous ftp

The `ftp` command (along with its server-side daemon, `ftpd`) provides a simple way to transfer files over a network. When you start `ftp`, you point it at the server machine from which you want to copy files. `ftp` connects to the server, prompts you to enter your name and password, and then presents a shell-like interface to allow you to list the files available on the remote server and to retrieve the ones you want. The `ftp` protocol is not specific to UNIX, so it's possible to copy files from almost any other kind of computer using `ftp`.

See page 514 for more information about SMTP.

Sometimes you must have an account on the remote machine in order to copy files, but many `ftp` servers allow you to log in with the name "anonymous" rather than your actual user name. At most sites, any password is accepted; it is customary to use your Internet email address as the password so that the site's administrator knows who is accessing the server. A few sites require an email address that can be verified via SMTP as a password. Anonymous `ftp` is one of the most common ways that software and documents are distributed on the Internet.

Throughout this book, we have occasionally said that software package so-and-so is available via anonymous `ftp` from a particular host. Now we will finally tell you how to get these goodies. The following session illustrates an `ftp` session to ftp.wustl.edu, a large `ftp` archive run by Washington University in St. Louis. If you do not have the name server running, you must either have ftp.wustl.edu in your host tables or know its IP address and use that in place of the machine name in the `ftp` command below.

```
% ftp ftp.wustl.edu
Connected to ftp.wustl.edu.
220 ftp.wustl.edu FTP server (Version 2.0) ready.
Name (ftp.wustl.edu:garth): anonymous
331 Guest login ok, send your e-mail address as password.
Password: garth@boulder.colorado.edu   /* does not echo */
230-
230-  This system may be used 24 hours a day, 7 days a
230-  week.  The local time is Sun Apr 17 17:03:49 1994.
230-
230-  All transfers to and from wuarchive are logged.
230-  If you don't like this then disconnect now!
```

```
230-
230 Guest login ok, access restrictions apply.
ftp> ls
200 PORT command successful.
150 Opening ASCII mode data connection for file list.
lost+found
mirrors
bin
decus
...
README
techreports
files.1st.Z
ls-lR.Z
226 Transfer complete.
224 bytes received in 0.022 seconds (10 Kbytes/s)
ftp> binary
200 Type set to I.
ftp> get files.1st.Z
200 PORT command successful.
150 Open BINARY connection for files.1st.Z (2911507 bytes)
226 Transfer complete.
local: files.1st.Z remote: files.1st.Z
2911507 bytes received in 64 seconds (44 Kbytes/s)
ftp> quit
221 Goodbye.
```

The file transfer took 64 seconds for a 2.9 megabyte file. Your mileage will vary; this transfer was Sunday afternoon, but at 10 a.m. Monday morning, allow more time.

files.1st.Z is a list of files available on the archive server. It is in a compressed format that must be decoded with the **uncompress** command. Since compressed files contain binary data, the **binary** command was used above to prevent **ftp** from dropping the most significant bit of each byte during transmission (some versions of **ftp** enter this mode automatically). To unpack the file, run

```
% uncompress files.1st.Z
```

See page 621 for more information about compression.
compress and **uncompress** are included with most UNIX systems. Lately, a more efficient compression system called "zip" has gained popularity. Zip files usually end in **.z**, **.gz**, or **.zip**. Most versions of UNIX don't include commands that handle zip files; you might need to **ftp** them from an archive site and compile them. One implementation of zip, called **gzip**, is included on the CD-ROM.

When a number of files are to be distributed together, they are often combined into a single file with **tar**, and then the **tar** file is compressed.[2] For example, to unpack a file called `perl.tar.Z` in the current directory, use the commands

```
% uncompress perl.tar.Z
% tar xvf perl.tar
```

Every since the Internet became a Big Media Event in 1993, it has been almost impossible to log into well-known `ftp` sites due to limitations on the number of simultaneous users. The following `expect` script can help; it attempts to log in at one minute intervals and turns control over to you once a successful connection has been established. This example is for ftp.wustl.edu; other sites may need slightly different procedures.

```
#!/usr/local/bin/expect
spawn /usr/ucb/ftp
expect "ftp> "
while 1 {
    send "open ftp.wustl.edu\r"
    expect "Name*: " {send "anonymous\r"}
    expect {
        "Password:" {send "[exec whoami]@\r"; break}
        "fail" {expect "ftp> ";send "close\r";expect "ftp> "}
        timeout {send_user "Can't log on, sorry.\r"; exit}
    }
    sleep 60
}
interact
```

For more information about `expect`, see page 390.

Setting Up an Anonymous ftp Server

In order to let others share your software via anonymous `ftp`, you must create an account for the fake user ftp, configure its home directory, and set up the `ftp` server daemon, `ftpd`.

See page 708 for more information about `inetd`.

`ftpd` is managed by `inetd` and therefore must have an entry in the `/etc/inetd.conf` and `/etc/services` files. When an anonymous login is made, `ftpd` does a `chroot` system call to make files outside of `~ftp` invisible and inaccessible. This enhances security, since `ftpd` must run setuid to root to manipulate privileged socket ports.

To allow anonymous `ftp` from your site, take the following steps:

- Add the user ftp to your regular password file.
- Create subdirectories `bin`, `etc`, and `pub` beneath `~ftp`.
- Copy the `ls` program to the `~ftp/bin` directory.
- Copy `/etc/passwd` and `/etc/group` to `~ftp/etc`.

---

2. It is much more effective to `compress` a `tar` file than to `tar` a set of compressed files.

- Edit the **passwd** and **group** files as described below.
- Replace all passwords in **~ftp/etc/passwd** with stars.
- Set the proper permissions on files and directories under **~ftp**.

No one needs to log in to the ftp account, so use a star as ftp's password. It's also a good idea to specify **/bin/false** as ftp's login shell.

Since an anonymous **ftp** session runs **chroot**ed to **~ftp**, the subdirectories **bin** and **etc** must provide a copy of all the commands and configuration information needed by **ftpd**—once the **chroot** has been done, **~ftp/bin** and **~ftp/etc** will masquerade as **/bin** and **/etc**. In most cases, **ftpd** uses only the **ls** command; copies of the **/etc/passwd** and **/etc/group** files should be put in **~ftp/etc** so that **ls** can provide the proper symbolic names for owners and groups.

See page 543 for more information about password security.

The **passwd** file under **~ftp** should only contain the users root, daemon, uucp and ftp. You must replace the passwords with stars since this copy of the **passwd** file will be available to people who use your **ftp** server. Even if the passwords are encrypted, there is still a risk involved in allowing other people to discover them.[3]

For added security, make **~ftp/bin/ls** execute-only by setting its mode to 111. This prevents clients from copying away the binary and scrutinizing it for weaknesses.

The files you want to make available should be put in **~ftp/pub**.

If your system uses shared libraries and your **ls** command is not statically linked, you may need to copy or hard-link extra files into **~ftp** to provide a proper execution environment, since the files that contain the shared libraries aren't normally accessible after a **chroot**.

 Solaris requires **ls** to be put in **~ftp/usr/bin**; **~ftp/bin** should be a symbolic link to **usr/bin** (*not* a symbolic link to **~ftp/usr/bin**, as this path will be unresolvable after a **chroot** has occurred). Solaris is a shared-library system, and fifteen extra files must be installed under **~ftp** to get **ls** to work. Refer to the **ftpd** manual page for instructions. A copy of **/etc/netconfig** should be put in **~ftp/etc**.

 Under HP-UX, you must put a copy of the **/etc/logingroup** file in the **~ftp/etc** directory.

 IRIX 5.2's **ftpd** requires a patch to prevent an annoying disconnect problem after multiple files have been transferred.

 SunOS uses shared libraries, so some additional files must be put in **~ftp** to make **ls** work. **ld.so** and the most recent **libc.so** should be copied or linked from **/usr/lib** to **~ftp/usr/lib**. You must also cre-

---

3. On some systems, you must run **mkpasswd passwd** after modifying the password file.

ate the directory ~ftp/dev and create a device file there with the command mknod zero c 3 12.

On DEC's OSF/1 systems, the /etc/sia directory should be copied into ~ftp/etc/sia.

Permissions on the various files and directories are quite important. We recommend that permissions be set as shown in Table 20.1.

Table 20.1   Recommended permissions under ~ftp

File	Owner	Mode	File	Owner	Mode
~ftp	ftp	555	~ftp/etc/passwd	root	444
~ftp/bin	root	555	~ftp/etc/group	root	444
~ftp/bin/ls	root	111	~ftp/pub	root	755
~ftp/etc	root	555			

Archive Servers

There are thousands of anonymous ftp servers on the Internet. Anything you might want is probably there, but how do you find it? The easiest way is to go to an "information supermarket."

There is a group of large archive servers that collect materials from other sources. These servers tend to be well-known and relatively permanent. Popular files and software packages can usually be found on one of these servers. The servers are systematically organized, so it's usually not difficult to find what you're looking for. Two of the better-known sites are ftp.uu.net and ftp.wustl.edu.

Archie

Another way to locate files on the Internet is to use a service called Archie, which provides a database of the files available via anonymous ftp. Archie began as a project of the McGill University School of Computer Science in Canada, but more database servers have been added as Archie has grown more popular.

Each month, the master Archie server goes out snooping on the Internet. It uses the standard ftp protocol to list the files on each server. Since the archive sites don't need to do anything special to help Archie along, Archie's records are usually fairly complete.

Archie doesn't copy files or look at their contents; the final product of the search is a database that maps filenames to the names of ftp servers. This is often adequate if you know what you're looking for.

There are several ways to access the Archie database. The first is to telnet to an Archie server (try archie.rutgers.edu, archie.unl.edu, or archie.ans.net in the United States). Log in as "archie". You will be transferred to a program that lets you search the database. For example, this sessions shows how to find archive sites with information about the Kerberos security system:

```
archie> prog kerberos
# matches / % database searched:  68 /100%
Host crl.dec.com  (192.58.206.2)
Last updated 07:44  8 Apr 1993
    Location: /pub/athena
      DIRECTORY rwxr-xr-x      512  Sep  2  1991    kerberos
Host mcsun.eu.net   (192.16.202.1)
Last updated 06:54 20 Mar 1993
    Location: /newsarchive/comp/protocols
      DIRECTORY rwxrwxr-x     2048  Mar 20 04:58    kerberos
    Location: /network/athena
      DIRECTORY rwxrwxr-x      512  Mar 20 04:08    kerberos
  ...
```

The second line shows that 68 exact matches were found on the word "kerberos." It is possible to match substrings, too, but it takes longer.

Two matches are shown above: crl.dec.com and mcsun.eu.net. Both of these sites have directories called **kerberos** that are accessible via anonymous **ftp**. In theory, it would be best to select a source that is "close" to you; however, the logical structure of the Internet is different from its physical structure, and apparent distances can be deceiving. You might have to go through a network in San Jose to reach a site on the other side of town.[4]

A second way to access Archie is through the Archie email server at archie@ans.net. If you don't have direct access to the Internet (or would simply prefer not to log in directly) you can send email to the server with your search requests in the body of your message. The syntax is similar to, but not exactly the same as, the login-style Archie syntax. A list of results will be returned to you via email. Send "help" in the body of a message to get detailed instructions for using the Archie server.

A version of the **archie** *command is included on the CD-ROM.*

Yet another way to get to Archie is to use an Archie client that runs as a command on your local machine. This is more convenient than picking a server, connecting to it, logging in, and using the interactive software; in fact, it's as simple and natural as a local **grep**, though it takes longer.

Client programs are available for a variety of systems; often, you can **ftp** them from the same machines that provide Archie service. All of these access paths will give you the same results; it's just a bit nicer to let a local command do some of the work for you.

---

4. In any case, you'll probably find that "all the good stuff's in Finland."

The Wide Area Information Service

Archie lets you search the entire world of `ftp` servers in a relatively superficial way. There is another service, the Wide Area Information Service (WAIS), which lets you perform an in-depth search on the information maintained by a single server.

Though you might not guess this from the long-winded WAIS documentation, performing a WAIS search is similar to `grep`ping through a set of files. WAIS provides a few more bells and whistles than `grep`, but you don't usually need to care about the details. WAIS servers typically use indexes to reduce search times, and in fact, the items in an index need not be taken from the documents they describe. For example, an index could contain the English text description of a binary data file.

WAIS searches do give you one neat thing that `grep` doesn't: an indication of how well each of the results matches your search criteria. These relevance ratings are normalized to a scale of 1 to 1,000, with the most relevant document assigned the value 1,000. Once you've found a document you like, WAIS can use its relevance-computing ability to find other documents that are similar.

As in the case of Archie, there are a couple of ways to use WAIS. The simplest is to `telnet` to quake.think.com and log in as "wais". This will take you to a simple WAIS client which allows you to search a variety of other servers. A better way to access WAIS is to obtain a client program that you can run locally. These are available for several platforms and can be obtained via anonymous `ftp` from think.com.

Since WAIS servers are independent, the problem of finding an appropriate server for the items you want arises once again. A master list of WAIS servers is maintained at the Thinking Machines Corporation, the epicenter of WAIS development. To find a server that might hold the kind of documents you are looking for, search the directory-of-servers database at quake.think.com. Remember that you are searching descriptions of the servers' contents and not the contents themselves. General searches are more likely to point you in the right direction.

Gopher

It's something of a chore to wade through the different services we've just described. Each of them has its own interface, its own servers, and so on; you need to have a pretty good idea how the whole scheme works before you can find what you're looking for quickly.

There is yet another service, Gopher, which ties these other services together. When you connect to a Gopher server, you're given a list of items to choose from. Choosing an item will either show you another list of choices, give you a file, perform a search, or log you into another computer. For example, the list of top-level items at the University of Minnesota, where Gopher originated, looks like this:

```
 1. Information About Gopher/
 2. Computer Information/
 3. Discussion Groups/
 4. Fun & Games/
 5. Internet file server (ftp) sites/
 6. Libraries/
 7. News/
 8. Other Gopher and Information Servers/
 9. Phone Books/
10. Search lots of places at the U of M
11. University of Minnesota Campus Information/
```

The items marked with a slash take you to other lists. Item #10 prompts you for keywords to search for, then gives a list of the results.

The clever thing about Gopher is that it uses a connectionless protocol. Each list can be served by a different computer, and a Gopher item can point anywhere on the Internet. It looks like a hierarchy to the user, but actually it's an arbitrary graph that you can enter at any point. The "Other Gopher and Information Servers" item provides links to the top levels of many other systems.

This linking feature is heavily used by most Gopher servers. Typically, the administrator of a Gopher site will add entries for the interesting resources that the site provides, and will also provide some links out to related Gopher servers and gateways. This scheme creates the illusion that every server is packed with information and resources, when in fact it may actually be providing only a small portion of the data. The effort a site spends on organizing links to other places in Gopherspace (as it is known) is often as valuable as the actual data it provides.

Much of the power of Gopher comes from gateways that map the functions of `ftp`, Archie, and WAIS into the Gopher model of interaction. Under the "Internet file server (ftp) sites" item, for example, you can choose an `ftp` server, browse the hierarchy of files provided by that server, and transfer the files that you want, all without leaving Gopher. Gopher's search facility maps fairly well onto both Archie and WAIS, and the gateways to these services allow you to browse or copy the documents your search locates.

To enter Gopherspace, you need client software. Software for many systems is available via `ftp` from boombox.micro.umn.edu. It's very easy to implement a Gopher client, so if you can't find Gopher software that works on a particular machine, you might want to write your own.

Just as anonymous `ftp` has Archie and WAIS has the directory-of-servers map, Gopherspace has a searching service called Veronica: Very Easy Rodent-Oriented Net-wide Index to Computerized Archives. Most Gophers provide a link to Veronica—look under "other Gophers."

The World-Wide Web

But wait, there's more. The World-Wide Web, one of the more recent additions to the Internet fracas, develops the idea of Gopher even further. Like Gopherspace, the World-Wide Web consists of many independent-but-interlinked servers. As users browse the "information space" of the web, they are seamlessly shifted from one server to another.

The WWW protocol specifications are available via `ftp` from info.cern.ch.

The main difference between Gopherspace and WWW is that the Web's fundamental building blocks are hypertext documents rather than unembellished lists of links. Although the basic idea of both systems is the same, WWW dresses up the technology with a rich document formatting language and a more general access model.

As you'd expect, there are numerous gateways from WWW into the Gopher, WAIS, Archie, and `ftp` domains. To complicate matters, some WWW clients understand these other services directly, providing a kind of one-stop interface to the entire Internet.

The most widely-used WWW client is called Mosaic. It is distributed by the National Center for Supercomputing Applications, and an X Windows version is included on the CD-ROM. Other versions are available via anonymous `ftp` from ftp.ncsa.uiuc.edu.

An alternative to Mosaic known as Netscape has recently been released by Mosaic Communications Corporation, a group of renegade engineers who used to work for NCSA. Netscape allows you to see and manipulate web pages as soon as their contents begin to arrive, rather than making you wait until the transfer has completed as other browsers do. This makes Netscape feel much faster than Mosaic, and it works especially well over slow network connections such as SLIP lines. Netscape is a commercial product, but individuals can use it without charge. It's available via anonymous `ftp` from ftp.mcom.com.

A WWW page as displayed by Mosaic is shown in Exhibit B (next page).

The Big Picture

Because many of the Internet navigation services provide the same kinds of information, it's often hard to tell them apart. The many gateways among services also add to the confusion.

It's easier to understand how the services relate to each other if you remember the order in which they were created: `telnet`, `ftp`, Archie,

Exhibit B   A World-Wide Web page as displayed by Mosaic

WAIS, Gopher, Veronica, and World-Wide Web. Each new service generally tried to both outdo and subsume the previous services. Exhibit C illustrates the general evolution.

Services near the top are the most recent; they provide gateways to the services underneath them.

20.5 CONNECTING TO THE INTERNET

To obtain the very latest information about connecting to the Internet, contact InterNIC Information Services via `ftp`, Gopher, or World-Wide Web at internic.net. Or send email to info@internic.net. Or call the Information Services referral desk at 1-800-862-0677 (908-668-6587 if outside the United States).

To connect to the Internet, you need three things: a "partner" that's on the Internet, a physical link, and some communication hardware.

Exhibit C Internet service conspiracy unmasked

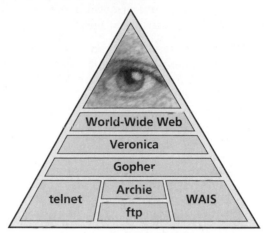

The partner is usually an Internet provider organization. Some providers are set up as not-for-profit groups, but most are hot-for-profit. The provider acts as a gateway between your network and the Internet. Providers also usually handle routing and domain-name issues for you. Some large providers in the United States are listed in Table 20.2; a complete list is always available from the InterNIC.

Table 20.2 Providers of Internet service in the USA[a]

Name	Phone	Email
Alternet	1-800-4UUNET3	alternet-info@uunet.uu.net
ANS	1-800-456-8267	info@ans.net
HoloNet	1-510-704-0160	support@holonet.net
PSINet	1-800-82PSI82	info@psi.com
SprintLink	1-800-877-SPLK	info@sprintlink.net

a. Source: InterNIC Information Services

You might be able to browbeat a university or business partner into connecting you to the Internet. This is a good deal if you can get it.

The physical link is usually a telephone line. If you're planning to use a modem as your communication hardware, you have the option of using a garden-variety voice line and simply dialing into the provider as you would dial up any other modem. This is cheap and requires no special setup; you don't even need to tell the phone company what you're using the line for, at least in the United States.

Unfortunately, even fast modems don't approach the bandwidth of a true network. If you decide to go with a modem, you'll be limited to a few tens of thousands of bits per second. It sounds like a lot, but after network latency and protocol overhead have taken their toll, the bulk transfer rate is only about one and a half kilobytes per second.

For faster speeds, you need a specially-installed telephone line and faster equipment. A voice line is good up to about 25 Kb/s; a DDS (Digital Dataphone Service) leased line handles around 56 Kb/s. High-grade lines are classified as T1, T2, or T3, and carry 1.5, 6, or 45 Mb/s, respectively. Some vendors offer "fractional T1" circuits which provide a variable amount of bandwidth between DDS and T1 in increments of 64 Kb/s. Fractional T1 is usually cheaper than DDS, too.

A DDS line is generally "fast enough" and is fine for a small site. A larger site may need a higher-bandwidth line because many people want to use the Internet at once. T1 is good enough for almost all sites. T2 is rarely used, and T3 is used mostly by backbone networks.

There is a large jump in price between a voice line and a leased line. A DDS line runs in the low hundreds of dollars per month; T1 and T3 are in the range of $500 and $5,000 per month. The distance between the endpoints of the line can affect its price significantly.

If you use a modem and a voice line for your Internet connection, you'll generally use a workstation as the Internet gateway. The gateway machine can run either the SLIP or the PPP protocol to encapsulate IP packets for transmission over the phone line. See Chapter 19 for more information about configuring such a system.

On higher-speed links, management of the connection is usually done with a special piece of routing hardware that you connect directly to your network and to the leased line. Your service provider will explain the available options.

20.6 RECOMMENDED SUPPLEMENTAL READING

Dozens of Internet books have been published in the last year. Unfortunately, a lot of them are "instant book" attempts to cash in on the Internet-as-media-event phenomenon. We advise careful shopping.

> KROL, ED. *The Whole Internet: User's Guide and Catalog.* Sebastopol: O'Reilly & Associates, 1992.

Ed Krol's book was one of the first books about the Internet, and like most of the O'Reilly books, it's a solid effort with plenty of technical information. Now in it's second edition, we think it's still one of the best books available.

21 *Electronic Mail*

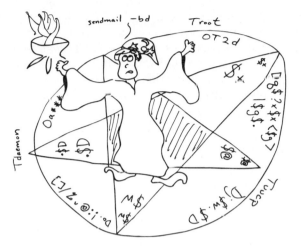

21.1 INTRODUCTION

Only a few years ago, electronic mail (email) was used mostly by computer nerds. Today almost all departmental communication occurs by email rather than by telephone, memo, or face-to-face discussion. When email is broken, the secretaries are the first to complain.

The growth of the Internet has made email both popular and almost universally available. For example, to get a message to her mother-in-law in Budapest, Evi sends mail to a cousin at a university who delivers the message on his way home from work. The wait to get a telephone installed in Hungary is about six years, but email arrives in seconds.

Email has introduced some interesting social behavior. It seems to be less formal than paper, and people therefore tend to say more directly what they mean and feel. It is also somehow less personal and more removed than voice contact, and so rage and frustration sometimes emerge. Email "flames" result, in which two people exchange messages they would never speak aloud or write on paper to each other.

For example, one of our users was easily upset and used to abuse the administrators regularly. The only defense seemed to be to save his messages and send them back to him a few weeks later when he had cooled down. He was appalled at the things he had committed to print.

Mail systems are complex. You need only examine the RFCs that specify how a mail system connected to the Internet should behave to realize that mail, while simple in concept, is complicated to implement. RFC822 describes what a mail message on the Internet should look like and sets the standards for both addresses and headers. The scary-looking lines that precede an actual message comply with RFC822 and are therefore understood by all programs involved in the transmission of mail.

See page 456 for a bit of history about the various revisions of sendmail.

Most of this chapter deals with the configuration of **sendmail**, the UNIX program that parses and routes electronic mail. **sendmail** was originally written by Eric Allman at the University of California, Berkeley. It has existed in three major versions: version 5 (V5), IDA, and version 8 (V8). However, **sendmail** is only one piece (although from a sysadmin's point of view, the most important piece) of the electronic mail puzzle.

21.2 MAIL SYSTEMS

A mail system consists of three distinct components: a "user agent" that lets users read and compose mail, a "transport agent" that forwards messages among machines, and a "delivery agent" that places messages in the receiving users' mailboxes. Exhibit A shows the relationship of these components.

Exhibit A   Mail agents in context

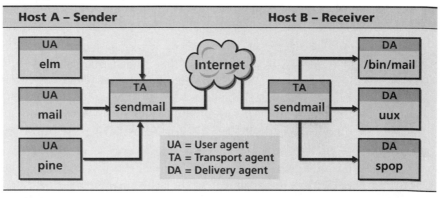

X.400, ISO's answer to RFC822 (CCITT's, really) was originally billed as an imminent replacement for UNIX mail systems based on **sendmail**. However, its complexity has relegated it to use within Europe (where it was invented) and the United States Government (where "standards" sometimes overshadow functionality and performance).

An X.400 address resembles a property list in an inventory system. For example, the X.400 address

```
/I=j/S=houldsworth/OU=ste0906/O=icl/P=icl/A=gold_400
  /C=gb/@x400gw.datacraft.com.au
```

corresponds loosely to the RFC822 address

houldsworth@icl.gb

The following opinion of X.400 performance recently appeared on one of the IETF mailing lists:

```
So, it took it from Aug 22 to Sept 1 to wander around
several X.400 systems, but once it got to the TCP/TP
world, it got from Australia, to Sun, to me via 11
intermediate systems in 15 minutes. Guess we know who
knows how to build fast and reliable e-mail systems,
don't we? Nope, isn't us IETF people. Must be them X.400
people, who have invented an online version of "The
check's in the mail." My hat's off to them, I now have
yet another excuse for not getting work done...
```

The Internet specifications require each site to define an alias called "postmaster" that refers to the people who maintain the email system. This alias is not required at X.400 sites and often is not implemented. Some X.400 sites use an alias called "helpdesk" for this purpose.

User Agents

ATT's **/bin/mail** was the original user agent. Several alternatives now exist; the freely-available agents are listed below, along with their original sources. Some vendors also supply a user agent based on a graphical user interface (such as Sun's **mailtool** or the **xmh** and **exmh** front ends for **mh**); we don't include these in our list. MIME (Multi-Purpose Internet Mail Extensions) is a standard for including multimedia objects in mail messages. It is supported by some user agents.

- **/bin/mail** from AT&T
- **/usr/ucb/mail**[1] from BSD
- **mh** from the Rand Corporation
- **pine** by Laurence Lundblade, Mike Seibel, and Mark Crispin
- **emacs** mail from GNU
- **mush** by Dan Heller at Berkeley
- **elm** by David Taylor at Intuitive Systems

elm, mh, and pine are included on the CD-ROM. Some user agents support a system-wide configuration file that sets defaults for all users. Individual users can override these defaults by setting up a personal configuration file in their home directories.

Table 21.1 (on the next page) shows the startup files for the mail readers listed above. The locations and even the names of the global configuration files are sometimes vendor-specific.

---

1. **/usr/ucb/mail** is sometimes called **/bin/mailx** or **/bin/Mail** on ATT systems.

Table 21.1   User agent configuration files

User Agent	System	Personal
bin/mail	–	–
ucb/mail	Mail.rc	.mailrc
pine	pine.conf	.pinerc
elm	–	.elm/*
mh	–	.mh_profile and .maildelivery
xmh	–	.mh_profile and .maildelivery

For example, a quick check on SunOS and HP-UX showed all of these:

```
/usr/lib/Mail.rc
/usr/lib/Mailrc
/usr/lib/mail/mailrc
/usr/lib/mailx/mailrc
```

Transport Agents

A transport agent must accept mail from a user agent, understand the recipients' addresses, and somehow get the mail to the correct hosts for delivery. A transport agent should also accept incoming mail from other transport agents. Many transport agents speak the SMTP protocol (Simple Mail Transport Protocol) defined in RFC821.

There are several transport agents for UNIX (MMDF, zmailer, smail, and upas, among others), but sendmail is the most comprehensive, most flexible, and most widely used. In this chapter, we will discuss only sendmail.

Delivery Agents

A delivery agent is responsible for accepting mail from a transport agent and actually delivering it to the appropriate recipients. Mail can be delivered to a person, to a mailing list, to a file, or even to a program.

Each type of recipient may require a different agent. /bin/mail is the delivery agent for local users. uux and spop are delivery agents for users at remote sites that use UUCP or POP to receive mail.[2] /bin/sh is the delivery agent for mail going to a file or to a program.

Mail Addressing

Local addressing is simple because a user's login name is a unique identifier. But when an addressee does not have an account on the local machine, addressing and delivery become more complicated.

---

2. POP stands for Post Office Protocol. PCs and Macs use it to interface to UNIX mail systems.

See page 674 for an overview of UUCP addressing.

There are basically two kinds of email addresses: route-based (relative) and location-independent (absolute). Route-based addressing requires the sender to know the intermediate machines that a message should travel through to reach its destination. Location-independent addressing simply identifies the final destination. UUCP addresses are route-based, while Internet addresses are (usually) location-independent.

The general form of Internet mail address is

```
user@host
```

where the @ separates the user name from the host specification. Mail is delivered to *user*'s mailbox on the machine *host*.

A UUCP address consists of a list of hosts the message must traverse to reach its final destination. The elements of the list are separated by exclamation points, which are sometimes called "bangs." For example, in the UUCP mail address

```
mcvax!uunet!ucbvax!hao!boulder!lair!evi
```

the destination is the machine lair and the recipient is the user evi. Each machine in the chain has a direct UUCP connection to the two machines on either side. For example, the machine ucbvax must have connections to both hao and uunet. UUCP address chains can be quite long, but now that use of the Internet is widespread, the real whoppers are seldom seen anymore. When UUCP-based email was the norm, administrators had a large part of the UUCP backbone map imprinted on their brains.

This same address expressed in the Internet fashion is evi@lair, or more properly, evi@lair.cs.colorado.edu. Mixed addresses are possible. For example, if UUCP connected lair to the rest of the colorado.edu domain, the address might take the form

```
lair!evi@boulder.colorado.edu
```

Since email addresses have no parentheses for expressing precedence, the address is ambiguous. Would you interpret it as

```
(lair!evi)@boulder.colorado.edu
```

or as

```
lair!(evi@boulder.colorado.edu)
```

That is, should the message go to the machine boulder first, or should it go to lair? Today, most mail systems give precedence to @ over ! and would send the message to boulder.

A special route-based form of Internet address, called a "route address," produces addresses such as

```
<@site1,@site2,...,@siteN:user@final-site>
```

This monstrous syntax sends a message to *user* at the host *final-site*, but it is required to go first to *site1*, then to *site2*, and so on. RFC821 required that mail transport agents support route addresses; the new RFC1123 which supersedes it now condemns their use. Much of the complexity of **sendmail** configuration files comes from the necessity of handling such addresses.

Route-based addressing is rather like requiring anyone who wishes to send a letter to know not only the recipient's postal address but also all the intermediate post offices the letter might pass through. The post office long ago relegated responsibility for the storage and use of routing information to the transport agent.

Another special punctuation mark you may see in email addresses is a percent mark ("%"), which represents an early form of Internet route addressing used during the transition from the original ARPANET to the Internet. It is like a deferred "@". An example:

```
user%host1%host2@host3
```

The mail is sent to *host3*, which forwards it to *host2*, which sends it to *host1*, which delivers it to *user*.

Reading Mail Headers

Every mail message starts with several lines called headers that contain information about the message. Most user agents hide the uninteresting headers from you, but there is usually an option to make the agent reveal them all.

The headers on a mail message tell a lot about where the message has been, how long it stayed there, and when it was finally delivered to its destination. Below is a typical mail message (generated by **sendmail**) interspersed with comments that describe the purpose of the various headers and identifying the programs that added them. The line numbers at the left are for reference in the following discussion and are not part of the message. Some lines have been folded to allow the example to fit on the page.

```
1: From acser@goliat.eik.bme.hu Fri May 13 07:05:35 1994
```

The first line was added by **/bin/mail** during delivery to separate this message from others in the recipient user's mailbox. Mail readers recognize message boundaries by looking for a blank line followed by the characters "From "; note the trailing space. This line does not exist until the message is delivered, and it is distinct from the "From:" header line.

```
2: Received: from nag.cs.Colorado.EDU (nag.cs.colorado.edu
       [128.138.250.20]) by piper.cs.colorado.edu
       (8.6.9/8.6.9) with ESMTP id HAA01229 for
```

```
        <evi@piper.cs.colorado.edu>; Fri, 13 May 1994
        07:05:34 -0600
    3: Received: from goliat.eik.bme.hu (goliat.eik.bme.hu
        [152.66.115.2]) by nag.cs.Colorado.EDU
        (8.6.5/8.6.5) with SMTP id HAA05062 for
        <evi@kinglear.cs.colorado.edu>; Fri, 13 May 1994
        07:05:24 -0600
    4: Received: by goliat.eik.bme.hu id AA14919
    5:    (5.67a/IDA-BME-1.5 for evi@kinglear.cs.colorado.edu);
        Fri, 13 May 1994 15:05:08 +0200
```

Lines 2-5 document the passage of the message through various systems en route to the user's mailbox. Each machine that handles a mail message adds a Received line to the message's header. Lines two and three appeared as very long lines; lines four and five represent one Received entry but were actually transmitted as two lines, with the second indented to indicate that it is a continuation of the previous line.

Each of these Received lines includes the name of the sending machine, the name of the receiving machine, the version of **sendmail** (or whatever transport agent was used) on the receiving machine, the message's unique identifier while on the receiving machine, the recipient, the date and time, and finally, the offset from Greenwich Mean Time for the local timezone. This data is collected from **sendmail**'s internal macro variables; see page 471 for a discussion of the procedure **sendmail** uses to format header lines.

Reading from bottom to top, we see that this particular message was first posted on the machine goliat.eik.bme.hu (running **sendmail** V5.67 plus IDA extensions) where it had ID AA14919. The queue ID of a message identifies it if it must be saved for later delivery, either because the destination host is down or because the sending machine is too busy to deal with it immediately.

See page 339 for more information about MX records. From there, it went to nag.cs.colorado.edu via the Internet, even though the message was addressed to evi@kinglear.cs.colorado.edu (see header line nine). A quick check with **nslookup** or **dig** shows that kinglear has an MX record that points to nag, causing the delivery to be diverted.

The machine nag was running **sendmail** V8.6.5, and it identified the message with queue ID HAA05062 while it was there. The message was then forwarded to piper.cs.colorado.edu rather than kinglear due to a mail-handling feature known as *aliasing* that is described in detail starting on page 449.

Aliases play an important role in the flow of mail. An alias maps a user name to something else, for example, to the same user at a different machine, to a group of users, or even to an alternate spelling of the user's name. It is actually not possible to determine why the message was diverted using only the example headers; as with MX records, you must seek external sources of information.

The machine piper, which was running **sendmail** V8.6.9, delivered the message (which has queue ID HAA01229 locally) to evi's mailbox.

```
6: From: "Cser Andras (18-20)" <acser@goliat.eik.bme.hu>
```

Line 6 shows the sender's full name and email address; the (18-20) is probably an office number.

```
7: Message-Id: <199405131305.AA14919@goliat.eik.bme.hu>
```

Line 7 contains the message ID, which is different from a queue ID and is unique within the world-wide mail system. It is made up of the date and time (in this case, 1:05 p.m. on May 13, 1994), a dot, the letters AA, the process ID of the **sendmail** handling the message on the originating system, an @, and finally, the fully-qualified domain name of the originating host. Version 8 of **sendmail** has added an additional letter in front of the AA to guarantee that the queue ID portion (an "A" plus the current hour) is unique in any 24-hour period. This makes it easier to write scripts that glean statistics from log files on a daily basis.

```
 8: Subject: USENIX '94: Arrangments for Andras Cser
 9: To: evi@kinglear.cs.colorado.edu
10: Date: Fri, 13 May 1994 15:05:07 +0200 (MET DST)
```

Lines 8-10 are standard. Although a Subject header is not required, most user agents include it. The To line contains the address of the primary recipient or recipients. The Date line shows the date and time that the message was sent.

If we look at the date stamps on the Received lines, we can see that the message began its journey on Friday, May 13 at 3:05:07 in the afternoon (Budapest time). It arrived in **sendmail**'s hands on the sender's machine one second later. The message traveled over the Internet to Colorado, arriving at 7:05:24 a.m., 16 seconds later (as measured with a different clock). It spent 11 more seconds (again, a different clock) in transit in Colorado before finally arriving in evi's mailbox.[3]

```
11: X-Mailer: ELM [version 2.4 PL23]
```

Line 11 identifies the sender's user agent (here, **elm**).

```
12: Status: RO
```

The final header line, Status, is added at the receiving end by the **ucb/mail** user agent and indicates that this message has been read by the recipient and is old.

---

3. Many sites synchronize their system clocks to a universal time standard using the NTP protocol. See page 717 for details.

```
13: Message body was here.
```

Exhibit B illustrates this message's journey through the mail system. It shows what actions were taken, where they happened, and what programs performed them.

Exhibit B   A message from Hungary

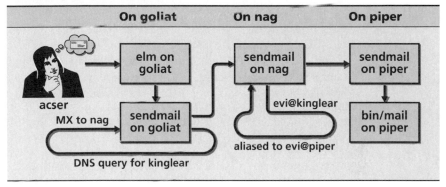

As you can see, **sendmail** is the real workhorse in this process. It handles the message from the time it leaves **elm** in Budapest until it arrives on piper for local delivery.

Not all headers in a mail message are well defined. You can add almost anything you want, as long as you don't accidentally co-opt a standard keyword. By convention, the names of any extra headers you add should start with "X-" so that the possibility of a collision is minimized. Some users have added message headers like X-Wotd (word of the day) and X-Fruit (fruit of the day) that are filled in by a program that selects randomly from a list of words, fruits, jokes, etc.

Transport agents (such as **sendmail**) generally ignore but pass along headers that they do not understand. V5 and IDA capitalize headers; V8 leaves them alone.

The Spool Directory

Users' mailboxes are usually kept in the directory **/var/spool/mail** (BSD) or **/var/mail** (ATT) in files named after the users' login names.

This directory is created during the installation of the operating system. It should have permissions set to mode 775 (with group owner mail), or, if the OS supports the sticky bit for directories, to mode 1777.[4]

---

4. On most systems, the sticky bit on a directory prevents users from removing each other's files. Usually, write permission on the directory is all that is needed to delete files.

Mail Philosophy

The mail philosophy we outline in this chapter is almost mandatory for keeping the administration of medium and large sites manageable. However, it is also appropriate for small sites. The two main concepts that lead to easy administration are:

- A master mail machine
- A mail home for each user

Avoid reinventing the wheel; mail is too complicated to make that practical. Find a **sendmail** configuration file that is close to what you need, steal it, and modify it to fit your situation. Some of the example configurations in both the IDA and V8 distributions will fit most sites. Watch out for vendor-supplied config files—they sometimes assume a homogeneous environment that uses only the vendor's own tools.

Using a master mail machine

A single machine at your site should be designated as the master mail machine. Other machines can forward any mail they don't understand to the master. Most of the machines at your site should have a simple, relatively stupid mail configuration; only the master should deal with bizarre addresses. It goes without saying that the master should be a machine that is relatively stable and reliable.

In the most extreme configuration of this type, other machines can forward all their mail to the master for delivery. However, allowing everyone to deliver simple Internet mail will reduce the master's load and make the mail system less vulnerable to a single point of failure.

Tables of hosts and routing information need only be maintained on the one "smart" machine. Out-of-date configuration files on other machines may result in some inefficiency, but will not result in any lost or misdelivered mail. **sendmail** with an out-of-date config file might forward a message to the master machine when it could have delivered it directly, had its config file been up to date.

A master mail machine can also hide the local structure of your organization and present a consistent image to the outside world. All users at our site can be addressed as user@cs.colorado.edu, even if they do not have a login on the machine cs.colorado.edu. Aliases, which implement this feature, are discussed in the next section.

Only the config file on the master machine needs to be maintained on a regular basis. The slave config files can all be identical and will seldom require attention. At large sites, a three-tiered (or deeper) hierarchy with a master, sub-masters, and slaves may be appropriate. Small sites may choose to just disable mail on all machines but the master.

Using mail homes

It is convenient for users to be able to read mail on a single machine, even if they have logins on several different systems. This can be accomplished with aliasing or with the "maildrop" field of the user database (`sendmail` version 8 only; see page 476). The aliasing scheme we use allows the alias files to be the same on all machines within an administrative domain. This is a big win from the administrator's point of view. (We assume that login names and UIDs are unique across all machines, a policy we recommend highly.)

Some sites centralize mail by exporting the `/var/spool/mail` directory using NFS. Locking problems with NFS files can cause users to lose mail or to have their spool files garbled. Finger pointing between NFS, `sendmail`, and the delivery agents with regard to proper locking does not help the poor user whose mailbox has been corrupted (`sendmail` is always innocent, since it never delivers mail to a user's spool file).

Some NFS implementations (such as those on dedicated NFS file servers) include a lock manager that works correctly. Most implementations either do not support locking or support it improperly. Some sites just ignore the locking problem and hope for the best, while others require users to read mail on the file server.

NFS partitions shared by both ATT and BSD systems illustrate another potential problem. Delivery under ATT is done by putting mail in a file owned by the login "mail" and then using ATT's `chown` system call to give the file to the appropriate user. BSD's version of `chown` does not allow this; only the superuser can change the ownership of files. If your file server is a BSD system and your master mail machine is an ATT system, you may have problems.

Mail Aliases

Aliases allow mail to be redirected by either the system administrator or by individual users. They can be used to define mailing lists (which include multiple recipients), to forward mail among machines, or to allow users to be referred to by more than one name.

Aliases can be defined in three different places (unfortunately, with three different syntaxes):

- In a user agent's configuration file
- In the system-wide aliases file, `/etc/aliases`
- In a user's forwarding file, `~/.forward`

The mail system first looks for aliases in the user agent files, then in the `aliases` file, and finally in the user's forwarding file.

Here are some examples of aliases in the `aliases` format:

```
nemeth: evi
evi: evi@mailhub
authors: evi,garth,scott,trent
```

The first line says that mail sent to "nemeth" should be delivered to the user evi on the local machine. The second line says that all mail to evi should be delivered on the machine mailhub, and the third line says that mail addressed to "authors" should be delivered to the users evi, garth, scott and trent. Recursion is supported, so mail sent to "nemeth" actually ends up going to "evi@mailhub".

See Chapter 18 for more information about NIS.

Global aliases are defined in **/etc/aliases** (**/usr/lib/aliases** on some systems, **/usr/lib/mail/aliases** under IDA). The location of the **aliases** file is specified in the **sendmail** configuration file. V8 allows multiple **aliases** files for sites that have both NIS aliases and regular aliases, or for sites that have both site-wide aliases and machine-specific aliases.

The format of an entry in the **aliases** file is

```
local-name: recipient1,recipient2,...
```

where `local-name` is the original address to be matched against incoming messages and the recipient list contains either recipient addresses or the names of other aliases. Indented lines are considered continuations of the preceding lines.

From mail's point of view, the **aliases** file supersedes **/etc/passwd**, so the entry

```
david: david@somewhere-else
```

would prevent the local user david from ever getting any mail. Therefore, administrators and **adduser** tools should check both the **passwd** file and the **aliases** file when selecting new user names.

The **/etc/aliases** file should contain an alias named postmaster that forwards mail to whoever maintains the mail system. An alias for automatic messages from **sendmail** must also be present; it's usually called Mailer-Daemon or Mailer-Agent, and is often aliased to postmaster. You should redirect mail to root to your site's administrators or to someone who logs in every day. The bin, sys, daemon, nobody, and hostmaster accounts (and any other pseudo-user accounts you set up) should also have aliases that forward mail to a human.

sendmail detects alias loops that would cause mail to be forwarded back and forth forever by counting the number of Received lines in a message's header and returning it to the sender when the count reaches a preset limit (usually 17).[5] Each visit to a new machine is called a "hop" in **sendmail** jargon; returning a message to the sender is known as "bouncing" it. The previous sentence, properly jargonized, would be, "Mail bounces after 17 hops."

Special Kinds of Aliases

In addition to lists of users, aliases can refer to:

- A file containing a list of addresses
- A file to which messages should be appended
- A command to which messages should be given as input

The `:include:` directive allows the members of an alias to be taken from an external file rather than listed directly in the **aliases** file. The file can then be local to one machine rather than global to all the machines that share the **aliases** file. It can also be changed locally without requiring intervention by the system administrator responsible for the global **aliases** file. For example:

```
sa-book: :include:/usr/local/adm/usah.readers
```

If the target of an alias is an absolute pathname (double-quoted if it includes special characters), messages are appended to the specified file. For example:

```
complaints: "/dev/null"
```

The file must exist and be either world-writable, setuid but not executable, or, if referenced from a `.forward` file, owned by the original recipient. For files owned by root, use mode 4644 or 4600, setuid but not executable. On some systems, it is sufficient for the file to be writable by the user "mail."

An alias can also route mail to the standard input of a program. This is specified with a line such as:

```
autoftp: "|/usr/local/bin/ftpserver"
```

It's easy to create security holes with this feature if the mail-receiving program is not careful. For example, an old version of the **majordomo** program (for maintaining mailing lists) called the **system** library routine, which if used with a return address containing a semicolon could give you a root shell. **majordomo** is written in **perl**, which is where the real weakness is. **perl** uses **system** rather than **exec** when executing programs destined for the shell. Be sure you know the program you are implicitly trusting as root.

---

5. 17 is the default. You can change this when you compile **sendmail** (V5 or IDA) or set it with the h option in the config file under V8.

Some typical aliases a system administrator might use are:

```
# Required aliases⁶

postmaster: trouble, evi
postmistress: postmaster
MAILER-DAEMON: postmaster
root: trouble, trent
usenet: news
news: trouble, garth

# include for local trouble alias
trouble: :include:/usr/local/adm/trouble.alias
troubletrap: "/usr/local/adm/logs/troublemail"
tmr: troubletrap,:include:/usr/local/adm/tmr.alias

# sysadmin conveniences
diary: "/var/log/diary"
info: "|/usr/local/bin/sendinfo"

# class aliases that change every semester
sa-class: real-sa-class@nag
real-sa-class: :include:/usr/local/adm/sa-class.list
```

In this example, we would like users from all over campus to be able to send mail to a single alias "trouble" whenever problems occur. Problem reports should always be routed to an appropriate group of local system administrators. In particular, we'd like to set up the mail aliases so that

- Trouble mail always goes to an appropriate group.
- A single version of the aliases file is used on all hosts.
- Individual admin groups control their own distribution lists.
- A copy of all trouble mail goes to a local log file for each group.

The configuration above satisfies these goals by taking the definition of the trouble alias from a file on each machine. Mail to trouble@anchor and mail to trouble@boulder would end up in different places even though anchor and boulder use the same **/etc/aliases** file.

Trouble mail is usually handled on one particular machine in each locale. For example, the **trouble.alias** file on a slave machine could contain the address

```
trouble@master
```

to make trouble mail go to the appropriate master machine.

When a trouble message is resolved, it is sent to the alias "tmr," which stands for "trouble mail readers." The tmr alias archives the message via the troubletrap alias and also sends it to a list of users taken from a

6. A white lie. Only postmaster is really required.

file on the master machine. Adding novice administrators to the tmr list is a great way for them to see the support questions that arise, the administrators' replies, and also the proper sycophantic tone that should be used with users (i.e. customers).

queuemh is included on the CD-ROM. This mechanism is just the tip of the iceberg of a complete trouble mail tracking system called **queuemh**, which is based on the **mh** user agent.

Mail Forwarding

The **aliases** file is a system-wide config file that should be maintained by an administrator. If users want to reroute their own mail, they can do so by creating **.forward** files in their home directories. A **.forward** file is often used when a user wants to receive mail on a particular host or when someone leaves your site and wants to have mail forwarded to a new location. A **.forward** file consists of a single line of comma-separated addresses. For example,

```
evi@vangogh.cs.berkeley.edu
```

or

```
\mcbryan, "/home/mcbryan/archive", mcbryan@f1supi1.gmd.de
```

In the first example, mail for evi is not delivered on the local machine, but is instead forwarded to the machine vangogh at Berkeley. The second entry is from a user who does not trust mail systems and wants his mail replicated in three places: the regular mail spool on the local machine, a permanent archive of all incoming mail, and a temporary address in Germany where he is traveling at the moment.

For temporary changes in mail routing, use of a **.forward** file is preferable to use of the global **aliases** file. The overhead (computer time and people time) required to change the system-wide aliases is quite high. A user's **.forward** file should be owned by the user and not be world writable. **sendmail** ignores **.forward** files on which the permissions look suspicious.

Permanent changes of address should go in the **/etc/aliases** file because a user's home directory and files will eventually be removed.

sendmail V8 has a feature that handles permanent email changes a bit more elegantly. If the user is aliased to user@newsite.REDIRECT, mail will be returned to the sender with a notification of the new address.

V8 can be configured to support a central directory for **.forward** files (set with the J option). This is more efficient for **sendmail**, but is not what users expect. Fortunately, if the central directory does not contain a **.forward** file for a user, the user's home directory is also checked.

An entry in the global **aliases** file takes precedence over an entry in a .**forward** file. Since these files are maintained by different people, care must be taken not to inadvertently create mail loops. If a user on a network has a mail home (and therefore an entry in the global **aliases** file), that user cannot use a .**forward** file to reroute mail to another machine that shares the same aliases. For example, at the University of Colorado, where we use a site-wide **aliases** file, an entry such as

```
evi: evi@boulder
```

and a .**forward** file on the machine boulder containing

```
evi@tigger
```

would create a loop. Mail addressed to evi would be forwarded to boulder, where the .**forward** file would cause it to be sent to tigger, where the **aliases** file would cause it to be forwarded back to boulder... After 17 hops, the mail would be returned to the sender.

Notifying a user of a mail loop is challenging if your primary mode of communication is email. Mail to *user* will deliver the message on the local machine, regardless of what the system-wide **aliases** file or the user's .**forward** file may say. If this is where the user expects to read mail, fine; otherwise send mail to the postmaster to report the loop. You may have to use two or more backslashes to get one of them past the shell and into **sendmail**.

The Hashed Alias Database

Since entries in /**etc**/**aliases** are in no particular order, it would be inefficient for **sendmail** to search this file directly. Instead, a hashed version of the **aliases** file is constructed.

The files derived from /**etc**/**aliases** are called /**etc**/**aliases.dir** and /**etc**/**aliases.pag**. The **dir** file is an index for the **pag** file, in which the data actually resides. Every time you change the **aliases** file, you must rebuild the hashed database with the **newaliases** command. **newaliases** is really just **sendmail** in disguise with command-line flags (**-bi**) that tell it to rebuild the database.

It can take several minutes to run **newaliases** on a large aliases file; it's best to run it at night when fewer users are impacted. Save the error output if you run it automatically, as you might have introduced formatting errors. **sendmail** suspends the delivery of mail while rebuilding the alias database.

See Chapter 18 for more information about NIS. V8 **sendmail** supports a new database format for the **aliases** file. Access seems faster and the database file is smaller. When you compile V8, you must include database library support for either the **dbm/ndbm** routines or the new Berkeley **db** routines, or both. If both are included and **sendmail** needs to create a database file, it will use the **db** routines. If you are using NIS, it will *create* both but *use* only the **db** version. The **db** library can be **ftp**ed from ftp.cs.berkeley.edu; look in **/ucb/4bsd**.

Mailing Lists

Mailing lists are usually specified in the **aliases** file but maintained in an external file. There are standard naming conventions that are understood by some versions of **sendmail** and also by special mailing list maintenance packages. Experienced users have also come to rely on them. The conventions are illustrated in the following examples:

```
mylist:  :include:/var/adm/aliases/mylist
owner-mylist: mylist-request
mylist-request: evi
owner-owner: postmaster
```

mylist is the name of the mailing list; the members are read from the file **/var/adm/aliases/mylist**. Errors from mailing to the list are sent to its owner, evi, as are requests to join the list. The indirection from "owner" to "request" to evi is useful because in V8 the owner's address goes out with each message; mylist-request is more appropriate than the owner's actual name. Errors in messages to the owner-mylist alias (really, evi) would be sent to owner-owner.

If you use a site-wide aliases file, you need to add an extra level of indirection pointing mylist to myreallist@master, so that the data file containing the list of members only needs to exist in one place.

There are several software packages that automate the maintenance of mailing lists. They typically allow users to add and remove themselves from the list, obtain information about the list, obtain files through email, etc. A few of the free ones (along with **ftp** sites) are:

- **majordomo**, from ftp.great.circle.com
- **almanac**, from oes.orst.edu
- **ListProcessor**, from cs.bu.edu

21.3 SENDMAIL: RINGMASTER OF THE ELECTRONIC MAIL CIRCUS

sendmail is the most complex and complete mail transport system in common use. It was written by Eric Allman while a student at Berkeley. Eric had recently taken a computer science course in which he used production systems, so he decided to tackle the mail delivery problem with a similar approach. At the time, he thought he was attacking a fly with a sledgehammer and was intending to move to a simpler technique once he understood the problem better.

As it turned out, **sendmail**'s generality allowed Eric to keep up with the fast-paced world of email standards. Several important standards were just taking form and were often changing every week. He came to realize that the fly was in fact an elephant and that his sledgehammer was just barely adequate.

sendmail can adapt to the whims of standards-makers partly due to the flexibility of its configuration file, which allows **sendmail** to meet the needs of a very diverse community of users. The rest of this chapter is primarily devoted to the understanding and construction of this configuration file, the infamous **sendmail.cf**. In reading various materials about **sendmail** to sharpen our config file tools, we came across adjectives like unapproachable, daunting, picky, cryptic, onerous, infamous, boring, confusing, tedious, ridiculous, obfuscated, and twisted.

sendmail is a transport agent, a program that interfaces between user agents and delivery agents. It is itself a delivery agent for the Internet. **sendmail**'s list of chores includes:

- Controlling messages as they leave the user's keyboard
- Understanding the recipients' addresses
- Choosing an appropriate delivery or transport agent
- Rewriting addresses to a form understood by the delivery agent
- Reformatting headers as required
- Passing the transformed message off to the delivery agent

sendmail also generates error messages and returns messages to the sender if they are undeliverable.

The History of sendmail

sendmail has existed in three major versions. **sendmail** V5 was written by Eric Allman in 1983. The latest version is V5.67; it can be obtained via **ftp** from ftp.uu.net.

*IDA **sendmail** is included on the CD-ROM.*

The IDA **sendmail** enhancement kit was written by Lennart Lövstrand at the University of Linköping in Sweden in 1987. Lennart was in the Computer Science Department, which in Swedish is the Institutionen för Datavetenskap; hence the name IDA. IDA is currently maintained by Neil Rickert from the University of Northern Illinois and Paul Pomes from the University of Illinois, Urbana Champaign. The current version is called UIUC IDA **sendmail** and is available from vixen.cso.uiuc.edu.

***sendmail** V8 is included on the CD-ROM.*

sendmail V8 is Eric Allman's 1993 update, which incorporates many of the features of IDA. The current version (V8.6.9) is available via anonymous **ftp** from ftp.cs.berkeley.edu.

As of this writing, most vendors' implementations of **sendmail** are derived from version 5, but an increasing number of sites are now using version 8 or IDA, especially in situations where the computing environment is heterogeneous.

See page 339 for more information about MX records.

`sendmail` as shipped by many vendors has security holes, does not use MX records, and does not always interoperate correctly in a heterogeneous environment. Vendors often customize a particular version of `sendmail` and then are reluctant to upgrade their base system to include current revisions. See the table on page 458 for information about the versions of `sendmail` shipped with our six example systems.

Version 5 is the basis for both version 8 and IDA `sendmail`. Eric Allman stopped maintaining V5 in 1987, about the time that IDA was born. Lennart Lövstrand developed IDA to simplify the configuration file for the common cases that every site must handle. IDA configuration files are typically 20 lines instead of hundreds. But of course, under the covers are the same long, complex config files we all know and hate.

In the course of simplifying the configuration file, many changes and extensions were added to the `sendmail` program itself; to run IDA, you must replace both the binary and the config files.

In 1991, Eric returned to Berkeley from private industry and had time to revisit `sendmail`. Soon after, he was reviewing Bryan Costales' draft manuscript of a `sendmail` book. The book and `sendmail` began a leapfrog game. Bryan would document a limitation of `sendmail` 5 or applaud a feature of IDA in a chapter of the draft. Eric would review the chapter and then fix or extend `sendmail`. Bryan would then update that chapter, and the next, and the next...

Finally, both the book and 4.4BSD needed to come out, and things stabilized with 800 pages published by O'Reilly and `sendmail` 8 in 4.4BSD. All programs in 4.4BSD are version 8.1, so `sendmail`'s numbering went from production V5 and beta-only V6 directly to V8.

RFC1123 defines the email requirements for hosts on the Internet.

Version 8 includes and generalizes many of the IDA extensions, supports RFC1123 conditionally (mandatory items are done, along with most, but not all, optional items), speaks ESMTP (Extended Simple Mail Transport Protocol), and includes the new Berkeley database files. Network performance (in terms of bandwidth) has been souped up, and security and DNS support have been improved.

Since the underlying syntax of the configuration file has changed only slightly, and since we expect vendors to move, albeit slowly, to version 8, we have chosen to base our discussion of `sendmail` on V8 and to note differences between it and V5 or IDA. Both IDA and V8 use the `m4` macro processor to allow easy configuration of the standard cases; for most sites, this "config lite" is all that you need.

However, we will also cover the syntax and semantics of the V5-style configuration file produced by **m4**. If there is a problem with your configuration, you'll have to base your debugging on a basic understanding of the raw, unadulterated config file.

Vendor-Supplied Versions of sendmail

sendmail as shipped by your vendor tends to be pretty lame. There are many holes, security problems, and incompatibilities with heterogeneous systems. We suggest that you seriously consider starting over with either V8 or IDA. Six months ago we would have recommended IDA for production sites and relegated V8 to universities and other brave souls. But V8 is now quite stable and is more secure than V5 or IDA.

gcc and its related tools and libraries are included on the CD-ROM.

IDA handles DECnet and V8 doesn't, but if you do not need DECnet support we recommend that you install V8 and ignore your vendor's offering.[7] However, small sites without dedicated administration staff may want to stick with their systems' defaults. In order to install either IDA or V8 **sendmail**, you must have a C compiler.

Table 21.2 lists the version of **sendmail** shipped with each of our example systems. In many cases, it was impossible to determine the actual **sendmail** base, so the general vintage is reported.

Table 21.2 **Vendors' versions of sendmail**

System	Code Base	Config Base
Solaris 2.4	Circa January '91	Circa February '83[a]
HP-UX 9.0	BSD 5.65	–
IRIX 5.2	IDA 5.65	Circa April '93
IRIX 4.2	BSD 5.21	–
SunOS 4.1.3	BSD 3.67	Circa February '83[a]
OSF/1 2.0	Looks like IDA	Circa 1991-'92
BSDI 1.1	BSD 8.6.5	Version 8.6.4

a. Yup, that's February 1983!

Solaris and SunOS ship a separate **sendmail.mx** that uses DNS MX records. It is not installed by default, but it does exist in the same directory with the default **sendmail** binary. Please use MX records; they are kinder to the network.

HP-UX ships the **sendmail** binary in **/usr/lib/sendmail** with mode 444. Mail fails because it cannot execute **sendmail**. No config file is shipped. Hello, anybody home?

7. Paul Vixie has a version of the **mail11** DECnet mailer that works with V8; **ftp** it from gatekeeper.dec.com.

IRIX 4.2 ships as its default a version of **sendmail** that does not support MX records and, like Sun, includes an MX version in the same directory. There is a wonderfully-commented sample config file that tells you exactly what needs to be changed and why. It is the best we have seen.

 OSF/1 seems to be based on IDA with major modifications by Paul Vixie and Fred Avolio to support DECnet (aka "King James **sendmail**")

BSDI is the only one of our six example systems that uses V8.

Modes of Operation

sendmail can run in several modes, which are selected with the **-b** flag. **-b** stands for "be" or "become" and is always used with another flag that determines the role **sendmail** will play. The legal values are listed in Table 21.3.

Table 21.3   Command-line flags for sendmail's major modes

Flag	Meaning
-bd	Run in daemon mode.
-bi	Initialize hashed aliases (same as newaliases).
-bp	Print mail queue (same as mailq command).
-bz	Freeze the configuration file (not in V8).
-bt	Enter address test mode.
-bs	Enter SMTP server mode (on standard input).

"Freezing" the config file means storing a memory image of **sendmail** after it has read the file. This made sense for ancient DEC hardware on which I/O was relatively cheap and processor time was expensive. But on modern hardware, it should not be used. It does not exist in V8.

When **sendmail** is run in daemon mode, the **-q** flag is usually specified. It sets the interval at which the mail queue is processed.

If you expect incoming mail to arrive via the network, **sendmail** should be run in daemon mode. In this mode, **sendmail** listens on network port 25 and waits for work. **sendmail** is often started at boot time from one of the **/etc/rc*** or **/etc/init.d/*** scripts with

```
/usr/sbin/sendmail -bd -q1h
```

to specify that it should act as a daemon and also process any queued messages once an hour. Traditionally, lock files in the queue directory are removed before **sendmail** is started:

```
cd /var/spool/mqueue; rm -f [lntx]f*
```

Newer versions of **sendmail** do not require this.

sendmail normally tries to deliver messages immediately, without saving them in the queue. But if your host is too busy or the destination machine is unreachable, **sendmail** will queue the message and try to send it again later. Every time **sendmail** processes the queue, it forks a child process, so don't set the queue-processing time too short. RFC1123 recommends at least 30 minutes between runs.

sendmail reads its configuration file, **sendmail.cf**, only at startup. Therefore, **sendmail** must be killed and restarted when you change the config file. Sending a hangup signal does not usually work.[8]

Both V8 and IDA create a **sendmail.pid** file containing **sendmail**'s process ID. This allows the process to be killed with

```
kill `head -1 sendmail.pid`
```

In V8, the **sendmail.pid** file has two lines: one with the PID and one with the command used to start **sendmail**. This is a nice feature, but it requires the use of **head** rather than just **cat** to extract the PID. Under IDA, the location of the PID file is **/etc/sendmail.pid**; in V8 it is a compile-time parameter that defaults to **/var/run/sendmail.pid** for newer BSD systems and to **/etc/sendmail.pid** for others.

The Mail Queue

Mail messages are stored in the queue directory when the machine is too busy to deliver them immediately or when a destination machine is unavailable. The queue directory is usually **/var/spool/mqueue** and usually has owner root and mode 711 or 700.[9]

When a message is queued, it is saved in pieces in several different files. Each filename has a two-letter prefix that identifies the piece and then a random ID built from the process ID of **sendmail**. This ID is not a constant because **sendmail** is constantly forking. The six possible pieces are shown in Table 21.4.

The **qf** file contains not only the message header but also a record of recipients, the sender, dates for returning it as undeliverable, priority in the queue, and the reason it's in the queue. Each line begins with a single-letter code that identifies the rest of the line.

Each message that is queued must have a **qf** and **df** file. All the others are used by **sendmail** during attempted delivery. When a machine

---

8. A couple of vendors have modified **sendmail** so that it rereads the config file on receipt of a hangup signal; check your manuals.

9. If the recipient of a mail message is a **csh** script, the spool directory must have mode 711 or, in version 8, the D= mailer clause must specify a directory with (at least) execute permission in which the script can be run.

Table 21.4 **Prefixes for files in the mail queue**

Prefix	File Contents
qf	The header of the message and control file
df	The body of the message
lf	A lock file for the message (empty and obsolete)
nf	Obsolete, used by older sendmails to avoid a race condition
tf	Temporary version of the qf file when delivery has failed again
xf	Temporary transcript file of error messages from mailers

crashes and reboots, the startup sequence for **sendmail** should delete the **lf**, **nf**, **tf**, and **xf** files.

The mail queue provides several opportunities for things to go wrong. The filesystem can be full (avoid putting the **/var/spool/mqueue** and **/var/spool/news** directories on the same partition), the queue can be clogged, or orphaned mail messages can be stuck in the queue.

V8 **sendmail** has added an option to help manage disk space. When the filesystem that contains the mail queue gets too full, mail will be rejected with a "try again later" error until there is more space.

See page 339 for more information about DNS MX records. If a major mail hub goes down, its MX backup sites may become overloaded with thousands of messages.[10] **sendmail** can fork too many copies of itself and thrash the machine to death. To handle a temporarily clogged queue, you need to move the clog aside, continue processing new mail as usual, and run a separate copy of **sendmail** on the clogged queue after things quiet down. For example:

```
# kill `head -1 sendmail.pid`
# mv queue cloggedq       /* To another FS if necessary */
# mkdir queue             /* Set owner/perms, too */
# /usr/lib/sendmail -bd -q1h &
```

When things settle down, run **sendmail** with the following flags:

```
/usr/lib/sendmail -oQ/var/spool/cloggedq -q
```

These flags point **sendmail** at the clogged queue directory and specify that **sendmail** should process it immediately.

For giant clogs, consider using the last digit of the message ID to separate messages into different queues, as shown in the following script.

10. A few years ago, Sun Microsystems decided to change its mail routing from direct-to-workstation addresses to division-wide gateways. The queue lengths on these gateways became so long that mail to the employee across the hall was taking more than a day to arrive. Unclogging these queues required hardware upgrades of all the gateway machines on a very tight schedule.

```
#!/bin/csh -f
foreach suffix (0 1 2 3 4 5 6 7 8 9)
   mkdir clog${suffix}
   mv ?f*${suffix} clog${suffix}
   sendmail -oQclog${suffix}
end
```

The point at which the queue becomes clogged depends on the site and the hardware that **sendmail** is running on. Your workstation and the mail hub for UUNET, which processes 200,000 messages a day, will have different definitions of a clogged queue. See the section *Mailer Statistics* on page 510 for information about measuring your traffic levels.

21.4 CONFIGURING SENDMAIL

sendmail's actions are controlled by a single configuration file (usually `/etc/sendmail.cf` or `/usr/lib/sendmail.cf`) called the config file for short. It allows **sendmail** to be customized for each host without being recompiled. The config file determines **sendmail**'s

- Choice of delivery agents
- Address rewriting rules
- Mail header formats

The file format was designed to be easy to parse, since **sendmail** must read and understand it every time it starts up. This has made it a bit lacking in warm, user-friendly features. Maintenance of the config file is the most significant administrative chore related to electronic mail.

Every version of **sendmail** uses a config file. IDA and V8 simplify the configuration process by using **m4** to create it. The next section discusses the config file and illustrates each command or construct.

If you're running V8 or IDA, you won't normally need to know about config files at the level of detail given here. You can build the **m4** files to describe your configuration by choosing an example that is close to what you want and modifying it a bit. You will only need to delve into the real config file if you are debugging a thorny problem or you are growing your mail site in bizarre ways. If you have standard needs and are not a masochist, skip ahead to the sections on configuring V8 or IDA on page 488.

Two key pieces of documentation are the book *sendmail* by Bryan Costales (with Eric Allman and Neil Rickert) and the paper *Sendmail Installation and Operations Guide* by Eric Allman. We will often refer to *sendmail* as a source for more information and will refer to it as "the **sendmail** book." Likewise, we will refer to Eric's installation paper as "the installation guide."

The Raw Configuration File

The only way to really understand the `sendmail.cf` file is to liken it to a frog in high school biology and dissect it piece by piece. That is what the following sections will attempt to do, and like that poor frog, there will be a few unidentified parts that just are.

The config file is organized into three general sections:

- Definitions of symbols, classes, options, and parameters
- Address rewriting rules
- Definitions of mailers (delivery agents)

General Syntax

`sendmail` commands begin in column one. The first character of a line determines the type of command and the format of the rest of the line. Each line is a complete command, except for lines beginning with spaces or tabs, which are continuations of preceding lines. Lines beginning with a pound sign ("#") are comments; blank lines are also treated as comments. The characters

```
<   >   (   )   "   \
```

have special meanings for `sendmail`. Any attempt to change their meaning with the config file is doomed to failure.

Config file commands are listed in Table 21.5.

Table 21.5   Command codes used in sendmail.cf

Code	Function
D	Defines a macro variable (single-valued)
C	Defines a class variable (multi-valued, like a set)
F	Defines a class using the contents of a file
O	Sets options
H	Defines a header
P	Defines message precedence classes
T	Defines trusted users (obsolete in V8)
V	Sets config file version number (only in V8)
K	Defines database file (only in V8, IDA uses option K)
S	Introduces a set of rewriting rules
R	Defines a rewriting rule within a set
M	Defines a mailer (delivery agent)

We will cover each command (with examples) in the next few sections.

The configuration file allows an administrator to define symbols, options, classes, priorities, and other configuration parameters for mail delivery. The commands to do this usually precede the meat of the config file, the address rewriting rules. Since these commands are fairly easy to understand, they sometimes give **sendmail** virgins a healthy dose of overconfidence.

The D Command: Define a Symbol

Variables (they are called macros in the **sendmail** documentation) are named with a single character and are defined using the D command. The syntax is:

```
DXvalue
```

For example, the definition

```
DJfoo
```

defines the variable J to contain "foo".

sendmail itself uses all of the lowercase letters and even some punctuation symbols; therefore, any additional macro definitions that you supply should have uppercase names.

Macro values (obtained with the syntax $x) are normally evaluated as **sendmail** reads the config file. In V8 and IDA, the evaluation can be deferred by referring to the value using the syntax $&x, which substitutes the value at run time whenever it is actually used. Some macros (such as the current sender of a message) are "magic"; they are always set and evaluated at run time regardless of the syntax you use.

sendmail macros have many uses. Some of them are defined, initialized, or referenced automatically by **sendmail**, while others are ignored unless you explicitly refer to them within the config file. Many macros have special behaviors associated with them; don't expect all macros to behave the same way, and remember that assignments can have non-obvious consequences.

Some of the macros with preordained meanings are listed in Table 21.6. We have included new ones and important ones, but see the installation guide for a complete list. In V8, all predefined macros have default values where appropriate; in V5 and IDA, some of them must be set.

Many of these variables are hardwired into **sendmail**. Some are universal (e.g. the date), some are site-wide (e.g. the domain name), and some pertain only to the current message (e.g. the sender's address).

In V5 and IDA, the value of $j was usually fully qualified but not always. V8 sets $w to the hostname portion, $m to the domain part, and $j to the fully-qualified domain name. V8 tries to figure these out from the system, but if your system is particularly uncooperative, V8 will fail and you will have to set $m and $j explicitly.

Table 21.6   Built-in variables[a]

Name	Meaning	Name	Meaning
a	Origination date (RFC822)	n	Daemon name (for errors)
b	Current date (RFC822)	o	The set of "operators"
c	Hop count	p	`sendmail`'s process ID
d	Current date (`ctime`)	q	Sender address format
e	SMTP entry message	r	Protocol used
f	Sender (From) address	s	Sender's hostname
g	"Envelope" sender	t	Current time (numeric)
h	Recipient host	u	Recipient user
i	Queue ID	v	`sendmail` version
j	Fully-qualified hostname	w	This site's hostname
k	UUCP site name (V8, IDA)	x	Full name of sender
l	Format of UNIX From line	z	Recipient's home directory
m	DNS domain name (V8)	_	Validated sender address (V8)

a. Adapted from the installation guide.

Here are some examples:

```
# delimiter (operator) characters
Do.!:@^%/[]
# format of a total name
Dq$?x$x<$g>$|$g$.
```

The first example defines the special symbols that **sendmail** will recognize as separator characters in addresses.[11] The second example uses the conditional form of a macro with syntax:

```
$?X true $| false $.
```

If the variable X is defined, then the *true* clause is evaluated. Otherwise, *false* is processed. The $| (else) clause is optional, and the $. (the dot is part of the token) terminates the conditional macro expansion. Armed with this knowledge, let's attack the line of gibberish that defines the q macro, the format of the sender's address.

It translates into $x, the full name of the sender (if defined), followed by <$g>, the sender's address relative to the recipient. This might expand to something like

```
Evi Nemeth <evi@cs.colorado.edu>
```

if the variable x is defined and to

```
evi@cs.colorado.edu
```

if not.

11. Don't include any of **sendmail**'s special characters (see page 463) in the list of delimiters. Strange behavior will result.

The C Command: Define a Class

A class of symbols (for example, "all directly-connected UUCP hosts") can be defined using the C command. The syntax is:

```
CXmembers
```

where *X* is the single-character name of the class and *members* lists the values to be added to the set. The members of a class are separated by spaces and may span lines. In V8 and IDA, the values may contain multiple tokens and may include macro variables. As usual, **sendmail** reserves most of the lowercase letters, so you should use only uppercase names. Macros and classes have separate namespaces; there is no relationship between the macro A and the class A. Here are some examples of the C command:

```
CUuunet lair
CGtigger
CGanchor
Cw$k
CSxor.com coop.net woz.org
```

See page 479 for more information about tokens.

The first line defines a class U with two members: uunet and lair. The second and third lines define a class G with two members: tigger and anchor. Either way of specifying multiple values is acceptable. The last two lines illustrate the V8 and IDA class extensions. The first includes a macro and the second consists of values with multiple tokens in the **sendmail** addressing sense (for example, woz.org is three tokens).

Classes are often used to define groups of machines that need to be handled in the same way, such as PCs whose mail should go to a gateway machine for forwarding. Membership in class X is expressed by $=X being true; exclusion from class X causes $~X to be true. These forms are used in the rewriting rules discussed starting on page 476.

The F Command: Define a Class from a File

F is identical to C in principle, except that the list of members is read from a file. The format to use while reading the file is specified using **scanf** notation. If not stated, it defaults to %s. For example:

```
FV/usr/local/lib/sendmail/vms.hosts
FU/usr/lib/uucp/Systems %[A-Za-z0-9_-]
FW|/usr/local/bin/gethosts              /* IDA only */
```

The first example defines V as the class of machines whose names are contained in the file **/usr/local/lib/sendmail/vms.hosts**, to be read with the default **scanf** format string %s. This method is best for a long list of hosts; if there are only a few hosts, use the C command.

See Chapter 30 for more information about the UUCP Systems file.

The second line defines the class U, the directly-connected UUCP hosts, as the contents of the UUCP **Systems** file read with a **scanf** format that eliminates comment lines and everything after the first blank. This will pick off just the host names.

This method of determining UUCP hosts does not require changing the configuration file when new hosts are added; they will automatically be included the next time **sendmail** is restarted. If you are using a frozen config file (which we do not recommend), you must re-freeze before restarting **sendmail**.

The third example defines class W to contain the standard output of a command, in this case **/usr/local/bin/gethosts**. This is only supported in IDA **sendmail**; it's omitted from V5 and V8 for security reasons. Be careful: **sendmail** runs as root. We strongly recommend that you *not* use this form (it's implemented as a **popen** in the IDA code).

The O Command: Set Options

The O command sets options in much the same way as D defines macros. The syntax is

```
OXvalue
```

where *X* is the single-character option name and there is no space between the name and the value.[12] Options can also be specified on the **sendmail** command line with the **-o** flag

Option values may be strings, integers, Booleans, or time intervals. There are many, many options, and practically every upper and lowercase letter has been used.

The examples below illustrate features of **sendmail** that are either new with V8 or are generally important from a system administrator's point of view (or in some cases, both).

The A option: sources of alias information

The A option can take the following forms:

```
# location of the aliases file
OA/etc/aliases
OAnis:mail.aliases@nisdomain
```

See Chapter 18 for more information about NIS.

The first form sets the location of the system-wide **aliases** file. In V8, multiple sources for alias information are supported; if the second form is also present, **sendmail** will first look in **/etc/aliases** and then in the NIS map called **mail.aliases**.

---

12. Version 8.7 will allow option names that are longer than one character.

The T option: queue timeout

The T option sets the amount of time that messages can remain in the queue before being returned to the sender as undeliverable.

```
# default timeout interval
OT5d
```

In this example, the timeout is set to five days. In **sendmail** V8, the notation 5d/4h means that the sender is notified of the delivery problem after four hours, but that delivery attempts continue for five days. If your master mail machine goes down for any length of time, the value of this option should be increased and **sendmail** should be restarted.

The r option: read timeouts

Read timeouts were forbidden in RFC821, the document that defined the SMTP protocol used by **sendmail** to exchange messages over the Internet. They are now required by RFC1123, which supersedes it. V8 allows separate timeouts to be specified for each step of the protocol exchange using the r option. This is a very important new feature that prevents **sendmail** from hanging when trying to talk to a recalcitrant partner across the Internet. Instead, **sendmail** will time out and enqueue the stuck message for later delivery. Formerly, **sendmail** would seem to wait forever when a network link went down after an SMTP conversation had started. Actually, it used a single timeout (usually two hours) for each step of the protocol negotiation.

The x and X options: load control

The x and X options allow **sendmail**'s behavior to be modified based on the system's load average. There are three ways that **sendmail** can handle messages:

- Accept messages and process them immediately (low load)
- Queue messages for later processing (moderate load)
- Refuse connections completely (high load)

The x and X options designate the load averages that define the boundaries between these actions. For example, the statements

```
Ox8
OX12
```

would make **sendmail** start to enqueue messages when the load average reached 8 and refuse connections at load averages of 12 or above.

The p option: enable security features

V8 **sendmail** supports a privacy/security option, p, that can be used to effect a modest increase in security. Table 21.7 lists the values that it accepts. More than one value can be used at once; values should be separated with commas.

Table 21.7   Values of the p option (V8 only)

Value	Effect
novrfy	Disables the VRFY command in SMTP
noexpn	Disables the EXPN command in SMTP
needmailhelo	Insists on a HELO exchange before a MAIL command
needvrfyhelo	Insists on a HELO exchange before a VRFY command
needexpnhelo	Insists on a HELO exchange before an EXPN command
restrictmailq	Restricts who can run the mailq command

The VRFY and EXPN commands are the same in V5 and IDA; they are distinct (as was intended) in V8. VRFY just checks to be sure that the given address is valid, while EXPN expands the address using both the global aliases file and users' `.forward` files on the remote machine. This may give away more information that you are comfortable with, especially if you have a company-wide alias called "everyone" or "engineering." The option

```
Opnoexpn
```

would disable the EXPN command in the SMTP mail transport protocol. As a result, mail sent to an alias would be delivered as usual, but no one would be allowed to snoop by connecting to port 25 and expanding the alias to see its members.

A HELO exchange allows **sendmail** to verify that the machine at the other end of the SMTP connection is who it claims to be; that is, that its IP address, when looked up in DNS, yields the same hostname that was specified with HELO. This makes it slightly more likely that the machine at the other end has not been recently rebooted and had its hostname set to one that you trust.

To deny EXPN and require HELO, use

```
Opnoexpn,needmailhelo
```

The **mailq** command lists the messages in the **sendmail** queue. By default, any user can run **mailq**. To restrict access to this command, turn on the restrictmailq value of the p option. For example, with

```
Oprestrictmailq
```

set, only users in the group that owns the queue directory can print the mail queue.

The P option: bounce control

The P option sends undeliverable mail to the local postmaster as well as returning it to the sender; under V8 and SunOS, only the headers are sent to the postmaster so that the sender's privacy is respected.

Mailing list options

The a option controls locking when the hashed **aliases** file is rebuilt; it tattles if the hashed version is out of date with respect to the source file. The D option rebuilds the hashed file whenever necessary. D and a together do it safely; don't use D alone.

Option C checkpoints the queue for mailing lists so that no duplicates are sent if **sendmail** dies. This only works in V8.

The y and Z options allow fine-tuning of message priorities and are quite important on hubs that handle large mailing lists or a lot of mail.

Performance options

Option d sets **sendmail**'s delivery mode. It accepts the values i (interactive delivery), b (background delivery), and q (enqueue only). The config file entry Odi is typical and also reminds us of a very good bar and Mexican restaurant near the Keystone ski area, the Old Dillon Inn.

sendmail uses TCP to send messages on the Internet. Unfortunately, setting up and tearing down a TCP connection for each message is a bit expensive. V8 supports connection caching, in which an open connection is not closed immediately after a message is delivered, but is held open in anticipation of another message for the same site.

Cached connections are controlled by the options k (size of the cache, in connections) and K (how long an idle connection is cached). Small values are suggested. The defaults are two connections and five minutes, respectively. Even one cached connection will give you a noticeable improvement in performance.

The n option: verify aliases

Option n tells **sendmail** to validate the RHS of aliases when rebuilding the alias database. This costs rebuild time, but it does find errors.

A complete table of **sendmail**'s options and their appropriate values can be found in either the **sendmail** book or the installation guide.

The P Command: Define Message Precedence

Every mail message is assigned a priority as it enters the **sendmail** queue. The priority is based on the time the message was submitted, the message's size, the number of recipients, the number of times delivery has already been tried, and the message's specified precedence value (if any).

The precedence value determines the class of service. It can be set for a message by including a Precedence header. Some user agents require additional headers to be listed in their configuration files. Some allow you to type headers directly into a message, and some provide no way to add them at all. Your mileage may vary.

The `sendmail` config file defines the meanings of the various precedence classes using the P command, which has the syntax

```
Pname=number
```

Negative numbers imply that no error message will be sent if the message is undeliverable. V8 has modified this policy and sends an error back to the sender but does not return the body of the original message. Some typical P entries are:

```
Pspecial-delivery=100
Pfirst-class=0
Pbulk=-60
Pjunk=-100
```

The T Command: Set Trusted Users (not in V8)

A trusted user, set by

```
Tuser1 user2 ...
```

can override the sender address using the **-f** flag. This may be necessary, for example, if a delivery program cannot deliver a message and wants to return an error message to the sender. In the `sendmail.cf` file distributed by vendors, the trusted users are usually root, daemon, uucp, and news. As well as allowing respectable users like daemon to impersonate someone else in mail messages, the trusted user concept gives the system administrator the opportunity to demonstrate a thorough knowledge of the manual by sending mail as someone else.

The H Command: Set Header Format

Mail headers produced by `sendmail` can be very verbose and can use more space than the message itself. Verbose headers are useful for debugging, but a bit redundant for everyday use. Some mail readers let users choose the headers they want to see and suppress the rest. The headers are still part of the message, but are not printed by default.

Headers are defined with the H command, using the syntax:

```
Hname: format
```

The headers are included with each outgoing message. The *name* field is not limited to a single letter, but should either begin with "X-" or come from a fixed list (see the **sendmail** book for the complete list).

Some header fields apply only if the message is sent on the Internet, or with UUCP, or is delivered locally. The program that does the actual delivery is called the delivery agent or mailer. Mailers have flags associated with them that turn on individual features or behaviors within **sendmail**. To allow the expression of dependencies on mailers, a conditional form of the H command exists:

```
H?flags?name: format
```

If the mailer that will deliver a message uses one of the specified *flags*, then the header line will be included. A list of mailer flags and their meanings is given on page 487. Here is a short example:

```
H?P?Return-Path: <$g>
```

This line says that if a message goes out via a mailer that uses the P flag, the following header line should be included:

```
Return-Path: <envelope-sender>
```

For example:

```
Return-Path: <evi@cs.colorado.edu>
```

The header line below does not contain the conditional clause (based on mailer flags) and so it will always be included:

```
HReceived: $?sfrom $s $.$?_($?s$|from $.$_) $.by $j
   ($v/$Z) $?r with $r$. id $i$?u for $u$.; $b
```

A deciphering dictionary for the macros mentioned in this header is given in Table 21.8.

Table 21.8 Decoding guide for our example header

Macro	Meaning	Value
$s	Sender's hostname	
$_	Validated sender address	evi@localhost
$j	Fully-qualified hostname	eclipse.cs.colorado.edu
$v	Version of **sendmail**	8.6.9
$Z	Version of config file	8.6.9
$r	Protocol (null for SMTP)	
$i	Queue ID	VAA01729
$u	Recipient	evi
$b	Date	Sat, 4 Jun 1994 21:03:26 -0600

It looks even more forbidding than the conditional header, but armed with the table of **sendmail**'s macros and a sample from a mail message, we can easily decipher it.

```
Received: (from evi@localhost) by eclipse.cs.colorado.edu
    (8.6.9/8.6.9) id VAA01729 for evi; Sat, 4 Jun 1994 21:
    03:26 -0600
```

Recall that a conditional macro has the format

```
$?X true $| false $.
```

The blow-by-blow of the hard part is shown in Exhibit C.

Exhibit C   The hard part

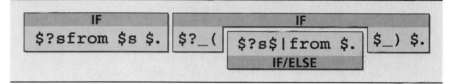

It contains an "if" on the variable $s and an "if/then/else" (with an empty "then" part) nested inside an "if" on the variable $_. In this particular example, $s is not defined, so

```
$?sfrom $s $.
```

has no effect. The variable $_ is defined, so the clause

```
($?s$|from $.$_)
```

is activated. It is an if/then/else form in which we take the else branch because the variable $s is not defined. This then reduces to

```
(from $_)
```

which yields the result

```
(from evi@localhost)
```

If you use a central trouble mail queue (as described on page 452), you may find a Reply-To header useful, although not all user agents obey it. It can be set to address a user's reply back to the trouble queue rather than to the individual who responded to the message. For example:

```
From millert@nagina.cs.Colorado.EDU Sun Mar 14:54:50 1993
...
Reply-To: trouble@kinglear.cs.colorado.edu
Date: Sun, 14 Mar 1993 18:53:48 -0700
From: "Todd C. Miller" <millert@nagina.cs.Colorado.EDU>
```

While this piece of mail is from millert and would normally be routed to him if the recipient replied to it, the Reply-To header will overrule this behavior and the message will go to trouble, not millert.

The Reply-To header line is specified in the configuration file for the user's mail reader. For **mh**, the following line in **Mail/replcomps** inserts a Reply-To header in each outgoing message:

```
%<(lit)Reply-To: trouble@nag.cs.colorado.edu\n%>\
```

The V Command: Set Configuration File Syntax Version

The syntax allowed in **sendmail**'s config file has changed as **sendmail** has evolved. V8 makes this explicit with a new command, V, that identifies the version of the syntax you are using.

There are actually three distinct version numbers floating around trying to confuse you:

- The **sendmail** version, set with the v macro
- The config file version, set with the Z macro
- The config file syntax version, set with the V command

Table 21.9 describes the five versions of the config file syntax that are currently defined.

Table 21.9   Versions of the configuration file syntax understood by V8

Version	Description
1	Original config files from V5 sendmail
2	Adds a "." to the end of fully-qualified hostnames
	Adds flexibility in the handling of local hostnames
3	Allows comments anywhere in the config file via "#"
4	Same as version three
5	Changes $w to be the relative, not fully-qualified, hostname

If you use an older configuration file with a V8 **sendmail** binary, you should include the V command within the config file so that **sendmail** will interpret the configuration correctly.

The version directive also accepts an optional vendor designation that vendors are encouraged to use if they modify the syntax or semantics of the config file. For example,

```
V5/Berkeley
```

identifies Berkeley's flavor of the version 5 config file syntax. Don't confuse syntax version 5 with **sendmail** version 5.

The K Command: Define Keyed Database (V8 Only)

IDA introduced keyed database files via the K option; V8 added a command, K, to define them. Both implementations speed lookups and add flexibility to some rewriting operations. Typical uses include:

- Mapping login names to full names
- Mapping UUCP hostnames to UUCP paths
- Mapping hostnames of non-Internet machines to their relays
- Mapping pseudo-hostnames to fax numbers
- Mapping pseudo-hostnames to digital pager numbers
- Looking up special mailer info for particular hosts

The syntax of the K command is:

```
Kmapname mapclass arguments
```

mapname is the name by which the database will later be referred to in the config file; it is not limited to a single character as other **sendmail** names often are.[13]

mapclass specifies the type of database you are defining. V8 supports both the **dbm/ndbm** database routines and the new **db** library from Berkeley, among others. Common *mapclass* values are: dbm, btree, hash, host, and nis. **sendmail** must be compiled with the supporting library routines for any classes you use.

The pseudo-mapclass dequote is used internally to attempt to remove quotes; the syntax of the resulting address is checked, and if it's legal the quotes are removed.

The exact arguments depend on *mapclass*, but usually only the filename containing the database needs to be specified. In rewriting rules, the expression to refer to a value in a database looks forbidding at first:

```
$(mapname key $@ parameters $: default $)
```

Only the *mapname* and *key* arguments are required. *parameters* and *default* are optional. The other tokens are just separators. The meaning of the expression is, "Look up *key* with *parameters* in the *mapname* database. If the lookup fails, use *default* as an answer." Most databases just use the key without any parameters or defaults; in this case the search expression is just

```
$(mapname key $)
```

V8's database mechanism is quite general, and you may find it useful in a variety of situations. There is one standardized database you should be aware of. It contains additional information about users and goes by the **sendmail** name of "userdb."

---

13. IDA databases defined with the K option are named with a single letter.

The userdb is a central repository of user information. It includes information such as users' mail homes, full names, addresses, and telephone numbers. It was envisioned as a more flexible and more powerful mechanism for handling aliases, but has more commonly been used to map login names to full names for header rewriting.

Entries in the database are of the form:

```
login:field-name          value
```

Whitespace separates the *field-name* from the *value*. Field names are listed in Table 21.10.

Table 21.10   Lexicon of the V8 userdb

Field	Contents
mailname	Host's official mail name, goes on From: line
maildrop	Delivery address for the user
mailsender	User's envelope name (for mailing lists)
fullname	User's full name
office-*	Address, phone, and fax at office
home-*	Address, phone, and fax at home
project/plan	Project and pointer to plan file

sendmail only uses the first four fields; the others are anticipating a new **finger** program. Here are some sample entries from a hypothetical **/usr/local/adm/userdb** file.

```
:default:mailname      cs.colorado.edu
trent:maildrop         trent@xor.com
trent:fullname         Trent R. Hein
hein:maildrop          trent
evi:fullname           Evi Nemeth
evi:maildrop           evi@piper.cs.colorado.edu
```

The database is constructed using the **makemap** command, which is a part of the new BSD database system and is included with the V8 distribution. For example:

```
makemap btree /etc/userdb.db < /usr/local/adm/userdb
```

Rewriting Rules

We have now gotten the skin off the frog and are ready to proceed with the real meat of the configuration file, the rewriting rules. Rewriting rules are used to transform addresses from one form to another. We will first describe the syntax, then proceed to dissect several rulesets as applied to some sample addresses.

`sendmail` accepts addresses in many forms. Its goal is to rewrite these addresses into a generic form where the user, host, and domain can be unambiguously identified. From the host and domain portion of the address, the correct mailer program is determined.

V8 and IDA consider each recipient address in two contexts: as an "envelope address" that determines where the message goes and how it gets there, and as a "header address" that is primarily cosmetic but does determine if the recipient can reply to the mail.

Interpreting addresses seems like a simple task when the address is

```
evi@cs.colorado.edu
```

But what if it's

```
@boulder,@sigi:haidozo!evi%wasteheat%moose@snake
```

Some mail addresses have no obvious operator precedence, and thus are difficult to parse correctly. Much of the "magic" in the config file is used to take care of hard problems like operator precedence and scoping.

Rewriting rules have three parts, separated by tabs: the left-hand side (LHS), the right-hand side (RHS), and an optional comment field. When an address matches the LHS of a rule, it is rewritten as specified by the rule's RHS. The separators *must* be tabs; spaces do not work. Snarfing config lines with a mouse and pasting them into another **xterm** window can teach you a painful lesson about spaces vs. tabs.

The S Command: Start a New Ruleset

Rewriting rules are grouped into "rulesets," each of which is designated by a number. The S command introduces a ruleset. For example,

```
S3
```

marks the beginning of ruleset three. Ruleset three would continue until another **sendmail** S command was encountered. In V8, there may be up to 100 rulesets (numbered 0 to 99); V5 and IDA support only 30 by default. This value can be changed by recompiling **sendmail**. Ruleset numbers are rather arbitrary; however, rulesets zero through four are applied in a predefined order.

Addresses are passed through rulesets using a syntax that will be described shortly. In general, every rule in a set is applied to the current address; an address may be rewritten several times within a ruleset. The rulesets are applied in the order shown in Exhibit D (next page).

Ruleset three is the first ruleset applied to all addresses. It tries to put addresses into the canonical form

```
local-part@host-domain-specification
```

Exhibit D   Order of application of standard rulesets

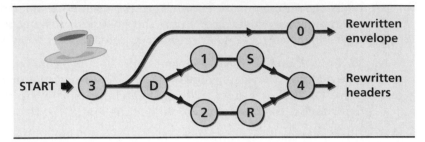

It also adds the tokens < and > to help "focus" on the destination host. For example, ruleset three might rewrite addresses as follows:

```
evi@cs.colorado.edu    to    evi<@cs.colorado.edu>
hao!boulder!evi        to    boulder!evi<@hao.uucp>
```

Ruleset three is probably the hardest ruleset to understand; if you are trying to figure out the config file, you might want to start elsewhere.

Ruleset zero decides what the destination really is and which mailer program (delivery agent) should get the message there. It resolves the destination address into a triple (*mailer*, *host*, *user*) that forms the envelope for the message. However, ruleset zero does not change the destination address in the header.

The ruleset labeled D in Exhibit D is not a real ruleset but rather an internal edit performed by **sendmail** when it receives an unqualified address (one that does not contain an @hostname part) from a remote site. It adds the sender's domain. For example, in the headers

```
From: trent@xor.com
To:   evi@cs.colorado.edu
Cc:   beth
```

the address "beth" is fine at xor.com, but ambiguous when received at cs.colorado.edu. Beth will receive the original message, but what if evi replies to both trent@xor.com and "beth"? Should **sendmail** treat it as beth@xor.com or as beth@cs.colorado.edu? **sendmail** normally interprets unqualified names as local addresses, so beth@cs.colorado.edu would be assumed. But in fact, that's the wrong answer.

The best way to prevent this problem is to rewrite "foreign" addresses when they first enter the mail system. In this example, we'd like to transform "beth" into "beth@xor.com" before the mail is processed locally. If the delivery agent has flag C set, ruleset D will take care of this by adding the sender's domain (here, xor.com) before the address escapes into the main body of rulesets.

Rulesets one and two rewrite sender and recipient addresses, respectively. By the time an address has reached ruleset one or two, a decision about where and to whom the message is going has already been made. The effects of rulesets one and two are purely cosmetic and will not influence delivery of the message.

IDA **sendmail** first introduced the idea of splitting the rewriting of the envelope from that of the message headers and having rules specified for each. Rulesets one and two are applied to the envelope in IDA, while rulesets five and six process sender and recipient headers.

A mailer can request that additional rulesets be invoked on the sender and recipient addresses, both for the envelope and for the headers. These rulesets are identified in the specification of the mailer; they are denoted R (recipient) and S (sender) in Exhibit D.

Ruleset four rewrites all addresses, usually from internal to external form. It is the final rewriting and often undoes the focusing added by ruleset three.

There are many other standard rulesets that are called as subroutines from the top-level rulesets described above.

The R Command: Define a Rewriting Rule

This section describes the actual rewriting rules. These rules are the constructs that give **sendmail** its reputation for being inscrutable and hard to configure. First we will look at the anatomy of a rewriting rule and explore the magic tokens used on the left and right-hand sides. Then we will inspect some examples and common blunders.

Before an address is modified by rewriting rules, it must first be parsed. Parsing is a computer jargon word that means reading an input string, dividing it into parts (called tokens), and determining the type of each token. In the case of email addresses, tokens are recognized as the separators defined in the o macro and the strings between them. Typically, the separators are:

```
!   .   :   @   %   /   [   ]
```

For example, the address evi@cs.colorado.edu contains seven tokens:

```
evi   @   cs   .   colorado   .   edu
```

Rewriting rules usually contain pattern-matching expressions called wild cards. The tokens that are matched by a particular wild card can be referred to by the sequence number of the wild card: $1 is the first, $2 is the second, and so on. For example, if the left hand side (LHS) of a rule looks like:

```
wildcard1@wildcard2
```

then the address

```
evi@cs.colorado.edu
```

would match it, with evi becoming $1 and cs.colorado.edu becoming $2. Such a match is called an indefinite match; the literal match of @ to @ is called a definite match.

Each rewriting rule lives on a line by itself and has the syntax:

```
RLHS <tab> RHS <tab> comment
```

If an address matches the LHS of the rule, then the RHS replaces the address. When there is a match, the rule is reapplied until it fails.[14] The syntax of pattern-matching tokens used in the LHS is summarized in Table 21.11. The Debug column shows the characters that **sendmail** V5 prints to represent each wild card token in debug mode; IDA and V8 repeat the entire rule to provide context.

Table 21.11 LHS pattern-matching tokens

Token	Debug	Meaning
$@		Match zero tokens (V8 only)
$-	^R	Match exactly one token
$+	^Q	Match one or more tokens
$*	^P	Match zero or more tokens
$X		Match value of macro variable X
$&X		Match value of variable X at run time
$=X	^SX	Match any token in class X
$~X	^TX	Match any token {not} in class X

The tokens X and $&X$ are *not* considered wild cards because macro variables are evaluated before pattern matching occurs. A fixed string will already have been substituted by the time the rule is executed. This means that the matched text cannot be referred to as $1, $2, etc. Miscounting is a common mistake that **sendmail** will not alert you to. Use the X syntax again on the RHS to obtain the macro's value.

The new V8 wild card $@ is usually used alone to match null input.

sendmail ignores spaces on both the LHS and RHS of a rule, and the readability of the pattern and subsequent action to take can be greatly improved with a liberal smattering of spaces. For example,

```
$+%$-@$+
```

is much harder to read than

```
$+ % $- @ $+
```

---

14. Infinite loop alert! The special RHS tokens $= and $@ override this behavior.

The pattern-matching algorithm that compares addresses to rewriting rules uses a minimal match anchored at both ends. By "anchored," we mean that it starts at the beginning and matches all the way to the end. For example, when matching an address such as

```
evi%rupertsberg%anchor@boulder.colorado.edu
```

against an LHS pattern of

```
$+ % $+
```

sendmail would choose the token evi as the first indefinite match and rupertsberg%anchor@boulder.colorado.edu as the second. But when matched with

```
$+ % $- @ $+
```

it would first choose evi, be unable to match completely, and then back up and try matching evi%rupertsberg against the first $+. This choice would allow a complete match.

Table 21.12 illustrates the application of several rules to the address evi@cs.colorado.edu. The values of the indefinite tokens are also do scribed relative to each rule.

Table 21.12   LHS rules applied to evi@cs.colorado.edu

Rule	Result
$*	$1=evi@cs.colorado.edu
$+	$1=evi@cs.colorado.edu
$-	Does not match, more than one token
$+ @ $+	$1=evi, $2=cs.colorado.edu
$+ % $+	Does not match, no %
$+ ! $+	Does not match, no !
$- @ $+	$1=evi, $2=cs.colorado.edu
$+ @ $-	Does not match, more than one token after @
$+ @ $- . $D	$1=evi, $2=cs
$+ . $+	$1=evi@cs, $2=colorado.edu
$+ . $+ . $=T	$1=evi@cs, $2=colorado, $3=edu

The two rules involving $D and $T will match assuming that $D has been properly defined as colorado.edu and that $T (the list of top-level DNS domains) includes the edu domain.

The RHS of a rule can contain any of the indefinite tokens matched from the LHS, arbitrary text, the values of macro variables, and some special symbols as well. These are summarized in Table 21.13, which appears on the next page.

Table 21.13 Special symbols in the RHS

Token	Debug	Meaning
$X	—	Use value of macro variable X
$?X yes $| no $.	—	Conditional macro
$n	^U n	Use indefinite token n from LHS
$>n	^Y n	Call ruleset n
$[hostname$]	^] hostname	Canonicalize hostname
$(mapname key $)ᵃ	—	Lookup key in database mapname
$#mailer	^V mailer	In ruleset 0, resolve to mailer
$@host	^W host	In ruleset 0, specify host to mailer
$:user	^X user	In ruleset 0, specify user to mailer
$@	^W	As a prefix, terminates ruleset
$:	^X	As a prefix, terminates rule

a. Or the more complete version, $(mapname key $@ args $: default $).

$n corresponds to a match of an indefinite token ($-, $+, $*, $=, or $~) from the LHS of a rule. The numbering starts at one and refers to the value of the nth indefinite token of the matching address. The value of n can range from one to nine. A match of a literal or definite token, such as the @ symbol, does not increase the count.

Other rulesets can be called as "subroutines" using the syntax $>n. The tokens following $>n on the RHS are passed to ruleset n as the address to be processed.

$[hostname$] causes hostname to be looked up in DNS and replaced with a fully-qualified canonical name. The starting hostname can be a local name, a fully-qualified name, or an IP address in square brackets.

In the expression for a database lookup, mapname is the name of the database (assigned with the K command), key is the value to look up, and args and default are optional. See page 475 for more details.

The last five entries in Table 21.13 have special uses. In ruleset zero, the forms $#mailer, $@host, and $:user inform **sendmail** of the mailer that should be used to deliver a message and identify the destination and recipient. The determination of these three pieces of information is one of the main goals of the rule-evaluation procedure.

As the first token on the RHS, $@ and $: determine the flow of control. When a rule matches the current address and the address is rewritten according to its RHS, the rule is applied again and again as long as the LHS continues to match. A $@ token on a rule's RHS terminates both the current rule and the entire ruleset and returns the rest of the RHS to the calling ruleset. A $: terminates the current rule and continues with the next rule in the ruleset.

sendmail applies a ruleset's rules in order. Each rule is reapplied as long as it matches and its RHS doesn't start with a $@ or $: escape. Once a rule no longer matches, the next rule in the ruleset is considered. Every time a rule matches, the address that sendmail is working on is rewritten before it is given to the next rule. If an address reaches the end of a ruleset without escaping early due to a $@ prefix, then the ruleset terminates and returns the address in its current form. If the ruleset was invoked with $>, sendmail resumes processing within the "parent" ruleset. If the terminated ruleset was invoked spontaneously by sendmail, processing continues as shown in Exhibit D on page 478.

If your configuration file contains a rule that continues to match forever, sendmail will go into an infinite loop. Older versions just hang; IDA and V8 detect the loop, print an error message via syslog, and then hang. An example of a rule that would cause an infinite loop is:

```
R $+      $1.$D      Add our domain
```

This rule would add the domain ($D) to the address many times over.

Examples of Rewriting Rules

Armed with this friendly notation for rules, let's look at some examples. In the samples that follow, we will use evi@cs.colorado.edu as the input address. We first show each rule and then, beneath it, the match that is tried on the LHS. If the match succeeds, the composition of the RHS is also shown. The rules and addresses are spaced so that corresponding portions line up.

The debugging information that would be printed by sendmail V8 if debugging were turned on at level 21.12 (see *Testing and Debugging* on page 511) is also shown below the matching.[15]

```
R $+ @ $+                   $: $1 < @ $2 >

LHS: $+   @ $+
     evi @ cs.colorado.edu

RHS: $: $1  < @ $2            >
        evi < @ cs.colorado.edu >

Debug:   -----trying rule: $+ @ $+
         -----rule matches: $: $1 < @ $2 >
         rewritten as: evi < @ cs . colorado . edu >
```

Note that the $: on the right-hand side is required or we would end up with many sets of nesting angle brackets and an infinite loop. This rule (from ruleset three) focuses on (adds angle brackets around) the *host.domain* part of the address.

15. We consider "2112" by Rush to be optimal music for debugging rulesets.

```
R $+ < @ $+ >                $@ $>96 $1 < @ $2 >

LHS: $+   < @ $+             >
     evi < @ cs.colorado.edu >

RHS: $@ $>96 $1   < @ $2                >
            evi < @ cs.colorado.edu >

Debug:   -----trying rule: $+ < @ $+ >
         -----rule matches: $@ $> 96 $1 < @ $2 >
         -----callsubr 96
         rewrite: ruleset 96 input: evi<@cs.colorado.edu>
```

The input address for this rule is the output of the previous rule. The angle brackets are already in place, and the rule does match. Ruleset 96 is called using the notation $>96. The portion of the RHS following the 96 is the address handed to ruleset 96. In this case, it simply reproduces the input address. The prefix $@ on the RHS terminates the current ruleset after ruleset 96 completes.

```
R $* < @ $* $~P > $*    $: $1 < @ $[ $2 $3 $] > $4

LHS: $*   < @ $*            $~P > $*
     evi < @ cs.colorado. edu >

RHS: $: $1  < @ $[ $2 $3 $]       > $4
        evi < @ cs.colorado.edu. >

Debug:   -----trying rule: $* < @ $* $~P > $*
         -----rule matches: $: $1 < @ $[ $2 $3 $] > $4
         rewritten as: evi < @ cs . colorado . edu . >
```

The class P contains the single character ".". It is used in this rule to determine if the domain part of the address has a final dot, as DNS would like it to have. If there is no trailing dot, one is added.

```
R $+ < $+ @ $+/>       $#local $:$1

LHS: $+  < $+ @ $+ >
     evi < ???

Debug:   -----trying rule: $+ < $+ @ $+ >
         ----- rule fails
```

This rule fails to match because our input address does not have one or more tokens between the < and the @ as the $+ in the LHS demands. This rule comes from ruleset zero; the notation on the RHS specifies the local mailer and user.

```
R $* < @ $* > $*       $#smtp $@ $2 $: $1 <@ $2 > $3

LHS: $*   < @ $*             > $*
     evi < @ cs.colorado.edu. >
```

```
RHS: $#smtp $@ $2              $: $1 <@$2>              $3
            cs.colorado.edu.  evi <@cs.colorado.edu.>

Debug:  -----trying rule: $* < @ $* > $*
        -----rule matches: $# smtp $@ $2 $: $1 < @ $2 > $3
        rewritten as: $# smtp $@ cs . colorado . edu .
                      $: evi < @ cs . colorado . edu . >
```

This rule, also from ruleset zero, selects the SMTP mailer with a destination host of "cs.colorado.edu." and user "evi@cs.colorado.edu.".

Common Ruleset Blunders

One of the pitfalls in dealing with **sendmail**'s configuration file is that an address you want to build a special rule for is often rewritten several times before it reaches any new rules you introduce. As a result, when it finally gets there, it doesn't match. Rulesets can be called recursively, directly or indirectly, and the path an address takes through the config file is often not clear. With all this bouncing between rulesets, it's no wonder your poor little address is unrecognizable by the time it reaches the new rule you wrote for it.

Ruleset three is always applied first; it adds the angle brackets around the relevant host and domain to help other rules parse the address. Ruleset three often calls other rulesets. Ruleset zero, which decides where a message is going, is invoked after ruleset three.

When ruleset zero chooses a (*mailer, host, user*) triple for delivery (sometimes after calling other rulesets to help) the address is said to become "resolved." If ruleset zero cannot resolve an address, it is considered unreachable and the message is returned to the sender.

Some of the features of **sendmail.cf** that tend confuse novices are:

- Each rule is potentially an infinite loop.
- Pattern matching in rulesets is conservative if there are choices of how large a bite to match.
- Rulesets are applied neither in numerical order nor in the order in which they appear in the config file.
- An address arriving at a rule may not be what you expect due to earlier rules having messed with it.

sendmail contains powerful debugging and trace code to help you spy on addresses as they wind through the config file; see page 511 for more details. If you're lucky, V8 or IDA may protect you from having to use it.

The M Command: Define Mailers

Mailers, the programs used to actually deliver a message, must be described in the config file.

The format of a mailer specification is:

```
Mname, P=prog, F=flags, ..., A=args
```

The *name* may be any string (yes, it can be longer than one character). The strange comma-separated clauses that follow it are various mailer options, called "equates" in the documentation. The P= and A= clauses must be present, but all other options are, well, optional. The A= clause must be last because it can include embedded spaces and perhaps commas. Although we have shown only single-letter option names above, some of them are actually words. For example:

```
Mlocal, Path=/bin/mail, ...
```

The various options are explained in Table 21.14.

Table 21.14 Mailer options

Option	Value
P	Program to call
F	Flags for sendmail and the mailer program
S	Additional rulesets to use for the sender address
R	Additional rulesets to use for recipient addresses
E	Characters that mark the end of line
M	Maximum allowable message size
A	Arguments with which to call the mailer
4	Force user identity (V8.7 only)

Mailers are chosen in ruleset zero, where all addresses are ultimately resolved. The mailer specified with $#*mailer* must refer to a mailer defined in an M command.

Two mailers, local and prog, must be defined. These mailers handle mail to local users and to local UNIX programs, respectively. In addition, several special mailers are often defined: error for generating error messages when mail is returned, *file* for sending mail to a file (V8 only), and *include* for sending to a mailing list (V8 only).

The P field specifies the path to the program that will act as delivery agent. The value of P must be an absolute path or the string [IPC].[16]

See page 339 for more information about MX records.

If no user ($u) is specified in the argument vector (A=), then both the sending host and the receiving host are on the Internet and the SMTP protocol should be used between their respective **sendmail** daemons to

16. [IPC] was named in the early days of sockets; it stands for "Inter-Process Communication." V5 uses [IPC] for the Internet mailer. IDA and SunOS use [TCP], and V8 uses [IPC] but recognizes [TCP] as well.

transfer the message. Before a connection is established, **sendmail** on the sending host calls the DNS system to see if there are MX records for the receiving host. If there are, the message is diverted to the host with the highest MX priority (lowest MX value). In V8, MX expansion can be overridden by changing the host specified in the $@*host* phrase of ruleset zero to $@[*host.domain*]. This feature is intended for use by sites with strict firewall machines.

The F option specifies the flags associated with the mailer. They have either a preset meaning to **sendmail** or may be invented locally to control header lines. There are a zillion flags; complete documentation can be found in the **sendmail** book or the installation guide. Some common flags are listed in Table 21.15.

Table 21.15   Mailer flags

Flag	Meaning
D	Mailer wants a Date header line.
E	Escape lines in the message that begin with From using ">".
F	Mailer wants a From header line.
M	Mailer wants a Message-Id header line.
P	Mailer wants a Return-Path header line.
S	It is safe to execute the mailer as root.
X	Add an extra dot to lines beginning with a dot.
l	This is a local mailer.
m	Mailer can send to multiple recipients in one transaction.
n	Do not insert a "From " line (mailer will do it).
s	Strip quote characters from address.
u	Preserve uppercase in user names.
x	Mailer wants a Full-Name header line.
7	Strip message body to seven bits.

Options S and R (returning to Table 21.14, *Mailer options*) specify the rulesets for rewriting the sender and recipient addresses, respectively. They are specified as either R=*N* in V5 or as R=*envelope*/*header* in V8 and IDA. Each of *N*, *envelope*, and *header* must be a ruleset number.[17]

The E option specifies the end-of-line character(s), usually either \n for a newline or \r\n for a carriage return followed by a newline. The first is used for non-SMTP mailers, and the second for SMTP.

The M option specifies the maximum size of a message in bytes. Zero means that the size should not be limited, which is the default.

A is the argument vector for **sendmail** to use when calling the mailer program. It usually needs to include the host ($@) and user ($:) fields of

---

17. If they are zero, no rewriting is done (ruleset zero is *not* called).

the address-resolution triple from ruleset zero. **sendmail** puts these values into two of its lowercase macro variables: $h for the host and $u for the remote user name.

When these are used in the argument vector, they are expanded just before the mailer is called, not at startup time like other variables that a site might define. As we said before, macros often behave in strange and wonderful ways.

If the mailer speaks SMTP, then $h should be the only parameter in the argument vector. For other remote mailers, both $h and $u are used. The local mailer usually needs only $u. Other parameters may be used in IDA or V8; see the installation guide for details.

Here are some common mailer specifications (these are from V8):

```
Msmtp, P=[IPC], F=mDFMuX, S=11/31, R=21, E=\r\n, A=IPC $h
Mprog, P=/bin/sh, F=lsD, A=sh -c $u
M*file*, P=/dev/null, F=lsDFMPEu, A=FILE
M*include*, P=/dev/null, F=su, A=INCLUDE
```

Let's dissect the first one. It is a specification for a mailer called smtp. The program is listed as [IPC], indicating that **sendmail** itself should deliver the message across the network using SMTP. Mailer flags m, D, F, M, u and X are set; see Table 21.15 for their meanings. The sender's envelope address will be sent to ruleset 11, and the header address will go through ruleset 31. The recipients' addresses are sent to ruleset 21. Lines are terminated with a carriage return followed by a newline. Finally, the argument vector IPC $h means to use SMTP to contact the host in the macro variable $h.

21.5 CONFIGURATION USING THE M4 PREPROCESSOR

Now that we have explored the syntax of the raw configuration file, we will introduce the IDA and V8 changes. Both IDA and V8 have boiled down the configuration process to the selection of just a few lines that enable the features that are appropriate for your site.

We will first describe **m4** very briefly, then move on to V8 and IDA configuration. Finally, we will show example configurations for each system at three distinct sites:

- A small site on the Internet (xor.com)
- A client machine at a larger site (the University of Colorado)
- The hub machine at that same site

V8 and IDA share many features. We describe the two systems separately, but they are then compared and contrasted on page 510 in classic term-paper form.

m4 is a macro preprocessor. It was originally intended as a front end for programming languages that would allow the user to write more readable (or perhaps more cryptic) programs. **m4** is powerful enough to be useful in many input transformation situations, and it works very nicely for **sendmail** configuration files. **m4** macros have the form:

```
name(arg1, arg2, ..., argn)
```

There should be no space between the name and the beginning parenthesis. Left and right single quotes are used to quote strings as arguments. Note that **m4**'s quoting conventions are different from those of other languages you may have used, as left and right quotes are different characters.[18] With today's compiler-building tools, one wonders how **m4** survived with such a rigid and exotic syntax.

m4 has some built-in macros, and users can also define their own. The most common built-in macros used in **sendmail** configuration files are listed in Table 21.16.

Table 21.16   **m4 macros commonly used with sendmail**

Macro	Function
define	Defines a macro named *arg1* with value *arg2*
undefine	Discards a previous definition of macro named *arg1*
include	Includes file named *arg1*
dnl	Discards characters up to and including the next newline[a]
divert	Manages output streams

a. This speeds up **m4** but clutters the config file; our examples omit it.

Both V8 and IDA **sendmail** have defined lots of complicated macros to handle common configuration situations. They have been given uppercase names. V8 requires a version of **m4** that is newer than the original UNIX version 7 code from Bell Labs. The versions of **m4** from System V, BSD releases since Net/2, and GNU are all OK. Under SunOS 4.1.X, you have to use the **m4** in **/usr/5bin**.

21.6 V8 Configuration

sendmail V8 is included on the CD-ROM.

The V8 distribution includes several directories of **m4** snippets. The distribution has a **src** directory that contains the files needed to build the **sendmail** binary and a **cf** directory that contains everything needed to configure it. In the **cf** directory are a **README** file and several subdirectories, listed in Table 21.17 (next page).

18. The quote characters can actually be changed with the changequote macro, but it's better not to tamper with the syntax. You'll just confuse the next person that has to maintain the file.

Table 21.17   V8 configuration directories

Directory	Contents
cf	Sample mc files for hosts at Berkeley (macro files)
domain	Sample m4 files for various domains at Berkeley
feature	Fragments of m4 files to implement various features
hack	Dubious special features
m4	The basic config file and other core files
ostype	OS-dependent file locations and quirks
mailer	m4 files that describe common mailers
sh	makeinfo script to determine user name and hostname
siteconfig	Sample m4 files for specifying UUCP neighbors

The **feature**, **ostype**, **m4** and **mailer** subdirectories contain the definitions of the **m4** macros used in the V8 configuration language. The other subdirectories contain sample files that illustrate common setups.

To build a **sendmail.cf** file for a host, create a file *hostname*.**mc** in the **cf** directory (see page 505 for an example). It will need some boilerplate from the **m4** directory, a few macros from the **feature** directory, an **ostype** file to identify the locations of key files (such as the aliases file), and some mailer definitions. If you are configuring a large site, you can create a file to hold your site-wide defaults in the **domain** directory; individual hosts can then include the contents of this file. Not every host needs a separate config file, but each group of hosts that play the same role (server, client, etc.) will probably need its own configuration.

m4 is used to compile the **mc** file into a real **sendmail.cf**:

```
m4 hostname.mc > hostname.cf
```

V8 does almost all the work for you. Conveniently, the **ostype** directory contains files for about 20 versions of UNIX, including our six example systems. The **ostype** files list the locations of the aliases file, the spool directory, and the statistics file. They also set local mailer flags and any other nonstandard details specific to a particular OS. The file for SunOS 4.1 is empty, since its values are the defaults. Other files are usually five or six lines long.

In the sections below, we will describe some of V8's features, show you how to change the values of options and parameters, and build a simple config file from scratch.

Even if you use V8, you will still have to make several configuration decisions for your site. As you read about the features described below, think about how they might fit into your site's organization. A small site will probably have only a hub node and leaf nodes and thus will need only two versions of the config file. A larger site may need a central hub, some second-level hubs, and leaf nodes.

Whatever the complexity of your site and whatever face it shows to the outside world (exposed, behind a firewall, or behind a UUCP gateway, for example), there are likely to be some appropriate ready-made configuration snippets in the **cf** directory just waiting to be customized and put to work.

The following constructs are presented in somewhat random order.

The define Macro

define is part of the **m4** language. It is used by V8 to reset options and macro variables when the default values are incorrect. The locations of key files and directories needed by **sendmail** can be specified with the define keyword. For example,

```
define(`ALIAS_FILE', `/usr/lib/aliases')
```

See Chapter 18 for more information about NIS.
specifies the location of the system-wide aliases file. This information is usually included in the **ostype** files and should only be defined if you need to override the default for your OS. V8 supports multiple alias files, either to allow both a file and an NIS database, or to facilitate splitting aliases between global and local files. For example,

```
define(`ALIAS_FILE', `/etc/aliases,nis:mail.aliases')
```

would search the file **/etc/aliases** first, and if that failed, would then try the NIS map called **mail.aliases**. The locations of several other items can also be specified:

```
define(`HELP_FILE', `/usr/lib/sendmail.hf')
define(`QUEUE_DIR', `/var/spool/mqueue')
define(`STATUS_FILE', `/usr/lib/sendmail.st')
```

Config file options (the O command) and macros (the D command) can be set via special **m4** macros. An almost complete list of macros and options accessible as **m4** variables is given in the **sendmail** book, in the appendix on V8 configuration. The default values are correct for most sites.

Some examples:

```
define(`confMESSAGE_TIMEOUT', `5d/24h')
define(`confPRIVACY_FLAGS', `noexpn')
```

The message timeout parameter determines how long a message will remain in the mail queue if it cannot be delivered. The default value is 5d/4h, which makes **sendmail** attempt delivery for five days but notify the sender of problems after only four hours.

See page 470 for more information about privacy options.

The first line resets the notification period from four hours to 24 hours in the case of mail that is in the queue but not yet delivered. The next line sets the privacy flags to disallow the SMTP EXPN command. The privacy option takes a comma-separated list of values.

The VERSIONID Macro

RCS and SCCS are revision-control systems. RCS is included on the CD-ROM.

You should maintain your config files with RCS or SCCS, not only so that you can back out to an earlier version but also so that you can identify the versions of the **m4** files that go into making up the config file. Use the VERSIONID macro to embed version information automatically. The syntax for RCS is:

```
VERSIONID(`$Id$')
```

and for SCCS it is:

```
VERSIONID(`%W% (identification) %G%')
```

The actual version information will be filled in by RCS or SCCS as you check in the file. It will appear in the final **sendmail.cf** file as a comment. This can also be useful if you forget where you put the **sendmail** distribution; often the location of files is dictated by available disk space and not by filesystem design logic. In the SCCS form, `%W%` expands to the filename and version and `%G%` to the last modification time. Replace the *identification* token with a string that identifies your site.

The OSTYPE Macro

Files in the **ostype** directory are named after operating systems and can be pulled in using the OSTYPE macro. It is a bit hard to find all the default values, so we have summarized them for you in Table 21.18.

A site with heterogeneous machines must choose between leaving files where vendors put them and using a different **ostype** file for each architecture, or moving everything to site-specific locations and thus having every host's mail defaults be the same regardless of architecture. The second option is appealing from an administrative point of view, but it must be carefully tested to make sure that vendor-supplied commands that touch the mail system will still work.

It's easy to add files to the **ostype** directory: just model the new files on ones that are already there. There are already files for our six reference platforms; these are listed in Table 21.19.

The MASQUERADE_AS Macro

The MASQUERADE_AS macro allows you to specify a single identity that other machines hide behind. All mail appears to emanate from the designated machine or domain. This configuration permits all users at a

Table 21.18   **Default values of V8 macros**

Variable	Default Value
ALIAS_FILE	/etc/aliases
HELP_FILE	/usr/lib/sendmail.hf
STATUS_FILE	/etc/sendmail.st
QUEUE_DIR	/var/spool/mqueue
LOCAL_MAILER_PATH	/bin/mail
LOCAL_MAILER_FLAGS	lsDFM
LOCAL_MAILER_ARGS	mail -d $u
LOCAL_SHELL_PATH	/bin/sh
LOCAL_SHELL_FLAGS	lsDFMeu
LOCAL_SHELL_ARGS	sh -c $u
USENET_MAILER_PATH	/usr/lib/news/inews
USENET_MAILER_FLAGS	rlsDFMmn
USENET_MAILER_ARGS	inews -m -h -n $u
USENET_MAILER_MAX	
SMTP_MAILER_FLAGS	mDFMuX
SMTP_MAILER_MAX	
UUCP_MAILER_PATH	/usr/bin/uux
UUCP_MAILER_FLAGS	mDFMhuU
UUCP_MAILER_SIZE	100000
FAX_MAILER_PATH	/usr/local/lib/fax/mailfax
FAX_MAILER_MAX	100000

Table 21.19   **OSTYPE files for common systems**

System	File	Usage
Solaris	solaris2.m4	OSTYPE(`solaris2')
HP-UX	hpux.m4	OSTYPE(`hpux')
IRIX	irix.m4	OSTYPE(`irix')
SunOS	sunos4.1.m4	OSTYPE(`sunos4.1')
OSF/1	osf1.m4	OSTYPE(`osf1')
BSDI	bsdi1.0.m4	OSTYPE(`bsdi1.0')

site to use a generic email address. For example, user@cs.colorado.edu works for all users in the cs.colorado.edu subdomain. Of course, you must have unique login names across the whole subdomain.

Some users and addresses (such as root, postmaster, hostmaster, trouble, operations, Mailer-Daemon, etc.) should be exempted from this behavior. They can be explicitly excluded with the EXPOSED_USER macro. For example, the sequence

```
MASQUERADE_AS(cs.colorado.edu)
EXPOSED_USER(root)
EXPOSED_USER(postmaster)
```

would stamp all mail as coming from cs.colorado.edu unless it was sent by root or postmaster; in these cases, the mail would carry the name of the true originating host. While this option only rewrites the headers and does not touch the envelope, it has implications for mail that is later replied to. The machine that represents cs.colorado.edu must know how to deliver all users' mail, even mail for users that do not have a login there.

The FEATURE Macro

The FEATURE macro allows you to enable several common options by including **m4** files from the **feature** directory. The syntax is:

    FEATURE(keyword)

where keyword corresponds to a file keyword.**m4**. See the directory itself and the **README** file for a definitive list of features. A few common ones are described below

The use_cw_file feature

The **sendmail** class w contains all the hostnames that are equivalent to a host's canonical name. This class can include nicknames, any X terminals that boot from the host, and perhaps diskless clients of the host, network devices that aren't real UNIX hosts, and the like. The feature use_cw_file defines class w from **/etc/sendmail.cw** (the exact filename is obtained from the confCW_FILE macro). Devices that have names on the network but cannot receive mail should use MX records and the **cw** file to route their mail to a real host.

The redirect feature

When people leave your organization, you usually either forward their mail or let mail to them bounce back to the sender with an error. The redirect feature provides support for a more elegant way of bouncing mail. If Joe Smith has graduated from oldsite.edu to newsite.com, then enabling redirect with

    FEATURE(redirect)

and adding the line

    smithj: joe@newsite.com.REDIRECT

to the aliases file will cause mail to the user smithj to be returned to the sender with an error message which suggests that they try the address joe@newsite.com instead.

The nodns feature

If your site does not use DNS, you must turn on the nodns feature.

The always_add_domain feature

Mail to a local address that is not fully qualified (for example, "evi") is rewritten as evi@*hostname*.cs.colorado.edu when this feature is on. It is appropriate when you share spool directories between machines that do not share an aliases file (which, incidentally, you probably shouldn't do). Mail to an alias that is not known everywhere would be fully qualified on the originating machine and therefore replyable.

For example, suppose anchor and piper in the cs.colorado.edu domain share the same **/var/spool/mail** directory but the alias "pigdog" exists only on piper and not on anchor. Mail to pigdog on anchor would be undeliverable but mail to pigdog on piper would be fine. Users that read mail from the shared mail directory would find that if they read mail on piper everything was fine, but on anchor they could not reply to a message that included a carbon copy to the pigdog alias.

The nullclient feature

This feature is for a host that should never receive mail directly and that sends all outgoing mail to a central server. Including

```
FEATURE(nullclient, server)
```

will route all mail through the specified *server*. The nullclient feature overrides many other features. It is appropriate for leaf nodes at a small site with a central mail machine. At larger sites, the mail load on the hub machine must be considered. You may want to adopt a hierarchical approach.

The notsticky feature

By default, mail to a local user (addressed to user@*localhost*) is expanded with system-wide aliases and **.forward** files, but not the V8 userdb. The notsticky feature makes **sendmail** look in the userdb, too. The original intent was that the userdb would specify a user's maildrop, but many sites are using it to accomplish a full-name to-login-name mapping. These sites should use the notsticky feature.

The MAIL_HUB and SMART_HOST Macros

If you want to forward all mail to a central server for delivery, assign MAIL_HUB the value *mailer:host*, where *mailer* is the agent to use to reach the designated *host*. If no delivery agent is specified, smtp is used. For example:

```
define(`MAIL_HUB', `smtp:mailhub.cs.colorado.edu')
```

The SMART_HOST designation causes a host to deliver local mail, but punt external mail to SMART_HOST. This can be used by UUCP hosts not directly connected to the Internet, or perhaps by machines behind a firewall that cannot use DNS directly. Its syntax parallels MAIL_HUB; the default delivery agent is UUCP. For example:

```
define(`SMART_HOST', `uucp:mailhub.cs.colorado.edu')
```

The LOCAL_* Macros

If you really need to get your hands dirty and write some exotic new rules to deal with special local situations, you use a set of macros prefaced by LOCAL_. For example, to add a rule to ruleset zero:

```
LOCAL_RULE_0
# comment about new rules
R new rule
R another new rule
```

The lines following the LOCAL_RULE_0 macro are placed in ruleset zero just after the boilerplate. A complete list of the LOCAL_ macro names appears in the files **cf/m4/cf.m4** and **cf/m4/proto.m4**, and also in the **sendmail** book.

The MAILER Macro

A MAILER macro must be included for each delivery agent needed in the config file. A complete list of supported mailers can be found in the directory **cf/mailers**. Currently, local, smtp, fax, pop, usenet, and uucp are supported. The syntax is:

```
MAILER(local)
MAILER(smtp)
```

The first line includes the local and prog mailers; the second line includes smtp, esmtp, and relay. uucp includes several flavors of UUCP mailers. POP is the Post Office Protocol defined by RFC1460. It's used by PCs and Macs that need to access mail on a UNIX host.

The usenet mailer provides an email interface to Usenet news. To use it, verify the values of the USENET_MAILER_* macros in the table of defaults on page 493 or in the **ostype** file for your architecture. Send mail to *newsgroup*.USENET to post an article. Some sites add a mailer argument that identifies the local organization. For example,

```
-o "Organization: University of Colorado"
```

added to the USENET_MAILER_ARGS line would add an Organization header to each news article.

flexfax is included on the CD-ROM. The fax mailer integrates Sam Leffler's **flexfax** package into the mail system. Mailing to user@destination.fax will send the body of the message as a fax document. The destination is typically a phone number. To allow symbolic names as destinations (rather than just phone numbers) use a keyed database file or the /etc/remote and /etc/phones files.

flexfax and sendmail must be glued together by installing a script from the flexfax distribution in /usr/local/bin. You must also change the value of the FAX_MAILER_PATH macro if necessary.

ghostscript is included on the CD-ROM.

Human intervention is still needed to deliver incoming faxes from the spool area to a user's mailbox. Fax documents can be converted to Post-Script (by flexfax) and viewed with the GNU package ghostscript. flexfax is available via anonymous ftp from ftp.sgi.com.

Any tuning of mailer-related macros such as USENET_MAILER_ARGS or FAX_MAILER_PATH must precede the line that invokes the mailer itself, or the old values will be used. For this reason, MAILER declarations usually come last in the V8 config file.

The SITE and SITECONFIG Macros

See Chapter 30 for more information about UUCP.

The SITE and SITECONFIG macros are used to specify UUCP neighbors. The growth and commercialization of the Internet have accelerated the demise of UUCP. Well-connected UUCP sites of the past had hundreds of UUCP neighbors; now, they mostly serve as gateways to the Internet for a relatively few UUCP sites.

See Chapter 19 for more information about SLIP.

The paradigm has shifted. Rather than having an extensive UUCP network that parallels the Internet, we have occasional UUCP hosts that connect to the nearest Internet host. Mail from one UUCP host to another typically goes to the Internet via UUCP, across the Internet via SMTP, and then to its destination via UUCP again, often without requiring a long-distance telephone call. Many sites use their modems for SLIP instead of UUCP and become full members of the Internet community.

UUCP diehards use Internet-style addresses and count on sendmail and DNS to do the right thing. V8 sendmail has UUCP support (via the SITECONFIG and SITE macros) that reflects the modern architecture and provides a clean way for a site to organize its UUCP hierarchy.

There are two forms of the SITECONFIG macro. The first is for UUCP hosts that are directly connected, and the second is for UUCP hosts that are connected to another host at your site. For example, if there were UUCP connections to boulder.colorado.edu and anchor.cs.colorado.edu, then anchor would have two SITECONFIG entries: one for its direct UUCP neighbors and one for the remote UUCP neighbors accessible via boulder. There would be a similar set of entries on boulder. Any other host at Colorado would have two remote entries: one pointing to boulder and one to anchor. Other hosts could also use a UUCP_RELAY entry to forward traffic to a smarter machine.

The first form (for direct UUCP connections) is:

```
SITECONFIG(`filename', `uucpname', `class')
```

This line says that the UUCP neighbors of this host (whose UUCP name is *uucpname*) can be found in **cf/siteconfig/***filename***.m4**. The value of *class* should be U.

The contents of *filename*.**m4** are a sequence of SITE designations:

```
SITE(neighbor1)
SITE(neighbor2)
```

The second form is used to specify the UUCP neighbors of other hosts at your site and has the format

```
SITECONFIG(`filename', `otherhost', `class')
```

where *otherhost* is the fully-qualified domain name of the host with direct UUCP connections, **cf/siteconfig/***filename***.m4** is the list of SITE macros for those remote neighbors, and *class* is any class except U, usually W for the first host, X for the next one, Y for the next, and so on. Most sites have very few UUCP hubs (often, zero) and so should not run out of letters.

UUCP mail to one of these hosts would first go via SMTP to *otherhost* and would continue from there via UUCP.

For example, in the anchor/boulder scenario presented above, anchor might have the entries:

```
SITECONFIG(`anchor.uucp', `anchor', `U')
SITECONFIG(`boulder.uucp', `boulder.colorado.edu', `W')
```

boulder's corresponding entries are:

```
SITECONFIG(`boulder.uucp', `boulder', `U')
SITECONFIG(`anchor.uucp', `anchor.cs.colorado.edu', `W')
```

And piper's would be:

```
SITECONFIG(`boulder.uucp', `boulder.colorado.edu', `W')
SITECONFIG(`anchor.uucp', `anchor.cs.colorado.edu', `X')
```

If piper wanted to simply punt to anchor:

```
define(`UUCP_RELAY', `smtp:anchor.cs.colorado.edu')
```

The files **anchor.uucp.m4** and **boulder.uucp.m4** would contain lines such as:

```
SITE(hao)
SITE(nbires)
```

The DOMAIN Macro

The DOMAIN directive allows site-wide generic information to be specified in one place (**cf/domain/**_filename_**.m4**) and then referred to in each host's individual config file with

    DOMAIN(_filename_)

The filename is usually chosen to describe your site; for example, our file for the Computer Science Department is called **cs.m4**. Small sites do not usually need a domain file, but larger sites often use them for references to relay machines (for UUCP or BITNET mail), site-wide privacy options, and references to a user database. Examples of typical entries in the domain file follow.

Relay definitions include the type of relay and an _agent:host_ specification as the second argument. For example,

    define(`UUCP_RELAY', `smtp:csn.org')

would cause all mail that was sent to user@host.UUCP (or rewritten to that form by **sendmail**) to be sent to the host csn.org via the smtp delivery agent. Relays must be defined for the .UUCP and .BITNET pseudo-domains if these addresses are to work properly.

The userdb described on page 476 is usually a site-wide database and is therefore appropriate for inclusion in a domain file. If it was built with

    makemap btree /etc/userdb.db < /usr/local/adm/userdb

then you might add the following line to your _sitename_**.m4** file:

    define(`confUSERDB_SPEC', `/etc/userdb.db')

If you choose to override your vendors' defaults and put the aliases file in the same place on every machine, that place should also be defined in the domain file. For example:

    define(`ALIAS_FILE', `/usr/lib/aliases')

Building a V8 Configuration File

Now that we have described many of V8's ready-made constructs, let's build a no-frills V8 config file for a leaf node, foo.com, which is on the Internet. We will call the **m4** file **foo.mc** and put it in the **cf/cf** subdirectory of the **sendmail** distribution. The compiled configuration file will be called **foo.cf** in that directory and will be installed in either **/etc** or **/usr/lib** as **sendmail.cf**.

Some boilerplate must go in each file. If you have comments in your file, the first line has to be

    divert(-1)

which throws away any spurious garbage on the **m4** output streams. Then come the comments. The next line must be

```
include(`../m4/cf.m4')
```

which brings in the definitions of all the macros we need to use. This path assumes that we are building our host **mc** file in **cf/cf**, where the examples are located in the distribution. We usually move the examples aside and start with an empty **cf** directory to reduce clutter.

A VERSIONID line (here using RCS) completes the boilerplate:

```
VERSIONID(`$Id$')
```

In many cases, specifying the OS type and mailers will complete the configuration:

```
OSTYPE(`sunos4.1')
define(`confCOPY_ERRORS_TO', `postmaster')
MAILER(local)
MAILER(smtp)
```

Here, we also set the option that will send a copy of the headers of any bounced mail to the local postmaster. This allows the postmaster to intervene when the problem is at the local site.

If you change your mind about a configuration line in **foo.mc** and want to comment it out temporarily, you might be tempted to put a # at the beginning of the unwanted line. This does not work. The # is not directed to **sendmail**, but rather to **m4**; unfortunately, **sendmail** V8 disables **m4** comments to gain consistency between different versions of **m4**.

To build the real configuration file, just run the **mc** file through **m4**:

```
m4 foo.mc > foo.cf
```

Then install **foo.cf** in the right spot. The right spot depends on your operating system and is set in the file **conf.h** or **pathnames.h** in the **src** directory of the **sendmail** distribution. There are multiple definitions there controlled with ifdefs, so yours may not be the first occurrence of the string "sendmail.cf".

Complete examples follow the IDA configuration section on page 505.

21.7 IDA CONFIGURATION

IDA is included on the CD-ROM.

Like V8, IDA requires not only IDA-style **m4** configuration files but also a new **sendmail** binary. You can obtain the most recent distribution from uxc.cso.uiuc.edu.

The distribution has a **src** directory where **sendmail** should be built. It also has a **cf** directory of configuration examples and **m4** files. The

`Sendmail.mc` file there is the core of the IDA configuration system. It plays much the same role that `cf.m4` does in V8.

IDA **sendmail** was developed at the Department of Computer and Information Science at the University of Linköping, Sweden. Major IDA innovations were the extensive use of **m4** to simplify the configuration language, separate rewriting rules for the envelope and header, and the introduction of **dbm** databases.

Almost all IDA config file specifications are of the form:

```
define(option, value)
```

often followed by a `dnl` macro (delete to newline) to flush garbage characters. The comments in `Sendmail.mc` provide a complete list of such features. The **OPTIONS** file in the distribution contains a partial list with descriptions. We will discuss only the most popular constructs.

IDA Database Files

IDA includes several **dbm** databases designed to help **sendmail** do the right thing. The basic format of the input is:

```
value key [key] ...
```

To specify a database in the **m4** configuration file, use

```
define(dbname, filename)
```

where `filename` has the format listed above. Database files are usually in LIBDIR (`/usr/lib/mail` by default) and have the same name as the macro, but in lowercase letters. Database definitions correspond to the K option in the raw **sendmail** config file. IDA database names must be a single letter; in V8, they can be strings.

The MAILERTABLE Database

The MAILERTABLE database helps resolve addresses to the appropriate mailer/host pair. Include it with:

```
define(MAILERTABLE, LIBDIR/mailertable)
```

It is used to specify what to do with pseudo-domains such as BITNET and DECnet, or to handle exceptions. Standard rules from **sendmail.mc** can resolve Internet addresses and directly-connected UUCP addresses, but cannot know about local exceptions or quirks. The MAILERTABLE is a convenient way to collect all the local knowledge about which hosts can be reached and how to reach them.

The format of the input is

```
mailer,host    domain
```

where *domain* is a partial or fully-qualified domain; partial domains begin with a dot. Some examples:

```
TCP,vaxf.colorado.edu        .BITNET
TCP,cubldr.colorado.edu      .DECNET
TCP,mroe.cs.colorado.edu     cu-cs.UUCP
```

Mail addressed to user@host.BITNET would be sent to vaxf using the TCP transport agent. The machine vaxf presumably knows how to handle BITNET mail. The separator between the mailer and host can be any of the following characters:

```
,   :   !
```

The comma is used for Internet addresses and the other separators are for UUCP addresses. The host that matches a partial domain, such as .BITNET, is available as %s. The following entry uses that fact to re-route DECnet mail:

```
Dmail,%s                     .DECNET
```

IDA supports DECnet addresses; V8 doesn't. IDA calls the Internet mailer TCP, while V8 calls it smtp. Both use the program designation [IPC].

The DOMAINTABLE Database

DOMAINTABLE is used to fully qualify domain names. **sendmail** and DNS should do this automatically. The DOMAINTABLE may be needed at a site that is partly Internet-connected and partly UUCP-connected.

The GENERICFROM Database

The GENERICFROM table allows login names to be rewritten in the form *firstname_lastname* (or some other version of a user's full name) on the From line of outgoing mail headers. Some mailers include a full name but get it from the GECOS field of the password file. Since users can modify this field, the values there are not always reliable, especially at universities, where this field sometimes becomes a social or political statement.

The GENERICFROM table is usually created automatically from the aliases file. A GENERICFROM database gives you control of the content of headers, at the cost of perpetual maintenance to keep the database file up to date.

Defining GENERICENVELOPE or GENERICTO will apply the mappings to the envelope and to the To and Cc addresses as well. These two options are not commonly used, perhaps because they imply that your user database contains the email address of everyone to whom your local users send mail.

The ALIASES File

The location of the aliases file can be specified by:

```
define(ALIASES, /usr/lib/aliases)
```

If not explicitly defined, the location defaults to LIBDIR/**aliases**.

The ALWAYSADDDOMAIN Macro

To ensure that no mail escapes your site without fully qualified host-names, you can define ALWAYSADDDOMAIN:

```
define(ALWAYSADDDOMAIN)
```

In V8, this behavior is the default.

The PSEUDODOMAINS Macro

PSEUDODOMAINS is used to declare pseudo-domains such as BITNET and UUCP that do not exist in DNS yet need to be handled by the mail system. A declaration such as

```
define(PSEUDODOMAINS, `BITNET UUCP')
```

allows the mail system to accept addresses of the form *host*.UUCP. The MAILERTABLE database tells **sendmail** what to do with them (that is, it tells what host to forward them to and which mailer to use).

The PSEUDONYMS Macro

PSEUDONYMS are additional names by which the local host is known. Pseudonyms can also be other hosts that share your mail spool. You should always include localhost and localhost.*domain* as pseudonyms. Other candidates include nicknames (DNS CNAMEs), the names of associated X terminals, and diskless workstations that boot from you. Values specified via PSEUDONYMS become part of **sendmail** class w.

Old workstations are often converted into X terminals by booting them with a special kernel. Unfortunately, mail addressed to user@oldhost will still exist years after this change is made due to out-of-date aliases and the hard-to-configure behavior of other users.

The UUCPNODES Macro

The UUCPNODES directive can be used to specify your site's direct UUCP neighbors. It is often specified as a pipe:

```
define(UUCPNODES, |uuname|sort  u)
```

This line defines a class variable that will contain the standard output of the command pipeline. It is initialized when **sendmail** starts; therefore, if you add or change an entry in your UUCP neighbors file (**L.sys** or **Systems**), you will have to kill and restart **sendmail** for the change to be seen by the mail system.

IDA **sendmail** has macros for several other UUCP-related features; see the IDA documentation for more details.

The HIDDENNET and HIDDENNETHOST Macros

For reasons of security and convenience, sites often make it appear that all mail originates from a fixed site-wide address. A HIDDENNET clause defines a class containing hosts that should hide behind the host listed as the HIDDENNETHOST. At some sites, the designated host is called mail.*domain* or just *domain*.

```
define(HIDDENNET, hosts-to-hide)
define(HIDDENNETHOST, visible-host)
```

The *hosts-to-hide* may be listed explicitly (separated with blanks), read from a file (if the value begins with a slash), or obtained from the output of a program (if the value begins with a "|").

For example, at the University of Colorado, everyone in the Computer Science Department can receive mail as user@cs.colorado.edu. Mail is forwarded to an appropriate local host via the global aliases file.

Only message headers are affected, never envelopes. To hide your entire DNS domain behind a host, use the directives HIDDENDOMAINHOST and HIDDENDOMAIN instead of the HIDDENNET versions.

The LOADAVEQUEUE and LOADAVEREJ Macros

The load averages at which to queue or refuse mail default to 7 and 11, respectively. To set new values, use

```
define(LOADAVEQUEUE, new-value)
define(LOADAVEREJ, new-value)
```

Setting either value to zero disables the feature; normal delivery will be attempted at all load averages. This is bad.

The TIMEOUT Macro

The length of time that a message may remain in the queue is specified with the TIMEOUT variable; the default is two days. Values are expressed with units of days, hours, or minutes using the suffixes d, h, and m. For example,

```
define(TIMEOUT, 5d)
```

resets the timeout to five days.

The RELAY_HOST and RELAY_MAILER Macros

When **sendmail** cannot deliver mail, perhaps because its config file is not smart enough, or because an essential service like DNS is not available, it will use RELAY_MAILER to forward the mail to RELAY_HOST, if both variables are defined. The RELAY_HOST should have an extensive mailer table and should be able to handle most mail.

The SPOOLDIR Macro

The SPOOLDIR macro specifies the location of the directory where mail is queued pending delivery. It defaults to **/usr/spool/mqueue**.

Building an IDA Configuration File

An IDA configuration file is as simple as a V8 file. The boilerplate is the file **Sendmail.mc**, which must be included as the last item in your **m4** input file. Mailers do not have to be explicitly included. Macros exist for most built-in **sendmail** parameters you might want to override. As with V8, you must compile your IDA config file with **m4** to produce a full-fledged **sendmail.cf**.

21.8 CONFIGURATION FILE EXAMPLES

As our first example, we will look at the V8 and IDA configuration files for a small company, xor.com, that is directly connected to the Internet. The sample files are not one-for-one compatible, but they try to accomplish roughly the same ends. In particular, the privacy options of V8 are not available in IDA.

The host xor.com is the gateway to the Internet, and all other hosts on XOR's network will hide behind this host (all outgoing mail will be stamped as being from xor.com). There are no UUCP connections.

V8 Configuration for a Small Site

The V8 configuration file for xor.com is listed below. XOR's configuration file is called **xor.com.mc**. It contains:

```
divert(-1)

# V8 configuration file for xor.com
# sendmail 8.6.9, trent, may, 1994

include(`../m4/cf.m4')
VERSIONID(`$Id$')
OSTYPE(`sunos4.1')
define(`confPRIVACY_FLAGS', `noexpn')
define(`confMESSAGE_TIMEOUT', `5d/72h')
FEATURE(use_cw_file)
```

```
MASQUERADE_AS(xor.com)
EXPOSED_USER(`root postmaster hostmaster')
MAILER(local)
MAILER(smtp)
```

See Chapter 19 for more information about SLIP. **/etc/sendmail.cw** contains a list of hostnames that must be mapped to the name xor.com. Some are aliases, and some are domains without any actual hosts that want to receive mail under their own names. The notification time on undeliverable mail has been extended to three days because XOR has part-time SLIP hosts that might go away for the weekend and not connect to download their mail.

IDA Configuration for a Small Site

The IDA configuration for xor.com follows:

```
# IDA configuration file for xor.com
# sendmail 5.67b+IDA, trent, jan, 1993

define(DEFAULT_HOST, xor.com)
define(FORCE_NAMED)
define(TIMEOUT, 5d)
define(PSEUDONYMS, chimchim.xor.com xor.com xor localhost)
include(Sendmail.mc)
```

DEFAULT_HOST is used instead of HIDDEN_HOSTS to map the name of the main server, chimchim.xor.com, to the domain name xor.com. The hosts listed in the PSEUDONYMS line would be in the **sendmail.cw** file in the corresponding V8 configuration.

Our next example is for a client host at a larger site. For V8 configuration, two files are used. Domain-wide aspects of the configuration are set in *domain*.**m4**, and host-specific details are set in *host*.**mc**.

V8 Configuration for a Larger Site

The file **cs.m4**, below, contains the common definitions for the entire cs.colorado.edu domain. The userdb specification lists Hesiod, a database service built on top of DNS, that is used here to map login names to full names for message headers. The headers from all bounced mail are routed to the postmaster as well as being returned to the sender.

```
divert(-1)

# Use RCS or your changes will disappear.
# Sendmail 8.x domain file, cs.m4 for CS Dept machines.
# Used with an ostype file to set default locations.

divert(0)
VERSIONID(`$Id$')
define(`UUCP_RELAY', `boulder.colorado.edu')
```

```
define(`BITNET_RELAY', `rutgers.edu')
define(`confUSERDB_SPEC', `hesiod')[19]
define(`confCOPY_ERRORS_TO', `postmaster')
FEATURE(always_add_domain)
FEATURE(redirect)
```

This domain file is used with a specific file for each type of host: client, server, or master. The client file is quite simple, since only the OS type might change from host to host:

```
divert(-1)

# Use RCS or your changes will disappear.
# Client Sendmail 8 configuration file for cs machines
# Many default values set in ../domain/cs.m4

include(`../m4/cf.m4')

VERSIONID(`$Id$')
DOMAIN(cs)
OSTYPE(bsd4.4)
MAILER(local)
MAILER(smtp)
MAILER(usenet)
```

The server hides its clients (with an MX record), many of which might be machines that were real in a former life but were later converted to be X terminals and are no longer capable of receiving mail. This is accomplished with the use_cw_file feature. The server's configuration:

```
divert(-1)

# Use RCS or your changes will disappear.
# Server Sendmail 8 configuration file for cs machines
# Many default values set in ../domain/cs.m4

include(`../m4/cf.m4')

VERSIONID(`$Id$')
DOMAIN(cs)
OSTYPE(sunos4.1)
FEATURE(use_cw_file)
MAILER(local)
MAILER(smtp)
MAILER(usenet)
```

The following configuration, for the master mail hub machine, increases some of the limits and uses a domain table to fix up any unqualified names that slip through.

---

19. The word hesiod here where a filename is expected is understood by **sendmail**, which will call Hesiod search primitives to access the userdb.

```
divert(-1)

# Use RCS or your changes will disappear.
# Master Sendmail 8 configuration file for cs machines
# Many default values set in ../domain/cs.m4

include(`../m4/cf.m4')
VERSIONID(`$Id$')
DOMAIN(cs)
OSTYPE(hpux)
MAILER(local)
MAILER(smtp)
MAILER(usenet)
MAILER(fax)

# increase limits
define(`confQUEUE_LA', `15')
define(`confREFUSE_LA', `30')
define(`confMESSAGE_TIMEOUT', `7d/24h')
define(`MCI_CACHE_SIZE', 3)
FEATURE(use_cw_file)
FEATURE(domaintable)
```

IDA Configuration for a Larger Site

Here is the IDA configuration for a client:

```
# Sendmail configuration file for anchor's clients
define(ALIASES, /etc/aliases)
define(ALWAYSADDDOMAIN)
define(FORCE_NAMED)
define(HIDDENNET, $w)
define(HIDDENNETHOST, anchor.cs.colorado.edu)
define(RELAY_HOST, mailhub.cs.colorado.edu)
define(RELAY_MAILER, TCPMAILER)
include(Sendmail.mc)
```

The IDA configuration for the cluster server contains a PSEUDONYMS entry for each of its clients; we have truncated the list here.

```
# Sendmail configuration file for cluster masters
define(ALIASES, /etc/aliases)
define(ALWAYSADDDOMAIN)
define(FORCE_NAMED)
define(HIDDENNET, $w)
define(HIDDENNETHOST, anchor.cs.colorado.edu)
define(PSEUDONYMS, anchor.colorado.edu
    bass.cs.colorado.edu becks.cs.colorado.edu
    xx.cs.colorado.edu ... )
define(RELAY_HOST, mailhub.cs.colorado.edu)
define(RELAY_MAILER, TCPMAILER)
include(Sendmail.mc)
```

And finally, the IDA configuration for the mail master machine. This machine has UUCP connections and serves as the relay host for others in the domain.

```
# Config file for mail/uucp-hub machine, UUCP name cu-cs

define(ALIASES, /etc/aliases)
define(ALWAYSADDDOMAIN)
define(HIDDENDOMAIN, cs.colorado.edu)
define(FORCE_NAMED)
define(LOADAVEQUEUE,15)
define(LOADAVEREJ,30)
define(TIMEOUT, 7d)
define(TRUSTEDUSERS, infosrv)
define(PSEUDODOMAINS, bitnet uucp)
define(PSEUDONYMS, cs.colorado.edu cs.cs.colorado.edu
    mroe.cs.colorado.edu trouble.cs.colorado.edu
    cu-cs.cs.colorado.edu uucp.cs.colorado.edu ...)
define(ALTERNATENAMES, mcbryan.cs.colorado.edu)[20]
define(UUCPNAME, cu-cs)
define(UUCPNODES, |uuname|sort|uniq -u)

####### Define dbm lookup tables
define(DOMAINTABLE, LIBDIR/domaintable)
define(PATHTABLE, LIBDIR/pathtable)
define(GENERICFROM, LIBDIR/generics)
define(MAILERTABLE, LIBDIR/mailertable)
define(UUCPXTABLE, LIBDIR/uucpxtable)

####### Deliver mail to localhost!user to ourself
CU$k
Cw$k.UUCP

####### Can't do anything without this:
include(Sendmail.mc)
```

The cryptic lines CU$k and Cw$k.UUCP are **sendmail** config commands that will not be touched by the **m4** preprocessor. $k is the UUCP name of the local host. These lines add that name to the classes U and w.

21.9 A Comparison of V8 and IDA

IDA initially simplified **sendmail** configuration for the easy cases. V8 extended its ideas to cover some of the exceptional situations as well. IDA was born in a UUCP world; V8 assumes that the Internet is the default environment.

20. ALTERNATENAMES is a variation of PSEUDONYMS. Mail to a pseudonym is delivered to the local host, but mail to an alternate name is looked up in the local host's mailer table for further delivery through another transport agent. At the time that this file was in use, mcbryan.cs.colorado.edu was connected by a UUCP link.

Not all directives have exact counterparts in the two systems. The correspondences between some selected V8 and IDA macros are illustrated in Table 21.20. Sometimes a command in one dialect corresponds to two or more commands in the other dialect. The divisions in Table 21.20 indicate logical groupings. Shaded groups are equivalent to one another; the individual commands within them are not.

Table 21.20 Comparison of V8 and IDA

V8	IDA
`define(ALIAS_FILE, `*`filename`*`)`	`define(ALIASES, `*`filename`*`)`
`define(QUEUE_DIR, `*`filename`*`)`	`define(SPOOLDIR, `*`filename`*`)`
`define(confMESSAGE_TIMEOUT, 5d/4h)`	`define(TIMEOUT, 5d)`
`define(confQUEUE_LA, 15)`	`define(LOADAVEQUEUE, 15)`
`define(confREFUSE_LA, 30)`	`define(LOADAVEREJ, 30)`
`define(confCOPY_ERRORS_TO, postmaster)`	`define(POSTMASTERBOUNCE)`
`FEATURE(use_cw_file)`	`define(PSEUDONYMS, `*`host1`*`,...)`
`define(confUSERDB_SPEC, `*`filename`*`)`	`define(GENERICFROM, `*`filename`*`)`
`MASQUERADE_AS(`*`server`*`)`	`define(HIDDENNET, `*`hostnames`*`)`
`EXPOSED_USER(root)`	`define(HIDDENNETHOST, `*`server`*`)`
`EXPOSED_USER(postmaster)`	`define(HIDDENDOMAIN, `*`domain`*`)`
`FEATURE(mailertable)`	`define(MAILERTABLE, `*`filename`*`)`
`define(BITNET_RELAY, `*`mailer`*`:`*`host`*`)`	`define(PSEUDODOMAINS, BITNET)`[a]
`define(UUCP_RELAY, `*`mailer`*`:`*`host`*`)`	`define(PSEUDODOMAINS, UUCP)`[a]
`SITECONFIG(`*`uucp-file`*`, `*`myname`*`, U)`	`define(UUCPNODES, neighbors)`
`SITE(`*`neighbor`*`) (in `*`uucp-file`*`)`	
`define(SMART_HOST, `*`mailer`*`:`*`host`*`)`	`define(RELAY_HOST, `*`hostname`*`)`
`define(MAIL_HUB, `*`mailer`*`:`*`host`*`)`	`define(RELAY_MAILER, `*`mailer`*`)`

a. Use with `MAILERTABLE`.

21.10 MAILER STATISTICS

sendmail can collect statistics on the number and size of messages it has handled. The data are organized by mailer and displayed with the **mailstats** command. **sendmail**'s S option specifies the name of the file in which statistics should be kept; its presence in the config file and the existence of the specified file turn on the accounting function.

The default location for the statistics file is **/etc/sendmail.st**, but many sites move it to **/var/adm** or **/var/mail**. The data are cumulative since the creation of the statistics file. If you want periodic statistics, you could periodically rotate and reinitialize the file from **cron**.

Four values are recorded: messages and bytes received (labeled `msgsfr` and `bytes_from`), and messages and bytes sent (`msgsto`, `bytes_to`). These values include both local and off-site mail.

For example:

```
Statistics from Wed Mar 2 10:42:12 1994

M   msgsfr  bytes_from   msgsto  bytes_to  Mailer
0      0           0K      460       466K  prog
1      0           0K     1393      6097K  *file*
3   6141       20835K       13        14K  local
4  85520      492560K   174490    827112K  smtp
6      7          45K       79       274K  relay
7      0           0K        6        12K  uucp
=========================================
T  91668      513440K   176441    833975K
```

21.11 TESTING AND DEBUGGING

V8 and IDA configurations are to some extent pre-tested, and you probably won't need to do low-level debugging if you use them. However, a complicated environment may sometimes need a custom configuration.

sendmail provides one of the richest sets of debugging aids known to UNIX, with debug flags that are not simple Booleans or even integers but two-dimensional quantities $x.y$, where x chooses the topic and y chooses the amount of information to display. 0 gives no debugging, and 127 wastes many trees if you print the output. Topics range from 0 to 99; currently, 60 are defined.

If **sendmail** is invoked with a **-d**$x.y$ flag, debugging output comes to the screen (standard error). Several important values of x and some Eric-suggested values for y are shown in Table 21.21.

Table 21.21 Debugging topics

Topic	Meaning and Suggestions
8	Show DNS name resolution (try y=7).
11	Trace delivery (shows mailer invocations).
12	Show local-to-remote name translation.
17	List MX hosts.
21	Trace rewriting rules. Use y=2 or y=12 for more detail
27	Show aliasing and forwarding (try y=4).
60	Show database map lookups.

checksendmail is included on the CD-ROM.

Rob Kolstad has written a **perl** script called **checksendmail** that invokes **sendmail** in address test mode on a file of test addresses that you supply. It compares the results to those expected. This script lets you build a test suite of your site's typical addresses and test new versions of the configuration file to be sure you haven't inadvertently broken anything that used to work.

Testing Rewriting Rules

sendmail can be run in test mode, in which only address rewriting is shown; no delivery of mail is actually performed. The command

```
sendmail -bt -Cnew-config
```

will use the file ./new-config instead of the normal configuration file. In this mode, you enter the rulesets you want to test followed by an address. For example:

```
3,0 evi@cs
```

In real life, ruleset three is always applied first. V5 sendmail always includes it in test mode, even if you don't request it. To see where the message is really going, use ruleset zero, which determines the address on the envelope. To see the exact effect of a single rule, run sendmail in test mode with debugging enabled. Two transcripts follow, one without debugging and then a fragment with debugging.

```
% sendmail -bt
ADDRESS TEST MODE (ruleset 3 NOT automatically invoked)
Enter <ruleset> <address>
> 3,0 evi@eclipse
rewrite: ruleset  3    input: evi @ eclipse
rewrite: ruleset 96    input: evi < @ eclipse >
rewrite: ruleset 96 returns: evi < @ eclipse . cs .
   colorado . edu . >
rewrite: ruleset  3 returns: evi < @ eclipse . cs .
   colorado . edu . >
rewrite: ruleset  0    input: evi < @ eclipse . cs .
   colorado . edu . >
rewrite: ruleset 98    input: evi < @ eclipse . cs .
   colorado . edu . >
rewrite: ruleset 98 returns: evi < @ eclipse . cs .
   colorado . edu . >
rewrite: ruleset  0 returns: $# local $: evi
```

Ruleset three focuses on the destination host, enclosing it in angle brackets. It then calls ruleset 96 to get that host's canonical name from DNS. Finally, ruleset zero calls ruleset 98 (empty in our configuration) and then resolves to the local mailer with user name evi. We ran this session on eclipse, so the local mailer is appropriate.

Trying the remote address eric@okeeffe.berkeley.edu with debugging turned on, we get:

```
# sendmail -bt -d21.6
ADDRESS TEST MODE (ruleset 3 NOT automatically invoked)
Enter <ruleset> <address>
> 3,0 eric@okeeffe.berkeley.edu
```

```
rewrite: ruleset  3   input: eric @ okeeffe . berkeley .
   edu
rewritten as: eric < @ okeeffe . berkeley . edu >
-----callsubr 96
rewrite: ruleset 96   input: eric < @ okeeffe . berkeley
   . edu >
rewritten as: eric < @ vangogh . CS . Berkeley . EDU . >
rewritten as: eric < @ vangogh . CS . Berkeley . EDU . . >
rewritten as: eric < @ vangogh . CS . Berkeley . EDU . >
rewrite: ruleset 96 returns: eric < @ vangogh . CS .
   Berkeley . EDU . >
rewritten as: eric < @ vangogh . CS . Berkeley . EDU . >
rewrite: ruleset  3 returns: eric < @ vangogh . CS .
   Berkeley . EDU . >
rewrite: ruleset  0   input: eric < @ vangogh . CS .
   Berkeley . EDU . >
-----callsubr 98
rewrite: ruleset 98   input: eric < @ vangogh . CS .
   Berkeley . EDU . >
rewrite: ruleset 98 returns: eric < @ vangogh . CS .
   Berkeley . EDU . >
rewritten as: eric < @ vangogh . CS . Berkeley . EDU . >
-----callsubr 95
rewrite: ruleset 95   input: < > eric < @ vangogh . CS .
   Berkeley . EDU . >
rewritten as: eric < @ vangogh . CS . Berkeley . EDU . >
rewrite: ruleset 95 returns: eric < @ vangogh . CS .
   Berkeley . EDU . >
rewritten as: eric < @ vangogh . CS . Berkeley . EDU . >
rewritten as: $# smtp $@ vangogh . CS . Berkeley . EDU .
   $: eric < @ vangogh . CS . Berkeley . EDU . >
rewrite: ruleset  0 returns: $# smtp $@ vangogh . CS .
   Berkeley . EDU . $: eric < @ vangogh . CS . Berkeley .
   EDU . >
```

See Chapter 16 for more information about DNS.

Our address was okeeffe.berkeley.edu, but **sendmail** intends to send it to vangogh.cs.berkeley.edu. What happened? A quick check of DNS with the **nslookup** command shows:

```
Non-authoritative answer:
Name:     vangogh.CS.Berkeley.EDU
Address:  128.32.130.2
Aliases:  okeeffe.berkeley.edu
```

okeeffe has retired, and "okeeffe" is now a CNAME record for vangogh.

Verbose Delivery

mail can be run with the **-v** flag, causing it to display the steps taken by **sendmail** to deliver the message.

`mail -v` output looks like this:

```
lair> mail -v eric@chez.berkeley.edu
Subject: just testing, please ignore
hi
.
Cc:
eric@chez.berkeley.edu... Connecting to mailhost (ether)..
220-anchor.cs.colorado.edu Sendmail 8.6.9/8.6.9/CSops
    ready at Sun, 29 May 1994 20:06:32 -0600
220 ESMTP spoken here
>>> HELO lair.cs.colorado.edu
250 anchor.cs.colorado.edu Hello lair.cs.colorado.edu
    [128.138.198.19], pleased to meet you
>>> MAIL From:<evi@lair>
250 <evi@lair>... Sender ok
>>> RCPT To:<eric@chez.berkeley.edu>
250 <eric@chez.berkeley.edu>... Recipient ok
>>> DATA
354 Enter mail, end with "." on a line by itself
>>> .
250 UAA20699 Message accepted for delivery
>>> QUIT
221 anchor.cs.colorado.edu closing connection
eric@chez.berkeley.edu... Sent
```

The **sendmail** on lair connected to the **sendmail** on anchor, which connected to chez.berkeley.edu. Each machine talked the SMTP protocol to negotiate the exchange of the message.

Talking in SMTP

You can make direct use of SMTP (Simple Mail Transport Protocol) when debugging the mail system. To initiate an SMTP session, **telnet** to TCP port 25. This is the port on which **sendmail** listens when run in daemon (**-bd**) mode. Some SMTP commands are shown in Table 21.22.

There are only 14 commands in the whole language, so it is quite easy to learn and use. It is not case sensitive. The complete specification for SMTP is included in RFC821 (also, see RFC1123). RFC1425 extends SMTP to ESMTP; **sendmail** V8 and HP's version of **sendmail** are trendily bisexual and speak both SMTP and ESMTP.

Logging

See Chapter 12 for more information about syslog.

sendmail uses **syslog** to submit error and status messages. **syslog** labels its severity levels from "debug" (the lowest) to "emerg" (the highest). **sendmail** uses facility "mail" and levels "debug" through "crit"; messages are tagged with the string "sendmail".

Table 21.22   SMTP commands

Command	Function
HELO *hostname*	Identifies the connecting host.
MAIL From: *revpath*	Initiates a mail transaction (envelope sender)
RCPT To: *fwdpath*[a]	Identifies envelope recipients
VRFY *address*	Verifies that *address* is valid (deliverable)
EXPN *address*	Expands aliases and .forward mappings
DATA	Begins the message body[b]
QUIT	Ends the exchange and closes the connection
RSET	Resets the state of the connection
HELP	Prints a summary of SMTP commands

a. There may be multiple RCPT commands for a message.
b. The body is terminated by entering a dot on its own line.

The L option, specified on the command line or in the config file, determines the severity level that **sendmail** will use as a threshold for logging. High values of L imply low severity levels and cause more information to be logged. An approximate mapping between L values and **syslog** severity levels is given in Table 21.23.

Table 21.23   Relationship between option L and syslog levels

L	Levels	L	Levels
0	No logging	3,4	notice
1	alert or crit	5-10	info
2	crit (V8) notice (V5, IDA)	>=11	debug

V5 and IDA log some events at level notice and do not use L = 7, 8, or 10. Recall that a message logged to **syslog** at a particular level is reported to that level and all those above it. The /etc/syslog.conf file determines the eventual destination of each message.

21.12 SECURITY AND PRIVACY

sendmail has long had a reputation for creating security loopholes. The worm that stormed the Internet in November, 1988 attempted (successfully, in many cases) to exploit weaknesses in **sendmail**, although it used other break-in methods as well. Known security problems have been fixed in current **sendmail** releases from Berkeley, but many vendors' UNIX products still use older, uncorrected versions. It is important for you to keep up to date with new **sendmail** releases.

Forgeries can easily be accomplished by speaking SMTP to **sendmail**. A student at our site was recently frustrated with the members of his senior project team. He tried to send mail to his teammates as his instructor, telling them he knew that they were not pulling their weight and that they should work harder. Unfortunately, he made a syntax error and the message bounced to the instructor. **sendmail** V8's use of the RFC1413 IDENT protocol told us who he was. Moral: avoid syntax errors when sneaking around.

It is possible to impersonate any user in mail messages. Be careful if mail messages are your organization's authorization vehicle for things like keys, access cards, and money. You should warn administrative users of this fact and suggest that if they see suspicious mail that appears to come from a person in authority, they should verify the validity of the message. This is doubly true if the message asks that unreasonable privileges be given to an unusual person. Mail authorizing a grand master key for an undergraduate might be suspect!

sendmail V8 has made a modest attempt to improve security and privacy. During an SMTP session, it is possible to require a HELO exchange in which the caller is identified by the callee before the next step of the protocol exchange is taken. You can configure **sendmail** so that the EXPN command is disabled, and can also restrict use of the **mailq** command to certain users.

identd is included on the CD-ROM.

V8 uses the IDENT protocol. It does a callback to the sending host to ask the **identd** running there for the login name of the user sending the mail. If **identd** is not running on the remote host, nothing is learned. If the remote machine is a single-user workstation, its owner could configure **identd** to return anything. But if the remote host is a large, multiuser machine such as that found at many university computing centers, then **identd** will return the user's real login name for **sendmail** to put in the message's header. In the case of the student mentioned above, **sendmail** V8 included the following lines in the bounced message:

```
The original message was received at Wed, 9 Mar 1994 14:51
-0700 from student@benji.Colorado.EDU [128.138.126.10]
```

But the headers of the message itself told a different story:

```
From: instructor@cs.Colorado.EDU
```

In addition, **sendmail** V8 has tightened up its actions when processing **.forward** files and **aliases** entries that send mail to a program. It runs as the "controlling user" (the recipient) when following **.forward** files, and acts as the file owner when going through an :include:. The controlling user must have proper permissions through the directory hierarchy, rather than just relying on **sendmail**'s ability (when running as root) to read any file.

Two other systems are available to enhance the privacy of email: PEM, Privacy Enhanced Mail, and PGP, Pretty Good Privacy. PGP is more or less a home-brew system, while PEM is a standards-track system described in RFCs 1421 through 1424.

These emerging standards offer a basis for email confidentiality, authentication, message integrity assurance, and non-repudiation of origin. PEM is designed to work independently of the transport agent and within the context of the RFC822 message format. As a result, PEM messages can be carried by regular transports such as `sendmail` and then decoded at the receiving end. At this point, PEM is mostly experimental. If you'd like to join the PEM developer's mailing list, send mail to the address pem-dev-request@tis.com.

PGP was developed by Philip Zimmermann of Boulder, Colorado as a poor man's encryption package. It was made available on the Internet with instructions that stated the US export policy for encryption-related software and asked that it be copied only within the United States. His request was followed for about five minutes.

At the time of this writing, Philip Zimmermann has been under criminal investigation for two years, but has not yet been indicted. The case is currently at the federal grand jury level, and the cost of Philip's legal defense is skyrocketing.

PGP is available from MIT's `ftp` site at net-dist.mit.edu for US distribution only. Look in the directory `pub/PGP`. For a commercial version of PGP, contact ViaCrypt in Phoenix, Arizona (1-602-944-0773).

21.13 RECOMMENDED SUPPLEMENTAL READING

Here are some other sources of information you may find useful:

> COSTALES, BRYAN, with ERIC ALLMAN AND NEIL RICKERT. *sendmail*. O'Reilly, 1993.

Bryan Costales' book is the definitive tome—800 pages' worth. It includes a tutorial as well as a very complete reference section. The book reads well in the open-to-a-random-page mode, which we consider an important feature for a reference book.

> AVOLIO, FREDERICK M. and PAUL A. VIXIE. *Sendmail Theory and Practice*. Digital Press, 1995.

From a preprint of this book, we got the impression that it addresses the "why and how" of `sendmail`, while the Costales book talks more about the "what." This 250-pager takes a high-level approach, with the apparent goal of transforming folks who are afraid of `sendmail` into fearless, `sendmail`-hacking drones. If you have to integrate DECnet and UNIX mail systems, this book has very complete coverage of the problems you will encounter and their solutions.

The man page for **sendmail** describes its command-line arguments. An overview can be found in *Sendmail: An Internetwork Mail Router*, by Eric Allman.

Installation instructions and a good description of the configuration file are covered in *Sendmail Installation and Operation Guide* (also by Eric Allman), which can be found in the **doc** subdirectory of the **sendmail** version 8 distribution. This document is quite complete and has a nice section on the differences between versions 5 and 8.

Changes in Sendmail Version 8 (also in the **doc** directory) focuses on the transition from V5 to V8. If you are considering upgrading to V8, this paper is a good starting point for testing the waters. Each of these documents is included on the CD-ROM.

Electronic Mail Addressing in Theory and Practice (aka *The Postmaster's Last Will and Testament*) by Lennart Lövstrand was first published on Usenet in 1987. It also appeared as a technical report from the University of Linköping, Sweden. It is the definitive reference for IDA.

RFC822 describes the syntax of messages and addresses in a networked mail system, and RFC1123 describes host requirements. These are in a sense the functional specifications to which **sendmail** was built.

RFC821 defines SMTP (Simple Mail Transport Protocol), the protocol that **sendmail** speaks, and RFC1425 extends it to ESMTP. RFC974 describes MX records in the Domain Name System and their relationship to mail routing. All of these RFCs are included on the CD-ROM; they can also be obtained via **ftp** from ds.internic.net.

 22 *Network Management*

22.1 INTRODUCTION

Because networks increase the number of interdependencies among machines, they tend to magnify problems. As the saying goes, "Networking is when you can't get any work done because of the failure of a machine you have never even heard of."

Network management is the art and science of preventing network meltdowns. It generally includes the following tasks:

- Fault detection for networks, gateways, and critical servers
- Schemes for notifying an administrator of problems
- General monitoring, used to balance load and plan expansion
- Documentation and visualization of the network
- Administration of network devices from a central site

On a single Ethernet, it is generally not worthwhile to establish formal procedures for network management. Just be sure to test the network thoroughly after installation, and check it occasionally to be sure that its load is not excessive. When it breaks, fix it.

As your network grows, management procedures should become more systematized. On a network consisting of several different cables joined with bridges or routers, you may want to start automating management tasks with shell scripts. If you have a WAN or a complex local network, you should consider buying dedicated network management stations with special software.

In some cases, the sophistication of your network management system will be dictated by your organization's need for reliability. At many sites, a problem with the net brings all work to a standstill. It may be cheaper to install an expensive network management system than to experience even an hour of down time.

22.2 DETECTING NETWORK FAULTS

Networks tend to exist in one of three basic states: working, broken, and working but with a high error rate or high latency. Complete breakdowns often occur when a gateway or router crashes, when a user connects something to the network incorrectly, or when an inaccurate IP route is installed.

Partial breakdowns are often electrical in nature. Bad terminators or cables, confused network interfaces, and ill-fitting connections can all result in intermittent problems. Another source of partial breakdowns is excessive traffic. Gateways can overload and start to drop packets, and even individual cables can become saturated and error-prone.

Fault detection is perhaps the most important feature of a management system. Luckily, it is also one of the easiest features to implement on your own. Advanced systems can also help to characterize faults; for example, in addition to telling you that a certain network has become unreachable, a good system might also tell you that the router that provides access to that network has crashed.

Checking Connectivity with ping

See page 273 for more information about ping.

The lowly **ping** command is the foundation of many sites' fault detection systems. It's embarrassingly simple, but in many situations it is all you need. Despite what vendors may tell you, a network management system need not be complex, obscure, and expensive.

ping uses the low-level ICMP "echo request" facility to send a packet on a round trip from one machine to another. The packet is routed using the usual IP mechanisms, and a successful round trip indicates that all networks and gateways lying between the source and destination are working "correctly," at least to a first approximation.

A series of pings can also provide an estimate of the reliability of the network. Echo request packets are not reliably delivered, so intermittent faults will often cause some packets to be dropped. The ratio of successful round trips to packets sent is a good indication of how well the network is performing.

ping can be used to check the status of individual hosts as well as segments of the network. Even if the network is completely operational, the death of a server can send clients into an unusable state.

However, there are some caveats. First, it is hard to distinguish between the failure of a network and the failure of a server using only the `ping` command. A failed ping just tells you that *something* is wrong.

Second, a ping does not guarantee much about the target machine's state. The kernel responds to pings at a very low level. A successful ping means only that the target machine is powered on and has not experienced a kernel panic. Higher-level methods must be used to verify the availability of services such as NFS and DNS.

Following Up on a Failed Ping

Suppose that a ping fails, indicating that something is amiss on the network. What do you do next? You can usually find out more information without too much trouble.

See page 278 for more information about traceroute.

First, use the `traceroute` command to find out exactly what's happening to the packets you send. You may find from `traceroute` that your packets are being misrouted. Or, you may discover that an intermediate network is simply dropping them, most likely indicating that a gateway is down. You might also find that packets cannot be delivered beyond the last gateway: either there is a problem on the destination network, or the target host is down.

Let's look at a couple of examples:

```
% traceroute piper
traceroute to piper (128.138.204.4), 38 byte packets
  1   netblazer (128.138.243.113)  216 ms   201 ms   199 ms
  2   engr-gw-cr (128.138.243.120)  !N  !N  !N
```

The !N notation indicates "network unreachable." In this case, it means that the host engr-gw-cr (actually, it is a dedicated router) has no idea how to get to the 128.138.204 subnet where piper lives. The problem is with the routing table on engr-gw-cr; either the static routes are wrong, or dynamic protocols have failed to propagate a route to the target net.

```
% traceroute dynamo.bio.colorado.edu
traceroute to dynamo.bio.colorado.edu (192.52.106.1)
  1   engr-gw-cr (128.138.243.120) 3 ms 8 ms 2 ms
  2   cu-gw.Colorado.EDU (128.138.138.1) 9 ms 16 ms 17 ms
  3   biogate.bio.Colorado.EDU (192.51.2.1) 42 ms 33 ms 35 ms
  4   ot-gw.bio.Colorado.EDU (192.100.8.1) 50 ms
      labring.bio.Colorado.EDU (203.180.23.5) !N !N
  5   dynamo.bio.Colorado.EDU (192.52.106.1) 42 ms !N 61 ms
```

In this example, biogate is multiplexing traffic for the 192.52.106 network through both ot-gw and labring. The labring gateway has a routing problem similar to engr-gw-cr in the previous example, while the packets traveling through ot-gw are forwarded correctly. The result is that some packets get through to dynamo while others do not.

A star ("*") in `traceroute`'s output indicates a gateway that did not respond to a probe in the allotted time. When you see stars, try using the `-w` option to increase `traceroute`'s time budget; it takes an argument in seconds. If that fixes the problem, inspect the timing information to see where latency is being introduced. It won't necessarily be at the link that was "failing" before you increased the wait time. The time budget applies to the entire round trip, so it's possible for a gateway to introduce a delay without causing an immediate timeout.

A slow link does not necessarily indicate a malfunction. Some physical networks have a naturally high latency. Sluggishness may also be a sign of congestion on the receiving network, especially if the network uses a CSMA/CD technology (such as Ethernet) in which repeated attempts to transmit a packet are made. Inconsistent round trip times would support such a hypothesis, since collisions increase the randomness of the network's behavior.

If a gateway consistently produces stars, it may simply be down. Another possibility is that its implementation of IP does not handle hop counts correctly, thus preventing it from ever returning reasonable data to `traceroute`.

If stars appear sporadically at a gateway, this may indicate a transient fault in one of the networks leading up to that gateway. The most likely explanation is congestion, although that is not the only possible answer. `traceroute` relies on low-priority ICMP packets, which many routers are smart enough to drop in preference to "real" traffic. Even if the network is too congested for `traceroute` to work properly, some packets may be getting through with no problem. A few stars shouldn't send you into a panic.

```
% traceroute -q 4 guano
traceroute to guano.batman.net (128.116.254.113)
 1   netblazer (128.138.243.113) 97 ms 92 ms 89 ms 90 ms
 2   engr-gw-cr (128.138.243.120) 92 ms 99 ms 87 ms 86 ms
 3   128.116.114.1 (128.116.114.1) 99 ms * 75 ms 86 ms
 4   guano.batman.net (128.116.254.113) * * 92 ms 94 ms
```

See Chapter 16 for more information about DNS.

Here, the `-q 4` option causes `traceroute` to do four queries at each gateway rather than three. Intermittent problems start to occur when probing the host 128.116.114.1 (its identity is shown as a number because it has not been entered into DNS). In general, problems will appear at all gateways past the point of failure, since packets that don't make it across the fault show up as stars no matter what gateway is being probed.

It's likely that the problem in this example lies on the link between the hosts engr-gw-cr and 128.116.114.1; however, this is by no means certain. It could be that the link between netblazer and engr-gw-cr is at fault and that `traceroute` was simply lucky. To pin down the problem, you need to send a statistically significant number of packets down the wire. This is generally easiest to do with `ping`.

The new-style `ping` *is included on the CD-ROM.*

If you have a recent version of the `ping` command, an intermittent network problem usually shows up as a discontinuity in the ICMP sequence numbers.[1] To track down the cause of disappearing packets, first run `traceroute` to discover the route that packets are taking. Then ping the intermediate gateways to discover which link is dropping packets.

For example, in the situation above, you might first verify that the path to engr-gw-cr is operating reliably:

```
% ping engr-gw-cr 56 100
PING engr-gw-cr.cs.colorado.edu: 56 data bytes
64 bytes from 128.138.243.120: icmp_seq=0. time=311. ms
64 bytes from 128.138.243.120: icmp_seq=1. time=244. ms
...
64 bytes from 128.138.243.120: icmp_seq=99. time=233. ms
----engr-gw-cr.cs.colorado.edu PING Statistics----
100 packets transmitted, 100 packets received, 0% loss
round-trip (ms)  min/avg/max = 222/237/311
```

The arguments to `ping` specify a payload of 56 bytes (the default) and ask that 100 packets be sent. Since this link looks OK, you could then continue on to test the link all the way to 128.116.114.1:

```
% ping 128.116.114.1 56 100
PING 128.116.114.1: 56 data bytes
64 bytes from 128.116.114.1: icmp_seq=0. time=348. ms
64 bytes from 128.116.114.1: icmp_seq=2. time=290. ms
...
64 bytes from 128.116.114.1: icmp_seq=99. time=281. ms
----128.116.114.1 PING Statistics----
100 packets transmitted, 77 packets received, 23% loss
round-trip (ms)  min/avg/max = 228/240/305
```

The problem has now been tracked down to one particular link. The network fault will generally lie on the link between the last gateway that can be pinged without loss of packets and the gateway beyond it.

Checking for Errors with netstat

To properly evaluate a network's traffic and collision rate, you need either a dedicated sniffer or a machine that supports a sniffer-like com-

---

1. The Solaris and SunOS versions of `ping` use the `-s` flag to request this form of output.

mand such as **tcpdump**, **etherfind**, or **snoop**. However, you can get a rough estimate of the collision rate with the **netstat** command.

See page 274 for more information about netstat.

netstat provides access to a variety of network-related reports. The most useful display for assessing the general state of the network is the interface status report obtained with **netstat -i**.

```
% netstat -i
Name  Net/Dest       Ipkts    Ierrs    Opkts    Oerrs   Collis
le0   cu-cs-capp   5723088     5429  4784052     1527    66651
ie1   cu-cs-cr     1394095     1200  1472943       16    82987
lo0   127.0.0.0     279422        0   279422        0        0
```

Some columns have been removed from this example to save space.

Ipkts and Opkts report the number of packets that have been received and transmitted on each interface since the machine was booted. Ierrs and Oerrs show the number of input and output errors; many different types of errors are counted in these buckets, and it is normal for a few to show up.

Errors should be less than 1% of the associated packets. If your error rate is high, compare the rates of several neighboring machines. A large number of errors on a single machine suggests a problem with that machine's interface or connection, while an error rate that is high everywhere most likely indicates a problem with the media. The error counts on gateways are good numbers to check when investigating a "roach motel" network, one where packets check in but don't check out.

The Collis column gives the number of collisions that were experienced while sending packets.[2] This number should be interpreted as a percentage of the total output packets (Opkts). In the example above, the collision rate on le0 is about 1.4% and the collision rate on ie1 is 5.6%. A "normal" value is less than 1%, and anything over 3% indicates problems. The network served by ie1 is overloaded.

An interface can be monitored in real time by naming it with the **-I** option and supplying a monitoring interval in seconds. For example:

```
% netstat -I ie1 5
    input    (ie1)       output
packets  errs  packets  errs  colls
13971549 1216  14757869 16    831629
512      0     99       1     27
464      1     94       0     4
516      0     101      0     6
452      1     87       0     6
336      0     71       0     0
...
```

2. This field has meaning only on broadcast-based networks such as Ethernet.

Columns summarizing the total activity of all interfaces are also printed; these have been removed for clarity. The first line of output is a summary of all packets received and sent since boot. Subsequent lines list the activity for each five-second interval. The current collision rate is running about 10% percent—break out the sniffer!

Automated Network Testing

On a small or medium-sized network, you can encode your understanding of the network's topology in a pinging script that you run out of `cron`. The script should verify that important gateways and servers are reachable, and should notify you if problems are found. You might want to run such scripts from a couple of strategic locations within the network for more comprehensive coverage.

Because `ping` puts additional load on the network, pinging scripts shouldn't be run too frequently. A ten minute interval between executions is probably a good compromise between loading the network and delaying the discovery of faults.

It is expensive to use `traceroute` in an automated script. If you want a script to provide more than just raw information about `ping` failures (for example, if you want it to deduce that an entire network is unreachable based on an inability to reach several hosts), you're better off writing down explicit checks based on your network topology than trying to generalize dynamically. Beware of checking for exact routes if your site uses a routing protocol, since routes may vary over time.

See page 670 for more information about dealing with runaway processes.

Another thing to check might be the load average or CPU utilization on important machines. A runaway process can effectively take a server out of commission without making it stop responding to pings. The 15 minute load average reported by `uptime` is generally the best basis on which to raise a CPU-related alarm.

Networks sometimes suffer from temporary glitches. A bridge may become momentarily confused and drop a series of packets. A workstation may spew broadcast packets, momentarily jamming other traffic. In general, any problem that fixes itself does not require your attention and should not be flagged by a pinging script. When a script detects problems with the network, it's best to have it sleep for twenty seconds or so, then perform the checks again. Only if both attempts fail should an alarm be raised.

We suggest that you add some random delay to your scripts so that checks do not occur at the same time each hour. Network glitches can happen on a regular schedule if they are caused by commands run out of `cron` or by other peculiarities of your organization. For example, at a university, it may be common for a lot of users to log in immediately after a certain class. You're more likely to discover such events if you test the network at random intervals.

22.3 FAULT REPORTING

See Chapter 12 for more information about syslog.

Once a fault has been detected, there are a variety of ways to bring it to the attention of a system administrator. The most flexible way is to log the fault through `syslog` and allow the routing of the report to be controlled by `syslog`'s configuration file. This scheme provides you with a variety of notification options that are already implemented and debugged—no need to roll your own.

Another common way to get attention is to have the pinging program report faults via email. This solution is somewhat unsatisfactory because mail may not be read immediately. By the time you realize there's a problem, you may already have anxious users calling you on the phone. On the other hand, email does permit a large amount of information about the fault to be included in a report. You might want to combine `syslog` and email to get the best features of both schemes.

Make sure that network faults can't prevent themselves from being reported. You'll get best results by putting your pinging scripts topologically close to your mail or `syslog` server.

One problem with both email and `syslog` is that they require administrators to be logged on before they can be notified of network faults. They don't provide much help outside of normal work hours or when administrators are away from a terminal. If your network needs round-the-clock support, you can use a beeper to notify a staff person of problems. Just dial it with a modem.

tpage, a set of paging tools, is included on the CD-ROM.

Most paging services allow a telephone number to be displayed on the target beeper. This function can be exploited to provide an encoded summary of the network problem. Some services support text, allowing you to dream up even more ingenious ways to persecute your staff. For example, you could forward mail from a particular alias (say, "emergency") to the beeper. There are freely-available tools that allow you to control an alpha pager from a regular modem.

22.4 PLANNING FOR RELIABILITY

Once a fault has been discovered, the design of your network will affect the time needed to diagnose and correct it. If your site relies heavily on the network, you must keep emergency operations in mind as you plan and extend it.

The general principles of network architecture are described in Chapter 15, *Network Hardware*. Although the design of highly fault-tolerant networks (like those used for financial trading and deployment of production databases) is too specialized to describe here, there are a few things you can do to make your network more resistant to failure at a relatively low cost:

- Divide networks into small, electrically separate pieces.
- Add redundant connections among networks.
- Distinguish between backbones and user networks.
- Keep spare parts, equipment, and network tools available.
- Set up backup servers (for DNS, NIS, etc.) on each segment.
- Use a smart routing protocol.
- Make disaster-recovery plans ahead of time.

The basic idea is to keep pieces of the network as independent from one another as possible. When a failure occurs, you want to make sure that it affects the smallest possible number of users. Since a high proportion of network failures stem from the misadventures of users, you must limit users' ability to interfere with one another.

For example, if you have a single thinnet loop serving thirty offices, you are asking for trouble. A confused user that breaks the connectivity of the cable or installs a bad connector will bring down the entire net. And don't expect that user to come to you for help; often, the user will not realize that there is a problem, and if he does, he may think that *you* have done something to take the net off-line that just happened to coincide with his changes.

This is bad for the other users on the cable, but the problem will be even worse if the network is used by other networks as a gateway to the outside world. Try to maintain a distinction between backbones and user networks. For various reasons, there may be political pressure to put workstations on a backbone; be forewarned and resist.

See page 305 for more information about network testing hardware.
Unless you have a TDR[3] or other electrical testing equipment, you may have to track down a cable problem by inspecting each connection to make sure that it is OK. It's often helpful to ask the people in each office how recently they have made changes. If nothing is obviously wrong, start checking for bad hardware. This can take a long time; portable debugging equipment can speed up the process.

It helps if you are able to short-circuit the network at a few key points; that way, you can test several offices at a time. The most efficient approach is a binary search. Divide the network in half, and see which half works. Then divide the injured portion, and so on. Another good place to split the network is between political domains. This allows blame to be assigned so that finger-pointing can begin immediately.

---

3. Time-domain reflectometer, an instrument that locates cable faults.

Technologies such as 10BASET (twisted-pair Ethernet) have an inherent advantage in protecting users from one another because they use a central "concentrator" to which all machines are connected in a star formation. There is no common cable that can be loused up by an individual user. Other versions of Ethernet all require the network to look like a long, unbroken cable; token ring nets use a cable arranged in a loop. In either case, one bad apple spoils the whole net.

Repeaters and bridges can be used to electrically insulate sections of the network from each other. For thinnet, there are multiport repeaters that act somewhat like 10BASET concentrators. Thinnet segments are connected in a spoke-like fashion, and any segment can go bad without affecting the others.[4]

The same principles that lead to high electrical reliability (small, insulated networks) can also apply to logical reliability. The networks that are best at handling traffic are those in which the cables are as independent as possible from one another. In practice, this means using routers to connect subnets, not bridges or repeaters.

If your network is complex enough to have more than just a single backbone net, you may want to consider adding more gateways among networks than are strictly needed for connectivity. This provides you with an alternate way to route traffic in the event of a problem. Loops are especially prized, since traffic can be routed around the failure of any individual net. In addition to providing for network emergencies, you can use any "extra" links to improve throughput and reduce latency.

See page 253 for more information about routing protocols.

On a network with loops or redundancies, be sure to use a routing protocol that is up to the task. For now, this means OSPF. RIP may not handle redundant nets properly, though you can use it to distribute routes discovered via other protocols if you use `gated`.

In addition to designing a reliable network, you should also do your part to prepare for a network outage. Keep plenty of cables, connectors, and spare parts around, and always have the proper tools handy. Network cabling tools are expensive, but it's wise to buy a set and learn how to use them even if an outside contractor does your initial wiring. If you can afford to keep a spare for bridges and concentrators, it might be worthwhile to do that (though these parts are generally reliable). For routers, it's generally cheaper to get an "instant service" contract; it takes a while to swap routers anyway.

Network documentation is a great comfort in times of stress. Chapter 32, *Policy and Politics*, describes some easy ways to keep your network documentation current.

4. Well, in most cases...

22.5 NETWORK MANAGEMENT PROTOCOLS

Over the last five years, network management issues have been much in vogue with commercial vendors and standards organizations. The most significant results have been the development of a couple of standard device management protocols and a glut of high-level products that exploit them.

Network management protocols provide a standard way of probing a device to discover its network connections, configuration, and general health. In addition, the protocols allow some of this information to be modified, so that network-level management can be standardized across different kinds of machinery and performed from a central station.

RFCs are included on the CD-ROM.
The most common management protocol used with TCP/IP is called SNMP, Simple Network Management Protocol. It was originally specified in RFC1067 and later accepted as a standard in RFC1157. True to its name, SNMP is very basic; it defines only a hierarchical namespace of management data and a way to read and write the data at each node. Most of SNMP's complexity lies above the protocol layer in the conventions for constructing the namespace and the conventions for formatting data items within a node. SNMP is widely supported.

Another protocol known as CMIS/CMIP has been tagging along with the Internet community for almost as long as SNMP, but has had relatively little impact. CMIP is similar to SNMP, but is generally acknowledged to be a better and more flexible protocol. However, it is also an ISO standard, and current implementations for TCP/IP depend upon several layers of nasty ISO emulation code. There was an effort several years ago (CMOT) to recast CMIP as a TCP/IP protocol, but the project didn't seem to get very far and has now been abandoned.

CMIP's future is closely tied to that of the other ISO protocols. At one time, it looked like political factors might force the adoption of the ISO protocols in the United States. However, that day is past; ISO and CMIP will probably stay dead.

Yeah, So What?

Since SNMP and CMIP are only abstract protocols, you need both a server program (an "agent") and a client to make use of them. Clients range from simple command-line utilities to dedicated management stations that graphically display networks and faults in eye-popping color.

Dedicated network management stations are the primary reason for the existence of management protocols. Most products let you build a topographic model of the network as well as a logical model; the two are presented together on-screen, along with a continuous indication of the status of each component.

Just as a chart can reveal the hidden meaning in a page of numbers, a network management station can summarize the state of a large network in a way that's easily accepted by a human brain. This kind of executive summary is almost impossible to get any other way.

When a problem occurs, a good management station pulls together information from various sources to form a theory of what happened. The failing component can often be identified with some degree of specificity. Many products also include a trouble-ticket system that helps you manage your team's response to each problem.

A major advantage of management-by-protocol is that it promotes all kinds of network hardware onto a level playing field. UNIX systems are all basically similar, but routers, gateways, and other low-level components are not. With SNMP or CMIP, they all speak the same language and can be probed, reset, and configured from a central location. It's nice to have one consistent interface to all the network's hardware.

However, all of these features have their price, both in money and in complexity. Despite what vendors may say, network management protocols are most at home in large sites. And like most large-scale proposals, they are either worth doing right or not worth doing at all. If you're going to start using one of these systems, be sure to get all the necessary toys. Don't attempt a half-baked implementation; you'll just end up deciding that the results do not justify the effort.

22.6 SNMP: THE SIMPLE NETWORK MANAGEMENT PROTOCOL

Many vendors ship an SNMP agent as part of their basic OS. RFC1470, a catalog of network management tools, lists some vendors that sell commercial implementations of SNMP agents.

CMU's implementation of SNMP is included on the CD-ROM.

Free SNMP clients are rare. Some simple utilities for dealing with individual machines are available from CMU. Unfortunately, most vendors sell SNMP-based network management software as a separate product and so do not like to give you anything useful for free.

When SNMP first became widely used in the early 1990s, it started a mini gold rush. At least thirty companies have come out with client-side software packages. A lot of them appear to be of questionable value, and it's unlikely that all will survive for another five years. Choose carefully. We especially like Hewlett-Packard's OpenView and NetMetrix.

The SNMP Namespace

The SNMP data space is, at least in theory, both universal and extensible. Large portions are set aside for future expansion, and vendor-specific additions are localized and monitored to prevent conflicts. The basic format of the namespace is called the SMI (Structure of Management Information) and is described most recently in RFC1155.

The SMI specifies a hierarchy that is very much like a filesystem. However, a dot is used as the separator character, and each node is given a number rather than a name. By convention, nodes are also given text names for ease of reference, but this is really just a high-level convenience and not a feature of the hierarchy (it is similar in principle to the mapping of hostnames to IP addresses). The path to a node is called the Object Identifier or OID for short.

The basic data types that an SMI node can contain are integer, string, and null. These can be combined into sequences of basic types, and a sequence can be instantiated repeatedly to form a table.

The root of the SMI hierarchy is broken into a subtree administered by CCITT (the International Telegraph and Telephone Consultative Committee), a subtree administered by ISO, and a subtree administrated jointly by ISO and CCITT. These trees are assigned the numbers 0, 1, and 2, respectively, with the logical names "ccitt", "iso", and "joint-iso-ccitt".

Management Information Bases

The actual contents of the namespace are assembled from pieces called MIBs (Management Information Bases) which describe the various domains of data accessible via SNMP. The top levels of the SMI hierarchy are used for delegation of authority among political groups and generally don't contain useful data. In fact, it is not until you reach the OID iso.org.internet.dod.mgmt (numerically, 1.3.6.1.2) that administrable objects for TCP/IP begin to appear.

The basic SNMP MIB for TCP/IP (MIB-I) was specified in RFC1066 and defines access to basic management data: information about the system, its interfaces, address translation, and protocol operations (IP, ICMP, TCP, UDP, and EGP). A later and more complete reworking of this MIB called MIB-II is defined in RFC1213. Most vendors that provide an SNMP server support MIB-II. A sampling of nodes from the MIB-II namespace is presented in Table 22.1 on the next page.

In addition to the basic MIB, there are MIBs for various kinds of hardware interfaces and protocols. There are MIBs for individual vendors and MIBs for particular hardware products. RFC1155 specifies the rules and procedures for installing a new MIB in the hierarchy.

A MIB is only a convention about the naming of management data. It must be backed up with code that provides access to this data in order to be useful. Code for the basic MIB comes with most SNMP servers. Some are extensible to include supplemental MIBs, and some are not.

Table 22.1   Selected OIDs from MIB-II

OID[a]	Type	Contents
system.sysDescr	text	System info: vendor, model, OS type, etc.
system.sysLocation	text	Physical location of the machine
system.sysContact	text	Contact info for the machine's owner
system.sysName	text	System name, usually full DNS name
interfaces.ifNumber	int	Number of network interfaces present
interfaces.ifTable	table	Table of info-bits about each interface
ip.ipForwarding	int	1 if system is a gateway, otherwise 2
ip.ipAddrTable	table	Table of IP addressing data (masks, etc.)
ip.ipRouteTable	table	The system's routing table
icmp.icmpInRedirects	int	Number of ICMP redirects received
icmp.icmpInEchos	int	Number of pings received
tcp.tcpConnTable	table	Table of current TCP connections
udp.udpTable	table	Table of UDP sockets with servers listening

a. Relative to iso.org.internet.dod.mgmt.mib-2.

SNMP Protocol Operations

There are only four basic operations defined on the SMI namespace: get, get-next, set, and trap. Note that there are no facilities for navigating or discovering the namespace; every request must include a fully qualified path to the data being referred to.

Get and set are the basic operations for reading and writing data to a node in the SMI hierarchy. Get-next is used to read the contents of tables, with one table row being returned for each request.

A trap is an unsolicited notification, from server to client, that reports the occurrence of an interesting event or condition. Several standard traps are defined, including "I've just come up" notifications, traps that report the failure or recovery of a network link, and traps for various routing and authentication problems. Many other not-so-standard traps are in common use, including some that simply watch the values of other SNMP variables and fire off a message when a specified range is exceeded. The mechanism by which the destinations of trap messages are specified depends on the implementation of the server.

Since SNMP messages may potentially modify configuration information, some security mechanism is needed. Unfortunately, version one of the SNMP standard outlines only a minimal security framework. The concept of an SNMP "community" is defined; it is basically a role that a client may claim when reading or writing data. In effect, the community name is a password.

In mid-1993, version two of the SNMP standard was proposed in RFCs numbered 1441 through 1452. Among other things, it provides for a more specific security model and for bulk retrieval of tables. New versions of the SMI and basic MIB are also provided. As of this writing, no vendor yet supports version two. However, the freely-available SNMP implementation from CMU is version two compliant. Do not confuse SNMP protocol version two with MIB-II.

The SNMP Documentation Swamp

There are over 54 RFCs related to SNMP, not counting those that have been updated or superseded. To help you sort out the morass of information, the most helpful of the RFCs are listed in Table 22.2. Obsolete RFCs are not listed, but you will often see them referred to in documentation.

Table 22.2   The most useful SNMP-related RFCs for administrators

RFC	Date	Title (may be abbreviated)
1155	5/90	SMI for TCP/IP-based Internets
1157	5/90	A Simple Network Management Protocol (SNMP)
1212	3/91	Concise MIB Definitions
1213	3/91	MIB for Management of TCP/IP-based Internets: MIB-II
1351	7/92	SNMP Administrative Model
1352	7/92	SNMP Security Protocols
1441	5/93	Introduction to Version Two of SNMP
1442	5/93	SMI for Version Two of SNMP
1443	5/93	Textual Conventions for Version Two of SNMP
1445	5/93	Administrative Model for Version Two of SNMP
1446	5/93	Security Protocols for Version Two of SNMP
1450	5/93	MIB for Version Two of SNMP
1452	5/93	Coexistence Between Versions One and Two of SNMP
1470	6/93	FYI on a Network Management Tool Catalog
1503	8/93	Algorithms for Automating Admin. in SNMPv2 Managers
1592	3/94	SNMP Distributed Protocol Interface Version Two

In addition, MIBs for specific device types and protocols are documented in the RFCs shown in Table 22.3 (next page).

Specifics for Various Operating Systems

HP-UX, IRIX, and DEC's OSF/1 all come with SNMP agents pre-installed. All of these systems support MIB-II, although there are occasional lapses in coverage, particularly with respect to support for exterior routing protocols. Consult your manuals for specifics.

Our other three example systems do not include SNMP support. However, commercial implementations are readily available. A list can be found in RFC1470. Since the specifications for commercial products

Table 22.3   Supplemental MIBs

RFC	Item	RFC	Item
1230	IEEE 802.4 Token Bus	1512	FDDI
1231	IEEE 802.5 Token Ring	1513	Token Ring extensions
1243	AppleTalk	1514	Host resources
1253	OSPF	1559	DECNET Phase IV
1315	Frame relay DTEs	1565	Service monitoring
1354	IP forwarding tables	1566	Mail monitoring
1381	X.25 LAPB	1567	X.500 monitoring
1382	X.25 Packet layer	1593	SNA APPN nodes
1389	RIP Version 2		

change so rapidly, we will not include them here; current information is available from ftp.wustl.edu in the directory `doc/noctools`.

_(hp)_ HP-UX's **snmpd** is configured in `/etc/snmpd.conf`. Comments are introduced with a pound sign ("#"). Five different keywords can be used within **snmpd.conf**, as illustrated in the following example:

```
# SNMP configuration file for host "turbine".
get-community-name: cuslug
set-community-name: cuslug
trap-dest: anchor
trap-dest: piper
location: Building 2, upstairs next to undergrad lounge
contact: Rupert Eastridge, 555-1234
```

The `get-community-name` and `set-community-name` keywords list the SNMP communities that are allowed to read and write data values. There may be more than one instance of each. However, access control cannot be subdivided; any name listed in any `set-community-name` statement is valid for any supported operation.

The `trap-dest` keyword specifies the name or IP address of an SNMP client that is to receive trap notifications. There may be several of these, and all traps are sent to all destinations.

The `location` and `contact` keywords allow free-format information about the machine to be made available via the MIB-II sysLocation and sysContact OIDs. The location and contact information can also be specified on **snmpd**'s command line.

You can control the amount of logging that **snmpd** generates with

   snmpd -m _logmask_

The _logmask_ should be a bitwise OR of your choice of option flags listed in Table 22.4. **-m 0** disables logging.

Table 22.4   **Option flag values for HP-UX snmpd**

Flag	Meaning	Flag	Meaning
0	Disable logging	8	Log SNMP transactions
1	Log authentication failures	16	Log added objects
2	Log errors	32	Dump all packets in hex
4	Log configuration requests	64	Log trace messages

Unfortunately, HP's `snmpd` does not use `syslog`. The default log file is `/usr/adm/snmpd.log`; an alternate can be specified with `-l` *log*.

 IRIX's `snmpd` can be configured to start at boot time by running the command `chkconfig snmpd on`. It can also be started by hand.

The file `/etc/snmpd.auth` is used for security configuration. Lines in this file have the form

```
{accept|reject}   hostname:community/operation ...
```

A star ("*") can be used to stand in for all hosts or all communities; unless you want undergraduates in Australia rebooting your router, we don't recommend this configuration. Multiple hosts or communities may be separated with a comma. The *operation* field may be left blank to indicate all operations. It's usually specified as `get` to designate certain hosts or communities as read-only.

IRIX's `snmpd` reports problems using `syslog`. Normally, only messages of level "err" or above are reported. The `-l` *loglevel* option can be used to vary the amount of information that is logged. The `-d` option sets various debugging options.

OSF DEC's SNMP agent has been segmented into several different processes and configuration files. The system is a bit complicated and unwieldy compared to other implementations, but it is also extensible. New MIBs and code to support them can be integrated into the basic framework.

The components are listed in Table 22.5 (next page). In DEC-speak, a "MOM" is a Managed Object Module, a program that implements a MIB.

See the man page for `snmpsetup` for information about adding additional MOMs to the system.

In the default setup, there are two configuration files of interest: the `/etc/eca/snmp_pe.conf` file, which configures the basic SNMP protocol engine, and the `/etc/eca/internet_mom.conf` file, which sets options specific to MIB-II. You can edit these files directly or use the supplied `snmpsetup` script.

Table 22.5   I want my MOM: components of DEC's SNMP server

Component	Function
snmp_pe	Implements the basic SNMP protocol
mold	Registers and queries MOMs on behalf of snmp_pe
internet_mom	A MOM that implements the standard MIB-II
trn_mom	A MOM for token ring, as specified in RFC1231
fddi_mom	A MOM for FDDI, as specified in RFC1285
snmpsetup	A hand-holding script for configuring the system
momgen	A developer tool used when writing new MOMs

Three kinds of statements can appear in **snmp_pe.conf**. An SNMP community is defined with the community statement:

```
community name ipaddr type
```

The *name* field names the community, and the *type* field specifies the access afforded to it. *type* can be readonly, readwrite, writeonly, or none. The *ipaddr* field provides a crude form of authentication: if it is an IP address in normal dot notation, only the specified machine may access the SNMP agent using this community name. If the field contains 0.0.0.0, no address check is performed.

A trap statement specifies a management station to which trap notifications should be sent:

```
trap name ipaddr
```

The name field specifies the trap community; it does not allow different kinds of traps to be sent to different stations. The *ipaddr* must be specified in numeric dot notation.

The optional statement

```
no_auth_traps
```

prevents "authentication failure" traps from being generated. If it is not present, the traps are sent to all defined trap communities.

The **internet_mom.conf** file specifies the text in the sysLocation and sysContact OIDs, along with the interval at which interfaces should be polled to make sure they are still alive, in seconds. These three values should be placed on separate lines, in this same order. Lines beginning with a pound sign ("#") are comments. For example:

```
# internet_mom.conf file for host turbine
Building 2, upstairs next to undergrad lounge
Rupert Eastridge, 555-8834
60
```

The CMU Tools

The CMU SNMP distribution is included on the CD-ROM.

Even if your system comes with its own SNMP server, you may still want to compile and install the client-side tools included in the SNMP package from CMU. They are about the only free tools currently available. Unfortunately, they seem to contain some questionable code and will not compile on all systems.

The most useful client-side tool is **snmpnetstat**. It emulates the behavior of **netstat**, except that it displays statistics for the host whose name you specify on the command line rather than the local host. This is more convenient than logging in to the remote host to display its network status. The **-c** *community* argument should also be supplied if the receiving host's SNMP server requires it.

There are minor differences between **snmpnetstat** and **netstat**. A few obscure features of **netstat** are not supported. **snmpnetstat** does allow an optional *interval* argument, which lets you watch the behavior of a host over time. Other major options are listed in Table 22.6.

Table 22.6   Major command-line options for snmpnetstat

Option	Meaning
-i	Show the status of network interfaces
-I *intf*	Show the status of one particular interface
-r	Show the routing table
-s	Dump per-protocol statistics

snmpnetstat's output is close enough to **netstat**'s for administrators, but probably not close enough for consumption by picky shell scripts. For example:

```
% snmpnetstat -i pelagius
Name    Mtu       Ipkts Ierrs    Opkts Oerrs
lo0     1536       2029     0     2035     0
en0     1500       3169     0     3395     0
```

A variety of other commands are provided for querying portions of the SNMP namespace. They're basically just testing tools, not production-quality commands for administrative use.

22.7 RECOMMENDED SUPPLEMENTAL READING

ROSE, MARSHALL T. *The Simple Book: An Introduction to Management of TCP/IP-based Internets.* Englewood Cliffs: Prentice Hall. 1991.

CARL-MITCHELL, SMOOT and JOHN S. QUARTERMAN. *Practical Internetworking with TCP/IP and UNIX.* Addison-Wesley. 1993.

LEINWAND, ALLAN AND KAREN FANG. *Network Management: A Practical Perspective*. Addison-Wesley. 1993.

HUNT, CRAIG. *TCP/IP Network Administration*. Sebastopol: O'Reilly & Associates. 1992.

Security

23.1 INTRODUCTION

UNIX was not designed with security in mind, and for that reason no UNIX system can be made truly secure. Throughout history, UNIX systems have regularly been broken into, beaten, brutalized, corrupted, commandeered, compromised, and illegally **fsck**ed.

There *are* things you can do to make your system somewhat more resistant to attack. Even so, several fundamental flaws in the UNIX model ensure that you will never reach security nirvana.

- UNIX is optimized for convenience and doesn't make security easy or natural. UNIX was designed by researchers, for researchers, and its philosophy stresses easy manipulation of data in a networked, multi-user environment.

- UNIX security is effectively binary: you are either a powerless user, or you're root. UNIX facilities such as setuid execution tend to confer total power all at once. Slight lapses in security can compromise entire systems.

- Most administrative functions are implemented outside the kernel, where they can be inspected and tampered with. Hackers have broad access to the system.

The first edition of this book was published just months after the 1988 "Internet Worm," which gained national attention after catching a large number of sites (including ours) off guard. At the time, it seemed like Robert Morris, Jr., the worm's author, had unleashed an inexcusable plague on the neighborly Internet community.

In reality, the worm caused little actual damage and increased security awareness on the Internet more than any other event to date. Once again, we were painfully reminded that good fences make good neighbors. A number of excellent tools for use by system administrators (as well as a formal organization for handling incidents of this nature) have come into being as a result.

There are many known security holes in UNIX that will never be fixed, and others that have been fixed by some vendors but not by all. In addition, many sites are a release or two behind, either because localization is too troublesome or because they do not subscribe to their vendor's software maintenance plan. When a vendor fixes a security hole, the window of opportunity for hackers does not disappear overnight.

Remember, too, that

$$\text{Security} = \frac{1}{\text{Convenience}}$$

The more secure your system, the more miserable you will be.

If you discover a security problem, do not tell anyone about it except trusted system administrators, the contact person at your software vendor, and CERT (the Computer Emergency Response Team; see page 558).

23.2 THE SEVEN COMMON-SENSE RULES OF SECURITY

Effective system security has its roots in common sense, and is a lot like dealing with an infestation of mice in your house. Here are seven rules you might use:

- Don't leave things that are likely to be interesting to mice lying on the kitchen table overnight. Cheese and peanut butter are excellent mouse-getters.

- Plug the holes that mice are using to get into the house. If they can't get in, they won't bother you.

- Don't provide places for mice to build nests within the house. Piles of dirty clothes on the floor make good nests.

- Set mouse traps along walls where you often see mice out of the corner of your eye.

- Check traps daily to re-bait them and to dispose of squashed mice. Full traps don't catch mice, and they smell.

- Avoid using commercial bait-and-kill poisons to deal with the situation. These can leave you with dead mice in your walls or kill your dog. Traditional snap traps are best.[1]

- Get a cat!

You can use these same seven rules (well, slightly modified) to secure your UNIX systems. Here's how you might rewrite them:

- Don't put files on your system that are likely to be interesting to hackers or nosy employees. Trade secrets, personnel files, payroll data, election results, etc., must be handled carefully if they're on-line. Reasonable security can be attained by using `compress` and then `crypt` on sensitive files; see page 557.

- Plug holes that hackers can use to gain access to your system. Read bulletins from your vendor, the security mailing lists discussed at the end of this chapter, and Usenet newsgroups that provide reports of and patches for security holes.

- Don't provide places for hackers to build nests on your system. Hackers often break into one system and then use it as a base of operations to get into other systems. World-writable anonymous `ftp` directories, group accounts, and accounts with poorly chosen passwords all encourage nesting activity.

- Set basic traps on systems that are connected to the Internet. Tools such as `tripwire`, `crack`, and COPS (described starting on page 549) will keep you abreast of infestations.

- Monitor the reports generated by these security tools. A minor problem that is ignored in one report may grow into a catastrophe by the time the next report is sent.

- Teach *yourself* about UNIX system security. A number of high-priced security "consultants" will happily come to your site and instill terror in you and your management about the insecurity of your systems. They'll explain that for only $50K they can make your site secure.

  Unfortunately, their solutions will often leave you with dead mice in your walls and kill your users' productivity. Traditional know-how and common sense are the most important parts of a site security plan.

- Prowl around looking for unusual activity. Investigate anything that seems unusual, such as odd log messages or changes in the activity of an account (more activity, activity at strange hours, or perhaps activity while the owner is on vacation).

---

1. Actually, politically correct mouse relocation methods vary. Consult your manuals.

23.3 SECURITY PROBLEMS IN THE /ETC/PASSWD FILE

See page 86 for information about /etc/passwd.

The contents of /etc/passwd determine who can log in and what they can do once they get inside. This file is the system's first line of defense against intruders. It must be scrupulously maintained and free of errors, security hazards, and historical baggage.

Password Checking and Selection

It is important to verify on a continuous (at least weekly) basis that every login has a password. Entries in the /etc/passwd file that describe pseudo-users like "daemon" which are used but never logged in to should have a star ("*") in the password field.

Several specialized software packages exist to check /etc/passwd for security problems, but the command

```
awk -F: '{ if ($2 == "") print $1 }' /etc/passwd
```

suffices just as well for finding null passwords. A script that performs this check and mails you the results can be run by **cron** every week. An added measure of security can be implemented by writing a script that checks /etc/passwd daily against a version from the previous day and mails any differences to you. You can then verify that any modifications are legitimate. /etc/passwd and /etc/group must be readable by the world, but writable only by root.

UNIX allows users to choose their own passwords, and while this is a great convenience it leads to many security problems. When users are given their logins, they should also be provided with instructions for choosing a good password. They should be told not to use their name or initials, or the name of a child or spouse. Passwords derived from personal data such as a telephone number or address are easily broken. Hackers routinely check for profanity and words such as "sex," "love," and "money" using dictionaries of common passwords.

Passwords are normally changed with the **passwd** command. Two replacements for this command (**npasswd** and **passwd+**) are included on the CD-ROM. They force users to select reasonably secure passwords.

Passwords should be at least seven characters long and should include numbers, punctuation, or changes in case. Passwords should not be chosen from a dictionary. Nonsense words, combinations of simple words, or the first letters of words in a memorable phrase make the best passwords. Of course, "memorable" is good but "traditional" is risky. Make up your own phrase.

 Solaris includes a version of **passwd** that forces users to adhere to certain common-sense rules, like not using their login names as passwords. You can customize the rules for the construction of passwords in the file **/etc/default/passwd**.

Group Logins and Shared Logins

Any login that is used by more than one person is bad news. Group logins (such as "demo") are sure targets for hackers to homestead. Don't allow them at your site.

See page 724 for some additional comments on shared logins.

Likewise, don't allow users to share logins with family or friends. If little Johnny needs a login to work on his science project, give him one with that stated purpose. It's much easier to take away Johnny's login when he abuses it than to get rid of Dad and his account, especially at government sites.

At most sites, "root" is a group login. Dangerous! We recommend using the **sudo** program to control access to rootly powers. See page 52.

User Shells

Do not use a script as the shell for an unrestricted (passwordless) login. Passwordless logins should be used only as a facility for running small, non-interactive utilities such as **date**, **sync**, or **lpq**.

Shadow Passwords

See page 550 for more information about password guessing.

Traditionally, each line in **/etc/passwd** consists of seven fields; the second field contains a string that represents the user's encrypted password. Since **/etc/passwd** must be world-readable for commands like **ls** to work, the encrypted password string is available to all users on the system. Evildoers can encrypt selected dictionaries or words and compare the results with the strings in **/etc/passwd**. If the encrypted strings match, a password has been found.

How much of a threat is this? In the 80s, there was at least one way to decrypt passwords post-haste,[2] but run-of-the-mill hackers had to be content with using the **crypt** library routine[3] to encrypt dictionary words for comparison. A "fast" machine in the 80s could do a few hundred encryptions per second. Recently, a Thinking Machines CM-200 with 64K processors was clocked at 424,000 **crypts** per second. That means that all passwords of six characters or less could be discovered in two days, and all seven-character passwords in four months.[4]

---

2. Evi Nemeth broke the Diffie-Hellman key exchange often used with DES in 1984, using a HEP supercomputer. Although DES is thought to be mathematically secure, the short key lengths in common use offer relatively little security.

3. Not to be confused with the **crypt** command, which uses a different and less secure encryption scheme.

4. On most systems, only the first eight characters of a password are significant.

This result is frightening, and it suggests that user access to encrypted password strings really ought to be restricted. A common way to do this is to put passwords in a separate file that is readable only by root, leaving the rest of /etc/passwd intact. The file that contains the actual password information is then called the shadow password file (often, it is /etc/shadow). Eventually, every UNIX vendor will be forced to implement shadow passwords. The current status of our six example systems is shown in Table 23.1. In some cases, shadow passwords are part of an add-on security package that costs extra money.

Table 23.1 Shadow passwords

System	Got 'em?	System	Got 'em?
Solaris	Yes	SunOS	No
HP-UX	No	OSF/1	No
IRIX	Yes	BSDI	Yes

Password Aging

There are utilities available to implement what is called password aging. These systems force users to change their passwords periodically. While this may seem like a good idea at first glance, it has several problems. Users often become resentful at having to change their passwords, and since they don't want to forget the new password, they choose something simple that is easy to type and remember. Many users switch between two passwords each time they are forced to change, defeating the purpose of password aging.

See page 52 for more information about sudo.

Nevertheless, the root password should be changed regularly. A root password should roll easily off the fingers so that it can be typed quickly and cannot be guessed by watching the movement of fingers on the keyboard.[5] At our site most people use sudo rather than the real root password, but we select the password carefully all the same.

Rootly Entries

The only distinguishing feature of the root login is its UID of zero. Since there can be more than one entry in the /etc/passwd file that uses this UID, there can be more than one way to log in as root.

A common way for hackers to install a back door once a root shell has been obtained is to edit new root logins into /etc/passwd. Since programs like who and w refer to the login name stored in /etc/utmp rather than the UID that owns the login shell, they cannot expose hackers that appear to be innocent users but are really logged in as root.

---

5. Some piano players can read fingers very effectively. Really!

The defense against this subterfuge is an **awk** script similar to the one used for finding logins without passwords:

```
awk -F: '{if ($3 == 0) print $1}' /etc/passwd
```

You could adapt this script to find entries with suspicious groups, or UIDs that are the same as those of key people within your organization.

You should also check for **passwd** entries that have no user name, or that have punctuation as a user name. These entries may seem nonsensical, but they will often allow you to log in.

23.4 SETUID PROGRAMS

Programs that run setuid, especially ones that run setuid to root, are prone to security problems. The setuid commands distributed with UNIX are theoretically secure; however, security holes have been discovered in the past and will undoubtedly be discovered in the future.

Writing Setuid Programs

The surest way to minimize the number of setuid *problems* is to minimize the number of setuid *programs*. If you must write something that's setuid, keep the following rules in mind as you code.

Don't write setuid shell scripts (for any shell). The purpose of a shell is to let users configure the environment to their taste. This is exactly what you don't want when running setuid. You need to have complete control over the execution of your code and not be affected by monkey wrenches thrown in by a user. Although a shell spawned to execute a script doesn't necessarily read the user's shell configuration files, there are other ways that it can be influenced: for example, by the user's environment variables, by the contents of the current directory, or by the way the script is invoked.

Don't use library routines that invoke a shell. Just because you code in C doesn't mean that you've escaped the dangers of the shell. Library routines that start up slave shells are almost as dangerous as setuid shell scripts. Fortunately, there are only a few of these. The most commonly-used routines are **popen** and **system**.

Don't use the **execlp** *or* **execvp** *library routines.* **execlp** and **execvp** are interfaces to **execve** that duplicate the path-searching functionality of a shell. The idea is that you can specify just a simple command name instead of a complete pathname and have the routine look through your search path to find the command. This is dangerous because users have control over their paths; if you use these routines, your code can be forced to execute whatever command a user wants.

Use full pathnames to identify files. In a similar vein, don't rely on any kind of searching mechanism to find files or programs. Each time you refer to a file from within a setuid program, you must be sure that you are getting the file you want. This means using absolute pathnames or setting the path at the beginning of the program.[6]

Don't setuid to root unless you need to. If all you need to do is restrict access to a file or database, there is no reason to make your code setuid root. Instead, make an entry in **/etc/passwd** for a pseudo-user whose only reason for existence is to own the restricted resources, and let your program setuid to that user. Follow the normal pseudo-user conventions: use a low UID, put a star in the password field, and make the pseudo-users's home directory be **/dev/null**.

Don't make setuid programs world-readable. There are separate permission bits for reading and executing. Use this to your advantage by setting up your setuid programs so that they can be executed but not read. This prevents prying eyes from finding out how your code works and exploiting its weaknesses.

Suppose there is a line in your code that reads

```
date_stream = popen("date","r");
```

Anyone who has read permission on the binary can use the **strings** command to find printable sequences in the file, including the string "date." A possible line of attack has now been made clear.

Don't put secret back-door escapes in your code. Historically, it has been common for UNIX programs to contain secret features for debugging, performing administrative chores, or spawning setuid shells. Needless to say, these features don't stay secret for long.

Finding Setuid Programs

A hacker who has breached the security of your system will sometimes create private setuid shells and utilities that allow access to other accounts. For example, having a setuid version of a shell is equivalent to knowing the root password. Watching for clandestine setuid programs helps to catch intrusions early.

The command

```
/usr/bin/find / -user root -perm -4000 -print |
    /usr/ucb/mail -s "Setuid root files" netadmin
```

would mail a list of all setuid root files to the user "netadmin." On some systems, **ncheck** can also be used to look for setuid programs.

---

6. The default path for root should not contain "." or any world-writable directories.

23.5 IMPORTANT FILE PERMISSIONS

There are many files on a UNIX system that must have particular permissions to avoid security problems. Some vendors ship software with permissions set for their own "friendly" development environment. These permissions may not be appropriate for you.

The special file `/dev/kmem` allows access to the kernel's address space. It is used by programs such as `ps` that need to look at kernel data structures. This file should only be readable by the owner and group members, not by the world. Programs that need to access this file should be setgid to the group that owns the file, usually "kmem."

Some vendors carelessly distribute systems with `/dev/kmem` publicly readable. This is a major security problem because a competent programmer can then look for things like unencrypted passwords in the kernel data structures and buffers. If your system has `/dev/kmem` publicly readable, change this immediately. If the change causes any programs to stop working, make those programs setgid to the group that owns `/dev/kmem`.

`/etc/passwd` and `/etc/group` should not be world-writable. They should have owner root and mode 644. The group should be set to some system group, usually "daemon." The `passwd` command runs setuid to root so that users can change their passwords without having write permission on `/etc/passwd`.

See page 429 for information about setting up an `ftp` *server.*

Directories that are available via anonymous `ftp` should not be publicly writable. Such directories create a nest for hackers to distribute illegally copied software and other sensitive files. If you manage an `ftp` archive that allows submissions, be sure to screen the submissions directory regularly.

Setting up anonymous `ftp` usually involves copying a skeleton password file into `~ftp/etc/passwd` so that `ls` will work correctly. Make sure to remove the encrypted password strings.

Device files for hard disk partitions are another potential source of problems. Having read or write permission on a disk device file is essentially the same as having read or write permission on every file in the filesystem it represents. Only root should have both read and write permission. The group owner sometimes gets read permission to perform backups, but there should be no permissions for the world.

23.6 MISCELLANEOUS SECURITY ISSUES

The sections below present some miscellaneous security-related topics. Most are either features that are useful to you as an administrator or misfeatures that can provide nesting material for hackers if they are not kept in check.

Remote Event Logging

See Chapter 12 for more information about syslog.

The `syslog` facility allows log information for both the kernel and user processes to be forwarded to a file, a list of users, or another host on your network. Consider setting up a secure host that acts as a central logging machine and prints out security violations (the auth facility) on a hardcopy printer. This prevents hackers from covering their tracks by rewriting or erasing log files.

Secure Terminals

Some systems can be configured to restrict root logins to specific "secure" terminals. It's a good idea to disable root logins on channels such as dialup modems. Often, network pseudo-terminals are also set to disallow root logins.

The secure channels are usually specified as a list of TTY devices or as a keyword in a configuration file. Table 23.2 shows the relevant configuration files on our six example systems.

Table 23.2   Restricting root login by TTY

System	Control file	System	Control file
Solaris	/etc/default/login[a]	SunOS	/etc/ttytab
HP-UX	/etc/securetty	OSF/1	/etc/ttys
IRIX	–	BSDI	/etc/ttys

a. See also /etc/default/su.

/etc/hosts.equiv and ~/.rhosts

These files define hosts as being administratively "equivalent" to one another, allowing users to log in and copy files between machines without typing their passwords. If you permit the use of this feature, you become vulnerable to viruses.

The safest approach is to create `/etc/hosts.equiv` and `~/.rhosts` for each user (including root) as a zero-length file. It is easier to assess what the state of a file was at 3:00 a.m. if it exists and is untouched than to assess the state of a non-existent file. This can be crucial when tracking intruders. Since users can edit their own `.rhosts` files, you will have to check periodically to ensure that the files remain empty.

See Chapter 16 for more information about DNS.

If you *must* use these files, set strict policies about what they can contain. In the case of `/etc/hosts.equiv`, allow only hosts that share login names and UIDs, and use fully-qualified DNS hostnames. Relaxing this rule could prove disastrous, as user "arlene" on another system would be able to read a local arlene's files. For ~/.rhosts, allow only fully-qualified names of local hosts (no user names).

 All versions of SunOS through 4.1.3 were shipped with a "+" token in /etc/hosts.equiv. This is a gaping security hole, since it means that a user with the login name "joe" at the University of Florida can log in to an account at the University of Colorado by the same name without being asked for a password. For years (quite literally), the software folks at Sun Microsystems shrugged off our calls to them on this issue, calling it a "feature." Not!

Security and NIS

You can read more about NIS in Chapter 18, Sharing System Files.

Other than the title of this section, these words should never be used together. The Network Information Service (NIS, formerly the Yellow Pages) is a Sun database distribution tool that many sites use to maintain and distribute files such as /etc/group, /etc/passwd, and /etc/hosts. Unfortunately, its very nature of "easy information access" makes it tasty hacker bait. A later replacement for this system (called NIS+) makes a feeble attempt to address the security problems of NIS. You'd be safer not to run either form of NIS at your site.

expect is included on the CD-ROM.

A more secure and reliable way to distribute these files is to create a login such as "netadmin" and place the most recent copies of these files in ~netadmin. Then, periodically run (from cron) an expect script on each client machine to ftp, sanity check, and install the most recent versions. See page 390 for more information.

Security and NFS

See page 369 for specific information about securing your NFS exports.

Security and sendmail

See Chapter 21 for more information about sendmail.

sendmail is a massive system, a large part of which runs as root. As a result, it has often been subject to the attacks of hackers and numerous vulnerabilities have been exposed over time. Make sure that you're running the most up-to-date version of sendmail on all your systems. *All versions of sendmail released prior to Berkeley version 8.6.9 (released April, 1994) have known vulnerabilities.* That includes the sendmail shipped with all vendor's operating systems produced before this date, as well as IDA sendmail.

23.7 SECURITY POWER TOOLS

Some of the neat avoidance chores mentioned in the previous section can be automated with freely-available tools. Here are a few of the tools you'll want to look at. New tools are usually put in the CERT security tools archive at cert.org (in the directory **pub/tools**) and announced on the cert-tools-list mailing list.

COPS: Audit System Security

COPS (the Computer Oracle and Password System) is a set of programs that monitor various areas of UNIX system security. COPS warns you of potential problems via email; it makes no attempt to fix them. A list of the items monitored includes

- File, directory, and device permissions and modes
- The contents of **/etc/passwd** and **/etc/group**
- The contents of system startup and crontab files
- The writability of users' home directories

Once you install COPS, you will get a nightly security report similar to the following:

```
ATTENTION:
Security Report for Sun Nov 14 20:24:00 MST 1993
from host raja.xor.com

Warning!  Root does not own the following file(s): /etc
Warning!  "." (or current directory) is in root's path!
Warning!  /var/spool/mail is _World_ writable!
Warning!  /etc/utmp is _World_ writable!
Warning!  User randy's home directory /home/staff/randy
   is mode 0777!
Warning!  Password file, line 8, no password:
runmailq::33:10:,,,:/home/staff/runmailq:/bin/csh
Warning!  Password file, line 2964, no password:
wp::31777:11:White Pages/CCSO,,,:/home/staff/wp:/bin/csh
Warning! /usr/bin/uudecode creates setuid files!
Warning!  Password Problem: Guessed: beth shell: /bin/csh
```

COPS is included on the CD-ROM.

COPS provides a number of other features, including the Kuang expert system, which attempts to intuit devious ways that regular users could attempt to become root. Run COPS before one of your users does.

crack: Find Insecure Passwords

crack is included on the CD-ROM.

Since most vendors still distribute systems that leave encrypted passwords in plain view, naughty hackers can easily compare them with an encrypted dictionary. One way to head off this attack is to make the comparison yourself and force users to change passwords that you have broken. **crack** is a tool that uses a number of common password-guessing techniques to expose poorly-chosen passwords. Be careful; **crack** stores the broken passwords as plain text.

tcpd: Protect Internet Services

tcpd is included on the CD-ROM.

tcpd, often referred to as the "TCP wrapper" package, allows you to log connections to TCP services such as **telnet**, **rlogin**, and **finger**. In addition, it allows you to restrict which systems can connect to these services. Both of these features can be very handy when tracking or controlling unwanted guests.

tcpd is easy to install and doesn't require modifications to existing network programs. You simply modify your **/etc/inetd.conf** file to execute **tcpd** instead of the actual program. **tcpd** then does any necessary logging and security checks before executing the real daemon. For example, if your **/etc/inetd.conf** originally contained the line:

```
telnet stream tcp nowait root /etc/in.telnetd in.telnetd
```

You could change this to:

```
telnet stream tcp nowait root /usr/etc/tcpd in.telnetd
```

The resulting log file (configured in **/etc/syslog.conf**) would look something like:

```
Nov 12 08:52:43 chimchim in.telnetd[25880]: connect from
   rintintin.Colorado.EDU
Nov 12 19:19:44 chimchim in.telnetd[15520]: connect from
   catbelly.com
Nov 12 23:48:45 chimchim in.telnetd[19332]: connect from
   atdt.xor.com
Nov 13 20:14:57 chimchim in.telnetd[2362]: connect from
   130.13.13.11
```

 HP-UX includes a version of **inetd** that has most of these features built in. It is configured in the file **/usr/adm/inetd.sec**.

tripwire: Monitor Changes to System Files

tripwire is included on the CD-ROM.

tripwire monitors the permissions and checksums of important system files, so that you can easily detect files that have been replaced, corrupted, or tampered with. For example, **tripwire** makes it easy to determine that an intruder has replaced your copy of **/bin/login** with one that records all your users' passwords in a clandestine file. Like COPS, **tripwire** should be set up to mail you a nightly report. A typical **tripwire** report looks like this:

```
### Phase 1:   Reading configuration file
### Phase 2:   Generating file list
### Phase 3:   Creating file information database
### Phase 4:   Searching for inconsistencies
###
### Total files scanned:    2988
```

```
###        Files added:        1
###        Files deleted:      0
###        Files changed:      2432
###
### After applying rules:
###        Changes discarded: 2430
###        Changes remaining: 1
###
changed: -rwxr-xr-x root  16384 Oct 11 13:51:17 1990
   /usr/etc/reboot
###
### Phase 5: Generating expect/observed pairs
###
### Attr          Observed (is)        Expected (should be)
### ===========   =============        ====================
/usr/etc/reboot
     st_ctime:  Nov 25 11:15 1993  Aug  4 21:21 1991
```

In this example, **tripwire** reports that the inode change time of **/usr/etc/reboot** is different than on the previous day. This may be an indication that a wily hacker has replaced the vendor's version of **/usr/etc/reboot** with one that contains a surprise waiting to be found the next time **reboot** is executed. Comparing the checksum of the executable with the version on the distribution tape can confirm or deny this as potential hacker droppings. Since some hackers are wily enough to rig the checksums on modified files, **tripwire** uses two different checksum methods.

23.8 Kerberos: A Unified Approach to Network Security

Gaining illicit access to a networked machine is often all too easy. Security can be foiled by such simple flaws as passwords transmitted across the network in plain text and users who have hundreds of machines in their ~/.rhosts files. The Kerberos system, designed at MIT, attempts to address some of the issues of network security in a consistent and extensible way.

Kerberos is an authentication system, a facility which "guarantees" that users and services are in fact who they claim to be. The security of Kerberos is based on cryptography; Kerberos uses the DES encryption algorithm to construct nested sets of credentials called "tickets." Tickets are passed around the network to certify your identity and to provide you with access to network services. Effectively, Kerberos provides the security of passwords without requiring you to actually type your password every few minutes.

Each Kerberos site must maintain at least one physically secure machine (called the authentication server) to run the Kerberos daemon.

This daemon issues tickets to users or services that request authentication based on credentials they provide, such as passwords. In Kerberos, passwords are always transmitted in an encrypted form.

Tickets are granted using a "name" of three parts:

- The *principal* name, which is the user or service's name (for example, the user "holly" or the service "NFS").

- The *instance* name, which is the specific case of the principal. For a user this is usually null. For a service, it is the name of the machine on which the service runs.

- The *realm* name, which is the name of the group served by the authentication server.

For example,

```
fred@CS.COLORADO.EDU
```

would be the user fred's Kerberos name in the Computer Science Department at the University of Colorado. In this realm, fred can request a ticket that allows him to do such things as log in to other machines without a password. After a fixed period of time (usually eight hours), the ticket expires and these privileges are revoked. This scheme provides a way to implement passwordless network logins without the risks of ~/.rhosts and /etc/hosts.equiv.

Vendors are beginning to distribute Kerberos as a part of their standard releases. Table 23.3 shows the current state of affairs. Systems with "Kerberos stubs" come ready to work with Kerberos if you have already set up an authentication server. But just as buying a cable-ready television doesn't get you HBO, you must still obtain a copy of Kerberos from an outside source if you are starting from scratch.

Table 23.3   Kerberos availability by vendor

System	Entire?	Stubs?	System	Entire?	Stubs?
Solaris	No	Yes[a]	SunOS	No	No
HP-UX	No	No	OSF/1	No	No
IRIX	No	No	BSDI	Yes	–

a. You must ftp the rest of the distribution from athena-dist.mit.edu.

Kerberos offers a better network security model than ignoring network security entirely. Unfortunately, it is plagued with holes, from windows that remain "authenticated" for hours while the user is at lunch, to passwords that are stored in plain text on the authentication server. In the end, you may find that taking other precautions described in this chapter provides a more-than-adequate level of security for your users.

23.9 PACKET FILTERING

In addition to protecting individual machines, you can also implement security precautions at the network level. The basic tool of network security is the packet filter.

A packet filter limits the type of traffic that can pass through your Internet gateway (or through a gateway that joins fiefdoms *within* your organization). You specify which destination addresses, port numbers, and protocol types are acceptable, and the gateway simply discards any packets that don't meet the profile. Filtering is supported by dedicated routing hardware such as that made by Cisco and Wellfleet. It may also be available in software, depending on the machine you're using as a gateway and its configuration.

Packet filtering should not be your primary means of defense against intruders. It's only appropriate as a supplemental security measure. The use of packet filters (sometimes called "firewalls," although this is an overused and almost meaningless term) often provides a false sense of security; if a filter lulls you into relaxing other safeguards, it will have had a *negative* effect on the security of your site.

Every host within your organization should be individually secured with tools such as COPS, **crack**, **tcpd**, and **tripwire**. Otherwise, you are simply building a structure that has a hard crunchy outside and a soft chewy center. On the Internet, it doesn't take many licks to get to the center of that bonbon.

Ideally, local users should be able to connect to any Internet service they want, but machines on the Internet should only be able to connect to a limited set of local services. For example, you may want to allow **ftp** access to an archive server and allow SMTP (email) connections to a mail server.

Almost all "well-known" services are associated with a network port in the **/etc/services** file (or its vendor-specific equivalent). The daemons that provide these services bind to the appropriate ports and wait for connections from remote sites.[7] Most of the well-known service ports are "privileged," meaning that the port numbers are in the range 1 to 1,023 and that they can only be used by a process running as root. Port numbers 1,024 and higher are referred to as "non-privileged" ports.

Service-specific filtering is based on the assumption that the client (the machine that initiates a TCP or UDP connection) will use a non-privileged port to contact a privileged port on the server. For example, if you wanted to allow only inbound SMTP connections to a machine with the address 192.108.21.200, you would install a filter that allowed TCP pack-

---

7. In many cases, **inetd** does the waiting for them. See page 708 for more information.

ets destined for that address at port 25 and permitted outbound TCP packets from that address to anywhere.[8] The way in which such a filter would be installed depends on the type of router; consult your manuals.

See page 427 for more information about ftp. Some services, such as `ftp`, add a twist to the puzzle. `ftp` actually has two connections open when transferring a file: one for commands and the other for data. The client initiates the command connection, and the server initiates the data connection. Ergo, if you want to use `ftp` to retrieve files from the Internet, you must permit inbound access from all non-privileged TCP ports, since you have no idea what port might be used to form an incoming data connection.

This tweak largely defeats the purpose of packet filtering, since some notoriously insecure services (for example, X11 at port 6,000) naturally bind to non-privileged ports. This configuration also creates an opportunity for curious users within your organization to start their own services (such as a `telnet` server at a non-standard and non-privileged port) that they and/or their friends can access from the Internet.

The most secure way to use a packet filter is to start with a configuration that allows nothing but inbound SMTP, then liberalize the filter bit by bit as you discover useful things that don't work. Some extremely security-conscious sites use two-stage filtering. In this scheme, there is one machine that's gatewayed to the Internet and also a second packet filter that lies between that gateway and the rest of the local network. The idea is to leave the outer gateway relatively open and to make the inner gateway very conservative. If the machine in the middle is administratively separate from the rest of the network, it can be used to provide a variety of services on the Internet with reduced risk.

The most secure way to handle the `ftp` dilemma is to allow `ftp` to the outside world only from this single, isolated host. Users can also log in to the `ftp` machine when they need to perform other network operations that are forbidden from the inner net. Since replicating all user accounts on the ftp server would defeat the goal of administrative separation, you may wish to create `ftp` accounts by request only. Naturally, the `ftp` host should run a full complement of security-checking tools.

Although this configuration does provide a little more security, it is inconvenient for users. It creates a barrier to widespread use of the Internet within your organization. If you want to maximize the value of your Internet connection, we recommend that you emphasize convenience and accessibility when deciding how to set up your network. Tools such as COPS, `crack`, `tcpd`, and `tripwire` allow much of this flexibility without the need for a strong set of packet filters.

8. Port 25 is the SMTP port as defined in `/etc/services`.

23.10 SECURITY AND BACKUPS

*See Chapter 11 for
more information
about backups.*
Regular system backups are an essential part of any site security plan. Make sure that all partitions are regularly dumped to tape and that you store some backups offsite. If a significant security incident occurs, you'll have an uncontaminated checkpoint to restore.

Since anyone can read the contents of a tape once it's mounted on a drive, store your backup tapes under lock and key.

23.11 TROJAN HORSES

Trojan horses are programs that aren't what they seem to be. An example of a Trojan horse was a program called `turkey` that was distributed on Usenet a few years ago. The program said it would draw a picture of a turkey on your terminal screen, but actually it deleted files from your home directory.

Be wary of software that you do not get from a reputable distributor, especially software from `ftp` servers or Usenet. This doesn't mean that you should never use such software; in fact, some of the best UNIX software is in the public domain (or more commonly these days, "freely distributed," which is essentially public domain with an attitude).

If you want to be sure that a particular package is kosher, you can always read every line of the source code to be sure it doesn't do anything dangerous. Or, if you'd rather have a life, you can use the principle of "safety in numbers."

When a new package is released, keep a copy but wait a few weeks to see how others in the UNIX community react. If the response is, "Gee, this `turkey` program ruined my life," don't install it. This scheme works because programs are seldom both useful and malignant. If problems don't surface soon, the software is probably not *too* harmful.

Another thing you can do is stick to heavily-used archive sites such as ftp.uu.net. These mega-archives are professionally administered, and since they serve many users (some of whom pay real money for access) problems are likely to be exposed quickly.

In general, don't install public domain programs that you don't have source code for. Binaries are OK for platform-specific programs, but most pure UNIX software is intended to run on a variety of computers, and the distribution of binaries is therefore impractical. Missing source code with no good reason is a very, very suspicious sign.

Of course, be especially wary of programs that claim they need to run setuid, and don't run new programs when you are logged in as root.

23.12 SMART TERMINAL PROBLEMS

Many "dumb" terminals have built-in intelligence that allows them to operate independently of a host computer. Although UNIX does not take advantage of these features, some of them can cause security problems. In particular, many terminals can be sent control sequences that cause them to echo back text as though it had been typed at the keyboard. If this feature is used to echo UNIX commands, the commands will be executed by whoever is logged in on the terminal. If root is logged in, the security of the entire system is compromised.

This bug is often referred to as the "25th line bug" because on many terminals the characters that are echoed back appear on the status line, line 25. One defense against this line of attack is to use **mesg n** to prevent anything, including the dreaded control sequences, from being sent directly to the terminal. Unfortunately, **mesg n** also prevents **write** and **talk** from working, and it doesn't keep the control sequences from being delivered to you through other routes, such as email. The problem can also be avoided by having smart terminals emulate older, dumber terminals that do not support a 25th line.

23.13 DATA ENCRYPTION WITH CRYPT

The **crypt** utility can be used to encrypt any files you don't want prying eyes to see. If you want to encrypt a whole directory hierarchy, first use **tar** or **cpio** to pack it into a single file.

cbw, the Crypt Breaker's Workbench, is included on the CD-ROM.

crypt uses a rotary cipher that is easy to break, and there are publicly-available tools that help to break it. The attack involves making incremental changes to the decryption settings and checking to see if they make the result more or less intelligible. To counter this attack, you can run **compress** on your data before using **crypt**. This makes it hard for a person to judge when they are getting close to decrypting your file, since compressed data looks like random noise.

crypt requires a "key" that becomes essentially a password for the encrypted file. The key cannot be recovered, so the use of **crypt** should not be taken lightly. **crypt** allows the key to be specified on the command line, but it's not wise to use this option because a timely **ps** or **w** can then display it. The editors **ex** and **vi** allow you to edit encrypted files using the **-x** option.

See page 517 for more information about PGP.

Many systems provide alternatives to **crypt** that use better encryption algorithms such as DES, the Data Encryption Standard. PGP, a freely-available encryption system by Philip Zimmermann, uses the IDEA algorithm, which is believed to be even stronger than DES. **man -k crypt** will show the encryption programs available on your machine.

23.14 CERT AND SCC

CERT advisories are available via anonymous ftp from cert.org.

In response to the uproar over the 1988 Internet worm, the Defense Advanced Research Projects Agency (DARPA) formed the Computer Emergency Response Team (CERT). The CERT Coordination Center (CERT/CC) is located at CMU's Software Engineering Institute (SEI). Although CERT's charter includes some degree of problem solving, in reality CERT lacks the ability to investigate problems or discipline offenders, and so is little more than a clearing house for vendor security patches and security tool announcements. These patches and announcements are called "CERT advisories." New advisories are posted to the newsgroup comp.security.announce.

If you are involved in a security-related incident, you should report the matter to CERT. They can be reached by phone at (412) 268-7090 or by email at cert@cert.org. Provide as much information as you can. CERT suggests that the following questions be answered in incident reports:

- What are the names of the hosts that were compromised at your site? What kind of machines are they, and what operating systems (including revision numbers) are they running?

- Have security patches been applied to the hosts? If so, were patches applied before or after the intrusion?

- Which user accounts were compromised?

- Were other hosts or sites involved in the intrusion? Have you contacted those sites about the problem? If other sites are involved, what is their contact information? If CERT is to contact the other sites, can your contact information (name, email address, and phone number) be given to the other sites?

- Have any law enforcement agencies been contacted?

- Is there an audit trail or log file that relates to the problem?

- What assistance would you like from CERT?

For MILNET (United States Military) users, there is a CERT-equivalent organization called SCC (Security Coordination Center) that provides a way to communicate security-related information to management personnel at DDN (Defense Data Network) facilities.

You can reach the SCC by calling (800) 235-3155 (7:00 a.m. to 5:00 p.m. PST), or by sending email to scc@nic.ddn.mil. For 24 hour coverage, call the MILNET trouble desk at (800) 451-7413 or AUTOVON 231-1713.

23.15 SECURITY MAILING LISTS

There are a number of Usenet groups and Internet mailing lists that provide real-time information about security problems. You should monitor at least a couple of them, perhaps sharing responsibility for monitoring them all with other administrators at your site.

Table 23.4   Sources of security information

Name	Subject	How to get it[a]
unix-security	General security	M security@cpd.com
security-misc	General security	G comp.security.misc
virus-list	Viruses	G comp.virus
sgi-bugs	IRIX bugs	G comp.sys.sgi.bugs
hpux-list	General HP-UX	G comp.sys.hp.hpux
solaris-list	Solaris 2.X	G comp.unix.solaris
sun-managers	Sun admin	M sun-managers-request@eecs.nwu.edu
ACM risks	Evils of technology	G comp.risks
cert-tools	New security tools	M cert-tools-request@cert.org
cert-advisory	CERT advisories	M cert-advisory-request@cert.org
		G comp.security.announce

a. M = mailing list (contact address is listed), G = Usenet newsgroup

23.16 RECOMMENDED SUPPLEMENTAL READING

CHESWICK, WILLIAM R. AND STEVEN M. BELLOVIN. *Firewalls and Internet Security.* Reading, MA; Addison-Wesley. 1994.

SEELEY, DONN. *A Tour of the Worm.* USENIX Conference Proceedings, San Diego, Winter 1989, pp. 287-304.

RITCHIE, DENNIS M. *"On the Security of UNIX."* May 1975. Reprinted in *UNIX System Manager's Manual*, 4.3 Berkeley Software Distribution. University of California, Berkeley. April 1986.

MORRIS, ROBERT, and KEN THOMPSON. *"Password Security: A Case History."* Communications of the ACM, 22 (11): 594-597, November 1979. Reprinted in *UNIX System Manager's Manual*, 4.3 Berkeley Software Distribution. University of California, Berkeley. April 1986.

GRAMPP AND MORRIS, *"UNIX Operating System Security."* AT&T Bell Labs Technical Journal, 63(8), October, 1984.

THOMPSON, KEN. *"Reflections on Trusting Trust."* in *ACM Turing Award Lectures: The First Twenty Years 1966-1985.* Reading, MA: ACM Press (Addison-Wesley). 1987.

GARFINKEL, SIMSON, and GENE SPAFFORD. *Practical UNIX Security.* Sebastopol: O'Reilly & Associates, 1991.

STOLL, CLIFFORD. *The Cuckoo's Egg.* New York: Doubleday, 1989.

STEIN, JENNIFER G., CLIFFORD NEUMAN, and JEFFREY L. SCHILLER. *"Kerberos: An Authentication Service for Open Network Systems."* USENIX Conference Proceedings, Dallas, Winter 1988, pp. 205-211.

SECTION THREE

BUNCH O' STUFF

24 *Usenet News*

24.1 INTRODUCTION

Usenet is a software system that distributes messages ("articles") to many sites around the world. It is not really a type of network, but rather a set of protocols, file formats, and affiliations among sites. The actual transport of messages usually occurs via the Internet or UUCP.

Usenet is similar to electronic mail, except that all articles are publicly readable. It's also similar in many respects to the "message boards" of on-line services such as CompuServe and America Online. However, it operates on a much larger scale. Usenet has more than 3,000,000 readers at 80,000 sites, and many subject areas ("newsgroups") receive hundreds of articles a day.

24.2 THE DISTRIBUTION OF NEWS

Most news is transmitted using the Network News Transfer Protocol (NNTP), which runs on top of TCP/IP. Originally, UUCP was used as the transport layer, but that is becoming increasingly rare.

Each news site has one or more *feeds* from which news is obtained and zero or more *clients* to which news is sent. The distribution of news is not centralized; articles ("postings") may originate at any site, and are simply propagated both "upstream" and "downstream" by the Usenet software. Each site that receives news is responsible for correctly preparing it to be resent to all the sites that it feeds.

563

Over 75 megabytes of news are posted each day. This is a staggering figure, and the amount of incoming data creates some formidable management problems. It has become very expensive (in terms of disk space) to create a stockpile of news articles. News sites typically allow articles to remain on the system for only a few days before they are deleted ("expired").

See page 567 for more information about C-News and INN.

In order to run news at your site, you need a Usenet software package (usually C-News/NNTP or INN) and one or more interactive news-reading packages. The Usenet software manages the flow of news articles to and from your site, while the readers provide user-level access to the database of articles.

24.3 NEWSGROUPS

Usenet articles are categorized into newsgroups. Each newsgroup is dedicated to the discussion of one particular topic, which may be as broad as the UNIX operating system (comp.unix) or as narrow as Celtic culture (soc.culture.celtic).

It is not necessary or even possible for users to read everything posted to the Usenet. There are over 5,000 newsgroups, and some of them receive upwards of a thousand messages a day. News-reading programs allow users to "subscribe" to the groups they are interested in, and some even provide ways of hiding particular threads of discussion inside groups. Even with all this help, it can take an hour or more to read 20 active newsgroups.

A lot of the articles posted to Usenet are computer-related: operating systems, software, human interfaces, programming languages, hardware, etc. This is perhaps a natural consequence of the fact that many Usenet readers are computer professionals. But there are also are newsgroups for skydivers, scuba divers, glider pilots, cooks, Buddhists, woodworkers, nudists, and almost any other category you can think of.

Most newsgroups are "unmoderated," which means that anyone can post an article. Some unmoderated groups feature high doses of irrelevant material and personal animosity. Groups with a technical bent usually maintain a high signal-to-noise ratio, but more socially-oriented newsgroups frequently degenerate into free-for-alls in which little useful information is exchanged.

Perhaps five percent of newsgroups are moderated. Instead of posting articles directly to a moderated newsgroup, users must send them to a moderator for review. Every article that appears in a moderated group has been personally approved by the moderator. Some moderators forward individual articles, while others condense them into digests that are posted as a single article. Most news readers provide the same interface for posting to an unmoderated group and submitting an article to a moderator. It is rare for a moderator to actually reject an article, since the mere threat of review tends to weed out spurious messages.

Like directories in the filesystem, newsgroups are organized into a hierarchy. The name of a newsgroup is analogous to the full pathname of a file, except that the separator character is a dot instead of a slash. The similarity between these two is intentional and convenient; news is stored in a tree of directories whose names are formed by translating dots to slashes.

At the top level of the news hierarchy are the core news classes listed in Table 24.1. Some top-level classes (for example, gnu and bionet) are distributed on a by-request basis and may not be available everywhere.

Table 24.1   Top-level newsgroup classifications

Name	Contents
alt	Alternative groups (alt.drugs, alt.sex, etc. – by request only)
bionet	Biotechnology groups
biz	Business groups
clari	International news wire in Usenet format
comp	Computer-related and source code distribution newsgroups
gnu	The Free Software Foundation
k12	Lower education (kindergarten through high school)
misc	Miscellaneous (items for sale, jobs offered or wanted)
news	Groups that discuss Usenet itself, its content and transport
pubnet	Public bulletin boards
rec	Discussions of recreational activities (skiing, hiking)
sci	Scientific and mathematical topics, new research, etc.
soc	Not-so-serious discussions (singles, college)
talk	Generally serious discussions (abortion, religion, philosophy)

Underneath each class is an arbitrary number of subdivisions. A subdivision may be a newsgroup in its own right, may have other subdivisions inside it, or both. For example, misc.consumers covers material of interest to consumers in general. Typical fare ranges from product reviews to consumer horror stories. This group also has a subgroup misc.consumers.house which addresses issues specific to real estate. The more subtopics in the name of a group, the more focused it is.

24.4 ALT: THE FORBIDDEN HIERARCHY

More than any other part of Usenet, the alt hierarchy has developed a widespread reputation in the network community. This is due to its liberal group creation policy: if you want to create a new group, you will generally be permitted to do so.[1] As a result, alt tends to be a catch-all for groups that didn't fit in elsewhere, either categorically or socially.

Alt is home to some fascinating groups, such as alt.dessert.toppings, alt.culture.austrian, alt.beer, alt.tv.brady-bunch, and the ever-popular alt.fan.dan-quayle. In the true spirit of free speech, however, alt contains many groups that might be deemed inappropriate for children, such as alt.sex.bestiality.barney,[2] alt.sex.watersports, and even the steamy alt.binaries.pictures.erotica.furry. You get the idea.

Clearly, it might be wise to partition some of this material from the under-18 crowd. Unfortunately, this separation is not well supported by Usenet and the Internet. Although it is possible to accept individual groups or subtrees of alt, it is safest to accept no part of the alt hierarchy if you provide computing resources to minors.

While alt is the largest moral majority offender, it is certainly not the only one. Newsgroups such as rec.arts.erotica are hidden in many dark corners throughout the Usenet tree. In addition, there is nothing to stop Joe Random Sicko from posting an inappropriate message to the otherwise "safe" k12 hierarchy.

Common sense might suggest that material like that found on the Internet is already available on playgrounds and soccer fields around the world, but it also suggests requiring parents to sign consent forms when any minor is given access to the Internet—even access that has been deemed "safe." There's always `ftp`.

Even if your site is a company with no underage users, you may still end up with an alt argument on your hands. Most of the enlightened world considers newsgroup suppression to be a form of censorship. But others contend that carrying alt is a waste of corporate resources or that certain groups are offensive to a specific gender, race, religion, or sexual preference. Now that's an argument you'll never win.

24.5 USENET: ASSET OR LIABILITY?

The classic Internet debate often centers around Usenet and its various offerings. Many members of upper management are convinced that engineers or secretaries who read news for an hour every day are "wasting time." In our view, this claim is unjustified.

Usenet often provides the irresistible bait that encourages Interphobes (those who are terrified of the Internet) to learn about the Internet and

---

1. See the group alt.config for information about creating a newsgroup in alt. Other hierarchies have more restrictive policies that usually involve a formal voting mechanism. Check news.groups to determine the current practice for your favorite hierarchy.

2. It's the thought that counts.

its various offerings, both for work and for pleasure. Once a secretary impressively produces a crucial tax form at the last minute by pulling it off the net, managers may think twice about their reservations.

Engineers and other technical staff often use Usenet as a sounding board for ideas and research. Perhaps management would rather build a fancy printed-matter library with outrageously expensive video conferencing hardware?

24.6 FAQs AND ARCHIVES

Well-focused groups usually maintain a Frequently Asked Questions (FAQ) file that collects answers to various common questions. In addition, FAQs often provide an overview of the topic that the group is devoted to and a list of locations (if any) where the group is archived.[3] Before posting to *any* group, try to find its FAQ and read it thoroughly. This will help you avoid irritating other readers by asking questions that have been asked thousands of times before. It will also keep you from looking stupid.

FAQs are usually posted to their respective groups once a month or so, and they are also posted to the group news.answers. If you're impatient, the host rtfm.mit.edu keeps an archive of all known FAQs which you can access via anonymous `ftp`.

24.7 CLARINET

Clarinet is a company that offers an "electronic newspaper" in Usenet format called ClariNews. ClariNews contains a wide variety of materials, from the AP and Reuters news wires to special features on science, technology, stock quotes, and the computer industry, just to name a few.

Clarinet charges a fee to provide this service to your desktop. They have a variety of pricing structures, with special pricing for educational institutions, overseas customers and public access systems or BBSs. Site licenses range from less than $4 per user per month for fifteen users to $1 per user per month for larger sites.

To obtain a feed, call Clarinet at 1-800-USE-NETS for more information, or email info@clarinet.com.

24.8 USENET SOFTWARE

News software is not a standard package, but it is "freely available." The software is not in the public domain, but distribution is unlimited. Two implementations can be found on the CD-ROM.

---

3. That is, where the articles are kept permanently on-line for reference.

C-News and NNTP

The most common and versatile news software actually consists of two separate packages joined together: the C-News system written largely by Henry Spencer, and the NNTP transport package written at Berkeley. Both are included on the CD-ROM, along with instructions on how to fit them together. C-News is responsible for storing incoming articles and deciding to what other sites they should be forwarded; NNTP is used to transmit them to remote neighbors.

INN

The InterNetNews (INN) package was written by Rich $alz as a complete replacement for the C-News/NNTP package combination in use at most sites. It uses the standard NNTP protocol to communicate with other sites and can talk to sites running either C-News or INN. INN is more efficient at managing a large news feed because it keeps a lot of information in memory.

INN is the best choice for a news package today if you have a fairly large feed and have a machine with lots of real memory (> 64MB) that you can dedicate as a news server. In a smaller environment, C-News is probably the best choice.

Setting Up News at your Site

Initial setup is by far the hardest part of news administration. Once the news software is installed and news has begun to flow, only occasional checkups are necessary. In general, setting up a news server involves the following steps.

First, you must allocate disk space to store the Usenet article tree. This should be at least a separate partition (**/var/spool/news**), and more than one partition if you intend to get a full feed (for example, one partition for alt, one for comp, and one for all the rest). Partitions should be placed on separate physical drives to optimize throughput.

To figure out how much space to allocate, you must first decide how many days of articles you want to keep on-line. To keep four days of articles, you would need 75MB/day * 4 days = 300MB, plus about 50% "slop." Ergo, a 450MB partition would provide adequate space.[4]

Second, obtain and install one of the news software packages (either INN or C-News/NNTP). These packages are responsible for accepting incoming news from your feed sites and storing it in the article tree. The basic news packages also serve individual articles to local clients, expire

---

4. Keep in mind that traffic is growing about 50% per year, so these numbers may or may not be appropriate by the time you read this.

old articles, and feed articles to downstream sites. Instructions for installing INN are given below.

Next, you need a news feed. Contact your Internet service provider or other system administrator "friends" to request one. It is common for sites to charge you a reasonable fee ($20-$100 per month) for the hassle and resources required to provide the feed.

Once you've found a feed, you must tell the upstream site the name of your news server and the groups or subtrees you want to receive. You will also need to know the name of the feed server so that you can propagate postings and other upstream traffic back to it. Enter all this information into your configuration files.

At this point, you can start the news daemon (or daemons) and wait for news to begin arriving. Watch log files carefully for the first hour or so until you are certain that you are correctly receiving and storing news.

Once news is up and running, you'll need to run maintenance and cleanup scripts (such as `news.daily`, see page 574) out of `cron`.

To read news, you'll need some client software. See page 574 for a survey of the most popular clients. The last step is to announce the availability of news to your users. Be sure to including a lecture about proper behavior (basically, "Don't be a jerk"). Then take cover.

24.9 INSTALLING INN

INN (pronounced "eye en en") can easily handle a very large news flow, provided that you have adequate computing resources (a > 20-30 MIPS machine with at least 64MB of physical memory). Given the growth of Usenet traffic, this will soon be a requirement at all sites that want to receive a reasonable number of newsgroups.

Obtaining INN

The first step in installing INN is to obtain the source code. It can be found on the CD-ROM and is also available from ftp.uu.net. The following sections assume that you've successfully uncompressed and un-`tarr`ed the file (if necessary) and that the result has been placed in a directory we'll call `$inn`.

Printing the INN Installation Documentation

Once you've unpacked the INN distribution, the first thing to do is to print out the official tutorial, *Installing InterNetNews*. We've summarized its contents in the sections that follow, but when in doubt, the distributed document should be considered authoritative.

The installation document is in **roff** format and uses the **-ms** macros. The distributed file comes in two parts that you'll have to concatenate before you can print. Assuming you have the **psroff** command to translate **roff** into PostScript and a PostScript printer named spud-lw, the following commands could be used to print the instructions:

```
% cd $inn
% make Install.ms
% psroff -Pspud-lw -ms Install.ms
```

Configuring INN

INN learns about its environment (where commands live, what library routines to use, etc.) via a master config file called **config.data**. Editing this file is the hardest but most essential step in the installation procedure. A template called **config.dist** is included in the INN distribution; copy it to **config.data** before you start editing.

config.data is processed by a command called **subst** which is distributed with INN. Much like **cpp** or **m4**, **subst** does token textual substitution. Here are some typical entries from the **config.data** file:

```
_PATH_NEWSLIB           /usr/local/news
_PATH_LOGFILE           /var/log/news/news
_PATH_ERRLOG            /var/log/news/errlog
_PATH_MOST_LOGS         /var/log/news
_PATH_SERVERPID         /usr/local/news/innd/innd.pid
_PATH_NEWSFEEDS         /usr/local/news/newsfeeds
_PATH_HISTORY           /usr/local/news/history
_PATH_INNDHOSTS         /usr/local/news/hosts.nntp
_PATH_ACTIVE            /usr/local/news/active
```

These lines define the paths to many of the files used by INN. You should skim through the entries in the distributed template and change the ones that you know are different on your system, such as the locations of log files, commands, or libraries.

Installing InterNetNews has a section near the back which details suggested changes for operating systems such as Solaris, HP-UX, IRIX, and BSDI. Since many of these changes are obscure (for example, changes in certain type declarations), you should refer to the distribution document if you're running a common system.

Compiling INN

Once you've finished tinkering with **config.data**, you'll need to run **make** to compile and install the INN programs and control files.

This can be done with the following commands.

```
% cd $inn
% make world
% make install
```

With luck, after a few minutes of compiling and file copying, the INN package will be properly installed in your destination directory (usually `/usr/local/news`).

The INN Cast of Characters

INN consists of a number of programs that perform specific tasks and a set of files that control them. The most important INN programs are:

innd   The "ringmaster" of INN. It runs as a daemon, listens on the NNTP port (TCP port 119), and accepts connections from feed sites as well as from local news-reading clients. Local connections are handed off to **nnrpd**.

nnrpd   This is a specialized daemon that services local clients; it is invoked by **innd**.

expire   Using `expire.ctl` as a guide, **expire** removes old articles from the article tree. Eventually, they are also removed from the article database.

nntpsend   **nntpsend** and its helper **innxmit** work together to transmit articles to neighbors, both up- and downstream. **nntpsend** is the front end, and the actual work is done by **innxmit**.

ctlinnd   **ctlinnd** sends "hints" to **innd**. For example, "I just changed file X, so you should go reread it now."

Important INN control files are listed in Table 24.2. These files usually live in `/usr/local/news`.

Table 24.2   Important INN control files

File	Purpose
`active`	Lists all active newsgroups, the oldest and newest article number for each, and each group's posting status
`expire.ctl`	Controls expiration, on a per-group basis if desired
`newsfeeds`	Specifies which articles to feed to downstream sites
`nnrp.access`	Lists machines permitted to read news from this server
`hosts.nntp`	Lists upstream and downstream sites allowed to connect via NNTP to transfer batches of articles

You must edit all five of the files listed in Table 24.2 before starting the news system for the first time.

The active file

The **active** file lists the groups that the news system knows about. It also contains a record of the article numbers that are on-line for each group, the acceptance and posting status of each group, and any group aliases that exist. There must be one line in this file for every valid newsgroup at your site. A typical entry might look like this:

```
alt.abortion.inequity 0000013258 0000013208 y
```

This line describes the newsgroup alt.abortion.inequity. Article number 13,208 is the oldest article on-line, and article number 13,258 is the newest. Thus, the next incoming article for this group would be assigned the number 13,259. The trailing y indicates that this group is accepted from feeds and that posting is allowed from this site. Valid options for this field are listed in Table 24.3.

Table 24.3 Newsgroup status option codes

Option	Meaning
y	Group is accepted and postable
n	Group exists but not at this site (not accepted/no postings)
m	Group is moderated (accepted but postings go somewhere else)
x	Group is accepted, but posting is not allowed
j	Articles in this group are not kept, only passed on
=alias	Group has been renamed to *alias*

When you initially set up your news server, you should request a copy of the upstream **active** file and replace the two middle fields with 0s. This can be done with **awk** as follows:

```
cat upstream.active | awk '{ printf("%s 000000000
    000000000 %s\n", $1, $4) }' > active
```

The expire.ctl file

expire.ctl is used by the **expire** program, which removes old articles when their time has come. Once an article has been removed, a record of its message ID is kept for a while longer so that the article can be rejected if a feed site offers it again. This helps to avoid duplicate postings. An initial **expire.ctl** file might look like this:

```
/remember/:14
*:A:3:4:5
```

The remember line is special and indicates that we should hold on to message IDs of old articles for 14 days. Subsequent lines specify when the bodies of articles in particular groups should be removed from the system. The fields have the meanings listed in Table 24.4.

Table 24.4 Decoding guide for example expire.ctl file

Field	Meaning
*	All newsgroups
A	All newsgroup types (moderated and normal)
3	Minimum number of days to keep articles
4	Default number of days to keep articles
5	Maximum number of days to keep articles

In this example, all newsgroups are treated alike. But there can be many configuration lines, each of which applies to a different set of newsgroups. When an article falls between the minimum and maximum retention times, its Expires header line is used to determine its life. If an articles has no Expires header, the default time is used.

The newsfeeds file

The **newsfeeds** file indicates how articles should be redistributed to upstream and downstream sites. There must be one line in this file for every site you exchange news with. The **newsfeeds** file has a powerful syntax that can be used for many situations, from UUCP feeds to article-at-a-time feeds via mail. Refer to the man page for **newsfeeds** for detailed information.

A simple entry for an NNTP feed to a remote site might look like this:

```
news.acme.com:comp.*,rec.*:Tf,Wnm:news.acme.com
```

The line starts with the name of the remote site, here, news.acme.com. The second field lists the groups that should be fed. In this case, the comp and rec hierarchies are sent. The third field specifies how article information should be "handed off" to **nntpsend** or an equivalent transport program. `Tf,Wnm` indicates that a list of articles should be written to a file in **/var/spool/news/out.going**, which is correct for feeds that use **nntpsend**. Finally, news.acme.com is specified as the host that **nntpsend** should contact to transmit the articles.

nntplink is included on the CD-ROM

nntplink, an alternative to **nntpsend**, can be used as a more efficient bulk transfer method for large sites. The **newsfeeds** man page illustrates the use of **nntplink** as a transfer program.

The nnrp.access file

nnrp.access controls server access by local news-reading clients. The only hosts listed in this file should be those that belong to your organization. An entry that would allow reading and posting from all hosts in the xinet.com domain might look like this:

```
*.xinet.com:Read Post:::*
```

The last three fields allow per-user posting and group access restrictions (not used here). See the man page for **nnrp.access** for details.

The hosts.nntp file

hosts.nntp specifies which remote hosts are allowed to transfer articles to the local site. Both upstream and downstream sites should be listed in this file. Some examples:

```
xor.com:
cronkite.cs.umd.edu:
news.colorado.edu:
```

Starting Up INN

A special script, **inndstart**, is used to start **innd**. It's usually located in **/usr/local/etc**. Once **innd** has started, you can use **telnet** to verify that it's alive:

```
% telnet localhost nntp
Trying 127.0.0.1 ...
Connected to localhost.xor.com.
Escape character is '^]'.
200 news.xor.com InterNetNews server INN 1.4 Dec-93 ready
```

Monitoring Article Flow

After **innd** has been running for a while (and the feed to you has been turned on at the remote site), you can use **tail -f** to examine the log, which is usually **/var/log/news/news.log**. Entries look like this:

```
Jun 14 00:16:34.536 + cs.umd.edu
    <2tikil$4e0@news1.svc.portal.com> news.colorado.edu
```

This entry indicates that an article with message ID

```
<2tikil$4e0@news1.svc.portal.com>
```

was received from cs.umd.edu and fed to news.colorado.edu.

If the news system encounters trouble, it will write details of the problem to the file **/var/log/news/errlog**.

Daily Chores

The **news.daily** script should run out of **cron** once a day to clean up log files, run **expire**, etc. Add an entry like this to news' crontab:

```
6 4 * * * /usr/local/news/bin/news.daily >/dev/null 2>&1 &
```

24.10 NNTP-Based News Readers

The NNTP protocol (RFC977) functions both as a way for news servers to talk among themselves and as a way for end-users to access the local news database (one article at a time). In the past, news was often read directly out of files in the spool directory. These days, most news readers understand NNTP.

See page 375 for more information about the performance of NFS.
Some sites use NFS to cross-mount the article tree from the news server. Since NFS is based on UDP and thus does no congestion control, this is a horrible idea. Accessing articles via an NNTP daemon is much kinder to your network.

The sections below describe some of the more popular news readers.

rn: Read News

rn is included on the CD-ROM.
rn is the traditional UNIX-based news reader. It provides basic news and posting (via **Pnews**) capabilities. Its command structure is somewhat cryptic, and it lacks creature comforts offered by other clients.

When you start up **rn**, it first prints a list of newsgroups that you have subscribed to, along with the number of unread articles in each. This information is based on your `~/.newsrc` file, which **rn** updates as you read articles. Next, **rn** asks if you want to subscribe to any new groups that have been created since you last read news.[5] Finally, it prompts you for the newsgroup you want to read first.

rn generally has a sour, UNIX-like flavor. It lacks the point-and-click feel of more modern news readers.

trn: A Threaded Version of rn

trn is included on the CD-ROM.
trn is a close cousin of **rn**. In fact, it looks exactly like **rn** except for one major enhancement: **trn** maintains a database (called a thread database) of all the subjects currently being discussed in each group. When reading news, a user can elect to follow a thread, reading all articles about a specific topic at once. This is much nicer than reading the articles in the essentially random order in which they arrived.

nn: No News is Good News

nn is included on the CD-ROM.
The goal of **nn** is to help you plow through a large volume of news in a relatively short period of time, quickly sifting the wheat from the chaff. Like **trn**, **nn** is thread-based. It also adds the innovation of presenting subject lines for your selection before moving on to the full articles.

Most news readers assume you want to read every article unless you specify otherwise; **nn** assumes that you don't want to see an article unless you specifically ask for it. **nn** maintains its own database of news information so that all operations are blindingly fast.

---

5. There can be hundreds of new groups. The N key says no to all of them.

tin: Yet Another News Reader

tin is included on the CD-ROM.

In the same vein as `nn`, `tin` is a heavily `curses`-based news reader that allows users to choose groups or articles from a menu, and also via a highlighted bar that can be moved up and down the screen with the arrow keys. `tin` has more creature comforts than most other newsreaders and supports everything from threads to the ability to "tag" a group of articles, save them to a file, concatenate them, remove their headers, and `uudecode` them all in one step. This is handy when reading a newsgroup such as alt.binaries.pictures.tasteless.

xrn: An X Windows News Reader

A somewhat cumbersome point-and-click news interface, `xrn` is an X11 application that provides pull-down menus, drag-and-drop text editing, and all the other comforts of a windowing system on your desktop. Unfortunately, `xrn` does not support threading.

24.11 Maintenance Strategies

Because of its chronically high disk activity, the news system makes disk backups be much larger than they ought to be. This is especially problematic if your news directory is on the same disk partition as users' home directories, since such partitions must be dumped often.

See page 142 for more information about inodes.

The solution is to make a separate filesystem on which to keep news. You may find that creating a number of news partitions on physically separate drives will dramatically boost your system's performance, since the kernel can then schedule disk arm movements more efficiently. You may also want to format filesystems for news with more inodes than usual, since the news database consists of numerous small files and directories.

Keep in mind that your news neighbors depend on you to keep your system running correctly. If you take your system down without telling your feeds, they will continue to queue news for transmission to your site. It does not usually take long before the backed-up news traffic starts to cause problems. Likewise, machines that you feed will wonder what is going on. Always notify your news connections of potential downtime and problems. Keep contact information off-line.

24.12 News-Reading Chores for System Administrators

Some newsgroups are so useful to a system administrator that we consider reading them to be practically mandatory. The following sections introduce a few of them. They are hard to prioritize and are not listed in any particular order. Unless marked, they are unmoderated.

news.announce.important (moderated)

This group carries information of vital importance to all news-reading users. Postings to this newsgroup are required to be really important, so it is rare to see anything here more often than every year or so.

news.admin

This is a forum for administrators of news software. Important information about the news software and Usenet in general usually comes in through this group.

comp.unix.questions

This newsgroup is a forum for questions and answers about UNIX. In theory, the material posted to this group should be hardware-independent, but in real life many of the questions relate to problems with specific versions of UNIX and specific kinds of hardware. Some of the material is obscure, but you will find that much of it pertains, if only indirectly, to you and your system.

If you have a system-independent question that your manuals cannot help you with, this is a good place to try and find an answer. If your question is better suited to a more focused newsgroup, don't post it here. As a general rule, you should learn to recognize the types of questions that are appropriate for a given newsgroup through a week or two of observation before posting anything.

comp.unix.wizards

This newsgroup is kind of an older sibling to comp.unix.questions, but the material discussed is more kernel-oriented. It isn't directly related to system administration, but it can give you a good feel for what is going on inside your machine.

One of the nice things about this newsgroup is that operating system bugs are often reported here as they are found (hopefully, not often). A patch that you can apply to your kernel if you have source code is often supplied along with the bug report, allowing you to increase the reliability of your system in a relatively painless way. But remember to beware of any patch!

comp.sources.unix (moderated)

Source code for use on UNIX systems is posted here. Almost any kind of program can appear, from spelling correctors to text formatters to programming languages to utilities for use with other packages such as UUCP. The code is free and is in the public domain.

*A program that cre-
ates shell archives
(**shar**) is included
on the CD-ROM.*

Most code posted to comp.sources.unix (as well as the other source newsgroups) is packed using a format called a shell archive or "shar" for short. This packing scheme allows multiple files to be placed inside a single file for transmission and then unpacked at the destination by running the file through **sh**. Before invoking **sh** on a file, be sure that all the header information has been trimmed off, as **sh** won't understand it and will gag on the file. And of course, beware of Trojan horses. Some additional comments about the safety of software obtained from Usenet are given on page 556.

comp.sources.misc (moderated)

This is a group for software that doesn't fit into other source code groups. Either it is not of interest to the general public (numerical analysis routines), or it isn't written in C (non-C programs are welcome in most newsgroups, but tend to be scoffed at), or it is for a specific computer that doesn't have its own source code newsgroup.

comp.sources.bugs

Bug reports and fixes for source code distributed through Usenet are posted here.

comp.sources.wanted

In this newsgroup are heard the pleas of people who are trying to find out if code exists to do a particular job, or who are trying to locate a copy of a package that they know exists. Think of this group as a kind of bank: every time you help someone else to get what they need, you are morally entitled to make a request. If the other person's question is not likely to be of interest to the general Usenet community, reply by email rather than posting a response.

Sometimes, it is painfully obvious that the person trying to locate source code is lazy and is trying to get someone else to do the work by posting on Usenet. This is bad because numerous people are liable to reply to easy questions: some to give the answer, and others to complain about how the poster shouldn't have asked the question. Don't get involved in this kind of situation—not as an asker or answerer, and especially not as a whiner.

comp.sys.*machine* and comp.sys.*machine*.digest (moderated)

These are moderated and unmoderated forums for general discussion of a particular machine or architecture. Most commercial systems are represented in the unmoderated groups, but only the more popular ones also have moderated versions. There are a few anomalously-named groups; for example, comp.sys.sun is moderated.

comp.unix.admin

This group is for general discussions of UNIX administration issues. There are often pointers to other, more specific discussion groups.

24.13 FUN NEWSGROUPS YOU MIGHT FIND INTERESTING

Table 24.5 lists some newsgroups that you might find entertaining or instructive in your spare time (or useful for debugging news).

Table 24.5   Some newsgroups

Group	Description
comp.sources.games	Recreational software (moderated)
misc.forsale	Short, tasteful postings about items for sale
misc.invest	Investments and the handling of money
rec.arts.bonsai	Dwarfish trees and shrubbery
rec.arts.movies.reviews	Movie reviews (moderated, surprisingly good)
rec.arts.startrek.info	Trekkish fandom (moderated)
rec.autos.sport	Discussion of organized, legal auto competitions
rec.bicycles.rides	Tours and training or commuting routes
rec.crafts.winemaking	The tasteful art of making wine
rec.food.drink	Wines and spirits
rec.humor.funny	Jokes that are sometimes funny (moderated)
rec.motorcycles	Motorcycles and related products and laws
rec.music.gdead	A group for (Grateful) Dead-heads
rec.photo	Photography and darkroom techniques
rec.sport.boxing	Boxing in all its pugilistic facets and forms
talk.bizarre	The unusual, bizarre, curious, and often stupid

24.14 RECOMMENDED SUPPLEMENTAL READING

O'REILLY, TIM and GRACE TODINO. *Managing UUCP and Usenet*. Sebastopol: O'Reilly & Associates, 1990.

TODINO, GRACE and DALE DOUGHERTY. *Using UUCP and Usenet*. Sebastopol: O'Reilly & Associates, 1990.

KANTOR, B. AND P. LAPSLEY. *Network News Transfer Protocol: A Proposed Standard for the Stream-Based Transmission of News*. RFC977. 1986.

HORTON, M. AND R. ADAMS. *Standard for Interchange of USENET Messages*. RFC1036. 1987.

25 *Printing and Imaging*

Flakiest Program of the year

25.1 Introduction

When we wrote the first edition of this book, the most common printers were ASCII line printers. Laser printers were new, expensive, and rare. High-resolution output devices required custom driver software and formatting programs.

Today, line printers are practically antiques. Almost every place you find a computer you will find a laser printer, and there are numerous "standards" for page description.

With all of these changes in technology, you might expect that the UNIX printing systems would have changed dramatically. Unfortunately, they have not. The old line printer spooling systems have simply been hacked and overloaded to try to support the new technology.

All major vendors use essentially the vanilla BSD spooling system (`lpd`, `lpc`, `lpr` and friends), the ATT spooling system (`lpsched`, `lpadmin`, `lp` et al.), or a combination of both. This chapter starts off with a brief description of the terminology involved in printing, then describes the BSD and ATT printing systems. Next we provide a section on getting the systems to work together in a network, and finally, a discussion of some common software associated with printing.

Table 25.1 lists our reference operating systems and brief description of their printing systems.

Table 25.1   Various operating systems' printing software

System	Printing System
Solaris	ATT with some completely random extensions
HP-UX	ATT with some useful extensions
IRIX	ATT and BSD, with all commands trying to do both
SunOS	Pure BSD
OSF/1	BSD plus an ATT front end
BSDI	BSD with a few minor enhancements

If you are trying to determine what kind of system you have, check to see which scheduler is present (`lpd` or `lpsched`) rather than looking at the queuing commands. Many systems provide command-line interfaces that mimic the other system. For example, HP-UX provides an `lpr` command, but uses the ATT printing system.

AIX for IBM workstations is based on ATT UNIX, but IBM uses home-grown printing software that is different from the standard systems. We will not cover the AIX printing system.

POSIX has chosen yet another system in their pitiful attempts at standardization. It is based on the Palladium printing system from MIT's Project Athena. Rumor has it that even MIT does not use this system.

25.2 MINI-GLOSSARY OF PRINTING TERMS

While an overview of current printing technology is beyond the scope of this book, we will try to give you enough information to respond when someone begins haranguing you in printer jargon.

spooler A spooler is a system that receives print jobs, stores them, prioritizes them, and sends them out sequentially to a printer. A user-level command is used to submit jobs to the spooler.

dpi Most modern printers are bitmap devices, meaning that the actual output is composed of rows of weensy dots. A printer's *dpi* is the number of dots per inch. Generally speaking, the higher the dpi, the better print quality. Sometimes a printer's resolution is asymmetric; a notation such as "300 x 600 dpi" indicates a horizontal resolution of 300 dpi and a vertical resolution of 600 dpi.

PDL Most printers accept input in one or more "page description languages" that specify the images to be placed on the page in an abstract way PDL descriptions are usually more efficient to transmit than raw images, and they are easier for applications to generate. They also have the benefit of being device and resolution-independent.

bitmap   Sometimes you need to print images that cannot be easily described using a PDL. In these cases, you use a bitmap, which is a set of data that specifies which dots are filled in and which are not (or what color each dot is, in the case of a color image).

pbmplus, a bitmap conversion package, is included on the CD-ROM.

As with PDLs, there are several competing formats for storing bitmaps. Every PDL supports at least one format. Since bitmaps are usually very large, they are often compressed. There are a plethora of tools for translating between different bitmap formats.

RIP   A RIP (Raster Image Processor) is a system that accepts documents in one or more PDLs and converts them to a bitmap format appropriate for a particular output device. When high-quality output devices first became available, ripping (converting a PDL document to a bitmap) was done on the host machine. Later, it became common to put the RIP in the printer. As printing systems have become more advanced and ripping has become more compute-intensive, RIPs have been moving back to the host machine.

PostScript   PostScript is by far the most common PDL found on UNIX systems. PostScript was designed by and is licensed from Adobe Systems Incorporated. Almost all page layout programs can generate PostScript, and many printers can accept PostScript input directly.

ghostscript, a free PostScript RIP, is included on the CD-ROM.

PostScript is actually a full-fledged programming language. PostScript programs can be read with a text editor and can be recognized by the plenitude of parentheses and slashes. PostScript files generally start with the characters %!. Although this is not required by the language itself, some versions of the UNIX printing software look for these characters when attempting to classify print jobs.

HPGL   HPGL is the Hewlett-Packard Graphics Language, another PDL. It was originally used to drive pen plotters and now just won't die. Most CAD programs can generate HPGL, and many large-format output devices understand it. Since HPGL was designed for plotters, it is best suited for line drawings such as mechanical designs and architectural plans. HPGL text consists of strings of two uppercase letters followed by optional comma-separated arguments.

PCL PCL, or Printer Command Language, is HP's alternative to PostScript. It is found almost exclusively on HP printers and is quite common in the PC world. UNIX applications usually cannot generate PCL, but most HP devices can be purchased with a PostScript option. It's often possible to upgrade an older PCL printer to PostScript using an add-on cartridge from a third-party vendor such as Pacific Page.

QuickDraw QuickDraw is a graphics language used on Apple Macintosh systems. Macintosh supports PostScript printers using a driver that converts QuickDraw to PostScript. Cheap Mac printers that do not have RIPs of their own are supported by translating QuickDraw directly to bitmaps.

roff roff is not a PDL but rather a text formatting language. Most UNIX documents (for example, the man pages) are formatted with roff. Periods at the beginnings of lines and weird-looking commands such as

```
.so macros
.CT 25 "Printing and Imaging"
.S0 "Introduction"
```

are sure signs of roffery. roff was designed in the era of character terminals, when it was impossible to see what a document really looked like without formatting and printing it. Even though roff is seldom used for new work, there are still many legacy documents left in this format.

Originally, each output device had a special version of the roff command: troff for the CAT phototypesetter, vtroff for the Versatec electrostatic plotter, etc. Just as the roff format was in its death throes, there arose a specification for ditroff, device-independent troff. This command generated files in an intermediate language which was actually a full-fledged PDL.

groff is included on the CD-ROM.

Despite roff being old and crusty, you will probably want to have some way to print roff documents, if for no other reason than to print man pages. Since roff must be licensed from its owner, some vendors have chosen to pre-format their manuals and to sell roff as an extra-cost item. See page 614 for information about groff, a free version of roff.

25.3 BSD PRINTING

BSD's printing system is somewhat crude. It supports only relatively simple operations, is hard to maintain, and sometimes just doesn't work right. Its saving grace is that it extends well to large, heterogeneous networks, allowing many computers to share printers.

In the discussions that follow, we assume that the printer hardware has already been physically connected to a host or the network. See Chapter 8, *Serial Devices*, for information about connecting serial printers, and Chapter 15, *Network Hardware*, for information about connecting devices to a network.

An Overview of the Printing Process

Under BSD, all access to printers is controlled by the `lpd` daemon (usually located in `/usr/lib`) and the `lpr` program. `lpr` accepts data to be printed and puts it in a spooling directory, where `lpd` finds it and prints it out. `lpr` is the only program on a UNIX system that can queue files for printing. Other programs that cause files to be printed (for example, `pr` and `ditroff`) do so by calling `lpr`.

When `lpr` is executed, it gathers together the data to be printed and information about how the job should be handled. There are three sources for this handling information: the command-line arguments supplied to `lpr`, the environment variables of the process that executes `lpr`, and the system's global configuration. In some cases, all three are potential sources for the same piece of information.

A case in point is the selection of the printer to which the job should be sent. If a `-P`*printer* argument is passed to `lpr`, *printer* becomes the destination. Otherwise, the environment is checked to see if PRINTER is defined, and if so, its value is used. If all else fails, the job is submitted to the system-wide default printer. Almost all printing-related commands understand the `-P` argument and the PRINTER environment variable, including `lpq` and `lprm`.

As soon as `lpr` knows to which printer the current job is headed, it looks the printer up in `/etc/printcap`, the system's printer information database. This file tells `lpr` the name of a directory where print jobs for that printer should be placed. This "spool directory" is usually `/var/spool/`*printername*.

`lpr` creates two files in the spool directory for each job. The first file's name consists of the letters `cf` (control file) followed by a number that identifies the job.[1] This file contains reference and handling information

---

1. The `cf` file is actually called `tf` ("temporary file") while `lpr` is in the process of accepting a job. After the file has been written, `lpr` changes its name from `tf`*xxx* to `cf`*xxx*.

for the job, such as the identity of the user that submitted it. The numeric portion of the filename allows space for only three digits, so the printing system becomes confused if more than 999 jobs are queued.

The second file's name begins with **df** (data file) followed by the same number. This file contains the actual data to be printed. After the file has been spooled, **lpr** notifies the **lpd** daemon of the job's existence.

When **lpd** receives this notification, it consults the **printcap** file to determine whether the destination is local or remote.[2] If **printcap** says that the printer is connected locally, **lpd** checks to be sure there is a printing daemon running on the appropriate queue, and creates one (a copy of itself) if there is not.

If the requested printer is connected to a different machine, **lpd** opens a connection to the remote machine's **lpd** and transfers both the data and the control file. **lpd** then deletes the local copies of these files.

Scheduling for print jobs is done on a first-in, first-out (FIFO) basis, but the system administrator can modify the printing agenda using the **lpc** program if desired. Unfortunately, there is no way to permanently instruct the printing system to give preferential treatment to jobs spooled by a particular user or machine.

When the job is ready to print, **lpd** creates a series of UNIX pipes between the spool file and the printing hardware through which the data to be printed is transported. In the middle of this channel **lpd** installs a filter process that can review and edit the contents of the data stream before it reaches the printer.

Filter processes may perform various transformations on the data, or do nothing at all. Their chief purposes are to provide formatting for special applications and to support any device-specific protocols that may be required for dealing with a particular printer. A printer's default filter can be overridden on the **lpr** command line.

The /etc/printcap File

/etc/printcap is the BSD printing system's master database. A printer must be described there before jobs can be submitted to it.

/etc/printcap uses the same format as the **/etc/termcap** and **/etc/remote** files. The first item in each entry is a list of names for the printer, separated by a vertical bar ("|"). This is followed by a number of configuration settings separated by colons, each of which is of the form

2. Actually, the **lpd** started from **/etc/rc** doesn't do any real work; it just waits for network connections and makes copies of itself to handle each request. When we talk about **lpd** doing something, we mean that some copy of **lpd** does it.

xx=string, *xx*, or *xx#number*, where *xx* is the two-character name of a parameter and *string* and *number* are values to be assigned to it. When no value is assigned, the variable is Boolean and its presence indicates "true."

The null statement is acceptable; two colons may be placed side by side. It is helpful to begin and end each line with a colon to make subsequent modifications easier. Comments in **/etc/printcap** are introduced with a pound sign ("#"). Entries may span several lines if intermediate lines are terminated with a backslash. Continuation lines are, by convention, indented.

The syntax of **/etc/printcap** is illustrated by the following short example. A more complete example is given starting on page 593, after the discussion of the **printcap** variables.

```
# Apple LaserWriter remote printcap. CS Department.

anchor-lw|cer|1-56|LaserWriter Plus in cer lab:\
    :lp=:sd=/var/spool/anchor-lw:rm=anchor:rp=anchor-lw:\
    :lf=/var/adm/lpd-errs:
```

From the first line, we can see that cer, anchor-lw, 1-56 and "Laser-Writer Plus in cer lab" are all equivalent names for the same printer. While you may give your printers as many names as you like, you should include at least three forms of the primary name:

- Short name – three or four characters, easy to type (e.g., cer)
- Full name – hostname and type of printer (e.g., anchor-lw)
- Descriptive name – other information (e.g., "LW Plus in cer lab")

Jobs submitted to the printing system without a specific destination are routed to the first printer with "lp" as one of its aliases. You should not use "lp" as a printer's primary name, as this will make it difficult to change the default printer.

Printcap Variables

The many **printcap** variables are well documented in the **printcap** manual page, so we'll discuss only the useful ones here. Most of the variables fall into six basic categories:

- File and directory specifications
- Remote access information
- Printing filters
- Communication settings
- Page information
- File and directory specifications

All **printcap** entries should include at least a specification of the spool directory (the sd variable) and the error log file (lf).

sd: spool directory

Each printer should have its own spool directory. All spool directories should be in the same parent directory (usually /var/spool), and should have the same name as the full name of the printer they serve (anchor-lw in the preceding example). A spool directory is needed even if the printer being described lives on a different machine; spooled files are stored locally until they can be transmitted for printing.

When you install a new printer, you must create the spool directory by hand. Permissions should be 775, with both owner and group daemon.

The spool directory for a printer also contains two status files: lock and status. The status file contains a one-line description of the printer's state. This information is maintained by lpd and referred to by the lpq command. The lock file is used to prevent multiple invocations of lpd from becoming active on a single queue, and to hold information about the active job. The permissions of the lock file are manipulated by lpc to control spooling and printing on the printer.

lf: error log file

See Chapter 12 for more information about log files.

One error log may be shared by all printers; it may be placed anywhere you like. When a log entry is made, the name of the offending printer will be included. The log file above is /var/adm/lpd-errs. Even remote printers should have log files, just in case there is a communication problem with the remote machine.

lp: device name

The device name for the printer must be specified when the printer is local. For a printer that is connected through a serial, parallel, or SCSI port, this is the file in the /dev directory that refers to the printer. If the printcap entry addresses a network printer (that is, a printer on your LAN, not just a "remote" printer; see page 614), the lp variable will usually be a pointer to a dummy file.

lpd uses an advisory lock on the lp file to determine if the printer is in use. Even if the printer is really accessed through a network connection, you should provide a value for the lp variable. You should specify a unique file that exists and lives on a local disk.

If the printer can send status information back to the host through the specified device file, the Boolean variable rw should be specified to request that the device be opened for both reading and writing.

af: accounting file

If you intend to charge for printer use or just want to keep tabs on how much your users are printing, you should enable accounting for the printer by specifying an accounting file. The accounting file need only be specified on the machine where the printer is physically connected, since accounting records are not written until a job is actually printed.

Accounting information is summarized with the **pac** command. See page 645 for more information about **pac**.

rm and rp: remote access

In most situations, you will want to access a printer from more than one machine on your network. Even if the printer is a network device, you should pick a single machine to be responsible for communicating with the printer. All other machines should forward jobs to the designated handler. This allows **lpd** to take care of queueing the jobs in order rather than having several machines constantly squabbling over control of the printer. It also gives you a single place to look when printing is not working.

"Remote" machines (machines that are not directly connected to the printer) have a simple **printcap** entry that tells where to send the job, as in the example on page 586. The rm variable specifies the machine to which jobs should be sent, while the rp variable gives the name of the printer on that machine. The details of remote printing, as well as some specific examples, are described starting on page 593.

At first glance, the **/etc/printcap** file seems to be an administrative nightmare because the entries that describe a local printer are different from those that describe a remote printer. Each host with local printers seems to need a customized **printcap** file. However, with a bit of cleverness in defining the rp variable, a universal **printcap** file can be constructed. For example, consider the following two entries:

```
cso|csoffice||7-7|postscript|PostScript|cso:\
    :lp=:sd=/var/spool/lpd/cso:mx#0:rm=sigi:rp=cso_real:\
    :lf=/var/adm/lpd-errs:ty=HP LaserJet 4M Plus:

cso_real|Real local entry for sigi's cso:\
    :lp=/dev/cso:sd=/var/spool/lpd/cso_real:\
    :if=/usr/local/cap/cso:af=/var/adm/cso_real.acct:\
    :tc=sigi_generic:
```

The first is a remote description of a printer called cso attached to the host sigi. The second is a local description of a printer called cso_real on sigi. They are actually the same printer. All users should refer to the printer by its network name, cso. Even on the machine where the printer actually lives, jobs will be "transferred" over the network to the queue associated with the local entry. Be sure to use different spool directories for the two **printcap** entries, just as if two different printers were being described.

of, if, nf: printing filters

Filters perform a number of functions. The default printing filter (usually `/usr/lib/lpf`) fixes up various non-printing sequences and writes out an accounting record, if appropriate. In the early days of UNIX, filters were often relied upon to perform various formatting tasks, but this practice is not as widespread as it once was. The only special filters you really need to worry about are those for handling **troff** output, TeX output, and screen dumps.

If you have a character-only printer, you don't really need to be concerned with filters, and if you have a laser printer, typesetter, or plotter the necessary filters will usually be provided with the printer's software. If you need to configure a printer that you don't have any software for, you will have to read through the details of the various filters in the rest of this section. Otherwise, skip ahead and live in blissful ignorance.

Filters are usually just shell scripts that call a series of translation programs. The filter program must accept the print job on standard input, translate the job to a format appropriate for the device, and send the result to standard output.

If the user does not specify a filter when executing **lpr**, either the `if` (input filter) or the `of` (output filter) will be used. The names are deceptive, as both are actually used to send data to a printer.

If an `if` entry occurs in `/etc/printcap`, but no `of` entry exists, the device will be opened once for each job, and the filter will be expected to send one job to the printer and exit.

If an `of` entry occurs, but no `if` entry exists, **lpd** will open the device once and call the filter program once, sending all the jobs in the queue in a big clump. This is good for devices that take a long time to connect to; however, such devices are rare.

If both an `of` and an `if` are listed in `/etc/printcap`, the output filter will be used to send the banner page (and it will be called even if banners are turned off), and the input filter will be called to send the job. This combination is too confusing for mere mortals. Avoid it.

If you have to write new filters, stick to using `if` filters, as they are easier to debug. Input filters get called with numerous arguments which vary among implementations. The most interesting are the user name, host machine, and accounting file name. If you wish to do accounting for the printer, the input filter must generate the accounting records and append them to the accounting file. If you want to restrict access to a printer (for example, to deny printing to the user "guest" on any machine), the input filter must also take care of that, as **lpd** has no built-in way to restrict individual users from printing.

To try to clarify the uses of filters, we will look at a very simple example of an `if` filter. The following example is for a PostScript printer connected to a serial line on the local machine:

```
#!/bin/csh -f
/usr/local/bin/textps $* | /usr/local/bin/psreverse
```

Since the printer is serially connected, **lpd** takes care of opening the device with the correct modes, as specified in **/etc/printcap**. The first program called is **textps**, which looks at the input and decides if it is PostScript (which our printer expects), and if not, converts it to Post-Script. It gets all the filter arguments that were passed (the `$*`), and is expected to generate accounting records from that information. The second program, **psreverse**, reverses the order of the pages so that they come out in a proper stack.

br: baud rate

If your printer is connected to a serial port, you will need a `br` entry. A serial printer is like any other piece of hardware; for correct operation, it and its host computer must agree on a common set of communication parameters such as speed, parity, and flow control. Configuration of a printer is much like the configuration of a terminal. See Chapter 8 for general information about serial devices and cabling.

There are three settings you control through **printcap**: the baud rate, the "flag" bits, and the "local mode" bits. The baud rate is the speed at which communication occurs (in bits per second), and is a simple integer. Since it is a numeric value, you use the pound sign ("#") to set it. For example, `br#9600` sets the baud rate to 9,600 bps.

Baud rate can only assume the standard values 50, 75, 110, 134.5, 150, 200, 300, 600, 1200, 1800, 2400, 4800, 9600, 19200, and 38400. Some of these values are no longer in common use. The speed you select will depend on the speeds at which the printer is capable of receiving data, the speed at which the printer actually prints, the speed of the serial port, and the quality of your connection cables.

It is not useful to run the communications to a printer much faster than the rate at which it can print. While most printers are smart enough to tell their host to stop sending data when their internal buffers are full, you increase the number of interrupts the host must handle and may reduce the reliability of the connection.

fc and fs: flag bits

The settings for flag and local mode bits (below) are also integers, but each bit within the number modifies the behavior of the port in its own way. Setting up these parameters correctly requires that you look up the meaning of each bit in the `tty` man page (section four, *not* section one) and add up the values for the bits you want to set or clear. Settings need only be specified on the machine the printer is connected to.

The flag bits set parity, flow control, duplex, buffering, and mechanical delays. Table 25.2 shows the meanings of the most important bits.

Table 25.2   Flag bits for a serial printer

Name	Value[a]	Function
FF1	0040000	Delays 2 seconds after form feed
CR1	0010000	Delays 0.08 second after carriage return
CR2	0020000	Delays 0.16 seconds after carriage return
TAB1	0002000	Delays after tabs (varies with distance)
NL1	0000400	Delays after newline (varies with column)
NL2	0001000	Delays 0.1 second after newline
EVENP	0000200	Even parity allowed and generated on output
ODDP	0000100	Odd parity allowed and generated on output
RAW	0000040	Passes characters through serial port immediately
CRMOD	0000020	Outputs linefeed as "carriage-return linefeed"
ECHO	0000010	Echo (full duplex)
LCASE	0000004	Uppercase on output, lowercase on input
CBREAK	0000002	Semi-raw buffering mode (see RAW)
TANDEM	0000001	Automatic software flow control

a. In octal.

There are two variables that can be assigned when adjusting the flag bits: `fc` and `fs`. `fc` (flag clear) specifies the bits that should be turned off, and `fs` (flag set) specifies the ones that should be turned on. Bits assigned to neither variable assume default values. It is meaningless (but amusing) to both set a bit and clear it.

 If you are using a built-in serial port on a Sun, use the **eeprom** command to set the hardware flow control correctly.

The values assigned to `fc` and `fs` are computed by adding up (in octal) the values listed in Table 25.2. An octal number may be entered directly into `/etc/printcap` by prefacing it with a zero.

Suppose you want to allow both even and odd parity, enable automatic flow control, and disable full-duplex communication. You would want to set ODDP, EVENP, and TANDEM, and clear ECHO. Since ODDP + EVENP + TANDEM = 0100 + 0200 + 0001 = 0301, you would use `fs#0301` to set these bits and `fc#010` to clear ECHO.

The various delay bits are for use with old impact printers that do not have internal buffers, such as Teletypes. Since it takes these printers much longer to perform carriage return, newline, and tab operations than to simply print a character, they may drop characters following these operations if the host computer does not pause to let them catch up. Be sure to clear delay bits on printers that don't need them.

Parity is not usually significant for printers, so EVENP and ODDP should either be both on or both off.

Setting the TANDEM bit lets the host computer issue flow control characters to the printer. This is useful only for smart peripherals like laser printers that both send status messages back to the host and also understand how to do output flow control.

The `tty` manual page explains the meaning of each flag bit in detail.

xs and xc: local mode bits

The difference between the flag bits and the local mode bits is that local mode bits configure the serial driver and flag bits configure the actual communication link. The configuration method for both is the same, with variables xc and xs analogous to `fc` and `fs`.

Most of the mode bits are intended for use on interactive video terminals and so are not relevant to printer configuration. The three bits you might want to set are listed in Table 25.3.

Table 25.3   Local mode bits for a serial printer

Name	Value	Description
LLITOUT	000040	Suppress output translations
LDECCTQ	040000	Only <Control-Q> restarts output after <Control-S>
LCRTBS	000001	Backspace on erase rather than echoing erase

You will probably want to set LLITOUT to keep the serial driver from meddling with any output codes that are destined for the printer. LCRTBS is used for impact printers that need overstrike capability for printing underlined text (e.g., `nroff` output). LDECCTQ is used in handling flow control. If the printer uses the standard <Control-S>/<Control-Q> flow control characters this bit should be set to minimize any interference that might be caused by line noise.

pw, pl, py, and px: page size information

Some filters need to know the size of the output page so they can do cropping and line folding correctly. For character printers, the `pl` and `pw` variables specify the page length and width in lines and characters, respectively.

For high-resolution printers, the analogous variables are `py` and `px`, which are specified in pixels. Some printers can act in either mode, so both sets of variables should be specified.

Miscellaneous printcap variables

Table 25.4 is a short summary of some other printcap variables with which you should be familiar.

Table 25.4   Miscellaneous /etc/printcap variables

Name	Type	Meaning	Default
tf	string	String that causes printer to form feed	<Control-L>
fo	bool	Send form feed when device is opened?	no
mc	num	Maximum # of copies allowed for job	0 (no limit)
mx	num	Maximum file size of job (in blocks)	0 (no limit)
sc	bool	Suppress multiple copies?	no
sf	bool	Suppress form feeds?	no
sh	bool	Suppress printing of burst page header?	no

Printcap extensions

A nice feature of the **lpr/lpd** system is that it does not mind if you supply values for non-standard **printcap** variables. Often, when a particular printer needs more configuration information than the base system defines, extra variables can be stuck in **printcap** for the printer's filters to use.

For example, the output filter for a network printer might need to know the network name of the device. The **printcap** entry for the printer might contain an entry such as:

```
:nn=laser.colorado.edu:\
```

Using **printcap** extensions like this allows all of the configuration information for a printer to be stored in one convenient place. If you see variables in the **printcap** file that are not discussed in the **printcap** manual page, you should check in the documentation for the printer drivers for their meanings.

A Sample /etc/printcap Entry

In this section we will look at local and remote printcap entries for an Apple LaserWriter named "gutenberg" ("gb" for short) connected to the machine sigi. Our intent is merely to give a taste of what a "real" entry is like rather than to fully explain every nuance.

The local printcap entry on sigi is as follows.

```
gutenberg|gb|7-24|CS LaserWriter OT7-24:\
     :lp=/dev/gutenberg:sd=/var/spool/gutenberg:\
     :lf=/var/adm/gutenberg-log:af=/var/adm/gb.acct:\
     :br#19200:rw:fc#0000374:fs#0000003:xc#0:xs#0040040:\
     :mx#0:sf:sb:if=/usr/local/lib/ps/psif:\
     :of=/usr/local/lib/ps/psof:gf=/usr/local/lib/ps/psgf:\
     :nf=/usr/local/lib/ps/psnf:tf=/usr/local/lib/ps/pstf:\
     :rf=/usr/local/lib/ps/psrf:vf=/usr/local/lib/ps/psvf:\
     :cf=/usr/local/lib/ps/pscf:df=/usr/local/lib/ps/psdf:
```

The printer has four separate names, one of which is the room number. This is useful if you know where you want your output to be printed, but don't remember the name of the printer there. The device file that represents the printer is identified as **/dev/gutenberg**; this file is actually a link to the serial port **/dev/tty01**. The spool directory is **/var/spool/gutenberg**. The log file is **/var/adm/gutenberg-log**, and accounting information is kept in **/var/adm/gb.acct**.

Gutenberg's serial line is run at 19,200 baud. Since LaserWriters are intelligent printers can send status information back to the host computer, the rw option is given to specify that **/dev/gutenberg** should be opened read/write.

The flag bits configure the port for no parity, no character buffering, full duplex with no echo, bidirectional flow control, no translation of new-line characters, and both uppercase and lowercase text. The local mode bits prevent the serial driver from doing output translation on control characters, and specify that only a <Control-Q> may be used to restart output after a <Control-S>.

The mx variable is set to zero to allow files of any size to be printed, as is appropriate for a printer with graphics capabilities. sf suppresses form feeds, and sb asks for only short banners to be printed.

The rest of the variables assigned in this entry are filter programs for various types of output. The default is **/usr/local/lib/psof**, and the filter that does accounting is **/usr/local/lib/psif**.

On a remote machine, the entry for gutenberg is much shorter:

```
gutenberg|gb|7-24|CS LaserWriter OT7-24:\
     :lp=:sd=/var/spool/gutenberg:\
     :rm=sigi:rp=gutenberg:\
     :lf=/var/adm/gutenberg-log:mx#0:
```

The spool directory and error log file are named the same as on sigi. No accounting file is specified, since all accounting is done on the printer's local host. The mx variable is set here because file size checks are done when a job is spooled. The rm variable identifies the printer's host as sigi, and the rp variable explains that sigi knows the printer as "gutenberg." More details about remote printing can be found in the cross-platform printing section that starts on page 609.

Controlling the Printing Environment

Day-to-day maintenance of the printing system requires that you know how to use only three commands: `lpq`, `lprm`, and `lpc`. `lpq` lets you examine the queue of jobs waiting to be printed on a particular printer, and `lprm` lets you delete one or more of these jobs, erasing their stored data files and removing any reference to them within the printing system. Both of these commands are available to users, and both work transparently across a network.

`lpc` lets you make a number of changes to the printing environment, such as disabling printers and reordering printing queues. Although some of its functions are available to users, `lpc` is primarily an administrative tool.

lpq: View the Printing Queue

`lpq` is normally used with a `-P` option, although other command-line arguments may be used to restrict which jobs are shown. Output from `lpq` looks like this:

```
% lpq
anchor-lw is ready and printing
Rank    Owner    Job  Files                 Total Size
active  garth    314  domain.2x1.ps         298778 bytes
1st     kingery  286  standard input         17691 bytes
2nd     evi       12  appendices               828 bytes
3rd     garth     13  proc                   43229 bytes
4th     scott     14  periodic               16676 bytes
5th     garth     16  standard input           489 bytes
```

The first column tells you what order the jobs will be printed in. This is rather superfluous since the output lines are always in order, with the active job on top and the last job to be printed on the bottom. If the first job is listed as 1st rather than active, there is no printing daemon running for the printer.

The second column tells you which user spooled the job. The third column gives the job identification number for each job; this is important to know if you intend to manipulate the job later using `lprm` or `lpc`. The fourth column lists the files on the `lpr` command line used to spool the job. If the spooled data came in via a pipe (as the first and fifth jobs did above), this column will say standard input. The fifth and final column tells you the size of the job. This number is the size of the job before it is sent to the filter program, and gives no information about how many pages long a job will be or how long it will take to print.

lprm: Remove Jobs

The most common form of lprm is lprm *jobid*, where *jobid* is the job identification number as reported by lpq. lprm *user* removes all jobs belonging to *user*. lprm without arguments removes the active job. lprm - removes all the jobs you submitted; if you are root, it removes every job in the queue. No ordinary user may remove another user's jobs; however, the superuser may remove any job. Perversely, lprm fails silently but produces output on success. If you don't see something like

```
dfA621xinet dequeued
cfA621xinet dequeued
```

it means you did not invoke lprm correctly.

The printing system maintains a notion of the origin of a job as well as the user who spooled it, and lprm's matching process takes both into account. Thus garth@boulder is not equivalent to garth@sigi, and neither can remove the other's jobs. Some systems (such as Suns) are even more cagey about removing jobs and don't allow the superuser to remove jobs over the network.

Trying to lprm the active job can cause problems on some printers (especially laser printers using Adobe's TranScript software). The filter process for the job doesn't get properly notified of the termination, causing the whole system to come to a grinding halt with the filter process holding an exclusive lock on the printer's port, preventing other processes from using the printer.

The only way to fix this situation is to use ps to identify filter processes and kill them off by hand. lpc is not of use in this situation. Rebooting the system will always cure a hung lpd, but this is a drastic measure. Before you resort to a reboot, kill and restart the master copy of lpd.

lpc: Make Administrative Changes

The lpc command can perform the following functions:

- Enable or disable queuing for a particular printer
- Enable or disable printing on a particular printer
- Remove all jobs from a printer's queue
- Move a job to the top of a printer's queue
- Manipulate the lpd daemon
- Get printer status information

lpc won our award for "flakiest program of 1989." It was also awarded this honor in 1985, 1986, 1987, and 1988. lpc has not really gotten any better, but other truly flaky programs (like Sun's automounter) have come into widespread use, and lpc is no longer at the top of the heap.

When the printing system is running smoothly, **lpc** works just fine. But as soon as a filter gets stuck or some other minor problem appears, **lpc** wigs out completely. And it lies: it sometimes claims to have fixed everything while in reality having done nothing at all. You may have to fix things up by hand or even power-cycle your equipment when printing gets badly snarled.

lpc cannot be used across a network. It is normally used interactively, although it may be invoked in a one-shot mode by putting an interactive command on the **lpc** command line. Once inside **lpc**, the following commands are available:

help [*command*]

The **help** command without arguments shows you a short list of all available **lpc** commands. With an argument, it shows a one-line description of a particular command.

enable *printer*
disable *printer*

These commands enable or disable spooling of jobs to the named printer. Users who attempt to queue files will be politely informed that spooling has been disabled. Jobs that are already in the queue are not affected. This operation is performed by simply setting or clearing group execute permission on **/var/spool/***printer***/lock**.

start *printer*
stop *printer*

start enables and **stop** disables printing on the named printer. Jobs may still be spooled when a printer has been stopped, but will not be printed until printing is restarted. **start** and **stop** operate by setting or clearing owner execute permission on **/var/spool/***printer***/lock**. They also kill and start the appropriate daemons for the printer. **stop** allows the active job to complete before disabling printing.

abort *printer*

abort is just like **stop**, but it doesn't allow the active job to complete. When printing is re-enabled, this job will be printed over again.

down *printer message*
up *printer*

These commands affect both spooling and printing. They are used when a printer is really broken or has to be taken off-line for an extended period. The *message* parameter supplied to **down** can be as long as you like (on one line) and need not be quoted; it will be put in the printer's **/var/spool/***printer***/status** file and shown to users who run **lpq** You'll normally want to use this to register a short explanation of why the printer is unavailable and when it will be back in service. The **up** command reverses the effect of a **down**.

clean *printer*

This command removes all jobs from the printer's queue, including the active job. Since the printing daemon for the queue will still hold references to the files of the current job, UNIX will not really delete them and the current job will complete.

topq *printer jobid*
topq *printer username*

The first form moves the specified job to the top of the printer's queue. The second form promotes all jobs belonging to *username*.

restart *printer*

restart is used to restart a printing daemon that has mysteriously died. You'll know that the daemon is dead when **lpq** tells you "no daemon present." Although you might think **restart** would have the same effect as a **stop** followed by a **start**, it does not; **restart** will fail to re-start a printer that has a filter still running.

status *printer*

This shows you four things about the named printer: whether or not spooling is enabled, whether or not printing is enabled, the number of entries in the queue, and the status of the daemon for that printer. If there are no entries in the queue, you'll see something like this:

```
lpc> status cer
cer:
    queuing is enabled
    printing is enabled
    no entries
    no daemon present
```

The fact that there is no daemon present is not a cause for concern; per-printer daemons go away after the queue is empty and aren't restarted by the master copy of **lpd** until another job is spooled.

File Size Limits

The mx **printcap** variable lets you set a limit on the amount of data that can be spooled at one time. If all your users are knowledgeable and directly accountable, don't use this feature. Some people have legitimate reasons for printing huge files.

On the other hand, naive users sometimes do incredible things like try to print binaries. This is a bad situation because binaries tend to contain form feed characters and other miscellaneous data that the printer is sure to misinterpret. Even a small binary file can use reams of paper. Some versions of `lpr` try to protect against this by examining the input file, but such a heuristic approach is never perfect. Fortunately, binary files tend to be fairly large. If you expect to have problems with naive users, you can experiment with restricting maximum file size.

Another thing to consider when using file size limitations is the type of printer. With an ASCII-only line printer you can be sure that the number of characters spooled approximates the actual number of characters to be printed—but what about laser printers and plotters? If bitmaps are being downloaded to the printer, it may take several hundred thousand characters to describe a single page. Our advice is not to use size limitations on anything but line printers.

On some systems, mx defaults to some value other than 0 (no limit), and an explicit mx#0 entry is necessary to allow large jobs. Note that like baud rate, mx is a numeric field, so although mx=0 looks like a valid entry (and will produce no error messages), it will not change the setting of the mx variable.

25.4 ATT PRINTING

The ATT printing system was originally more robust and usable than the BSD system. Unfortunately, it was not designed with network printing in mind, and it has not scaled well. Most of the vendors that use it have made numerous changes, some that add useful functionality, and some that are purely gratuitous. We discuss the standard system, with many vendor specific notes. Attempts to make the system function over the network are described starting on page 609.

Overview

A user who wants to print something must either use the `lp` command or a command that invokes `lp` indirectly. `lp` takes input and places it in a file in the spool directory appropriate for its final destination. The `lpsched` daemon determines when and where a particular file should be printed, then executes an interface program that formats the data and outputs it to the correct printer. Table 25.5 (on the next page) gives a brief description of the commands in the ATT printing system.

Destinations and Classes

A destination has a name, which consists of up to 14 alphanumeric characters and underscores. In addition to being named, a destination may belong to zero or more *classes*. A destination is usually a printer, but it does not have to be. For example, a destination could be an ordinary text file that needs to be appended to by many users. The printing

Table 25.5 ATT printing commands

Command	Function
accept	Starts accepting jobs for a device
cancel	Cancels a queued or printing job
disable	Disables printing to a device
enable	Enables printing to a device
lp	Queues jobs for printing
lpadmin	Configures the printing system
lpmove	Moves jobs from one device to another
lpsched	Printer scheduling daemon
lpshut	Disables lpsched
lpstat	Shows the status of the system
reject	Stops accepting jobs for a device

system could be used to avoid a situation in which two people attempt to add to the file at the same time.

A class is a group of destinations that all serve the same purpose in some way. For example, if a site had two printers in the same room, they could be placed in a class. lpsched would direct output for that class to whichever printer became available first. Class names have the same restrictions as destination names.

In the rest of this chapter the word "printer" will be used to refer to destinations, even though a destination is not necessarily a printer.

A Brief Description of lp

lp is a user-level command that is used to queue data for printing. lp makes a copy of the data to be printed (which may come either from named files or from standard input) and places it in a file or set of files in the spool directory. The spool directory for a destination is usually **/var/spool/lp/request/**_dest_ where _dest_ is the name by which lp knows the printer or class of printers.

The file(s) are named _xxxn_, where _n_ is a job identification number assigned by lp and _xxx_ varies from system to system. This filename is used to identify the job both to the user and internally to the printing system. We will henceforth refer to this name as the job identification (jobid, for short).

If the **-d** _destination_ option is specified to lp, the input is queued for output to _destination_, where _destination_ is either a printer or a class. If the **-d** option is not used, lp checks the LPDEST environment variable and uses its contents as the name of the output device. If this environment variable is not set, lp queues the data for output to the default device if one has been specified by the system administrator, or rejects the request if there is no default device. (The default device can be set with `lpadmin -d`.)

lpsched and lpshut: Start and Stop Printing

`lpsched` is a daemon that takes the files placed in the spool directory by `lp` and sends them to an appropriate device as soon as one is available. `lpsched` keeps a log of each file it processes and any errors that occur, usually in `/usr/spool/lp/log`. When `lpsched` is started, it moves `/usr/spool/lp/log` into `/usr/spool/lp/oldlog` and starts a new log file. A log file looks something like this:

```
***** LP LOG: Jul  6 12:05 *****
pr1-107          garth   pr1     Jul  6 12:10
pr-112           scott   pr1     Jul  6 12:22
pr-117           evi     pr2     Jul  6 12:22
pr1-118          garth   pr1     Jul  6 12:25
pr1-119          garth   pr1     Jul  6 13:38
pr-132           evi     pr1     Jul  6 13:42
```

The first column is the jobid of each job. The second column is the user that requested the job. The third column is the actual printer the job was sent to, and the last column is the time that the job was queued.

On the system in this example, there are two printers: pr1 and pr2, both of which are in the class "pr." The user garth always specified the specific printer pr1, so that's where his jobs were always sent. The users scott and evi, on the other hand, specified the class pr, so their jobs were sent to the first available printer in that class.

If jobs disappear from the system or other problems occur, the log file is the first place you should look to try to determine the problem.

Solaris places some of the `lp` commands normally found in `/usr/lib` in the `/usr/sbin` directory. Some (but not all) of the files normally found in `/usr/spool/lp` are found in `/etc/lp`. `lpsched` has been carefully hidden in `/usr/lib/lp`. Logs are in `/var/lp/logs`.

To stop `lpsched` for any reason (to run `lpadmin`, for example), type `/usr/lib/lpshut`. When `lpsched` is not running, no jobs will actually be printed, though `lp` may still be used to queue jobs for printing. Any jobs in the process of being printed when the daemon is stopped will be reprinted in their entirety when the daemon is restarted. To restart the daemon, simply type `/usr/lib/lpsched`.

The file `/usr/spool/lp/SCHEDLOCK` is a file that is created to make sure only one copy of `lpsched` is running. If `lpsched` is stopped by any means other than `lpshut`, `SCHEDLOCK` must be removed by hand before `lpsched` can be restarted.

lpadmin: Configure Printing Environment

The `lpadmin` command is used to tell the printing system about your local printer configuration. It is used to give each printer a name, to create classes, and to specify the default printer. All the `lpadmin` command really does is create text files in `/usr/spool/lp`. However, these files are a good place to practice the old adage, "Look but don't touch." You should not try to edit these files directly because they are very format-sensitive and break easily.

Most `lpadmin` commands will not work when `lpsched` is running, so `lpsched` must be stopped with `lpshut` before `lpadmin` is used.

Solaris wants `lpsched` to be running during most administrative commands. There appears to be no method to this madness.

Before the printing system can output jobs to a particular printer, it must be told that the printer exists. To add a new printer, execute

```
/usr/lib/lpadmin -pprinter -vdevice { -eprinter | -mmodel
    | -iinterface } [ -cclass ... ] [{ -l | -h }]
```

where *printer* is the name of the printer (both internally in the queuing system and at the level of user commands) and *device* is the file that the printer is associated with. *printer* is limited to 14 alphanumerics and underscores. *device* is usually a special file in **/dev** (for example, **/dev/pr1**), but it can be any file.

The flag **-e**, **-m**, or **-i** is used to tell the queuing system which printer interface program should be used. The printer interface program is responsible for actually formatting jobs before they are sent to the printer. (*Interface Programs* on page 607 goes into more detail.)

The interface program can be specified in three ways:

-e*printer* In this case, *printer* is the name of an existing printer. This method of specifying the interface program is useful if you are adding a printer that is exactly like an existing one. The `lpadmin` command makes a copy of the interface program with the new destination's name.

-m*model* With this option, *model* is a type of device that your system has an interface program for. Refer to your system documentation or look in the directory **/usr/spool/lp/model** to determine which models your system supports.

When a model file is specified, `lpadmin` makes a copy of the file **/usr/spool/lp/model/***model* in **/usr/spool/lp/interface/***destination*.

-i*interface* With the **-i** option, *interface* is the full pathname of a program that is to be used as the inter-
face script. Most versions of **lpadmin** will make a
copy of the interface program, so if you want to
change it after you have run **lpadmin**, you need to
change the copy in **/usr/spool/lp/interface**,
not your original.

 HP-UX allows you to specify programs that return status information
and cancel printer jobs. These programs can be specified like interface
scripts, but different option prefixes are used (**-ocm** and **-osm** supply
cancel and status model scripts, respectively).

Solaris requires you to specify what type of input your device can handle with the **-I** option. The input programs reject input that is not of
one of the correct types, so if you do not specify any type, your printer is
useless. **-I postscript,simple** works well for PostScript printers.
For line printers, use **-I simple**. Solaris stores interface programs in
/etc/lp/interfaces rather than **/usr/spool/lp/interface**.

In addition to the required flags, **lpadmin** accepts these options:

-c*class* where *class* is the name of a class that the printer
should be included in. Any number of classes may
be specified for a given printer. If a class is specified
that does not exist, it will be created. The name is
limited to 14 characters.

-1 may be specified to tell **lpsched** to automatically
disable the printer when it starts up. This option is
intended to be used when the printer is a login terminal (hence the **-1**), but it can also be used for a
device that is only attached to the system occasionally. Before any output can be sent to a printer
specified with the **-1** option, the printer must be
enabled (see page 606). The **-h** option, the default,
specifies that the printer is hardwired. It can be
used to disable the **-1** option.

lp will not accept requests for a new printer until it is told to do so with
the **accept** command. See page 605.

Some versions of Solaris default to accepting jobs when you first install
a printer with **lpadmin**.

lpadmin can be used to modify the specification of an existing printer
by specifying **-p***printer* and any options you wish to change. In general, **lpadmin** should not be used while **lpsched** is running. However,
the device file can be changed with **-v** without stopping **lpsched**.

The **-x***printer* flag may be used to remove a printer. If *printer* is the only member of a class, then that class is also removed. Neither a printer nor a class may be removed if it has jobs queued for output. The **lpmove** and **cancel** commands may be used to remove jobs queued for a printer. If you are having trouble getting **lpadmin -x** to remove a printer, see page 608.

To remove a printer from a class, use the **-r***class* flag. The **-r** flag does not remove the printer; it just removes it from the class. If the specified printer is the only member of *class*, the class is removed.

When the flags to a command could refer to multiple objects, a quoted, comma-separated list of destinations can be used in place of a single object. For example,

```
lpstat -p"pr1,pr2"
```

would give the status of pr1 and pr2. Table 25.6 summarizes the flags understood by **lpadmin**.

Table 25.6   lpadmin flags

Flag	Function
-d*dest*	Makes *dest* the system default destination
-x*dest*	Removes *dest* from the printing system
-p*printer*	Specifies printer to which other options apply
-c*class*	Adds *printer* to *class*
-r*class*	Removes *printer* from *class*
-e*dest*	Copies interface program from *dest* for *printer*
-i*interface*	Makes *interface* the interface program for *printer*
-m*model*	Makes *printer* use the interface program for *model*
-h	Indicates that *printer* is hard-wired
-l	Indicates that *printer* is a login terminal
-v*file*	Appends output for *printer* to *file*

Here are some examples of **lpadmin** commands, with brief explanations of what they do:

```
/usr/lib/lpadmin -ppr1 -v/dev/tty06 -mdumb -cpr
```

This tells the printing system that a printer to be called pr1 is connected to **/dev/tty06**, that the printer should be in the class pr, and that the interface program for dumb printers should be used.

```
/usr/lib/lpadmin -ppr2 -v/dev/tty07 -epr1 -cpr
```

Here a printer connected to **/dev/tty07** is added. It is also a member of the class pr. The printer is named pr2, and it uses the same interface program as pr1.

```
/usr/lib/lpadmin -ppr2 -v/dev/tty01
```

This command notifies the system that pr2 is now connected to `tty01` rather than `tty06`. All other parameters of pr2 remain the same.

```
/usr/lib/lpadmin -dpr
```

Sets the system default destination to class pr.

```
/usr/lib/lpadmin -ppr1 -rpr -cfast
```

Removes printer pr1 from class pr and adds it to class fast.

```
/usr/lib/lpadmin -xpr1
```

Removes printer pr1 completely. This also removes the class fast if pr1 was its only member.

cancel: Remove Print Jobs

`cancel` allows jobs that are queued or being printed to be canceled. `cancel` can either be invoked with a job number (this can be determined with `lpstat`, see page 606) or by printer name. If a printer is specified, the job currently being printed is canceled.

For example, `cancel 576` would cancel job 576, and `cancel pr1` would cancel the job currently on printer pr1. `cancel` is usually owned by the pseudo-user lp with group bin and mode 6775 so that any user can use it to cancel jobs that are obviously bogus. If someone who did not send a job cancels it, mail is sent to the job's owner. If users abuse this privilege, the mode of the command may be set so that it does not run setuid.

accept and reject: Control Spooling

If a printer will be unavailable for a long time (for example, due to hardware failure), spooling to that device should be disabled so that users who are unaware of the situation do not fill up the queue. This is done with the `reject` command. For example,

```
/usr/lib/reject -r"pr1 will be down until Tuesday" pr1
```

would cause `lp` to reject requests for pr1:

```
% lp -dpr1 afile
lp: cannot accept requests for destination "pr1"
    -- pr1 will be down until Tuesday
```

The `-r` flag is optional, but it is a nice way to tell users the reason that the printer is rejecting requests. `accept` *printer* tells `lp` to begin accepting requests for *printer*. `accept` must be executed once for each new printer added with `lpadmin` because new printers are configured to reject requests by default.

`accept` and `reject` may be given a class name instead of a destination name to enable or disable spooling for an entire class.

enable and disable: Control Printing

The `disable` command tells `lpsched` to stop sending jobs to a particular printer. Unlike `reject`, `disable` does not stop `lp` from queuing jobs for the printer. However, queued jobs will not be output until the printer is re-enabled with the `enable` command. `disable` does not normally abort printing of current job, but the `-c` option can be used to request this behavior. Like `reject`, `disable` supports a `-r` flag that allows you to explain why a printer is disabled. For example, to disable printing on pr1, use the command:

```
/usr/lib/disable -r"Being cleaned, back in 5 minutes" pr1
```

To restart printing, type:

```
/usr/lib/enable pr1
```

lpmove: Transfer Jobs

Sometimes it is necessary to move jobs queued for one printer or class to another printer. This is accomplished with `lpmove`. `lpmove` is run with a list of jobids and the name of a new printer. For example,

```
/usr/lib/lpmove pr1-324 pr1-325 pr2
```

would move the jobs numbered 324 and 325 from the queue for printer pr1 to the queue for printer pr2. `lpmove` can also be given a printer or class as a source; for example,

```
/usr/lib/lpmove pr1 pr2
```

would move all jobs queued for pr1 to the queue for pr2. When `lpmove` is used in this way, it has the side effect of executing a `reject` on the printer of origin. In the preceding example, `lp` would no longer accept requests for pr1. `lpmove` cannot be used when `lpsched` is running.

lpstat: Get Status Information

The `lpstat` command shows the status of the printing system. If executed without any arguments, it gives the status of all jobs that belong to the user who executed it. With a `-p` argument, `lpstat` gives information on the status of a particular printer. For example,

```
% lpstat -ppr1
pr1 is now printing pr-125. enabled since Jul 4 12:25
```

shows the status of printer pr1. The status of `lpsched` can be determined with `lpstat -r`; for example,

```
% lpstat -r
scheduler is running
```

shows you that everything is OK. Table 25.7 lists the flags for `lpstat`.

Table 25.7   lpstat flags

Flag	Function
-r	Shows the status of the `lpsched` daemon
-d	Shows the default destination
-c*class*	Lists the members of *class*
-o*arg*	Shows the status of output requests for *arg*[a]
-u*user*	Shows the status of jobs submitted by *user*
-p*printer*	Shows the status of *printer*
-v*printer*	Lists the output device associated with *printer*
-a*dest*	Shows the acceptance status of *dest*
-s	Shows a summary of status information
-t	Shows all status information

a. *arg* can be a printer, a class, or a jobid.

Interface Programs

An interface program must take information from a file that `lpsched` specifies, format it, and send the formatted data to its standard output. The interface program is also responsible for setting the correct modes on the output device and for generating headers and trailers if they are desired. Interface programs are usually shell scripts, but they can be executable binaries, too.

The interface program for each individual printer is kept in the file `/usr/spool/lp/interface/`*printer*. A user-supplied interface program specified with `lpadmin -i` should be owned by the pseudo-user lp and group owner bin, and should have mode 644.

`lpsched` calls interface programs with the following arguments:

```
jobid user title copies options file [file ...]
```

Where:

- *jobid* is the job identification that is given by `lp`
- *user* is the user to whom the job belongs
- *title* is an optional title supplied by the user
- *copies* is the number of copies to print
- *options* are user-supplied options
- The *files* are full pathnames of files to be printed

All of the arguments are supplied each time the interface program is executed, but some may be null strings. The interface program gets its standard input from `/dev/null` and both standard output and standard error are directed to the destination device as specified by the `lpadmin -v` command.

Unlike BSD, where there are different interface programs for different file formats, ATT requires interface programs to handle all the kinds of data that the printer can accept (and to fail nicely if unrecognizable input is received). For this reason, interface programs are usually just shell scripts that process their arguments and call other programs to do the real work of formatting.

Essentially, the interface script is responsible for the entire output stage of the printing system. While this makes customization easy, it also leads to different printers behaving in very different ways.

An interface program should exit with a 0 on successful completion, and with an integer in the range 1 to 127 if an error is encountered. If a job fails, the interface script should attempt to reprint it. If a serious error occurs, the interface program should **disable** (see page 606) the printer. If you are having erratic printing problems, you can probably find the cause in the interface script.

What to Do When the lp System is Completely Hosed

Sometimes, attempts to configure and unconfigure printers will leave the `lp` system hopelessly confused. The system stores its configuration information in random files in `/usr/spool/lp`. Configuration files vary among implementations; they are seldom documented and often not human-readable.

If you somehow create a printer that is confusing the system, the best solution is to remove the destination completely and start over. Sometimes the system can be so confused that even this is hard.

The following brute-force technique will often rescue you from this sort of situation. Here we will try to remove the printer *dest*. Don't do this if *dest* is not unique.

```
# lpshut
# lpadmin -xdest
# find /usr/spool/lp -name dest -exec rm -rf {} \;
# lpsched
# lpstat -t
```

The first two commands turn off the scheduler and attempt to remove the printer using the USDA-approved method. If the system is confused, `lpadmin -x` may fail. The **find** command removes all interface programs and spool directories for the printer. `lpsched` restarts the scheduler, and `lpstat` checks to be sure there are no more references to *dest* within the printing system.

25.5 CROSS-PLATFORM SPOOLING

In most organizations there will be multiple printing devices and multiple hosts where printing can be initiated. To simplify your job as system administrator, you should try to set up your network so that a few hosts control all of your printers. Other machines should simply transmit jobs to the main printing machines. This setup can save you a lot of work because you will not have to keep a close eye on the printing system on every machine. In addition, when there is a printing problem you will have relatively few configurations to investigate.

See page 614 for more information about network printers.

Some printers contain full-fledged network interfaces, allowing them to sit directly on a network and accept jobs using one or more protocols. Even for these printers, it is a good idea to pass all jobs through a single print queue. Many networks have a mix of systems running **lp** and **lpr**, as well as different vendors' modifications to the basic printing systems.

 SGI has chosen to provide complete versions of both the **lp/lpadmin** and **lpr/lpd** systems. This can get quite confusing, since the user-level commands have all been modified to act correctly depending on the type of printer. For example, you can use **lp** to spool jobs to **lpd** queues, and vice versa with **lpr** and **lpadmin**. If you are going to print to or from remote machines under IRIX, it is easiest to use the **lpr/lpd** system. It is vanilla BSD.[3]

Most versions of **lp** have been extended to accept input from remote **lpd** queues, and most versions provide a way to send jobs to a remote **lpd** queue. Unfortunately, almost every system supports these features differently. We will provide some common examples, but you may still have to take a careful read through your system documentation to see how to do this.

If you have problems debugging a remote printer connection, there are six (yes, six) places you have to look to track down the problem:

- The system log file on the machine hosting the printer, for messages about permission problems

- The system log file on the sending machine, for name resolution and permission problems

- The print daemon log file on the printing machine, for messages about bad device names, incorrect formats, etc.

- The print daemon log file on the sending machine, for missing filters, unknown printers, missing directories, etc.

- The printer log file on the printing machine, for errors in transmitting the job

---

3. The BSD printing software is optional under IRIX. Be sure to load it at installation time.

- The printer log file on the sending machine, for errors about pre-processing or queuing the job

When setting up remote printers, you should always keep in mind that there must be a queue for the job to go to on the requesting machine, a way to decide where to send the job, and a method of sending the job to the remote machine. On the printing machine, there must be a place to queue the job, sufficient permissions to allow the job to be printed, and a way to output to the device.

Before you start tracking down a network printing problem, make sure you can print from the printer's local machine.

In the following examples, we will be trying to print from a machine called "client" to a machine called "server," which has a printer called pr1 connected to it. We will set up a remote print queue called rpr1 on the client machine.

Spooling to an lpd System from an lpd System

On systems with **lpr**, this is done by adding an **/etc/printcap** entry on the remote machine. For example, on client we would add:

```
rpr1|lp|8-6|LaserWriter IIg, called pr1 on server:\
    :lp=:rm=server:rp=pr1:sd=/var/spool/rpr1:mx#0:
```

We would then create the spool directory on client:

```
# mkdir /var/spool/rpr1
# chown daemon /var/spool/rpr1
# chgrp daemon /var/spool/rpr1
# chmod 755 /var/spool/rpr1
```

On server, we'd make sure that client is listed in **/etc/hosts.equiv** or **/etc/hosts.lpd** (which gives access only for printing). The parsing of **hosts.lpd** is not as robust as the parsing of the **hosts.equiv** and **hosts** files. Often, you must use the primary name of the machine. For example, if **/etc/hosts** contained

```
131.6.6.6  client.foo.com client cl1
```

you would have to put client.foo.com in **hosts.lpd** to get the desired result, as client or cl1 would not work (though they should). If you allow access via **hosts.equiv** or **hosts.lpd**, all printers on the server will be equally accessible. If you want per-printer controls, you must implement them in the print filter.

After setting this all up, we verify that we can print on server:

```
# lpr -Ppr1 /etc/printcap
# lpq -Ppr1
```

Check to see that the job becomes active and prints. If this is all working correctly, we then enable printing on the client and try it out:

```
# lpc enable rpr1
# lpc start rpr1
# lpr -Prpr1 /etc/printcap
# lpq -Prpr1
```

Most likely, there will be something that does not work correctly. The status messages produced by lpq may prove enlightening. If not, check the six log files listed above to try to track down the problem.

Spooling from HP-UX to an lpd Printer

HP-UX has added some of the functionality of lpd to the lpsched daemon. This allows you to queue jobs to lpd printers without writing your own complicated interface script and driver. To set it up (using the same names as the last example), we run these commands on the HP-UX side:

```
# /usr/lib/lpshut
# /usr/lib/lpadmin -prpr1 -mrmodel -v/dev/null -ormserver
  -orpr1 -ob3
# /usr/lib/accept rpr1
# /usr/lib/enable rpr1
# /usr/lib/lpsched
```

The lpadmin command makes a queue called rpr1 that spools to pr1 on the server. We would still have to add client to server's hosts.equiv or hosts.lpd, as above. Note that lpadmin takes care of making the spool directory with the right permissions.

Spooling from an lpd System to lpsched on HP-UX

HP-UX also provides the ability to accept jobs from lpr/lpd systems. This is done with a daemon called rlpdaemon. rlpdaemon is usually started at boot time, but can be run from inetd. It accepts jobs from hosts listed in hosts.equiv or /usr/spool/lp/.rhosts.

Spooling to and from Solaris

Solaris uses a command called lpsystem to manipulate the printing permissions. Before you can send or receive jobs, you must enable the operation using lpsystem. When you do this, you use the -t option to specify the type of printing the remote machine has. For systems that will accept jobs via lpd (all BSD systems and HP-UX), use the type bsd. For machines running Solaris, use s5.

As of Solaris 2.4, the system is shipped with printing access allowed to and from all machines.

Since this is probably not what you want, you should execute:

```
# lpsystem -r +
Removed "+".
```

which removes permissions for the magic cookie "+", denoting all machines. You can get a listing of the state of network printing with `lpsystem -l`. Errors are logged to `/var/lp/logs/lpNet`.

If you want to configure spooling from Solaris to a remote printer, you use `lpadmin`, specifying the remote printer as *server!printer*.

```
# lpsystem -t bsd server
server has been added
# lpadmin -p rpr1 -s server!pr1 -I and -T unknown
# accept rpr1
```

If the remote system was another Solaris machine, we would substitute **s5** for **bsd** in the arguments to `lpsystem`. The next thing to do is to check for error messages with

```
# /bin/lpstat -t
```

As of Solaris 2.4, the configuration above does not work properly.

If you want to allow your Solaris machine to accept connections from remote machines, consult the *Routine System Administration Guide*.

25.6 THE LESSER EVIL?

In this chapter, we have complained extensively about both the BSD and ATT systems. Unfortunately, you will have to use at least one of these systems, and in many cases both. Table 25.8 provides a simple chart to aid the transition from one system to the other.

Table 25.8 Comparison of ATT and BSD printing systems

ATT	BSD	Function
lp	lpr	Submits jobs for printing
lpsched	lpd	The printing daemon
lpshut	–	Stops the printing daemon
lpstat	lpq	Checks the status of a queue
cancel	lprm	Removes jobs from a queue
lpmove	–	Moves jobs among queues
lpadmin	/etc/printcap	Configures the printing system
accept	lpc enable	Enables queueing
reject	lpc disable	Disables queueing
enable	lpc start	Starts printing to a device
disable	lpc stop	Stops printing to a device
–	lpc topq	Re-orders jobs in the queue

It should be evident from Table 25.8 that most functionality is available in both systems. If you have a choice about which system to use, the report card shown in Exhibit A may help you make that choice. It is based on the systems as they were shipped in 1994.

Exhibit A   **Printing report card**

YOUR WORK SHOWS LITTLE IMPROVEMENT.

PLEASE TRY HARDER NEXT YEAR!!!

BOULDER VALLEY ADMINISTRATIVE DISTRICT				FINAL REPORT
Student: UNIX	Solaris	HP-UX	IRIX	BSD[a]
Local Printing	C	B–	B	C
Net Send	F	A	F	A+
Net Receive	F	B	C+	A
Reliability	D+	B	B	C

Code: 555-21-4266
Home Room: Ritchie

0 38000 04920 0

☑ Parent-teacher conference requested

a. Any flavor: includes SunOS, OSF/1, BSDI, and part of IRIX.

25.7 COMMON PRINTING SOFTWARE

Although BSD and ATT both provide adequate systems for queuing, monitoring, and outputting printing jobs, neither of them provides much of the format translation necessary to drive modern printers. Most vendors have at least one set of tools that sits on top of the printing system to provide these features. Sometimes these tools are included in the OS, but more often they are extra-cost add-ons. Third-party and freely distributed packages are also in wide use.

Our purpose in this section is not to tell you everything you need to know about these packages, but just to let you know what functionality they advertise.

TranScript

Originally written by Adobe, TranScript is a set of filters that translate some common formats to PostScript. This package was quite popular as an add-on to SunOS, although different versions of it pop up on other OSs. It includes filters to translate text files to PostScript, as well as handling `roff` files and usually the bitmap format of the platform it is running on. TranScript is available from Adobe and from some vendors.

NeWSPrint

NeWSPrint is a RIP package from Sun that includes translation from various formats to PostScript (like TranScript), as well as a PostScript screen viewer. It is not a particularly robust package, but if you buy a raster printer (such as a SPARCprinter) from Sun, you will have to have it. It is available on SunOS and Solaris.

Impressario

Impressario is essentially like NeWSPrint, only for IRIX platforms. It also provides a graphical front-end to the printing system.

JetDirect

This is a package from HP that lets you send jobs via TCP/IP to newer HP printers connected to the network. It does not include a RIP.

groff

groff is included on the CD-ROM.

`groff` is a set of `roff` formatters from GNU. It is available as source code from many `ftp` sites. It allows you to convert `roff` format to PostScript, or to preview it on a display running X11. If `roff` is a separate purchase item on your system, you should definitely get `groff`. It will probably take less time to install and work better than your vendor's add-on package.

ghostscript

ghostscript is on the CD-ROM.

`ghostscript` is a freely-distributed PostScript interpreter that allows you to view PostScript files on your screen. If you need to drive some sort of raster output device and you don't want to spend the money for a commercial driver, `ghostscript` is a good starting point for building your own driver. Be forewarned that this is a very complicated process.

CAP and K-Spool

See page 282 for more information about AppleTalk.

CAP and K-Spool allow you to accept print jobs from Macintosh computers, and to print to AppleTalk printers from your UNIX queue. CAP (the Columbia AppleTalk Package) is free and is available from most large `ftp` sites. K-Spool is a commercial product made by Xinet.

mpage

mpage is included on the CD-ROM.

`mpage` is a text-to-PostScript converter that lets you place multiple logical pages on a single physical page. This is a great tree saver when you are printing things like source code, where you don't need big type and large margins.

25.8 NETWORK PRINTERS

Jobs that include bitmapped images, especially color images, are quite large. By hanging printers right on the network, data can be sent to them much more quickly than to serial or parallel printers (but not as fast as SCSI printers, which are also becoming popular). Unfortunately, there is no standard way for these printers to communicate with UNIX.

Before you purchase a network printer, make sure that you can get software that will allow one of your machines to drive it. Make sure you add the cost of the software (if any) to the cost of the printer before making your decision.

25.9 POSTSCRIPT PRINTERS

There are a few caveats that generally apply to PostScript printers.

- PostScript printers contain a CPU. The faster the CPU, the faster your job will image. Printer speeds are quoted in pages per minute that the marking engine can print, but some CPUs are not fast enough to keep the engine working at full speed.

- If the software that drives the printer does not read and log PostScript errors, you will not know why some jobs do not print. For this reason, only connect PostScript printers to bi-directional interfaces (i.e. not most parallel interfaces).

- PostScript interpreters require a lot of memory, and if your PostScript is complicated, you may run out of it. The error message returned may or may not be enlightening. For example, messages such as

```
error: insufficient memory
vmerror 343443 stack underflow: offending command /sew
stack overflow -- offending command _]ew
```

will be returned by different printers if they run out of memory. Although PostScript is relatively portable, not all printers can successfully image complex documents.

- PostScript printers have a certain number of fonts. Some fonts are built into the printer, while others are loaded into memory. If you print a job that uses a font that is not in the printer's ROM and is not included in the job, the printed output will use the Courier font. Printers that appear identical (same brand) may not have the same fonts.

- If you print lots of bitmaps or are buying a color printer, a serial interface will not provide acceptable throughput.

- If a job won't print, try previewing it on your screen.

- It is not unusual for applications to occasionally generate bogus PostScript. Different PostScript interpreters may generate different error messages for the same problem.

25.10 PRINTER PHILOSOPHY

The main things to expect when dealing with printers are troubles and frustrations. If all else fails, just be glad it's not MS-DOS.

Use Printer Accounting

You should enable printer accounting even if you don't plan to charge for printer use. The overhead is very slight and you get to see exactly who is using the printer. It also gives a good indication of the various sources of print jobs, a good thing to know when you are configuring new printers.

Use Banner Pages Only When Necessary

The printing system can preface each job with a page showing various pieces of information associated with the job. This header page can be useful on printers that are used by many different people, but it is a waste of time and paper for light-duty printers or printers used by only a few people. If you don't need it, suppress it by setting the Boolean printcap variable sh true on BSD systems, or simply don't have your interface script generate a banner on ATT systems.

Provide Recycling Bins

All kinds of computer paper are recyclable. You can use the boxes that paper comes in as recycling bins. Post a sign asking that no foreign material (like staples, paper clips, and newspaper) be discarded there.

Provide Previewers

Users will often print a document, find a small error in the formatting, and end up re-printing the whole job. This waste of paper can easily be avoided by providing software that allows users to see how the printed output will look on their screens.

Previewing is built into many modern WYSIWYG editors, but if your users are addicted to an older typesetting system, you will need to provide some other way to preview documents.

For random PostScript documents, you can use **ghostscript**. For **roff**, **xditsee** is quite nice; for TeX, try **xdvi**. After you have provided the necessary previewers, you will need to train your users to use them. A good use of printer accounting records is to check for cases in which the same document is printed repeatedly.

Buy Cheap Printers

Printer technology is mature. You don't need to spend a lot of money for great output and reliable mechanics.

Don't splurge on an expensive "workgroup" printer unless you really need it. There's no difference in the output, and a medium-grade "personal" printer can often be just as fast and just as reliable, not to mention tens of pounds lighter. A ten-page-per-minute printer can serve about five full-time writers; you'd be much better off buying five $1,000 printers for a group of 25 writers than one $5,000 printer.

In general, never buy a printer (or a hard disk, or memory) from a computer vendor. They will fleece you. The best deals are likely to be PostScript printers manufactured for the PC and Macintosh markets. We have found both HP and Apple printers to be superior products, and both brands are very cheap.

Keep Extra Toner Cartridges on Hand

Laser printers occasionally need their toner cartridges replaced. It's a good idea to buy replacements before you need them. Streaks and grayish areas on the printed output are signs that the printer is running out of toner. Before you replace a cartridge, remove it from the printer and try gently rocking it to redistribute the remaining toner particles. You can often get another hundred pages out of a cartridge this way.

Rather than replacing cartridges with new ones, you can often get them refilled by a third party. Good shops will clean the cartridge and replace the imaging drum in addition to adding more toner. This service is expensive, but it's cheaper than buying new cartridges. We have usually found refurbished cartridges to be as good as new.

26 *Disk Space Management*

26.1 INTRODUCTION

It has been said that the only thing all UNIX systems have in common is the login message asking users to clean up their files and use less disk space. No matter how much space you have, it isn't enough; as soon as a disk is added, files magically appear to fill it up.

Both users and the system itself are potential sources of disk bloat. Chapter 12, *Syslog and Log Files*, discusses various sources of logging information and the techniques used to manage them. This chapter focuses on space problems caused by users and the technical and psychological weapons you can deploy against them.

If you do decide to add a disk, refer to Chapter 9 for help. Even if you have the option of adding more disk storage to your system, it's a good idea to follow this chapter's suggestions. Disks are cheap, but administrative effort is not. Disks have to be dumped, maintained, cross-mounted, and monitored; the fewer you need, the better.

26.2 DEALING WITH DISK HOGS

In the absence of external pressure, there is essentially no reason for a user to ever delete anything. It takes time and effort to clean up unwanted files, and there's always the risk that something thrown away might be wanted again in the future. Even when users have good intentions, it often takes a nudge from the system administrator to goad them into action.

On a PC, disk space eventually runs out and the machine's primary user must clean up to get the system working again. But on a UNIX machine, many users can share a disk. When space gets low, users sometimes try to ignore the problem as long as they can in the hope that someone else will "break" first. It's often hard to convince users that they should remove any of their precious files until the disk is actually full or overflowing. Some users keep large junk files around just so that they'll have something to delete when the disk fills up and they can no longer get any work done.

It does not work to send mail to all users asking them to clean up their files or to post a message about the problem in `/etc/motd`. These methods don't assign responsibility to specific people. To get action, you have to find out who the disk hogs are and let them know that *you* know they are the source of the problem.

spacegripe is included on the CD-ROM.

You can do this automatically with a script that calculates disk usage for each user, identifies those whose consumption is above a certain threshold, and sends polite mail requesting that they clean up their files. We call our version of this script `spacegripe`. Since `spacegripe` needs to forage in users' home directories, it must be run as root. You can set the threshold at which mail is sent by replacing the number 10,000 with the maximum number of disk blocks someone can have without being pestered.

`spacegripe` is quite polite and precise, but alas, it is generally ignored by our user community. It's most effective the first time a user receives a message; after that, the novelty wears off and subsequent messages are often deleted without being read. Since the mail does not come from a real person, it's perceived as being only slightly more personal than a broadcast message.

No one likes to be labeled as one of the top ten disk hogs, especially if disk space is tight enough that other users are having trouble getting their work done. We have found that publishing such a list is by far the most effective way of "persuading" users to clean up. Whenever a list of disk hogs is posted in `/etc/motd`, the disk space situation miraculously improves.[1]

If some users do not reduce their disk usage even after being publicly denounced, you will have to deal with them on a person-by-person basis. Be gentle; a friendly message from an administrator has ten times the impact of an automated reminder.

Another option for automation is to compress files that are larger than a certain threshold and that have not been accessed recently, say in

---

1. At sites where every user has a workstation, people tend to stay logged in all the time and therefore never see the contents of `/etc/motd`. Public email is a good substitute.

thirty days. This is an invasive tactic and it is not 100% safe, since users' files must be modified. However, it does free up a lot of disk space and is worth considering in extreme cases.

See page 621 for more information about compression.

A perl script called **compressfs** is included on the CD-ROM; it performs the compression chores and then sends email to each user whose files were compressed to explain what has happened.

When you ask users to clean up, you will get better results if you provide an easy way for them to store files off-line. A tape drive in a public area allows users to archive infrequently-used files with minimal help from you. In a semi-public setting such as a university, you might want to consider selling tapes. DAT and QIC tapes can be hard to find, and it takes some familiarity with the media to know what to buy. At minimum, attach information to the tape drive that describes what kind of media to buy, where to find it, and how much it costs.

26.3 HOG DETECTION

Information about disk usage can be obtained with the **quot** command, which shows each user's total number of files and disk blocks on each filesystem. For example, **quot -f /dev/sd4c** produces

```
blocks    files   user
------------------------
/dev/sd4c (/home/anchor):
112180    2501    markey
66340     3254    drew
63258     1267    weinberj
53874     5918    christos
45192     9761    jules
. . .
```

The **quot** command is *not* related to the quota system discussed later in this chapter. **du** summarizes the disk usage within a directory hierarchy. For example, **du -s /home/anchor/*** yields

```
blocks   user
---------------
112325   markey
66332    drew
63258    weinberj
53874    christos
47311    jules
. . .
```

The numbers reported by these commands are in "disk blocks." Unfortunately, folks and filesystems can't seem to agree on how big a block is. Table 26.1 shows the block sizes for various operating systems, in bytes. Block size is actually a parameter of each filesystem, but many commands don't take this fact into consideration. Files with holes[2] should not be expanded when measuring file sizes, but on some systems, with some commands, they are. Database files created by **dbm** always contain holes and are usually only 25% of their apparent size.

Table 26.1   Block sizes used by various commands

System	du	df	quot
Solaris	512[a]	512[a]	1024
HP-UX	1024	1024	2048
IRIX	512[a]	512[a]	1024
SunOS	1024	1024	1024
OSF/1	512[a]	512[a]	1024
BSDI	512[b]	1024	–

a. You can get 1K blocks with the **-k** option.

b. Uses environment variable BLOCKSIZE, if defined.

The HP-UX manual page claims that **quot** uses 2,048-byte blocks, which is true for **quot -h**, but not true for the **-f**, **-c**, and **-v** options. HP-UX provides the Berkeley version of **df** under the name **bdf**.

quot counts all files belonging to a user; **du** counts all files in a particular directory. Users can own files outside their home directories, and there can be files in users' home directories that don't belong to them. Thus, there may be a discrepancy between the numbers reported by **du** and **quot**. Holes in files and the counting algorithm for symbolic links also influence the reported sizes.

26.4 DATA COMPRESSION

Most UNIX systems provide at least one set of utilities for data compression and expansion. These utilities usually include a compression program, an expansion program, and a program that dynamically expands for viewing. Some common program sets are the **compress** family, the **gzip** family, and the **pack** family.

gzip is a GNU thing. It's included on the CD-ROM.

The best compression ratios are achieved with **gzip**, but it is fairly slow and not all systems provide it. There are some compatibility problems with early versions of the command, so if you use **gzip** it is wise to standardize on the most recent version.

2. A file that is created by a program that writes a byte, seeks out a megabyte, and then writes another byte is called a file with a hole in it. Should it occupy two bytes on the disk or a million and two? Files with holes are usually stored with the holes compacted; they are sometimes expanded by programs that either measure their size (**du** under ATT) or archive them (**tar** or **cpio**).

compress is peppier than gzip and is universally available; its compression is pretty good, too. pack is obsolete and should not be used if you have a choice. It is even faster than compress, but it provides relatively poor compression. Table 26.2 compares the performance of the compress, gzip, and pack commands.

Table 26.2   Comparison of compress, gzip, and pack

Input	compress		gzip		pack	
	Saved[a]	Time	Saved[a]	Time	Saved[a]	Time
2.1MB English text	57.8%	16.3 s	61.4%	50.0 s	38.9%	8.8 s
1.8MB Binary file	50.0%	14.2 s	61.9%	43.2 s	25.1%	8.1 s
3.3MB C code	60.4%	24.1 s	74.0%	51.4 s	35.5%	14.3 s
2.6MB Encrypted	*none*		*none*		*none*	

a. Percentage of original size removed. Bigger numbers indicate better compression.

Encrypted data does not compress.[3] Superficially, it appears to be random data and thus fools the compression algorithms, which look for patterns. There are other kinds of data that do not compress or that compress poorly; for example, DNA sequencing information. Compressed files generally cannot be compressed again.

Large files that are only accessed occasionally are good targets for compression. When deciding whether to compress a file, you must decide whether the savings in disk space warrant the CPU time and the hassle that it takes to compress and expand the file.

26.5 SKULKER SCRIPTS

skulker is the name usually given to a script that goes around the disk, controlling the size of system logs, removing abandoned junk files, and checking for security breaches. skulker scripts are usually run by cron either daily or weekly.

The junk files that skulker should remove vary from system to system. Editor checkpoint and backup files, core files, and certain by-products of compilation are generally safe to remove, but there is always a chance that someone will unknowingly name an important file to match one of skulker's specifications and have it deleted. Your site's deletion policies should be documented in a public place so that users will not be surprised when their files disappear.

Cleaning the Filesystem on page 176 gives examples of commands that might be used in a skulker script. Many of the security-related com-

---

3. Actually, it gets bigger when you try to compress it.

mands described starting on page 549 are also good candidates for inclusion in a **skulker**.

26.6 TUNEFS: SET FILESYSTEM PARAMETERS

The **tunefs** command is used to alter the layout policies on a particular filesystem. **tunefs** doesn't change the filesystem's contents; it simply modifies the way in which future write operations will be handled.

The following filesystem parameters can be adjusted with **tunefs**:

- The rotational delay between groups of blocks in a file
- The maximum number of blocks in a single transfer
- The number of blocks a file may claim from a cylinder group
- The amount of disk space to reserve as overhead

Theoretically, you can manipulate these parameters (and others specified when the filesystem is constructed) to achieve better filesystem performance. Unfortunately, most modern hard drives are geometrically more complex than UNIX expects, and the kernel's optimizations are often less than perfectly effective. Some settings make a difference and some don't; most sites don't bother to fiddle with the defaults.

The overhead or "reserve" setting is still a useful tool, however. If this parameter is set to a value other than zero, the filesystem conceals a percentage of the available disk space. The default reserve is 10%, causing writes to fail when the filesystem becomes 90% full. The remaining 10% of space can only be used by root.[4]

This accounting trick allows the filesystem to keep pockets of free space together so that new files can be written out in large chunks, boosting performance. On a full disk with no reserve, throughput can be three times slower than on a disk that's 90% full.

If you're completely out of disk space, can't delete anything, and can't add more storage to the system, you might consider shrinking the filesystem reserve to free up more space. The command

```
tunefs -m pctfree device
```

sets the reserve percentage for the filesystem located on *device* to *pctfree*. Some systems also support an **-o** option to instruct the filesystem to optimize for fastest readback (**tunefs -o t** *device*) or least fragmentation (**tunefs -o s** *device*). When the reserve is pared to under 10%, fragmentation is usually more important.

tunefs alters information stored in a filesystem's superblock. Since the superblock is cached in memory while the filesystem is in use, **tunefs**

---

4. If root does use some extra space, **df** will report the disk as being more than 100% full.

should only be used on an unmounted filesystem. Otherwise, your changes will be clobbered the next time the cached superblock is written out. If you want to change the parameters of the root filesystem, run the **sync** command a couple of times, use **tunefs** to edit the superblock, and then do a **reboot -n** to reboot without any more **sync**s. This is best done from single-user mode.

 HP-UX provides a nifty **-v** option to view a filesystem's current parameters. It also provides a **-A** option, which forces backup copies of the superblock to be edited as well as the master.

 Most versions of the **tunefs** manual page mention that you can tune a filesystem, but you can't tune a fish. However, under OSF/1 you can apparently tune a fish.

BSD's **dumpfs** command prints out the superblock of an existing filesystem. It can be used to examine the filesystem's state before you start making changes.

26.7 DISK QUOTAS

If you can keep your disk space under control using informal methods such as peer pressure and periodic audits, that is usually the best way to run the system. But if these techniques fail, you may need to install disk quotas to force your users to comply with "reasonable" limitations on their use of disk space.

Quotas allow you to limit the number of inodes and disk blocks that can be allocated to each user. The number of inodes roughly determines how many files a user can own. The disk block limitation controls the total amount of filesystem space a user can allocate.

Each limit is specified as two numbers: a *soft limit* after which the user is warned about the impending quota violation, and a *hard limit* that determines the absolute limit on the resource. Users are supposed to stay under their soft limits when not logged in.

To keep users from simply ignoring the soft limits, the quota system keeps track of how long someone has exceeded them. After a certain amount of time (often three days by default), the soft limit is enforced as rigidly as the hard limit, and nothing useful can be done until the user cleans up. At this point, the time limit is reset and the user can exceed the soft limits with impunity once again.

 BSDI and OSF/1 support group quotas as well as user quotas, allowing you to limit the disk space consumed by a particular project or class of people. This is a nice feature because it gives you a way to protect different groups from each other's abuse while still leaving the space management within each group up to peer pressure and negotiation.

On systems without group quotas, disk partitioning can be used to achieve a similar effect. For example, separate partitions for students and faculty will stop faculty from taking so much space that students have none left. This provides rather gross control, since partitions are often a few hundred megabytes and house many individual users.

 HP-UX provides only halfhearted support for disk partitioning, and does not support group quotas.

See Chapter 4, The Filesystem, for more information about chown. Group quotas don't work well when users are in multiple groups; they can simply rotate among groups to evade the quotas. Another sneaky way for users to avoid quotas is to use the chown command to give away their files to other users. Quotas originated in BSD, which doesn't allow chown to be used by anyone but root. The ATT version of chown is a little different and does allow the owner of a file to give it away. In these days of Chinese-menu operating systems, it is not unheard of to see BSD's quotas and ATT's chown on the same system. There is usually a flag that can be set at kernel configuration time to disallow the use of chown by generic users.

 HP-UX addresses the "chown vs. quotas" problem as part of a more general facility for controlling access to quasi-root-like privileges. Read the man page for setprivgrp for more details.

Quotas are useful not only to control true disk hogs, but also to stop runaway user programs that might otherwise fill the disk by mistake. Quotas provide a fine level of control, but require more maintenance than other means of controlling disk usage. Frantic users who cannot save their edit sessions become a constant administrative chore when disk space is tight.

See Chapter 29 for more information about disk performance. Quotas can also reduce filesystem throughput by up to 30%. Since disk bandwidth has a dramatic effect on overall system performance, quotas can sometimes make a machine act sluggish. To minimize the performance cost of quotas, don't install them on the root partition, where most system-related disk activity occurs.

Quotas are handled on a per-user per-filesystem basis. If there is more than one filesystem on which a user is able to create files, quotas must be set for each one separately. If no quotas have been set for a particular user on a given filesystem, no default limit is applied. By convention, a limit of zero is also interpreted to mean "unlimited."

How Quotas Work

Quota information for a filesystem is kept in a file called quotas in the filesystem's root directory. The quotas file contains the limits placed on each user and also a summary of the amount of space consumed by each of the system's users.

On systems that support group quotas, there are two summary files: **quota.user** and **quota.group**. For brevity, we speak in this chapter as if there were only one file; you may have to repeat instructions that apply to the quota files if your system has group quotas.

The **edquota** command edits the per-user or per-group limits defined in the quota file or files. **quota** and **repquota** print out information about users' quotas and their current use of disk space.

The kernel normally updates the **quotas** file whenever filesystem operations change the number of disk blocks that a user is consuming. However, system crashes and other irregularities can introduce small errors into the summary file.

The **quotacheck** command examines a filesystem block by block to calculate the current disk usage, then updates the **quotas** file with an accurate summary. It is normally run with the **-a** flag at boot time, causing it to check every mounted filesystem declared to have quotas in the system's filesystem table (usually **/etc/fstab**). **quotacheck -v** prints a list of all users and their disk usages (a la **quot**). Most systems also understand **quotacheck -p**, which makes **quotacheck** examine filesystems in parallel in the manner of **fsck**.

HP-UX provides an even fancier **-P** option, which checks filesystems only when they appear to need it. This can save a lot of time.

The kernel doesn't automatically enforce quotas just because a filesystem contains a file called **quotas**; quotas have to be explicitly turned on after a filesystem is mounted using the **quotaon** command.

Enabling Quotas

Since quotas are a feature of the filesystem, they must be implemented in the kernel. Most systems today are shipped with quotas already enabled. Unfortunately, some are not—on these systems, you must build a new kernel that includes the quota code.

Chapter 13, *Configuring the Kernel*, describes the process of building a new kernel. To enable quotas, you usually add a line like

```
options QUOTA
```

to the new kernel's configuration file. After editing the config file, rebuild the kernel as described in Chapter 13 and reboot.

In addition to having quotas defined in the kernel, your system must explicitly start up quotas when the system boots. This involves running the **quotacheck -a -p** and **quotaon -a** commands[5] after local filesystems have been mounted (these commands do not work on unmounted

_____
5. The **-a** flags apply the commands to all filesystems for which they are appropriate.

filesystems). This can be done from an `rc` startup script or from `/etc/inittab`, depending on how your system's startup routine works. Refer to Chapter 2, *Booting and Shutting Down*, for specifics.

A typical sequence of commands to mount, validate, and enable quotas on all filesystems is

```
/usr/etc/mount -a > /dev/console 2>&1
echo -n 'checking quotas:' >/dev/console
/usr/etc/quotacheck -a -p >/dev/console 2>&1
echo ' done.' >/dev/console
/usr/etc/quotaon -a
```

 HP's version of **mount** understands quotas and turns them on automatically when a filesystem that supports them is mounted. HP-UX still provides the **quotaon** command, but it needn't be used at boot time.

Setting Up Quotas on a Particular Filesystem

Two steps must be taken to enable quotas on a filesystem. First, the **quotas** file must be created and configured, and second, the filesystem must be declared as using quotas in the filesystem table.

The **quotas** file should be owned by root. It should have read and write permissions for root and none for anyone else. For example, for a filesystem mounted as **/users**, you could create the **quotas** file with the following commands:

```
# touch /users/quotas
# chown root /users/quotas
# chmod 600 /users/quotas
```

These commands create an empty **quotas** file that you can populate with summary information by running **quotacheck** *devfile*, where *devfile* is the block device file (in **/dev**) on which the filesystem lives.

The filesystem table (usually **/etc/fstab**, sometimes **/etc/vfstab** or **/etc/checklist**) contains information about how disk partitions are set up and the uses to which they are to be put. Just as **mount** reads the table to find information about which filesystems should be mounted at startup time, **quotaon** and **quotacheck** read the table to find out which filesystems have quotas enabled.

Partitions on which you have not yet instituted quotas will normally have a line in the filesystem table that looks something like

```
/dev/ra0q /users      rw  1  2
```

The third field contains the code rw, meaning that the partition is to be mounted for both reading and writing (on your system, this field may contain additional options). To configure the filesystem for quotas, you either replace `rw` with `rq` (read/write with quotas), or you add the additional option `quota`, depending on the system. See page 630 for platform-specific information.

Systems that provide both user and group quotas may use the `rq` convention; however, they also use options `userquota` and `groupquota` to explicitly enable each flavor of quota. Both of these options can take an argument indicating the pathname to the appropriate quota control file. The default names are **quota.user** and **quota.group**; there's usually no reason to change them.

Once you have set up a filesystem for quotas, you can reboot the system to make quotas take effect, or you can run **quotaon** *filesystem* to turn them on by hand. Since the format of the **fstab** file is rather picky, we recommend rebooting. A syntax error you introduce when enabling quotas may go undetected until a power failure months later.

edquota: Set Quotas

Once your filesystems are set up to support quotas, you can assign limits to specific users and groups with the **edquota** command.

edquota *user* will put you into **vi** (or whatever editor is specified in the EDITOR environment variable) to edit the quotas for that user on each mounted filesystem that is currently configured for quotas. You can specify multiple users, but since you will not be given any indication of which user's quotas you are editing at any given time, this is not very useful. The command

    edquota -p *proto-user user* ...

sets *user*'s quotas to be the same as those of *proto-user*. Multiple users may be specified, but only one prototype user.

We maintain logins for a number of pseudo-users that are used only as disk quota prototypes. We used to have pseudo-users with several different quota allocations for each of about four different categories of account. This soon became too complex, so we simplified it to a three-level system: small, medium, and huge.

If your system supports group quotas, the command

    edquota -g *group*

or the command

    edquota -p *proto-group* -g *group*

will set the quotas for *group*. **edquota -t** is sets the amount of time that a user can stay over the soft quota limit before the system cracks down and enforces it. A variety of different time units are supported.

quota and repquota: View Quotas

To see the quotas set for a particular user, use the command

```
quota user
```

This command gives quota status information for filesystems on which *user* is over quota; complete information about quotas on all filesystems can be obtained by adding the **-v** flag. Individual users can find out their own quota information using the **quota** command, but only the superuser can see the quotas of other people.

login executes the **quota** command whenever a user logs in, thus warning the user about any quota problems that exist. This can cause annoying delays, especially with remote filesystems.

The **repquota** command produces a disk usage report similar to that of **quot** and **quotacheck -v**, but it also reports each user's quotas.

Quotas and NFS

See Chapter 17 for more information about the Network File System.

When filesystems are cross-mounted on a network, the implementation of quotas remains local to the machine that serves each filesystem. A client machine isn't responsible for doing any quota-related processing. But since quotas are checked on the server before each operation, quota limits are still enforced.

Most systems provide a simple daemon called **rquotad** which allows quota information to be queried over the network. It's used mostly to make the **quota** command work correctly for remote filesystems, so that users can be warned when they are over quota.

26.8 DISK OVERFLOWS

A filesystem that is completely full should be attended to as soon as possible. An overflow on a root, **/usr**, or **/var** partition is more important than one on a non-system partition, but no disk should be allowed to fester in an unusable state.

First, find out what caused the filesystem to overflow. If you have been keeping an eye on the filesystems and keeping them under 90% full, it is most likely some sort of runaway program that is filling the disk. Do a **ps** and look for suspicious processes. If you find the culprit, suspend it, inspect and possibly remove the files it was making, and apprise the process's owner of the situation.

If the overflow was not caused by a runaway program, you will need to remove some files to give breathing room for the filesystem until you can get people to clean up. If the overflowing filesystem is **/var**, remove whatever looks like junk in **/var/tmp** and truncate log files if you don't need to keep them for accounting. Check for kernel core dumps in the

`/usr/crash` or `/var/crash` directory if your system supports them; these can often be huge. If the problem is on a user filesystem, it may be harder to find things to delete, but core files are a good place to start.

You can use the `find` command to identify large files that have been recently created or modified. Here's a typical example:

```
find / -xdev -mtime -7 -size +200 -print
```

The exact syntax of the `find` command varies from system to system. This example is from SunOS; it lists files in the root partition that are larger than 100K and that have been modified in the last week. If you often have problems with overflowing disks, you might try running this command from `cron` every night and mailing yourself the results (perhaps with a higher size threshold).

26.9 SPECIFICS FOR VARIOUS OPERATING SYSTEMS

 Quota-related commands are in `/usr/sbin`. Solaris does not support group quotas; quota information is kept in a single `quotas` file. The filesystem table is in `/etc/vfstab`. Use the `rq` option to request quotas on a particular filesystem.

 Commands are in `/etc`. The mount table is `/etc/checklist`. Filesystems with quotas are marked with the option `quota`; `noquota` is also defined but is optional. HP-UX keeps track of the times when filesystems are gracefully unmounted, or when commands are used that might invalidate the quota summary information. This information is used to implement `quotacheck -P`, which acts like `quotacheck -p` but does no unnecessary work. `setprivgrp` can be used to set the behavior of the `chown` command. Group quotas are not supported.

Commands are in `/usr/etc`. Group quotas are not supported. The filesystem table is in `/etc/fstab`; use the `rq` option to request quotas on a particular filesystem. `quotacheck -n` *numusers* extends the size of the `quotas` file to accomodate *numusers* users. `quota -n` limits the display to local filesystems. IRIX does not have `tunefs`.

The filesystem table is `/etc/fstab`; `quota` and `noquota` options are used to turn quotas on or off. Commands are in `/usr/etc`. Group quotas are not supported.

Commands are in `/usr/sbin`. Group quotas are supported. The filesystem table is `/etc/fstab` and the `rq` option is used to request quotas, along with `userquota` and `groupquota` (see page 628).

 Commands are in `/sbin`. The filesystem table is in `/etc/fstab`, and `userquota` and `groupquota` are used to enable user and group quotas. The `rq` option is not used. The `quot` command is not supported.

27 *Hardware Maintenance*

27.1 INTRODUCTION

Many years ago when dozens of programmers shared a single VAX, on-site vendor maintenance was essential. If *the* machine was down, no one could get anything done. The 90s have brought an influx of desktop workstations and a move away from single points of failure. As a result, it is often possible to use the "fly by the seat of your pants" approach to hardware maintenance.

Maintenance rates are typically 10-12% of a component's list price per year. If you can afford a maintenance contract from the manufacturer or a reputable third-party vendor, by all means use it. If not, you can soon develop a sense of the ways in which machines fail and create a maintenance plan of your own.

See page 743 for more information about retiring hardware.

If you keep a log book, a quick glance at the records for the last six to twelve months will give you an idea of your failure rates. It's a good idea to keep a careful record of failures and replacements so that you can accurately evaluate the different maintenance options available to you. Some parts fail more often than anticipated by the manufacturer, so contracts are sometimes not only convenient but also financially advantageous. But remember, there comes a time when all hardware should be replaced, not maintained. Know your hardware and let it go gracefully when its time has finally come. You might even consider donating outdated equipment to your local university or school. For them, equipment is rarely too old to be useful.

Desktop workstations usually contain wave-soldered motherboards with "no user-serviceable parts inside." These are cheap and very reliable. However, when something does go wrong, the whole motherboard must often be replaced.

The best maintenance scheme is probably the "selective warranty" strategy. Disk drive manufacturers offer warranties up to five years long, and some memory SIMMs even come with a lifetime guarantee. Many workstations have at least a year of warranty. When purchasing new equipment, shop around for the best warranty—it will save you money in the long run.

The rest of this chapter offers some hints on handling and maintaining hardware. Some of these suggestions will most likely void your manufacturers' warranties. *Follow our advice at your own risk.*

27.2 BOARD-HANDLING LORE

In these days of single-board computers, you rarely need to get into the guts of a system to install or remove circuit boards. PC-based systems are perhaps an exception, as they seem to require at least four or five add-on boards to reach workstation standards (SCSI, sound, video, network, memory... Hmm, what's on that motherboard anyway?).

Circuit boards should be handled gently, not dropped, not have coffee spilled on them, books piled on them, etc. Most customer engineers (those friendly repair people that come with your maintenance contract) are ten times rougher on boards than seems reasonable.

Static Electricity

Electronic parts are sensitive to static electricity. To handle boards safely, you must ground yourself before and during installation. A ground strap worn on the wrist and attached to a special mat that you kneel on (most computers require you to show proper respect!) will isolate you properly.

Remember that you need to worry about static when you first open the package containing a printed circuit board, not just when you perform an installation. This is particularly true if the office where you receive your mail (and might be tempted to open your packages) is carpeted; carpet generates more static electricity than a hard floor.

One way to reduce static on carpeted floors is to purchase a spray bottle at your local Wal-Mart and fill it with one part Downy fabric softener to three parts water. Spray this on the carpet (but *not* on computing equipment) once a week to keep static levels low. This procedure also leaves your office area with that April-fresh scent.

Reseating Boards

Many hardware problems can be fixed by simply powering down the equipment, reseating its interface cards (SCSI, Ethernet, etc.) and powering it back up. To reseat a card, pull it out from its "seat" (usually a high-density connector) and then reinstall it. If this works temporarily but the same problem comes back a week or a month later, it probably means that the electrical contact between the card and the motherboard is poor.

If the card uses an edge connector, take it all the way out and clean the contacts with a pencil eraser. Don't use an eraser that is old and hard; if your eraser doesn't work well erasing pencil marks from paper, it won't work well on electrical contacts either. Try to keep your fingers off the contacts. Just "erase" them with the pencil (a mild abrasive), brush off the eraser droppings, and reinstall the card.

Some motherboards (especially those of the PC variety) still have socketed ICs. Over time, the connections in the sockets deteriorate, mostly because of vibrations from fans. You can press firmly on the top of the chips with your thumb (after you've donned a grounding strap, of course) to tuck them in.

27.3 MONITOR MAINTENANCE

The monitor is often the least reliable component of modern computer systems. Many monitors have brightness and convergence adjustments that are accessible only from the circuit board. Unfortunately, monitors often use internal charges of tens of thousands of volts that can persist long after the power has been disconnected. Because of the risk of electric shock, we recommend that you have your monitors adjusted by a qualified technician.

If you are adventurous enough to attempt the job yourself, be very careful. Use insulated tools that have been specifically designed for this purpose. They can be obtained from most electronics stores.

27.4 MEMORY SIMMs

Most of today's hardware accepts memory in the form of SIMMs (Single Inline Memory Modules) rather than individual chips. SIMMs range in size from 256K to 64MB, all on one little card.

If you need to add memory to a workstation or server, you can usually order SIMMs from a third-party vendor and install them yourself. Don't buy memory from workstation vendors; they will soak you 'til you're good and soggy.[1]

---

1. Unless it's part of a package deal; some of these deals are OK.

If you install your own SIMMs, keep these two rules in mind:

- High-density memory is more sensitive than anything else to static electricity. Make sure you're well grounded before opening a baggie full of memory.

- The connector that's used to attach SIMMs to the motherboard varies from machine to machine. SIMMs usually snap in easily enough, but you need a special tool to remove them once they've been installed. It always looks tempting to use a ballpoint pen or a paper clip to release the fasteners, but this approach often ends up damaging the connector.

SIMMs are frequently a candidate for the pencil eraser cleaning technology described earlier in this chapter.

27.5 Preventive Maintenance

Some pieces of hardware have filters that must be regularly cleaned or changed. Clogged filters impede the flow of air and may result in overheating, a major cause of equipment failure. It is important to keep the air vents on all equipment open and unobstructed. It is not uncommon to find books or newspapers lying on top of a computer's vents; in these cases, we recommend repeatedly punching the perpetrator in the shoulder until it really starts to hurt.

Anything with moving parts may need regular lubrication, cleaning, and belt maintenance. Old line printers are prime candidates, as are old tape drives and disk drives (but all disks made within the last five years or so are totally sealed and maintenance free). Listen for squeaks from your older equipment and pamper it accordingly.

Tape drives usually require regular cleaning. Exabyte and DAT drives are cleaned by inserting a special cassette; other formats may need manual cleaning with Q-Tips and alcohol. See the descriptions of various tape media beginning on page 180 for specific instructions.

27.6 Maintenance Contracts

Several major companies offer hardware maintenance on computer equipment that they do not manufacture. These vendors are often very anxious to displace the manufacturer and get their foot in the door, so to speak. You can sometimes negotiate very attractive maintenance contracts by playing a manufacturer against a third-party provider. If possible, get references on all potential maintenance vendors, preferably from people you know and trust.

It is rare for any maintenance provider to diagnose problems beyond the board level. There is an old joke: "How many customer engineers does it take to fix a flat tire? Four—one to replace each wheel." It is not unusual for a customer engineer to simply swap boards until the system starts working again.

A typical maintenance call involves several steps, and its nature depends on the type of service.

On-Site Maintenance

If you have an on-site maintenance contract, the repairman will bring spare parts directly to your machine. Guaranteed response time varies between four and twenty-four hours; it's usually spelled out in the contract. Response times during business hours may be much shorter than at other times of the week.

Board-Swap Maintenance

A board swap program requires you and your staff to diagnose problems, perhaps with the help of hotline personnel at the manufacturer's site. After diagnosis, you call a maintenance number, describe the problem, and order the necessary replacement board. It is usually shipped immediately and arrives the next day. You then install the board, get the hardware back up and happy, and return the old board in the same box in which the new board arrived.

The manufacturer will often want to assign a return authorization number to the transaction. It should be written on the shipping documents and sent back with the bad board.

Warranties

The length of the manufacturer's warranty should play a significant role in your computation of a machine's lifetime cost of ownership. Three months' warranty is standard for computers, but warranties of a year or more are not uncommon.

In a university environment, it seems to be much easier to get federal funding for capital equipment than for support personnel or maintenance. We have occasionally requested an "extended warranty" option on new hardware (which could also be described as long-term prepaid maintenance) to convert equipment dollars to maintenance dollars.

If you order a computer system from several vendors, the parts will not necessarily arrive at the same time. The warranty period should not start until the equipment is all there and the system has been installed. Most vendors are cooperative about delaying the beginning of the warranty period (for a month or two). With many pieces of hardware, the biggest maintenance and reliability problems occur quite soon after installation. Hardware failures that occur within a day or two of installation are referred to as "infant mortality."

27.7 ENVIRONMENTAL FACTORS

Back in the old days of central machine rooms, a proper environment meant large air conditioners, raised floors, Halon fire-control systems, and power conditioners. These days, many computers live in peoples' offices and must survive on building air conditioning (often turned off at night and on weekends), unconditioned power, and a healthy dose of papers and books on cooling vents. When you put a computer in an office, keep in mind that it will steal air conditioning that is intended for humans. In extreme cases, you may want to put the offending machine in a room with its own air conditioner.

Power Supply

Computer hardware would like to see nice, stable, clean power. In a machine room this means a power conditioner, an expensive box that filters out spikes and can be adjusted to provide the correct voltage levels and phases. In offices, surge protectors placed between machines and the wall help to insulate hardware from power spikes.

Our Electrical Engineering Department once maintained a lightning generator. It was originally used for research, but later in life it became a demonstration tool for entertaining parents and prospective students. The surge when the lightning machine went off would bring down our entire machine room. After the first such demo and our subsequent screams and curses, we were informed of impending strikes and took machines down for the duration. Machines should also be taken down and left down during natural lightning storms.

You might want to consider putting your servers and network infrastructure equipment on an Uninterruptable Power Supply (UPS). Good UPSes have an RS-232 interface that can be attached to the machine to which they supply power. This allows the UPS to warn the computer that the power has failed and that it should shut itself down cleanly before the batteries run out. We've had fantastic luck with UPSes manufactured by BEST Power Technology. They're not the least expensive, but they are very nice products.

See page 45 for more information about shutdown procedures.

One study has estimated that 10% of the electrical power consumed in the United States is used to run computers. Traditionally, UNIX boxes were based on hardware and software that expected the power to be on 24 hours a day. These days, only servers and network devices really need to be up all the time. Desktop machines can be powered down at night if there is an easy way for users to turn them off (and you trust your users to do it correctly).

At the very least, ask users to turn off monitors and laser printers when they go home—these are the biggest power hogs. When buying new equipment, look for an Energy Star certification. It indicates that an item complies with EPA guidelines for energy-efficient operation. For example, Energy Star monitors must be able to automatically shut off their displays after a certain period of inactivity.

Temperature

The ideal operating temperature for computer equipment is 64 to 68 degrees, with about 45% humidity. This does not coincide with the ideal operating temperature of a computer user. Temperatures above 80 degrees in the computer room imply about 120 degrees inside machines. Commercial-grade chips have an operational range up to about 120 degrees, at which point they stop working; beyond about 160 degrees, they break.

Humidity

The ideal humidity for most computer hardware is in the range of 40% to 60%. If the humidity is too low, static electricity becomes a problem. If it is too high, condensation can form on the boards, causing shorting and oxidation.

28 *Accounting*

28.1 INTRODUCTION

Accounting is an anachronism. Back in the good old days of expensive timesharing hardware[1], the use of accounting was common. Today, it is used primarily to provide an audit trail for tracking security break-ins, and perhaps to monitor disk and printer usage or to convince management of the need for more resources.

The UNIX kernel and various system programs keep accounting records for CPU time, login sessions, printer usage, modem usage, and a number of other system resources. A system administrator must wade through the megabytes of collected data and decide what to archive, what to keep temporarily, and what to throw away.

Accounting data files can grow quickly and will overflow the disk if not truncated regularly. Management of log files in general, including accounting files, is covered in Chapter 12, *Syslog and Log Files*.

The disk space consumed by these data files is one of the main costs of accounting. Another potential cost is reduced system performance. In particular, process accounting requires an additional write to disk for each process. On some older systems this seemed to have a perceptible effect, but on modern systems the impact is negligible.

1. A one-MIPS Vax 11/780 cost between $200,000 and $300,000 in 1980.

The accounting systems are quite different under ATT and BSD, but both systems measure essentially the same data. The BSD system has a few C programs that summarize single quantities of interest, while the ATT system is built on shell scripts that collect and summarize the data into comprehensive reports. System administrators tend to write scripts that take the output of the available tools and convert it to a format that suits their needs.

28.2 WHY BOTHER WITH ACCOUNTING?

The most obvious reason for accounting is to bill for resources used. This is appropriate for commercial providers, but not usually for in-house installations. Government contractors may be required to keep detailed accounting information.

Universities that purchase computers with federal research dollars are often required by their funding agencies to keep accounting records if they charge research grants for use of the computing infrastructure. In the past it was common to charge a "sales tax" based on usage. But as accounting fell out of favor and the volume of data saved to protect against a possible audit became unmanageable, many sites changed their charging algorithm to an "income tax" on research grants, thus sidestepping accounting altogether. This approach has even survived a couple of audits.

See Chapter 23 for more information about security. The most compelling reason to maintain accounting records remains the discovery of unauthorized use. Hackers[2] are out there, and accounting records are often the only way a site can tell if it has been attacked.

28.3 WHAT TO MEASURE AND ARCHIVE

Connect-time records written by `login` to the `wtmp` file are often the most helpful accounting records for tracking misuse. CPU accounting information written by the kernel to the `acct` or `pacct` file is of less value, because only the names of commands are recorded, not their arguments. Printer accounting is useful if you either charge for printing or provide a "reasonable" amount of printing without charge. Records of disk usage are used to browbeat users into cleaning up their files.

Before truncating accounting files, you may want to create a permanent record by archiving summaries to disk or tape. Raw accounting data files, summaries of their contents, and some log files may all need to be archived if records are required for a possible audit.

---

2. Or more accurately, "crackers." A person that breaks into a computer system used to be called a hacker, but these days "hacker" just as often denotes a prodigious, but possibly inelegant, coder. Technical lexicographers had to come up with a new word for the bad guys. For example, "Stay away from my network, you honky cracker!"

Four broad philosophies exist for archiving these files:

Conservative   Archive all accounting files and most log files to tape. Store tapes in a secure location.

Sensible   Archive summary accounting files to tape or disk. Rotate other accounting files, overwriting them as the rotation sequence wraps around. Keep at least a month's worth of raw data to facilitate tracking if security problems arise.

Carefree   Restart all accounting and log files periodically and throw away the old ones.

None   Turn off accounting as much as possible and truncate files nightly out of **cron**.

Choose a philosophy that fits your site's requirements.

28.4 ACCOUNTING IN A NETWORKED ENVIRONMENT

In an environment with lots of workstations on a local area network, separate accounting on each workstation can be a real nightmare. Programs run out of **cron** can collect and summarize data locally; if further summaries by host are required, you must build a tool that can be run from a central host.

An example of such a tool (for printer accounting using BSD's **lpr** system) is a pair of scripts we call **pachelper** and **pacmaster**, which are included on the CD-ROM.

28.5 ACCOUNTING UNDER BSD

In BSD, accounting files were traditionally located under **/usr/adm**. A few years ago, Sun reorganized the filesystem and introduced the **/var** directory for files that vary on a per-host basis. This allowed directories such as **/usr** to be made machine-independent. With this organization, local files are concentrated in only a few places rather than being scattered randomly throughout the filesystem.

Many vendors have followed Sun's lead, and accounting files now often live in **/var/adm**. As an aid to old-timers and old software, there is often a symbolic link from **/usr/adm** to **/var/adm**.

CPU Accounting

CPU accounting must be enabled in the kernel, and then can be turned on by the **accton** command. **accton** *filename* turns accounting on (*filename* must identify an existing file) and **accton** with no arguments turns accounting off.

accton is usually executed at boot time from one of the system startup scripts. Accounting data is kept in **/var/adm** in a file called **acct** or, on later systems, **pacct**. The name was changed to suggest process accounting, not to break all your accounting programs, although that may be a secondary effect. You can theoretically specify a different file-name as an argument to **accton**, but if you don't use the default file-name, commands such as **lastcomm** may break. **lastcomm** can be used to verify that process accounting is working; it shows every command that has been executed, organized by user or by terminal port.

Process accounting data grows by megabytes per day on a busy system. Each process has a record that includes its UID, elapsed CPU time, average memory use, I/O summary, and several other details. Accounting records are written as each process completes; a program that never terminates does not produce an accounting record.

The **sa** command summarizes CPU data, either by user (typically to the file **/var/adm/usracct**) or by command (to **/var/adm/savacct**). It has a zillion options, most of which have to do with the sort order of the final output and the uninteresting processes to ignore.

Two useful options are **-m** to summarize by user, and **-s** to summarize by command and reinitialize the raw data file. **sa -s** should be run at least daily to control the size of **/var/adm/pacct**.

The user-centric output looks like this:[3]

```
# sa -m
user    #commands   CPU-min   io-operations   memory used
-----------------------------------------------------------
root        61038   676.14cpu    41532937tio   77683440k*sec
daemon       8365    27.00cpu     3619385tio     291491k*sec
sys           224     1.26cpu      813849tio      11414k*sec
yiyan         226     2.82cpu      239285tio     242423k*sec
giffard        46     1.41cpu      227312tio     247336k*sec
nikki         187     0.53cpu       35722tio       9419k*sec
...
```

Column one is the login name of the user. Column two is the total number of commands that the user executed. Column three is the CPU time (user plus system) consumed, in minutes. Column four is the total number of I/O operations performed, and column five is the average memory used, measured in kilobyte-seconds.

sa -s summarizes CPU use by command, producing the following output. It also truncates **/var/adm/pacct** to zero length.

---

3. Accounting commands tend to produce very wide reports. We have in some cases made slight adjustments to fit as much information as possible into the examples.

```
# sa -s
#commands          CPU time                  I/O  memory command
------------------------------------------------------------------
198939  992142.01re 4594.91cp       945avio    648k  TOTALS
   163    6818.52re 2915.13cp       960avio     29k  perl
  1808  186951.93re  166.22cp      2871avio   1357k  in.rlogi
    19    1671.62re  163.05cp   2578356avio   4509k  xlock
 19253    2000.08re  124.47cp       332avio    956k  sendmai*
   167    7600.94re   97.71cp     21363avio   3612k  emacs
   401  130627.88re   74.80cp      5101avio   2493k  xterm
  3685  242328.77re   63.87cp       641avio    853k  csh
 28673 -157505.92re   32.77cp        16avio     53k  sh
    43     598.05re   24.74cp     39600avio   5225k  ***other
  1097     166.93re   24.43cp      6928avio   1910k  sendmail
  . . .
```

Column one is the number of times the command has been executed. Columns two and three are the real time (wall-clock time) and CPU time (user and system), both in minutes. Column four is the average number of I/O operations per command execution. Column five is the memory usage in kilobytes averaged over the CPU time execution period. Column six is the command name.

The first line contains the totals for all commands. (The word TOTALS isn't really part of **sa**'s output; we added it for clarity.) The ***other entry represents all commands with unprintable characters in their names and all commands that were executed only once.

Command names are truncated to eight characters; an asterisk after a command name means the process was run by root. There are often two entries for common rootly commands: one for regular users executing the command and one for root executing it.

Values are kept in a special floating point format that can wrap around; note the elapsed time entry for **sh**. This example is on a SunOS system where the virtual memory accounting is suspect. 29K average memory usage for **perl** certainly looks low!

The system automatically suspends accounting if the filesystem where accounting data is written becomes too full. When space becomes available on the filesystem again, accounting is restarted.

If the machine crashes or is rebooted, processes that were running are not recorded in the CPU accounting file. A sneaky user could avoid CPU accounting by having a program sleep indefinitely upon completion so that it is always still running when the machine is rebooted.

You might ask, "Who cares about the CPU cycles, memory usage, and so on? Hardware is cheap, and it costs the same whether it's running or sitting idle." Well, here is an example of using process accounting to tackle a serious breach of security:

When the Internet Worm hit in the Fall of 1988, it created several mischievous processes called -sh. A ps of the system looked normal, but the load average was going through the roof. Very short-lived processes are hard to spot and understand using ps; we ran sa -s to summarize the existing accounting data and truncate the raw data file. After five minutes we ran sa again and noticed that the -sh processes were getting all the CPU time. We then knew what processes to kill to attempt to get things under control again.

Two factors were crucial in our analysis and control of the situation:

- We immediately tried to get (and eventually got) a high-priority root shell using the **nice** command, so our commands did not take minutes to complete when the load average pushed 100.

- Accounting was running so that we could look at the process accounting data. If you choose not to run accounting, it should still be compiled into the kernel so you can turn it on if need be.

Connect-Time Accounting

Connect-time accounting is turned on by the existence of the data file /var/adm/wtmp. Login, port, and login/logout times are recorded.

With the advent of window systems and pseudo-terminals, connect-time accounting has become a poor indicator of use. A user logged in to a remote host from several windows is counted multiple times. But a user that accesses the host via **rsh** and runs **xterm** is not counted at all. If you have a workstation in your office and you leave yourself logged in for weeks at a time from several windows, you can record over 100 hours a day of connect time.[4]

The **ac** command summarizes the data in **wtmp** by person (-p) or by day (-d), and should be run monthly. A quick glance at the output may alert you to unexpected login activity; for example, unexplained use by an employee on vacation or by an inactive account. The **wtmp** file should be rotated or truncated when **ac** is run. (Note that while **sa** truncates the pacct file unless told not to, ac never truncates **wtmp**.) The per-person summary looks like this:

```
# ac -p
login   connect-hrs
------------------
neves         19.46
weaver         0.13
```

---

4. Does your site pay overtime?

```
dwight          2.67
jacques         3.51
...
total         759.14
```

A list of login names can also be given. For example:

```
# ac -p evi trent root
login   connect-hrs
------------------
evi            21.03
trent          24.70
root            0.02
total          45.75
```

The output of **ac -d**, which summarizes by date, illustrates that the weekends are periods of lighter usage.

```
# ac -d
date            connect-hrs
-----------------------
Nov  1   total     126.70
Nov  2   total     170.98
Nov  3   total     198.19
Nov  4   total     140.47
Nov  5   total     122.83
Nov  6   total      58.92
Nov  7   total      89.93
Nov  8   total     131.55
```

These options can be combined. For example:

```
# ac -dp lane
date            connect-hrs
-----------------------
Aug  1   total      8.87
Aug  2   total      7.71
Aug  5   total      4.45
```

The **last** command can be used to determine the actual times that a user logged in and out. Its output can be keyed to a particular user or to a port, which is useful for tracking intruders, finding overworked or broken terminals, and monitoring dial-up modem usage. For example, the command **last lane** shows details on user lane's usage:

```
# last lane
lane   ttyp    hartree.cs.colo Thu Aug 5 15:02-19:28 (04:26)
lane   ttyp4   lair.cs.colorad Mon Aug 2 18:44-20:38 (01:54)
lane   ttyp3   lair.cs.colorad Mon Aug 2 18:44-20:38 (01:54)
lane   ttyq8   hartree.cs.colo Mon Aug 2 14:16-16:15 (01:59)
lane   ttyp4   lair.cs.colorad Sun Aug 1 19:17-22:14 (02:57)
lane   ttyp1   lair.cs.colorad Sun Aug 1 19:16-22:13 (02:57)
```

The double entries come from a window system configured to start a remote login session in two windows at once.

```
# last ttyd0
Ufossa        ttyd0                     Fri Aug 6 13:44-13:53 (00:09)
Uicarus       ttyd0                     Fri Aug 6 13:36-13:36 (00:00)
Ueddie        ttyd0                     Fri Aug 6 13:16-13:19 (00:02)
Upathome      ttyd0                     Fri Aug 6 12:47-12:48 (00:00)
Upathome      ttyd0                     Fri Aug 6 11:45-11:46 (00:00)
```

These are all UUCP hosts; five years ago when home users typically had only ASCII terminals (and when dial-up ports were on workstations rather than concentrated at terminal servers as they are today), this list would have included more real users. For security reasons, it is useful to run `last` on the dial-up ports every so often to look for unusual events (unexpected users or users at unexpected times).

Printer Usage

See Chapter 25 for information about /etc/printcap.

The line printer daemon `lpd` records printer usage if a printer's entry in `/etc/printcap` has the `af` variable defined and the designated file exists. By convention, printer accounting data files are usually called `/var/adm/`*printer*`-acct`. They list the number of pages printed for each job, the hostnames where the jobs originated, and the user names of the jobs' owners. The information is summarized by the `pac` command; use it at least monthly. For example:

```
# /etc/pac -Pgutenberg
Login                   pages/feet   runs      price
alpo:ross                    29.00      2     $  0.58
anchor:zweifel              114.00      2     $  2.28
axon:paul                     7.00      1     $  0.14
blue:brookmak                 6.00      6     $  0.12
blue:sanders                  1.00      1     $  0.02
columbine:carolyn            44.00     40     $  0.88
columbine:harriet            42.00      7     $  0.84
...
total                       731.00    161     $ 14.62
```

The notation `alpo:ross` refers to user ross on host alpo. The `pac` command takes a flag `-pprice` which sets the price per page in dollars. The default is two cents per page. `pac` does not charge per run, so header pages are not included in the `price` column. There are several other options to `pac`; as always, consult your manual.

It is the responsibility of the printer's input filter to generate accounting records. On PostScript printers, unless the filter actually queries the printer for its page count before and after the job, the page counts are extremely suspect.

Dial-Out Usage

The `tip` and UUCP family of commands (BSD version) record the login name, date, time, phone number, and status of all calls made through a dial-out modem. The information is in **/var/adm/aculog**, which is a text file. Sample log entries are shown below (with lines wrapped to fit).

```
uucp:daemon (Sun Oct 31 18:31:03 1993) <interlink,
   5551234, telebit> call completed
uucp:daemon (Mon Nov  1 08:58:35 1993) <uswestpaging,
   5555678, telebit> call completed
uucp:staff (Mon Nov  1 09:37:07 1993) <t38, , /dev/cua0>
   call completed
uucp:staff (Mon Nov  1 09:38:56 1993) <t38, , /dev/cua0>
   call terminated
```

`interlink` and `uswestpaging` are entries in **/etc/remote** that describe modem characteristics, ports, phone numbers, and so on.

If you allow users to talk directly to a modem via a `dialer` entry in the **/etc/remote** file, then `tip dialer` will circumvent accounting, since `tip` does not directly cause the phone number to be dialed and therefore cannot write an appropriate log entry.

There are no standard tools that summarize the **aculog** file, but **grep** can be used to identify long distance calls. The phone company usually provides itemized bills for long distance calls that can be matched against your `tip` log files.

Unfortunately, most modems can be put into command mode via a special sequence of characters and pauses. A thief can circumvent accounting by calling a local number, sending the modem's break sequence, and then instructing the modem to hang up and redial unbeknownst to `tip`. The break sequence is usually configurable, so you might want to make it something nonstandard if you allow general access to modems.

Summaries

Table 28.1 details the files that store accounting data on BSD-ish systems. The owner, group, and mode (shown here in octal) of the accounting data files are important; any program used to reinitialize these files should be sure to **chown**, **chgrp**, and **chmod** appropriately.

Table 28.2 summarizes the BSD accounting commands.

28.6 ACCOUNTING UNDER ATT

Most versions of ATT UNIX contain a fairly complete accounting system implemented with C programs and **sh** scripts. These scripts are typically run daily and monthly by **cron**. All accounting is done under the

Table 28.1   Summary of BSD accounting files

Data	Filename	Type	Owner	Group	Mode
CPU, Memory	`acct` or `pacct`	Binary	root	system	644
Connect time	`wtmp`	Binary	root	system	644
Printer usage	`lp-acct`	Text	daemon	daemon	644
Dial-out usage	`aculog`	Text	uucp	daemon	660

Table 28.2   Summary of BSD accounting commands

Data	Command	Frequency to run
CPU, Memory	`accton`	During boot
	`sa`	At least daily
	`lastcomm`	As needed
Connect time	`ac`	Monthly
	`last`	As needed
Printer usage	`pac`	Monthly for each printer

login adm with home directory `/var/adm`; accounting information is kept in `/var/adm/acct`. The accounting programs and scripts are usually in `/usr/lib/acct`.

Setting Up Accounting

On most systems, accounting does not run by default, so you must set it up. The accounting programs may even be unbundled (either sold separately or included with standard distribution but separately installed).

To see if you have the accounting system on-line, look in the directory `/usr/lib/acct`. If it's empty, go back to the distribution CD-ROM. Otherwise, make sure that the adm login exists. If it does not, you can create it by adding the following line to `/etc/passwd`:

```
adm:*:4:4:Administrative Login:/var/adm:/bin/sh
```

adm traditionally has UID four, but that is arbitrary. It's best to look on the distribution and observe the UID of all the accounting programs and configuration files. After creating the adm login, make sure that the directory `/var/adm/acct` exists and is owned by adm. `/var/adm` should include a `.profile` file with the following contents:

```
PATH=/usr/lib/acct:/bin:/usr/bin
```

You should also create the subdirectories **night**, **sum**, and **fiscal** in `/var/adm/acct`.

Accounting information is not gathered until the **startup** command is executed. To start accounting automatically on a system using BSD-style

/etc/rc files, such as HP-UX, add the following line to the appropriate section of the **rc** file:

```
/bin/su - adm -c /usr/lib/acct/startup
```

The **/usr/lib/acct/shutacct** command turns off accounting; some systems need to have it done specifically during the shutdown process, and some do it automatically.

For systems using ATT-style **init** levels to specify the actions to take when going multi-user (for example, Solaris), the following shell script added to **/etc/init.d** and hard-linked to the **rc2.d** directory would turn accounting on and off as the machine came in and out of multi-user mode.

See Chapter 2, *Booting and Shutting Down*, for more information about starting services at boot time.

```
#!/bin/sh
# rc script to start and stop accounting

case "$1" in
'start')
    if [ -x /usr/lib/acct/startup ] ; then
        echo "accounting started."
        /usr/lib/acct/startup
    fi
    ;;

'stop')
    if [ -x /usr/lib/acct/shutacct ] ; then
        /usr/lib/acct/shutacct
    fi
    ;;

*)
    echo "Usage: /etc/init.d/acct { start | stop }"
    ;;
esac

exit 0
```

A copy of this script is included on the CD-ROM. IRIX 4.0 includes a similar script, but IRIX 5.2 and Solaris 2.4 do not. Sometimes the script exists in **/etc/init.d** but the link to **rc2.d** is missing.

In order for the system to charge properly for system usage, you must tell it which hours you consider "prime time" and which days you consider holidays. This is done in the file **/usr/lib/acct/holidays**. A sample **holidays** file follows.

```
* Prime/Nonprime Table for Accounting System
*
* Year    PrimeStart  NonPrimeStart
  1994      0900         1800
*
    1       Jan 1        New Year's Day
   35       Feb 4        AT&T vs. UC Lawsuit Settled
  231       Aug 19       ucbvax Retired
  323       Oct 31       Halloween
  325       Nov 2        Anniversary of the Internet Worm
  359       Dec 25       Christmas Day
```

All lines starting with a star are comments. The first non-comment line specifies the current year (in this case 1994), and the start and end of prime hours. In this example, prime hours are from 9:00 a.m. to 6:00 p.m. Prime time must be a contiguous block of time; all other times are considered non-prime. There is no way to have more than two classes of service (prime and non-prime) or to have more than one block of prime time per day (for example, prime time from 10:00 a.m. to 5:00 p.m. and again from 7:00 p.m. to 10:00 p.m.).

The rest of the lines in the file list the days that you consider holidays, which are treated the same as weekends. The fields are:

yearday monthday description

Both a C program and a **perl** *script to compute Julian dates are included on the CD-ROM.*

Of these, only *yearday* (the Julian date) is actually used by accounting programs. Obviously, the **holidays** file must be updated each year. If accounting is run with an out-of-date **holidays** file, a mail message will be sent to users adm and root, and log entries will be written. If you don't use accounting to charge people for computing services, don't worry too much about the contents of the holidays file. It only needs to contain the line specifying the current year and prime time hours in order to keep the log files from filling with error messages.

See Chapter 10 for more information about **cron.**

Running **startup** tells the system to start archiving accounting data, but it does not cause the data to be processed. The following **cron** entries, usually placed in adm's crontab with **crontab -e adm**, support both daily and monthly processing of accounting. They run accounting in the wee hours of the night, when users won't be disturbed.

```
# daily and weekly accounting chores
#
0 4 * * * /usr/lib/acct/runacct 2>/var/adm/acct/nite/d2log
0 1 * * 4 /usr/lib/acct/dodisk
0 * * * * /usr/lib/acct/ckpacct
#
# monthly accounting
#
0 2 1 * * /usr/lib/acct/monacct
```

What Accounting Does

The **runacct** program generates several files that contain daily accounting information and stores them in **/var/adm/acct/sum**. The only files that are of any real interest are the report files.

There are report files for each day since **monacct** was last run called **rprt***mmdd* where *mm* is the month and *dd* is the day. These reports can be printed out if you want a record of daily accounting. The reports contain summaries of terminal usage, command usage, disk usage, and time of last login. The format of the reports is self-explanatory.

If **runacct** does not run to completion because the system crashes, it must be restarted by hand. The manual page gives a complete description of how to restart **runacct** so it picks up where it left off. **runacct** writes error messages to **/var/adm/acct/nite/fd2log** (or whatever file you specify in the **cron** entry that starts **runacct**). For example:

```
acctcms: Hash table overflow. Increase CSIZE
***UPDATE /etc/holidays WITH NEW HOLIDAYS***
acctprc2: INCREASE A_USIZE
```

 Unfortunately, only the **holidays** file can be updated by mere mortals. CSIZE is the size of a hash table defined in **acctcms.c**; it cannot be changed unless you have source code, and its value is usually 1,000. A_USIZE is the maximum number of logins and is set in **acctdef.h**, usually to 500; it also requires access to the source code to change. Solaris has boosted these constants to more reasonable values.

Error messages are also written to **/var/adm/acct/nite/log***mmdd*, where *mm* is the current month and *dd* the current day. For example, the file **log0601** contains

```
***UPDATE /etc/holidays WITH NEW HOLIDAYS***
acctcon1: RECOMPILE WITH LARGER A_TSIZE
```

Again, you must have source code to fix most errors.

The **dodisk** program collects disk usage information. In the example above, **dodisk** is only run once a week on Thursdays; it uses a bit of CPU and I/O bandwidth, and for many users the results are not very volatile. The data is stored in **/var/adm/acct/nite/disktacct** and is merged into the file **daytacct** by the **runacct** script.

See page 620 for more information about du.

The **ckpacct** command monitors the process accounting data file **pacct** (in either **/usr/adm** or **/var/adm**) and splits it up when it gets larger than a certain size, usually 1,000 **du**-sized blocks. **ckpacct** also monitors free space on **/usr** or **/var** and disables accounting if there are fewer than 500 free blocks.

Such monitoring makes sense if the monitor watches the filesystem on which the `pacct` file lives. Under SunOS, `/usr` is watched, but `pacct` is in `/var/adm`, usually on a separate partition. Fortunately, `ckpacct` is a script and so you can change `/usr` to `/var` to fix this problem.

`monacct` summarizes the daily reports for the previous month, stores summaries in `/var/adm/acct/fiscal/fiscrpt`*mm* (where *mm* is again the month), and restarts the summary files in the **sum** directory. If you want to charge users for their usage, you can write a simple `perl` or shell script that examines the monthly summaries and generates invoices for each user.

In addition to the information that is collected automatically when accounting is turned on, the **chargefee** program allows you to assess additional fees on specific users. This is useful if you want to charge for something that you did for them, such as loading a tape. You could use the command

```
/usr/lib/acct/chargefee joe 10
```

to charge the user joe for ten accounting units (the meaning of units is completely arbitrary). All fees that are charged with **chargefee** will appear in the report files, so you can include them in invoices.

Ideally, you should not have to worry about the nitty-gritty of how data files are processed. However, if you want to modify the way that accounting works, or if something is not working correctly, you may have to investigate its inner workings. The accounting system keeps a lot of internal files in `/var/adm/acct/nite` and `/var/adm/acct/sum`. Descriptions of the various commands and data files can be found in the documentation. Table 28.3 (next page) describes the files usually found in the directory `/usr/lib/acct`. Entries with a program in parentheses at the end of the description field are not run directly, but rather by the designated program.

This is an impressive array of accounting artillery. However, very few of the commands are used directly by a system administrator. Daily and monthly summaries are normally handled out of **cron**. Occasionally, accounting will fail to run to completion, but the ATT accounting system does a good job of letting you restart it.

`runacct` produces the daily summaries. It is usually invoked so that its error output is sent to `/var/adm/acct/nite/fd2log` (file descriptor two is the standard error channel). If there is something wrong with accounting, diagnostic messages will show up in this file. If you ignore accounting and have something misconfigured, the file can grow quite quickly. Keep an eye on it. Also, periodically inspect the other output files beneath `/var/adm/acct`.

Table 28.3 Summary of ATT accounting files in /usr/lib/acct

	Command	Type	Description
Administration	`startup`	sh script	Runs at boot time to enable accounting
	`accton`	Program	Turns on process accounting
	`turnacct`	sh script	Turns on accounting to `/usr/adm/pacct`
	`shutacct`	Program	Turns off accounting and logs to `wtmp`
	`chargefee`	sh script	Charges specific users
	`holidays`	Text file	List of holidays
	`nulladm`	sh script	Reinitializes files and checks ownerships
	`remove`	sh script	Cleans up `/usr/adm/acct/sum`
Time	`acctcon1`	Program	ASCIIfies connect-time records (`runacct`)
	`acctcon2`	Program	Converts to `tacct` format (`runacct`)
	`lastlogin`	sh script	Updates last login record in `sum/loginlog`
	`acctwtmp`	Program	Adds boot record to `wtmp` file
	`fwtmp`	Program	Fixes dates in `wtmp` when changed by `date`
	`wtmpfix`	Program	Recognizes/repairs a bad `wtmp` file
CPU	`ckpacct`	sh script	Restarts `pacct` file if it is too big
	`acctcms`	Program	Makes command usage records (`runacct`)
	`acctprc1`	Program	Makes process records (`runacct`)
	`acctprc2`	Program	Makes process records (`runacct`)
Disk use	`acctdisk`	Program	Makes disk usage records (`dodisk`)
	`acctdusg`	Program	Makes disk usage records (`dodisk`)
	`diskusg`	Program	Generates disk accounting data by user
	`dodisk`	sh script	Takes a snapshot of disk usage
Reports	`runacct`	sh script	Summarizes daily data
	`acctmerg`	Program	Merges processed records (`runacct`)
	`prctmp`	sh script	Prints session record file
	`prdaily`	sh script	Prints previous day's accounting summaries
	`prtacct`	sh script	Prints accounting records from `tacct` files
	`monacct`	sh script	Produces monthly reports

Printer Accounting

See Chapter 25 for more information about printing.

ATT systems do not have printer accounting, although the spooler records print jobs in the file **/var/spool/lp/logs/requests**. The number of bytes printed is recorded, but not the number of pages, so the information is essentially useless for accounting purposes. If you want true printer accounting like that provided by the BSD **pac** command, it must be built into the printer interface scripts used in the **lp** system.

28.7 SPECIFICS FOR VARIOUS OPERATING SYSTEMS

Most vendors use BSD- or ATT-style accounting without much modification. Tables 28.4 and 28.6 detail the locations of accounting data files and the commands supplied by vendors to administer them.

Table 28.4 **File and command locations by vendor (ATT)**

File	Solaris	HP-UX	IRIX
ATT commands	`/usr/lib/acct`	`/usr/lib/acct`	`/usr/lib/acct`
ATT reports	`/var/adm/acct`	`/usr/adm/acct`	`/var/adm/acct`
`acct` or `pacct`	`/var/adm`	`/usr/adm`	`/var/adm`
`wtmp`	`/var/adm`	`/etc`	`/var/adm`
`pac`	–	–	`/usr/etc`

Solaris is straight ATT, with no **sa**, **ac**, or **pac** to be found. There is no `/usr/etc` either. The holidays file is in `/etc/acct`, carefully moved to its own directory so that any old accounting scripts expecting it to be in `/usr/lib/acct` will break without warning.

Table 28.5 describes four bonus commands in `/usr/lib/acct` that join those from Table 28.3. The last two of these commands account for users who are logged in while accounting is being run.

Table 28.5 **Bonus commands in Solaris**

Command	Type	Description
`acctcon`	Program	Combines `acctcon1` and `acctcon2` programs
`acctprc`	Program	Combines `acctprc1` and `acctprc2` programs
`closewtmp`	Program	Fakes entries for users logged on during accounting
`utmp2wtmp`	Program	Adds `wtmp` records for users currently logged on

HP-UX uses ATT-style accounting and 4.3BSD-style logging via **syslog**. Accounting is a separate subsystem and must be explicitly loaded from the software distribution. Commands are in `/usr/lib/acct`; raw data files are in `/usr/adm` with summaries in `/usr/adm/acct`. Accounting must be started in `/etc/rc` to begin collecting data.

IRIX uses ATT-style accounting with commands in `/usr/lib/acct` and the data summarized in `/var/adm/acct`. It supports both ATT and BSD printing; the **pac** printer accounting program is included.

IRIX distinguishes between an empty data file for a configured service and an unconfigured service. The directory `/etc/config` contains files representing each service; the command **chkconfig** checks to see if the service is configured or not. If **acct** contains the word on and crontab entries are as below, accounting data will be collected and summarized.

```
# runacct processes connect, fee, disk, and process
# accounting files
0  4  *  *  1-6   if /etc/chkconfig acct; then
  /usr/lib/acct/runacct 2> /usr/adm/acct/nite/fd2log; fi
```

```
# ckpacct checks the size of /usr/adm/pacct
5  *  *  *  1-6   if /etc/chkconfig acct; then
   /usr/lib/acct/ckpacct; fi
# monacct creates summary files in /usr/adm/acct/fiscal
0  5  1  *  *    if /etc/chkconfig acct; then
   /usr/lib/acct/monacct; fi
```

Table 28.6   File and command locations by vendor (BSD)

File	SunOS	OSF/1	BSDI
accton	/usr/lib/acct	/usr/sbin/acct	/usr/sbin
sa	/usr/etc	/usr/sbin	/usr/sbin
acct or pacct	/var/adm	/var/adm	/var/account
usracct	/var/adm	/var/adm	/var/account
savacct	/var/adm	/var/adm	/var/account
ac	/usr/etc	/usr/sbin	–
wtmp	/etc	/var/adm	/var/log
pac	/usr/etc	/usr/sbin	/usr/sbin
ATT reports	/usr/lib/acct	/var/adm/acct	–
ATT commands	/var/adm/acct	/usr/sbin/acct	–

SunOS uses ATT-style accounting but also includes the BSD commands for login, process, and printer accounting. As shipped, data files are in **/var/adm/acct** and programs and scripts are in **/usr/lib/acct**. Accounting must be configured into the kernel in order for process accounting data to be kept. The variable SYSACCT must be defined; see Chapter 13, *Configuring the Kernel*.

The accounting data files were traditionally beneath **/usr/adm**, which Sun has linked to **/var/adm**. SunOS has an additional accounting command not in the general ATT list from the previous section: **getname**. **getname** is an undocumented command that looks up a user in **/etc/passwd**. It is used by several scripts in **/usr/lib/acct**.

OSF/1 uses ATT-style accounting, but has moved the commands from **/usr/lib/acct** to **/usr/sbin/acct**. DEC's OSF/1 2.0 includes the BSD accounting commands in **/usr/sbin**. Older versions had the man pages but not the commands (except for **pac**).

Accounting on BSDI is BSD-style with commands in **/usr/sbin**; the **ac** command is missing. Process accounting information is archived in **/var/account/acct**. Login information is in **/var/log/wtmp**.

29 *Performance Analysis*

29.1 INTRODUCTION

Many administrators are convinced that their systems could run twice as fast, if only they knew how to properly tune them to release their vast, untapped potential. In reality, this is almost never true.

One common fantasy of advanced administrators involves tweaking the kernel variables that control the paging system and the buffer pools. Once upon a time, there were situations in which this was necessary and prudent. These days, it is usually a bad idea. The most likely result is that you will *reduce* your system's overall performance and not even be aware of what you've done, all the while congratulating yourself on being such a clever kernel hacker.

Modern kernels are pre-tuned to achieve reasonable (though admittedly, not optimal) performance under a variety of load conditions. If you try to optimize the system based on some random measure of performance, the chances are high that you will distort the system's behavior relative to other performance metrics and load conditions. It seems easy to get results, but the gains are usually illusory.

In particular, take everything you read on Usenet with a tablespoon of salt. In the area of system performance, you will see superficially convincing arguments on all sorts of topics. However, most of the proponents of these theories do not have the knowledge, discipline, and time required to design valid experiments. Popular support means absolutely nothing; for every hare-brained proposal, you can expect to see a Greek chorus of, "I increased the size of my buffer cache by a factor of ten just like Joe said, and my system feels MUCH, MUCH faster!!!" Right.

System performance is not entirely out of your control. It's just that the road to good performance is not paved with "magic" fixes and romantic kernel patches. The basic rules are:

- Don't overload your systems or your network. UNIX gives each process an illusion of infinite resources. But once 100% of the system's resources are in use, UNIX has to work very hard to maintain that illusion, delaying processes and often consuming a sizable fraction of the resources themselves.

- Waste not, want not. Don't squander the available performance on unnecessary features (disk quotas and CPU accounting are common performance offenders). Write efficient scripts and programs, and do system work late at night from `cron`.

29.2 WHAT YOU CAN DO TO IMPROVE PERFORMANCE

Here are some specific things can you do to improve performance:

- You can make sure the system has enough memory. As we will see below, memory size has a major influence on performance.

- You can correct problems of usage, both those caused by users (too many jobs run at once, inefficient programming practices, jobs run at excessive priority, and large jobs run at inappropriate times of day) and those caused by the system (quotas, CPU accounting, unwanted daemons).

- You can organize the system's hard disks and filesystems so that load is evenly balanced, maximizing I/O throughput.

- You can monitor your network to be sure that it is not saturated with traffic and that the error rate is low. Networks can be supervised with the `netstat` command, described on page 274. See also Chapter 22, *Network Management*.

- You can configure the kernel to eliminate unwanted drivers and options, and to use tables of an appropriate size. These topics are covered in Chapter 13, *Configuring the Kernel*.

- You can tune the filesystem's layout policies for individual disks. See *Tuning Filesystems* on page 668.

- You can identify situations in which the system is fundamentally inadequate to satisfy the demands being made of it.

These steps are listed in rough order of effectiveness. Adding memory and correcting problems caused by users can make a huge difference in performance. You might see some improvement from organizing the system's disks correctly and from correcting network problems. The other factors may or may not make any difference at all.

29.3 FACTORS THAT AFFECT PERFORMANCE

Perceived performance is determined by the efficiency with which the system's resources are allocated and shared. The exact definition of a "resource" is rather vague. It can include such items as cached contexts on the CPU chip and entries in the address table of the memory controller. However, to a first approximation, only the following four resources have much effect on performance:

- CPU time
- Memory
- Hard disk I/O bandwidth
- Network I/O bandwidth

All processes consume a portion of the system's resources. If there are still resources left over after active processes have taken what they want, the system's performance is about as good as it can be.

If there are not enough resources to go around, processes must take turns. A process that does not have immediate access to the resources it needs must wait around doing nothing. The amount of time spent waiting is one of the basic measures of performance degradation.

CPU time is one of the easiest resources to measure. There is always a constant amount of processing power available. In theory it is 100% of the CPU cycles, but overhead and various inefficiencies make the real-life number more like 95%. A process that's using more than 90% of the CPU is entirely CPU-bound and is consuming most of the system's available computing power.

Many people assume that the speed of the CPU is the most important factor affecting a system's overall performance. Given infinite amounts of all other resources, or certain types of applications (numerical simulations, for example), a faster CPU *will* make a dramatic difference. But in the everyday world of workstations and graphical user interfaces, CPU speed is relatively unimportant.

The real performance bottleneck on UNIX systems is disk bandwidth. Because hard disks are mechanical systems, it takes tens of milliseconds to locate a disk block, fetch its contents, and wake up the process that's waiting for it. Delays of this magnitude overshadow every other source of performance degradation. Each disk access causes a stall worth millions of CPU instructions.

Because UNIX provides virtual memory, disk bandwidth and memory are directly related. On a loaded system with a limited amount of RAM, you often have to write a page to disk to obtain a fresh page of virtual memory. Unfortunately, this means that using memory is often just as expensive as using the disk. Swapping and paging caused by bloated software is performance enemy #1 on most workstations.

Some systems attempt to replace disk transfers with CPU time by compressing pages as they are swapped out. A compression ratio of 2:1 is achievable in many cases and allows two memory pages to be packed onto one disk page. This trick is also used by some PC software.

See page 375 for some NFS performance-tuning suggestions.

Network bandwidth resembles disk bandwidth in many ways, due to the latencies involved and the fact that a high proportion of network traffic is NFS. However, networks are atypical in that they involve entire communities rather than individual computers. They are also susceptible to hardware problems and overloaded servers.

29.4 GIVING YOUR SYSTEM A PERFORMANCE CHECKUP

Most performance analysis tools tell you what's going at a particular point in time. However, the number and character of loads will probably change throughout the day. Be sure to gather a cross-section of data before taking action.

ATT systems seem to have better monitoring tools than BSD systems. The tools are all integrated into the **sar** command; BSD systems have a random selection of independent tools, many of which provide the same information. **sar** can also be run periodically from **cron** to accumulate data over a long period of time.

Analyzing CPU Usage

There are three kinds of CPU data you might want to gather: overall utilization, load averages, and per-process CPU consumption.

Summary information can be obtained with **vmstat** on BSD systems and **sar -u** on ATT systems. Both commands take two arguments: the number of seconds to monitor the system for each line of output, and the number of reports to provide. For example:

```
% sar -u 5 5
13:33:40    %usr    %sys    %wio    %idle
13:33:45      4      58      27      11
13:33:50      7      83       9       0
13:33:55      9      77      13       0
13:34:00      2      25       3      71
13:34:05      0       0       0     100

Average       4      49      10      36
```

sar -u reports the percentage of the CPU's time that was spent running user code (%usr), running kernel code (%sys), and idling. Idle time is charged to the %wio category if there are processes blocked on high-speed I/O (disk, usually) and to the %idle column if not.

vmstat prints a variety of information, with the CPU-related columns at the end:

```
% vmstat 5 5
procs              page                faults        cpu
r b w    re   mf pi po fr do sr   in   sy   cs   us sy id
0 0 0     0    0  0  0  0  0  0    4   22   19    2  1 97
1 0 0    67    2  0  0  0  0  0   26  751   52   53 47  0
0 0 0    96    0  0  0  0  0  0   39 1330   42   22 71  7
0 0 0    16    0  0  0  0  0  0   84 1626   99    7 74 19
0 0 0     1    0  0  0  0  0  0   11  216   20    1 11 88
```

Some columns have been edited out of this example. We will defer discussion of the paging-related columns until later in this chapter. The first line of **vmstat**'s output summarizes activity since boot time.

User, system, and idle time are shown in the us, sy, and id columns. CPU numbers that are heavy on user time generally indicate computation, while high system numbers indicate that processes are making a lot of system calls or performing I/O (**vmstat** shows the number of system calls per second in the sy column under faults). The cs column shows context switches per interval, the number of times that the kernel changed which process was running.

 Solaris provides both the **sar** and **vmstat** commands. **sar** is also available in DEC's OSF/1 as an installation option.

Large-scale CPU statistics allow you to determine whether there is fundamentally enough CPU power to go around. If the CPU usually spends part of its time in the idle state, there are cycles to spare. Upgrading to a faster CPU won't do much to improve the overall throughput of the system, though it may speed up individual operations.

As you can see from these examples, the CPU generally flip-flops back and forth between full-on use and complete idleness. Therefore, it's important to observe these numbers as an average over time. The smaller the monitoring interval, the less consistent the results.

On a workstation with only one user, the CPU generally spends 99% of its time idle. Then, when you go to scroll one of the windows on your bitmap display, the CPU is floored for a few seconds. In this situation, long-term average CPU utilization is relatively meaningless.

The second CPU statistic that's useful for characterizing the burden on your system is the "load average," the average number of runnable processes. In general, the load average includes processes waiting for disk and network I/O, so it is not a pure measure of CPU use. However, it does give you a good idea of how many pieces the CPU pie is being divided into. The load average is obtained with the **uptime** command:

```
% uptime
2:07pm up 4:02, 5 users, load average: 0.95, 0.38, 0.31
```

Three values are given, corresponding on most systems to the five, ten, and fifteen-minute averages. Under OSF/1, the averages are for the last five seconds, half-minute, and minute.

Generally, the higher the load average, the more important the system's aggregate performance becomes. If there is only one runnable process, that process will generally end up bound by a single resource (commonly disk bandwidth or CPU). The peak demand for that one resource becomes the determining factor in performance.

When more processes share the system, loads may or may not be more evenly distributed. If the processes on the system all consume a mixture of CPU, disk, and memory, the performance of the system is less likely to be dominated by constraints on a single resource. In this situation, it becomes most important to look at average measures of consumption such as total CPU utilization.

See page 70 for more information about priorities.

Workstations do not deal well with load averages over about 3.0. A load average of this magnitude is a hint that you should start to look for ways to artificially spread the load, such as asking users to run long processes at night or using **nice** to set process priorities.

Another way to view CPU usage is to run the **ps** command with arguments that let you see how much of the CPU each process is using (**-aux** for BSD, **-elf** for ATT). More likely than not, on a busy system, at least 70% of the CPU will be consumed by one or two processes. (Remember that **ps** consumes some CPU itself.) Deferring the execution of the CPU hogs or reducing their priority will make the CPU more available to other processes.

*See page 81 for a more thorough discussion of **top**.*

An excellent alternative to **ps** is a program called **top**. **top** presents about the same information as **ps**, but in a "live" format that lets you watch the status of the system change over time.

The Cost of Virtual Memory

Memory is usually managed in pages of at least four kilobytes. They are sometimes called "page clusters" if they are larger than the page size supported by the CPU or memory controller. Disk blocks are usually smaller than memory pages (1K or 512 bytes), so the kernel has to associate several disk blocks with each page that's written out.

In general, UNIX tries to manage the system's memory so that pages that have been recently accessed are kept in memory and less active pages are paged out. This is known as an "LRU" system since the least recently used pages are the ones that get rotated to disk.

It would be very expensive for the kernel to really keep track of all page references, so most versions of UNIX use a statistical technique for managing memory known as the clock algorithm. It's much cheaper than a true LRU system, but produces similar results.

The kernel maintains a *free list* of pages that are eligible to be paged out. When memory is low, pages are placed on the free list seemingly at random. (Actually, there is a defined order, so the "clock" hand points to every page equally often.) As a page is placed on the free list, its address mapping is unwired from the memory controller so that the next time a process attempts to access it, a fault is generated.

If a "freed" page is referenced before being paged out (called a "soft" fault), the kernel takes it off the free list and rewires its address mapping. The page is then safe until the next pass of the page-freeing clock. On average, infrequently referenced pages don't get rescued; their contents are eventually written out to disk and they are then recycled.[1]

Demand for memory varies, so the kernel can run the page-freeing clock at different speeds. If there is plenty of memory, the clock does not run at all, thus sparing the system the overhead of processing soft page faults. When the demand for memory is extreme, the clock runs at high speed and pages must be rescued in a shorter amount of time to avoid being paged out.

The virtual memory (VM) system depends on the lag between the time when a page is placed on the free list and the time when it's actually paged out to sort active pages from inactive pages. Therefore, it has to predict future paging activity in order to select an appropriate speed for the paging clock. If the clock runs too slowly, there might not be enough pages on the free list to satisfy demand. If too fast, the kernel spends excessive time processing soft page faults.

Since the paging algorithm is predictive, there is not necessarily a one-to-one correspondence between page-out events and page allocations by running processes. The goal of the system is to keep enough free memory handy that processes don't have to actually wait for a page-out each time they make a new allocation.

Swapping is handled somewhat differently from paging. It's also done predictively, but on the basis of accurate per-process records rather

---

1. It is not always necessary to save the contents of a page that's being recycled; text pages and other pages that can be retrieved from their original sources are simply discarded.

than statistical estimates. If memory is scarce and a process is known to have been idle for a long time (tens of seconds), it makes sense to write out all its pages at once rather than waiting for the paging algorithm to collect them.

It is a very bad sign if the kernel forcibly swaps out runnable processes. This is called thrashing or "desperation swapping," and it indicates an extreme memory shortage. In this situation, it's likely that a substantial portion of the system's resources are being devoted to memory housekeeping rather than to useful work.

A similar VM pathology can occur when two large processes compete for the CPU. When the first process gets to run, it brings in a group of its own pages, forcing out some of the second process's pages. Then the second process runs and reinstates its own pages at the expense of the first process. Neither process gets much work done.

Even processes running at a low CPU priority can be sneaky page thieves. For example, suppose you're running a simulation at very low priority (high **nice** value) on your workstation, while at the same time reading mail in a terminal window. As you pause to read a message, your CPU use falls to zero and the simulation is allowed to run. It brings in all of its pages, forcing out your shell, your window server, your mail reader, and your terminal emulator. When you type **n** to go on to the next message, there is a long delay as a large chunk of the system's memory is turned over. In real life, a high **nice** value is no guarantee that a process won't cause performance problems.

Locality of reference is essential for good VM behavior.[2] A text editor that keeps 4MB of data in sequential order is less likely to cause trouble than a 1MB program with a random access pattern. Some other programming practices that can lead to memory problems are neglecting to free memory that is no longer in use ("leaking") and randomly intertwining memory structures that are not logically related.

Analyzing Memory Usage

On a workstation, your best memory analysis tools are your ears. The amount of paging activity is generally proportional to the amount of crunching you hear from the disk. On most disks it's the seeking of the heads that you actually hear, but the correspondence is good enough to give you a general idea of what's going on.

There are basically two numbers that quantify memory activity: the total amount of active virtual memory and the paging rate. The first

---

2. "Locality of reference" means that data or instructions that are frequently accessed together are stored adjacent to each other in a process's address space. Good locality tends to minimize the number of memory pages in active use.

number tells you how much total demand for memory there is, while the second suggests what proportion of that memory is actively used. The goal is to reduce activity or increase memory until paging remains at an acceptable level. Occasional paging is inevitable, so don't worry about trying to eliminate it completely.

The amount of swap space in use can generally be determined with **pstat -s** on BSD systems and **swap -1** under ATT. **sar -r** can also be used on ATT systems (as always, with arguments to specify the monitoring interval), but for some reason it gives results that are not entirely consistent with **swap -1**.

```
% pstat -s
110224k allocated + 13556k reserved = 123780k used,
   163000k available
```

```
% swap -1
swapfile            dev  swapl   blocks    free
/dev/dsk/c0t0d0s1   32,1     16   164400  162960
```

```
% sar -r 5
17:58:52 freemem freeswap
17:58:57     361   179616
```

pstat shows the swap sizes in kilobytes, while **swap -1** and **sar -r** use 512-byte disk blocks. This **pstat** output is from SunOS; pure BSD versions produce slightly more verbose output showing the fragmentation of the swap area. The sizes quoted by these programs do not include the contents of core memory, so the total amount of virtual memory is approximately:

```
VM = size of real memory + amount of swap space used
```

 HP-UX has a dedicated command called **swapinfo** that provides a detailed analysis of the system's swap areas.

 Installation of **sar** is optional on OSF/1 systems; **pstat** and **swap** are not provided. However, there is an extra option (**-s**) to **swapon** that shows the current status of the swap areas. For example:

```
% swapon -s
Total swap allocation:
    Allocated space:        30576 pages (238MB)
    Reserved space:          4274 pages ( 13%)
    Available space:        26302 pages ( 86%)

Swap partition /dev/rz8b:
    Allocated space:        30576 pages (238MB)
    In-use space:            4274 pages ( 13%)
    Free space:             26302 pages ( 86%)
```

On BSD and HP-UX systems, paging statistics are obtained with **vmstat**:

```
% vmstat 5 5
procs      memory                   page
r b w    avm     fre  re at   pi  po   fr  de   sr  ...
0 1 0      0     280   0  0   64  80  208   8   82  ...
1 0 0      0     576   1  2   88  64   96   0  115  ...
0 1 0      0     328   2  0  112  96  224   0  178  ...
1 0 0      0     608   1  0   64  32   72   0    0  ...
0 1 0      0     440   0 12  128  16  152   0   65  ...
```

OSF

CPU information has been removed from this example. OSF/1's **vmstat** command produces output in a substantially different format; some fields have the same names but different contents. There may be other subtle differences among systems. Check your documentation.

Under the `procs` heading are shown the number of processes that are immediately runnable, blocked on I/O, and runnable but swapped. If the value in the `w` column is ever non-zero, it is likely that the system's memory is pitifully inadequate relative to the current load.

In theory, the `avm` column gives the number of active kilobytes of virtual memory, where "active" means that it belongs to a process that has run within the last 20 seconds. However, this example is from SunOS, which never shows a value in the `avm` field. The `fre` column tells the number of kilobytes on the system's free list; values lower than 3% of the system's total memory generally indicate problems.

The next seven columns give information about paging activity. All columns represent average values per second. Their meanings are:

- `re` – number of pages reclaimed (kept off the free list)
- `at` – number of pages attached (recovered from the free list)
- `pi` – kilobytes paged in
- `po` – kilobytes paged out
- `fr` – kilobytes placed on the free list
- `de` – kilobytes of "predicted short-term memory shortfall"
- `sr` – number of pages scanned by the clock algorithm

The `de` column is the best indicator of serious memory problems. If it often jumps above 100, the machine is starved for memory. Unfortunately, most versions of **vmstat** don't show this number.

vmstat -S shows statistics for swapping rather than paging.

The apparent inconsistencies among the memory-related columns are for the most part illusory. Some columns count pages, while others use kilobytes. The clock algorithm is not responsible for all frees, as some pages may be voluntarily released by processes. All values are rounded averages. Furthermore, some are averages of scalar quantities while others are average deltas. For example, you can't compute the next value of `fre` from the current `fre` and paging information, because the paging events that determine the next average value of `fre` have not yet occurred.

Solaris systems use **sar** to get the low-down on paging activity. **sar -g** gives information about page-outs, and **sar -p** provides similar information for page-ins. Page-out data are generally more interesting.

A page-in does not necessarily represent a page being recovered from the swap area. It could be executable code being paged in from a filesystem or a copy-on-write page being duplicated, both of which are normal occurrences that do not necessarily indicate a shortage of memory. On the other hand, page-outs always represent data being forcibly ejected by the kernel.

```
% sar -g 5 5
20:27:52  pgout/s ppgout/s pgfree/s pgscan/s %ufs_ipf
20:27:57    1.80    11.60    13.20    20.40    0.18
20:28:02    4.20    26.20    32.80    47.20    0.49
20:28:07    1.20     7.00     9.80    19.20   36.54
20:28:12    1.80     9.80    12.20    27.80   62.90
20:28:17    1.80    10.18    14.77    34.73   35.64
```

The `pgout` and `ppgout` columns list the number of page-out requests and actual page outs per second (in clusters). `pgfree` is the number of pages put on the free list and `pgscan` is the number of pages scanned.

Other versions of **sar** show paging information differently. HP-UX's **sar** does not provide any paging-related displays; use the **vmstat** command instead. IRIX provides only a summary of memory faults. It can be accessed with **sar -p**.

If your system has a constant stream of page-outs, you need more memory. But if paging happens only occasionally and does not produce annoying hiccups or user complaints, it can be ignored. If your system falls somewhere in the middle, further analysis should depend on whether you are trying to optimize for interactive performance (e.g., a workstation) or to configure a machine with many simultaneous users (e.g., a compute server).

On an interactive machine, you may want to consider the cost of paging in terms of latency. Most systems that swap to a single SCSI disk can handle about 40 disk transfers per second. The exact figure will depend on the kind of disk you are swapping on; also, see the next section for more information about optimizing your swap partitions.

If half the operations are page-outs, you can figure that every 20 page-outs cause about one second of latency. If 30 page-outs must occur to let you scroll a window, you will wait for about 1.5 seconds. User interface researchers claim that an average user perceives the system to be "slow" when response times are longer than seven tenths of a second.

Analyzing Disk I/O

Most systems allow disk throughput to be monitored with the **iostat** command. Like **vmstat**, it takes optional arguments to specify an interval in seconds and a repetition count, and its first line of output is a summary since boot. Like **vmstat**, it also tells you about how the CPU's time is being spent.

```
% iostat 5 5
       tty              wd0           sd0        cpu
 tin tout sps tps msps  sps tps msps  us ni sy id
   2    9   2   0  0.5    3   0 20.3   0  0  0 99
   1  252   0   0  0.0  614  40 16.9  27  0 14 59
   1  321   0   0  0.0  511  45 16.7  17  0 12 71
   0   15   0   0  0.0  419  27 19.9  11  0  8 80
   1  191   0   0  0.0    3   0 25.0   0  0  0 99
```

Columns are divided into topics (in this case, four: tty, wd0, sd0, and cpu), with the data for each topic presented in the fields beneath it. **iostat** output tends to be slightly different on every system.

The tty topic presents data concerning terminals and pseudo-terminals. This information is basically uninteresting, although it might be useful for characterizing the throughput of a modem. tin and tout give the average total number of characters input and output per second by all of the system's terminals.

Each hard disk has columns sps, tps, and msps, indicating sectors transferred per second, total transfers per second, and milliseconds per seek. One transfer request can include several sectors, so the ratio between sps and tps tells you whether there are a few large transfers or lots of small ones. Large transfers are more efficient. Calculation of seek times seems to work only on specific drives and sometimes gives bizarre values (the values in this example are reasonable).

Some systems support **iostat -D**, which gives the percentage utilization of each disk:

```
% iostat -D 5 5
          sd1            sd2            sd3            sd5
 rps wps util   rps wps util   rps wps util   rps wps util
   0   0  1.3     0   0  0.3     0   0  0.5     1   1  4.2
   9   8 41.1     1   0  1.8     1   0  2.4     6   8 34.8
  11   4 48.4     0   1  2.0     0   0  0.0     3  11 32.6
   8   0 15.6     0   0  0.0     0   0  0.0     3   0  9.2
   0   0  0.0     0   0  0.0     0   0  0.0     0   0  0.0
```

Here, volumes are quoted in reads and writes per second.

The cost of seeking is the most important factor affecting disk drive performance. To a first approximation, the rotational speed of the disk and the speed of the bus it's connected to have relatively little impact. Modern disks can transfer several megabytes of data per second if they are read from contiguous sectors, but can only perform about 50 to 100 seeks per second. If you transfer one sector per seek, you can easily realize less than 2% of the drive's peak throughput.

Consequently, the most important statistic to watch for in `iostat`'s output is the number of transfers per second (the `tps` column for plain `iostat` or the sum of `rps` and `wps` for `iostat -D`). You can assume approximately one seek per transfer. Disk access is always slow, but if the number of transfers starts to reach 40 or 50 per second, it can be even slower than necessary due to overloading. (However, keep in mind that programs will sometimes try to read a lot of data in sequence, usually maxing out the drive. The important numbers are the average demand versus the average capacity of the drive.)

Seeks are more expensive when they make the heads travel a long distance. If you have a disk with several filesystem partitions, and files are read from each partition in a random order, the heads will have to travel back and forth a long way to switch between partitions. On the other hand, files within a partition will be relatively local to one another. When partitioning a new disk, you may want to consider the performance implications and put files that are accessed together in the same filesystem.

To really achieve maximum disk performance, you should put filesystems that are used together on different disks. Although it depends on the bus architecture and device drivers, most computers can manage multiple disks independently, dramatically increasing throughput. For example, system binaries (`/usr`), home directories, and `/tmp` can profitably be put on different disks.

If you have a lot of disks, you may be able to boost performance even further by installing more than one disk controller or SCSI bus. The effectiveness of this technique will depend on the architecture of your system. Check your hardware documentation or consult your vendor.

If your site receives Usenet news, be sure to divide up the news database among several disks, if possible. News is an extreme disk pig, and you'll definitely notice the difference. See page 576 for more information about the storage of news.

It's especially important to split the swap area among several disks if possible, since paging tends to slow down the entire system. All systems support this configuration using either the **swapon** command, the **swap** command, or a kernel configuration option (see page 229). Many systems support both dedicated swap partitions and swap files on a formatted filesystem. Dedicated partitions are more efficient; do not use swap files if you have a choice.

Some systems allow you to set up **/tmp** as a "memory-based filesystem," which is essentially the same thing as a PC RAM disk. A special driver poses as a disk, but actually stores data in memory. This may reduce the average amount of memory available for general use, but it makes the reading and writing of temporary files blindingly fast. It's generally a good deal. For more information, see the man page for **tmpfs** on Solaris or SunOS, or the man page for **mfs** on OSF/1 and BSDI.

See Chapter 26 for more information about quotas.

Some software degrades the system's performance by delaying basic operations. Two examples are BSD disk quotas and CPU accounting. Quotas require a disk usage summary to be updated as files are written and deleted, while CPU accounting writes a data record to an accounting file whenever a process completes. Disk caching helps to soften the impact of these features, but they may still have a noticeable effect on performance and should not be enabled unless you really use them.

See Chapter 28 for more information about accounting.

Tuning Filesystems

See page 623 for a longer discussion of tunefs.

The **tunefs** command can be used to alter the filesystem's layout policies on each partition. The parameters set by **tunefs** affect localized layout such as the interleave factor and the maximum number of contiguous blocks; they affect seek patterns only indirectly.

On some systems, under some conditions, judicious use of **tunefs** can marginally increase your disk performance. However, you must do experiments for each filesystem. You cannot generalize "correct" numbers for your system or even for each disk. Furthermore, the filesystem's model of a hard disk doesn't really match modern hard disks very well, so the parameters you set with **tunefs** have only a partial correspondence with reality.

tunefs parameters only affect the layout of files as they are written. To "optimize" a partition, you must make a level zero dump, re-initialize the partition, set the parameters, and then reinstall all the files.

pstat: Print Random Statistics (BSD)

Another useful tool available on BSD systems is the **pstat** command. It dumps the contents of various kernel tables in an almost human-readable form. There is no unifying theme to the information **pstat** can display; it is just a gopher for tidbits maintained by the kernel.

The following displays are available under BSDI; some systems may have more or fewer:

- A dump of the inode table (`-i`)
- A dump of the text table (`-x`)
- A dump of the process table, gorier than `ps` (`-P`)
- A dump of the open file table (`-f`)
- Status information for all terminals (`-t`)
- Information about a particular process (`-u`)
- Information about swap space usage (`-s`)
- Information about how full the kernel's tables are (`-T`)

One of the most useful of these displays is the table usage summary produced by the `-T` option. The information you get looks like this:

```
% pstat -T
121/364   files
85/158    inodes
34/74     processes
21/38     texts
70/169    00k swap
```

The numbers separated by slashes represent current use versus the total size of each table. For example, this system is currently running 34 processes, but an additional 40 processes could be started. Note that the limit on texts is distinct from the limit on processes; you could have 74 processes but only 38 separate texts active at once. Unlike the other values, the `inode` entry refers to a cache. A cache can be pruned or cleared at any time, so it can't cause problems by filling up.

`pstat -T` is useful for determining the optimal value of `maxusers` when configuring the kernel. Unfortunately, `pstat -T` only shows you a small fraction of the things that are affected by `maxusers`, so you must still allow a generous margin of safety in your configuration. See Chapter 13, *Configuring the Kernel*, for more information.

29.5 Help! My System Just Got Really Slow!

In previous sections, we've talked mostly about issues that relate to the average performance of a system. Solutions to these long-term concerns generally take the form of configuration adjustments or upgrades.

However, you will find that even properly configured systems are sometimes more sluggish than usual. Luckily, transient problems are often easy to diagnose. 90% of the time, they are caused by a greedy process that is simply consuming so much CPU power or disk bandwidth that other processes have been stalled.

You can often tell which resource is being hogged without even running a diagnostic command. If the system feels "sticky" or you hear the disk going crazy, the problem is most likely a disk bandwidth or memory shortfall.[3] If the system feels "sluggish" (everything takes a long time, and applications can't be "warmed up"), the problem may be CPU.

The first step in diagnosis is to run **ps** or **top** to see if there are any obvious runaway processes. Any process that's using more than 50% of the CPU is very likely to be at fault. If no single process is getting an inordinate share of the CPU, check to see how many processes are getting at least 10%. If there are more than two or three (don't count **ps** itself), the load average is likely to be quite high. This is, in itself, a cause of poor performance. Check the load average with **uptime**, and check to see if the CPU is ever idle using **vmstat** or **sar -u**.

If there appears to be no contention for CPU, look to see how much paging is going on with **vmstat** or **sar -g**. All disk activity is interesting: a lot of page-outs may indicate contention for memory, while disk traffic in the absence of paging may mean that a process is monopolizing the disk by constantly reading or writing files.

There's no direct way to tie disk operations to processes, but **ps** can narrow down the possible suspects for you. Any process that is generating disk traffic must be using some amount of CPU time. You can usually make an educated guess about which of the active processes is the true culprit.[4] Use **kill -STOP** to test your theory.

Suppose you do find that a particular process is at fault—what should you do? Usually, nothing. Some operations just require a lot of resources and are bound to slow down the system. It doesn't necessarily mean that they're illegitimate. It is usually acceptable to **renice** an obtrusive processes that is CPU-bound. But be sure to ask the owner to use the **nice** command in the future.

Processes that are disk or memory hogs can't be dealt with so easily. **renice** generally will not help. You do have the option of killing or stopping a process, but we recommend against this if the situation does not constitute an emergency. As with CPU pigs, you can use the low-tech solution of asking the owner to run the process later.

BSD systems allow a process's consumption of physical memory to be restricted with the **setrlimit** system call. This facility is available in the C shell via the built-in **limit** command.

---

3. That is, if it takes a long time to switch between X Windows applications or to start scrolling a window, but performance is acceptable when repeating a simple task.

4. A large virtual address space or resident set used to be a suspicious sign, but shared libraries have made these numbers less useful. Most versions of **ps** are not very smart about separating systemwide shared library overhead from the address spaces of individual processes. Many processes wrongly seem to have megabytes of active memory.

For example,

```
% limit memoryuse 2m
```

causes all subsequent commands that the user runs to have their use of physical memory limited to two megabytes. This is roughly equivalent to **renice** for memory-bound processes. You might tactfully suggest that repeat offenders put such a line in their .cshrc files.

If a runaway process doesn't seem to be the source of poor performance, there are two other possible causes to investigate. The first is an overloaded network. Many programs are so intimately bound up with the network that it's hard to tell where system performance ends and network performance begins. See Chapter 22 for more information about the tools used to monitor networks.

Some network overloading problems are hard to diagnose because they come and go very quickly. For example, if every machine on the network runs a network-related program out of cron at a particular time each day, there will often be a brief but dramatic glitch. Every machine on the net will hang for five seconds, and then the problem will disappear as quickly as it came.

Server-related delays are another possible cause of performance crises. UNIX systems are constantly consulting remote servers for NFS, NIS, DNS, and any of a dozen other facilities. If a server is dead or some other problem makes it expensive to communicate with, the effects can ripple back through client systems.

For example, on a busy system, some process may use the **getpwuid** library routine every few seconds or so. If an NIS glitch makes this routine take two seconds to complete, you will likely perceive a difference in overall performance.

29.6 RECOMMENDED SUPPLEMENTAL READING

LOUKIDES, MIKE. *System Performance Tuning.* Sebastopol: O'Reilly & Associates, 1990.

30 *UUCP*

30.1 INTRODUCTION

UUCP (UNIX-to-UNIX copy) is a set of programs and protocols that allow computers to communicate over serial connections, networks, or ordinary telephone lines. It supports two operations: file copying and remote command execution.

The history of UUCP, like that of Internet networking, dates back to the steamy dawn of UNIX computing. Over time, UUCP has been adapted for several generations of now-obsolete communications hardware. By now, UUCP contains more historical grotesquerie than useful code. However, it's still the most widely-used way for two UNIX systems to communicate using modems.

See Chapter 19 for more information about SLIP and PPP. The functions of UUCP are a subset of those offered by Internet networking, and interest in UUCP has dwindled as it has become easier and cheaper to set up Internet connections. Even for computers whose connection to the outside world is through a modem, dial-up Internetworking systems such as SLIP and PPP may offer a better way of connecting two computers. UUCP is in an odd state where it is too obsolete to bother improving, and yet not quite obsolete enough to actually go away. We expect that there will be continued use of UUCP throughout the 90s.

There are, broadly speaking, two sorts of UUCP. The more common these days is HoneyDanBer UUCP, which is named after its authors: Peter Honeyman, David A. Nowitz, and Brian E. Redman. HoneyDanBer

UUCP is usually associated with ATT-ish versions of UNIX, although a number of BSD systems have also appropriated parts of it. The other kind of UUCP is closely related to the original V7 UUCP; it's associated with BSD and older ATT systems. The differences between the two are mostly superficial.

The two UUCP's have, over time, become inbred. Several vendors have formulated hybrid systems that include the features of both. It has also been common for vendors to switch flavors of UUCP between releases. For these reasons, it is hard to make general statements about what kind of UUCP you should expect to find on what systems.

In the first edition of this book, we discussed UUCP in relatively thorough detail. But due to the waning importance of UUCP, the proliferation of nonstandard systems, and the publication of several excellent UUCP books, we now cover only the features of UUCP that seem useful and relevant to modern computing. If you want to learn more about the UUCP arcana, the book *Managing UUCP and Usenet* by Tim O'Reilly and Grace Todino is a good reference. A full citation is given on page 704.

30.2 UUCP vs. SLIP and PPP

See Chapter 19 for more information about SLIP and PPP. UUCP is a batch system. If your modem connection is down more often than it is up, UUCP may be preferable to SLIP or PPP for some applications. UUCP is primarily used to transport electronic mail and Usenet news; if that's all you want your communication link to do, UUCP is both simpler and more secure than the IP-based alternatives.

UUCP was designed with slow serial lines in mind and is considerably more efficient at pumping information across a pair of modems than IP. If you make long-distance modem calls or share one phone line between voice and data, UUCP might suit your needs well.

If you're paying to connect to a service provider, UUCP may also be dramatically cheaper than SLIP, depending on your level of use. The price of SLIP connections is falling, but it still has a long way to go before it's within the reach of everyone.

SLIP and PPP offer dramatically more functionality than UUCP. It is theoretically possible for UUCP to be of some use other than mail and news, but in reality this just doesn't happen. For a taste of the goodies that come with Internet access, see Chapter 20.

You don't necessarily need to choose between SLIP and UUCP. With a little extra configuration work, you can run them both on the same modem. On the other hand, if you're going to go to the trouble and expense of setting up a SLIP or PPP connection, you might as well use it for everything and forget about UUCP.

30.3 AN OVERVIEW OF UUCP

In order to contact another site using UUCP, you must make prior arrangements with that site's administrator. You must tell your system how to contact the other site, and the other site must be configured to permit this contact. Once configuration is complete, the two computers can call one another without human supervision. This setup is usually called a UUCP "connection," even though the two computers are actually connected only on occasion. The sites you communicate with are called UUCP "neighbors."

UUCP operations are initiated with the **uux** and **uucp** commands. **uux** executes command on a remote system and **uucp** copies files. **uux** and **uucp** both create a file that describes the operation to be performed, which is then saved away in UUCP's work queue (`/var/spool/uucp` on most systems). Actual transmission of the jobs is handled by a separate process, **uucico**.[1] You, the site administrator, specify how often **uucico** is to be run.

UUCP does not directly support forwarding of files or command sequences; you may only communicate with machines to which you have established direct connections. However, transactions may involve more than one directly-connected host. For example, you may copy a file directly from one neighbor to another.

Since both mail and news require third-party forwarding, these systems provide their own forwarding facilities. Each time a mail message or news article makes a hop from one machine to another, it re-enters the mail or news system for further routing.

Both mail and news make use of remote command execution rather than file copying. Mail messages and news articles are sent as standard input to special mail- and news-receiving programs that try to determine their ultimate destinations. These programs accept the materials for local use or feed them back to UUCP for retransmission to another site (often, they do both).

30.4 UUCP ADDRESSES

Addressing systems are generally either route-based or destination-based. "Go straight through two lights, then hang a right at the House of Foam," is a route-based address; it tells you how to get somewhere by giving you a complete list of instructions. "900 Memory Lane" is a destination-based address. It only tells you *where* to go; you have to use a map or directory to figure out *how* to get there. UUCP is one of the last outposts of route-based addressing.

---

1. UNIX-to-UNIX copy in, copy out. Any similarity to "garbage in, garbage out" is incidental.

Commands in the UUCP system use the syntax *sitename!target* to identify remote files and commands. Mail and news have adopted a similar syntax for the specification of indirect UUCP paths. The basic and extended syntaxes are similar enough that we consider them together under the generic heading of "UUCP addresses."

A UUCP address consists of a list of names separated by exclamation points (or as UNIX hipsters call them, "bangs"). The last name (the target) is a user name, filename, or command name, depending upon whether the address is a mail address, file copy address, or remote command execution request. All other names leading up to the target are UUCP site names. The list of sites specifies a sequence of UUCP hops that can be followed to get to the appropriate machine. If the address is to be used with a native UUCP command, there can usually only be one site specified.

For example, the mail address

```
foo!bar!roger
```

would route mail to somebody named Roger on the host "bar" via the host "foo."

In the past, the UUCP world was a vast sprawl of randomly-connected sites. The use of long paths for mail and news was common, and all kinds of special mapping systems and path-computing algorithms were used to figure out efficient routes from one place to another.

Of late, Internet connectivity has become so common that this thicket of UUCP paths is largely gone. Most UUCP connections are now supplied by commercial vendors that are connected directly to the Internet. These vendors usually provide one-hop news service, and they help with email routing by translating between the Internet and UUCP domains. In effect, the UUCP connection is a sort of private link between the vendor and the client site. From the perspective of the outside world, the client site appears to be on the Internet. Consequently, indirect UUCP paths are seldom seen anymore.

30.5 User-level UUCP

Two programs can enqueue UUCP requests:

- uucp – copy files between hosts
- uux – execute commands on a remote host

The following sections describe these commands in detail. Although we speak of the commands as though they were meant for human users, it is more common for them to be invoked by other programs and scripts.

uucp: Copy Files

uucp is similar to cp, except that the locations of files are specified using UUCP syntax. Each path begins with a system name, followed by an exclamation point and a (possibly remote) filename. If the system name is null, the path is assumed to refer to a file on the local system and the exclamation point is optional. The filename must be specified in one of the following formats:

- A full pathname   (e.g., **/usr/dict/words**)
- A pathname beginning with ~*user/*   (e.g., **~evi/proposal**)
- A pathname beginning with ~/   (e.g., **~/explain**)
- A relative pathname   (e.g., **bin/bustbladder**)

The use of tildes ("~", and actually, you must call them "twiddles" if you want to be cool) to specify pathnames should be familiar from the shell. "~" denotes the user's home directory, and ~*user* is the home directory of *user*. Tildes are interpreted on the specified system, so these expressions may mean something different from what you expect. For reasons that will become clear later, the "current user" used to evaluate expressions such as ~/*file* isn't necessarily you; this syntax often proves too treacherous for real-life use.

The full pathname syntax means about what you would expect: the name is simply looked up on the appropriate system. The relative pathname syntax is trickier because **uucp** always inserts the absolute pathname of the local directory from which it is run in front of the relative pathname. For example, if you **cd** to **/staff/garth** and execute

```
uucp akelei!files/exabyte exabyte
```

uucp will try to copy the file **/staff/garth/files/exabyte** from the system akelei into **/staff/garth/exabyte** on the local machine, probably not what you want.[2]

The **uucp** command accepts a number of flags that modify its behavior in insignificant ways. You can have it send you mail when the copy is complete, force it to make a copy of local files rather than use the actual files themselves (in case you want to delete the files immediately), allow it to create directories as needed for storage of the transferred files, etc. It does *not* accept the **-r** flag to copy a directory hierarchy recursively.

One thing that you must keep in mind when using any UUCP command is that the operations you request will ultimately be performed by a

---

2. Various shells interpret "!" and "~" as metacharacters, so they must be backslashed on the command line if they are to reach **uucp** unmodified. We have omitted this detail for clarity in this chapter's examples. If you get an error message like "event not found," you have probably omitted a backslash.

uucico process with UID and GID different from your own. Files you want to manipulate must be world-readable or world-writable.

For example, if you want to copy a file from a remote system into your home directory, you must give write permission on your home directory to everyone—this is *not* recommended. To copy files from the local system to a remote system, you must give read permission on them to the world. Files that UUCP creates are usually owned by the pseudo-user uucp, not by you, no matter where they are located. If you have uucp copy a file into your home directory, you will probably be able to read it but not modify it. You will have to copy the file to a different filename and then delete the original (which you can do because you have write permission on your home directory, even if not the file).

Because of all these permission and ownership headaches, there is a special world-writable directory, usually /var/spool/uucppublic, available for use with UUCP. It is analogous to the system-wide /tmp directory in that anybody can put files there, but it is intended for use primarily when performing UUCP operations. You can have uucp put transferred files here for you to pick up later.

Since /var/spool/uucppublic is used for temporary storage of files that are on their way into or out of the system, it has a tendency to accumulate unwanted junk files. As with /tmp, you should run a cleanup script out of cron to delete these files. See *Cleaning the Filesystem* on page 176 for more information about how to do this.

uux: Execute Commands on Other Systems

uux is used to initiate remote command execution. uux accepts shell-style command strings in which each file or command name is a network path, specified in the same syntax used by uucp. uux understands the shell metacharacters ">", "<", "|", and ";". Since the command string must appear to uux as a single argument, it should be quoted on the command line.

For example, the command

```
uux '!diff hal!/usr/jack/rabbit moon!/res/hare > !diffs'
```

invokes the local command diff on the files /usr/jack/rabbit from the machine hal and /res/hare from the machine moon, sending the output of the command to the file diffs on the local machine.

30.6 UUCP Data Transport

Inter-machine communication is managed by the uucico program. There are a variety of programs in the UUCP system for queuing requests and querying the state of connections, but only uucico can make actual transactions. When two systems have a UUCP "conversation," a copy of `uucico` runs on each machine.

`uucico` can operate in two modes: master and slave. At any given time, one of the two `uucico` processes plays each role. The two `uucico`'s switch roles occasionally so that large outgoing or incoming jobs do not block data flowing in the other direction.

In master mode, `uucico` attempts to deal with requests that have been queued on the local system. Satisfying these requests may involve sending a file to the slave site, requesting a file from the slave site, or requesting execution of a program at the slave site. The designation of master and slave is independent of the current sender or receiver of information; if the master has requested a file from the slave, it will be both the master and the receiver. In slave mode, `uucico` listens to the orders issued by the remote site and attempts to carry them out.

To initiate a conversation, a `uucico` process on one machine must contact another machine and start up a remote `uucico` process to communicate with. This is usually done by making a special login account on the remote machine that uses `uucico` as its login shell. This way, the calling `uucico` need only log in to the remote machine in order to establish a `uucico`-to-`uucico` connection.

As soon as the two `uucico` processes have been connected, they negotiate a communication protocol to use during the subsequent conversation. The standard protocol used over telephone lines is called the "g" protocol, and every version of UUCP understands it. Other protocols exist, but they are mostly intended for use on reliable circuits. The "g" protocol is fully error-correcting, so transferred data are guaranteed to arrive at their destination intact.[3]

30.7 SETTING UP UUCP

Setting up UUCP is not difficult, but some of the steps can be time-consuming. Two sorts of tasks are involved: tasks that are performed once when the system is first set up, and tasks that you must repeat each time you acquire a new UUCP neighbor.

We will go through the steps in the order you need to complete them when setting up your first UUCP connection. You may be able to parallelize some steps; read through the entire procedure before starting.

- Identify your UUCP software.
- Verify software configuration.
- Connect modems.
- Describe your modems to UUCP.

3. Ha!

- Enter telephone prefix codes.
- Prepare an access control specification.
- Find a UUCP neighbor.
- Make a login for the new neighbor.
- Make an **L.sys** or **Systems** file entry for the neighbor.
- Debug the connection.
- Configure your mail system to use UUCP.
- Set up automatic calling using **cron**.

Identifying your UUCP Software

There are three important directories in the UUCP system:

- **/usr/lib/uucp** – for storage of executables and config files
- **/var/spool/uucp** – for storage of jobs and temporary files
- **/var/spool/uucppublic** – for use by users

Most of UUCP's user-level commands are kept in **/usr/bin**.

You may find that your system has bonus UUCP directories. On some systems, **/usr/lib/uucp** has been moved to **/etc/uucp**. You might also find that the UUCP spool directory is **/usr/spool/uucp** rather than **/var/spool/uucp**.

In this chapter, we'll refer to UUCP directories by the most commonly-used pathnames. If your system is set up differently, you'll need to remember to map each path that we mention to its local equivalent.

Take a look at the contents of your **/usr/lib/uucp** directory. Do you see files named **Devices**, **Dialcodes**, **Dialers**, **Permissions**, or **Systems**? If so, your UUCP is HoneyDanBer-ish. If you see files named **L-devices**, **L-dialcodes**, **L.cmds**, **L.sys**, or **USERFILE**, your UUCP is BSD-ish. If you see none of these files, or a combination of both sets, your system is nonstandard (or, in technical terminology, "weird").

On some systems, UUCP software is considered optional and must be specifically loaded from the distribution CD-ROM (or tapes) when you install the system. Your manuals will explain, perhaps.

If the **/usr/lib/uucp** directory exists but contains only the commands **uucico**, **uuclean**, and **uuxqt**, then your system is probably set up without any example configuration files to look at.

A brief summary of the files usually found in **/usr/lib/uucp** is shown in Table 30.1 on the next page. There isn't exactly a one-to-one mapping from BSD to HoneyDanBer, but the two systems are fairly close. Honey-DanBer also provides several commands that have no BSD equivalents (not all UUCP commands are shown in the table).

Table 30.1 Files in the /usr/lib/uucp directory

BSD	HDB	Purpose
L-devices	Devices	Specifies types of available modems
	Dialers	Modem dialing instructions
L-dialcodes	Dialcodes	Phone number database
L.aliases		Lists hosts that change their names
L.cmds	Permissions	Lists commands available via uuxqt
USERFILE	Permissions	Filesystem access specifications
L.sys	Systems	List of UUCP neighbors, login scripts
uucico	uucico	Manages inter-machine communication
uuclean	uuclean	Cleans up spool directory
uuxqt	uuxqt	Remote command execution server

Verifying your Software Configuration

Everything in **/usr/lib/uucp** should be owned by the user uucp, and the programs stored there should be setuid to this account. In addition, **/var/spool/uucp** and **/var/spool/uucppublic** should be owned by uucp and should have group owner daemon. Check these ownerships carefully, as several vendors ship with bogus permissions.

In **/usr/lib/uucp**, no file should be writable by anyone but its owner (the uucp account), and the files **L-devices**, **L-dialcodes**, **L.cmds**, **L.sys**, **Devices**, **Dialcodes**, and **Systems** (whichever are present) should be readable only by the owner.

The **/var/spool/uucp** directory should have the permissions:

```
drwxr-xr-x 13 uucp daemon    512 Jul 15 02:32 uucp
```

Inside **/var/spool/uucp**, all subdirectories should have mode 775. The BSD log files should have the permissions

```
-rw-r--r-- 1 uucp daemon     71 Jul 15 23:20 ERRLOG
-rw-rw-r-- 1 uucp daemon 662326 Jul 16 19:25 LOGFILE
-rw-rw-r-- 1 uucp daemon 301847 Jul 16 19:25 SYSLOG
```

and the HoneyDanBer permissions should be

```
drwxr-xr-x 2 uucp daemon    512 Feb  8 1990 .Admin/
drwxr-xr-x 2 uucp daemon    512 Feb  8 1990 .Corrupt/
drwxr-xr-x 6 uucp daemon    512 Feb  8 1990 .Log/
drwxr-xr-x 2 uucp daemon    512 Feb  8 1990 .Old/
drwxr-xr-x 2 uucp daemon    512 Feb  8 1990 .Sequence/
drwxr-xr-x 2 uucp daemon    512 Feb  8 1990 .Status/
drwxr-xr-x 2 uucp daemon    512 Feb  8 1990 .Workspace/
drwxr-xr-x 2 uucp daemon    512 Feb  8 1990 .Xqtdir/
```

/var/spool/uucppublic should exist, should be owned by user uucp and group daemon, and should have mode 777.

*See Chapter 6 for
more information
about creating user
accounts.* If your system does not have the correct permissions or ownerships, you
may need to add the uucp login before you can continue. Use an asterisk
as uucp's password, since no one will be logging in to the account.[4]
uucp's home directory should be **/var/spool/uucppublic**, and its
shell should be **/usr/lib/uucp/uucico**. The UID should be within
the range you reserve for pseudo-users (usually less than 100).

Connecting Modems

UUCP uses modems in the same way that other modem-using programs
do, so everything should be set up as described in Chapter 8, *Serial
Devices*. Device files should be owned by user uucp and group daemon,
and should have mode 664; these ownerships and permissions are also
those correct for use with **tip** and **cu**. Either one of these programs can
be used to verify that the modem is connected correctly and that you
can dial out to other sites.

If you plan to use the same modem as both a dial-in and a dial-out line
for UUCP, there are some additional tasks that you must perform. Refer
to Chapter 8.

Describing your Modems to UUCP

UUCP only pays attention to its own configuration files. Even though you
may have had to edit **/etc/ttys**, **/etc/remote**, **/etc/inittab**, or
other system-wide configuration files to set up your modems, you still
need to give UUCP its own copy of the information.

There are a variety of standards in the modem world. Different modems
can't necessarily be controlled the same way, nor can they always communicate with each other. These incompatibilities give rise to two separate problems. The first problem is that you can't necessarily use the
same modem to communicate with all of your UUCP neighbors. UUCP
solves this problem by allowing you to specify explicitly what kind of
modem should be used for each neighbor.

The second problem is that UUCP itself must be able to control your
modems in order to place calls, set communication speeds, and detect
problems. Different versions of UUCP solve this problem in different
ways. HoneyDanBer provides the **Dialers** file, where instructions for
controlling modems are encoded in a standard format. Some UUCPs
have a file called **/etc/acucap** or **/usr/lib/uucp/modemcap** that
serves the same purpose; it's patterned after **/etc/termcap**. In BSD
UUCPs, there is a standard set of modem types that are supported; if
support for your modem isn't compiled into the code, you're out of luck.

4. Some sites use "uucp" as the generic login for all clients. This works, but we recommend
giving each system its own login. This helps to control access to your system and lets you
disable one site's login without disabling everyone else's. See page 692.

But fear not. Almost any modem you are liable to encounter will conform to the Hayes command syntax, and it is highly unlikely that you will need to perform any special configuration. If you're not sure exactly what kind of modem you are dealing with, try your system's "Hayes-compatible" setting first. This will work in 95% of cases.

Modem information is stored in **/usr/lib/uucp/L-devices** on BSD systems and in **/usr/lib/uucp/Devices** on HoneyDanBer systems. The formats are slightly different, but both files record more or less the same information: the type of modem being used, the device file through which it can be accessed, and the modem's speed.

In most versions of UUCP, the UUCP configuration files (**L-devices** and **Devices** included) share a common syntax for comments and continuation lines. Lines beginning with a pound sign ("#") are ignored, and lines ending with a backslash are joined with the following line before interpretation. Check to be sure your system supports continuation lines before using this feature. Also, be sure to start each configuration line in the first column, since some versions of UUCP are confused by initial spaces.

Each line in **L-devices** (or **Devices**) represents one piece of equipment that can be used to connect to other computers. The format for modem entries is much the same in both files; we will describe the BSD **L-devices** format and note differences for HoneyDanBer.

Each line in **L-devices** looks like:

    type device dialer speed brand chat

In your system's documentation, these fields are probably referred to by different names: *caller*, *device*, *call unit*, *class*, *dialer*, and *chat*. Some of the fields in **L-devices** are used in different ways depending on what type of device is being described, and so the field names in standard documentation are more vague. We'll only be discussing modems here, so we've chosen explicit names for clarity.

Fields are separated by whitespace and have the following meanings:

type   The *type* field indicates what sort of device the line describes. For modems, this field should contain the letters ACU, which stand for "Automatic Calling Unit." Some other codes you might see here (in BSD) are DIR for a dedicated serial line and TCP for an Internet link. TCP links are provided mainly to ease the transition from UUCP to Internet; you simply change ACU to TCP when you become an Internet site, and data addressed to UUCP neighbors will be delivered over the Internet.[5]

5. As long as your neighbors are running uucpd.

device   The *device* field specifies the name of the device file through which the connection is to be made. For a modem this is something like **/dev/cua0** (often a link to **/dev/ttya** or whichever serial port your modem is connected to).

dialer   This field is obsolete. Put a dash or the word unused here as a place holder.[6]

speed   The *speed* field tells how fast a modem can communicate, in bits per second. In BSD, modems that support several speeds (and most do) must have multiple entries in **L-devices**, each with a different speed.

          If your UUCP is HoneyDanBer-ish, you can directly specify a range of speeds in the *speed* field; for example, 300-9600. You can also use the word Any to specify that a modem is fast enough to use for any site.

brand   This field identifies the particular brand and model of modem. For modern modems, this field usually contains hayes. (hayestone and hayespulse can also be used in BSD to specify touch-tone or pulse dialing).

          Some old releases of SunOS use a modification of the *type* field instead of a separate *brand* field. On these systems, you'd use a type of ACUHAYES instead of type ACU and brand hayes.

          On HoneyDanBer systems and others with user-configurable brand definitions, the value of the *brand* field identifies an entry in **Dialers**, **acucap**, or **modemcap**.

chat   The *chat* is a miniature script used to gain access to the communications device. Usually you don't have to put anything in this field, but it can be useful if the modem lies on the other side of a data switch. It can also be used to send a command string to the modem to put it in Hayes-compatible mode, if that is not the default.

          The format of the chat script is identical to that of the login script used in the **L.sys** or **Systems** file, but since scripting is rarely used in **L-devices**, we will delay a discussion scripts until page 696. Some versions of BSD-style UUCP do not allow a chat script. In Honey-DanBer, you must use the **Dialers** file to specify the script for a device.

6. In the past, the device that dialed the telephone was often different from the device that communicated over the connection once it was established. To use UUCP in these situations, two device files had to be specified. But these days, modems have dialers built in.

As you can see, the only really interesting tidbits in the **L-devices** file are the device file and speed of the modem. But sometimes, a modem has other important properties that UUCP must be made aware of. For example, you might own only one or two modems that speak a certain high-speed protocol. To connect to a neighbor with this high-speed protocol, you need a way to identify modems so that UUCP knows they are appropriate for use with that neighbor.

This kind of information can be sneaked into **L-devices** or **Devices** by adding a non-numeric prefix to the front of the *speed* field. For example, if a modem understands the MNP-5 error correction protocol at 19,200 bits per second, you might put MNP19200 in the speed field. In other UUCP configuration files, you can specify that an MNP19200 modem is needed to talk to a particular site. UUCP just matches up the letters, so you may pick your own prefix conventions.

Suppose your site has a Hayes modem (**/dev/cua0**) that runs at 1,200 and 2,400 baud and a Telebit modem (**/dev/cua1**) that understands advanced protocols such as V.32bis, V.42bis, and MNP-5 at speeds up to 19,200 bps. **L-devices** might look like this:

```
ACU     /dev/cua0     unused     1200      hayestone
ACU     /dev/cua0     unused     2400      hayestone
ACU     /dev/cua1     unused     T19200    hayestone
```

Entering Telephone Prefix Codes

All versions of UUCP have a macro facility that allows you to define text names for phone numbers and prefixes of phone numbers. BSD-ish systems store this information in **/usr/lib/uucp/L-dialcodes**, and HoneyDanBer puts it in **/usr/lib/uucp/Dialcodes**. The format is the same: each line lists a name and a phone prefix, separated by whitespace. For example,

```
# Phone number for Ubob (Bob Watson's consulting company)
#
ubob_phone 555-2368
```

defines ubob_phone to mean the phone number 555-2368. In the **L.sys** or **Systems** file, where UUCP neighbors are defined, you could list the phone number for this site as ubob_phone instead of 555-2368.

This facility allows you to put the phone number for a site in a publicly-readable location. **L.sys** and **Systems** contain account names and passwords for remote sites, so they must be readable only by the UUCP agents and root. Phone numbers can sometimes help users to debug a connection when no system administrator is available, so it is often nice to put them in a separate file.

Conversely, you may want to use the dialcodes file to hide long-distance billing codes. For example, if `genacct` is defined to access a long distance service and bill the call to the general expenses account, then something like `genacct1-303-555-2368` can be used from **L.sys** or **Systems** to specify both the phone number and the billing.[7]

Preparing an Access Control Specification

See Chapter 23, Security, for a more general discussion of security issues.

It is not a good idea to give your neighbors free run of your system via UUCP. All versions of UUCP allow you to specify which files your neighbors may access via the **uucp** command and which commands they may execute via **uux**. You should plan and implement a UUCP security strategy before you establish any UUCP connections.

BSD and HoneyDanBer handle UUCP security in completely different ways. BSD uses two files in `/usr/lib/uucp`, `USERFILE` and `L.cmds` (sometimes `L-cmds`), to control access to files and commands, respectively. HoneyDanBer uses the file `/usr/lib/uucp/Permissions` to specify both kinds of security.

We will treat the two systems separately in the discussion below. But before we launch into the specifics, let's discuss some general principles of UUCP security.

The main thing to keep in mind is that even though a remote site might have no more access to your site than a local user, this is usually enough to compromise the security of your installation. Even if system files can't be directly written to, they can be copied away for remote analysis and scrutinized for weaknesses. And on most systems, some user files are sure to be available for casual browsing.

It is safe to permit unrestricted access to `/var/spool/uucppublic`. But think carefully before allowing access to any other part of the system. If you must make additional files available, be as restrictive as you can; don't allow access to `/var` just so that a remote site can get to the `/var/spool/news` directory, for example.

See Chapter 24 for more information about Usenet news.

All your precautions will be nullified unless remote command execution is also carefully restricted. Unless you're involved in a special situation, any access to commands other than **rmail** (for receiving email), and **rnews** (for receiving news) is highly suspect.

Both flavors of UUCP allow permissions to be set on a per-site or per-user basis (except for **L.cmds** in BSD, which applies to all sites). A tricky feature of UUCP security is that access depends on several different con-

---

7. Most modems will ignore the dashes, but you can insert special punctuation marks if your modem understands them. For example, a comma signifies a pause in the Hayes command language. Refer to Chapter 8, *Serial Devices*, for more information.

ditions, not just one fact such as the identity of the remote system. In various situations, the role played by **uucico** (master or slave), the identity of the requesting user, the login name under which a remote site logged in, and the initiator of the telephone call can all make a difference in the computation of permissions.

Permissions that seem to say clearly, "Remote site wasteheat can never access anything outside **/var/spool/uucppublic**" often don't say that at all. You must be conversant with the subtleties of these configuration files in order to make them mean what you want them to mean.

Because of all this nastiness, you may find that the following sections attempt to teach you more about UUCP security than you really care to know. If you just want to use a secure, boilerplate configuration, here's what to do. Under BSD, set up the **USERFILE** like this:

```
unused,    /var/spool/uucppublic
,unused    /var/spool/uucppublic
```

and **L.cmds** like this:

```
PATH=/bin:/usr/bin:/usr/ucb:/usr/local/lib/news
rmail
rnews,Error
```

On a HoneyDanBer system, set up the **Permissions** file like this:

```
MACHINE=OTHER COMMANDS=rnews:rmail
```

BSD Security: USERFILE and L.cmds

USERFILE restricts the files that are available for access, while **L.cmds** restricts the programs that may be run via **uux**. In addition to restricting the access allowed to remote systems, these files also restrict the access that users have to the local system when using UUCP commands. For example, suppose that your system name is "jove" and that someone on one of your UUCP neighbors executes

```
uux '!cat jove!/etc/passwd !myfile | jove!mail evi'
```

Permission to execute the **cat** command on the remote system (meaning the system that originated the command) must be granted by the **/usr/lib/uucp/L.cmds** file on the remote system. Likewise, permission to access **myfile** on the remote system must be granted by the remote system's **USERFILE**. Assuming that the remote system permits this command, its success on jove depends upon whether or not jove's **USERFILE** allows access to the **/etc/passwd** file and whether or not jove's **L.cmds** file allows access to the **mail** command. The argument **evi** in this example is neither a file nor a command, so it is not subject to any security checks. Note that it does not matter whether or not jove allows use of the **cat** command.

Format of the USERFILE

Each line in the USERFILE is of the form

```
loginname,systemname [c] pathname ...
```

loginname and *systemname* must be separated by only a comma. The other fields may have spaces or tabs between them.

When file access permissions are to be determined, the USERFILE is read sequentially until a line that applies to the current situation is found. For local **uucp** or **uux** processes, or when **uucico** is run in master mode, the file is searched for a line that has a *loginname* field identical to the login name of the current user. When **uucico** runs in slave mode, it is the *systemname* field that is examined instead; a line is selected when this field matches the actual name of the remote site (*not* the site's login name, e.g., "moto" rather than "Umoto"[8]).

If no matching lines are found, the first line with an empty field in the appropriate spot is used. If there is more than one matching line, the first matching line is used.[9] Either of the two first fields may be empty on any line. In some versions of BSD, both fields may be empty.

The character c (callback) that follows the *loginname* and *systemname* fields is to be either entered literally or left out. It has meaning only in the case where the program examining the USERFILE is a slave-mode **uucico** process. If the c is present, the connection between the local and remote **uucico**s is broken and the local **uucico** attempts to call the remote system back immediately, using its own idea of the remote system's telephone number. This provides a degree of security against impostors, yet ensures that either side of the connection may initiate a conversation.

The pathname list consists of directories or prefixes that filenames must begin with to be accessible by the remote system. For example, the directory name **/var/spool/uucppublic** in this field would allow access to any file within that directory or one of its subdirectories.

To illustrate the subtleties of the USERFILE, imagine that there are two sites that jove talks to: one called "goodsite" and one called "badsite." Assume that we'd like to allow goodsite to access files anywhere underneath the **/usr** or **/etc** directories, but we want badsite's access restricted to **/var/spool/uucppublic**. Since goodsite has access to sensitive information, we want to be sure that it is not impersonated and we'll put it on callback status.

---

8. By convention, UUCP logins begin with a capital "U" to distinguish them from real users. See page 692 for more information about the naming of UUCP logins.

9. Actually, there are some versions of UUCP that use the last matching line.

Imagine further that there is a user "badguy" on the local system who we suspect of subversive activities. We'd like to prevent him from shipping out the system's files, but we want everyone else to have free run of the system. Here's what the **USERFILE** should look like:

```
Ugoodsit,goodsite   c /etc /usr
Ubadsite,badsite    /var/spool/uucppublic
badguy,unused       /dev/null
,unused
unused,             /var/spool/uucppublic
```

The line that gives permissions for badsite is not strictly necessary, since those permissions match the defaults specified for other systems on the fifth line. However, it is wise to include such a line in case you decide to liberalize the default access permissions. You might forget to rescind badsite's default permissions at that time.

Login and system names specified as unused are given to prevent matching of null fields. It is important to provide the login names of the remote sites as well as their system names, since some remotely-executed programs may attempt to forward files or execution requests by executing the **uucp** or **uux** commands.

This example setup is dangerous in several ways. To begin with, you shouldn't give permissions on **/etc** or **/usr** to external sites. And unfortunately, new contacts will by default have access to all files on the system when remote command executions they request cause **uucp** or **uux** to be executed, because of line four. But without line four, local users couldn't access their own files when using **uucp** or **uux**.

Format of the L.cmds File

/usr/lib/uucp/L.cmds contains a list of commands accessible via remote command execution, and, optionally, a list of directories in which to search for these commands. The default directories are **/bin**, **/usr/bin**, and **/usr/ucb**. If you intend to run news, you should add the directory that contains news commands (**/usr/lib/news/bin** or **/usr/local/bin**) by adding a configuration line of the form

```
PATH=/bin:/usr/bin:/usr/ucb:/usr/local/bin
```

to the **L.cmds** file.

Command names in **L.cmds** are listed one per line, and may have the optional suffixes ",Error" and ",No", indicating that acknowledgment messages are to be sent to the initiator of the command request only in the case of an error, or never, respectively.

Typically, the **L.cmds** file allows execution of the commands **rmail** and **rnews**. **rmail** is the mail-receiving program used in conjunction with

UUCP, and **rnews** is the standard receiving program for Usenet news. **rnews** should be specified as `rnews,Error`. If there are other commands that you want to include in your **L.cmds** file, you should be sure that they do not have any kind of built-in shell escape facility, and the shells themselves should be off limits.

HoneyDanBer Security: Permissions

`/usr/lib/uucp/Permissions` is essentially no different in purpose and scope from its BSD equivalents, but it uses a flexible file format that provides for a few more bells and whistles. HoneyDanBer UUCP is much more secure than BSD in its default configuration.

Be careful with the syntax of this file, as small errors can cause unintelligible permission errors in other parts of the UUCP system. Luckily, HoneyDanBer provides the **uucheck** command which, with the **-v** option, can be used to explain how the contents of the Permissions file will be interpreted.

Statements in the **Permissions** file are sequences of *name=value* clauses separated by whitespace. Long lines can be broken using the backslash convention, and multiple values for a name may be separated with colons. The properties that may appear as names are listed in Table 30.2. The "When" column indicates whether a property applies when the local system is the caller (the initiator of the conversation), the callee, or both.

Table 30.2   Properties in /usr/lib/uucp/Permissions

Property	When	Value
MACHINE	Caller	Machines this statement applies to
LOGNAME	Callee	Login names this statement applies to
VALIDATE	Callee	List of system names OK for this login
READ	Both	Directories the remote site can read files within
WRITE	Both	Directories where files can be deposited
NOREAD	Both	Exceptions to READ
NOWRITE	Both	Exceptions to WRITE
REQUEST	Both	Can remote site ask for your files? (yes/no)
SENDFILES	Callee	OK to perform locally-requested tasks? (yes/call)
COMMANDS	—	List of commands the remote site may execute
CALLBACK	Callee	Call the remote site back immediately? (yes/no)
MYNAME	Both	System name alias

In order to determine whether a particular operation should be permitted, **uucico** searches the **Permissions** file for a line that is applicable to the current situation. When the local site is the caller, **uucico** searches for a line with a MACHINE clause that matches the system name of the system that was called. When the local site is the callee, **uucico** looks for a LOGNAME clause containing the account name that the remote site used to log in.

There are two exceptions to this rule. First, when **uucico** wants to verify that a remote site's command execution request is legitimate by checking the value of COMMANDS, it looks for a matching MACHINE entry, even if the remote site initiated the call. Second, if no matching MACHINE or LOGNAME clauses are found during a permission search, a statement that specifies MACHINE=OTHER, if one exists, will be used.

The remaining properties specify various permission details. In the explanations below, we'll refer to the following two statements:

```
LOGNAME=Urhino:Ubob MACHINE=rhino REQUEST=no \
   SENDFILES=yes READ=/var/spool NOREAD=/var/spool/mail \
   WRITE=/tmp:/var/spool/uucppublic COMMANDS=rnews:rmail \
   CALLBACK=yes
MACHINE=akelei MYNAME=titan REQUEST=yes
```

A single statement may contain both MACHINE and LOGNAME clauses. Thus, properties described in the first statement apply to the site "rhino" whether or not rhino initiates a conversation (assuming that rhino logs in with the account name Urhino).

READ and WRITE list directories within which the remote site should be granted read and write permission. Reading and writing are always defined from the local site's perspective, regardless of who initiates a conversation. Normal UNIX file permissions still apply; even if UUCP allows a remote site to read files in **/usr/foo**, they might not be readable by the UNIX account that the remote site uses to log in. Both READ and WRITE default to **/var/spool/uucppublic**.

NOREAD and NOWRITE specify exceptions to READ and WRITE. It's often clearer to use these exception clauses to mask out certain directories than to explicitly list the directories' siblings in a READ or WRITE. In the first of the examples above, rhino and bob can read files from anywhere in **/var/spool** except **/var/spool/mail**.

REQUEST and SENDFILES control the transfer of files from the local site to the remote site. It is assumed that files may always be transferred in the other direction. REQUEST tells whether it's OK to transfer files at the remote site's request, and SENDFILES tells whether it's OK to transfer them at the local site's request.

There is a subtle difference between these two properties: if REQUEST is turned off, remote requests to transfer files will fail and be discarded. But if SENDFILES is turned off, it simply means "not now"; the files can be transferred later when the local site is the initiator of a subsequent conversation. That's why the opposite of yes is no for REQUEST and call for SENDFILES. The defaults are no and call. (In the example above, there's no way for rhino to ever get a file from the local site without someone at the local site sending it.)

COMMANDS lists the commands that a remote site may execute. The default value is compiled into UUCP and is implementation-dependent.

CALLBACK is only checked when a remote site dials in. If its value is yes, the conversation is aborted and the local site attempts to call the remote site. This provides a measure of extra security, since an impostor would have to take over the remote site's phone as well as its UUCP information. If CALLBACK is turned on, only MACHINE entries relating to particular host will be significant, since the local site will always be the caller by the time that the uucico processes begin to transfer files.

VALIDATE is a not-very-reliable way to check that a caller is who it claims to be. It checks the login name against the listed system names; if the caller's system name doesn't match, the connection is terminated.

The MYNAME property allows you to masquerade as a site with a different system name. The value should be set to the system name you would like to adopt. This can be useful when changing your system name; your UUCP neighbors won't all update their configurations immediately, and people in the outside world may persist in routing UUCP traffic using the old name.

Armed with this exciting information, we can now decode the example configuration shown earlier. From the first statement, we see that the system rhino can never request files from us, but that we are willing to send files queued as the result of local commands any time we talk to rhino. Any files under /var/spool can be sent, except for those in or beneath /var/spool/mail. Rhino can only write files in the directories /var/spool/uucppublic and /tmp. Rhino is on callback status, and may only execute the **rnews** and **rmail** commands. All of these conditions also apply to the system "bob" when bob calls us; when we call bob, the default settings are used.

The second statement says that when we call "akelei," we should pretend to be a site called "titan," and that we should let akelei request files from /var/spool/uucppublic (the default value of READ).

Finding a UUCP Neighbor

Before you can go much further with your UUCP configuration, you'll need a UUCP neighbor to talk to. It may take time to arrange a connection, so it's best to plan ahead.

In the past, obtaining a UUCP connection required begging skills, since local universities and businesses were often the only potential connection points. But these days there are companies that offer UUCP connections as a commercial service. The fees for a connection are usually reasonable, and it's now considered somewhat rude to cadge free UUCP connections from universities.

Even if you can obtain a free UUCP connection from another site, you may still be better off using a commercial supplier. Suppliers are usually well-connected to networks other than UUCP (including Internet), and it's therefore faster to get materials to their proper destinations. If your site is only accessible through an indirect chain of UUCP sites, your risk of experiencing problems is increased.

See Chapter 16 for more information about DNS.

Another nice feature of using a commercial UUCP provider is that the provider can use DNS magic to give the world the impression that you are on the Internet. bill@whitehouse.gov is a more respectable address than uunet!goatboy!bill. Silly, but true.

Most service companies charge a flat monthly fee for UUCP service. Usually, you must also reimburse them for telephone charges incurred on your behalf. News is usually available for an additional charge.

Two large providers are UUNET and PSI; both operate world-wide. Send email to info@uunet.uu.net or info@psi.com for more information.

Once you've arranged a connection of some sort, each site must give the other the following four pieces of information:

- The machine name of the local system
- The remote system's login name and password
- The phone number of the local system
- The name and phone number of the system administrator

You must also reach agreement on the calling schedule and the modem speeds and protocols to be used. You might want to ask if there are any unusual features of the remote site's login procedure.

Making a Login for a New Neighbor

A UUCP login need not be a full-fledged user account, so you don't have to perform all the steps outlined in Chapter 6, *Adding New Users*. It is usually sufficient to add a line to the `/etc/passwd` file or to the equivalent network administrative database.

We suggest that the login name for a remote system be the name of the system prefaced with a capital "U" and truncated to eight characters. This convention makes UUCP logins recognizable on sight, allows you to figure out the login for a particular site without maintaining an explicit table, and avoids problems with systems that are confused by long login names. For example, the login name for a machine called "watergate" would be "Uwaterga".

UUCP passwords should consist of random letters and digits, since no human needs to remember or type them.

All UUCP logins should share a single UID. This single-UID scheme avoids cluttering the pseudo-user UID range with UUCP logins and allows files created in **/var/spool/uucppublic** by one login to be read and rewritten by another. The shared UID should *not* be the same as the UID of the generic "uucp" login.

Once you've made the **/etc/passwd** entry for a new neighbor, use the **passwd** command (or **yppasswd**, if appropriate) to set a password for the remote system.

Making an L.sys or Systems Entry for a Neighbor

L.sys (BSD) and **Systems** (HoneyDanBer) are central to UUCP. These files, which are practically identical, contain the names, phone numbers, and passwords of all systems with which you communicate. They normally live in **/usr/lib/uucp**.

In some versions of UUCP, it is possible to receive calls from systems that are not listed in **L.sys** or **Systems**; however, it's never possible to place a call to another system without first entering the system's information in these files.

Because **L.sys** and **Systems** contain instructions for logging in to your UUCP neighbors, you must keep their contents confidential. Never give any permissions on these files to the world, and make sure that any backup copies are kept secure.

The format of an entry is

```
site times type speed phone chat
```

The fields have the following meanings:

site	This field specifies the remote computer's host name (*not* the remote computer's login name).
times	This field specifies the times at which a call may be initiated to the specified host. It doesn't place any restrictions on the times at which calls may be received from that host, however. See *Specifying when to call*, below, for instructions on filling out this field.
type	This field specifies the type of connection to be used. It is identical to the *type* field of the **L-devices** or **Devices** file, and should be ACU for a modem.

records the time at which the call was attempted. Depending on how you've configured the link, an attempt to retry the call might fail because uucico thinks that insufficient time has elapsed since the last attempt. You must remove the file **/var/spool/uucp/STST/**.*system* in BSD or **/var/spool/uucp/**.**Status/***system* in HoneyDanBer to get uucico to try the call again.

It is more difficult to monitor an incoming call. You will probably have to content yourself with looking at output from **ps** and **w** to trace the general flow of the conversation and to be sure that the remote system was able to log in without problems. If you are running HoneyDanBer and a remote site initiates a conversation with debugging turned on, some diagnostic information may be put in a file called **AUDIT** in the UUCP spool directory.

Configuring your Mail System to Use UUCP

Most versions of **sendmail** do not handle UUCP mail directly. Instead, they give UUCP-addressed mail to a special UUCP mailer (usually called **rmail**) for forwarding. The mail system does the address parsing and rewriting, and the UUCP mailer is responsible for examining the final result and forwarding it to the appropriate machine. On most systems, the UUCP mailer also receives incoming UUCP mail from other machines and submits it to the local mail system.

Chapter 21, *Electronic Mail*, describes the proper incantations for configuring **sendmail**. However, since UUCP addresses are stylistically different from other kinds of mail addresses, you may find it difficult to add UUCP to an existing installation. Unfortunately, some vendors' mail-handling tools make the process even harder than it needs to be.

These versions of **sendmail** *are included on the CD-ROM.*

We recommend installing either the IDA **sendmail** package or version eight of Berkeley **sendmail**. Both of these packages contain versions of **sendmail**, **/bin/mail**, and **rmail** that are designed to work together and make the UUCP configuration process easy.

See Chapter 16 for more information about DNS.

If you want email addresses for your users to look like Internet-style addresses rather than UUCP addresses, you need to have a UUCP neighbor on the Internet who can front for you. The Internet Domain Name System (DNS) allows the fronting machine to publish a mail exchanger (MX) record for you in much the same way that it publishes its own name. This will cause mail sent to you at the Internet-style address to be routed through your neighbor for forwarding via UUCP. Commercial UUCP vendors provide this service as a matter of course.

Testing UUCP mail is generally fairly easy. You can send mail to yourself that must travel through a remote host and back again to get to you, proving that you can both send and receive mail correctly. In the following examples, we'll assume that "lair" is the name of your neighbor and that your local system's name is "jove."

The first thing you should try is

```
mail -v lair!jove!yourname
```

This will let you watch **sendmail** chew on the address. A successful session looks something like this:

```
% mail -v lair!jove!garth
Subject: Hi garth
<Control-D>
Cc:
Null message body; hope that's ok

lair!jove!garth... Connecting to lair.uucp...
lair!jove!garth... Sent
```

If instead of this, **sendmail** tells you that it's "totally stumped," the problem lies in your `/etc/sendmail.cf` file. You need to review your UUCP mailing rules. If you get messages saying that the host lair is unknown, that probably comes from the UUCP system itself and requires that you go back to the configuration files in `/usr/lib/uucp` to try to figure out what is wrong.

You can use **uustat -slair** to verify that a job has been queued for the remote site. If everything looks good, force a call to lair with:

```
/usr/lib/uucp/uucico -r1 -slair -x5
```

It may take a minute or two for the message to get turned around, so you may have to force another call to pick up the incoming message. Once the second session has completed, wait another minute and then check your mailbox.

If there's no mail, you should check the contents of the UUCP log files in `/var/spool/uucp` (described starting on page 701). If the mail went out but didn't come back, the problem most probably lies with the address rewriting rules in your **sendmail.cf** file. Refer to Chapter 21, *Electronic Mail*, for help with debugging address rewriting rules.

If you configure **sendmail** to read the names of UUCP sites directly out of **L.sys** or **Systems**, be sure to restart **sendmail** when you add a new UUCP neighbor so that **sendmail** will become aware of it.[10]

Setting Up Automatic Calling using cron

Once you know that your UUCP system is functional, you need to set it up for automatic operation. The times you specify in **L.sys** or **Systems**

---

10. Actually, you'll need to restart **sendmail** no matter how you tell it about your neighbors.

tell when it's *permissible* to make a call, but the contents of this file don't cause calls to actually be made. You use the `cron` daemon for that.

The `cron` daemon executes programs at preset times. It is a whole topic in itself, and more information about how to use it is given in Chapter 10, *Periodic Processes*. Here, we will just present some boilerplate configurations that can be used directly or with only a little modification.

The timing of incoming calls is controlled by your UUCP neighbors. If you find that incoming calls arrive at inconvenient times, the only thing you can do is place your neighbors on callback status using `USERFILE` or `Permissions`. But actually, it's easier to just call the administrators of the offending sites and ask them to modify their calling schedules.

You do have control over the times when you initiate calls to other systems. The usual way to initiate calls is to run `uucico` in master mode (the `-r1` flag does this). With no other arguments, `uucico` scans its spool directories to discover for which systems work has been queued, and then makes calls to each of those systems, provided that the current time is within the range specified for each system in the `L.sys` or `Systems` file. If there is no work for a site, no call is placed.

`uucp` and `uux` will, by default, attempt to start up `uucico` whenever a job is queued for a remote system, unless the `-r` flag is included on the command line. Mail and news always use this option, so you have more control over their schedules than you do over the transfer times of operations initiated by users.

The simplest way to set up UUCP is to have `cron` run `uucico` in master mode every hour or so. The longest amount of time any job will spend sitting in your system's UUCP queue (assuming it is eligible to be transmitted) is the amount of time between executions of `uucico`.

On an ATT system, the crontab line for an hourly check will look something like this:

```
43  *   *   *   *    /usr/lib/uucp/uucico -r1
```

This line should be added to the configuration for the uucp account with `crontab -e uucp`. The BSD syntax is slightly different.

Calling only when there is outbound data for a site is fine as long as your neighbors are set up to call you when they have data for you. But if you call a site that doesn't call you, you have to be sure that a connection is made every once in a while regardless of whether or not you have work for it. There is no way for you to know whether or not there are jobs waiting on the other end without forcing the call.

It is only slightly harder to do a poll than it is to do a queue scan; the problem is that a separate command line is required for each system.

The -s*system* flag to **uucico** will cause the named system to be called regardless of whether or not there is work. This flag should be supplemented with **-r1** to ensure that **uucico** is started in master mode.

The easiest way to handle polling is to write a shell script and install it in your UUCP directory. If you do not poll many systems, you can hardwire their names right into the script; otherwise, you should have a script that accepts as arguments the names of systems to call. You should run this script out of **cron** just as you run **uucico** directly for non-polled sites. Some versions of UUCP provide such a polling command ready-made.

As a trivial example, the following script simply polls its arguments:

```
#!/bin/csh -f
# uucp.poll sitename1 sitename2 ... sitenameN
foreach site ($argv)
   /usr/lib/uucp/uucico -r1 -s${site}
end
```

If you were to use this script as part of a polling regime, you'd have a crontab line for each set of sites to be polled at once. For example:

```
00   7     *   *   *    /usr/local/etc/uucp.poll bog pika
23   7,16  *   *   *    /usr/local/etc/uucp.poll tiger luna
```

30.8 THE UUCP LOG FILES

See Chapter 12 for more information about the care and feeding of log files.

Most of the files in **/var/spool/uucp** are internal to the UUCP system and won't need to be configured or inspected. There are a couple of files and directories that may interest you, however. The information in these files tends to be extremely verbose, so you may wish to run some cleanup scripts out of **cron** to delete them every week or to compress them and move them somewhere else.

LOGFILE and .Log

In BSD-ish UUCPs, **LOGFILE** contains general information about UUCP activity on the local site and actions performed when connected with remote sites, whether or not the calls were initiated locally. Every time a UUCP remote command execution request is queued locally, a line of the following form is entered in the **LOGFILE**:

```
evi lair (7/19-21:52-5938) XQT QUE'D (rmail allspice!bob)
```

which shows the requestor (evi) the remote site (lair), the date, and the command to be executed.

In addition, information about the various calls that were attempted or received, whether or not they succeeded, and what went on during the conversations are also recorded here.

In ATT-ish UUCP, the `LOGFILE` information for each neighbor is separated into the files `/var/spool/uucp/.Log/uucico/`*neighbor* and `/var/spool/uucp/.Log/uuxqt/`*neighbor*. Most releases provide a command called `uudemon.cleanup` that gathers the logs at the end of each day and summarizes them into `/var/spool/uucp/.Old`.

SYSLOG and .Admin/xferstats

`SYSLOG` is used in BSD, and `.Admin/xferstats` in ATT. The format is the same. This file shows the size in bytes of each UUCP transaction, the name of the requestor, the site with which the transaction occurred, the time of the transaction, and the time needed to perform the transaction. For example, the line

```
news akelei (7/19-20:55) (553748130.51) sent data 8347
   bytes 38.85 secs
```

indicates that 8,347 bytes of news were transferred in 39 seconds.

ERRLOG and .Admin/errors

`ERRLOG` (`.Admin/errors` in HoneyDanBer) is used to record various errors that occur during the operation of the UUCP system. This file is the first place you should look when attempting to track down UUCP problems. A line from this file looks like:

```
ASSERT ERROR (uux) pid: 16140 (10/4-19:15) CAN'T OPEN
   D.sigiX00W0 (0)
```

Here, `uux` was unable to open a file that it expected to have access to. This may have been caused by someone removing the file by hand.

30.9 MISCELLANEOUS UUCP SUPPORT PROGRAMS AND FILES

There are several utilities supplied with UUCP for examining the job queue, finding the status of connections, and reading the logs in an organized way. These programs aren't really essential to the operation of UUCP, but they can be helpful in tracking down problems and in monitoring traffic.

uuclean: Sanitize the Spool Directory

`uuclean` is used to remove outdated cruft from the spooling area and to perform general housekeeping for the UUCP system. It can be used to remove all files over a certain age, and can select the files to be deleted on the basis of their names, which is useful if only files of a certain type (e.g., lock files) are to be removed.

`uuclean` is generally run out of `cron`, just like `uucico`. Normally, `uuclean` is run every 24 hours, and only the `-m` flag is supplied; this causes `uuclean` to do a general cleanup and to send mail to any users whose stale files were deleted.

uuq and uustat: Monitor the UUCP Queue

These two commands are similar, and most systems provide one or the other. The commands allow you to monitor the UUCP work queue, and they support a number of options to select only jobs having certain qualities, such as being destined for a particular system.

`uuq` and `uustat` can also be used by the administrator to delete jobs from the UUCP queue; to do this, the command must first be run in normal or verbose mode to provide the job names for each job, and then run again with the `-d` (for `uuq`) or `-k` (for `uustat`) flag to indicate which job is to be deleted.

uusnap: Show Status of Connections

This violent-sounding command displays the status of all UUCP connections that have work waiting for them on the local system. It shows the number of files and commands waiting to be handled, and the current status of the connection. If the status is blank, it means that the system has not yet been called; otherwise, it will say that the remote system is currently being talked to, or will show any problems or comments relevant to previous connection attempts.

uuname: Show UUCP Neighbors

Without any arguments, `uuname` shows the names of all known UUCP neighbors. With a `-l` flag, it shows the UUCP name of the local host.

To obtain the list of neighbors, `uuname` simply looks at the first field of each line in the `L.sys` or `Systems` file, hardly an amazing feat. However, it does handle comments and continuation lines, so it's useful for writing shell scripts. `uuname` is also useful because ordinary users do not have read permission on `L.sys` or `Systems`, so they need an intermediary, setuid program to search this file for them.

uupoll: Force a Call to a UUCP Neighbor

This command is used to force a telephone call to a remote system. Rather than using `uucico` with polling flags, as we've described in this chapter, it queues a job for the system and then attempts to start `uucico` normally. `uucico` sees that there is work and initiates a call.

uulog: The Command of a Thousand Faces

This command does different things under different versions of UUCP. Some versions of the UUCP system actually keep log information in separate files in the spool directory; this information is not compiled into `/var/spool/uucp/LOGFILE` until `uulog` is run. On these systems, `uulog` should be run at least once per day.

On other systems, log entries are written directly to the log files and the `uulog` command is used to search through these logs for information about particular systems. Consult the manuals for your system to find out what your `uulog` does.

30.10 SPECIFICS FOR VARIOUS OPERATING SYSTEMS

Except for BSDI, our example systems all use HoneyDanBer UUCP.

 Installation of UUCP is optional in Solaris. Refer to your system installation manuals for specific instructions. `/etc/uucp` is used instead of `/usr/lib/uucp`; the spool directory is `/var/spool/uucp`, and the public directory is `/var/spool/uucppublic`. If you use UUCP over modems, you will have the privilege of using `/etc/uucp/Devconfig` to configure protocol stacks. Refer to the comments in the file and read a book about STREAMS.

 HP-UX is a plain vanilla HoneyDanBer system. Configuration files are located in `/usr/lib/uucp`, and spool and public directories are in `/usr/spool/uucp` and `/usr/spool/uucppublic`.

 IRIX is similar to HP-UX. The `/usr/lib/uucp/Devconfig` file is used for configuration of protocol stacks.

 SunOS UUCP is essentially the same as that for Solaris. Installation is optional. Refer to your system's installation guide.

 Installation is optional. The system is mostly vanilla HoneyDanBer. A `uucpsetup` command is provided to assist with configuration.

 BSDI uses a version of BSD UUCP that has been enhanced to permit local customization. Configuration files are kept in `/etc/uucp`; the `/etc/uucp/CONFIG` file is used to declare the location of other directories. See the man page for `uuparams` for information about how to set up this file. The other directories default to `/var/spool/uucp` and `/var/spool/uucppublic`.

30.11 RECOMMENDED SUPPLEMENTAL READING

O'REILLY, TIM and GRACE TODINO. *Managing UUCP and Usenet.* Sebastopol: O'Reilly & Associates, 1990.

TODINO, GRACE and DALE DOUGHERTY. *Using UUCP and Usenet.* Sebastopol: O'Reilly & Associates, 1990.

KROL, ED. *The Whole Internet.* Sebastopol: O'Reilly & Associates, 1992.

 *Daemons*

31.1 INTRODUCTION

A daemon is a background process that performs a system-related task. In keeping with the UNIX philosophy of modularity, daemons are programs rather than parts of the kernel. Many daemons start at boot time and continue to run as long as the system is up. Other daemons are started when needed and run only as long as they are useful.

The words "daemon" and "demon" both come from the same root, but "daemon" is an older form and its meaning is somewhat different. A daemon is an attendant spirit that influences one's character or personality. Daemons aren't minions of good *or* evil; they are creatures of independent thought and will. As a rule, UNIX systems seem to be infested with both daemons and demons.

"Daemon" was first used as a computer term by Mick Bailey, a British gentleman who was working on the CTSS programming staff at MIT during the early 1960s.[1] Mick quoted the Oxford English Dictionary in support of both the meaning and the spelling of the word. Daemons made their way from CTSS to Multics to UNIX, where they are so popular that they need a superdaemon (`inetd`) to manage them.

This chapter presents a brief overview of the most common daemons. Not all of the daemons listed here are supplied with all versions of UNIX,

---

1. This bit of history comes from Jerry Saltzer at MIT, via Dennis Ritchie.

and not every daemon supplied with some version of UNIX is listed here. Besides making you more aware of how UNIX works, a knowledge of what all the various daemons do will make you look really smart when one of your users asks, "What does **xntpd** do?"

Before **inetd** was written, all daemons started at boot time and ran continuously (or more accurately, they blocked waiting for work to do). Over time, more and more daemons were added to the system. The daemon population became so large that it began to cause performance problems. In response, BSD developed **inetd**, a daemon that is responsible for starting other daemons as necessary. **inetd** was such a success that all major versions of UNIX now include it, and most new daemons run under its control.

There are many daemons that system administrators should be intimately familiar with, either because they require a lot of administration or because they play a large role in the day-to-day operation of the system. Many daemons that are described here in one or two lines have an entire chapter devoted to them elsewhere in this book. We provide cross-references where appropriate.

We will start this chapter by introducing a couple of very important system daemons (**init** and **cron**) and then move on to a discussion of **inetd**. Finally, we will briefly describe most of the daemons a system administrator is likely to wrestle with on our six example platforms.

31.2 ESSENTIAL DAEMONS

You will find **init**, **cron**, and **inetd** on every UNIX system.

init: The Primordial Process

init is the first process to run after the system boots, and in many ways it is the most important daemon. It always has a PID of 1 and is an ancestor of all user processes and all but a few system processes.

At startup time, **init** either places the system in single-user mode or spawns a shell to read the startup files. When the system is booted into single-user mode, **init** reads the startup files after the single-user shell is terminated with <Control-D>.

Chapter 8, Serial Devices, covers the care and feeding of your TTY ports.

After processing the startup files, **init** consults a configuration file (/etc/ttytab, /etc/ttys, or /etc/inittab, depending on the system) to obtain a list of ports on which logins should be expected. It opens the ports and spawns a **getty** process on each one.[2] If a port cannot be opened, **init** periodically issues complaints on the system

---

2. Except under Solaris. See page 123 for the sordid details.

console until either the port can be opened or it is removed from the list of active ports. On older systems, terminal ports were the backbone of the system. These days, they are something of a relic.

`init` also has the ghoulish task of exorcising undead zombie processes that would otherwise accumulate on the system. `init`'s role in this process is described on page 72.

Shutting down the system is accomplished by sending `init` an appropriate signal, usually SIGTERM, which makes it take the system to single user mode. This is the last step in most shutdown scripts. `init` is so essential to the operation of the system that an automatic reboot is initiated if `init` ever dies.

See page 48 for more information about killing `init`.

On some systems, `init` can be told to reread its control file by sending it a hangup signal (SIGHUP). Since `init`'s PID is always the same, you can simply run `kill -1 1`. The `-1` specifies a SIGHUP, and `1` is the PID of `init`. If you forget the `-1`, you will bring your system to a grinding halt.

The System V version of `init` is more complex than a traditional `init`. This `init` supports various "run levels" at which it can be started. The run levels determine what set of system resources should be enabled. There are usually eight levels: 0 to 6 plus "s" for single-user mode. The characteristics of each run level are defined in `/etc/inittab`, the format of which is described on page 121.

When the System V `init` starts up, it prompts the user to enter a run level (unless one is given as an argument). If "s" is specified, `init` enters single-user mode. Otherwise, it scans `/etc/inittab` for entries that are valid for the requested run level and executes their corresponding commands.

The `telinit` command is used to change `init`'s run level once the system is up. For example, `telinit 4` forces `init` to go to run level 4. `telinit`'s most useful argument is `-q`, which causes `init` to re-read the `/etc/inittab` file.

On systems where startup files are kept in `/etc/init.d` and linked to directories called `/etc/rcX.d`, bringing `init` to a particular level causes the scripts in the appropriate directory (`/etc/rcX.d`, where `X` is the new run level) to be run with the argument `start`. Scripts associated with the old run level are run with the argument `stop`.

For example, if `init` went from level 2 to level 3, all the scripts in `/etc/rc3.d` would be run with the `start` option. These facilities allow startup and shutdown to be handled in an orderly manner. Chapter 2, *Booting and Shutting Down*, gives a more detailed description of the System V `init` and the `inittab` file.

cron: Schedule Commands

cron is responsible for running commands at preset times. It accepts schedule files ("crontabs") from both users and administrators.

See Chapter 10, Periodic Processes, for more information about cron.

cron is frequently employed for administrative purposes, including management of accounting and log files, polling of UUCP neighbors, and daily cleanup of the filesystem. In fact, **cron** is so important to system administrators that we have devoted an entire chapter to it.

inetd: Manage Daemons

inetd is a daemon that manages other daemons. It starts up its client daemons when there is work for them to do and allows them to die gracefully once their tasks have been completed. To work under **inetd**, clients must observe some special conventions; if your system doesn't come configured to use **inetd** out of the box, it can't really be added after the fact without replacing many other programs.

inetd only works with daemons that provide services over the network. In order to find out when someone is trying to access one of its clients, **inetd** attaches itself to the network ports that would normally be managed by the quiescent daemons. When a connection occurs, **inetd** starts up the appropriate daemon and connects its standard I/O channels to the network port.

Many daemons can be used in either the traditional way (in which they are started once and continue to run until the system shuts down) or with **inetd**. Daemons discussed in this chapter are marked with an ⓘ if they are **inetd**-compatible.

Configuring inetd

inetd uses a configuration file (usually **/etc/inetd.conf**, but sometimes **/usr/etc/inetd.conf** or **/etc/servers**) to determine which network ports it should listen to. The format is the same on all platforms. Here's a sample:

```
ftp       stream tcp       nowait root   /etc/ftpd ftpd
telnet    stream tcp       nowait root   /etc/telnetd telnetd
shell     stream tcp       nowait root   /etc/rshd rshd
finger    stream tcp       nowait guest  /etc/fingerd fingerd
bootp     dgram  udp       wait   root   /etc/bootpd bootp -f
pop-2     stream tcp       nowait root   /etc/popper popper
pop-3     stream tcp       nowait root   /etc/popper popper
mountd/1  stream rpc/tcp wait   root   /etc/mountd mountd
mountd/1  dgram  rpc/udp wait   root   /etc/mountd mountd
...
```

The first column contains the service name. Service names are mapped to port numbers by consulting either the **/etc/services** file (for TCP and UDP services), or the **portmap** daemon (for RPC services). RPC (Remote Procedure Call) services are identified by names of the form *name/num* and the designation rpc in column three. In the example above, the last two lines are RPC services.

The second column determines the type of socket that the service will use: stream, dgram, or raw. In general, stream is used with TCP (connection-oriented) services, while dgram is used with UDP. raw is rarely if ever seen.

The third column identifies the communication protocol used by the service. The allowable types are listed in the **protocols** file (usually in the same directory as the **inetd** configuration file). The protocol is almost always tcp or udp. RPC services prepend rpc/ to the protocol type, as with rpc/tcp and rpc/udp in the example above.

If the service being described can process multiple requests at one time (rather than processing one request and exiting), column four should be set to wait, which will prevent **inetd** from constantly forking new copies of the daemon. This option is used with services that handle lots of small requests. If wait is not appropriate, put nowait in this field.

The fifth column gives the user name under which the daemon should run. If you do not trust a particular program or you know that it has security problems, you can run it as someone other than root to reduce your exposure. Of course, this only works for daemons that do not require rootly powers. In the example above, **fingerd** is run as "guest."

The remaining fields give the fully-qualified pathname of the daemon and its command-line arguments. The first argument should always be the short name of the program. This is not a peculiarity of **inetd** but a traditional UNIX convention that is normally hidden by the shell.

The services File

After adding a new service to **inetd.conf**, you may also need to enter it in the **services** file. This file is usually found in the same directory as **inetd.conf**; it is used by several standard library routines that map between service names and port numbers. For example, when you type the command

```
telnet anchor smtp
```

The port number for the "smtp" service is looked up in the **services** file. Most systems ship with all the common services already configured; you need only edit the **services** file if you add something new.

The **services** file is used only for bona-fide TCP/IP services; similar information for RPC services is stored in a separate configuration file, usually /etc/rpc.

Here are some selected lines from a **services** file (the original is about 70 lines long):

```
tcpmux        1/tcp                        # TCP port multiplexer
echo          7/tcp
echo          7/udp
...
smtp          25/tcp        mail
time          37/tcp        timserver
time          37/udp        timserver
rlp           39/udp        resource     # resource location
name          42/tcp                     # IEN 116
whois         43/tcp        nicname
...
```

The format of a line is

```
name        port/type  aliases       # comment
```

Services are generally listed in numerical order, although this is not required. _name_ is the symbolic name of the service (the name you use in the **inetd.conf** file). The _port_ is the port number at which the service normally listens; if the service is managed by **inetd**, this is the port that **inetd** will listen on.[3]

The _type_ indicates the protocol used by the service (in practice, it is always tcp or udp). If a service can use either UDP or TCP, a line for each must be included (as with the time service above). The _alias_ field contains additional names for the service (for example, whois can also be looked up as nicname).

Restarting inetd

See Chapter 12 for more information about syslog.

Changes to the configuration file do not take effect until you tell **inetd** to reread it. You do this by sending **inetd** a hangup signal. After signalling, wait a minute and then check the log files for error messages related to your changes (**inetd** records errors via **syslog**). You might want to try to contact any new services to be sure they work correctly.

portmap: Map RPC Services to TCP and UDP Ports

portmap maps RPC service numbers to the TCP/IP ports on which their servers are listening. When a program that supports RPC starts up, it registers itself with **portmap**, listing the services it supports and the port it is using. Clients query **portmap** to find out how to get in touch with an appropriate server.

---

3. Port numbers are _not_ arbitrary. All machines must agree about which services go with which ports; otherwise, requests will constantly be directed to the wrong port. If you are creating a site-specific service, pick a high number (in the thousands) that is not already listed in the **services** file.

This system allows a port to be mapped to a symbolic service name. It's basically another level of abstraction above the **services** file, albeit one that introduces additional complexity (and security problems) without solving any real-world problems. Many RPC programs are actually started via **inetd**, thus providing not one but two full layers of indirection and deceit.

If **portmap** dies, all the services that rely on it (including **inetd** and NFS) must be restarted. In practical terms, this means rebooting. The **portmap** daemon must be started before **inetd** in order for **inetd** to handle RPC services correctly.

31.3   THE BSD DAEMONS

The following group of daemons are found on BSD-style systems. Of the five, only two can really be considered daemons in the traditional sense of the word. **pagedaemon**, **swapper**, and **update** perform tasks at the kernel level rather than at the user-service level.

Although most modern systems have equivalent daemons that provide these services, we will only describe the BSD versions.

pagedaemon: The Paging Daemon

See page 660 for more information about virtual memory.

pagedaemon is a part of the BSD virtual memory system. When a page of virtual memory is accessed, a table is consulted to determine if the page is currently in physical memory. If not, a fault occurs and the **pagedaemon** is called to bring it into memory from the swap area.

The **pagedaemon** determines the location of the page within the swap space, then reads it into an available page of physical memory. If there are no physical pages available, **pagedaemon** makes room by writing out some other page to the swap device and updating the appropriate page table entries.

swapper: The Swapping Daemon

When many processes are running simultaneously, the system will begin to spend a lot of time processing page faults because each process has a certain number of pages that it accesses regularly. This condition is called thrashing, and it can seriously degrade performance.

The **swapper** monitors the number of page faults that occur in proportion to the number of memory references. If there are too many faults, the **swapper** starts to move entire processes out to the swap space. Swapped processes are completely removed from physical memory and are prevented from running for a comparatively long time (seconds).

The **swapper** continues to eliminate processes until the page fault rate falls to an acceptable level.

update: Synchronize Filesystems

See page 143 for more information about filesystem superblocks.

update executes the **sync** system call every 30 seconds. **sync** causes all "dirty" disk blocks to be written out, including filesystem superblocks, inode tables, and buffered data blocks.[4] This housekeeping minimizes the damage that can occur during a crash. On some early versions of UNIX, **update**'s function was performed by **cron**.

We know of one novice administrator who, while cleaning up the system's crontab files, removed the **update** function completely. The filesystem mess that resulted was monumental.

lpd: Manage BSD Printing

*A detailed description of **lpd** is given in Chapter 25.*

lpd is responsible for the BSD print spooling system. It accepts jobs from users and forks processes to perform the actual printing. **lpd** is also responsible for transferring print jobs to and from remote systems. **lpd** can sometimes hang and require a manual restart.

sendmail: Transport Electronic Mail

sendmail's tasks include accepting messages from users and remote sites, rewriting addresses, expanding aliases, and transferring mail across the Internet. **sendmail** is a very important and very complex daemon; refer to Chapter 21, *Electronic Mail*, for more information.

31.4 ATT DAEMONS

lpsched is really the only standard ATT daemon. But since ATT systems suffer from daemon envy, most releases include a large number of daemons from other systems.

lpsched: Manage ATT Printing

*See Chapter 25 for more information about **lpsched**.*

lpsched is the ATT version of the line printer daemon. It receives print jobs from the **lp** program and queues them for printing. When an appropriate device becomes available, **lpsched** forks a process to manage the actual printing.

31.5 RANDOM DAEMONS

The next group of daemons trace their heritage to neither ATT nor BSD. Some of them are found on almost every platform, while others are the exotic creation of a single vendor.

---

4. Actually, **sync** simply schedules these blocks to be written out; it doesn't guarantee that writing has completed by the time it returns.

snmpd: Network Management Server

*See Chapter 22 for
more information
about SNMP.*

snmpd responds to requests that use the SNMP (Simple Network Management Protocol) protocol. SNMP was designed to standardize some common network management operations.

rlpdaemon: Print from BSD to HP-UX

rlpdaemon is an HP-UX daemon that allows HP's ATT-ish **lpsched** system to accept print requests from BSD-style systems. See page 611 for more information about **rlpdaemon**.

glbd and llbd: Location Brokers

glbd (Global Location Broker Daemon) and **llbd** (Local Location Broker Daemon) maintain a database of the addresses of network and local services, respectively. These programs are designed to decrease the amount of network bandwidth used to locate network services. Since a typical lookup consists of a broadcast followed by numerous responses, a system like this could potentially reduce network traffic quite a bit. However, these services are not in widespread use.

31.6 NFS DAEMONS

The following daemons are part of the NFS file sharing system. We will give only a brief description of their functions here; Chapter 17 describes them in detail.

nfsd: Serve Files

nfsd runs on servers and is responsible for handling requests from NFS clients. **nfsd** does not really do much work: it simply accepts requests from remote machines and passes them on to the kernel. **nfsd** takes a single argument that specifies how many copies of itself to fork. There is some voodoo involved in picking the correct number of copies; see page 371 for specifics.

rpc.mountd: Respond to Mount Requests

rpc.mountd[5] accepts filesystem mount requests from potential NFS clients. It is responsible for verifying that each client has permission to mount the requested directories. **rpc.mountd** consults **/etc/exports** to determine which applicants are legitimate.

rpc.lockd and rpc.statd: Manage NFS Locks

While **lockd** and **statd** are two distinct daemons, they always run as a team. **lockd** is responsible for maintaining advisory locks (a la

---

5. The **rpc** prefix indicates that the daemon uses RPC. Some systems use it and some don't.

`flock`) on NFS files. `statd` allows processes to monitor the status of other machines that are running NFS. It is used by `lockd` to decide when to attempt to communicate with a remote machine.

 Almost every SunOS release has been followed by at least one `lockd` patch. If you are not running the latest release, make sure you have at least installed the most recent "jumbo NFS patch." Console messages starting with `klm_` are a good indication that you need a patch.

biod: Cache Blocks

See page 373 for more information about biod.

`biod` (block I/O daemon) is responsible for caching read and write requests on NFS clients. `biod` performs both read-ahead and write-behind buffering, which greatly improve the performance of NFS.

For example, when an NFS client requests three bytes from a file, a much larger chunk (usually 4K) is actually read. When the client reads the next three bytes, no network transaction needs to occur.

31.7 NIS Daemons

There are several daemons associated with Sun's NIS and NIS+ administrative database systems. Complete coverage of these systems is given in Chapter 18, *Sharing System Files*. Note that NIS and NIS+ are distinct and independent systems, despite their similar names.

ypbind: Locate NIS Servers

The `ypbind` daemon runs on all NIS clients and servers. It is responsible for finding an NIS server to which queries can be directed. `ypbind` does not actually process requests itself; it just tells client programs which server to use.

ypserv: NIS Server

`ypserv` runs on all NIS servers. There must be at least one machine running `ypserv` on every physical network because clients locate servers via broadcasting. `ypserv` accepts queries from clients and responds with the requested information.

ypxfrd: Transfer NIS Databases

`ypxfrd` allows NIS databases to be transferred to slave servers in an efficient manner. A slave initiates a transfer with the `ypxfr` command. Whenever a database is changed on the master, it should immediately be pushed out to all the slaves so that the servers are consistent with one another.

rpc.nisd: NIS+ Server

See Chapter 16 for information about DNS name service.

`rpc.nisd` is the NIS+ counterpart of `ypserv`. It must run on all NIS+ servers. If invoked with the `-B` option, `rpc.nisd` automatically forks `rpc.nisd_resolv`, which allows use of name service through NIS+.

31.8 INTERNET DAEMONS

We define "Internet daemons" very loosely to mean daemons that use Internet protocols to handle requests. Most Internet daemons actually spend the majority of their time servicing local requests.

comsat: Notify Users of New Mail

`comsat` is responsible for notifying users when new mail has arrived. When it receives an indication that there is new mail for a user and `/etc/utmp` shows that the user is logged on, `comsat` checks to see whether notifications have been enabled with `biff y`.[6] If so, `comsat` prints the beginning of the mail message on the user's terminal.

talkd: talk Server

Connection requests from the `talk` program are handled by `talkd`. When it receives a request, `talkd` negotiates with the other machine to set up a network connection between the two users who have executed `talk`. There are actually two flavors of `talk`: the original (at port 517) and a newer one from 4.3BSD (`ntalk`, at port 518). `ntalk` is not backward compatible and will not accept connections from `talk` clients. Most implementations of `talk` do not take byte sex into account, so connections between machines with different byte order often do not work. If you see the message

```
Checking for invitation on caller's machine.
```

it indicates that the two machines have incompatible `talkd`s.

rwhod: Maintain Remote User List

`rwhod` maintains information about the users that are logged in to machines on the network. `rwhod` collects this information for the local machine and broadcasts it; when it receives information from other hosts, it verifies that the information is reasonable and then puts it in the file `/usr/spool/rwho/whod.`*hostname*, where *hostname* is the name of the host that sent the information. The programs `rwho` and `ruptime` refer to this information.

By default, `rwhod` broadcasts every three minutes, so the information reported by `rwho` and `ruptime` is only approximately correct. `rwhod` is

6. The official explanation is that `biff` stands for "bark if from found." Biff was actually the name of Heidi Stettner's dog, who always barked when the mailman came.

very inefficient, so unless you have network bandwidth to burn and actually use the information, you should turn it off.

ⓘ ftpd: File Transfer Server

See page 429 for more information about ftpd.

ftpd is the daemon that handles requests from ftp, the Internet file transfer program. Many sites disable it, either because it is a resource hog or because they are worried about security. ftpd can be set up to allow anyone to transfer files to and from your machine.

ⓘ popper: Mailbox Server

popper is included on the CD-ROM.

The popper daemon implements the Post Office Protocol. This protocol is used by non-UNIX systems to send and receive UNIX-style electronic mail. It is available via anonymous ftp from ftp.cc.berkeley.edu.

ⓘ rlogind: Remote Login Server

rlogind is responsible for handling remote logins. When invoked by inetd, it tries to automatically authenticate the remote user by examining the contents of the /etc/hosts.equiv file and the user's ~/.rhosts file. If automatic authentication is successful, the user is logged in directly. Otherwise, rlogind executes the login program to prompt the user for a password.

ⓘ telnetd: Yet Another Remote Login Server

telnetd is very similar to rlogind, except that it uses the TELNET protocol. This protocol allows the two sides (client and server) to negotiate flow control and duplex, making it a better choice than rlogind for slow or unreliable links. Many non-UNIX systems support telnet.

ⓘ rshd: Remote Command Execution Server

Remote command execution requests from rsh and rcmd are handled by rshd. The authentication process enforced by rshd is similar to that of rlogind, except that if automatic authentication does not work, the request is denied without allowing the user to supply a password. rshd is also the server for rcp (remote cp).

ⓘ rexecd: Yet Another Command Execution Server

rexecd is similar to rshd, except that it does not perform any kind of automatic authentication; all requests must be accompanied by a user name and a password.

This server was used by some early networking programs, but it is no longer in widespread use.

ⓘ rpc.rexd: Yet a Third Command Execution Server

`rexd` is the RPC remote execution daemon. It is not used much and is riddled with security holes. You should make sure that `rexd` is commented out of your `inetd` configuration file. `rexd` is used by the `on` command, which will stop working when you disable `rexd`.

timed: Synchronize Clocks

A number of different time synchronization systems exist, and more than one time daemon is named `timed`. Most systems use essentially the same scheme. One or more machines are designated as masters. Their clocks are considered authoritative, and they negotiate with each other to agree on the "correct" time. Other machines are slaves; they periodically converse with a master to learn the time and then adjust their internal clocks.

The time between settings of a slave's clock is short enough that only slight adjustments are usually needed. Slaves will use the `adjtime` system call (if it is available) to smooth the adjustment of the system's clock and prevent large time leaps backwards or forwards.[7] It is especially harmful to set the clock back suddenly; time should be a monotonically increasing function.

The notion of "correct" time is rather nebulously defined. Some systems poll the network to get an average time value, while others simply declare one master correct by fiat.

xntpd: Synchronize Clocks Even Better

xntpd is included on the CD-ROM.

`xntpd` is a daemon that uses the Network Time Protocol (NTP, RFC1119) to synchronize a number of "peer" clocks to within milliseconds of each other. Servers are arranged in a hierarchal tree, each level of which is called a "stratum."

`xntpd` can access a number of reference time standards, such as those provided by WWV and GPS. As a result, `xntpd` provides a much more accurate way to set the clock on your UNIX machine than `timed`; clocks are not only synchronized, but also accurate. The current version of `xntp` can be obtained via anonymous `ftp` from louie.udel.edu.

routed: Maintain Routing Tables

`routed` maintains the routing information used by TCP/IP to send and forward packets on a network. `routed` deals only with dynamic routing; routes that are statically defined (that is, wired in with the `route`

---

7. `adjtime` biases the speed of the system's clock so that it very gradually falls back into correct alignment. When the system time matches the current objective time, the bias is cancelled and the clock runs normally.

command) are never modified by **routed**. **routed** is relatively stupid and inefficient, and we recommend using it only in a few specific situations. See page 266 for a more detailed discussion.

gated: Maintain Complicated Routing Tables

gated is included on the CD-ROM.

gated understands several routing protocols, including RIP, the protocol used by **routed**. **gated** translates routing information among various protocols and is very configurable. It can also be much kinder to your network than **routed**. Chapter 14 gives the succulent details.

gated was written by Mark Fedor at Cornell and is available via anonymous **ftp** from gated.cornell.edu.

named: DNS Server

named is the most popular server for the Domain Name System. It maps hostnames into network addresses and performs many other feats and tricks, all using a distributed database maintained by **named**s everywhere. Chapter 16, *The Domain Name System*, describes the care and feeding of **named**.

named (or more accurately, BIND, the system of which it is a part) is included on the CD-ROM.

nntpd: Transfer Usenet News

NNTP (Network News Transfer Protocol) is used to transfer news articles across the Internet. The protocol is sufficiently general to allow it to serve both as a back end for interactive users and as a mechanism for bulk propagation of news from machine to machine.

nntpd and C-News are included on the CD-ROM.

nntpd is a daemon that implements the NNTP protocol. It's usually used with the C-News package. As an interactive news server, it is driven by programs such as **rn** and **xrn** that maintain the illusion that news articles are stored on every machine.

As a bulk transfer agent, **nntpd** is driven by the news distribution software in much the same way that UUCP is driven for transfers via telephone. See Chapter 24, *Usenet News*, for more information about the transfer of news.

innd and nnrpd: Alternate NNTP Daemons

INN is included on the CD-ROM.

innd and **nnrpd** are a team of NNTP servers that come with the INN package written by Rich $alz. **innd** is in charge of connections to remote news sites, while **nnrpd** gets handed the more mundane task of serving local news readers. See the instructions starting on page 569 for information about setting up INN.

syslogd: Process Log Messages

*See Chapter 12 for more information about **syslog**.*

syslogd acts as a clearing house for status information and error messages produced by system software and daemons. Before **syslogd** was written, daemons either wrote their error messages directly to the system console or maintained their own private log files. Now they use the **syslog** library routine to transfer messages to **syslogd**.

ⓘ fingerd: Look Up Users

fingerd provides information about the users that are logged in to the system. If asked, it can also provide a bit more detail about individual users. **fingerd** does not really do much work itself: it simply accepts lines of input and passes them on to the local **finger** program.

finger can return quite a bit of information about a user, including the user's login status, the contents of the GECOS field in **/etc/passwd**, and the contents of the user's **.plan** and **.project** files.

*A recent version of **fingerd** is included on the CD-ROM.*

If you are connected to the Internet, anyone in the world can obtain this information. **fingerd** has enabled some really neat services (such as the Internet white pages), but some unscrupulous people have also used it for sleazy purposes, such as finding people to cold-call. Some sites have responded to this invasion by turning off **fingerd**, while others just restrict the amount of information it returns. If you choose to run **fingerd**, you should install a current version; a security hole in older **fingerd**s was exploited by the Internet worm.

ⓘ httpd: World-Wide Web Server

httpd and Mosaic are included on the CD-ROM.

httpd allows your site to become a server of World-Wide Web hypertext documents. **httpd** can send text, pictures, and sound to its clients. The most common **httpd** client is Mosaic, a point-and-click interface from the National Center for Supercomputing Applications. Another popular World-Wide Web client is called Netscape.

31.9 DAEMONS FOR DISKLESS CLIENTS

In the 1980s, the UNIX world was swept by a wave of diskless workstation mania. These machines booted entirely over the network and performed all their disk operations using a remote filesystem technology such as NFS. As disk prices dropped and speeds increased, the interest in diskless workstations quickly faded. The two main remnants of the diskless era are a plethora of daemons designed to support diskless computers and the bizarre organization of most vendors' filesystems.

While diskless workstations are not very common anymore, their booting protocols have been usurped by other devices. Most X terminals, some network terminal servers, and some network printers boot using a combination of the services listed below.

ⓘ bootpd: Boot Server

When a diskless client is powered on, it broadcasts a BOOTP request on the network. When **bootpd** hears such a request, it looks up the client's Ethernet address in the **/etc/bootptab** file. If it finds an appropriate entry, it responds by telling the machine its IP address and the file from which it should boot (usually via the TFTP protocol). **bootpd** does not handle the actual transfer of the boot file.

A **bootptab** file looks something like this:

```
global:\
     :sm=255.255.255.0:\
     :hd=/tftpboot:\
     :gw=131.106.3.1:\
     :ht=ether:
bigx:\
     :tc=global:\
     :ha=0000A7117D5F:\
     :ip=131.106.3.12:\
     :bf=Xncd19r:
smallx:\
     :tc=global:\
     :ha=0000A71199B6:\
     :ip=131.106.3.13:\
     :bf=Xncd15r:
```

The format is the same as that of the **termcap** and **printcap** files. The first entry lists global values that are inherited by the second and third entries (because they specify tc=global). The ha= clause specifies the hardware address of a machine.

For example, if a client with hardware address 0000A7117D5F broadcasted a BOOTP request, **bootpd** would tell it to use **Xncd19r** from the directory **/tftpboot** as its boot file (bf= and hd=, the latter inherited from the global entry). **bootpd** would also tell the client to use IP address 131.106.3.12 (ip=) and netmask 255.255.255.0 (sm=, also inherited from the global entry). At this point, **bootpd**'s job is done. The client machine would continue its boot procedure using some other protocol to obtain the boot file.

ⓘ tftpd: Trivial File Transfer Server

tftpd implements a file transfer protocol similar to that of **ftpd**, but much, much simpler. Many diskless systems use TFTP to download their kernels from a server. **tftpd** does not perform authentication, but it is normally restricted to serving the files in a single directory (usually `/tftpboot`). Since anything placed in the `tftpboot` directory is accessible to the entire network, it should contain only boot files and should not be publicly writable.

rarpd: Map Ethernet Addresses to IP Addresses

`rarpd` implements RARP, the Reverse Address Resolution Protocol. This protocol allows diskless machines to determine their IP addresses at boot time. `rarpd` runs on a server; one copy is generally started at boot time for each network interface that needs RARP support. `rarpd` uses the `/etc/ethers` and `/etc/hosts` files to determine appropriate mappings, so there is no need for a separate configuration file. RARP is a subset of BOOTP, but your hardware will dictate which protocol you must use (possibly both).

 Under SunOS, `rarpd` has been known to degrade the network performance of the servers on which it runs. Don't enable this daemon unless you actually have clients that depend on RARP to boot.

bootparamd: Advanced Diskless Life Support

`bootparamd` uses the `/etc/bootparams` file to tell diskless clients where to find their filesystems. `bootparamd` service is often used by machines that get their IP addresses via RARP and use NFS to mount their filesystems. The `bootparams` file looks something like:

```
exec    root=usenix:/home/export/root/exec \
        swap=usenix:/home/export/swap/exec
office  root=usenix:/home/export/root/office \
        swap=usenix:/home/export/swap/office \
        dump=usenix:/clients/dumparea/office
```

This example shows entries for two machines. Each entry must contain the machine name and the location of the root filesystem and swap area. An entry can also contain a location for crash dumps (as in the second entry).

In this example, the first entry specifies that the machine "exec" would mount `/usr/export/root/exec` from the machine "usenix" as its root partition. It would also use `/home/export/swap/exec` as its swap file. The swap file should be created with `mkfile` before it is used.

There is no need to specify other partitions in the `bootparams` map. Once a machine has mounted its root partition, it can read its own `/etc/fstab` file to find the locations of other filesystems. While each diskless machine must have its own root filesystem, it is quite common for many machines (of the same architecture) to share `/usr`.

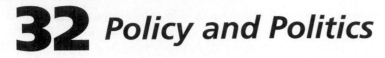

32 *Policy and Politics*

32.1 INTRODUCTION

This chapter covers some non-technical topics that are often included in an administrator's repertoire. In addition to discussing various issues of law and policy, we'll talk about some of the interpersonal aspects of system administration and the political intrigues that occur at UNIX sites.

While researching this chapter, we talked to big shots in the system administration world, in computer security, in the standards community, and in computer law. We were surprised that they all mentioned "signed, written policy" as being essential to a healthy organization.

UNIX and computer networks are both quite young—a mere 25 years old—yet they reflect social issues that have existed for thousands of years. In many cases, the legal and social institutions of the real world have been slow to adapt to the implications of new technology.

For example, there are well-defined laws and conventions regarding the privacy, use, and misuse of paper mail. But what about email? Is it private, or does the owner of the disk on which it is stored have a right to read it? If a computer forwards a message, is the computer's owner liable when the message turns out to be libelous or obscene?

Your car and TV are personal property; if they are stolen or damaged, liability is clear. But it's hard to apply the normal rules to a data file. After all, a file is only ones and zeros on a disk. Even when the file has been stolen (copied), it's still there.

Books are protected by copyright law, at least in the United States. But that protection is often irrelevant, since it's more expensive to photo-copy a book than to buy it at a book store. Software represents intellec-tual effort just as a book does, but it can be copied instantaneously, with little effort or expense.

As might be expected given the uncertainty surrounding these issues, many sites (not to mention governments) lack a well-defined policy for dealing with them. The situation seems even more explosive when you consider that computer networks threaten to replace both the postal service and the telephone company within the next few decades.

32.2 POLICY AND PROCEDURE

Policies and procedures should be written down, approved by manage-ment, and checked by lawyers. It's preferable if this is all done *before* they need to be used to deal with a thorny problem. Several different policy documents should exist:

- Administrative service policies ("We don't do Windows!")
- Rights and responsibilities of users
- Policies regarding administrators (users with special privileges)
- Guest account policy

Procedures in the form of checklists or recipes can be used to codify existing practice. They are useful for both new administrators and old hands. Several benefits of having standard procedures are:

- The chores are always done in the same way.
- The likelihood of errors is reduced.
- It's faster for the administrator to work from a recipe.
- The changes are self-documenting.
- There is a measurable standard of correctness.

Consider setting up procedures for:

- Adding a host
- Adding a user
- Localizing a machine
- Upgrading the operating system
- Installing a software package
- Installing software from the net
- Upgrading critical software (**sendmail**, **gcc**, **gated**, etc.)
- Backing up and restoring files

Many issues sit squarely between policy and procedure, for example:

- Who can have an account?
- What happens when they leave?

Often the "how" portion is the procedure and the "if" portion is the policy. Such things need to be written down so you can stay consistent and avoid falling prey to the well known four-year-old ploy of "Mommy said no, let's go ask Daddy!"

Some policy decisions are dictated by the software you are running or by the policies of external groups, such as Internet providers. Some policies are mandatory if the privacy of your users' data is to be protected. We call these topics "non-negotiable policy."

In particular, we feel that Internet addresses, hostnames, UIDs, GIDs, and login names should all be managed on a site-wide basis. Tools to help manage hosts (**addhost**) and user accounts (**adduser**) across administrative domains are included on the CD-ROM. You will have to modify them to fit your site, but they offer a reasonable starting point.

We feel strongly that logins should *never* be shared. It is a lot easier to enforce this policy if the temptation to share is removed. A guest machine with a liberal account creation policy provides an easy alternative to clandestine sharing.

Consider using an older machine as a guest system where a student's mom, an employee's spouse, or a visitor can have an account. Set a time limit on guest logins so that they can eventually be removed. Make the policy for use very explicit and have it signed by the user.

Other important policy issues that may have larger scope than just your local sysadmin group are:

- Security break-ins
- Group accounts
- NFS export controls
- Password selection criteria
- Removal of logins for cause
- Software piracy

Good channels of communication between administrative groups at large sites can prevent problems and help to develop trust and cooperation. Consider throwing a party as a communication vehicle.

Security Policies

What do you want to protect? Your data? Your hardware? Your ability to recover quickly after a disaster?

A copy of RFC1244 is included on the CD-ROM.

RFC1244, *Site Security Handbook*, is a 100-page document written in 1991 by a subgroup of the IETF. It advises sysadmins on various security issues, user policies, and procedures. It does not include a recipe for securing an Internet site, but it does give some valuable information.

RFC1244 suggests that you ask the following list of questions when formulating policy:

- Who is allowed to use the resources?
- What constitutes proper use?
- Who is authorized to grant access and approve usage?
- Who may have system administration privileges?
- What are the users' rights and responsibilities?
- What are the rights and responsibilities of an administrator?
- What do you do with sensitive information?

Whatever policy you adopt, it must be explicit, written down, understood, and signed by all your users. Enforcement must be consistent. A user may be a customer who has paid for computing services, such as a university student whose dad is a lawyer. Users can sue administrators for enforcing policy—be sure it's written down.

User Policy Agreements

Here are some explicit issues that should be addressed in a user policy agreement:

- Sharing accounts with friends and relatives
- Running password crackers[1] on the local `passwd` file
- Running password crackers on other sites' `passwd` files
- Disrupting service
- Breaking into other accounts
- Misusing electronic mail
- Looking at other users' files (if readable? writable? invited?)
- Posting to Usenet (never? with a disclaimer? anytime?)
- Importing software from the net (never? always? if you check?)
- Using system resources (printers, disk space, modems, CPU)
- Copying licensed software
- Allowing others to copy licensed software
- Other illegal activities: fraud, libel, etc.

Two sample policy agreements are included on the CD-ROM. One is aimed at undergraduates in a laboratory where a login is a privilege and not a right. It is the more militant of the two. The other document is for faculty, staff, and graduate students.

Administrator Policy Agreements

A policy document for administrators (and others with special status) must set guidelines for using root privileges and for honoring users' privacy. It is hard to respond to a user's complaint that mail is broken

---

1. For example, `crack`, which is an efficient program for guessing passwords; it is included on the CD-ROM. See page 550 for more information.

without looking at messages that have bounced. But a copy of the headers is often sufficient to characterize and fix the problem.

See page 52 for more information about sudo.

If your site uses a tool such as **sudo** for root access, it is essential that your administrators use good passwords and not share their logins with *anyone*. Consider running **crack** on sysadmins' passwords regularly.

For some administrators, the urge to show off rootly powers overcomes common sense. Gently suggest other career alternatives.

At some sites, having the root password is a status symbol, perhaps more valuable than a key to the executive washroom. Often, the people that have the password are engineers that don't need it or should not have it. One site we know offered all engineers the root password, but stipulated that any takers would have to wear a beeper and help others when it was required. Requests plummeted.

Another technique that we have had good success with is to put the root password in an envelope and hide it in a well-known place. Administrators generally use **sudo** to do their work; if they actually need the root password for some reason, they open the envelope. The root password is then changed and a new envelope is stashed.

Policy and Procedures for Emergency Situations

Decide ahead of time who will be in charge in the event of a security incident. Determine the chain of command in advance, and keep names and telephone numbers off-line. It may be that the best person to put in charge is an administrator from the trenches, not the director of computing services (who is usually a poor choice for this role).

We are accustomed to using the network to communicate and to access documents. However, these facilities may be unavailable or compromised after an incident. Store your contacts and procedures off-line. Know where to get recent dump tapes and what restore command to use without looking at **/etc/dumpdates**. Avoid talking to the media, especially if the incident is unfolding in real time.

The person in charge must have dictatorial powers. When the Internet worm hit us, no one was really in charge, so some undergraduate CS students who knew what to do took over. We delegated the task of talking to the media to the director of the Computing Center.

At one point, machines in another department were infecting the rest of campus. As soon as we would get clean, they would infect us again. We had already asked (and told) them to turn off their machines. When we returned, they insisted they needed to get work done (with a load average of 60 on a Sun3, it's hard to imagine what work they had in mind) and had turned the machines back on. After three rounds of turning them off only to discover them back infecting the rest of campus, we declared ourselves in charge and took their power cords.

32.3 LEGAL ISSUES

The federal government and several states have laws regarding computer crime. At the federal level, there are two:

- The Federal Communications Privacy Act
- The Computer Fraud and Abuse Act

Log files may prove to you beyond a shadow of a doubt that x did y, but to a court it is just hearsay evidence. Protect yourself with written policies. Electronic policy agreements may not hold up in court.

You may need a security policy in order to prosecute someone for misuse. It should include a statement such as:

```
Unauthorized use of University computing systems may
involve not only transgression of University policy but
also a violation of state and federal laws. Unauthorized
use is a crime and may involve criminal and civil
penalties; it will be prosecuted to the full extent of
the law.
```

We advise you to put a warning in `/etc/motd` (the message of the day) that advises users of your snooping policy. Ours reads:

```
Your keyboard input may be monitored in the event of a
real or perceived security incident.
```

Some connections do not see the message of the day; for example, `ftp` sessions and `rshed` copies of `xterm`. Users can also suppress the message by creating a file called `.hushlogin` in their home directories. You may want to ensure that users see the notification at least once by including it in the startup files you give to new users.

Be sure to specify that users indicate acknowledgment of the written policy by using their accounts. Explain where users can get additional copies of policy documents and post key documents on an appropriate bulletin board. Also include the specific remedies for non-compliance: deletion of the account, a million dollars in a Swiss bank account, first-born child, etc.

Suppose something naughty is posted to news from your site. If you are CompuServe, this is a problem. In a case called *Cubby v. CompuServe*, something libelous was posted. The judge ruled that CompuServe was not guilty, but found the moderator of the newsgroup to which it was posted negligent. The more you try to control information, the more liable you become.

You are safest if your site subscribes to all newsgroups and does not censor postings or prune the newsgroup hierarchy based on content. However, a technical reason for pruning (such as a lack of disk space) is probably OK. If you must prune, do it high in the tree. Removing all of alt is easier to justify than removing alt.sex.fetish.feet but not removing alt.sex.bestiality.hamsters.

This principle also applies to other interactions with the outside world. From a legal standpoint, the more you monitor your users' use of the Internet, the more you may be liable for their actions or postings. If you are aware of an illegal or actionable activity, you have a legal duty to investigate it and to report your findings to Big Brother.

System administrators should be familiar with all relevant corporate or university policies and should make sure that they are followed. Unenforced or inconsistent policies are worse than none, both practically and from a legal point of view.

32.4 SOME INTERESTING FACTOIDS

A summary of these results is included on the CD-ROM.

In 1992, Rob Kolstad and Jeff Polk surveyed LISA (USENIX's Large Installation System Administration Conference) attendees to determine how much time was spent on sysadmin chores and what level of support was required to maintain a site. The results of this survey of 152 full-time administrators appeared in the June, 1994 issue of the USENIX publication *;login:*. Here are some of the conclusions:

- Administrators work 47.5 hours per week, on average.[2]
- The average number of users per administrator is 82.
- 37% of an administrator's time is spent helping users.
- 24% of time is spent on system maintenance.

The variance of each of these average values was quite large. The responses came predominantly from large sites; there were an average of 4.6 administrators per site, along with 180 workstations, 460 PCs and Macs, and 200GB of disk space.

When reviewing the survey form, most administrators realized that they really did not know exactly how they spent their day. Almost all sites felt understaffed. It doesn't take too many whiny users for an 82-to-1 ratio to become oppressive.

32.5 SCOPE OF SERVICE

The services provided by an administrative support group must be clearly defined or users' expectations will not match reality.

---

2. This number may in fact be low since all responses over 70 hours per week were thrown out as not being sustainable.

Here are some issues to consider:

- Response time
- Service during weekends and off-hours
- House calls (support for machines at home)
- Weird (one of a kind) hardware
- Special-purpose software
- Janitorial chores (cleaning screens and keyboards)

In addition to knowing what services are provided, users must also know about the priority scheme used to manage the work queue. Priority schemes always have exceptions, but try to design one that covers most situations without them. Some priority-related variables are:

- The number of users affected
- The importance of the affected users
- The loudness of the affected users (squeaky wheels)

Our support group for faculty, staff, and graduate students has developed a set of documents that delineate their services, priority scheme, and contact mechanisms. This group of customers contains several levels of importance and squeakiness. The policy documents have been used for about a year with good, but not perfect, results. They are included on the CD-ROM.

32.6 TROUBLE REPORTING SYSTEMS

Our trouble reporting system uses an email alias called "trouble." At one time we were bombarded with trouble reports that were either incomplete or incomprehensible. We wrote a script that asked the user specific questions, such as:

- On what host does the problem occur?
- Is the problem repeatable?
- How important is it that the problem be fixed immediately?

The user rebellion started about an hour later. We had backed the system out within a day. Its only value seemed to be that with the furor over the script, many users actually read the questions it was asking and the quality of our free-form trouble reports improved.

Another site dealt with this problem by sending out a message explaining what information is important in a trouble report and showing examples of useless reports. When a useless report was received, it was answered with an apology ("Sorry, I don't have enough information to…") and a copy of the explanatory message. Users caught on quickly.

Our trouble system now uses the mh mail handler and several special commands for dealing with messages. This was not always true, but the proliferation of trouble messages that received either five answers (the easy ones) or no answers (the hard ones) caused us to switch to a mail system that can lock individual messages as an administrator deals with them, rather than locking a whole mailbox. The special commands we wrote tack status messages or "resolved, and here's the solution" messages onto the user's original report.

When a message is resolved, it is removed from the trouble queue and sent to a list of "trouble mail readers." Adding novice administrators and trainees to the tmr alias lets them familiarize themselves with the common problems and solutions, as well as the appropriate tone of messages to users.

See page 452 for a description of the aliases used to implement trouble mail. The complete system, `queuemh`, is included on the CD-ROM.

32.7 Financing Models

Many sites have a central department charged with providing computing support. It usually seems more expensive to use the central department than to do it yourself, but there are many hidden costs.

A disk drive can be purchased for only a few hundred dollars, but once it has been ordered, received, formatted, partitioned, filled with data, and backed up, the actual cost is much higher.

University departments with small computer operations use a variety of mechanisms to finance them:

- Income tax – a percentage of all research grants
- Property tax – a fixed charge for each machine
- Sales tax – fees based on CPU cycles or disk space used
- Head tax – fees assessed on each login

The mechanism is often dictated by the fine print in researchers' federal grant proposals.

Many departments bristle at central control of computing (Computer Science departments, for example), while others relish it. Princeton University tried to finance its network infrastructure by charging for IP addresses. The University of Colorado installed extra fiber while upgrading its telephone system and has made access to the campus network almost free.

A site that charges for access to the backbone network on a graduated scale (with a PC costing much less than a server or mainframe) will find its network growth very strange as the poor little PC becomes a gateway for the mainframe behind it on a local subnet.

32.8 MANAGING MANAGEMENT

Upper management often has no idea what system administrators do. Keeping a diary for a week that records what you do and how long it takes will surprise even you. This kind of documentation is essential when campaigning for additional staff or equipment. It can also be a source of power in day-to-day political squabbles. It may be wise to keep good records even in the absence of a particular goal.

Often a system administrator becomes the scapegoat for failures further up in the corporate food chain. In a small company, news of a new product often leaks out and the system administrator is held responsible. Blaming the administrator is easier than telling the stockholders the truth.

Email in a corporate setting is essentially public. If a large group such as "marketing" or "software" gets a piece of email, the press will get it too (if it's juicy enough). The link may not be direct. Tasty email is first shared with other co-workers, then former co-workers at other companies, and finally the entire world.

At a company where one of us once worked, persistent rumors goaded the Vice President of Manufacturing into sending mail to a group of employees in his division. It was untrue, said the mail, that the company was purchasing disk drives from a particular manufacturer only because he was sleeping with that manufacturer's sales rep. In fact, the Vice President claimed to be sleeping with someone else entirely. Needless to say, everyone at the company soon received a copy of that mail through one channel or another. By the next day, it was the toast of Silicon Valley.

Managers, especially non-technical managers, are often way off in their estimates of the difficulty of a task or the amount of time it will take to complete. This is especially true of troubleshooting tasks.

Try to set expectations realistically. Double or triple your time estimates for large or crucial tasks. If an upgrade is done in two days instead of three, most users will thank you instead of cursing you as they might have if your estimate had been one day.

It is sometimes hard for an administrator to get a written policy put in place. In that case, document existing practices and policy. For example, "We have eight licenses for Excel and 47 copies installed." Ask for money to buy more copies. If this fails, write a memo documenting the problem with a copy to upper management.

Fortunately, there is a shortage of good system administrators, so your job search should be short.

32.9 HIRING, FIRING, AND TRAINING

There are two approaches to building an administration staff:

- Hire experienced people.
- Grow your own.

Experienced people usually come up to speed faster, but there are always things you want them to unlearn. In order to do their job, they need root access. But you do not know them well and may not be willing to put your company's data in their hands.

It takes quite a bit of time and effort to train an administrator, and production networks are not an ideal training ground. But given the right person (smart, interested, curious, careful, etc.) the end result is often better.

We have developed two evaluation tools for experienced applicants. We used to call them "tests," but have found that some institutions are not allowed to test applicants. We no longer test; we evaluate and assess.

The first not-a-test, a written evaluation, asks applicants to rate their experience and knowledge of various system and networking tasks. The scale of familiarity is:

- Never heard of it (1)
- Heard of it, never did it (2)
- Have done it, could do it with supervision (3)
- Could do it without supervision (4)
- Could teach someone else to do it (5)

Embedded in the questions are several ringers. For example, in the hardware section is a question about RS-232 connectors followed by one about "MX connectors."[3] These bogus questions let you measure the BS factor in an applicant's answers. A four on the MX connectors would be suspect. After the not-a-test, you might ask innocently, "So, what do *you* use MX connectors for?"

The second evaluation is designed for use during a telephone interview. Questions are set up to elicit quick answers from someone who knows their stuff. We score +1 for a right answer, 0 for an "I don't know," and -1 for obvious BS or typing **man xxx** in the background.

These two schemes have been quite good metrics for us. The percentage of bogus questions we use is determined by our state hiring folks; one or two questions isn't enough. However, these evaluations do not address other key issues regarding a prospective administrator.

---

3. MX refers to a mail exchanger record in DNS, not to a serial connector.

- Will they get along with other members of the team?
- How is their user interface?
- Will they take direction?
- Are they on a growth curve with a positive slope?

A personal interview might answer some of these questions. A telephone conversation with references usually tells you more. Listen carefully; many people do not like to say anything bad about a former employee or co-worker. Be very suspicious if the applicant does not use recent employers for recommendations.

If you make a hiring mistake, fire early. You may miss a few late bloomers, but keeping people who are not pulling their own weight will alienate your other staff members as they take up the slack and clean up after the losers. In many organizations, it is very hard to fire someone.

You may have to collect data showing incompetence, give formal warnings, set performance goals, and so on. Often, firing is easy during an initial probationary period and nearly impossible after that. Make sure that initial evaluations are taken seriously.

The evaluation forms we use are included on the CD-ROM. Can you find all the bogus questions?

Attitude Adjustment

System administrators, especially those who are suffering from SAPS (System Administrator Personality Syndrome), often forget that they are service providers and that users are their customers. Many administrators secretly hold the opinion that the systems are theirs to play with and that users are a regrettable nuisance.

In some organizations, administrators are respected, treated as skilled professionals, and paid well. In others, they are looked upon as electronic janitors several castes below developers and engineers. Mistreated administrators commonly develop a surly, passive-aggressive attitude, never outright refusing to help, but always subtly letting you know (by tone of voice and body language) how much of an imposition every simple request is.

Some of the qualities of a good system administrator are contradictory. An administrator must be brash enough to try innovative solutions when stuck on a problem, but must also be careful enough not to try anything truly destructive. People skills and problem solving skills are both important, yet they seem to lie on orthogonal axes among many of the administrators we have known. One of our reviewers suggested that a "personable sysadmin" was an oxymoron.

A system administrator's job includes more context switches in a day than many jobs contain in a year. No wonder some administrators seem a bit spacy.

Operator Wars

New administrators often become the victim of what we call "operator wars," in which more experienced users alias `ls` to `logout` in their environments, send them mail bombs, and generally harass them and their inexperience. Administrators who forget to log out are especially tempting victims.

This is more prevalent at universities than at commercial sites, but it probably happens everywhere to some degree. While it seems fun, it can easily be carried too far and should be strictly discouraged. There are enough real whammos for a new administrator without adding more, even in jest.

When our new terminal multiplexer was installed, it had no inactivity disconnect. It was typical for a phone line to drop and leave a port with an active session on it, just waiting for the next random person to dial in. The number of times you ended up connected to someone else's shell was worrisome.

Needless to say, we disabled privileged logins from dial-ups through the campus data multiplexer, but not before several practical jokes and a few not-so-practical ones were played on unsuspecting users. Our policy documents now forbid taking advantage of someone else's login session, however it might be happened upon.

Iterative Refinement

An administrator will often think that a problem has been fixed, only to receive several more trouble reports as the task slowly gets done completely and correctly. This can happen because the user who first reported the problem did not describe it clearly or suggested the wrong solution. Equally often, it can happen because the administrator did not test the solution carefully.

Some common complaints include:

- Man pages and documentation not installed for new software
- Software not installed everywhere
- Software that turns out to be owned by the administrator

Testing is boring, but a busy administrator can often cut productivity in half by skipping it. Every trouble report costs time and effort, both for users and for the administrator. The job is not really done until all operational glitches have surfaced and been taken care of.

Users can become upset when a problem is not completely solved on the first attempt. Try to set their expectations appropriately. It is often useful to get the user who reported a problem to work with you in solving it, especially if the problem relates to an unfamiliar software package. You will obtain additional information and the user will be less likely to think of your relationship as adversarial.

32.10 War Stories and Ethics

This section contains war stories that illustrate the ethical dilemmas a system administrator may face. Some of the stories are our own, while others have been harvested from external sources, perhaps N^{th} hand and perhaps not entirely in their most accurate forms.

Boss's Mistake #1

A department chair incorrectly sent personnel data to all faculty instead of to the executive committee for which it was intended. He asked a student administrator who was working that weekend to edit faculty members' mailboxes and remove the message. Should the student do it? Should he refuse? Should he look at the message and decide for himself if it were really serious enough to warrant an invasion of privacy?

In this instance, the administrator did do as he was asked, but he demanded that the chairman send mail to the faculty members explaining what had happened. He also stipulated that there be a witness to watch him trim mailboxes and verify that he did not browse around while editing. This was a good solution and one that both the administrator and the chairman felt comfortable with.

Boss's Mistake #2

A new secretary at a large computer manufacturer in the midwest was new to UNIX and email. At the end of her first week, she sent her boss a message about how nice the job was and how everyone had been very helpful. Her command line was something like:

```
% mail boss I like my new job, everyone is so helpful,
    thank you. Working here for you will be really fun ...
```

The boss read the mail and responded with a jokingly rude and sexist remark about the size of her breasts. Other folks responded about the need to put a carriage return between the name of the recipient and the message itself. It seems "everyone" was an alias for all employees.

A few hours later, the head administrator (who by that time had seen both the secretary's message and the boss's response) got a call from the boss. The boss explained that he had made a mistake (R instead of r, perhaps) and needed copies of the message removed from everyone's mailbox—everyone being several thousand employees. Needless to say, the administrator refused.

Who to Fire

A novice administrator and an operator trainee discovered how to break into the Computing Center's student computers. These hosts were run by a different group that was somewhat looked down on for being too conservative. The rookies wanted to leave a back door. As they were about to edit the `/etc/passwd` file, they were advised by a senior administrator to use `vipw` instead of `vi`. After the back door was installed, the novices did not use it, but the senior administrator did and was caught. Who should you fire?

Our answer would be either all three, or just the senior administrator, who should have stopped the break-in when he became aware of it instead of aiding and abetting the installation of a back door. However, in this case the senior administrator was deemed too valuable to lose; the two rookies were fired instead.

We view this as a very bad management decision. If the limits of behavior are set by an employee's value rather than by a written policy that is consistently enforced, the company is vulnerable to litigation (to say nothing of disgruntled employees with assault rifles).

Horndog Joe

Joe, a new administrator at a major computer manufacturer, was infatuated with the receptionist and asked her out for a date. She always went out with newcomers once to show them around and welcome them to the area. Joe asked her out again but she refused. A week or so later, she mentioned to one of the senior administrators that the machine always told her she had new mail even when she didn't. Hmmm. The senior sysadmin checked log files and found that Joe was reading the receptionist's mail. What should you do?

- Fire him?
- Give him a strong talking to?
- Give him a mild talking to?
- Nothing?

The right answer was actually a question: Is there a written policy that says, "Don't read other peoples' email?" The answer was no. They opted for a strong talking to.

A few weeks later, it happened again. This time it seemed to be a different person reading the mail, Tom. The senior administrator called Tom in and confronted him with the evidence. But Tom was at a basketball game when the log files showed that the access had occurred.

Upon further investigation and after backtracking through several machines, the sysadmin discovered that Joe was the true culprit once again. Half an hour later, Joe was fired and the contents of his desk were on the curb.

A policy that allows for one warning is a license to steal until caught.

Electric Fence

System administration is often a weird mix of front-line fire fighting and managing various sub-departments such as wiring and operations. In our organization, the wiring staff is supervised by the system administrators. One bleak summer day, we hired a new wiring guy. We'll call him "Wally the Wirer" for purposes of this story.

Since wiring folks often need to run wires through other departments' ceilings, they need access to the entire building. Although we have an excellent card access system, various politically-inclined folks frown on members of the wiring crew having "God cards" (cards that will open any door), even though they generate a log message each time they are used. Instead, it's much easier to obtain master keys to the physical locks, which generate no log. Thus, political types don't have to worry about who was where; instead, they just don't know.

At first, we were very impressed with Wally. He usually got his work done in a reasonable amount of time, and it was usually good enough that we didn't have to redo it within a week. The most amazing thing was Wally's dedication. We'd often find him in the building doing "wiring" around the clock. One night after a 4 a.m. power outage, he was the first person on the scene, well ahead of the system administrators that had been paged from their homes.

Life in a 750,000 square foot building that houses six academic departments can often be surreal. Around this same time, some departments began having odd things happen to their computing equipment. One day, someone would walk in and find that all the memory had been quietly removed from his Mac. Another day, a laptop, a Mac, or a printer would simply vanish. At first, the departments didn't communicate their losses to each other; the campus police were incompetent, and there was no obvious pattern—or so we thought.

Then one day, another wiring guy was pulling some cable through a region that Wally had recently wired. Quite to his surprise, in the ceiling above the department chair's desk sat a Mac that had recently been reported as stolen. Wow, the thieves must have been startled and stashed it up there, we naïvely thought.

Equipment continued to disappear for over a year. Some administrators had put the pieces together all too well, but without concrete evidence nothing could be done. Finally, Wally didn't show up at work for a week and was fired. Curiously, the thefts stopped right around then.

Things that we might learn from this:

- It's better to issue "God cards" than master keys.
- Over-dedication to a job may be an indication of trouble.

Wedding Invitations

A sysadmin who was getting married and hadn't finished all the preparations for the wedding gave his best man (an administrator from another site) the key to his office and the root password to his workstation. The friend was to go into work and make last minute place cards for the tables at the reception. This violated lots of local policies and was noticed by other administrators because the common practice was to use the `sudo` command instead of logging in as root or using `su`.

The root password was the same on all machines, so the visitor had actually been given the root password and physical access to the entire site. But no damage was done.

The circumstances seemed special, but written policy was violated. The employee was a valuable member of the staff. What to do? He was somewhat reluctantly fired with cause; he fought it and lost.

Pornographic GIF Images

A student's high school buddy came down to visit the computer lab during the summer. The student showed his friend how to view GIF files and showed him the location of a few "interesting" ones. He installed the friend at the last workstation at the back of the room and then worked on his homework. When they were done, they left.

Some time later (days, probably) the Dean, accompanied by the basketball coach, was showing a promising recruit from Texas (a woman) around the campus. The Dean had a key to the labs and so instead of entering as the students do, with an access card, he entered at the back of the lab with his key.

The first workstation they saw was the one that the friend had viewed GIFs on. And thanks to the magic of screen savers, when the mouse was moved, a sexually explicit photograph appeared on the screen. Needless to say, the Dean and the basketball coach were furious; the student thought it was no big deal. The Dean demanded that all GIFs be removed from university-owned computers, that the student who left it on the screen be expelled from school, etc.

Our policy agreement, which the student had signed, said that you should not display pictures on your screen that would offend other people. The end result was that the student lost his login for a semester. The policy agreement was reviewed by the lawyers (who upheld our side, not the Dean's), and the whole incident was handled within the department. We apologized to the student recruit.

Migrating Data

A small Colorado business used a local service firm for hardware and software support. One evening, their system administrator was swapping out a disk on which the bearings were going bad. The service firm had supplied not only the replacement disk but also a large scratch disk so that the transfer could be made without going to tape and back again. The administrator installed the replacement disk and the scratch disk and rebooted.

He was surprised when the workstation booted from the replacement disk and claimed that the clock was 297 days off. Should he wipe the disk immediately? Should he look at the data? Should he just return the disk to the service provider? His first instinct was to wipe the disk without looking at it, but after some reflection it seemed better to check and see whose data it was so that the service provider could determine how it had slipped out with data on it.

A quick scan of the **passwd** file showed that the disk had previously belonged to this very same company. It contained not only the root partition with encrypted passwords, but also the company's development databases, new products, etc. In short, a large part of the assets of the company, a bit out of date, had arrived from the service provider on a replacement disk.

When asked, the service provider admitted that the way they tested disks was to copy data from one to another, regardless of whatever data happened to be on the source disk.

This incident illustrates a problem that is obvious with hindsight and also hard to fix. Whose responsibility is the data on a broken disk? It cannot always be wiped before being returned for repair. Service providers (and probably more importantly, peripheral resellers) do not see your data as valuable; they see only a broken or breaking disk.

As administrators, we are used to protecting our backup tapes. Broken disks are taken for granted and they shouldn't be. Whenever possible, a disk with valuable data should be wiped (a low-level format and verify should do it) before being returned for repair or trade-in. If it's too broken to reformat, make sure your service provider knows that it contains sensitive data that you would like deleted.

It is probably worthwhile to ask your service providers about their policy regarding customers' data. When they admit that they don't have one, act very surprised and shocked.

High-security US Government sites (defense installations, especially) are sometimes forbidden to let any computer equipment off-site, ever. It it breaks, they have to buy a new one. It may sound paranoid, but as this story illustrates, it is not without basis. The policy even applies to components such as CPU boards that wouldn't normally retain data. You never know where those Russkies might be hiding.

Bill Must Die!

A student left himself logged in on a machine in the Computer Science undergraduate lab while he went to his TA's office to pick up a document. While he was gone, someone typed in a mail message to

```
president@whitehouse.gov
```

which threatened to send President Clinton to a violent and spectacular death. The Secret Service called the next morning.

The student was a foreigner who had served in his country's militia as an encryption expert. He had also neglected to mention to the local system administrators that he received an acknowledgment from the White House for mail he had not sent. Things did not look good.

The system administrators spent the weekend collecting log files and card access records to determine what had happened. Luckily, the log files provided enough circumstantial evidence to convince the Secret Service that the student had probably been the victim of a stupid joke.

The student's command history file (`~/.history`, which included timestamps) showed that he was a regular user of `pine`. But the offending message had been sent using `mail`, with a sizable period of inactivity before and after the event. Most users cling tenaciously to a single user agent for reading and writing mail, so the discrepancy was highly suggestive of a compromised account.

As it turns out, threatening the President is a felony. Even though the foreign student was exonerated, the Secret Service investigation continues. They would still like to identify (and perhaps prosecute) the real author of the mail message.

Our recommendation: if you are going to try and assassinate the President, do not tell the Secret Service about your plans.

32.11 LOCAL DOCUMENTATION

Documentation is often pushed down in the priority queue in favor of "real work." It's quite easy to defer documentation because at the moment you should be writing it, you remember how to do the task in question. Any administration group that includes students probably has serious documentation extraction problems.

Local documentation serves many purposes. Have you ever walked into a machine room needing to reboot one server, only to face racks and racks of hardware, all alike, all different, and all unlabeled? Or had to install a piece of hardware that you've handled before, but all you can remember about the chore was that it was hard to figure out? Or gone through days of localizing a new machine to fit your environment, only to realize that you have forgotten a couple of crucial steps?

Local documentation should be kept in a well-defined spot, perhaps in `/usr/local/doc`. Some documentation is most appropriate as a paper booklet or as a sign taped to a piece of hardware.

All system consoles should bear printed instructions that list the hostname, boot instructions, architecture, and any special key sequence that's needed to reboot (L1-A on a Sun, for example). The hostname should be readable from across the room. The special key sequence may seem a bit silly, but many servers' monitors are snitched and replaced with an aging terminal when someone else's monitor dies. Trying to find L1-A on a VT100 can be a challenge.

The hostname should also be taped to other pieces of hardware that are associated with that machine: disk drives, modems, printers, tape drives, etc. If the host is an important citizen (for example, a major server or a crucial router), include the location of its circuit breaker. If a floppy disk or flash memory card is required for bootstrapping, point to its location.

Disk device names, partition tables, mount points, and the locations of backup superblocks should be taped to the disk drive itself.

Tape drives should have information about the device files and commands needed to access them. Again, the best place to store this information is on the drive itself. It's also a good idea to list the type of tapes the drive requires, the nearest place to buy them, and the price.

Printers should list their names, brief printing instructions, and the hosts that they depend on, if any. Printers have started to come with network interfaces and will soon be full citizens of the network.

See page 435 for more information about the World-Wide Web.

It's a good idea to prepare a printed document that you can give to new users. It should document local customs, the correct way to report problems, the names and locations of printers, the backup and downtime schedules, and so on. This kind of document can save an enormous amount of administration or user-services time. You can also make this information available via a World-Wide Web server.

In addition to this introduction to the local environment, documentation for common user commands is essential in a university environment where the user community is often transient and UNIX-illiterate. We have printed one-page crib sheets about the `vi` editor, `mail`, news, logging in and out, the X environment, and the use of man pages.

Network wiring must be scrupulously documented. Cables should be labeled, patch panels and wall outlets identified, and network devices marked. Never make it difficult for your wiring technician to keep the documentation up to date. Keep a pencil and forms hanging on the wall of the wiring closet, so that it's painless to note that a cable moved from one device to another. Data recorded this way can be transferred to on-line storage later.

A `diary` file associated with each machine that documents major events in its life (upgrades, hardware repairs, major software installations, etc.) provides a central place to review the status of a machine. You can construct an email alias that points to the file so that the diary can be carbon copied on mail sent among administrators. This is perhaps the most painless and least organized way of keeping records.

32.12 PROCUREMENT

At many sites, the system administration team and the purchasing team are totally separate. This is bad.

Administrators need to know about any new hardware that's being ordered in order to verify that it fits the current infrastructure and can be supported. They also need to be able to influence the specifications on purchase requests. Often, they can provide good information about the competence of vendors (especially third-party resellers) and the reliability of certain types of equipment.

A system administrator's participation is especially valuable in organizations that by default must buy from the lowest bidder (for example, government institutions and state universities). Most purchasing systems allow you to specify evaluation criteria for a bid which must be set prior to bid opening. Be sure to include escape clauses. Sample evaluation criteria that we used for a major workstation purchase a few years ago are included on the CD-ROM.

The incremental impact of an additional workstation is not fixed. Is it the 60th of that architecture or the first? Does it have enough local disk for the system files? Is there a spare network port to plug it into? Will it be in an area of the building that is accessible to the network? Is it a completely new OS?

Questions like these tend to emphasize a more fundamental question: Do you stay stagnant and buy equipment from your current vendor, or do you try the latest whizzy toy from a startup that might shake the world or might be out of business in a year? The nature of your organization may answer this one. It's not a simple "yes" or "no"; there is often a complex trade-off between the latest and greatest equipment and the machines that you are comfortable with and understand.

If you are allowed to negotiate with vendors (officially or otherwise) you can often do much better than your purchasing department. Don't be shy about quoting prices from other vendors for comparable equipment or inflating the size of expected purchases for the coming year. Being able to get an order out fast is useful at bean counting boundaries such as the end of a quarter or year. Orders submitted in the last week of June can often obtain a sizable additional discount just to make a department's quota look better. Another bargain time is just before new models are introduced; vendors want to reduce their inventory of the older products. This kind of vendor bashing is common at universities and may or may not be appropriate at companies and government institutions. But it is fun.

32.13 DECOMMISSIONING HARDWARE

Retiring a computer is often a painful ordeal. Stubborn users won't let go; weaning requires them to learn a new system or convert to new applications. Some sites convince themselves that they cannot afford a new system and force the staff to support the old one and keep it running. This usually ends up costing more than the new system would have. An aging VAX probably uses more electricity in a month than its salvage value. Yet its user community is likely to be adamant about the impossibility of turning it off.

A related problem at universities involves donations from businesses that would like to get a tax deduction. Often, the right answer is, "No thanks, we don't need 2,000 nine-track tapes and racks to put them in." One university in Budapest was recently given an IBM mainframe. Instead of saying no and buying fast PCs, they have now spent more than a year's budget on shipping and electrical wiring alone.

Every time hardware performance increases, software drags it back down, usually by getting bigger and more complex. Old hardware slows down if the new software is installed, sometimes to the point of becoming unusable. We have turned our older workstations into X terminals by booting a specially-tuned kernel. A Sun 3/50 with 4MB of memory would probably have trouble even booting as a stand-alone workstation with current UNIX software, but with its 19-inch monitor it makes a pretty good X terminal.

Because users and management are often reluctant to scrap obsolete equipment, you will sometimes have to take the initiative. Financial information is the most persuasive evidence. If you can demonstrate on paper that the cost of maintaining old equipment exceeds the cost of replacement, you will remove many of the intellectual objections.

A transition between systems can be eased by keeping both of them on-line. You can leave the old system powered on, but step down the level of support that your administrative group provides. You can also discontinue hardware maintenance on the old machine, allowing it to limp along until it dies of its own accord. Various incentives can be dangled in front of users to lure them onto the new system: better performance, next-generation software, etc.

Even a very old machine may find use as a print server or guest machine. If your organization is run for profit, it may be advantageous to donate older equipment to a university or school ("Hello? How would you like to have 2,000 nine-track tapes, with racks to put them in?"). Barring that, you may have to think of creative disposal methods. A Pyramid P90X that had been decommissioned found itself the primary piece of debris attached to our head administrator's car when he got married. Quite effective. Another use we have seen was during the annual Engineering egg drop contest, in which a raw egg is packaged so as not to break when dropped out of an eighth-story window.

32.14 MANAGEMENT OF DUMPS AND DATA

The security of dump tapes directly affects a company's bottom line. Senior management needs to understand what the backups are actually supposed to do, rather than what they want the backups to do. It may be OK to lose a day's work at a university Computer Science department, but it probably isn't OK at a Wall Street trading firm.

Dan Geer, a security consultant, said, "What does a backup do? It reliably violates file permissions at a distance." Hmmm.

When the World Trade Center was bombed, some firms that stored their backup tapes on-site lost both their main computer systems and their backup data.

There are businesses you can hire to store your backups off-site in locked, fireproof containers. You can also trade with a non-competitor, storing their backups at your site and yours at their site. An administrator can take the backup tapes home. (Maybe this should be the responsibility of the company president.) Today's media (4mm DAT and 8mm Exabyte) are so small that these are all reasonable alternatives.

Spot-check your backups once a week or once a month to be sure you can read them. Just restore a random file from the fifth dump on a tape. If this works, your dumps are probably OK. Do this step yourself; don't leave it up to the operator who made the dumps.

A major research firm in California had an operator who was too busy hacking to do dumps. He opened tapes, labeled them, and hung them on the racks without ever putting any data on them. This went on for two or three months until someone insisted on having a file restored.

What happened to him? Fired? No, he was given an internal transfer, but was eventually arrested and convicted on unrelated electronic fraud charges. Rumor has it he got 40 years.

The same thing (empty dump tapes) happened to us a few years ago. The dump meister was the wife of a valuable system administrator. Pleas to fire her fell on deaf ears until one of the boss's important files was lost and her monstrous charade was exposed.

32.15 SOFTWARE PATENTS

Software patents seem to be invading the computer industry. While they do not have much to do with system administration, we will sneak in a short diatribe anyway.

In the beginning, the patent office ruled that you could not patent a mathematical theorem. Then the theorem became an algorithm, and it still could not be patented. Then the algorithm was implemented in hardware, and that could certainly be patented. Firmware, maybe. Software, still no.

But patents can be appealed, and one of the lower courts liked software patents. Against its will, the patent office started issuing them, in some cases for applications that were filed 10-15 years earlier.

Unfortunately, the patent office has historically had scant comprehension of the state of the art in software and has issued many inappropriate (some would say, stupid) patents. Five different patents exist for the Lempel-Ziv data compression algorithm. That algorithm was published in a mathematical journal and was implemented and distributed in Berkeley UNIX. The concept of an include file is patented. The concept of a monitor that displays text is patented. The process of copying an image from memory to an on-screen window is patented. Several data encryption standards are patented. The concept of embedding advertising material in a user interface is patented.

Lotus won a "look and feel" patent for its user interface to a spreadsheet program. Image how it would be if the user interfaces for automobiles were patentable:

- Apple would own the steering wheel
- Lotus would own the foot pedals
- Hewlett-Packard would control the H shape for stick shifts
- Microsoft would control the brakes

Each car would have the controls in different places, doing different things. It might be difficult to drive a rental car.

The patent office is attempting to clean up its act, but the damage seems to have already been done in many cases. A major milestone was the recall (in the summer of 1994) of a patent belonging to Compton's New Media. This patent involved retrieval systems for data stored on CD-ROM. Some analysts considered it broad enough to cover 80% of all existing CD-ROM products, although this is probably an exaggeration. In the end, each of 41 claims was invalidated through a campaign on the part of software vendors to demonstrate the existence of prior art.

The discovery of prior art is the real weakness in the patent office's process. Patent applications are kept secret, and with very little software expertise in the patent office it is difficult for them to know which applications really represent new technology.

32.16 ORGANIZATIONS AND CONFERENCES

Several UNIX support groups, both general and vendor-specific, exist to help you network with other people that are using the same software. A brief list of organizations and our opinionated description of each is presented in Table 32.1. There are plenty of national and regional groups that are not listed in this table. Many of these organizations would probably take exception to our use of the word UNIX and insist that they are "open systems" folks.

Each organization produces membership publications and holds one or more conferences per year. USENIX holds one general conference and several specialized (smaller) conferences or workshops. UniForum, SUG, and AUUG have substantial trade shows with their conferences.

There are also several events with awesome trade shows and smaller technical programs, such as Interop and UNIX Expo. Interop's trade show is the premier, and its tutorial series is also of high quality; it has a networking focus and is not UNIX-specific.

Table 32.1   UNIX organizations

Name	What it is	Comments
USENIX	UNIX Users Group	Quite technical
SAGE	System Admin Guild	USENIX technical group
UniForum	UNIX Users Group	Management and marketing focus
SUG	Sun Users Group	Independent of Sun Microsystems
DECUS	DEC Users Group	Trying to shake their VMS heritage
EUROPEN	European UNIX Users	Includes national groups, mini UN
AUUG	Australian UNIX Users	Both technical and management
JUS	Japan UNIX Users	Both technical and management

Interop used to be an annual event that was eagerly awaited by techies and vendors alike. Now there are five Interops a year (a traveling network circus, so to speak) and the salaries of tutorial speakers have been cut in half. We will have to see if the quality survives. UniForum's and UNIX Expo's "technical" programs are oriented toward management and marketing people.

SAGE, USENIX's System Administrators' Guild, is the first national organization for system administrators. A section of the USENIX newsletter *;login:* is produced by SAGE; it contains administrative news, tips, reviews and announcements. SAGE has also produced a booklet of job descriptions for administrative positions. Together with USENIX, its parent organization, SAGE puts on the LISA conference each fall.

In addition to the national group SAGE, several local groups have been formed to help administrators interact with their peers more regularly. Some of these groups are Bay LISA in the San Francisco area, BackBay LISA in the Boston area, and $GROUPNAME in New Jersey.

The USENIX/SAGE LISA (Large Installation System Administration) conference (which denies that it's only for large systems) is the biggest, best, most technical, and most focused. It is held each fall, usually in California, and typically includes two days of tutorials and three days of technical sessions, invited talks, and help sessions. For information, send mail to conference@usenix.org or see the URL

```
http://www.usenix.org/about_sage.html
```

Recently, UniForum has added a system administration track to its tutorial offerings, and a UNIX group in the Washington DC area has held smaller conferences (called SANS) with an administrative bent.

The US computer industry has been economically depressed for the last few years, and the lack of cash has resulted in reduced attendance at various conferences and trade shows. This has put some organizations in jeopardy, and their offerings have diminished.

Mailing Lists

There are numerous mailing lists for administrators of specific systems. Some lists related to our six example systems are shown in Table 32.2.

Table 32.2   Platform-specific mailing lists

System	Subscription address
Solaris	sun-managers-request@ra.mcs.anl.gov
HP-UX	majordomo@cv.ruu.nl (say "subscribe hpux-admin")
SunOS	sun-managers-request@ra.mcs.anl.gov
OSF/1	majordomo@ornl.gov (say "subscribe alpha-osf-managers")
BSDI	bsdi-users-request@bsdi.com

32.17 STANDARDS

The standardization process helps us in some cases (modems from different manufacturers can talk to each other) and hurts us in others (OSI protocols, millions of dollars down the drain). Standards committees should not invent.

Standards are intended by some to codify existing practice and by others to delay a competitor or to reduce the amount of work required to bring their company's products into conformance. Standards have also been called a non-monetary trade barrier.

There are several standards bodies, both formal and informal. Each has different rules for membership, voting, and clout. From a system or network administrator's perspective, the most important are POSIX (the Portable Operating System Environment), ISO (the International Organization for Standardization), and the IETF (the Internet Engineering Task Force, described in *Internet Administration* starting on page 425). Summaries of emerging standards appear in the groups comp.std.unix and comp.org.usenix, and in the USENIX publication *;login:*.

POSIX has engaged itself for the last several years in defining a general standard for UNIX. Has this had any effect on commercially-available versions of UNIX? Yes: everything is more complicated now that vendors support both POSIX and their own original interfaces. POSIX .1 and .2 (now ISO 9945-1 and 9945-2) define the POSIX versions of the UNIX system calls and commands; .7, currently under development, addresses several common administrative tasks.

ISO certifies standards in various fields. In the UNIX arena, many of the ISO standards originate in lesser bodies such as ANSI (the American National Standards Institute) and the IEEE (the Institute of Electrical and Electronics Engineers). After the standards have had some "soak time," they are then promoted to international status.

Spec 1170 is the name given to the specification that will define what it means to be "UNIX." The UNIX trademark originally belonged to AT&T Bell Labs. It went from there to UNIX Systems Laboratories (a subsidiary of AT&T), then on to Novell, and finally to the X/Open consortium (now called the X/Open Company, Ltd.). It is rumored that Novell did not want to become embroiled in the legal disputes between AT&T and the University of California and so quickly gave the trademark away.

X/Open is a vendor consortium that does standards work. Full membership costs $500,000 a year. Limited membership that allows a vote on one standard rather than all standards is approximately $20,000 a year. In either case, it is unlikely that small organizations or individuals will be able to contribute to their standardization process.

If your product meets the Spec 1170 definition of UNIX and you have sufficient money, then you may call your product UNIX. X/Open claims that it is trying to capture existing practice in its standardization effort, rather than inventing. We hope it's true.

Many people feel that the standards process is not grounded in reality. Companies are the only organizations that can afford the cost of participation, but company representatives are often far from the technical trenches. Attendance at standards meetings has been declining for the last few years. Some standards organizations (in fact, most) receive a large portion of their income by selling copies of the standards documents, not for $20 (paper and reproduction costs) but for $400. An interested individual is unlikely to participate at that price.

USENIX and UniForum (UNIX user groups) fund a person to be an institutional representative. They do this not necessarily to shape the direction that a standard may be taking, but rather to inform the UNIX community of the status of standards work and to derail bogus standards as they start to emerge. The USENIX/UniForum standards representative collects input from many sources, the most notable of which are the "snitches."

A snitch is a technical person who attends a particular session and writes a snitch report. These snitch reports become the basis for the summary reports in the *;login:*. They have also been used by some of the attendees to understand what the standard is proposing and what's wrong with it.

32.18 SAMPLE DOCUMENTS

Several of the policy or procedure documents referred to in this chapter have been included on the CD-ROM in the file `policy.tar`. A list of filenames and their corresponding contents is given on the following page in Table 32.3.

Table 32.3 Policy-related documents on the CD-ROM

Filename	Contents
`ugrad.policy`	Undergraduate lab user policy agreement
`grad.policy`	Faculty and graduate student user policy agreement
`sysadmin.policy`	Administrator policy agreement
`localization`	Localization checklist
`eval.rfp`	Evaluation criteria for workstation RFP
`services`	CSOPS services, policies, and priorities
`sysadmin.survey`	Rob Kolstad's survey for administrators
`hiring.quiz1`	Rate your experience quiz
`hiring.quiz2`	Administrative knowledge quiz

About the CD-ROM

INTRODUCTION

The CD-ROM included with this book contains a variety of freely-available software, standards, documents, and examples. We have referred to many of these packages in the text; others are less specific to system administration, but invaluable in their own way. Explore and enjoy.

The software has been harvested from a variety of sources, including Usenet news archives, the Internet, and our own labs. Due to space constraints, we have pruned a few packages down to the most recent code base, or in some cases, to the most essential files. When binaries were provided with a distribution, we have included them on the CD.

The CD-ROM is formatted according to the ISO-9660 standard. It can be mounted on most UNIX machines, including all six of our example systems: Solaris, HP-UX, IRIX, SunOS, OSF/1, and BSDI. It can also be read on PCs and Macs.

We have not tested each package on all six systems, and we make no claims regarding the packages' usability or integrity. Compile, install, and use the software at your own risk. Bugs and problems should be reported to the author or maintainer of the package in question, not to us.

Your CD-ROM has been carefully sealed in Advanced Technology Vinyl to ensure its safety during transportation. It should reach you fresh and in perfect condition. Please send comments, suggestions, and complaints regarding the CD to

```
sa-cdrom@admin.com
```

The date your CD was harvested is printed on front of the disc. If the disc is more than a year old, some of the contents may be out of date. Updates will be available on an approximately yearly basis; to order the latest version, call 1-800-ADMIN-CD or send email to

```
cd-order@admin.com
```

We would like to acknowledge the assistance of Jim Lane, who did most of the work needed to make this CD-ROM a reality. Jim toiled for hundreds of hours transferring files, writing index entries, and preparing the data for mastering.

GETTING STARTED

To access this CD-ROM, you must first mount it as a filesystem. When in doubt, follow your vendor's instructions for mounting an ISO-9660 disk. Some quick hints for the "standard" configuration of each architecture are given below.

The file **manifest.txt** contains a one-line description of the various packages. Detailed information about each package can be found in the **index** directory. Files on the CD are organized into nine subdirectories; the contents of each directory are described in Table A.1.

Table A.1   CD-ROM contents by subdirectory

Directory	Contents
gnu	The GNU (Free Software Foundation) distribution
goodies	Miscellaneous UNIX tools
index	Extended descriptions of each package
mail	Packages related to electronic mail
network	Packages related to networking
news	Packages related to Usenet news
rfc	Request For Comments documents (Internet standards)
security	Packages related to UNIX security
sysadm	System administration tools

Files named ***.tar** must be unpacked with the **tar** command. To unpack the code for **sudo**, you might use the following commands:

```
% mkdir /tmp/sudo
% cd /tmp/sudo
% tar xvf /cdrom/sysadm/sudo.tar
```

Files named ***.txt** are ASCII text files that can be viewed with **cat** or **more**. Files called ***.ps** are PostScript files. These can be printed on any PostScript-compatible printer.

A FEW WORDS ABOUT VERSION NUMBERS

Some ISO-9660 drivers (in particular, the one included with HP-UX) append a "version number" to the end of each filename. For example, `ls /cdrom/mail` might produce:

```
cksendml.tar;1    ease.tar;1    elm.tar;1    idamail.tar;1
listserv.tar;1    mh.tar;1      pine.tar;1   pop.tar;1
sendmail.tar;1
```

instead of the usual

```
cksendml.tar      ease.tar      elm.tar      idamail.tar
listserv.tar      mh.tar        pine.tar     pop.tar
sendmail.tar
```

If your system handles CD-ROMs in this way, the version number is an authentic part of each filename. You must include it when trying to access a file. Beware: most shells assign a special meaning to semicolons. You'll need to "protect" them with a backslash. For example, to unpack the source code for `sudo` on a system that uses version numbers, you'd use the following commands:

```
% mkdir /tmp/sudo
% cd /tmp/sudo
% tar xvf /cdrom/sysadm/sudo.tar\;1
```

MOUNTING THE CD-ROM

Table A.2 shows the commands needed to mount the CD-ROM on our six example systems. These commands are for use on "typical" configurations; your mileage may vary.

Table A.2   Commands to mount an ISO-9660 CD-ROM

System	Command
Solaris 2.4	mount -F hsfs -o ro /dev/dsk/c0t6d0s0 /cdrom
HP-UX 9.0.5	mount -t cdfs -o ro /dev/dsk/c1d1s0 /cdrom
IRIX 5.2	Not needed, see comments
SunOS 4.1.3	mount -t hsfs -o ro /dev/sr0 /cdrom
OSF/1 2.0	mount -t cdfs -o noversion /dev/rz3c /cdrom
BSDI 1.1	mount -t iso9660 /dev/mcd0a /cdrom, see comments

Umount /cdrom

 The `t6` in the Solaris device file represents SCSI target 6. If your CD-ROM is addressed with a different target number, you'll need to adjust this. Note that `vold`, the volume manager, may mount a CD-ROM automatically when you insert it into the drive. See the man page for `vold` for more information.

Under IRIX, you simply insert the CD-ROM into the drive. IRIX will automatically mount it and display a CD icon on the desktop via **mediad**.

Use **/dev/mcd0a** for a Mitsumi CD-ROM drive or **/dev/sd1a** for a SCSI CD-ROM drive, where **sd1** depends on your system configuration. Check **dmesg** to find out which device corresponds to your CD-ROM drive.

QUICK INDEX TO THE CD-ROM

Table A.3 presents an abbreviated list of the CD-ROM's contents, along with a one-line description of each package. The "Page" and "Chap" columns point to the page and chapter in this book that are most relevant.

Although the CD-ROM includes most of the GNU distribution, GNU packages are not listed in this table. Look in the **gnu** directory for more information about these items.

Table A.3 lists packages according to their filenames on the CD (the **.tar** suffix is not shown). Due to the limitations of ISO-9660, the filenames and package names may be somewhat different.

Table A.3   Contents of the CD-ROM

Filename	Description	Page	Chap
addhost	Adds and removes hosts from a central database	359	16
adduser	Adds and removes user accounts	86	6
amanda	Network disk backup tool	–	11
amd	NFS automounter, superior to Sun's **automount**	379	17
archie	Queries **ftp** databases using Prospero	431	20
bind	Berkeley Internet Name Domain system (DNS)	315	16
cbw	The **crypt** breaker's workbench	557	23
cksendml	Checks **sendmail** configuration files	511	21
cnews	Usenet news transport and storage subsystems	568	24
compfs	Compresses entire filesystems	619	26
compress	Data compression utility	621	26
cops	Checks for possible security problems	550	23
crack	Tries to guess users' passwords	550	23
crippled	Safe shell for fake syslog user	214	12
cron	Runs commands at preset times	172	10
cslip	Compressed SLIP (Serial Line Internet Protocol)	408	19
dig	Domain Information Groper (DNS debugger)	356	16
ease	Precompiler for **sendmail** configuration files	–	21
ebackup	Automated remote backups to Exabyte	–	11
elm	An interactive mail system (user agent)	441	21
ether	Table of Ethernet numbers by vendor	289	15
expect	Controls interactive programs	390	18
facts	Miscellaneous dates and useful facts	176	10

Table A.3 Contents of the CD-ROM (*continued*)

Filename	Description	Page	Chap
flexfax	Fax modem support for UNIX systems	496	21
gated	Multi-protocol Internet routing daemon	267	14
glimpse	Index and search entire filesystems	–	–
gopher	Internet information server	433	20
idamail	IDA sendmail enhancement kit	500	21
inn	An implementation of the Usenet news system	568	24
jove	A lightweight, elegant version of emacs	–	–
julian	Computes Julian dates	649	28
listserv	Automatic mailing list maintenance utility	455	21
lynx	ASCII-based World-Wide Web browser	435	20
majrdomo	Automatically maintains Internet mailing lists	455	21
mh	RAND mail system (user agent)	441	21
mirror	Auto-fetch packages from remote ftp sites	427	20
mklabel	Makes labels for Exabyte tapes	190	11
mosaic	World-Wide Web browser for X Windows	435	20
mpage	Prints multiple pages per sheet on a PS printer	614	25
ncftp	Internet file transfer program	427	20
nfswatch	Monitors an NFS server	–	17
nn	Usenet news reader (No News is good news)	575	24
nntp	Network News Transfer Protocol server	568	24
nntplink	Network News Transfer Protocol linker	573	24
nov	Common newsgroup overview database	–	24
npasswd	Forces users to select secure passwords	542	23
ntp	Network time protocol daemon	717	31
nvi	ex, vi, and view text editors	4	1
pac	Scripts to help with printer accounting	640	28
passplus	Forces users to select secure passwords	542	23
pbmplus	Tools for converting bitmap formats	582	25
perl	Practical Extraction and Report Language	4	1
pidentd	Network authentication server	516	21
pine	Electronic mail with an easy user interface	441	21
ping	Sends ICMP echo request packets	273	14
plexus	World-Wide Web server written in perl	435	20
policy	Sample policy and procedure documents	749	32
pop	Post Office Protocol server	442	21
ppp	Point-to-Point Protocol server and client	412	19
rc	rc or init.d accounting startup script	648	28
rcs	The Revision Control System	492	21
rdist	Remote file distribution system	387	18
rn	Yet another Usenet news reader	575	24
rotz	Rotates and restarts log files	207	12
sendmail	Sends mail over the Internet (V8)	455	21
shar	Creates Bourne shell archives	578	24

Table A.3 **Contents of the CD-ROM (*continued*)**

Filename	Description	Page	Chap
snmp	Simple Network Management Protocol tools	537	22
space	A script that identifies disk hogs	619	26
sps	Extra-fast version of ps	78	5
sudo	Controls access to the root account	52	3
syslog	Comprehensive logging system	206	12
tcl	Tool Command Language	390	18
tcpd	Verifies and logs Internet service requestors	551	23
tcpdump	Packet sniffer implemented in software	279	14
tcsh	An enhanced C shell	90	6
template	Templates for IP address and domain requests	260	14
tin	Yet another Usenet news reader	576	24
top	Dynamically displays process information	81	5
tpage	Tools for controlling alpha pagers	526	22
tracert	Traces the route that IP packets follow	278	14
tripwire	Checks system files for tampering	551	23
trn	Usenet news reader with threads	575	24
ttcp	Measures performance of TCP/IP	272	14
uidswap	Changes user or group IDs	–	–
untamo	A daemon that limits logins and idle time	–	–
wais	Wide Area Information Service	433	20
wuftpd	A souped-up ftp daemon	429	20
www	World-Wide Web server	435	20
xmodem	Christensen protocol file transfer utility	–	8
zmodem	PC-to-UNIX transfer protocol	–	8

Colophon

This book was produced using FrameMaker 4 on a Macintosh Quadra 660AV. We provided "camera ready" Frame files for everything except the front and back cover and the copyright page.

Most illustrations were created with Adobe Illustrator 5.5. A few were modeled in MacroModel 1.5, then rendered with Strata StudioPro 1.0.

Cartoons were drawn by Tyler Stevens using pen and ink, then scanned with a Hewlett Packard ScanJet IIcx at 400 dpi. We edited and filtered them with Adobe Photoshop 2.5, then converted them to PostScript outlines using Adobe Streamline 3.0.

The body text is New Century Schoolbook. Headings, tables, and illustrations are in Frutiger. The fixed-width font is Courier.

First drafts of chapters were written with garden-variety text editors on several different UNIX systems. After two cycles of internal review, we transferred the chapters to Frame for editing and formatting.

Each formatted chapter was sent to a copy editor and to a group of external reviewers selected for their expertise and tact. The original author integrated review comments on a printed copy of the chapter, and these changes were then transferred to Frame by the Frame Person.

In general, we were happy with this platform, software, and method. Our main complaint is that once each chapter became a Frame file, it was impractical for anyone to manipulate it except the anointed Frame Person. There were several reasons for this, ranging from the problem of transporting fonts across platforms to the problem of standardizing the

757

formats so that more than one person could work on the text. Or perhaps the Frame Person simply enjoyed reducing the other authors to groveling weasels who had to beg and prostrate themselves for every little change. Maybe the Frame Person is going to have an unfortunate accident real soon now.

Table B.1 shows our ratings of the hardware and software products we used to prepare this book.

Table B.1 **Publishing report card**

Product	Grade	Comments
FrameMaker	B	Fast and powerful, but some rough edges
Adobe Illustrator	A+	One of the world's most perfect applications
Adobe Photoshop	A	Real nice. A little slow without tons o' RAM
Adobe Streamline	C	Works OK, but chokes on complex artwork
MacroModel	D	Great ideas, inconsistent implementation
Strata StudioPro	B	Renders well, but UI needs work. Imprecise.
HP ScanJet IIcx	B	Fast and sharp, but software is only so-so
HP LaserJet 4MP	A+	A great little desktop printer
Quadra 660AV	B+	Plenty fast, 13" monitor wasn't a problem

Index

We have alphabetized files under their last components. And in most cases, *only* the last component is listed. For example, to find index entries relating to the `/etc/passwd` file, look under `passwd`. Our friendly vendors have forced our hand by hiding standard files in new and inventive directories on each system.

About the Authors

Evi Nemeth is a member of the Computer Science faculty at the University of Colorado. Evi teaches tutorials at several conferences, including the USENIX LISA conference for system administrators. She also designed the networks for the new Computer Science buildings at Princeton University and Dartmouth College.

evi@cs.colorado.edu

Garth Snyder has worked at NeXT and Sun and holds a degree in Electrical Engineering from Swarthmore College. Garth is the President of Runway Solutions, Inc., a high-profile virtual corporation of questionable repute.

garth@cs.colorado.edu

Scott Seebass has worked on UNIX operating systems at a number of locations, including Interactive Systems and mt Xinu. He is currently the VP of Engineering at Xinet, a company that produces software to integrate Macintosh and UNIX systems. Scott received degrees in CS and Statistics from the University of California, Berkeley.

scott@xinet.com

Trent R. Hein worked on the MIPS port of 4.4BSD at Berkeley and was the third engineer hired at BSDI. He is currently Chief Network Architect at XOR Network Engineering, a Boulder consulting firm specializing in UNIX, TCP/IP, and the Internet. Trent received a B.S. in Computer Science from the University of Colorado.

trent@xor.com